When Jesus Came,
the Corn Mothers Went Away

When Jesus Came,

STANFORD UNIVERSITY PRESS
Stanford, California

the Corn Mothers Went Away

Marriage, Sexuality, and Power in New Mexico, 1500–1846

Ramón A. Gutiérrez

Stanford University Press
Stanford, California

© 1991 by the Board of Trustees of the
Leland Stanford Junior University

Printed in the United States of America
Original printing 1991

Last figure below indicates year of this printing:
12   11   10

Published with the assistance of the
National Endowment for the Humanities

CIP data appear at the end of the book

For my parents, Arthur and Nellie
and for my teachers,
Verena, Jane, Alan, Peter, and Ramón

Acknowledgments

This book could not have been written without the help, encouragement, and love of many individuals and institutions. Arthur and Nellie Gutiérrez, my parents, made it all possible, lifting my spirits and sustaining my life. My special thanks to them, and also to my history godfather, Alan Gerlach, who as my first teacher of Latin American history was the person most responsible for leading me into the profession.

The embryo of this book grew out of a course of doctoral studies at the University of Wisconsin in Madison under the direction of Peter H. Smith, Thomas E. Skidmore, Thomas J. McCormick, and Steve J. Stern. Over the years these men have been inspiring mentors, demanding critics, loyal counselors, and treasured friends. I find it difficult to express adequately my gratitude to Peter H. Smith. Had he not encouraged me continually, when it all seemed impossible, had he not been convinced that Chicano history was a legitimate field of historical research, when many others had their doubts, and had he not urged me to explore the history of kinship and sexuality to understand the dynamics of race and class, this book never would have been produced.

I owe a billion thanks to William B. Taylor for carefully reading and rereading my manuscript and every last footnote. With an immense knowledge of Latin American history and cultural anthropology, he offered me generous, gentle, and constructive criticisms. Along with his advice, bibliographic leads, and leading questions, he has honored me with his friendship, sustained me with his humaneness, and inspired me with his own scholarship.

Several friends and colleagues read various incarnations of this work, in part or whole, helped me polish its argument, and offered their unending encouragement. For all of this I thank Tomás Almaguer, George Reid

Andrews, Hal Baron, Evelyn Hu-DeHart, Nancy Farriss, Robert Frost, Sheldon Garon, Deena González, David Gutiérrez, Christine Harrington, Margaret Hedstrom, Steve Koblik, Murdo MacLeod, Michael Monteón, Vicki Ruiz, Harry Salzburg, David J. Weber, Richard White, and Allen Woll. I am especially indebted to Ramón E. Ruiz for his intellectual guidance and for his unswerving support; to George Lipsitz for his friendship and for his generous sharing of his immense knowledge of American history and cultural analysis with me; to Alfonso Ortiz for showing me the complexities of Pueblo Indian culture; to John Kessell for his encouragement and for his constant readiness to impart his encyclopedic knowledge of New Mexico's history and archives; and to Richard Trexler for sharing his truly brilliant published and unpublished work with me and for asking those difficult questions that have contributed greatly to my intellectual growth.

My intellectual debts to others are extremely large. Indeed, one of my greatest fears is that the individuals who have provided me with insights, sources, and methods will see their ideas in these pages without the full credit they so justly deserve. Without a doubt, my greatest intellectual debt is to Verena Martínez-Alier (a.k.a. Stolcke), whose brilliant book, *Marriage, Class and Colour in Nineteenth-Century Cuba*, first showed me the centrality of gender and sexuality in the creation and perpetuation of social inequalities. Equally important in my intellectual formation were Julian Pitt-Rivers' studies of honor and shame in the Mediterranean, Jane Collier's models of marriage in classless societies, and Raymond T. Smith's work on kinship ideology in Latin America. I thank them all immensely and hope that with this book I will give to others what they have given to me.

I had truly outstanding research assistance from Frank Long, Gerald Shenk, Brian McCormack, and Jackie Griffin. Deeanna Knickerbocker at the Center for Advanced Study in the Behavioral Sciences designed and typed all the tables and figures.

For generous access to archival materials I thank Myra Ellen Jenkins, Richard Salazar, and James Purdy at the New Mexico State Records Center and Archives; Stephanie Egar, Orlando Romero, Richard Rudisill, and Arthur Olivas at the Museum of New Mexico Library; Jan Barnhart at the University of New Mexico's Zimmerman Library; and Archbishop Robert F. Sánchez and Fray Angélico Chávez at the Archives of the Archdiocese of Santa Fe.

I am extremely grateful for financial support from the University of Wisconsin's Graduate School, the Danforth Foundation, and a prize fellowship from the John D. and Catherine T. MacArthur Foundation.

Portions of this book were written while I was a fellow at the Center for Advanced Study in the Behavorial Sciences at Stanford. I am grateful to the Center and all of its helpful staff, but especially to Gardner Lindzey, Robert A. Scott, Kay Holm, Kathleen Much, Lynn Gale, Patrick Goebel, Margaret Amara, Julie Schumacher, and Rosanne Torre. Financial support provided by the Andrew W. Mellon Foundation and the National Endowment for the Humanities (#FC 20029) made my years at the Center possible.

Finally, I want to thank Richard Flintorp and Timothy McDaniel for their friendship.

R.A.G.

Contents

Tables and Figures

Figures

When Jesus Came,
the Corn Mothers Went Away

Introduction

Herein is a social history of one remote corner of Spain's colonial American empire, the Kingdom of New Mexico, between 1500 and 1846. Using marriage as a window into intimate social relations, this study examines the Spanish conquest of America and its impact on one group of indigenous peoples, the Pueblo Indians. The European defeat of America's Indians has been told many times before. What dominates the written record are the visions of the victors. We have numerous panegyrics to their daring, to their strength, and to their valor. We have learned apologias of the conquest by the clergy and intelligentsia, as well as chronicles of its blackest moments, the stuff from which legends were spun. Rarely have we been privy to the vision of the vanquished. Many historians since 1492 have been content to leave in blindness those "savages" the conquistadores said lived in the darkness of idolatry. And even in the pages of those who have tried to rescue noble savages from oblivion, Indians have proven all too listless.

This book, then, is profoundly a project in point of view. It gives vision to the blind, and gives voice to the mute and silent. The conquest of America was not a monologue, but a dialogue between cultures, each of which had many voices that often spoke in unison, but just as often were diverse and divisive. The power dynamics of the conquest clearly favored the Spanish in the contest of cultures that began in 1492 and continues to this day. Each side of that discourse was hard-pressed to prove its superiority. As such, the historical process that unfolds here is a story of contestation, of mediation and negotiation between cultures and between social groups. This is not a history of Spanish men or of Indian men, or of their battles, triumphs, and defeats. It is a history of the complex web of interactions between men and women, young and old, rich and poor, slave and free, Spaniard and Indian, all of whom fundamentally depended on the other for their own self-definition.

For some time scholars have understood that marriage offers us a window into the social, political, and economic arrangements of a society. When people marry they create social alliances, establish a new social unit, change residence, exchange property, and gain rights to sexual service. In every culture marriage usually means adulthood. A daughter becomes a mother and a son a father. Universally, like tend to marry like. Thus when one asks the question, "Do we marry with them?," one fundamentally defines the local contours of class and status. Marriage is also about gender. The institution requires that there be a female and a male. How this marital relationship between two gendered individuals is culturally defined often becomes a gender representation of relations of domination and subordination in other realms. Marriage thus provides us with concrete instances when individuals and groups negotiate the meaning of their symbols in the process of social practice.

The analytic strategy employed here to untangle the complex meanings of marriage, particularly as it shapes gender and sexuality, has been profoundly influenced by the work of two cultural anthropologists, Jane Collier and Sylvia Yanagisako. Following their lead, this book is premised on the assumption that every society is a system of inequality. The task is not to explain why inequality exists, but rather to expose the different forms it has taken during a period of rapid social change, specifically the Spanish conquest of the Pueblo Indians beginning in 1539. The complex cultural meanings surrounding marriage are best understood through symbolic analysis and interpretation, a method that relates "symbols and meanings to other cultural symbols and meaning on the one hand, and to the forms of social life and experience on the other." Collier and Yanagisako maintain that symbols and meanings "are always evaluative . . . [and] encode particular distributions of prestige, power, and privilege." Distributions that have a temporal dimension remain stable or change as people create and recreate their social worlds.[1]

As a social history of New Mexico between 1500 and 1846 largely viewed through the institution of marriage, this book examines three models of marriage in three cultures during three contiguous historical periods—thus the organization in three parts. Part I explores marriage customs among the Pueblo Indians during the sixteenth century. At that time, the Pueblo Indians were a tribal society of horticulturalists known for the practice of serial monogamy and polygamy. We will explore how gift giving and marriage structured the obligations that perpetuated the basic inequalities in society, those between juniors and seniors and between successful and unsuccessful seniors.

Part II traces the history of the Spanish conquest of the Pueblo Indians, which began in 1540 with the expedition of Francisco Vásquez de Coronado into New Mexico. Here Franciscan clerical culture is examined, including its theories of personal transformation and evangelism and the concepts of hierarchy and inequality embedded in the model of mystical marriage that friars carried in their hearts. Also described is how this model of mystical marriage conflicted both with Indian ideas of marriage and with those of the Spanish soldiers, most of them bachelors who expected from their conquest the spoils of lust. As in Part I, where we explore how the competing interests of juniors and seniors and successful and unsuccessful seniors structured the discourse over marriage, in this part we also examine the tensions and conflicts among social and cultural groups. Thus we can explain why in 1680, when the Pueblo Indians revolted and drove the Spaniards out of New Mexico, their call to arms was a promise that "who shall kill a Spaniard will get an Indian woman for a wife, and he who kills four will get four women, and he who kills ten or more will have a like number of women." The second section of Part II traces the political and economic history that led to the revolt.[2]

Part III deals with marriage formation and control in the mature eighteenth-century colony that was reestablished with the 1693 reconquest of New Mexico. Here the book's focus shifts away from Pueblo-Spanish relations to those groups residing in Spanish towns and villages: the nobility, the landed and landless peasantry, and Indian slaves. Marriage in Spanish society was strictly supervised to assure the perpetuation of social inequalities. In this part of the book we see how and why this was so.

In each of the three historical periods discussed—the sixteenth, seventeenth, and eighteenth centuries—marriage is situated in its cultural context. During the 1680 Pueblo Revolt, much of the documentary record up to that date was destroyed. What remained in European and Mexican archives were some journals, expedition itineraries, and reams of paper reporting the jurisdictional squabbles between the Franciscans and the provincial governors over control of the Indians.

Consequently, the depth and breadth of coverage on many topics has been dictated by the limitations of the sources. The provincial records after 1693 are as complete as a historian can hope for and are particularly rich in documenting the private lives of Spaniards and acculturated Indians residing in Spanish towns, especially their concerns over honor and marriage. The Pueblo Indians by virtue of their *privilegios de cam-*

pana (special privileges they enjoyed as mission Indians) were exempt from the ecclesiastical marriage investigations that so vividly reported the texture of daily life in Spanish towns. As a result, we have only fragmentary bits of information on Pueblo Indian marital behavior, and almost nothing about how they interpreted Spanish concepts of honor. These facts also explain why in Part III of this book the Pueblo Indians, so much in the foreground in Parts I and II, move into the background.

Before beginning our historical narrative, some introductory remarks are necessary on the origins of the Pueblo Indians, on their spatial and linguistic distribution, and on the methods of historical reconstruction I have employed here.

The history of the Pueblo Indians began some eleven thousand years ago in what is today the U.S. Southwest. In an environment of savannas dotted by shallow lakes, humans hunted a variety of game (mammoth, horse, camel, bison, peccary, and deer) using simple projectile points. Sometime around 9500 B.C., a major climate change decreased the level of moisture, drying up many of the lakes and transforming the savannas into the treeless short-grass plains that now dominate the landscape. Once extensive varieties of animals declined. As this occurred, humans adapted by altering their mode of subsistence from large- to small-game hunting (deer, antelope, rodents, and birds) and by increasing their reliance on gathered plants (pine nuts, berries, grass seeds, and roots). The hunting and gathering culture that developed throughout the region is generally referred to as Desert Archaic Culture.[3]

The diffusion of agriculture from central Mexico was perhaps the greatest innovation experienced by people of the Desert Archaic Culture. Maize cultivation reached the Southwest around 2000 B.C. Two millennia passed before beans and squash entered the zone. By A.D. 700 domesticated cotton had also been introduced. Aside from demographic growth, the development of agriculture in the Southwest produced negligible changes in material life and culture. Nonetheless, by 500 B.C. the desert nomads began to construct permanent villages with durable houses and food storage pits. Shortly thereafter they began to manufacture pottery for cooking and storage.[4]

By 300 B.C., three regional adaptations had evolved from the Desert Archaic Culture. Each adaptation was suited to a particular ecological niche. In the pine-covered mountains of southwestern New Mexico and southeastern Arizona the Mogollon Culture developed. The Hohokam settled along the Salt and Gila river drainages in southern Arizona. The

Four Corners region, where modern-day Colorado, New Mexico, Arizona, and Utah meet, became home to the Anasazi.[5]

By the end of the first millennium A.D., the Anasazi—who are thought to be ancestral to the Pueblos—had constructed elaborate settlements, first at Chaco Canyon and in the San Juan River Basin in northwestern New Mexico, and later at Mesa Verde in southwestern Colorado and at Canyon de Chelly in northeastern Arizona, to name but a few sites. The Anasazi practiced intensive agriculture using irrigation through simple stream diversion and floodwater control, thus providing food surpluses for demographic expansion and labor specialization.[6]

Sometime around A.D. 1250, Anasazi villages were abandoned in a rather orderly fashion at a point of considerable technological development. The most convincing hypothesis for this abandonment hinges on soil erosion. As population grew, the ecological niches in which the Anasazi lived were overutilized, and the fallow cycle for soil rejuvenation was shortened. This triggered a chain reaction of soil erosion, crop failure, disease, and feuds, or so many archaeologists think. Amid the heightened social tensions, the Anasazi migrated to other areas. Some moved south and regrouped at Acoma. Others formed the Zuñi and Hopi Pueblos of western New Mexico and eastern Arizona. The remainder traveled southeast across the Continental Divide and established villages on the banks of the upper Rio Grande.[7]

What modern science explains through soil analysis, radiocarbon dating, and dendrochronology, the Puebloans explain otherwise. They say that the Anasazi abandoned their cliff dwellings because the serpent, their rain and fertility deity, mysteriously departed one night. The people felt helpless without their god. So they gathered their possessions and followed the snake's trail until it reached a river. There they built houses anew.[8]

The migration of the Anasazi in search of their rain deity bespeaks a migratory way of life that was widespread in the Southwest between A.D. 1250 and 1540. During this period thousands of small, dispersed pueblos ranging in size from 20 to 60 rooms were abandoned and replaced by a smaller number of large towns ranging in size from 200 to 750 rooms. This aggregation expanded the distance between towns. In western New Mexico and eastern Arizona, for example, the mean distance between a pueblo and its nearest neighbor was 7.4 km in the 1300s, increasing to 14.8 km by 1540. Similarly, the mean distance between pueblo clusters went from 74.3 km in the 1300s to 133.7 km in 1540.[9]

Archaeological remains for the years A.D. 1250 to 1500 tell of what must have been a massive building project. Hundreds of towns were built, intermittently occupied for 30 to 40 years, abandoned, then refurbished and reoccupied at a later date. In the Zuñi area alone, 13,000 rooms were built and abandoned between A.D. 1250 and 1400, prompting anthropologist Leslie Spier to characterize this period as one of "constant movement . . . a sort of milling around." The large pueblos that developed by 1400, were, by comparison to those fleeting settlements of the previous century and a half, relatively stable.[10]

The fluidity of the Pueblos between 1250 and 1400 is often explained as the predictable instability and fission that accompanies the centralization of dispersed segmentary lineages. In tribal, segmentary societies the best integrated and cohesive groups are the low-order units of the household and lineage. When a village consisting of a localized lineage enters a larger aggregation of similarly organized groups, the integrative mechanisms that unite the various segments so joined are weakly articulated and take some time to evolve. The solution to this problem is the creation of higher order units that cut across the primary segments and integrate the town as a whole, be it through exogamous marriages among lineages or the development of work groups, esoteric societies, or all-encompassing cults that promote ritualized reciprocal exchanges across segmentary units.[11]

A scenario such as the one discussed undoubtedly unfolded in the Pueblos between A.D. 1250 and 1400. Keith W. Kintigh's archaeological survey of the Zuñi region found that the two largest pueblos ever constructed appeared shortly after town aggregation began in A.D. 1250. These two towns were rapidly abandoned and towns of that size were never constructed again. Subsequent construction showed lower standard deviations in site size over those of the previous period, more uniformity in architectural plans, and less diversity in topographic setting. Kintigh concludes that A.D. 1250 to 1400 was a period of great experimentation, when Puebloans tested various mechanisms of social control and integration until they developed those institutions that insured relative stability in town life.[12]

Excavations at other Pueblo sites buttress Kintigh's hypothesis. Jesse W. Fewkes unearthed a decreasing proportion of kivas (male lodge houses and ritual chambers) to rooms over time, indicative, perhaps, of the development of town-wide, cross-cutting associations and task groups. Post A.D. 1450 kivas had larger numbers of ceremonial artifacts than during the preceding period. Those who study the origins of the Pueblo katsina cult, today the principal town-wide integrative ritual association, believe that the cult entered the Pueblos around A.D. 1350 to 1400 from north-

ern Sonora in Mexico. Katsinas are the collective ancestral dead, venerated as rain deities and artistically depicted as masked beings. Such
masked beings began to appear on kiva murals as part of a broader artistic revolution, also seen in pottery decoration, that emphasized complex,
asymmetrical, and curvilinear designs over previously simple, symmetri-
cal, and repetitive geometric forms. The numerous grain storage bins and
irrigation works constructed around A.D. 1350 indicate that the recession
of the Pueblo territory between A.D. 1250 and 1400 also involved a shift
from extensive to intensive agriculture, and with it, as theory suggests,
the development of crafts specialization.[13]

Pueblo prehistory still has to be worked out in considerable detail.
Intensive archaeological investigation has been conducted primarily in
what is called the Western Pueblo region, that area in western New Mexico and eastern Arizona where Acoma and the Zuñi and Hopi pueblos
are situated. The Eastern Pueblo region, defined by the pueblos located
along the banks of the Rio Grande and its main tributaries, was never as
thoroughly studied because this was the area of greatest Indian acculturation after the Spanish conquest. The Spaniards focused their extractive
colonizing project among the Eastern Pueblos because they had a year-
round supply of water and fish, more precipitation, abundant grain surpluses, numerous types of scrub brush and grasses for livestock grazing,
various species of small and large mammals for meat, and easily penetrated town walls. The Western Pueblos not only resisted the Spanish
more doggedly, but the ecological niches they occupied were less productive and thus less attractive to the conquistadores. The Western Pueblos
lived on arid mesas and steppes. They were dependent on dry farming
and whatever water they could divert from heavy rains. They had a
broader variety of cacti and scrub brush, but fewer grasses. Animal pro-
tein sources were roughly similar in both areas. Western Pueblos were
generally constructed on remote geologic formations and thus more de-
fensible. Understandably, the Spaniards constructed their towns among
the Eastern Pueblos. Modern scholars seeking to understand Pueblo prehistory naturally focused on the Western Pueblos as the area of least European acculturation. This accounts for the Western Pueblo bias in
archaeology and ethnography, as well as the pronounced, often counter-
productive, Western Pueblo–Eastern Pueblo dichotomy that has dominated scholarship since the 1870s. The east-west distinction is used here
primarily as the Spanish colonists saw it, as ecological zones.[14]

At the beginning of the sixteenth century the Pueblo Indians may have
numbered as many as 248,000, residing in 134 or more towns and villages throughout New Mexico and eastern Arizona. The spatial distri-

Map 1. Pueblo Language Families.

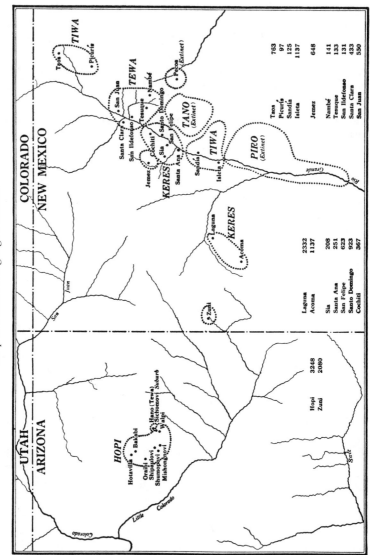

SOURCE: Adapted from Parsons, *Pueblo Indian Religion.*

bution of these villages is best imagined as a "T", with the head running north-south along the New Mexican banks of the Rio Grande, the stem extending westward into Arizona (see Map 1). Language was the main characteristic that differentiated Puebloans. In 1500 seven languages belonging to four families (Tanoan, Keresan, Zuñi, Uto-Aztecan) were spoken.[15]

The Tanoan language family was composed of Tiwa, Tewa, Piro, and Towa speakers who lived primarily on the banks of the Rio Grande or its main tributaries. The Tiwa pueblos of Taos and Picuris were at the northern edge of the Pueblo world in 1500. Thirty miles southwest of these was a group of Northern Tewa–speaking pueblos: San Juan de los Caballeros, Yugeuingge, Santa Clara, San Ildefonso, Pojoaque, Nambé, Cuyamunge, and Tesuque. Twelve miles southwest of present-day Santa Fe were the Southern Tewa (or Tano) pueblos of San Marcos, Galisteo, San Lázaro, and San Cristóbal. Separated by several hundred miles from their northern kin were the Southern Tiwa pueblos in the vicinity of present-day Albuquerque. Near what is today Bernalillo, the Spanish explorers reported a group of ten to twelve villages that they referred to collectively as Tiguex; only Puaray and Napeya were specifically named. Fourteen miles south of Albuquerque was Isleta, and due east on the eastern slope of the Sandia-Manzano Mountains were Chililí, Tajique, Quarai, Abó, and Gran Quivira. Fifty miles south of Albuquerque, back along the river plain, were the Piro pueblos of Alamillo, Pilabo, Senecu, and Trenaquel.[16]

The Towa-speaking pueblos were roughly located at the intersection of the "T" described above. Some 40 miles east of Santa Fe stood Pecos Pueblo, at the edge of the Great Plains. Fifty miles west of Santa Fe along the Jémez River were Giusewa (or San José de Jémez) and Amoxungua. Early Spanish explorers reported seven Towa pueblos in this area, but only the two noted here have been identified.[17]

The second major Pueblo language family was Keresan. All the Keres pueblos except Acoma were located near the Rio Grande, approximately 25 miles southwest of Santa Fe. These pueblos were, from north to south, Cochiti, Santo Domingo, San Felipe, Zía, and Santa Ana. Acoma Pueblo, perched atop a steep mesa some 60 miles west of Albuquerque, was the only Keres pueblo in western New Mexico until the foundation of Laguna Pueblo in 1697. The apparent diffusion of Pueblo cultural patterns from west to east via the Keres pueblos has led some to consider these speakers as a cultural bridge between the Eastern Pueblos and the Western Pueblos.[18]

Two additional Pueblo language families existed in western New Mexico and eastern Arizona, far removed from the dense settlements of the Rio Grande Valley. Speakers of Zuñi, a distinct language family, occupied pueblos 70 miles northwest of Acoma. When the Spanish first saw these villages in 1539 they thought they had found the mythical Seven Cities of Cíbola. Archaeological evidence indicates that only six, not seven, pueblos existed. From east to west, they were Kiakima, Matsaki, Halona, Kwakina, Kechipauan, and Hawikuh.[19]

Two hundred miles northwest of the Zuñi, in northeastern Arizona, stood the Hopi (or Moqui) villages of Uto-Aztecan linguistic extraction. In 1540, seven Hopi pueblos existed on four adjacent mesas. On Jeddito Mesa, the easternmost mesa, were Kawaiokuh and Awatobi; on First Mesa, Walpi; on Second Mesa, Mishongnovi, Shipaulovi, and Shungopovi; and on Third Mesa, Oraibi.[20]

For many years anthropologists thought that the contraction of the far-flung Pueblo world between A.D. 1250 and 1400 had been caused by the arrival of nomadic raiders, presumably Athapaskans. High defensive walls and the strategic emplacement of towns seemed to indicate this. Studies of Athapaskan migration from Alaska into the Southwest forced a rejection of this hypothesis. No Athapaskan remains dating to before A.D. 1525 have been found near the Pueblos. The scholarly consensus now is that Athapaskan nomads migrated south along the eastern range of the Rocky Mountains and arrived in the Southern Plains, just east of the Pueblos, around A.D. 1525. From there, undifferentiated bands of Athapaskans moved westward into New Mexico and Arizona in two directions. Across northern New Mexico and Arizona entered the people who would become known as the Navajo and Jicarilla Apaches. Across the southern portions of those states, forming a broad arch from east to west, entered ancestral Lipan, Mescalero, Chiricahua, and Western (i.e., White Mountain, Cibecue, San Carlos, Southern Tonto, Northern Tonto) Apaches.[21]

The first documentary mention of Athapaskans near New Mexico was made by the Spanish conquistador Francisco Vásquez de Coronado on the Plains just east of Pecos Pueblo in 1541. In 1583 Diego Pérez de Luxán reported "many Chichimecos, who are called Corechos" near the Hopi Pueblos, and another group of "neighboring mountain people" who were at war with Acoma Pueblo and known as "Querechos Indians who are like the Chichimecos." Ethnohistorians think these Indians may have been Navajos or Gila Apaches. By 1598 a much broader distribution of Apaches was observed by Don Juan de Oñate. Bison-hunting *apaches vaqueros*—so called, said Fray Jerónimo de Zárate Salmerón in 1626, "because they subsist on these cows"—were ranging near Pecos, beyond Picuris "from the Sierra Nevada toward the north and east," and in "the neighboring sierras and settlements" of Jémez. Fray Alonso de

Benavides in the 1620s estimated that the Apaches in the Kingdom of New Mexico (roughly the current states of New Mexico and Arizona) numbered "400,000 souls."[22]

The Spanish reported the presence of Athapaskan tribes—referred to generically as *apaches*—in close proximity to the Pueblos. Apaches occupied numerous *rancherías*, or loosely grouped clusters of dispersed huts, and ranged and raided seasonally, moving often in winter and less so in summer when they tended their crops. The only Apaches specifically named were the *apaches de nabaju*, the Navajo who hunted, gathered, raided, and farmed just like the other Athapaskans, but relied more heavily on farming. Fray Alonso de Benavides said in 1630 that the word *nabaju* meant "large cultivated fields." For the other Apacheans in New Mexico and Arizona, gathering was the dominant mode of existence, supplemented first by hunting and second by farming—exactly opposite priorities among the Navajo.[23]

The entry of peripatetic hunters and gatherers into Pueblo terrain created intense competition for hunting, foraging, and farming grounds. Athapaskans gathered food distributed over extremely wide geographic expanses by restricting the movement of non-Athapaskans. Those pueblos that were adjacent to invaded territory were forced into a greater reliance on agriculture and a circumscription of their hunting. A modus vivendi soon developed. Athapaskans bartered game and gifted the Puebloans to obtain farm products, but when necessary raided for what they wanted. The Pueblos hosted and even feasted the Athapaskans for obvious reasons: they were territorially constricted by them, were eager to curtail their raids, and desired their hunt products.[24]

Bear in mind while contemplating Pueblo and Apachean cultural geography that what we now recognize as discrete ethnic categories and tribal affiliations were in considerable flux during the sixteenth century because of the intrusions into the Pueblo world by Athapaskans after 1525 and by Spaniards after 1539. For some time the scholarly orthodoxy has been to project backward the modern reality of autonomous, fixed, and relatively permanent pueblos as if they had stolidly withstood the ravages of time without change. Modern Athapaskan tribal categories (such as Navajo, Jicarilla, Mescalero, or Chiricahua), which only emerged in the eighteenth century as a result of European contact, were likewise assumed to have a long and timeless past. Before we proceed to a discussion of Pueblo culture on the eve of European contact we must abandon these stereotypes.

The aggregation of Pueblo villages between A.D. 1250 and 1400 created a great deal of movement, uniting and then scattering groups in rapid succession. That is why every Pueblo origin myth is a history of a people wandering from one place to another, spurred to move by water shortages, soil infertility, disease, or factionalism. When Francisco Vás- quez de Coronado entered the region in 1540, he noted the ruins of numerous towns along his way. The warfare and displacement that oc- curred when Apacheans began competing with Puebloans for vital re- sources must have been extensive. That weaker pueblos were sent pack- ing is attested by Gaspar Castaño de Sosa's 1590 discovery near Santo Domingo Pueblo of two recently abandoned towns that had been beset by war. A Zuñi Indian told Fray Marcos de Niza in 1539 that the King- dom of Marata, which consisted of many towns, "has been and still was at war with the lord of the seven cities [Zuñi Pueblos]; that by this war Marata had been greatly reduced in power." Six decades later, Don Juan de Oñate found that with the exception of Acoma, no other pueblo stood where it had been observed by Coronado in 1540. Of the 134 Indian pueblos Oñate listed between 1598 and 1601, 43 remained by 1640, a scant 20 by 1707. The evolution of the pueblos as independent agricul- tural villages each marked by distinctive cultural traits is thus a product of Athapaskan constriction of the Pueblo world, accelerated and com- pounded by the Spanish conquest and their colonial design to fragment the native population through forced resettlement, strictly defined land tenure, and enforced isolation through travel restrictions.[25]

What happened to the Puebloans sent scurrying by Athapaskan war- riors or to those displaced lineages and clan segments that splintered from established towns? Historical examples help answer this question, as well as addressing the nettlesome problem of the development of dis- crete Apachean ethnic categories. Among the eighteenth-century Navajo and Western Apache it was not uncommon for lineage and clan segments to join or leave a particular band at any time of the year, be it the hunting, gathering, or farming season. Similarly, we know that throughout the seventeenth century Acoma, Taos, and the Zuñi and Jémez pueblos re- sisted Spanish domination, periodically rebelled, and when faced with su- perior forces took refuge among the nomadic Navajo and Apache for a period, before slowly returning to town life. The best example of this oc- curred during the 1680 Pueblo Revolt. Throughout the colonial period Puebloans at times abandoned their towns for a nomadic life whenever warfare, drought, or disease afflicted them, just as the Apache and Na- vajo entered towns when spurred by similar needs.

What I propose, then, is that the entry of Athapaskans and Europeans into the Pueblo world displaced small towns, lineages, and clan segments.

Such groups roamed around for a period before being incorporated into another town or larger nomadic band. How else can we explain the numerous *naciones* (literally "nations") or nomadic tribes reported by the Spanish between 1539 and 1700 that disappeared and were never mentioned again? There were once Cocoyes, Janos, Jocomes, Jumanos, Paducas, Sumas, and Teyas, to mention but a few. They are generally believed to have been conquered or absorbed by other tribes. The Spanish would not gain conceptual mastery over the native topography they conquered until the eighteenth century, so it was not until then that the Apachean tribal distinctions we know today became fixed.[26]

We turn shortly to Chapter 1, to a historical reconstruction of sixteenth-century Pueblo culture and social structure. The vantage point for this portrait is Acoma Pueblo, the oldest continuously settled town in the United States. Established perhaps as early as A.D. 1300 atop a steep rock formation in western New Mexico, Acoma has resisted ancient enemies, Spanish conquest, United States territorial annexation, and, more recently, modern technology. Acoma's oral traditions are rich and among the best recorded in the Pueblo world. Its origin myth is singular, in that it is the most etiological of Pueblo origin myths, exposing the workings of an entire cosmology. Cultural patterns found at Acoma are here elucidated and expanded upon with information first from the Hopi and Zuñi Pueblos, and only second from the rest.[27]

The methodology employed to construct this representation of the sixteenth-century Pueblo Indian world on the eve of European contact is simple. Approaching the voluminous heap of information on the Pueblos as a modern-day archaeologist of knowledge, I have bored down through the numerous layers of historical artifacts searching for certain themes, symbols, and practices. In the nineteenth and twentieth centuries these artifacts are ethnographies, archaeological site studies, collections of myths and traditions, and reminiscences about the "olden days." For the eighteenth century they are reports by friars and bureaucrats on the state of affairs in the Kingdom of New Mexico, as well as extensive civil and ecclesiastical court records. For the seventeenth and sixteenth centuries they are investigations on Indian revolts, litigation between church and state functionaries, chronicles of conquest, and explorers' narratives.

To explain how marriage historically has structured inequality, the themes that orient this rendering of sixteenth-century Pueblo culture have been gifting, relations between the generations and between the sexes, and gender and sexual symbolism. Historians interested in other topics, such as Pueblo irrigation practices or trade, would choose other coordinates for their excavations and undoubtedly advance very different hypotheses from those presented here.

Several theoretical dangers confound historical reconstructions. Presentism and a naive belief in the static timelessness of cultural forms constantly threaten to undermine such projects. Edward P. Dozier, the noted Pueblo anthropologist, offered scholars several cautionary axioms concerning the ethnographic present that merit repeating. Dozier believed that inferences about the past were most reliable when the temporal and spatial distance between a reconstructed site and a living site was short. The present and past could be compared only if both societies had similar sociocultural levels. Contemporary linguistic affiliations could not be imputed to the past. And finally, "some measure of how conservative the ethnologic culture had been over time should be established, insofar as possible." So judged, Dozier concluded, "the Pueblos would appear to mirror the past rather well." [28]

Skeptics can easily counter with a "new wine in old bottles" argument, pointing out that symbols and practices can remain constant even though their meanings change; meanings can remain identical despite a radical change in the outward appearance of symbols and practices. In order to surmount these objections, Chapter 1, "The Pueblo Indian World in the Sixteenth Century" is cast in dialogue with Chapter 2, "The Spanish Conquest of New Mexico," and Chapter 3, "Seventeenth-century Politics." Though Chapter 1 may at times seem based more on unsubstantiated assertions than on an extensive documentary base, rest assured that relations, symbols, and practices therein described are amply documented in Chapters 2 and 3. In a fundamental sense, Chapter 1 is a necessary starting point from which to chronicle changes in Indian society wrought by the Spanish conquest and not, like so many historical reconstructions, a timeless and static end in itself. Care has been taken not to advance hypotheses about the past for which there is only modern ethnographic evidence. Boring down through the layers of knowledge on specific topics, thus obtaining vertical depth and variation, should allow us to tell whether the wine in the bottles we find is merlot or burgundy, and if it has aged well. [29]

The theoretical grids for my empirical map of the sociocultural process in sixteenth-century New Mexico come largely from anthropology and sociology, from studies that offer paradigms for understanding how paleolithic hunters and gatherers were transformed into neolithic horticulturists and herders, and how inequality is structured in cultures where lineage modes of production dominate. Pueblo ethnographers undoubtedly will argue that the comparative method employed here to construct a Weberian ideal type for sixteenth-century pueblos does violence to the cultural integrity of the pueblos as we know them today. Nothing could be further from the truth. The cultural similarities that once existed among the Pueblos were never more pronounced than they were in 1500. The unique characteristics that modern anthropologists have come to identify with a particular pueblo or group of linguistically related pueblos are, in fact, post-Columbian developments. They were the result of post-conquest depopulation, of imposed town reaggregations, and particularly of the isolation imposed on each pueblo through Spanish vagrancy and land tenure laws. This largely explains the peculiarities in kinship and ceremonial organization that developed in each present-day pueblo.

Fred Eggan, whose *Social Organization of the Western Pueblos* still stands as the authoritative comparative study on the Pueblo Indians, believed that they once shared a common "social structure." Joseph G. Jorgensen reached a very similar, albeit more empirically rigorous conclusion, in his massive study in quantitative ethnology, *Western Indians*. Examining 172 tribes in Western North America and coding 292 cultural and 134 environmental variables, Jorgensen found that the Southwestern data clustered into four groups: Puebloans, Apacheans, Yumans, and Pima-Papago. Despite environmental variation, geographical dispersion, and linguistic differences, writes Jorgensen, the Pueblos "form one large group." This is a conclusion about the pre-Columbian past with which the eminent Pueblo anthropologist, Alfonso Ortiz, agrees. Based on his own meticulous research on the Tewa, he too asserts that an ancient common worldview still binds the Pueblos.[30]

With all of this in mind, let us turn to Acoma Pueblo's origin myth, which lays bare the origins and structure of the native world.

PART I

 The Sixteenth Century

I

The Pueblo Indian World in the Sixteenth Century

I am glad I have seen your nakedness;
it is beautiful;
it will rain from now on.
—Talashimtiwa, Hopi Indian from Oraibi, 1920

In the beginning two females were born underneath the earth at a place called Shipapu. In total darkness Tsichtinako (Thought Woman) nursed the sisters, taught them language and gave them each a basket that their father Uchtsiti had sent them containing the seeds and fetishes of all the plants and animals that were to exist in the world. Tsichtinako told the sisters to plant the four pine tree seeds they had in their basket and then to use the trees to ascend to the light. One grew so tall that it pushed a hole through the earth. Before the sisters climbed up the tree from the underworld, Thought Woman taught them how to praise the Sun with prayer and song. Every morning as the Sun rose, they would thank him for bringing them to the light by offering with outstretched hands sacred cornmeal and pollen. To the tones of the creation song, they would blow the offering to the sky, asking for long life, happiness, and success in all their endeavors.[1]

When the sisters reached the earth's surface it was soft, spongy, and not yet ripe. So they waited for the Sun to appear. When it rose, the six directions of the cosmos were revealed to them: the four cardinal points, the earth below, and the four skies above. The sisters prayed to the Sun, and as they did, Thought Woman named one of the girls Iatiku and made her Mother of the Corn clan; the other she named Nautsiti, Mother of the Sun clan.

"Why were we created?" they asked. Thought Woman answered, "Your father Uchtsiti made the world by throwing a clot of his blood into space, which by his power grew into the earth. He planted you within it so that you would bring to life all the things in your baskets in order that the world be complete for you to rule over it."

When the first day ended, the girls slept. They awoke before dawn to greet the Sun with a prayer on their lips and an offering of cornmeal and pollen. When Sun rose and gave them warmth, the sisters were very happy. Tsichtinako then took several seeds from their baskets and showed the sisters how to plant corn. With a dig stick she poked holes into Mother Earth and deposited seeds in her womb. The corn germinated and grew. When its ears were ripe and plump, Thought Woman showed them how to pick it, how to collect its pollen, and how to mill its kernels into the meal they would offer their father daily.

That night a flash of brilliant red light fell from the sky and when it touched the earth, it exploded into fire. "Your father Sun gives you fire to cook your food and to keep you warm," explained Thought Woman. "The fire's tongues will stay alive if fed branches from the pine tree that gave you passage from the underworld." From that day forward, Iatiku and Nautsiti had fire with which to cook corn. They flavored the corn with the salt they found in their baskets and ate to their hearts' content.

Next, Thought Woman taught the sisters how to give life to the animal fetishes in their baskets so that the animals would give them life in return. Mice, rats, moles, and prairie dogs were created and were given grasses on which to forage and multiply. The sisters cast pebbles in various directions and from these emerged mountains, plains, mesas, and canyons. From the seeds they next strewed about, pine, cedar, oak, and walnut trees grew and underneath them beans and squash sprouted and yielded their fruit. Rabbits, antelope, bison, and deer were dispatched to the open plains. To the mountains went the elk with their predators the lions, wolves, wildcats, and bears. Eagle, hawk, and turkey were cast into the sky, but turkey fell back to earth and never learned to fly. In the earth's waters fish, water snakes, and turtles were placed, and there they flourished and multiplied. Now Thought Woman told the sisters to kill an animal. "Roast meat and corn together and flavor it with salt," she instructed. "Before you eat, always pray and offer morsels of these to your father Uchtsiti who created the world and lives in the fourth sky above."

Tsichtinako cautioned Iatiku and Nautsiti to handle their baskets carefully. At first they did. But as they were giving life to the snakes one fetish fell out of a basket unnoticed and came to life of its own power as the serpent Pishuni. Pishuni bred selfishness and competitiveness between the sisters. Soon Nautsiti became sullen and refused to associate with Iatiku. When this occurred, Pishuni asked Nautsiti: "Why are you lonely and unhappy? If you want what will make you happy, I can tell you what to do. If you bore someone like yourself, you would no longer be lonely. Tsichtinako wants to hold back this happiness from you," he said.

Nautsiti believed Pishuni and agreed to meet him near a rainbow. On a rock near the specified rainbow, Nautsiti lay on her back, and as she did drops of rain entered her body. From this rain she conceived and bore twin sons. Father Sun had strictly forbidden the sisters to bear children, and when he learned that Nautsiti had, he took Thought Woman away.

When Nautsiti's sons grew up, the sisters separated. Nautsiti departed East with her favorite child; Iatiku remained with Tiamuni, the son Nautsiti disliked. Iatiku and Tiamuni eventually married and had many daughters to whom they gave clan names representing all the things that their father had given them at emergence: Sky, Water, Fire, and Corn.

After Thought Woman departed, Iatiku took earth from her basket and made the season spirits: Shakako, the ferocious spirit of winter, Morityema, the surly spirit of spring, Maiyochina, the warm spirit of summer, and Shruisthia, the grumpy spirit of fall. Iatiku told the people that if they prayed properly to these spirits they would bring moisture, warmth, ripening, and frost, respectively.

Next Iatiku, their Corn Mother, took dirt from her basket and created the katsina, the Cloud-Spirits or ancestor dead who were to live beneath a lake in the West at Wenimats. Tsitsanits (Big Teeth) was brought to life first as ruler of the katsina, then many other katsina were brought to life. Some looked like birds with long beaks and bulging eyes, others had large animal snouts, and still others were moon creatures with horns sticking out of their heads like lunar crescents. "Your people and my people will be combined," Iatiku told the katsina. "You will give us food from your world and we will give you food from our world. Your people are to represent clouds; you are to bring rain." Iatiku then took cornmeal and opened a road four lengths long so that the katsina could travel to Wenimats and along which they would return when called.[2]

"Now we are going to make houses," said Corn Mother. Suddenly a house made of dirt and trees grew out of the earth resembling in shape the mesa and mountain homes of the season deities. Each of Iatiku's daughters constructed a house for their children and when they were all ready, Iatiku laid them out into a town. "All is well but . . . we have no sacred place, we have no *kaach* [kiva]," Iatiku said. She taught the oldest man of the Oak clan how to build religious houses underneath the earth's surface to resemble Shipapu, the place of emergence.

The people did not have a father of the game animals, so Iatiku appointed a Shaiyaik (Hunt Chief), taught him the songs and prayers of the hunt, gave him an altar, and showed him how to make stone fetishes and prayer sticks to secure the power of the prey animals. Hunt Chief eventually became overburdened with work and so Corn Mother made Tsatia hochani (War Chief or Outside Chief) to rule over everything outside the pueblo. Iatiku gave him a broken prayer stick with four tails marked on four sides to extend from the earth to the sky. "When you hold [the prayer stick] clasped in your hands," Iatiku told Tsatia hochani, "you are drawing all the people together so they will not be scattered. With this you will have great power over all the rest of the people." Iatiku gave the War Chief twin sons, Masewi (Wren Youth) and Oyoyewi (Mocking Bird Youth), to assist him. The boys were the Twin War Gods, sons of Father Sun.

The people had never known sickness until the serpent Pishuni returned as a plague. The people tried to cure themselves, but could not. To break Pishuni's spell Iatiku created the *chaianyi*, the Medicine Man. The oldest man of the Oak clan was made Fire Medicine Man because fire was the strongest thing that Sun had given them and oak burned hottest. Corn Mother told Oak Man to go to North Mountain and there in a pine tree that had been struck by lightning he would find an obsidian arrowhead that would be his heart and his protection. She taught him how to make black prayer sticks as symbols of the night in which he would work, and then made him an altar. Iatiku taught the Medicine Man how to mix medicines and how to secure the power of bears to destroy disease-causing witches. "Now I will make you *honani* [corn fetish] so that you will remember me," Iatiku said to the chaianyi, "it will have my power." Into a corn cob she blew her breath along with a few drops of honey to symbolize all plant food. The cob was wrapped in four husks and dressed with the tail feather of a roadrunner and of a magpie to make it useful in prayers. Iatiku also placed turquoise on the corn fetish so that it would always have the power to make one attractive and loved.

Everything was ready for a cure so Iatiku said to Fire Medicine Man, "Let us try it out." For four days the medicine man did not touch women, salt, or meat, and only sang and prayed. On the fourth night he performed a cure. The people quickly recovered. When Iatiku saw this, she also created the Flint, Spider, and Giant Medicine Societies.

Eventually it came to pass that the young people no longer respected Iatiku. So she returned to Shipapu. After she departed, Outside Chief led the people in search of their home at Haako (Acoma), "the place where the echo returned clearest." They settled at White House for a while but the katsina refused to visit because the young had insulted Iatiku. Rain clouds would not form and famine came. Flint Medicine Man and an ordinary man worked very hard, prayed, and fasted, and finally got the katsina to visit, bearing rain and gifts.

Iatiku's people were happy for a long time until sickness again befell them. The War Twins believed that this was a sign from Iatiku that they should move to Haako, and so they did, gathering everything in four days and traveling until they reached Washpashuka. They settled there until the people began to quarrel. When this occurred, Outside Chief told the people that it was time to move again. They walked south for many moons until they reached Tule Lake. The people settled at Tule Lake for a while too. But after they suffered a severe famine there, they decided to continue their search for Haako.

They traveled south until they reached Dyaptsiam, a place of many turkeys and antelope. There they built a town. The people lived very happily until Outside Chief reminded the Medicine Men and the War Twins that they still had not reached Haako. The chiefs searched in the south and came upon a large rock. Outside Chief yelled out, "Haako!" and listened. Four more times he yelled and each time the echo came back clearly. After four days of preparation the people moved to Haako and were happy knowing that their journey had ended.

Pueblo Ideology

The origin myth of the Acoma Indians just presented likened human life to plant life. Seeds held the potential to generate life. When planted deep within Mother Earth and fertilized by the sky's vivifying rain, seeds germinated, grew into plants, and eventually bore seeds that repeated the cycle of life. Like a sprouting maize shoot rooted in the earth or a child coming forth from its mother's womb, so the Pueblo Indians described their emergence from the underworld.[3]

All of the Pueblos have origin myths that dramatically depict the ideological structure of their world. Myths express the values and ideals that organize and make people's lives meaningful. They explain how the universe was created, its various components, and the tensions and balances that kept it intact. Whether through the deeds of gods, the feats of heroes, or the abominations of monsters, the Pueblo origin myths expressed life's generic prospects: birth, marriage, sex, quarreling, illness, migrations, and death. The Pueblo Indians conceived their history as instances of these generic forms. When pestilence struck, when famine engulfed the land, or when invading warriors demanded submission, it was through comparison with patterns in remote mythological events that the particular was understood.

The Western mind's linear concept of time imposes chronology on all events and struggles to comprehend the causes and consequences of moments that have irrevocably altered history. Such a concept of time was alien to the Pueblo Indians until quite recently. Time to them was not linear but cyclic: in the words of Mircea Eliade, it eternally returned. No event was deemed unique or serendipitous; the particular was simply comprehended through those experiences of mythic progenitors. Like the life contained within a seed that sprouts, bears fruit, and dies, only to be reborn again from a seed, so the Pueblo Indians conceived of time and of their historical past.[4]

The structural principles of Pueblo culture were not a static set of symbolic oppositions but a dynamic process that unfolded and constantly created and recreated the basic cultural categories and relationships. "The system has an internal (structural) diachrony, of its nature temporal and changing," writes anthropologist Marshall Sahlins. "Structure is the cultural life of the elementary forms. Yet precisely as this diachrony is structural and repetitive, it enters into dialogue with historical time, as a cosmological project of encompassing the contingent event."[5]

Pueblo Rites

From birth until death every phase of a Pueblo Indian's life was marked by rites of transition and incorporation. Before children of either sex could be considered adults they needed a host of essentials. Girls needed religious fetishes, esoteric knowledge in curing, pottery production, household construction, basket making, and a husband. Boys likewise needed sacred fetishes, knowledge in hunting, warfare, curing, rain-conjuring, and a wife. Boys and girls, however, were incapable of obtaining these goods for themselves. Seniors had to secure them for their children and did so by offering gifts to those seniors who could provide the required goods. For example, four days after a child was born at Acoma, a medicine man had to present the infant to the rising sun, to give it a name, and to endow it with a perfect ear of corn, and if a boy, also with a flint arrowhead. Early on the fourth day, with four arm-gathering motions, the medicine man presented the child to the sun and gave it the sun's strength saying: "Now you have become a member of the _____ clan." When the medicine man returned the child to its mother he would announce: "Here comes [child's name] . . . she is bringing food, beads, game, and a long life into her house." The mother welcomed the abundance and prosperity her daughter brought with four arm-gathering motions. Then the medicine man sprinkled the baby's cradle board with medicines, attaching a perfect ear of corn, and if it was a boy, a flint arrowhead too. For the blessing and gifts the medicine man gave the child, the parents reciprocated with gifts of cornmeal and food.[6]

Thus when girls and boys began life they were already indebted to their parents for the payment of gifts to the medicine man on their behalf. As a result of this debt and the many others they would incur to reach adulthood, juniors had to reciprocate with obedience and respect toward their parents. Concretely, respect meant that girls had to work for their mothers grinding corn, cooking, and tanning hides; boys had to tend to the corn crops, hunt, and weave cloth. Seniors, by appropriating the products of their children's labor, obtained gift stuff to offer seniors of other households so that their children could receive those blessings, knowledge, and gifts they needed to become adults.[7]

Gift exchange in Pueblo society created dyadic status relationships between givers and receivers. A gift properly reciprocated with a countergift established the exchanging parties as equals, there being no further claim one could make of the other. If a gift giver initiated an exchange with a highly respected or knowledgeable person to obtain blessings, religious endowments, or ritual knowledge, such as when a parent offered a medicine man gifts so that he would present their child to the rising sun, the obligation created was fulfilled through a proper countergift. But if only one side gave and the other side could not reciprocate, the receiver out of gratitude had to give the presenter unending obedience and respect.[8]

The rules of reciprocity that governed gift exchange among the Pueblos are revealed in a variety of historical sources. The Acoma origin myth explains that when Tsichtinako gave life to Iatiku and Nautsiti, she presented each with a basket their father Uchtsiti had given them containing the seeds and fetishes of all the plants and animals in the world. As a result of this paternal gift the girls had to welcome him daily with songs and prayers, offering him the products of their labor—maize ground into cornmeal and sacred pollen. From the moment of their creation the Corn Mothers were indebted to their father for the baskets he had given them. Since they had nothing to give him in return, they did as Tsichtinako instructed, daily singing his praises and offering him food. Humans and animals, just like their mythic ancestors, were bound by these rules of reciprocity in gifting, noted Fray Alonso de Benavides in 1634:

If they went hunting, they would offer meal to the heads of deer, rabbits, hares, and other dead animals that they had in their houses, believing that this would enable them to catch much game. When they wanted to go fishing, they first offered meal into the river, hoping by this means to obtain a big catch. . . . Whenever they went to war they offered meal and other things to the scalps of the enemy nation which they had brought back as trophies of those they had slain.[9]

The debts children incurred by obtaining unreciprocated gifts from or through their parents created bonds of obligation they had to fulfill. As the Acoma myth notes, before the Corn Mothers even knew that they needed baskets, seeds, and fetishes to create life, their father had already fulfilled his duty to provide them with these things. So with children, before they became conscious that they needed gifts, parents had already overfulfilled their duty to provide them. Children had never reciprocated these gifts and were thus indebted to their parents, owing them respect and labor. The fact that juniors did not own the products of their labor and possessed nothing the seniors needed meant that if juniors were to continue to accumulate the things that conferred adult status they had to do as seniors commanded. Children exhibited respect for their elders when they did as they were told. Seniors would only endow respectful juniors, and no elder would ever listen to or speak up for a disrespectful junior.[10]

The Acoma origin myth also describes what could happen if the rules of reciprocity that governed gifting and structured generational obligation faltered. These themes surface in reference to the katsina, the beneficent rain spirits that represented the ancestral dead. In Pueblo thought, with increasing age one approached the godliness of katsina. The myth explains that the katsina first fought with the people, abandoned them, refused to shower them with rain and happiness, and ultimately severed the ties that bound them with the people because the young no longer respected the katsina and instead mimicked their gestures, burlesqued their dances, and refused to call them properly with gifts. Seniors scolded juniors for their disrespect, but the juniors continued to misbehave. When the katsina discovered this, they became very angry and refused to accept the peoples' prayer sticks. When the katsina finally visited they killed many people. The Twin War Boys retaliated by killing many katsina, explaining that they did so because "the katsina on their part should care for the people." The town chief told the Twins that the people were at fault because they had not respected the katsina. He urged the War Twins to use their magical powers to bring the katsina back to life. The Twins agreed because it was "by them [i.e., the katsina] that we have lived and been happy." The magic worked. The katsina came back to life. To teach the young the respect they had to show the katsina, that is, the reciprocity which regulated generational relations and labor exchange between juniors and seniors, every adolescent had to be initiated into the katsina cult and learn what death and destruction awaited those juniors who did not observe these rules.[11]

Marriage, the mark of transition from junior to senior status, was similarly enmeshed in gift exchanges. Girls married when they were about seventeen years old, said Hernán Gallegos in 1582, boys when they were about nineteen. This occurred in the standard boy-meets-girl way. The young man would then inform his parents that he wanted to marry. If the parents and kin agreed to the match, the senior members of his household gathered the necessary marriage-validating gifts on the boy's behalf. The willingness of elders to gather these gifts testified that the boy had been respectful of his elders, had toiled for them tirelessly, and had been obedient. Had he not, they could withhold the gifts he needed to present to his prospective in-laws, reminding him of his past failures and of their anger at him, much like when the katsina became angry at disrespectful juniors and refused to bless them.[12]

When the boy's elders had gathered their marriage-validating gifts, they took them to the girl's household. If the girl's kin agreed to the marriage and accepted the gifts, each person that accepted a gift had to give one in return. The gifts the bride's kin collected for her in-laws were usually taken to them on the fourth day after the initial gifts were received. Jane Collier characterizes this marital system as one of "equal bride-wealth" because "equal" amounts of wealth are exchanged between the boy's and girl's households to validate the marriage. When these exchanges were complete a marital rite followed.[13]

Hernán Gallegos observed such a marriage in 1582 and proposed that the gifts exchanged represented the Pueblo sexual division of labor.

[C]olored and ornamented blankets are set before the couple. The groom covers his bride with her blankets and she places his on him, in such a way that they clothe one another. . . . [T]he people place before the bride a grindstone, an olla, a flat earthenware pan (comal), drinking vessels, and chicubites. They also put a grinding stone in her hand. . . . [T]he gifts set before her, which are all entirely new, signify that with them she is to grind and cook food for her husband; that she is to prepare two meals every day for him, one in the morning and the other in the afternoon; that they are to dine and retire early, and rise before daybreak. . . . [B]efore [the groom] are placed a Turkish bow, spear, war club, and shield, which signify that with them he is to defend his home and protect his wife and children. They give him his crate (*cacoxte-cacaxtle*) and leather band (*mecapal*) for carrying burdens. Then they place a hoe in his hand to signify that he is to till and cultivate the soil and gather corn to support his wife and children.

The marriage ceremony Marcelo de Espinosa observed in 1601 was very similar and ended with a communal meal.[14]

Marriage was not conceptualized as a monogamous life-long tie. The Indians "make agreements among themselves and live together as long as they want to, and when the woman takes a notion, she looks for another husband and the man for another wife," asserted Joseph Brondate in 1601. Serial monogamy was the norm except among successful seniors who were always described as polygamous. Shortly we will see why.[15]

Marriage and procreation marked one as an adult. Children triggered a new cycle of indebtedness. But if because of few or sickly children a couple was unable to produce those socially desired goods exchanged as gifts, then these unsuccessful seniors would have to indebt themselves to successful seniors in order to provide their own children with the prerequisites for adulthood. Unsuccessful seniors who obtained gifts they could not reciprocate for their child from successful seniors were indebted to them and could be expected to render labor, respect, and obedience. Heads of successful households, by having numerous juniors as well as unsuccessful seniors whose labor they could appropriate to accumulate gift-stuff, were thus in a position to support large extended households consisting of secondary wives, widows, orphans, and strays.

These "papas," as the sixteenth-century Spanish explorers called the heads of successful households, were often polygamous. "The men have as many wives as they can support," wrote Gaspar Pérez de Villagrá in 1610. "I saw Indians who had five or six wives," attested Marcelo de Espinosa. Brondate concurred and added that the marital system was sexually asymmetrical: men could have several wives but "women have only one husband." On pondering why this was so, several Spaniards offered their theory for polygamy. Fray Alonso de Benavides observed among the Apache in the 1620s what Espinosa and Ginés de Herrera Horta in 1601 believed to be the case among the Pueblos: the number of wives one had depended "on rank, for it is a mark of prestige to have numerous wives."[16]

Pueblo seniors who became successful by virtue of their superlative skills and knowledge as hunters, warriors, rain-conjurers, or medicine men received many gifts from seniors who wanted their knowledge or their blessings for themselves or for their children. Successful seniors were the individuals best capable of community leadership because of the available wealth they stood prepared to offer the gods and unsuccessful seniors as gifts. This, then, was how gifting structured inequality both between juniors and seniors and between successful and unsuccessful households.

Relationships of superordination and subordination among the Puebloans were based on age and personal characteristics. Such societies are often called egalitarian because theoretically all men and women had equal access to those things a person of either sex needed in life, be it ritual blessings, esoteric knowledge, tools, land, or seeds. "I have not seen any principal houses by which any superiority over others could be shown," said Francisco Vásquez de Coronado in 1540, as he tried to assess the differences between the Aztecs and the Pueblos. Diego Pérez de Luxán visited the Hopi and Zuñi Pueblos in 1582 and concluded that no discernible differences in material trappings existed between the caciques, or chiefs, and others: "They are all equal." Age grading was one source of inequality in the Pueblos, but as one advanced through life and married, became a parent, a household head, and finally an elder, one's power and prestige also grew. Senior men, successful or unsuccessful, controlled social well-being. Senior women likewise commanded great respect and authority through ownership of the household, of its sacred fetishes, and of its seeds, whatever the household's size or productivity. "The old men are the ones who have the most authority," reported Hernando de Alvarado and Fray Juan de Padilla in 1540. Pedro de Castañeda observed that same year that the Hopi were governed "by an assembly of the oldest men." [17]

According to Jane Collier, "leadership is a creation of followership" among tribesmen. When a chief died or became so senile that he was no longer able to accumulate the gift-stuff to stage ceremonials and to indebt others, his following dissolved. The chief's children might be advantaged in obtaining ritual knowledge, blessings, and gifts, but every person who aspired to leadership had to obtain his own ritual knowledge, his own bride, and his own following. Leadership was not hereditarily based in one household or matrilineage until the eighteenth century, thus minimizing inherited inequalities. Additionally, the Pueblos prized generosity and equated conspicuous wealth with witchcraft. Chiefs were above all successful seniors who generously gifted those who sought their help and selflessly provided all the goods necessary to stage religious ceremonials through which the gods' blessings were obtained. [18]

The Pueblo Indians viewed the relations between the sexes as relatively balanced. Women and men each had their own forms of wealth and power, which created independent but mutually interdependent spheres of action. The corn fetish every child was given at birth and the flint arrowhead with which boys were endowed symbolized these relations and expressed the basic preoccupations of a people living in a semi-arid environment. Corn and flint were food and water, but they were also the cosmic principles of femininity and masculinity. Female and male combined as corn seeds and rain combined to perpetuate life. Corn plants without rain would shrivel and die; water without corn was no life at all. The ear of corn infants received represented the Corn Mothers that had given life to all humans, plants, and animals. At Acoma Pueblo this corn fetish is still called Iatiku, because it contains her heart and breath. For this reason too the Hopi called this corn fetish "mother." "Corn is my heart, it will be to [you] . . . as milk from my breasts," Zia's Corn Mother told her people. Individuals kept this corn fetish throughout their entire lives, for if crops failed its perfect seeds held the promise of a new crop cycle.[19]

If the corn ear represented the feminine generative powers latent in seeds, the earth, and women, the flint arrowhead represented the masculine germinative forces of the sky. Father Sun gave men flint arrowheads to bring forth rain, to harness heat, and to use as a weapon in the hunt. The noise emitted by striking together two pieces of flint resembled the thunder and lightning that accompanied rain. Rain fertilized seeds as men fertilized their women. Without rain or semen life could not continue. The flint arrowhead was the sign of the hunter and warrior. Sun gave his sons, the Twin War Gods, arrowheads with which to give and take away life. From flint too came fire. When men struck flint and created that gift Sun gave them at the beginning of time, they transformed that which was raw into that which was cooked. To the Pueblo Indians flint, rain, semen, and hunting were to male as corn, earth, and childbearing were to female. This idea is conveyed in the Hopi word *posumi*, which means both corn seed and nubile woman. We see this too in the ceremony Zuñi women perform to celebrate the sex of their babies. Over a girl's vulva the women place a large seed-filled gourd and pray that her sexual parts grow large and her fruit abundant. The boy's penis is sprinkled with water, and the women pray that it remains small. Men became very angry when they saw this ritual, for through it women asserted that their life-bearing capacity was immense in comparison to that of men. Men vigorously contested this claim in their rituals to vivify the earth, sporting large artificial penises to show women that their fructifying powers were really more immense, "singing about the penis being the thing that made the women happy."[20]

The natal home was the primary unit of affiliation in Pueblo society. Everyone belonged to a home. Humans, animals, deities, and even the natural forces were believed to each have a home within which they lived. In the sixteenth century the Pueblos were matrilineal, anchoring maternity to matrilocal households. "The houses belong to the women, they being the ones who build them," observed Espinosa in 1601.[21]

The household was preeminently a female domain of love and ritual. Women joined together to fashion houses out of the entrails of Mother Earth, setting her stones in charcoal ash and dirt mortar, assiduously building those multistoried edifices they still call home. Though houses were clustered together in hive-like compounds, each had its own entrance, a hearth for heat and cooking, sleeping rooms, and a room for the storage of seeds, sacred fetishes, and religious objects. The interior walls of a house were whitewashed and decorated with the clan's eponym. Reed mats for sleeping, pottery utensils for cooking and storage, and a mill stone for grinding corn were basic furnishings. When a household outgrew its space, usually when daughters married, adjacent rooms were added as vertical or horizontal extensions to the hearth.[22]

Towns were an aggregation of households. Each town contained anywhere from 50 to 500 houses grouped around a central plaza in which several kivas stood. Houses rarely had ground floor entrances; they were usually entered by ascending moveable ladders that connected the various terrace levels of a housing compound. This was supremely a defensive architectural design. If enemies attacked, town residents climbed up to the highest terrace, removed the ladders to the lower ones, and from these heights, pelted outsiders with arrows and stones. From these heights, too, women protected their homes, rallying assistance with smoke signals or by "lifting their hands to their mouths and letting out a loud cry which could be heard far away."[23]

The role men played in the construction of homes was rather limited. "The women mix the plaster and erect the walls; the men bring the [roof and support] timbers and set them in place," observed Pedro de Castañeda in 1540. Timber came from distant mountains outside of the town—the province of men and gods. Women owned the domestic hearth, exercised authority over those that lived within it, and at death passed on the edifice to their daughters. The female household head was custodian of its rights and possessions: the agricultural plots their husbands and sons worked, all food and seed reserves, and the sacred fetishes and ritual objects of the clan. The implication of these facts for domestic politics was clear to Fray Alonso de Benavides in 1634: "[The woman] always commands and is the mistress of the house, and not the husband."[24]

The typical household unit consisted of a grandmother and her husband, her sisters and their husbands, her daughters and their husbands, various young children, and perhaps an orphan, slave, or stray. Women were attached to their natal dwelling throughout their lives, said Hernán Gallegos in 1582, and did "not leave except when permitted by their mothers." Men moved from house to house according to their stage of life. During childhood boys lived with their mothers, and at adolescence they moved into a kiva to learn male magical lore. When they had mastered these skills, and were deemed worthy of marriage by their kin, they took up residence in their wife's home. A man nonetheless remained tied to his maternal home throughout his life. For important ceremonial events, men returned to their maternal households. When this occurred the household became a matrilineage. Matrilineages that acknowledged descent from a common ancestor, usually through ownership of a similar animal or spirit fetish, formed larger, primarily religious aggregations known as clans.[25]

When a child was born, the umbilical cord was buried—inside the household underneath the grinding stone if it belonged to a girl, outside in a cornfield if it belonged to a boy. This natal practice nicely delineated the sexual division of space and labor. The house and compound were female space invested with descendent earth-bound symbols. In the household women gave men their love and their bodies. They bore children, reared them, and engaged in that ritual activity that was at the core of kinship—feeding. Women fed their children, their mothers and grandmothers, their brothers and maternal uncles, and their husbands. Kinship was reckoned through genealogical principles—born of blood and substance. But just as importantly, kinship was created through feeding, what the Puebloans call "adoption." Any life or spirit form was transformed into kin through feeding. Thus women regularly fed the sun and prepared food for the katsina. They fed the household animal fetishes and the scalps of enemy dead to assure that they remained content. Before hunters carried the carcass of an animal into the pueblo, the women fed it, and by so doing adopted it into a household. This feeding assured that the animal's spirit would not haunt the hunter. When foreign chiefs and caciques were feasted, the social exchange of food that signified peace was accomplished through the role of women's feeding.[26]

Large portions of a woman's day were spent preparing meals for her household. Corn, beans, and squash were the main staples of the diet. Corn was the most important and symbolic of these. It was boiled whole, toasted on the cob, or dried and ground into a fine powder easily cooked as bread or gruel. Every day a woman and her daughters knelt before metates, grinding corn to feed their gods, their fetishes, and their kin. The women worked joyful at this task, observed Castañeda in 1540. "One crushes the maize, the next grinds it, and the third grinds it finer. While they are grinding, a man sits at the door playing a flageolet, and the women move their stones, keeping time with the music, and all three sing together."[27]

> Oh, for a heart as pure as pollen on corn blossoms,
> And for a life as sweet as honey gathered from the flowers,
> May I do good, as Corn has done good for my people

Through all the days that were.
Until my task is done and evening falls,
Oh, Mighty Spirit, hear my grinding song.

Within the household an age hierarchy existed, for as Hernán Gallegos observed in 1582, "women, if they have daughters, make them do the grinding." The production of pottery (e.g., storage jars, cooking utensils, ritual medicine bowls), moccasins, ceremonial apparel, and turkey-down blankets was also women's household work. Men appropriated and circulated some of these goods throughout the Southwest. Pottery was widely coveted and brought a handsome barter in hides, feathers, and meat.[28]

After feeding, the activity of greatest cultural import to Pueblo women was sexual intercourse. Women were empowered through their sexuality. Through sex women bore the children who would offer them labor and respect in old age. Through sex women incorporated husbands into their maternal households and expected labor and respect from them. Through sex women domesticated the wild malevolent spirits of nature and transformed them into beneficent household gods. Accordingly, then, sexuality was deemed essential for the peaceful continuation of life.

Female sexuality was theirs to give and withhold. In marriage a woman gave her husband her love and her body because of the labor he gave her mother, and because of all the marriage-validating gifts that had been given on her behalf to her in-laws. When women gave the gift of their body to men with whom no obligational ties existed, they expected something in return, such as blankets, meat, salt, and hides. For a man to enjoy a woman's body without giving her a gift in return was for him to become indebted to her in a bond of obligation.[29]

Erotic behavior in its myriad forms (heterosexuality, homosexuality, bisexuality) knew no boundaries of sex or age. Many of the great gods—the Zuñi Awonawilona, the Navajo First Man/First Woman, the Hopi Kawasaitaka katsina—were bisexual, combining the potentialities of male and female into one—a combination equally revered among humans. If the Indians sang of sex, copulated openly, staged orgiastic rituals, and named landmarks "Clitoris Spring," "Girl's Breast Point," "Buttocks-Vagina," and "Shove Penis," it was because the natural world around them was full of sexuality.[30]

Sexuality was equated with fertility, regeneration, and the holy by the Pueblo Indians, a pattern Mircea Eliade has found to be common to many societies. Humanity was dependent on sexuality for its continuation. The Acoma Indians say they were conceived when Pishuni, the serpentine deity of water, entered Nautsiti's body as rain. At the beginning of time, too, Thought Woman taught the Corn Mothers that maize would give them life if planted deep within Mother Earth's womb. When the clouds (men) poured down their rain (semen) the seeds (women) would germinate and come to life. The reader will recall that this is why a boy's penis was sprinkled with water at birth and a girl's vulva was covered with a seed-filled gourd.[31]

Modesty and shame were not sentiments the Pueblo Indians knew in relationship to their bodies. Before European contact they wore little clothing and were "entirely naked except for the covering of their privy parts." Women wore what resembled "table napkins, with fringes and a tassel at each corner, tying them around the hips." Most men left their genitals totally exposed; some tied their penis "near the prepuce with a maguey fiber" to protect it from evil spirits.[32]

Sexual intercourse was the symbol of cosmic harmony for the Pueblo Indians because it united in balance all the masculine forces of the sky with all the feminine forces of the earth. The solstitial rituals that renewed the union between Nautsiti and Pishuni from which the Acoma Indians were born culminated in sexual intercourse. Whenever the katsina visited, these Cloud-Beings brought fructifying rain so that seeds germinated, animals multiplied, and cosmic peace prevailed. What better way to celebrate fertility than by copulating with the katsina? And this is precisely what always happened, said Fray Nicolas de Chávez in 1660: "men and women have sexual intercourse in bestial fashion."[33]

Society was made whole through libidinous female sexuality. Through intercourse, outsiders (men from other towns or clans) became insiders (household and community members). This principle also operated in other domains: in female ceremonial associations, in the Pueblo scalp dance, and in animal butchering rites. Elsie Clews Parsons concluded in her monumental *Pueblo Indian Religion* that "all Pueblo women's societies . . . are genetically war societies." To see what these female societies tell us about the incorporation of outsiders, let us turn to the Hopi Pueblos where the vibrant ceremonies are best recorded.[34]

With the onset of menses Hopi girls were initiated into the clan-based Marau, Lakon, or Oaqol societies. Since the Hopi say that the Lakon and Oaqol ceremonies are derived from the Marau ceremony, let us focus on it. According to myth, the Marau Society was created by the Sun. He met a woman in the underworld and abducted her, and from their union came many children. Sun taught one of his sons the mysteries of the Wuwutcim (men's society) and one of his daughters those of the Marau.[35]

Twice a year, in January and in September, the Marau Society conducted a ceremony at which women officiated; at no other time did this
occur. The January ceremony, which celebrated female fecundity, sexuality, and reproduction, began with four days of prayer-stick making,
songs, prayers, and smokes. On the fifth day the society's initiates were
inducted with a hair-washing. Throughout the next two days the women
danced to awaken the sky's (men's) desires so that it would pour forth its
rain (semen). Dancing naked in a circle with their backs to the community, the women would fondle clay phalluses and taunt the men with lewd
songs to the clouds (rain, semen) and lightning (penis), repeatedly bend-
ing over to expose their genitals to the men. "Iss iss, iss iss," the men
would cry excitedly. "I wish I wish, I wish I wish!"—wishes the women
satisfied at the dance's end, cooling the passion of the men through intercourse, the symbol of cosmic harmony.[36]

The September Marau celebration was identical except for a ritual
confrontation between the society's women and two men who impersonated the Twin War Gods. While the women danced holding corn-stalks
with young ears of corn on them, the War Twins approached the circle
and shot arrows at a bundle of produce that represented the feminine reproductive earth. The arrows symbolized lightning (penis), and their
strikes germination (intercourse). The dancers then encircled the Twins
and fed them cornmeal, the substance of female labor, which when exchanged as a gift symbolized peace, established affinity, and incorporated
individuals into a household. When the dance ended, the women deposited the arrows at the shrine of the war gods.[37]

Warfare was a male activity among the Pueblos that was outside and
beyond the moral order of society. In the continuum of reciprocities that
regulated a pueblo, the taking of human life through violence was at the
negative end; gifting was at the positive end, signifying the avoidance of
war. Through the gifting of food and the offering of hospitality in the
form of intercourse women assured communal peace. Violence was domesticated and tamed through such female ritual. And through the issue
of women's bodies—children—foreigners and natives became one and
were incorporated into households.[38]

These ideas were expressed poignantly during the scalp dance performed by Pueblo women when their men returned from war. Women
would jubilantly greet returning war parties outside the pueblo, reported
Fray Atanasio Domínguez in 1776, and together with their men would
carry the scalps of the enemy dead, "singing on the way about the events
of the battle . . . [with] howls, leaps, shouts, skirmishes, courses back and

forth, salvos, and other demonstrations of rejoicing." When the scalps entered the pueblo, said Domínguez, "the women scornfully touch their private parts with the scalp." Another observer said that the women "bared their buttocks to it [the scalp]. They said it was their second and third husband and lay down on it as if having sexual intercourse. All of this was to take power away from the enemy." After the scalps had been robbed of their power in this way, they were attached to a large wooden pole and a dance was performed for them, which included much singing about the feats of battle and the prowess of Pueblo warriors.[39]

The Pueblos believed that an enemy's head and scalp were invested with the person's spirit; if not properly adopted, they would wreak havoc. To forestall this possibility, after the scalps were robbed of their power through intercourse, they were entrusted to women who fed them corn-meal and thereby incorporated into a household. Beneficent fetishes now, the scalps were considered potent rain makers. "We are going to have a little rain," the Keres say, "the scalps are crying."[40]

Finally, we see the cultural importance that feeding and sexual inter-course played in domesticating all those alien and dangerous forces out-side the pueblo in the deer butchering practices of the Acoma Indians. After the men killed a deer, usually through suffocation, they began the butchering by splitting open the deer's cavity. Then they removed the deer's penis, if it was male, or the vulva, if female, and placed the genitals in the stomach. This joining of genitals and stomach in a wild animal that is about to enter the village underscores the close symbolic association between sexuality and feeding. Women performed a similar rite for the deer when it entered the pueblo. First the women sexually taunted the dead deer with lewd speech, they "had" intercourse with it, fed it, and finally welcomed it into their home.[41]

The power women enjoyed by virtue of their control over the house-hold, feeding, and sexuality was rivaled by the power men enjoyed as a result of their control over the community's relationships with its gods, which made hunting, warfare, rain making, and trade possible. In fact, had Karl Marx known the sixteenth-century Pueblo Indians, his formula-tion of the base/superstructure relationship might have been inverted. Pueblo men would have told him that the religious superstructure un-questionably "determined" the economic base.[42]

"A man's place is outside of the house," Hopi women assert. As we saw, out in the fields they would bury a baby boy's umbilical cord, sig-nifying that that was the place for males. But this was the female's point of view. Men had a much more expansive notion of their space, which encompassed everything that was at the core and center of society, as well as everything that was outside and beyond it.[43]

Men's spatial location in village life correlated closely with their roles in the sexual division of labor. Three distinct but overlapping spaces were defined as masculine. The first zone was created through kinship and marriage obligations to women. Sons had to work their mothers' corn plots, brothers those of their sisters, husbands those of their mothers-in-law. "The men attend to the work in the cornfields," observed Gallegos in 1582. "The day hardly breaks before they go about with hoes in their hands." He continued: "The men bear burdens, but not the women." When wood was needed for the construction of a house or to stoke the cooking fires, the household's matriarch dispatched the men to "bring the firewood . . . and stack it up," noted Castañeda in 1540.[44]

The space outside and beyond the pueblo was authentically the province of men and gained meaning in opposition to the space men controlled at the symbolic center of the town. The male conceptualization of space outlined here comes from Pueblo origin myths. Bear in mind that such myths are products of the male imagination. They are sacred knowledge that men transmitted to other men and as such were profoundly political narratives. By outlining the organization of society in mythic times, detailing who helped whom emerge when and where, men asserted their spatial claims, their rights, and their precedence in their relationships both with women and with the members of other households and clans.[45]

The men of every pueblo considered their town to be the center of the universe and placed their main kiva at the vortex of a spatial scheme that extended outward to the four cardinal points, upward to the four skies above, and downward to the underworld. Kivas were usually round (sometimes square) subterranean structures that conjoined space and time to reproduce the sacred time of emergence. Located at the center of the kiva's floor was the *shipapu*, the earth's navel, through which the people emerged from the underworld and through which they would return.[46]

The kiva was circular to resemble the sky. A hole in the center of the roof, the only entrance and source of light, symbolized the opening through which the Corn Mothers climbed onto the earth's surface. The profane space outside and the sacred space within the kiva were connected by a ladder called "rainbow" made of the same pine tree the sisters had used to emerge. The kiva floor had a fire altar that commemorated the gift of fire, and a hollow, dug-out place that represented the door to the house of the Sun, the Moon, and the mountains of the four cardinal points. The walls had altars on which were placed stone fetishes representing all the animals and deities of the world. Around the entire base of the kiva was an elevated ledge covered with bear and lion skins known as "fog seats." When the spirits that lived outside the pueblo were invoked and came to participate in ceremonials, they sat on these. Men's claims to precedence over women lay precisely in this capacity to bring what was outside the village into its core during religious rituals, to communicate with the gods, and thereby to order and control an otherwise chaotic and hostile natural world.[47]

Radiating outward horizontally from the kiva toward the four cardinal points were a series of tetrads that demarcated the sacral topography. The outermost tetrad was formed by the horizontal mountain peaks in which the seasonal spirits lived. In between the horizon and the pueblo were the shrines of the outlying hills and mesas. Shrines were "heaps of small stones which nature [had] formed," reported Hernán Gallegos in 1582, or holes in the earth's surface that resembled navels. People "worshiped and offered sacrifices" at these places, said Diego Pérez de Luxán, when they were "weary from their journey or troubled with any other burdens." Within the town the tetrad was repeated as directional points that all ceremonial dance circuits touched. At the center of the pueblo, the kiva united the cosmic six directions. Men owned the kivas and the sacred fetishes, altars, masks, and ritual paraphernalia contained therein.[48]

The kiva, as the navel that tied the people with their gods, was the physical symbol of political society. Each pueblo was a theocracy. At the center of political life stood the cacique, the town chief or Inside Chief, who exercised broad authority over all matters. Around him stood men of superlative knowledge in hunting, warfare, medicine magic, and rain-conjuring who by virtue of their abilities had accumulated large followings as well as large amounts of gift-stuff with which they could stage communal rites and offer gifts to others on behalf of unsuccessful villagers. Next were the unsuccessful seniors, their veneration increasing with age. Young male aspirants to the religious knowledge that would translate into political power came next. And finally, at the margins, as men saw it, were women, children, slaves, and strays.[49]

The forces of dispersion that could destroy Pueblo society were centrifugal. The political discourse that religious ritual made possible was centripetal. Men mechanistically created cosmic harmony, a requisite for social peace, only by coming together in unison at the center. Junior men moved from the margins to the center to obtain the blessings and ritual knowledge that would bring them adult status, a wife, and social power. But unlike the path of the young toward the old, of the human toward the godly, which was symbolized by movement from the margins to the center, our journey through the male world of ritual goes in the opposite direction, from the center outward. This expository strategy helps us to localize social groups in space.

Presiding over the town's main kiva, the quasi-divine Inside Chief was simultaneously a lawgiver and a peacemaker, a war lord and a high priest. He symbolized cosmic harmony and the embodiment of those forces of attraction that constituted society. He conjoined the human and the divine, the cosmological and the political, the mythic and the historic, and organized those three functions on which Pueblo religio-political life depended: administration of the sacred, exercise of physical force, and control over well-being and fecundity.[50]

The Inside Chief controlled the sacred in Pueblo society. He was the town's chief priest, a direct descendant of the Sun, "the holder of all roads of men," and the person who brought order to an otherwise chaotic cosmos. The people "esteemed and venerated the sun above all things," said Hernando de Alarcón in 1540, "because it warmed them and made the seeds germinate." Associated with the sky's greatest deity, the cacique regulated life's rhythms and assured happiness, prosperity, and long life. Appropriately, the Zuñi town chief was called Sun Speaker (*Pekwin*), and the Hopi chief, Sun Watcher (*Tawawunitaka*).[51]

The religious system the Inside Chief administered was fundamentally monistic. Humans, animals, natural forces, and supernatural spirits were all intricately related in balanced ties of reciprocity. The cosmic harmony every person desired was subject to human mechanistic control. So long as people performed religious rites joyfully and precisely, careful that every prayer was word-perfect and full of verve, and that the ritual paraphernalia was exact to the last detail, the forces of nature would reciprocate with their own uninterrupted flow. The sun would rise and set properly, the seasons of the year would come and go, bringing rainfall and verdant crops in summer, and in the winter, game and snow.[52]

The cacique's central imperative was to keep the cosmos properly balanced so that humanity did not swerve from life's road. So long as the forces of evil that threatened to disrupt society were rendered impotent through ritual, peace and prosperity reigned. The Inside Chief accomplished this by calling together the men in the town's households and clans for ritual purposes and by acting as arbiter of law and order. As high priest, the cacique was the keeper of sacred time. From the heights of the town's dwellings he watched the courses of the sun and moon and with amazing accuracy announced the summer and winter solstices, the vernal and autumnal equinoxes, and all the dates for planting, harvest, initiations, and rain and curing rites. At appropriate points in the lunar year, the cacique entered the town's main kiva, and by ritually recreating the primordial time of emergence when humans and gods were one, and when all a town's clans, kivas, and esoteric societies were in harmony, he temporarily obliterated local enmities and tensions.[53]

Through these ceremonials (which women could watch but not participate in) the Inside Chief integrated the town into one communal whole. The fragmenting pull of clan, lineage, and household affiliations were suspended as each clan, village-wide kiva, and esoteric society (for example, hunt, war, rain, and medicine societies) contributed its special role to a ceremony or performed a certain dance in a dance complex. According to Gallegos, an ethos of unity prevailed at the ceremonies the town chief staged:

[T]he dancers rise and execute their movements, revolving to the rhythm of the music like clowns. They raise their hands toward the sun and sing in their language, with the cadence of the dance, "ayia canima." This they do with much unity and harmony, in such a way that though there are three hundred savages in a dance, it seems as if it were being sung and danced by one man only, due to the fine harmony and measure of their performance.[54]

Gifting and feasting were vital aspects of Pueblo ceremonialism. When the katsina were called, or when the hunt, war, rain, or curing deities were invoked, large amounts of food were offered to them by village chiefs so that they would reciprocate with blessings and success. The food collected at these events was shared by everyone. Modern investigators have discovered a clear relationship between the timing of rituals and the yearly food supply of most households. From January to March, when food reserves are lowest, the greatest number of communal redistributive rituals occur.[55]

The cacique's frequent promotion of communal peace through ritual was necessary because fragmentation constantly threatened to tear society asunder. Generations of anthropologists have long interpreted the Pueblo ideology of harmony and equilibrium as statements of fact rather than as a denial of man's greatest fear. If cosmic harmony was indeed the normal state of affairs, as Ruth Benedict and others thought, why the constant need to create ceremonial harmony? The answer lies in an inversion of the formula: factionalism was the normal state of affairs, and ceremonial harmony was the ideal men tried to create. Each pueblo was an aggregation of matrilineages, each with its own rituals, fetishes, and patron deities. Marital exogamy and cross-cutting lineage affiliations in kiva and esoteric societies fostered village integration. But in times of stress, whether caused by political, social, or environmental factors, communities splintered along lineage and household lines, leading to those town abandonments and population dispersals which were so rife in the Pueblo world between 1250 and 1600.[56]

If the Inside Chief's administration of the sacred was a harmonizing power, the antithesis—violence, human domination, and the negation of the community's moral order, what we will call physical force—was in the hands of the Outside Chiefs, war chiefs who protected the village from external, natural, and supernatural enemies.[57]

Protecting the village from enemies was perhaps the Outside Chiefs' most important duty. A decade rarely went by without war over women, land, water, salt, turquoise, or hunting grounds. A village with an abundant supply of any of these resources was always at risk of losing them. The threat was met in part by constructing impenetrable fortress-like towns. From the heights of the towns the war chiefs could easily spot intruders and marshal their defenses. The war chiefs also participated in hunts, salt expeditions, wood-gathering trips, and visits to sacred springs for waters. When a foreign bride entered a pueblo, it was the war chiefs who escorted her.[58]

The Outside Chiefs were the divine sons of Father Sun, Masewi (Wren Youth) and Oyoyewi (Mockingbird Youth), also known as the Twin War Gods, say the Acoma Indians. The Twins were conceived miraculously when an ordinary woman ate two pine nuts the Sun gave her. As youngsters the Twins were fearless warriors, roving the countryside, causing mischief, terrorizing others, and killing with those instruments of war their father had given them: bows, arrows, and flint arrowheads.[59]

The mythic tales of the Twin War Gods explained the use of force in Pueblo life. Physical force was born of the godhead through an act of copulation with a woman who represented the land's people. The sons were of their father's essence but were also his antithesis. At the center of society such brutish and terrorizing boys would have wreaked havoc. And so they were pushed to the peripheries as the Outside Chiefs to rule over all that was outside of the village. There, their violence befitted external threats to tranquillity. Localizing functions and social groups in space, we find that warfare was conceived of as marginal, young, and outside the pueblo, while the sacred was at the center, old, and inside the town.

The power of the Twin War Gods and their human personifications, the Outside Chiefs, was likened to the forces of nature. Astronomically, they were portrayed as falling stars, comets, and particularly Morning Star—all war symbols. Lightning and thunder were their arrows, sources both of destruction and germination. The Twins "made canyons with lightning, made mountain and rocks," explain the Hopi. When the earth was still a watery void they "cut channels through which the waters rushed away, wearing their courses deeper and deeper, thus forming the great canyons and valleys of the world."[60]

How was the Outside Chiefs' violence domesticated for community life? The problem is an important one because the war chiefs lived among their people and performed vital functions within their towns. The Acoma Indians say that because the Twins killed impetuously, without regard for the sanctity of life, the directional deities punished them. The boys and the gods were reconciled only when the boys promised to respect life and to perform the scalp dance every time they returned home from war with the heads, hearts, and scalps of enemy dead. As we saw, during the scalp dance females transformed the malevolent spirits of the enemy dead into beneficent community members through intercourse and feeding.[61]

Warfare was the most generalized masculine task in Pueblo society. Before boys could become men, they had to establish themselves as competent warriors. To do this, young men sought out a "warrior father" (usually the war chief or Outside Chief) of great bravery and skill to teach them the prayers, songs, dances, and esoteric lore that would give them power over enemies. Through offering the warrior father numerous gifts, aspiring warriors were gradually taught how to harness the power of the prey animals for success in battle. I want to emphasize the word gradually here, because knowledge was power, and as such it was in the interest of the warrior father to dispense his knowledge slowly. By so doing he maintained a large following and acquired numerous gifts with which he could indebt others and gather the means to stage large raids.[62]

Besides the town's main kiva, male ritual associations devoted to war, curing, hunting, and rain-making each had its own kiva that doubled as a lodge house. Warrior novices lived in the warrior society kiva and there their warrior father taught them bravery, endurance, and agility. Before the arrival of European horses in the Southwest, all warfare was conducted on foot, so running fast was also a cultivated skill.[63]

When men practiced war magic they had to have pure minds and hearts. For the four days before and after war, they refrained from sexual intercourse and purified themselves with sweat baths and emetic drinks. Offering smokes to the war gods and singing war songs, they prayed for success. To obtain the ferocity and strength of bears, the cunning of lions, and the sharp vision of eagles, the warriors took their war fetishes shaped in the likeness of animals, bathed them in human blood and fed them pieces of human hearts that had been torn from the breasts of enemies in previous victories. When all the ritual preparations for warfare were complete, the warriors marched into battle.[64]

Once a young man had proven himself by killing an enemy he was inducted into the warrior society through an ordeal. The Zuñi Bow War Society required its initiates to sit naked atop a large ant hill for a day and submit stolidly to the insects' bites. Members of the Hopi, Zuñi, and Tewa Cactus War societies whipped themselves with cacti. Such a be-numbing ordeal also marked the installation of a war chief.[65]

The opposing forces harmonized by the town chieftaincy—Inside Chief versus Outside Chiefs, center versus margin, old versus young, native versus foreign, law versus force—were dependent on the existence of fecundity and well-being. This third essential component of religious life was controlled competitively by three chieftaincies: the rain chiefs, the hunt chiefs, and the medicine men.

The chiefs who directed the hunt, rain, and medicine societies knew well the godly transmitted mysteries of life and death. Women might know the life-giving secrets of Mother Earth, seeds, and child-bearing, but through ritual men controlled the key to the positive and negative reciprocities in their world, which at any moment could be turned to life or death. The heart (which contained the breath and spirit of humans, animals, and deities) and blood were the symbols of the rituals staged by men to assure communal peace and fertility. Just as feeding was a central part of female ritual, so too men regularly gave life to their fetishes, bathing them in nourishing blood and symbolically feeding them bits of heart. Men also fed the earth with their own blood, whipping themselves crimson when they sought those blessings that assured fertility.

Rain was the Pueblo Indians' central preoccupation and the essential ingredient for fecundity. Men recognized that Mother Earth and women had immense capacities to bring forth life, but to realize this potential the sky had to fructify the earth with rain and men their wives with semen. Thus what the people worshipped most, said Hernando de Alarcón in 1540, was "the sun and water." Why did they worship water? According to Coronado it was "because it makes the maize grow and sustains their life, and that the only other reason they know is that their ancestors did so."[66]

The rain chief was one of the most powerful men in every village be-cause he knew how to conjure rain both by calling Horned Water Snake and the katsina. The Pueblos equated serpentine deities with rain. The Horned Water Serpent of the Pueblos united the vertical levels of the cos-mos. He lived both upon the earth and below it and so combined the masculine germinative forces of the sky (rain) with the feminine generative power of the earth (seeds). The phallic representations of Horned Water Snake were cloaked in feathers as a god of lightning and rain. The earliest Pueblo rock drawings depict him as a zigzag line with a horned triangular head and as a lightning snake attached to a cloud burst.[67]

Horned Water Serpent was also feminine and lunar. "Sun is male, Moon is female," maintain the Acoma Indians. The serpent's ability to shed its skin and to be born anew undoubtedly resembled the moon's birth and death every 28 days. In decorative motifs the measured zigzags of the lightning snake and the coiled spiral of the rattlesnake evoked those rhythms governed by the moon: the rains, the agricultural calendar, and a woman's menstrual flow. Water Serpent's horns, too, were lunar. Each horn represented the moon's crescent; with two, the lunar cycle was complete.[68]

Horned Water Serpent, then, provided the Pueblo Indians with fecundity and abundance by joining together the levels of the cosmos (sky/earth, earth/underworld) and social existence (male/female, life/death).[69]

The Pueblo Dead—the katsina—were also potent rain spirits tied to the living in bonds of reciprocity. It was the rain chief who knew how to call the katsina and did so by offering them prayer sticks and gifts, asking them to visit with rain, food, and fertility. Katsina lived at the place of emergence underneath lakes and on mountain tops. Missives to the katsina were dispatched as puffs of smoke, which as mimetic magic beckoned the cloud spirits to visit. At death Puebloans became clouds. That is why to this day the Hopi harangue their dead saying: "You are no longer a Hopi, you are a Cloud. When you get yonder you will tell the chief to hasten the rain clouds hither."[70]

The worship of the katsina was a model for generational reciprocities and an integrative cult, in that it cross-cut household and lineage affiliations and tied the town as a whole together. Katsina initiation for youth also marked the clear inception of differentiation of male and female roles. At Acoma, katsina initiation occurred during the winter solstice. To call the katsina, the men entered the town's main kiva and for four days prayed, sang, offered smokes, and made prayer sticks. Prayer sticks were six to twelve inches long, each painted with a human face and cloaked in feathers. Like the birds who were messengers between humans and gods, the feathered prayer sticks called the katsina.[71]

On the fourth day, the prayer sticks were offered to the katsina. Then the katsina initiates awaited Tsitsanits, the ruler of the katsina, in the main kiva. Brandishing a whip, Tsitsanits entered and struck each child four times until he drew blood. He attached a turkey feather to each child's hair and gave each a clan name. After the children received gifts from the katsina, they were told about how the katsina and the people had once fought because the young did not show them respect, about how much life had been lost, and about the calamities that would befall them if they showed the Cloud Spirits disrespect.[72]

With katsina initiation boys left their maternal household and moved into the masculine world of the kiva, where they gradually learned how to communicate with the spirits and gods by offering gifts to successful seniors. The knowledge gained was essential in keeping the fragile forces of the cosmos properly balanced. Castañeda observed in 1541 that the "young men live in the estufas [kivas]. . . . [I]t is punishable for the women to sleep in the estufas or to enter them for any other purpose than to bring food to their husbands or sons." Diego Pérez de Luxán reiterated the point in 1582, as did Fray Jerónimo Zárate de Salmerón when he wrote in 1623: "The women and young children sleep in [houses]; the men sleep in the *kiva*." Father Zárate implied that even after marriage, men continued to sleep in the kivas. This was not necessarily so. At marriage men moved into their mother-in-law's home. If the marriage failed and "a man repudiates his wife, he must come [return] to the estufa [*kiva*]," added Castañeda.[73]

Besides calling the katsina, the rain chief also staged the Snake Dance. The symbol of the rain chieftaincy was an eagle perched on a cactus devouring a serpent—what we now recognize as the Mexican national symbol. The eagle was the strongest bird in the sky; the serpent a water deity; the cactus a purificatory agent, a source of moisture in the desert, and its tunas symbols of human hearts on which the gods fed. The Snake Dance was "performed to bring rain . . . for their cornfields," explained a Hopi to Gallegos in 1582. Another said that the dance was "for rain to fall to water the earth, that planted things may ripen and grow large; that the male element of the Above, the *Ye*, may impregnate the female earth virgin, *Naasun*."[74]

Preparation for the Snake Dance began with the rain chief and his assistants purifying their bodies through emesis and flagellation—the pain serving as a route to ecstasy and the holy. Describing a Snake Dance in 1582, Gallegos noted that the participants flagellated themselves with cactus pods and then whipped the "lord" until they "drew blood, making him look like a flagellant. . . . [T]hey continue to dance and to give him . . . lashes until they make the blood flow as if he is being bled." Pueblo bloodletting performed two functions. Scientists today understand that the massive loss of blood can induce hallucinations. The delirium of such states allowed ritual celebrants to transcend their daily existence and enjoy close contact with the gods. The blood men ritually shed was also deemed a nutrient. In the beginning, say the Acoma Indians, the world was created from a clot of blood shed by Father Sun. From the Pueblos south to the Maya, bloodletting was tied to rulership and the mythology of cosmic order. As previously noted, the ritual accession of Pueblo war chiefs was marked by bloodletting. At every important religious event, men shed blood by flagellating themselves, by lacerating their penes, or by cutting incisions into various parts of their body, thus feeding the gods and expressing piety. Blood shed from the penis was particularly nourishing because it would bring rain.[75]

The focus of the Snake Dance observed by Gallegos in 1582 was on two large snakes that were kept specifically for this dance.

[T]he lord . . . takes them, and they creep up his arms and over his body, making a great deal of noise with their rattles, until they reach his throat. Then the flayed one rises and swings around quickly. The snakes fall to the ground, where they coil and are picked up by those who brought them. Kneeling, the two Indians put the reptiles in their mouths, and disappear through a little doorway.

The snake/rain, phallus/semen symbolism of the dance horrified the Europeans. One missionary fixated on the ceremonial fellatio performed on the rain chief; another on the snake wrestling, which ended when the snake "fondled his private."[76]

After warfare, hunting was the broadest male task in Pueblo society. Thus, after katsina initiation young men entered a hunt society. Men contributed meat to the maize diet at every pueblo, but it was at those villages dependent exclusively on rainfall for crop irrigation that hunting magic was most important. Boys learned hunting techniques by observing renowned hunters and by listening to their animal stories. When a boy killed his first rabbit, he was initiated into a hunt society and apprenticed to a hunt father who gradually taught him the prayers, songs, and magical ways of the hunt in return for gifts of corn and meat. The novice became a full member of the society when he captured a large game animal (deer, antelope, or mountain sheep). If by chance he killed a prey animal (bear, lion, or eagle), he automatically became a member of the warrior society, because hunting and warfare were considered very similar activities.[77]

Hunting practices for rabbit, antelope, deer, and buffalo were all very similar. We focus here on deer hunting because deer meat was the most abundant and highly prized, and because men thought of women as two-legged deer. A deer hunt was organized whenever food reserves were low, when a ceremonial was to be staged, or when the katsina were going to visit.

For four days the hunt chief led the hunt society's members in song, prayer, prayer-stick making, and smokes. During this time the eldest male of each household brought his lineage "offspring" animal fetish to the kiva and placed it next to the hunt chief's "mother" fetish on the society's altar. There the hunt chief empowered the fetishes with animal spirits for a successful hunt by bathing them in nourishing blood and feeding them small bits of the animal they were going to hunt. These fetishes contained the living heart and breath of the animals they depicted. When the hunt chief empowered them, he unleashed the fetish's heart and breath. The fetish's breath immediately pierced the heart of the hunted animal, sapped its soul's energy and immobilized it. In this state the hunted animal was easily overcome.[78]

During these four days, and for four days after the hunt, men were sexually continent. Hunters believed that animals disliked the smell of women and would not allow themselves to be captured by a man so contaminated. To rid himself of such odor, a hunter purified his body with emetic drinks and smokes. If a man was to accomplish his goal, neither his mind nor his heart could be dissipated by the thought of women.[79]

The hunt began on the fourth day. Transformed into the animals they hunted, the hunters donned deerskins with the head and antlers still attached. The hunt chief selected the hunting ground and dispersed the men around its edges, forming a large circle. Slowly the circumference of the circle tightened and the deer became exhausted. Finally the deer were wrestled to the ground and choked. A deer was suffocated so that its breath and spirit would be reborn as more game, and because only the skins of suffocated animals could be used as hunt costumes.[80]

The deer was immediately skinned and disemboweled. First its heart was cut out and its blood was fed to the animal fetishes the hunters carried in their pouches. Next the stomach was removed and opened. If a doe, its vulva was placed in the stomach and sprinkled with corn pollen; if a buck, the penis and testicles were similarly treated. The carcass was then carried back to the pueblo, where it was adopted into the hunter's maternal household through ritual intercourse and ritual feeding. "We are glad you have come to our home and have not been ashamed of our people," Acoma's women would tell the deer as they offered it cornmeal. The hunter's relatives rubbed their hands over the deer's body and then across their own faces to obtain its beauty and strength. Finally, the hunter purified himself with juniper smoke so that the deer spirit would not haunt him. The meat was divided between the hunt chief who had taught the boy how to hunt and the hunter's household of affiliation.[81]

A pueblo's prosperity was fundamentally dependent on the physical and psychological well-being of its members. Thus every village had several *chaianyi*, medicine men who cured illnesses and exorcised disease-causing witches who robbed human hearts of their breath and spirit. As knowledgeable herbalists, the *chaianyi* cured minor ailments; but if a disease seemed unique, longlasting, or particularly debilitating, witchcraft was its cause. Witches wrought calamities and illnesses by shooting objects into the body of their victim or by stealing their heart. Using tactics similar to those of hunters, witches sapped people of their strength by attacking their heart. Since witches plied their craft disguised as animals, medicine men had to fight them as animals. That is why *chaianyi* were known as bears (the fiercest animal humans knew) and their magic as "bear medicine." In such form medicine men could help people regain their health, winning back their heart and sucking out the objects shot into them by the witch.[82]

When an individual or a community was afflicted by disease, a cure by the medicine man known to have power over that illness was requested through gifts. For four days the medicine man prepared himself, smoking, making prayer-sticks, reciting the necessary prayers and songs, and abstaining from meat, salt, and sex. He made offerings at appropriate shrines, obtained water for medicines from sacred springs, erected an altar, and arranged on it fetishes, medicine bowls, and curing paraphernalia. When all was ready, the sick individual was placed on the floor before the altar. Near the patient, the medicine man made a circular sand painting representing all the powerful forces in the cosmos. Then, to obtain the power to cure from the "real" medicine men, the animals, he prayed to the bear fetish for the power of all the animals on earth, to the eagle fetish for the power of the animals in the air, and to the weasel fetish for the power of the animals in the ground. Each of these fetishes was fed and bathed in blood from the heart of the animal they represented. Wearing a bear claw necklace with four claws, and holding eagle plumes in each hand, the medicine man "whipped away" the disease with cutting motions. If a quartz crystal with which the person's body was examined revealed foreign objects, the medicine man sucked them out. If the patient's heart had been stolen, the *chaianyi* fought with the witches to retrieve it. When the ceremony ended, the patient drank medicines and returned home cured. If for some reason the patient died, the presumption was that the ceremony had not been properly conducted or that the *chaianyi*'s heart was impure.[83]

In sum, entering male ceremonialism from the edges and moving toward the center, we first find the chiefs who controlled well-being and fertility (rain, hunt, and medicine chiefs), then the Outside Chiefs who organized physical force, and finally at the core the Inside Chief who represented the sacred powers of attraction that constituted political society. Through apprenticeship in a town's various societies, junior men gradually learned the religious knowledge they needed to assure prosperity and guarantee their personal advance to senior status. Religious knowledge allowed men to harness and control those natural forces outside the pueblo, which the gods ruled, and to bring them peacefully into the core; it gave them the power to kill, and by so doing assured life. By carefully executing prescribed ritual formulas, they preserved the relationship of reciprocity that existed between men and the spirit world and kept the fragile structure of the cosmos intact.

Men envisioned a cosmos in which masculinity and femininity were relatively balanced. But the social world really was not so. In a largely horticultural society women asserted and could prove that they had enormous control and power over seed production, child-rearing, household construction, and the earth's fertility. Men admitted this. But they made a counterclaim that men's ability to communicate with the gods and to control life and death protected the precarious balance in the universe by forestalling village factionalism and dissent. The tendency of women to overproduce had to be properly controlled through the religious activities of men. Women's voraciousness for semen and the earth's infinite capacity to soak up rain sapped masculinity of its potence. This was indeed the case, explains Jane Collier, regarding gender concepts in "equal bridewealth" societies. On a daily basis women appropriated men's vital energies: the crops they planted, the children they engendered, and the meat from their hunts. Men thus frequently renewed their energies by segregating themselves from women and staging ceremonials to assure successful hunts, war, curing, and rain-making. Because potent femininity polluted and rendered male magic impotent, men abstained from sex with women for a prescribed period before and after their rituals. It is easy to understand the roots of these gender concepts in the social division of labor. The ecological constraints of the habitat in which men pursued their productive activities made their world precarious. Who could predict defeat in battle, disease, factionalism, drought, or poor hunting? [84]

It is as part of this contestation between the sexes over the cosmic power of men and women, and the masculine assertion that ritual give them a dominant hand, that we can best understand the place and function of the "third sex" in Pueblo life, the half-men/half-women, as the natives still know them, or the berdache (from the Arabic *bradaj*, meaning male prostitute), as the sixteenth-century Europeans called them. [85]

The berdache were biological males who had assumed the dress, occupations, mannerisms, and sexual comportment of females as a result of a sacred vision or community selection. Hernando de Alarcón in 1540 observed that in those villages where he found berdaches, they numbered four. Four was a sacred number to the Pueblo Indians; there were four horizontal directions, four seasons, four lengths to Wenimats, four days of preparation before ritual, etc. Alarcón was told that if one of the four berdaches died, "a search was made for all the pregnant women in the land, and the first born was chosen to exercise the function of women. The women dressed them in their clothes, saying that if they were to act as such they should wear their clothes."[86] Alvar Núñez Cabeza de Vaca observed berdaches during his 1523–33 trek across Texas and New Mexico: "I saw one man married to another and these are impotent, effeminate men and they go about dressed as women, and do women's tasks, and shoot with a bow, and carry great burdens . . . and they are huskier than the other men and taller."[87]

That the berdache were consistently described as men abnormally tall and heavy led Fray Juan Agustín de Morfi in the 1770s and Dr. William A. Hammond, the U.S. Surgeon-General, in the 1850s to wonder if they were intersexuals. Morfi pondered the matter and admitted uncertainty; Hammond uncovered the "facts," examining the genitals of an Acoma and a Laguna berdache. To Hammond's amazement, neither was a hermaphrodite. Both had large mammary glands, scant pubic hair, small penises ("no larger than a thimble," "not . . . over an inch in length"), and small testicles ("the size of a small filbert," "about the size of a kidney bean"). More significant were the comments Hammond elicited from the Acoma berdache: "He told me that he had nursed several infants whose mothers had died, and that he had given them plenty of milk from his breasts. I expressed my doubts of the truth of this assertion, but he persisted with vehemence that it was true . . . he informed me with evident pride, [that he] possessed a large penis and his testicles were 'grandes como huevos'—as large as eggs." Despite the physiological realities, the Acoma berdache believed herself (she was always referred to with the feminine pronoun) to possess the reproductive capacities of both male and female. Rising above the basic dualities that structured the world, she symbolized the coincidentia oppositorum, the joining of opposites that men created in ritual.[88]

Pre-menopausal women polluted male ritual and were thus excluded from active participation in all kiva-centered ceremonials. According to Gallegos, when men gathered to renew the universe or to recreate primordial time "only the men take part, the women never." The participants in these rituals "wore the masks and dress of both men and women even though they were all men," attested Don Esteban Clemente in 1660, even to the point of smearing the insides of their legs with rabbit blood to resemble menstrual discharge.[89]

Ritual female impersonators may not all have been berdaches, but the historical evidence does seem to indicate this. On the basis of the berdaches' role in Pueblo ritual we see again the male assertion that they controlled all aspects of human life. Women had power only over half of creation; through ritual men controlled its entirety—male and female—and were thus equal if not superior to women. Women obviously contested this claim.

The emphasis male ritual placed on village cooperation and social peace also explains in purely functional terms the meaning of the berdache. As sacred half-man/half-woman who conjoined all that was male and female, she was a living symbol of cosmic harmony. Castañeda witnessed a boy's initiation as a berdache in 1540 and described how the women endowed him with female clothing, turquoises, and bracelets.

Then the dignitaries came in to make use of her one at a time, and after them all the others who cared to. From then on she was not to deny herself to any one, as she was paid a certain established amount for the service. And even though she might take a husband later on, she was not thereby free to deny herself to any one who offered her pay.

Alarcón added that the berdaches who dressed and behaved like women "could not have carnal relations with women at all, but they themselves could be used by all marriageable youths. . . . They receive no compensation for this work . . . although they were free to take from any house what they needed for their living." As noted earlier, bachelors were residentially segregated in kivas until they married, ostensibly to master male esoteric lore, but also to minimize conflicts between juniors and seniors over claims to female sexuality that adult married men enjoyed. Sex with a berdache served a personal erotic need and a religious (political) end. So long as bachelors were having sex with the half-man/half-woman, the social peace they represented was not beset with village conflicts between men over women. This may have been why the Spaniards called the berdaches *putos* (male whores). European prostitutes initiated young men to sexuality and gave married men a sexual outlet without disrupting family, marriage, or patrimony.[90]

These, then, were the contours of Pueblo Indian society in the sixteenth century. Each pueblo was an aggregation of sedentary horticulturists living in extended matrilineal households, supplementing their existence through hunting and warfare. Elders controlled the organization of production and, through the distribution of its fruits as gifts and ritual blessings, perpetuated the main inequalities of life; the inequality between juniors and seniors and between successful and unsuccessful seniors. The household and all the activities symbolically related to it belonged to women; the kivas and the pueblo's relationships with its gods was the province of men. That said, we turn in Chapter 2 to discuss the arrival of the Spanish conquistadores in 1538 from the Indian point of view.

PART II

   The Seventeenth Century

2

The Spanish Conquest of
New Mexico

The Black Katsina Arrives

In May of 1539, as preparations were being made to call the katsina
to bring rain, the Zuñi warriors of Hawikuh spotted a black katsina
approaching from the west. The katsina was unlike any they had ever
seen before. He was large in stature, wore animal pelts, and was richly
adorned with large pieces of turquoise. He "wore bells and feathers on
his ankles and arms, and carried plates of various colors." Many Pima,
Papago, Opata, and Tarahumara Indians accompanied the katsina. They
called him Estevanico, a great healer and medicine man. The men showered him with gifts, and the women, hoping to obtain his blessings, gave
him their bodies. All along Estevanico's route, he constructed large prayer-
sticks (crosses) that he commanded everyone to worship.[1]

Hawikuh's cacique awaited the arrival of the black giant with great
foreboding. While still a day's distance from the village, Estevanico sent
the town chief a red and white feathered gourd rattle and a message that
"he was coming to establish peace and to heal them." When the chief saw
the rattle, he became very angry and threw it to the ground saying, "I
know these people, for these jingle bells are not the shape of ours. Tell
them to turn back at once, or not one of their men will be spared."[2]

Undaunted by what his messengers told him, Estevanico proceeded to
Hawikuh. The road to the village was closed symbolically with a cornmeal line, and when the black katsina crossed it, the pueblo's warriors
took him prisoner and confined him in a house outside the village. There,
"the oldest and those in authority listened to his words and tried to learn
the reason for his coming." The katsina told them that other white katsina, children of the Sun, would soon arrive. The cacique thought these

words were crazy, and when Estevanico demanded turquoise and women, he had him killed as a witch and foreign spy.[3]

The old men of the village huddled together in the kiva, pondering the meaning of what had been said and done. Repeatedly they asked, Who was this black katsina? Whence had he come? What did he want? Would more katsina shortly arrive, as Estevanico said? The old men were silent on these matters, as were the ancient myths. The answers to these questions would be found not in the Pueblo world but in a distant land across a sea in a place the black katsina called Castile. To that European kingdom we turn to learn more about these god-like creatures who appeared on Hawikuh's horizon in 1539.

Granada, Spain, 1492

On the morning of January 2, 1492, on the rim of the valley overlooking the Iberian city of Granada, at a place still called *El Sospiro del Moro*, stood Boabdil, Granada's last Moorish king. Etching the city's beauty in his memory through tear-filled eyes, he watched as a large silver cross was raised over the city and Christian military banners were unfurled on its walls. "You do well to weep like a woman for what you failed to defend like a man," Boabdil's mother told her son. Hours earlier he had surrendered the Alhambra, his palace, and marched outside the city's walls to submit to King Ferdinand of Aragón and to show obeisance to the king's wife, Queen Isabella of Castile.[4]

Boabdil's sad submission was a sweet victory for Ferdinand and Isabella, who through their 1469 marriage had united the crowns of the kingdoms of Aragón and Castile and thus amassed the fervor, the will, and the manpower to storm the infidel's last stronghold at Granada. Since 711 when Moorish armies swept across the Straits of Gibraltar and conquered the Iberian peninsula as far north as the Pyrenees, the Christian faithful had fought from their mountain havens in Asturias and slowly pushed the boundaries of Islam back to the south. For nearly eight centuries the Christians were at war with the Moors. Known as the *Reconquista*, these centuries of warfare were a series of expansive pulsations propelled by population pressures and a hunger for booty, constrained by geography and Muslim military might, and interspersed by periods of quiescence and coexistence. Through crusades and *cabalgadas* (hit-and-run raids), the Christians first plundered the infidel's domain, taking lands, livestock, gold, and slaves. Next, Christian culture and institutions were implanted, and when territory was sufficiently secure and new population pressures again mounted, another southward thrust onto the Moorish frontier began.[5]

The monumental fight against the infidel ended with the vanquishment of Islam in 1492. But habits of warfare forged over centuries die slow, wrote Francisco López de Gómara in 1523, and since the Spanish had long fought infidels, "the conquest of the Indies began when that of the Moors was over." Fate had it that Christopher Columbus, the man who extended the medieval epic of the Reconquest from the Old World to the New, witnessed Boabdil's submission, and shortly thereafter won royal support for his proposal to reach the Orient by sailing west across the sea. On August 2, 1492, Columbus set sail on an odyssey that many believed would end in the abyss. Braving those uncharted expanses of ocean which the medieval *mappae mundi* filled with fantastical beings— pygmies, giants, Amazons, and various headless creatures—Columbus reached the Bahamas on October 12 and from there sailed on to the island he named Española (Hispaniola).[6]

From Hispaniola the continents of North and South America were soon discovered. The stories of wealth and fantastic things to be found in the New World quickly filtered back to the Old, inflaming imaginations steeped in the mythical kingdoms and utopias of chivalric romance. Feverish with dreams of fame and fortune, flushed with the courage of errant knights, and guided by a determination to propagate their faith, Spaniards left Iberia to conquer the New World.[7]

The quests for gold, vassals, and souls were all realized. In 1519, Hernán Cortés, with a band of 400 soldiers of fortune, left Cuba for the eastern coast of Mexico and by 1521 had conquered America's richest empire, the Aztec state in the Valley of Mexico. From there adventurers departed in all directions, seeking for themselves the "other Mexicos" that legend held were still to be won. In 1521 Luis Marín went south to the land of Oaxaca. Pedro Alvarado ventured into Guatemala in 1523, and from there with Francisco Pizarro staged the 1532 conquest of the Inca Empire in Peru. Nuño de Guzmán, the first president of Mexico City's Audiencia, pushed north into the present-day Mexican states of Nayarit, Jalisco, and Sinaloa in 1529, cutting a bloody trail of depredation.

The dream of finding a new and more magnificent Mexico to the north seemed to materialize in March 1536. Nuño de Guzmán, out on a slaving raid in the valley of the Río Sinaloa, spotted four ragged Europeans. The four—Alvar Núñez Cabeza de Vaca, Alonso de Castillo Maldonado, Andrés Dorantes, and his black slave Estevanico—were the sole survivors of the aborted 1528 Narváez expedition to colonize Florida.

When their project failed they tried to return to Cuba on makeshift rafts but instead landed near Galveston, Texas. For the next six years the expedition's survivors traveled west across Texas and into the Rio Grande Valley just north of El Paso, skirting the headwaters of the Gila River in southern Arizona and finally turning south into Sinaloa where Guzmán encountered them. Cabeza de Vaca told Guzmán that the Ures Indians to the north had given him "five emerald arrowheads" and had described "towns of great populations and great houses." The significance of the "emeralds" (probably malachite) and the cities was immediately understood. Were these the Seven Golden Cities of Antilla (with its capital of Cíbola) told of by the sages?[8]

Hernán Cortés thought so and immediately set sail up the Pacific Coast in search of the Seven Cities. Viceroy Antonio de Mendoza also wanted to claim them and enlisted Fray Marcos de Niza, a Franciscan friar who had witnessed the conquest of Peru, to travel north to Cíbola. Fray Marcos left Culiacán, Mexico's northernmost outpost, on March 7, 1539, with the slave Estevanico as his guide. The company moved slowly, and on March 23, 1539, Estevanico rushed ahead to reconnoiter the country, promising to mark his path with crosses of varying sizes to indicate the magnitude of his discoveries. Every day Fray Marcos progressed, he was overcome with enthusiasm as he encountered larger and larger crosses. One day's distance from Cíbola (Hawikuh), Fray Marcos encountered Estevanico's companions fleeing from the town. They reported that Estevanico had been killed as a witch at Cíbola. They had barely escaped and would not accompany the friar any farther. Fray Marcos nonetheless pushed forward and on June 5 beheld Cíbola, writing in his journal that it was "a very beautiful city . . . bigger than the city of Mexico."[9]

Back in Mexico City by September 1539, Fray Marcos described a kingdom more magnificent than either Mexico or Peru. Every time he told of Cíbola's wealth, its splendor grew. And every time the tale was repeated, it was embellished even more, until there was no alternative but to conquer the Seven Cities of Gold. On January 6, 1540, Viceroy Antonio de Mendoza dispatched Francisco Vásquez de Coronado, the 29-year-old governor of Nueva Galicia, to conquer Cíbola. The expedition left Compostela in central Mexico in late February 1540 amid great jubilation and pageantry. It was, wrote Pedro de Castañeda, "the most brilliant company ever assembled in the Indies to go in search of new lands." Coronado was accompanied by Fray Marcos de Niza, 292 soldiers of European origin, 800 Mexican Indian allies, and enough livestock on the hoof to feed them all. With Coronado's departure, New

Spain's population sighed a breath of relief. Gone were the troublesome "young and idle persons" who had come to the New World seeking fame and fortune and "had nothing to do but eat and loaf." [10]

The expedition took over a month to reach Culiacán. Hardships and hunger constantly plagued the soldiers, and they began to grumble and curse. The road was not "level and good" as Fray Marcos had promised, nor was it paved with gold. But all the friar had to say was that he was leading them "to a land where they could fill their hands with wealth," and their nerves were calmed. At Culiacán Coronado divided his troops into two groups and pushed forward with Fray Marcos and 50 horsemen, leaving the slower infantry to trail behind. When, on July 7, 1540, they finally reached Cíbola in western New Mexico, Coronado was profoundly disappointed. Fray Marcos had "not told the truth in a single thing." [11]

The Katsina Return

The spirits of winter, spring, and summer had showered the Pueblos with happiness and prosperity. As they prepared to call the katsina to give them thanks for their crops in July 1540, strange messengers approached from the west carrying the prayer-stick (cross) of an unknown katsina. Speaking unintelligible words, the messengers indicated through signs that the katsina would soon arrive. [12]

The katsina approached amid a cloud of dust. The earth shook, the heavens showered fire (gunfire), large stones were hurled through the air like hail (stone mortars), and strange birds shrieked a deafening cry (trumpets). Riding atop ferocious monsters (horses), the katsina were bedecked in the sun's glittering radiance (gilded armor) and were crowned with feathers (plumed helmets). "Who were these gods?," the Indians along the route asked. Had they "sprung from the water or earth or descended from the sky"? One katsina (Pedro de Alarcón) pointed to the sun and said, "I came from the sun . . . I am its son." The old men did not believe him and asked, "how the sun could send [him] when it was high in the sky and never stopped"? The katsina explained "that it was true that the sun was high above and never stopped, but that they could see that at sunset and sunrise it came close to the earth where it dwelt; that they could always see it rise in the same place; that the sun had created me in that land where it rose." On hearing this the Indians "took maize and other grains in their mouths and sprinkled" the katsina with them, saying that this "was the way they offered sacrifice to the sun." [13]

Hawikuh's residents had been warned with smoke signals of the gods' approach and awaited them in fear. The Outside Chiefs greeted the kat-sina with "coldness . . . and mean faces" at the outskirts of town. When the katsina crossed the cornmeal line that closed the road, the Zuñis cut loose with a rain of arrows, lances, and stones. The Indians proved no match for the armored, gun-carrying horsemen, who charged to the battle-cry "Santiago." Within hours they commanded the town. That night the soldiers ate like hungry dogs, and as the Indians watched this, they wondered if the strange katsina truly were gods.[14]

The surrounding Pueblos waited fearfully, knowing that the mighty Zuñis had been conquered by "very fierce men who rode animals that ate people." The katsina demanded food and clothes and killed with light-ning sticks (harquebuses) the "sun had given [them] . . . which roared a great deal and spat fire." Everywhere the people were terrified by the loud report of these sticks and fell to the ground as if stunned. The Indians approached each monster (horse) with trepidation and spoke to it "as if it were a person." They "rubbed their bodies against the animals' haunches, raising their hands to heaven and blowing toward the sky," thus imparting a prayer that the monsters not hurt them. Before the prayer-stick (cross) the katsina constructed, the natives offered "powders [sacred cornmeal] and feathers, some even the blankets they were wearing. They did it with such eagerness that some climbed on the backs of others in order to reach the arms of the crosses to put plumes and roses on them. Others brought ladders, and while some held them others climbed up to tie strings in order to fasten the roses and feathers." With the passing of these events the old men recalled what had been foretold: strange katsina would come from the west and "the whole country would be conquered."[15]

Coronado Among the Pueblos

Just as the Indians made sense of the conquest through native cate-gories of thought and action, the Spanish conquistadores understood the world before them through their own cultural categories. Francisco Vásquez de Coronado named Cíbola "Granada," "because it has some similarity to it." A Piro pueblo was named Sevilleta because it resembled Seville. The trees of New Mexico were "like those of Castile," observed Hernando de Alvarado in 1640. Kivas were "mosques," dark-skinned In-dians were "Turks," their bows and arrows "Turkish bows," and their wives "Moorish women."[16]

From the conquistadores' perspective, the Pueblo Indians were an in-ferior breed close to savages: "a people without capacity," "stupid," and "of poor intelligence." Marveling at the houses he saw at the Zuñi pueblos in 1540, Coronado's comments are telling: "I do not think that they have the judgment and intelligence needed to be able to build these houses in the way in which they are built, for most of them are entirely naked." Surprised at how fiercely the Pecos Indians defended their homes, Gaspar Castaño de Sosa wrote that it was "a thing not to be believed, that uncivilized people should be so clever." Puebloans were judged intelligent only when they acquiesced to Spanish desires. The Tiwa Indians were "very intelligent," concluded Hernán Gallegos, because they were "willing to serve." [17]

Coronado's troops occupied Hawikuh from July until November of 1540 and from there reconnoitered the Tusayan (Hopi) pueblos of eastern Arizona, the Grand Canyon, and Quivira, a land east of New Mexico, which the Indians said was rich in gold, silver, and silks. The infantry that had been slowly marching north finally arrived at Hawikuh in late November 1540 and proceeded to Alcanfor Pueblo in Tiguex province (near Bernalillo) for the winter because it had abundant food. [18]

The intensity of that winter brought exploration temporarily to a halt. The troops huddled at Alcanfor rapidly succumbed to hunger and cold. Coronado's troops extracted blankets and corn from the Tiguex pueblos by force, and when the soldiers satisfied their lust with Indian women but gave nothing in return, the Indian men declared war. The Spaniards retaliated with their own war of blood and fire, ordering "200 stakes be driven into the ground to burn them alive." One hundred warriors were burned at the stake and hundreds more were massacred as they fled the Spaniards. [19]

When the spring thaw arrived, Coronado renewed his search for Quivira (villages of the Wichita Indians, in Kansas), which he beheld in August 1541. But there was no gold! Quivira's gold was a gigantic hoax fabricated by the Pueblos to get the Spanish out onto the plains where they would be more vulnerable to attack. [20]

Throughout the autumn and winter of 1541, Coronado's troops shivered in the cold, hungry and constantly engaged in Indian skirmishes. And so, when news reached Coronado in April 1542 that the Indians of Sonora were in rebellion, he and his forces abandoned New Mexico, bringing to a close the first period of Spanish interest in the area. When silver was discovered to the south near Zacatecas in 1548, the epoch of conquest that had begun with Cortés effectively ended. Energies formerly spent on pillage and rapine were now used to establish the mining towns of New Spain's northern frontier—Guanajuato, Querétaro, San Luis Potosí, and Durango. The fierce Chichimeca Indians that roamed beyond the silver mining frontier effectively curtailed exploration and settlement farther north, and for 40 years the boundary of New Spain lay at the edge of the mining towns.[21]

The Franciscan Century, 1581–1680

From 1581 to 1680, Franciscans provided the impetus for colonization in New Mexico. For most of this period the friars were virtual lords of the land. They organized the Indians into a theocracy that lasted until the Pueblo Revolt in 1680. What also differentiated the "Franciscan century" from the period of territorial conquest that preceded it was the promulgation of the 1573 Ordinances of Discovery, in which the king outlawed grand military expeditions such as those of Cortés and Coronado. "Discoveries are not to be called conquests," the Ordinance stated. "Since we wish them to be carried out peacefully and charitably, we do not want the use of the term 'conquest' to offer any excuse for the employment of force or the causing of injury to the Indian." Henceforth, only peaceful settlement directed by missionaries would be allowed into remote, hitherto uncivilized areas.[22]

The Franciscans' desire to carry the Gospel to New Mexico in 1581 was the logical outgrowth of the missionary enterprise they had begun in the Valley of Mexico in 1524. As the Indian *doctrinas* (parishes) they established to convert the natives were increasingly secularized and placed under episcopal control after 1572, the Franciscans had two choices. They could terminate their active ministry and retreat to conventual life or push into new missionary fields. The friars who entered New Mexico in 1581 chose the latter option, inflamed by millennial dreams and aglow with the spirit of apostolic renewal.[23]

Long after the conquistadores' dreams of pillaging gold from the Seven Cities of Antilla had been forgotten, a hypnotic spell beckoned the Franciscans to New Mexico. There, in a new missionary field—as would be the case in Texas during the early 1700s and in California after 1769—the most radical members of the order flocked to usher in Christ's second coming. In New Mexico, far from the corrupting influence of civilians, they would labor to fashion a theocracy, a utopia in which the Indians would "spend their time marching in processions and praising God with hymns and spiritual canticles."[24]

To realize these dreams, the Franciscans organized two expeditions to reconnoiter New Mexico: one, in 1581, was led by Fray Agustín Rodríguez, under the command of Francisco Sánchez Chamuscado; the other, in 1582, was led by Antonio de Espejo, and was ostensibly to rescue two friars who had remained in the Pueblos after the 1581 expedition. Both of these expeditions provided the Franciscans with a wealth of ethnographic information on the Pueblos. As the 1573 Ordinances of Discovery ordered, the friars collected data on the various tribes, on their languages and customs, and in particular on their social organization and ceremonial life. Once the contours of the native religious cosmos were understood, the European fathers were well prepared to stage their most spectacular thespian feat—the conquest.[25]

Glowing reports from the Franciscans about New Mexico reached King Philip II, and as a result, license was issued in 1595 to one of New Spain's most illustrious sons, Don Juan de Oñate, for the conquest and colonization of the Kingdom of New Mexico. "Your main purpose shall be the service of God Our Lord, the spreading of His holy Catholic faith, and the reduction and pacification of the natives of the said provinces," Oñate was instructed. Numerous delays ensued before the expedition finally departed from Zacatecas in January 1598. Only 129 of the necessary 200 soldiers had been mustered and their character, the viceroy lamented, was extremely "troublesome."[26]

The mostly young and single men who went to New Mexico were a rough-hewn group. Little is known of their social origins except what is reported on the muster rolls. More than half of the men, 71 to be exact, were under the age of 30. The rest were not much older; 34 were aged 30 to 39, 14 were between 40 and 49, and 10 were over 50. The youngest recruit was 15 and the oldest 60. Sharing origins similar to those of the Franciscans who would serve in New Mexico, roughly half of the soldiers declared that they were born in Spain, primarily in Andalusía and Estremadura. Another 50 or so gave New Spain as their birthplace, and a handful were from other countries. For example, Juan Griego was Greek, Antonio Rodríguez was Portuguese, and Rodrigo Velman was Flemish. Also included among the expedition's members were the wives, children, servants, and slaves of several of the officers.[27]

From the moment the Spaniards reached the banks of the Rio Grande in New Mexico on April 20, 1598, what the Indians saw and heard was but a well-choreographed political drama that was to teach them the meaning of their own defeat, of Spanish sovereignty, and of the social hierarchies that would prevail under Christian rule. The European actors in this conquest theater gave dazzling initial performances. The Indians attentively watched. At first they were a bit confused, but they soon understood the dramatic message. For the narrative of this drama was a triumphal history of the conquest of Mexico as the victors wanted it remembered. The Spaniards correctly assumed that the Pueblos had learned of the 1523 Aztec defeat through word of mouth. To fix in the

Indian mind that their own subjugation in 1598 was identical to the Aztecs' submission in 1523, various episodes of that earlier encounter were staged for them.

In time the actor-audience relationship of the 1598 conquest drama was reversed. The Indians became the actors and Spaniards smugly looked on. When the Indians performed the dances, dramas, and pantomimes of the conquest, they continually relived their own defeat, their own humiliation and dishonor, and openly mocked themselves with those caricatures of Indian culture the conquistadores so fancied. Today in many Pueblos these conquest dramas are still enacted in seventeenth-century attire. A highly ideological view of the conquest thus became an integral part of what we now brand native culture. How pleased Oñate and the Franciscans would have been if they could only have seen it. So let us take a look.[28]

Oñate entered New Mexico with some legendary characters and props. His soldiers marched under a banner with an image of "Our Lady of the Remedies," identical to the one Hernán Cortés had carried into Tenochtitlán in 1519. By Oñate's side was a group of Tlascalan Indian allies, like those who had befriended Cortés for his historic defeat of the Aztecs. There was also a native maiden named Doña Inés whom Oñate hoped would be seen by the Indians as "a second Malinche." Doña Inés, a native of Pant-ham-ba Pueblo (near Galisteo), had been abducted by Gaspar Castaño de Sosa during his unauthorized 1590 expedition into New Mexico and taken back to central Mexico. When Oñate obtained license to colonize the area he demanded of the King the "Indian woman who was brought from New Mexico." Oñate expected that just as the first Malinche had acted as Hernán Cortés' mistress, interpreter, and advocate before the native lords, so too would Doña Inés. Finally, there were twelve Franciscans who played the twelve Franciscan "Apostles" who in 1524 initiated Mexico's spiritual conquest.[29]

The first act of the New Mexican conquest drama took place near modern-day El Paso. There Oñate received four Indian emissaries from a nearby village and immediately dressed them as Spaniards, cloaking their nakedness and regaling them with gifts. Oñate thus conformed to the European diplomatic convention that an inferior host always donned the clothes of the superior guest. Eighty years earlier Montezuma, the Aztec emperor, had greeted Hernán Cortés in a similar fashion, wearing the red cap and seated in the chair Cortés had sent him. In 1598 Oñate played Cortés, enacting that earlier encounter.[30]

On April 30, 1598, Oñate had a chapel contructed. Solemn High Mass was celebrated, and after the sermon the soldiers enacted for the

Indians another historical episode in Mexico's conquest, the arrival of the twelve Franciscan "Apostles" in Mexico City in 1524 and the spectacular greeting they received from Hernán Cortés. Cortés gathered the lords and populace of Tenochtitlán to behold how he greeted the twelve Franciscans. Cortés approached the friars on his horse, dismounted, fell on his knees before them, and then kissed their hands and their hems. Cortés then ordered the caciques to do likewise. To edify the Puebloans in 1598, Oñate did as Cortés had done in 1524, again projecting an image of himself as the new Cortés. Oñate approached the friars, knelt, kissed their hands and hems, and then ordered the Indians to do likewise. In the play's closing scene the "simple natives . . . reverently approached on bended knee and asked to be received into the faith, being baptized in great numbers." New Mexico's friars insisted that such didactic gestures were "necessary, since it was the first time that [such a] proud and bellicose people had seen it." Indeed, kneeling before the Spaniards was a radical and humiliating gesture for the Puebloans. Never had they approached their leaders or their gods on bended knee. Now, not only were they expected to kneel before the Franciscans, but every time they greeted a priest they were to kneel and kiss his hands and feet. By so doing, said Fray Estevan de Perea, the Indians would "understand the true veneration that they should show the friars." When the drama ended, Oñate again fell to his knees, lifted his eyes toward heaven, and loudly prayed for the conversion of "these infidels [and for] . . . the peaceful possession of these kingdoms." Firing harquebuses to evoke the heat of battle and the force of the sun, Oñate ceremoniously erected a cross as a sign of Christ's victory over the enemy, and then moved on.[31]

Oñate's expedition traveled north along the Rio Grande to Santo Domingo Pueblo. There, in early July 1598, Oñate gathered the chiefs of 31 surrounding pueblos to have them swear obedience and vassalage to the king. Through Tomás and Cristóbal, two Mexican Indians who had been left at Santo Domingo during the 1590 Castaño de Sosa expedition, Oñate explained that the king had sent him for "the salvation of their souls, because they should know that their bodies had also souls which did not die even though the bodies did. But if they were baptized and became good Christians, they would go to heaven to enjoy an eternal life of great bliss in the presence of God . . . [if not] they would go to hell to suffer cruel and everlasting torment." The chiefs promised to obey Oñate as their temporal lord and Fray Alonso Martínez, the Franciscan commissary, as their spiritual lord. The Indians demonstrated this by kneeling and kissing first Oñate's hand and then Martínez's. The ceremony of submission at Santo Domingo ended with a Mass.[32]

From Santo Domingo, Oñate proceeded north to Ohke, renaming it San Juan de los Caballeros. Once all the chiefs of the surrounding villages had gathered here, he staged the medieval drama "The Christians and the Moors." The play, set in Reconquest Spain, depicted the theft of the Cross by the Moors, its heroic recapture by the Christian soldiers, and the final submission and acceptance of the Cross of Christ by the infidel. Oñate writes that when the play ended the chiefs swore obedience and vassalage, humbled themselves before the friars and returned to their pueblos accompanied by a friar who would preach the gospel to them. Oñate thrice warned that "if they failed to obey any of the *padres* or caused them the slightest harm, they and their cities and pueblos would be put to the sword and destroyed by fire." At last, New Mexico was nominally under Spanish control.[33]

Perhaps because bloody memories of their 1540–41 encounter with the Spanish "Children of the Sun" still lingered in the minds of Pueblo seniors, Oñate's conquest drama was not accorded an audience everywhere. Villages that knew well their vulnerabilities, such as Teypana (Socorro), Sevilleta, and Puaray, deserted their homes when the foreign katsina entered the outermost quarter of their world. The mightier, well-fortified towns received the conquistadores as they did other visiting tribes, gifting and hosting them as a sign of goodwill. At "the great pueblo of the Emes [Jémez]," wrote Oñate in his itinerary, "the natives came out to meet us, bringing water and bread." At Acoma "the Indians furnished us liberally with maize, water, and fowls." And at the Hopi Pueblos "the natives came out to welcome us with tortillas, scattering powdered flour over us and our horses as a sign of peace and friendship . . . and gave us a fine reception."[34]

The Spanish narratives of the conquest are silent on the hospitality the Indian women offered the "Children of the Sun." Because sanctity and sex were so closely related in the Pueblo world, it was common for men and women to give their bodies to persons they deemed holy, in order to partake of their supernatural power. Fray Alonso de Benavides mentioned this custom with great disgust in the 1620s, noting that when a group of Pueblo women re-entered their town after extensive ritual emesis, fasting, and flagellations, they did so "emaciated and feeble" but "confident that every man who beholds them will crave them and give them many blankets and other presents." This observation helps us understand how the Pueblos greeted Oñate's soldiers in 1598. Captain Gaspar Pérez de Villagrá tells us that "the natives brought a great number of beautiful many-colored blankets, which they gathered together, hoping to entice with them the Castilian women whom they liked and coveted." The Indian men desired sexual intercourse not only with the Spanish women, but with the soldiers as well. "If a youth in our company had not cried out for help, he would have been attacked," said Villagrá, because "these people are addicted to the bestial wicked sin [of sodomy]." [35]

The Pueblo women cooled the passion of the fierce fire-brandishing Spanish katsina through intercourse, and by so doing, tried to transform and domesticate the malevolence of these foreign gods. But the Spaniards as a group would interpret their subjugation of the Pueblos as a supreme assertion of masculine virility, and as such, would see 1598 as a sexual conquest of women. The soldiers did not report their sexual comportment during those initial months in New Mexico to their superiors, and shortly we will see why. The Franciscans painted a picture of horrors such as those they had seen in Moorish country. Fray Francisco Zamora swore before God that he had witnessed native men stabbed and knifed because the soldiers wanted their wives. "I know for certain that the soldiers have violated them [the women] often along the roads," Zamora wrote. Fray Joseph Manuel de Equía y Leronbe said that he had heard the conquistadors shouting as they went off to their debaucheries: "Let us go to the pueblos to fornicate with Indian women. . . . Only with lascivious treatment are Indian women conquered." Oñate granted his men such freedom in their exploits, complained another, that they continually abused the Indians, "entering their houses, taking their women, and causing them a thousand such annoyances and vexations." [36]

The soldiers' version of these same events in Pueblo country did not surface willingly, and then only belatedly in July 1601, when Don Francisco de Valverde, on orders from the viceroy, conducted an investigation of New Mexico's conquest. The soldiers recounted no exploits, admitted no faults. Rather, they spoke of the licentious Pueblo women who had "no vices other than lust." Normally, Spanish soldiers might have bragged about their sexual triumphs in words evocative of the terror of their victims—rape, vanquishment, violation. But in 1601 the conquistadores seemed to scratch their heads in collective befuddlement, wondering what had transpired between them and their Pueblo subjects. The Indians did not "care much whether or not their wives are faithful," attested Ginés de Herrera. The women had "absolutely no shame," said Marcelo de Espinosa. "The women are not faithful to their husbands, nor do the latter care about this or punish them," declared Joseph Brondate. To this Juan de Ortega added, an "Indian does not abandon his wife, nor does he punish her or show any particular ill feeling if she offends him." [37]

The generosity of Pueblo women and the seeming indifference of their husbands to their behavior would have made sense to the Spaniards if placed within the political context of gifts as diplomatic gestures that guaranteed blessings and peace. The Europeans understood the meaning of gifts. The cultural misunderstanding was in the gifting calculus of each society. Quite early in New Mexico's conquest the Spanish tried to ascribe to Indian gifts their own meanings and motives. At a Tiwa pueblo in 1581 Hernán Gallegos marveled that:

the inhabitants gave us much corn . . . and brought quantities of calabashes and beans for us to eat. We took a little, so that they should not think we were greedy nor yet receive the impression that we did not want it; among themselves they consider it disparaging if one does not accept what is offered . . . since we understood their custom, we took something of what they gave us. Moreover, we did this *to get them into the habit of giving freely without being asked.* Accordingly, they all brought what they could.

If the conquistadores understood as much about Pueblo gifting as they said they did, then their explicit goal in New Mexico was to teach the Indians that the native equations would be inverted. The Pueblo generational representation of inequality would remain, but no longer would gifts—the product of human labor—circulate among seniors on behalf of juniors, with proper reciprocation signifying equality. Rather, under Spanish civilian rule Pueblo seniors would be cast as "ignorant Indian children" who offered gift-stuff to their victorious "Spanish fathers" in return, as the soldiers saw it, for tutelage in the ways of civilization and those few "trinkets" Oñate always gave to the Indians for water, food, and love."[38]

What the Puebloans thought they gave as gifts, the *españoles* thought had been surrendered as tribute. Indeed, the surface calm that had greeted the colonizers erupted violently in December 1598, precisely over the meaning of Indian gifts and how cheerfully they should be surrendered.

On December 4, 1598, Captain Don Juan de Zaldívar and 31 soldiers, en route to the Zuñi pueblos, had stopped at Acoma for provisions. Zaldívar and his men were greeted at about four in the afternoon by a large number of the villagers "showing much satisfaction and joy." Because the place where the soldiers set up camp had neither wood nor water, seven soldiers ascended the steep mesa on which Acoma sits "to bring what the Indians might give." According to Captain Gerónimo Márquez, the Indians "sent only a small amount of water and wood. This witness thought they gave it unwillingly, so he and his men went down at once and told" Zaldívar. The next morning the chiefs "brought few tortillas and three or four fanegas of maize," but Zaldívar wanted flour. The Indians told him to return in a few days and the maize would be ground.[39]

On December 4, Zaldívar returned and climbed the mesa with eighteen soldiers to obtain the flour. When a soldier named Vivero stole two turkeys, a bird sacred to the Indians, and violated an Indian maiden, Acoma's warriors attacked, killing Zaldívar and twelve men. A few soldiers survived the fracas by jumping off the edge of Acoma's mesa to the sand dunes below. With the sentinels that had been left watching the horses they retreated to San Juan. Oñate encountered the survivors of Acoma's battle on December 13 as he was returning from Zuñi to San Juan. Immediately, plans were made to punish Acoma. If the colony was to survive, stern and swift action would have to be taken. Oñate reasoned that any hesitation might be interpreted by the Indians as a sign of weakness and might encourage other pueblos to similar rebellions.[40]

A punitive expedition of 70 soldiers—over half of the Spanish force in the province—set out for Acoma on January 12, 1599, under the command of Don Vicente de Zaldívar, the slain officer's brother. They reached the pueblo on January 21, and claim to have implored the Indians to surrender peacefully. Acoma's warriors are said to have jeered and responded with a volley of arrows and stones. For three days the Spanish mercilessly waged a certified "just war." During the heat of battle St. James came to the soldiers' aid, riding "a white horse . . . a spear in his hand." He killed the infidels "like a whirlwind," with "a maiden of most wondrous beauty," presumably the Virgin Mary, at his side. At one point the Indians sued for peace, offering 80 blankets and numerous turkeys as gifts, but Zaldívar would not accept them, preferring instead to punish Acoma. When the fighting ended, 800 Indian men, women, and children lay dead. Eighty men and 500 women and children were taken as prisoners to Santo Domingo to stand trial.

Several of Acoma's chiefs—Caoma, Xunusta, and Taxio among them—appeared before Oñate to explain their rebellion. "Why had they killed Zaldívar and his men?," Oñate asked Caoma. "Because they asked for such large amounts [of maize, flour, and blankets] they killed them." Xunusta answered the same question saying that "the Spaniards first killed an Indian, and then all the Indians became very angry and killed them." Why, on January 21, 1599, when Acoma was ordered to surrender, had the Indians refused? Taxio retorted that "the old people and other leading Indians did not want peace, and for this reason they attacked with arrows and stones." Xunusta added that "some Indians wanted to make peace but others did not, and because they could not agree, they would not submit." Why had the Indian women participated in the fighting? Taxio said that they threw rocks "because they were together with the men and therefore they took part in the demonstration and the fighting."[41]

Acoma's residents were found guilty of murder and failing to surrender willingly the provisions the Spaniards demanded. All men and women over the age of twelve were condemned to twenty years of slavery among New Mexico's settlers. In addition, all men over the age of 25 had one of their feet severed. Children under the age of twelve were distributed as servants to monasteries and households. Two Hopi Indians captured at Acoma each lost their right hand and were dispatched home as testaments of the Christians' wrath. Oñate hoped that with these punishments, Pueblo resistance to Spanish presence and demands would definitively cease. He was right. The Indians from various pueblos later testified that after Acoma's defeat they realized that they did not have the strength to resist the Christians.[42]

The colony struggled along, low on morale and provisions. Oñate informed the viceroy that if the colony was to survive, reinforcements were necessary. On Christmas eve, 1600, 73 men arrived. With these recruits Oñate finally had enough soldiers to pursue the riches of Quivira that had eluded Coronado. He set out onto the Great Plains in June 1601 and found exactly what Coronado had—nothing. Faced with Indian hostilities and exhausted troops, Oñate returned to New Mexico.[43]

Reaching San Gabriel (New Mexico's capital had been moved from San Juan to San Gabriel at the end of 1598) at the beginning of September 1601, Oñate found the town virtually deserted. Many of the kingdom's settlers had returned to New Spain, complaining that the province contained no precious metals, that the climate was harsh, that the natives were ferocious, that a drought in 1600 had caused widespread starvation, and that Oñate was a selfish, power hungry, and elusive manager of colonial affairs. The Franciscans, eager to limit the number of civilians in New Mexico, supported the settlers' grievances and chimed in with a few of their own. Oñate lived "dishonorably and scandalously with women . . . married and unmarried." He had been excessively harsh with the Indians, extracting food and clothing through torture, allowing his soldiers to abuse women, thereby severely hampering conversions. According to the friars the Indians understandably asked, "if [you] who are Christians cause so much harm and violence, why should [we] become Christians?" Unable to answer the question, the friars thought it best if the settlers left and the province remained a mission field.[44]

The viceroy found the charges against Oñate true and in 1607 ordered him to resign his governorship. For several years the crown pondered New Mexico's fate. Finally, in December of 1608, Friars Lázaro Jiménez and Isidro Ordóñez informed the king that seven thousand Puebloans had been converted and "others were clamoring for baptism." The royal conscience was stirred. New Mexico would be retained as a colony with a governor and 50 married soldiers. Exploration into outlying areas would cease. The friars were to occupy their time converting the Indians. And Don Pedro de Peralta, appointed governor in 1609, was to establish a Spanish town so that the colonists would "live with some order and decency." This he did in 1610 with the founding of Santa Fe as the kingdom's capital.[45]

Given the decisive role the Franciscans played in reawakening royal interest in New Mexico in 1581 and maintaining the area as a mission field in 1608, they believed that the kingdom had been saved providentially for them. In 1608 the Franciscans began constructing the theocracy they had long imagined among New Mexico's Indians.

Charismatic Domination

To understand how the Franciscans established their charismatic domination over the Pueblo Indians, let us return to the indigenous conception of order and power circumscribed by those three ideological functions of male ritual discussed in Chapter 1—the cacique or Inside Chief's control of law and the sacred, the Outside Chiefs' organization of force, and the promotion of fertility and well-being shared by the rain chiefs, the hunt chiefs, and the medicine men.[46]

When the friars entered New Mexico they attempted to portray themselves to the Indians as supermen who controlled the forces of nature—a portrayal that worked, attested Fray Gerónimo de Mendieta. So simple-minded had the Indians proven, wrote Mendieta in 1596, that they thought "we were gods or men from the sky . . . whom they received like angels without the least suspicion." The Spanish conquest was a cataclysm of unprecedented proportions for the Puebloans. Amid the chaos and excitement created by the arrival of the "Children of the Sun," accompanied by fire-brandishing katsina (soldiers) with animals at their command, stood the friars who were prepared to show the Indians through thespian acts that they were men of enormous magical power. The Indians were understandably awestruck. All the magic of the native chiefs had not halted the Christians' advance, and indeed seemed impotent against them. These Christian chiefs (friars) combined in one person what it took five native chiefs to accomplish.[47]

One of the first functions the friars assumed was that of potent rain chiefs. Because the Pueblo cosmology was not very different from that of the Indians of central Mexico, the friars were well aware of the symbolic power of rain in the Pueblo belief system. Thus the friars tried to time their arrival in New Mexico to coincide with the rainy season. No sooner had they set foot on the Rio Grande Valley in 1598 than a terrible tempest arose. It seemed as if the natural forces at Satan's command resisted the Christians' advance, wrote Gaspar Pérez de Villagrá, chronicler of the kingdom's settlement. "The sky darkened with heavy black clouds and the entire earth shook and trembled with the force of a mighty earthquake." The friars exorcized the clouds with their crosses and to the great "amazement of the Indians as well as the Spaniards," the storm immediately subsided. Later, when the friars entered San Juan Pueblo, they found the earth parched and the crops wilted for lack of rain. The friars constructed a cross, prayed for rain, and ordered the Indians to do likewise. Then, "while the sky was as clear as a diamond, exactly twenty-four hours after the outcry had gone up, it rained . . . so abundantly that the crops recovered." San Juan's inhabitants rejoiced and presented many feathers, corn meal, and other gifts to the crucifix and to the friars.[48]

The padres who aped rain chiefs also impersonated medicine men. Fray Gerónimo de Pedraza, a surgeon of some renown, took it upon himself to cure Quinía, a widely feared war chief who had been shot in the chest with an arrow by his own warriors because of his friendliness towards the Franciscans. Fra Gerónimo examined Quinía's infected wound, took a large copper medal with the images of the blessed Virgin Mary and Saint Francis, placed it over the wound and bound it tightly with a cord. The friar returned the next day and found that the medal had penetrated the wound and attached itself to the arrowhead. He untied the cord and out popped the medal and arrowhead in a stream of pus. Quinía speedily recovered and eventually sought baptism in 1627.[49]

But perhaps the most impressive medical "miracle" occurred in 1632 at Awatobi. The medicine men there were irritated by Fray Francisco de Porras' successes in curing minor ailments and decided to test his medicine magic. They presented to him a thirteen-year-old boy who had been blind since birth saying, "You go about deceiving us and disturbing the people with what you call a cross. If what you say about it is true, place it on the eyes of this boy; if he regains his sight, we shall believe everything you tell us; but if not, we will kill you or cast you out in shame." Fra Francisco fell to his knees, prayed for a miracle "for the confusion of all these infidels," and placed a cross over the boy's eyes. He took dirt, made a little mud with his own spittle, rubbed the mud on the boy's eyes and said *epheta*. Suddenly the boy saw! The Hopi proclaimed the friar a powerful healer. The medicine men retreated, muttering and promising revenge; a promise they made good on June 28, 1633, when they poisoned Fra Francisco.[50]

Equally daunting was the friars' animal magic, which far exceeded anything hunt chiefs could conjure. The only animals the Pueblos had domesticated were the turkey, for its feathers rather than for its meat, and the dog, as a beast of burden. The appearance of friars shepherding enormous flocks of docile animals, their escorts riding atop horses that were stronger, faster, and more obedient than any animal they had ever seen before, was quite astounding. The rapid reproduction of the European herds, which, according to a 1634 account by Fray Alonso de Benavides, nearly doubled every fifteen months, and the introduction of beef, pork, and mutton into the native diet marginalized the role of the hunt chiefs. Here was a permanent, year-round meat supply that, at least for the moment, was not the object of intense competition between neighboring villages and Athapaskan bands, or subject to the vicissitudes of the hunt chiefs' magic.[51]

The spatial organization of force that the friars and Spanish soldiers presented to the Indians meshed well with its indigenous counterpart. Force in the Indian world was exercised by the Outside Chiefs and their warriors, who protected the village from external enemies. Within the pueblo, force was culturally prohibited. There the Inside Chief, the symbol of cosmic order, ruled. To the Pueblo Indians force was young and outside society; the sacred was old and at the very center. Whenever the Franciscans established a parish to indoctrinate the natives, they tried to reproduce this spatial relationship between force and the sacred. The friars always insisted on keeping the soldier-settlers outside the Indian villages to minimize their corrupting influences, but not too far away should the friar require their assistance imposing mission discipline or extirpating idolatry.

From the Indians' perspective the Spanish governor and his young soldiers resembled an Outside Chief and warriors whom the friars could mobilize at a moment's notice. The soldiers repeatedly warned the Puebloans "that if they attempted to injure [the friars] . . . the governor would bring his army against them and burn their pueblos and lay waste their fields," said Fray Estevan de Perea. After all, the soldiers carried the forces of nature that gave warriors their power—lightning, thunder, and fire in the form of guns. A poignant example of how the Franciscans communicated the embodiment and spatial location of force under colonial rule comes from 1582 when the Rodríguez expedition entered New Mexico. One day three horses were stolen from the party and slaughtered by the Indians at Pueblo Malpartida (San Lázaro). The soldiers quickly apprehended the culprits and sentenced them to death. Fearing that the executions might spark rebellion, the friars devised a theatrical ploy to rescue the guilty from the chopping block. At a preordained moment, the friars would free the Indians and assail the soldiers, making the Indians believe that the friars had saved their lives. All went as planned. Just as the executioner's ax was to sever an Indian's head, "the friars came out in flowing robes and removed the Indians from the block. As we pretended that we were going to take them, the Indians who were watching immediately took hold of the said friars and Indians and carried them away to their houses. . . . Due to what had been done and attempted the natives became so terrified of us [sic]." In 1599 Don Juan de Oñate made explicit the intent of such rescues: "They [the Indians] will recognize the friars as their benefactors and protectors and come to love and esteem them, and to fear us." Indeed, from surface appearances it seemed that the Franciscans commanded a legion of ruthless and invincible warriors.[52]

The Franciscans also aggressively asserted their dominance over village affairs as Inside Chiefs. The Inside Chief embodied the sacred in Pueblo society, coordinating the various chieftaincies that promoted fertility, mobilizing force, and keeping sacred time. The Franciscans masterfully asserted their control over fertility and force, and by presenting themselves as ritual specialists before whom mortals had to kneel, the unmistakable conclusion was that the friars were Inside Chiefs who controlled the sacred. For after all, the Christian fetishes invested with power—be they crucifixes, statues, relics, or other sacred objects—were in the hands of the friars, as was the Holy Eucharist, the living presence of Christ in the community. To elucidate how the sacred was structured and conceived in colonial New Mexico, let us examine the structure of the Christian cosmology before returning to our narrative thread.

Space, objects, and time were the three dimensions that structured both the Pueblo and the Christian cosmologies. When Christians gathered together to ritualize their relations, it was on ground sanctified by the presence of sacred objects, at times that commemorated the life of Christ or those of his saints. The landscape the Pueblos inhabited was profane space by Christian standards. Certainly the physical geography was the handiwork of the Almighty, but before the land could be claimed for God and king, the false spirits that inhabited it had to be exorcised by Christ's redemptive matrix. Thus when Fray Marcos de Niza gazed on Hawikuh in 1539, he immediately christened the area and marked its possession with a cross. Don Juan de Oñate did likewise on reaching the Gulf of California while en route to New Mexico in 1597. He plunged into the ocean with sword in hand, cutting a cross into the water and proclaiming it "Christian territory." The ease with which New Mexico's topography was transformed into Christian space prompted Fray Juan de Prada to wonder whether the conquest was prophetic, for the Indians, almost as if by divine design, had located their villages in "the shape . . . of a cross."[53]

Since reverential objects were the most potent loci of the holy in Christianity, it was primarily through enclosure, through the construction of a church or an oratory, that space received its power. Placement of a church was not particularly important, except when its superimposition atop a native shrine or kiva served an instructional end. The things of greatest importance enclosed in a church were "the things of divine worship," noted Fray Lucas Maldonado. The Eucharist, tabernacle, altar stone, and images of Christ, Mary, and the saints were all objects essential for efficacious ritual. The friars brought these sacred objects to New Mexico to serve as the focus for the celebration of community. The mobile quality of these items allowed them to be moved to and fro, to be processed solemnly through town and countryside, and to be stolen and profaned. New Mexican churches, unlike their European counterparts, were rarely consecrated. Consequently, as soon as a church's *sacra* were removed, the edifice became but a hollow memory of its past.[54]

The mission church was a physical symbol of the celestial community in which humanity participated and by which it was sustained. The church was a ritual field for the experience of community when the faithful gathered as one to revere the sacred objects that embodied supernatural power. Logically, the edifice that represented this union was an architectural bulwark; its walls were massive, 3 to 4 feet thick and 25 to 30 feet high. Church interiors were spacious and unobstructed, and their parapets served a military function, offering its defenders cover against enemy fire. In times of war, the Christian community huddled together inside the church with their sacred objects. In times of festivity or natural disaster they sanctified the space in their village by processing outdoors with these objects.[55]

The hierarchy of power New Mexico's friars attributed to their holy objects is best studied by examining the spatial organization of the reredos, those ornamental screens that stood as backdrops for the main altar, as well as the division of space within the church. The main altar on which the Mass was celebrated was the center of Christian ritual. Through the miracle of the Mass, God was made man and bread and wine were transformed into the body and blood of Jesus Christ. This conjunction of the divine and the human, of the triune godhead and the community that filled the church, was visually represented in the union of the reredos and the altar. The reredos, divided horizontally into three ascending sections rising up behind the altar, was an image of the heavenly order and a visual representation of Christian theology and history. Reigning over the top was the Trinity, portrayed either as three persons each wearing the papal tiara, as a triangle surrounded by rays of light, or as the triangular eye of God in a sunburst. The reredos section below this was vertically subdivided into three niches (sometimes into two). The tier of Santa Fe's main altar in 1776 had in the center niche a statue of St. Francis, the church's patron saint, in the right niche St. Joseph, and in the left niche St. Didacus, a Franciscan saint. The lowest section of the screen, a physical extension of the altar, duplicated the spatial organization of the section above it. In the center niche of Santa Fe's altar was a statue of Our Lady of the Pillar of Saragossa, flanked by St. Dominic, founder of the Dominican Order, and by the theologian St. John Capistran "with a crucifix in his hand and a heretic at his feet." Below the center niche was the tabernacle, "as is customary on altar screens," said Fray Francisco Atanasio Domínguez, and over the tabernacle a crucifix. Here at a glance were the historic pillars of the Church—its theologians, founders of religious orders, saints, and members of the Holy Family, all hierarchically juxtaposed to the Trinity in a triangular space.[56]

The altar on which the redemptive sacrifice of the crucifixion was celebrated stood on a step known as the *predella*, which was "all adorned with relics," the physical fragments or clothing of holy dead. The reredos, the altar, and the predella formed the sanctuary. This concentration of holy objects was separated from the rest of the church by a communion rail beyond which only the priest and assistants could pass.[57]

The space that extended from the communion rail back through the church proper and out into its courtyard and cemetery was organized hierarchically according to worldly inequalities. One's proximity to the main altar and the Eucharistic table was a sign of one's standing in the terrestrial community. Closest to the altar sat the provincial governor. Throughout the seventeenth and eighteenth centuries, his seat was located on a dais outside the sanctuary in the left transept of Santa Fe's church. After the governor came the men of honor and might who bickered over where they would kneel in the church and squabbled over their proximity to the holy. Don Bernardino Bustamante y Tagle's family secured a place of prominence in church in the early 1700s by purchasing two small altars in Mexico City—one to Our Lady of Guadalupe and the other to St. Anthony of Padua—and having them installed in the transept of Santa Fe's Church. Behind the settlers came the Indian children; boys on the Epistle side of the nave, girls on the Gospel side. Next were their parents, standing as couples. And finally, widowers and widows formed another row in the church, careful always to leave "the passage free for the entrance of settlers."[58]

In death as in life, one's honor in the community determined where one's bones would rest in relation to the sacred objects. Close to the altar, at the foot of the predella in San Francisco de Sandía Church, were buried the bones of New Mexico's first martyrs, Fray Francisco López and Fray Agustín Rodríguez. When Fray Estevan de Perea died in 1639, he too was buried here beside his brothers. Citizens of wealth and power buried their dead as close to the altar as possible. Those of lesser means were buried farther back in the nave, and impecunious souls found rest outside in the cemetery. Fray Andrés García made this schema explicit in his 1768 chart listing interment prices in Santa Cruz Church. A transept burial close to the altar cost 19 pesos, nave burials cost 8, one at the back of the church cost 4, and burial in the cemetery cost 2 pesos. A church burial insured participation in the communion of saints and everlasting life. Only infidels and excommunicates were denied sacred resting ground. For New Mexico's colonists, whose common identity was shaped by their religion, to be denied burial near the sacred objects of the community was to relegate one's soul and memory to obscurity.[59]

Time was also thoroughly imbued with the holy. Much as a kiva's shipapu, altars, and fetishes recreated the time of Pueblo emergence from the underworld, so too the reredos that rose up behind the church's main altar brought as witnesses to Christ's sacrifice the saints who over the centuries had toiled to build Christianity. The cycle of Christ's life was the measure of time, marking the days and years. Don Juan de Oñate so reckoned time, noting in his journal that April 30, 1598, was the day of the ascension of our Lord," that May 10 was the feast of the Pentecost, that May 17 was the "day of the Holy Trinity," that May 21 was the "day of the Most Holy Sacrament," and so on. This concept of time inspired numerous toponyms. The Indian pueblo Oñate visited on June 24, 1598, was named San Juan Bautista because it was the feast of St. John the Baptist. Zía Pueblo was called St. Peter and St. Paul for a similar reason. When, as in 1599, conflict arose among the settlers as to the identity of the mounted soldier that had assisted the Christians during their infamous siege of Acoma, the Christian calendar became their final authority. Though the men who fought at Acoma were convinced that they had seen St. James, Fray Alonso de Benavides insisted that it could not have been. The battle occurred on January 25, the feast of the Conversion of St. Paul. Thus, Benavides argued, it was St. Paul and not St. James who had appeared to them.[60]

At no moment were space, objects, and time more perfectly conjoined than during the celebration of Mass. Then the high altar became a cosmic stage for the violent sacrifice of the crucifixion whereby Jesus, the son of God, was mocked and put to death at the behest of his Almighty Father. Through this sacrifice Christ atoned for humanity's sins, thereby restoring the covenant between God and mankind. Lest the congregation lose sight of the centrality of the Mass, churches were always illuminated to draw the eye to the sacrificial table. Naves were dimly lit, shadowy tunnels that stood in stark contrast to the luminescent altar and its brightly painted reredos. The directional force of the lighting immediately drew one's attention to the altar "as in a theatre."[61]

The Mass New Mexico's friars celebrated was a rite that promoted communal peace and social accord. Organized into three parts—introduction, canon, communion—the drama of the Mass unfolded as follows. The introduction began with a psalm on humanity's sinfulness; a general confession and absolution of sin followed. In the *Gloria* God's redemptive plan was announced, and the community responded by singing glory to Him on high and praying for peace on earth. The epistles, gospel, and Nicene Creed acclaimed the congregation's faith. The offertory followed and here began the canon proper and the sacrifice of the Mass.[62]

The offertory brought together the community's various parts, and in unison they presented the priest gifts of wine and bread. Spaniards and Indians, slave and free, male and female, the living and the dead, stood as one, suspending the earth's inequalities for union as one body in Christ. Together with the priest they prayed for a successful sacrifice: a sacrifice that represented the discord of mutual murder, its preclusion, and the peace that ritual murder made possible. Before a kneeling congregation, in magical formulas whispered over the bread and wine, the offerings were transformed into Jesus Christ. The priest elevated Christ's body first and then his blood for everyone to see.[63]

Before the consecration there had been prayers for the living; now there were prayers for the dead. The congregation affirmed its unity, praying the *Paternoster*, bidding each other reconciliation—avoidance of temptation and deliverance from evil. Next the priest performed the *Fractio panis*, the breaking of the bread by which the body of the crucified Christ embossed on the host's surface was shattered and torn apart. Uttering words evocative of sacrifice—"Grant peace in our days, that we may be helped by thy merciful assistance, always free from sin, and secure from all disturbance"—the celebrant split the host vertically in half, and then one of the halves again in half. Because the host as the body of Christ represented both the church and Christian society, the fraction symbolized the way in which the *corpus mysticum*, the mystical body of

Christ as an image of society, could be torn asunder. To preclude this possibility and to neutralize latent hostilities, the tearing of the host was followed immediately by the Pax, the Kiss of Peace. The friars were hesitant to offer women the Kiss of Peace, or for that matter to allow husbands to give it to their wives. So a pax-board (called *portapaz* or simply pax on church inventories) bearing the words "My peace I give to you," was passed among the faithful for everyone to kiss. Through this sacrificial rite the congregation as a whole was put, in the words of Godfrey Lienhardt, "at peace with itself." Amity among the faithful was reinforced by reciting the *Agnus dei*, thrice praying that the sacrificial Lamb of God grant the assemblage peace. Now the celebrant consumed the consecrated host, and if it was one of those rare occasions when the laity also received the Eucharist, they knelt at the communion rail to consume the body and blood of Christ. Finally, with a communal blessing, the Mass ended.[64]

Much in the same way that the town chief conjoined a pueblo's various clans during Pueblo ceremonials, and by recreating the primordial time of creation promoted peace in the community, so too the friars sought to preclude societal discord and unrest by celebrating the union made possible through the sacrifice of the Mass. Before marching into New Mexico, and always before marching into battle, Don Juan de Oñate instructed his soldiers to "make their peace with God" at Mass. If nothing else, Oñate continued, Mass and Communion would bring them good luck.[65]

For the Pueblos who saw how the friars controlled the sacred, mobilized force, conjured rain, healed the sick, and provided the community with meat, there was little doubt that the padres resembled mighty Inside Chiefs. Equally significant was the Franciscans' vow of perpetual chastity, a mark of immense spiritual strength to the Indians. "Continence . . . [was] essential to being *teshkwi*, sacred," writes Elsie C. Parsons. Pueblo men temporarily abstained from sex while practicing their ritual magic, but the idea that men would willingly pledge themselves to life-long chastity was truly astounding. Understandably some of the Indians responded to the presence of these new caciques by offering them gifts of food, labor, and respect to obtain their ritual blessings and gifts, as they previously had done with their own native chiefs. Others probably took a wait-and-see attitude toward the friars, and still others wanted nothing to do with these witches.[66]

The forceful conquest of the Pueblos by the Spaniards and the imposition of their Christian deities and leaders was a familiar process to the Indians. As a result of the warfare that had plagued their world, they understood very well the habits of victors: how they imposed their tribal gods, their chiefs, and their rituals. As we saw, the Pueblo female rituals, which celebrated the transformation of outsiders into insiders, of virile warriors into native chiefs, be it through fertility or scalp dances, attested to this. Ever since Franz Fanon wrote on African colonialism we have come to see as axiomatic the tendency for certain colonized adults to ally themselves with the colonizers. They do so at certain times but not at others, and in certain spaces but not in others.

It was thus to be expected that some of the native chiefs rapidly allied themselves with the Franciscans, subordinating their pantheon of gods to that which the Europeans brought. We see this poignantly in the words Sanaba, a native chief, allegedly uttered to Fray Alonso de Benavides in 1626 on presenting him with a gift of a soft deerskin decorated "with the sun and the moon, and above each a cross." "What did the picture mean?" asked Benavides. Sanaba explained:

Father, until now we have not known any benefactors as great as the sun and the moon, because the sun lights us by day, warms us, and makes our plants grow; the moon lights us by night. Thus we worship them as our gods. But, now that you have taught us who God, the creator of all things is, and that the sun and moon are His creatures, in order that you might know that we now worship only God, I had these crosses, which are the emblems of God, painted above the sun and the moon. We have also erected one in the plaza, as you commanded.

Benavides was deeply moved by the gift and "placed it on the high altar as a banner from the enemy as evidence of their high intelligence."[67]

Fray Estevan de Perea reported with great glee that in 1629 the chiefs of the Zuñi Pueblos presented themselves to Fray Roque de Figueredo asking "to be purified by the sacred ceremony of baptism." On the appointed day, before a specially constructed altar, Father Roque christened their "highest chief" with the name Agustín (it being the feastday of Saint Augustine). Agustín then turned to his people, exhorting them "to accept such a good law and such a good God . . . he had been baptized and had not died from it, but, on the contrary, that he felt such great rejoicing and courage in his heart that he considered himself to be much braver than before." On hearing this, Agustín's tribesmen were said to have also clamored for baptism.[68]

But such windfalls were rare. More common, said Fray Estevan de Perea in 1633, was for the Indians to receive the friars "with some coolness, because the devil was trying in all possible ways to impede and obstruct the promulgation of the divine law." Perea's work in the Hopi Pueblos had been particularly difficult because an Indian apostate from a Christian pueblo preceded him, announcing that "some Spaniards, whom they would meet shortly . . . with the tonsures and vestments were nothing but impostors and that they should not allow them to sprinkle water on their heads because they would be certain to die from it." [69]

This explained why, when Fray Roque de Figueredo arrived in Hawikuh in 1628, the town chief explained that neither he nor his people wished to become "wet-heads" (the Indian name for baptized Christians) "because with the water of baptism they would have to die." The Puebloans probably had death from diseases and labor drafts in mind. But Figueredo gave their words little thought and brazenly concluded that "the words of the demon are equivocal, he really wanted to say that they had to die for their guilt and sin, and for his domination." The cacique urged his people "to throw that foreign priest out," but as the friar's presence deeply divided the community, he was not expelled. [70]

We noted in passing, while discussing the 1599 trial of the Acoma Indians for the murder of thirteen Spaniards, how deeply divided and ambivalent the Indians were in their reception of the Christians. Xunusta explained that "some Indians wanted to make peace but others did not, and because they could not agree, they would not submit." Similar internal divisions greeted the Franciscans at many pueblos. We read about the assassination attempt on Quinía, the wounded war chief from whom Fray Gerónimo de Pedraza extracted an arrowhead. Quinía's fellow warriors tried to kill him because of his friendliness toward the friars. [71]

Not too surprisingly, at some pueblos civil war broke out. Pueblos were inherently prone to factionalism by their very structure; the stress of the conquest and Christianization only exacerbated latent rifts. The division between warriors and medicine men became so pronounced, said Fray Alonso de Benavides in 1626, that

The warriors attempted to reduce all the people to their dominion and authority; and the sorcerers [medicine men], by emulation and argument, persuaded them all that they were the ones who made the rain fall and the earth yield good crops, that they formed the clouds in the heavens, with that variety of colors which the sunset often gives them, and such other things, at which the warriors jeered greatly. This gave rise to civil wars among them, and countless numbers were slain. [72]

When a pueblo stood united against its friars the effects were unequivocal. The medicine men at Taos constantly bewitched their padres, adding urine and mouse meat to their corn tortillas, finally killing Fray Pedro de Miranda in 1631. Jémez likewise did not find the gospel "as sweet as honey"—a favorite Franciscan expression. They killed their friars, burned their church, and fled to the hills in 1623. Yet amid these and other such episodes of aggression, the 1632 behavior of the Zuñi warriors is instructive. The Zuñis killed Friars Francisco de Letrado and Martín de Arvide that year, decapitated and scalped the two, and took their hands and feet as trophies. If, as was customary, the women robbed these scalps of their power through intercourse, and adopted them into their households through feeding, the expectation was that the friars' spirits had been transformed into beneficent domestic gods. The only problem with this ritual formula and interpretation was that the Spaniards did not share it and avenged the death of the friars as they had promised, waging a war of blood and fire.[73]

The Franciscans' assault on the religious (political) structure of the Indian community to impose their charismatic authority was consciously coupled with an effort to disrupt the system of calculated gift exchange between juniors and seniors that structured inequality in Pueblo society. Before examining concretely how they accomplished this, we turn first to a discussion of Franciscan religious formation, for two reasons. First, the model of generational conflict that the life of St. Francis of Assisi, the Order's founder, offered men—that is, a youthful conversion and rejection of biological paternity for a spiritual father in heaven—was the ideal the friars consciously sought to emulate in their own lives and in the conversion of the Indians. Second, the model for personal transformation that the Franciscan Rule offered men to attain personal sanctity would explicitly double as their model of evangelism among the Indians.[74]

Franciscan Spiritual Formation

The Franciscans who came to New Mexico during the seventeenth century were a legion of highly disciplined ascetic virtuosi who had forsaken the world to bear witness to Christ. Heirs to the purificatory spirit of the Spanish Counter-Reformation, many of these mendicants were radicals who believed that Christianity could only be reinvigorated through the strictest interpretation of Franciscanism, with its emphasis on severity of discipline, mystical retreat, and abject poverty. As men who sought personal sanctity by emulating the life of St. Francis, vowing themselves as Francis had to a literal imitation of Christ, the Franciscans saw themselves as polemicists for spiritual life. By rejecting the male cult of sexual aggressiveness associated with warfare, by shedding the material trappings of wealth in a Spain that had grown fat on the spoils of the New World, and by forsaking the ties of kinship for a spiritual father in heaven, the friars hoped to critique the vainglories of the world, and thereby turn society to repentance.[75]

The method the Franciscan Order employed to simultaneously transform the "outer man" (behavior) and "inner man" (the soul), thereby
leading him to holiness, was elaborated in the *Instrucción y doctrina de
novicios Sacada de la de San Buenaventura* and the *Cartilla y doctrina
espiritual para la crianza y educación de los novicios que toman el hábito
en la orden de N. P. S. Francisco.* As the titles of these novitiate guides
indicate, they were largely based on St. Bonaventure's mystical tracts,
particularly *The Soul's Journey into God* and *The Triple Way, or Love
Enkindled,* and peppered with quotations from other classics of Spanish
mysticism. The personal re-formation elaborated in these guides was ter-
nary, consisting of first, purgation of the old self, second, an illumination
modeled on the exemplary lives of Christ and St. Francis, and third, a
mystical marriage or union between Christ (the Bridegroom) and the individual soul (the bride).[76]

The novice began his spiritual re-formation by purging himself of all
that was flesh and blood, all that one had or could have in the world.
"Like an Apostolic Serpent" the novice turned his back on the world,
"entered himself . . . shedding his old skin and dressing his nakedness
solely with tears of mortification and repentence." To tame the will and
to triumph in the war the flesh vigorously waged against itself, novices
were taught how to arouse the sting of conscience, how to sharpen that
sting, and how to direct it against the soul's enemies—the world, the
flesh, and the devil. The flesh, the major source of haughtiness and pride,
"had to be tamed, punished . . . and repressed with devout and continu-
ous prayer, with flagellations, vigils, fasts [and] abstinences from food
and drink."[77]

As men dead to the world, the friars' bodily techniques were to reflect
the Christ they carried in their hearts. Novice masters taught them how
to walk, sit, speak, and eat. If food brought them excessive pleasure, they
were to dull their palates as St. Francis had, mixing ashes into their food
or diluting it with water to make it tasteless.[78]

Next, novices were implored to root out concupiscence from their
hearts, a sin broadly defined as all carnality, curiosity, and vanity. Lust
was the ugliest of these sins because it "was a metaphor for all impurity,
for all worldliness." The chronicles of Franciscan sainthood read to or by
the novices were replete with men who exposed their bodies to snow and
icy pools of water to extinguish the libidinous flames that burned within
them, or to fire to numb and purify the stirrings of human desire. Novice
masters warned their neophytes that, in the words of Ecclesiastes (7: 26),
"more bitter than death I find the woman who is a hunter's trap, whose
heart is a snare and whose hands are prison bonds. He who is pleasing to

God will escape her, but the sinner will be entrapped by her." The only woman that should command their attention was the Blessed Virgin Mary, a woman whose sexual purity was intact.[79]

To triumph over concupiscence, the desire for worldly goods had to be "shunned as carefully as lust for women." Here the novice master impressed on his pupils the importance of poverty, a poverty that meant not only the rejection of material wealth but a "spiritual denudation" as well, eschewing all favor, praise, and honor.[80]

Once the novice had purged his old self and put a silence to human stirrings, he progressed to the next stage of spiritual development, illumination. Christ was the way, the truth, and the light; through Him novices were illuminated and filled with sanctifying grace. No man had more perfectly imitated Christ than St. Francis. Thus only by knowing Francis and modeling one's life after his would a novice come to know Christ; only by imitating both men would the novice die to his old self and pass over to the loving embrace of the Father.[81]

The various biographies the novices read to learn of the life of St. Francis told the story of Francis Bernardone, the son of a wealthy Assisi cloth merchant who had spent most of his teens as a rowdy pleasure-seeker, given to womanizing, wantonness, and buffoonery. Then, in 1204, at the age of 23, Francis suffered a profound psychological crisis marked by confusion, repeated bouts of illness, and a series of disturbing dreams. As a result of this crisis, Francis withdrew into prayer, meditation, and works of charity, eventually shedding the material symbols of his social status and repudiating his father for the Father in heaven.[82]

Having turned his back on the world, Francis dedicated his life to a literal and uncompromising imitation of Christ, preaching of perfect poverty and humility. Francis' love for the crucified Christ was so intense that when he meditated on the crucifixion he sobbed and sighed. So burning was his desire to imitate Christ, wishing to die like Him a martyr's death, that in 1219 he traveled to the Holy Land. Francis' martyr's crown was finally given to him on September 12, 1224. The crucified Christ in the form of a six-winged seraph appeared to him and imprinted the wounds of the crucifixion on his body. At last Francis bore on his body the crucified Christ that he carried in his heart.[83]

The life of St. Francis was the story of one man's psychological crisis and youthful religious conversion. Men and women who sought personal sanctity could, like Francis, put on the crucified Christ by embracing his Order's rule, rejecting the world's material trappings, and transforming their bodies, confident that by so doing, their souls would be led to salvation. Francis' stigmata proved that inner personal virtue could be known to others through external means. Thus for the Franciscans, example—especially literal example—more than preaching or appeal to reason, was the best way to lead souls to salvation.[84]

Novices were further illuminated by observing God's presence in nature. This idea that humanity could know God through nature greatly facilitated the incorporation of the Pueblo pantheon of animal deities into Christian ritual and accounts for most of the pastoral symbolism one finds in Franciscan mission iconography.[85]

Once illuminated, the novice progressed to the unitive stage of spiritual development. Here was the acme of self-absorption, when the novice turned within himself to marvel at God's presence in the operations of his will, intellect, and memory. When St. Francis reached this pinnacle of perfection he withdrew "into his interior and was totally carried into God." Those who beheld the ecstatic raptures of Francis' followers said that they "were rapt out of themselves, and lay as though dead and insensible to the world."[86]

As the soul (always referred to as Christ's bride) approached mystical marriage with her Bridegroom, Christ, she yearned for the security of his love, seeking the tranquility of His embrace through tribulation and suffering. Like the apostles who rejoiced in their pain and abuse, the friar showed his selfless love for those who despised and persecuted him by seeking a martyr's death.[87]

The desire for martyrdom in Franciscan ideology was a supreme act of charity akin to Christ's crucifixion, signifying that the friar so perfectly loved God that he willingly gave his life for his neighbor's salvation. "A servant of God ought always to desire to die and to end by the death of a martyr," St. Francis enjoined his disciples. Thomas of Celano tells us in the *Vita Prima* that Francis had sought martyrdom "not terrified by the fear of death, but rather *drawn by the desire for it*." Always the words of the evangelist Luke were on his lips: "whoever loses his life for my sake will save it."[88]

Through martyrdom, literal or figurative, the soul finally reached the summit of perfection, uniting with God in a spiritual marriage. The descriptions of this marriage in the Franciscan novitiate manuals were derived from two mystical traditions. The first, a joyful bridal lyricism inspired by St. Bernard of Clairvaux's sermons on the Song of Songs, described union with God through the metaphor of sexual intercourse.[89]

Listen as the bride (soul) cries out to her bridegroom (Christ): "enflame me and embrace me totally with the fire of your love so that my entire soul melts on you, flows on you, and is united perfectly with you." Passionately she begs "that He kiss me with a kiss of His mouth," with that kiss symbolizing their perfect union. When the Bridegroom beholds the soul's nakedness, "he pities her and spreads his cloak to cover her, saying that this is the moment reserved for lovers and for their sweet breasts, and he gives her wine to drink . . . from the cellar of divine love." Now she wishes only that He "penetrate her intimately and to the depth of her heart. She wishes that He whom she desires would not show Himself to her under an exterior form but that he come as an infusion into her, not that He appear to her but that He penetrate her." Pierced by the "lover's arrows," carried away on the "wings of love," enflamed by the "fires of love," she sings libations of praise, benediction, and adoration to her Spouse. Rapturously she utters, "O my Love! Ah, Love of my Life!" [90]

Such blissful descriptions of mystical marriage were intertwined with a second motif that focused on the wrenching pains of the crucifixion. Here union was the soul's death in Christ and their mutual passage into God the Father. Though this union was erotic, it was bathed in tears and harrowing groans of dolor. We hear Christ shouting from the cross, "My God! My God! Why have you abandoned me?," paradoxically torn by joy and despair as he approached his Father. St. Bonaventure described this union well when he wrote:

transformed into Christ by your burning love for the crucified, pierced by the nails of the fear of God, wounded by the spear of superabounding love, transfixed by the sword of intimate compassion, seek nothing, desire nothing, wish for no consolation, other than to be able to die with Christ on the cross. Then you may cry out with the apostle Paul: "With Christ, I am nailed to the cross. It is now no longer I that live, but Christ lives in me" (Gal. 2: 19–20). [91]

The incendiary passion of these lovers was a chaste one; a mere allegory on human love. "In order to eliminate all taint of carnality from our idea of our Spouse's love," St. Bonaventure warned novices, "the bride is called also a sister; for sisters are never the object of carnal love." [92]

But for men who joined the Franciscans having known carnal love either in or outside of marriage, or through popular literary and artistic works, the line between allegory and eroticism was indeed a fuzzy one. What was the novice to think when he awoke in the middle of the night aroused, having homoerotically dreamed of Christ's kisses and of His intimate embrace? Novice masters anticipated such moments and urged friars to give themselves fifteen lashes and enter Christ through his wounded side. "Place the eyes of our soul on the holiest wounds of your Redeemer and lord, hugging his cross, looking particularly at that holiest open wound and at the blood which flows from him, from his entire person, body and cross which he shed for us; supplicating with loving affection that he defend you from your enemies." [93]

It is easy to see the sublimation of sexual desire in the prayers, hymns, and sermons to Christ's wounds. Iconographically, as Virginia Reinburg has so splendidly demonstrated, images of Christ's wound were often disembodied, placed in reliquaries, and venerated not in a horizontal position, as we have come to know it, but in a vertical position so that the wound and its streaming blood could easily be read as vaginal lips and pubic hair. And if one has difficulty seeing the sublimated eroticism in the meditations to Christ's wound, dare to look at the mystical marriage depicted in Francisco de Ribalta's 1628 painting "Christ Embracing St. Bernard," which pulls back the veil of desire. In this painting a muscular Christ, his torso barely clad, his wounded side prominently displayed, sits atop angel-borne clouds and embraces the bride below Him. She (St. Bernard) stands agog, the whites of her eyes rapturously fixed upon Him. Much is suggested in the movement of their rumpled clothes, in the fluttering of the angels' wings, in the active and passive positions of the Bridegroom and his bride, and in the climactic excitement of the moment.[94]

But let us not stop to catch our breaths. Let us push on to tease the political from these descriptions of union with God. Among the Pueblo Indians sexual intercourse was a metaphor for politics. Coitus was the symbol of cosmic harmony created through the union of opposites (male-female, sky-earth, rain-seeds). So with the Franciscans for whom the purified eros of mystical union was the epitome of hierarchy and order in which the higher power took care of the lower, the lower aspired to the perfection of the higher, each according the other the reciprocal care of an ideal family.[95]

Franciscan Evangelism

Having examined the logic of the model of spiritual re-formation Franciscans embraced to attain personal sanctity and described the principles of hierarchy and order implicit in it, we are well prepared to discuss how this model doubled as the Franciscan model of evangelism among the Pueblos. If the Indians were to reach God, they too would have to be led through purgation, illumination, and union. This clearly emerges when the friars outlined their mission in New Mexico as that of leading the Indians "out from the darkness of paganism and the somberness of death" and into the "Father of Light."[96]

The purgation of the Indian's soul began with a systematic repudiation of Pueblo religion. The Indians had to renounce Satan, banish his earthly assistants (native chiefs), and forsake their superstitious beliefs and idols. To assure that the Indians did not cling to their idolatry the friars raided homes, confiscating katsina dolls, ceremonial masks, prayer sticks, and fetishes. Fray Alonso de Benavides boasted in the 1620s that on one day alone he had seized "more than a thousand idols of wood," which he incinerated before the assembled community with the derisive laughter of an iconoclast. The padres entered the kivas, profaned them, and built crosses on them to delimit a new sacred topography. Indians complained that such defilements put their gods to flight. The friars were delighted to hear this and boasted that they had driven the devil from his house.[97]

Once the visible forms of idolatry had been destroyed, the friars turned their attention to the wretched sins of the flesh. Sex in Pueblo society was a positively valued activity that assured social and cosmic reproduction. Few restrictions were placed on sexual pleasures, and certainly guilt and remorse were not associated with such activities. Ginés de Herrera Horta marveled in 1601 at the naturalness with which the Pueblos regarded their bodies, noting how they walked about "stark naked without any . . . indication of self-consciousness." The Old Testament book of Genesis explained that Adam and Eve had experienced shame because of the Fall. Yet, here was a people who went about naked without shame. Why was this? Pedro de Castañeda posed and then answered his own question in 1540, concluding that the Indians were born naked and thus "go about as they were born."[98]

But for Franciscans who had vowed themselves to celibacy out of a deep sexual guilt, the nexus between sexuality and the sacred in the Indian world was extremely repugnant. Descriptions of Pueblo sexual practices written by the friars must be read with this bias in mind. The Pueblos certainly were sexually spirited; of this there is no doubt. The ribaldry of their dances, which ended in intercourse, the sexual toponyms that demarcated their landscape, and the "lewd" behavior that transpired at incorporation rituals, be they with humans, scalps, or game, are all too well documented from various points of view to be dismissed as clerical anxiety. Pueblo songs, myths, and tales recount with great gusto the feats, liberties, and license of "night-prowlers" and "creeping-lovers" who routinely sought the affections of women. The Puebloans practiced serial monogamy and polygamy, and seemed undisturbed by sexual variance. The main distinctions the Christian lexicon had to describe Indian sexual practices were those of sin. Thus the Pueblo *berdaches*, those half-men–half-women who symbolized cosmic harmony, were simply *putos* (male whores) and *sodomitas* (sodomites) to the Spanish. Even the position in which the Indians copulated was "bestial," said the friars, because "like animals, the female plac[ed] herself publicly on all fours." Intercourse in this *retro* (from behind) position dishonored humans, lowered them to the level of animals, and violated natural law. What appropriately became known as the missionary position was the "natural manner of intercourse," advised the seventeenth-century Spanish theologian, Tomás Sánchez, "because this manner is more appropriate for the effusion of the male seed, for its reception into the female vessel." [99]

Should we be led by these descriptions to the conclusion the Franciscans wanted the readers of their letters, reports, and denunciations to reach, namely, that the Pueblos led lives of unbridled lust? I think not. Their comments were thick with clerical anxieties over the sinfulness of the flesh and served as a political justification for the regime of sexual repression they felt was necessary to lead the Pueblos to God. Anthropologists attest that every society has rules governing sexual comportment, especially about such things as incest. Thus when we read the 1660 Inquisitorial denunciation of Fray Nicolas de Chávez, which states that when the Pueblos staged the katsina dances they frolicked in sexual intercourse—"fathers with daughters, brothers with sisters, and mothers with sons"—we must ask: What rhetorical end did such a statement play in the contestation between Indians and Spaniards over the place and meaning of sexuality in a well ordered society? The friars clearly had an answer and thundered it wherever they preached. [100]

The laws of God commanded chastity before marriage, fidelity within the nuptial state, life-long indissoluble monogamy, and modesty and shame in all bodily matters. Men and women who practiced "bestial" activities, who wallowed in their pagan promiscuity, violating Christian laws of sexual morality, had to be publicly whipped, placed in stocks, and sheared of their locks. Only thus would the flesh be purged of its sinfulness. [101]

Excruciating as these punishments were, people were not so easily cowed into abandoning those practices—sexual or otherwise—that gave order to their cosmos. In all honesty the Franciscans had to admit as much. Try as they might to bridle Indian concupiscence, their successes were rather superficial. Reflecting in 1627 on his life's work among the Pueblos, Fray Tomás Carrasco concluded that it had been extremely "difficult to extirpate this evil [polygamy and promiscuity] from among them." He recounted how one day while imploring the Indians to live monogamously, a woman confused them by preaching against it. "A bolt of lightning flashed from a clear untroubled sky, killing that infernal agent of the demon right in the midst of those good Christian women who were resisting her evil teachings." Carrasco was elated that God had struck "the witch" dead. The Indians interpreted the event differently. For them, persons struck by the germinative force of lightning immediately became cloud spirits, thus confirming that what the woman said was morally true.[102]

Once purified, the Indians were ready to receive the illuminating light of the gospel. This stage on the road toward God required the total reorganization of Indian life through intensive religious, political, and economic education at a *doctrina* (Indian parish). Christianity was an urban religion that flourished best in towns and cities. Thus the first task of the Franciscans was to concentrate widely dispersed Indian villages. Three mission types (of occupation, penetration, and liaison), which corresponded roughly to levels of urbanization, were established. The first *doctrinas* in New Mexico were missions of occupation established among the Tewa (San Juan de los Caballeros, Santa Clara, San Ildefonso) and the Keres Indians (Santo Domingo), whose densely populated villages dotted the Rio Grande Valley. Once these groups were nominally subdued, itinerant preachers pushed into pagan areas, forming missions of penetration by concentrating small dispersed pueblos into larger towns. The missions of the Jémez area—San José Guisewa and San Diego de la Congregación—were formed in this way, gathering twelve hamlets into two towns. The entire Pueblo region underwent a similar transformation during the seventeenth century; 150 or so villages were reduced into 43. From the missions of penetration, missions of liaison were launched on the frontier. If their work was successful, they would eventually become missions of penetration, and finally missions of occupation.[103]

The transformation of the Indians into model Christians at the missions required radical alterations of the native social structure. So hand in hand with the friars' assault on the political structure of the Indian community was their effort to drive a wedge into the main relationship that structured inequality, the relationship between juniors and seniors and between children and their parents. The model of generational conflict that the Franciscans employed for this task was that offered by their founder, whose youthful conversion had led to a renunciation of his natural father for a spiritual Father in heaven. Men who embraced a religious vocation as Franciscans underwent a similar transformation and thus logically hoped that the Indian children to whom they ministered would likewise convert to Christianity and renounce their parents for the love and benefits the padres offered them.

Through baptism "God makes Himself known to souls," affirmed Fray Estevan de Perea. Through baptism the friars became spiritual fathers to the Indians, offering them a paternity that rivaled the act of physical conception. Like the biological parenthood created through the mingling of an ovum and sperm, so through baptism—a spiritual regeneration—a person was "born again a son of God as Father, and of the Church as Mother," asserted Aquinas in the *Summa Theologica.* "He who confers the sacrament stands in the place of God, whose instrument and minister he is, he who raises a baptized person from the sacred font . . . stands in the place of the Church." Cognizant of the paternal responsibilities the sacrament of baptism engendered, New Mexico's padres strove to "make the Indians understand that the friar [was] their spiritual father and love[d] them very much." Fray Roque de Figueredo frequently proclaimed his "fatherly love" to the Indians, as did Fray Salvador de Guerra, who rationalized some of the most barbaric excesses as "fatherly love." [104]

A century of proselytizing among New Spain's Indians had taught the Franciscans that Christianity could not be constructed easily atop pagan foundations. Certainly some Indian adults would become pillars of the church; the majority would not. If Christianity was to be planted firmly, it would be in the Pueblo youth. New Spain's Indian children were "the smartest and purest" found in the entire world, vaunted Fray Gerónimo de Mendieta. Once they matured and began to know women, "they lost their vigor" and became like the children of any other nation. The Pueblo youth were the image of godly innocence to the Franciscans. Snatched from the devil through baptism, their sexual purity still intact, these juveniles, they hoped, would become the saviors of society. The friars knew that if they could turn sons against their fathers and simultaneously win the youths' loyalties by convincing them that the paternity the padres offered was of greater value, a formidable cadre with which to extirpate idolatry and propagate the faith would have been forged. In Mexico City, in the Yucatán, and in New Mexico as well, the Franciscans tried to fashion a force to disrupt generational lines of authority in the native world. Fray Gerónimo de Mendieta stated the strategy well when he explained that the children became "the preachers, and the children were the ministers for the destruction of idolatry." [105]

Historians of Mexico's Christianization recognized the importance the Franciscans placed on the conversion of Indian youth, but failed to place their discussions of this process in the context of kinship politics. To Friars Toribio Motolinía, Bernardino de Sahagún, Gerónimo de Mendieta, and their missionary colleagues, the politics of kinship was what most occupied them at Indian *doctrinas.* By exorcising Satan through baptism and snatching babes still warm from their mothers' wombs, the Franciscans were engaging in a war for the hearts and minds of Indian children that they had no intention of losing. [106]

The time-tested strategy the Franciscans used to win the loyalty and obedience of the Pueblo children required first the humiliation of their parents, followed by gifts to the children calculated to endebt them to the friars. From the start of New Mexico's Christianization, the warriors of Christ were determined to show the young through naked displays of power just how impotent their fathers and native gods were before the padres.[107]

The humiliation of fathers before their own children was most demeaning when the friars emasculated the men, thereby symbolically transforming them into women. A clerical technique occasionally used to render an obdurate and cocksure Indian submissive was to grab him by the testicles and to twist them until the man collapsed in pain. Pedro Acomilla of Taos complained in 1638 that Fray Nicolas Hidalgo "twisted [his penis] so much that it broke in half," leaving Pedro without "what is called the head of the member." Francisco Quaelone and an Indian called "El Mulato" escaped Fra Nicolas' hand, but were buggered for their insubordination, a posture that the Spanish regarded as a sign of submission.[108]

Changes in the sexual division of labor wrought by the conquest were equally demeaning. Traditionally, men spun, wove, hunted, and protected the community. Women cared for hearth and home and undertook all building construction. The Spaniards established new work categories. Men were to toil in building arts, women were to weave, and hunting, warfare, and all native religious works were to cease. The sight of men performing women's work often provoked giggles. "If we compel any man to work on building a house," said Fray Alonso de Benavides, "the women laugh at him . . . and he runs away." Such men often took refuge among the Apaches and rarely returned to mission life.[109]

Equally humiliating were the religious dramas the friars staged at the missions. Whatever the text of these didactic plays and dances, the subtext ensconced in the generational casting (Indian children playing angels or Christians, the Indian adults playing devils, infidels, or enemies) was the defeat of Indian culture and the subordination of adults to Christianized youths.

If for the adults the friars had only the stick and the whip, for the children there were abundant carrots. We saw in Chapter 1 that parents extracted labor and obedience from their children by controlling the gifts children needed to present to other seniors if they were to obtain the symbols of adulthood—wives, esoteric knowledge, and allies. Whenever a person accepted a gift without offering one in return, a dyadic status relationship was established, obliging the accepting party to reciprocate with perpetual obedience and respect. The Pueblo theory of gifts helps us to understand why the Indians flocked to the missions and freely gave their labor to the friars. As men vowed to evangelical poverty the Franciscans offered seeds, livestock, manufactured goods, and an immense ritual arsenal to the Indians for which they wanted nothing in return. When Fray Francisco de Porras gave gifts to the Indians he always emphasized "that the friars came to give rather than to ask of them." Fray Roque de Figueredo told the Zuñi the same thing in 1628. He had come "not for the purpose of taking away their property, because he and the members of his order wished to be the poorest on earth, but rather he was bringing them help and . . . knowledge of the one true God." [110]

At the missions the friars offered young men livestock, meat, and education in animal husbandry in return for baptism and obedience of God's laws, just as the hunt chiefs before them had taught young men hunting techniques and hunt magic in return for corn and meat payments. Since animals disliked the smell of women and would not allow themselves to be captured by men who had recently copulated, effective native hunt magic was always dependent on temporary sexual abstinence. This fact was not lost on the friars, who distributed livestock to men who promised to live monogamously. In precolonial times seniors had enjoyed the most meat because juniors were always indebted until they reached adulthood. Now obedient and pious junior men were most favored by the friars. Thus in a few years, the introduction of European livestock eroded the hunt chiefs' authority, diminished the importance of hunting in Pueblo society, and totally transformed the age hierarchy on which meat distribution and consumption were based.

In the preconquest period, Pueblo seniors had given juniors wives by providing them with the marriage-validating gifts they had to present their senior in-laws before their marriage and the adult status it symbolized were acknowledged socially. The friars injected themselves into the control of marriage, too. Since the sacrament of matrimony was in their hands, it was only by accepting the gifts the padres offered and by reciprocating, accepting the laws of God and promising monogamy and marital fidelity, that juniors obtained wives. We will see in Chapter 3 that the friars' control of marriage and their imposition of monogamy were the tyrannies that most angered Pueblo men and became the most persuasive reasons for revolt.

The Franciscans' appeal to the Indians as powerful fathers was coupled with an appeal to the Indian women. The friars wanted the women to think of them as feminine nurturing mothers. Fray Juan de Talaban often called his followers to the mission in warm compassionate terms, telling them of God's love and how he would suckle them with the mother's "milk of the Gospel." Fray Juan de Prada spoke of nursing the Indians at "the bosom of the Church." The maternal metaphors the Franciscans used to describe their apostolate among the Pueblos had been employed in Christianity since at least the twelfth century, relying on the symbolism of female breasts, the mouth, and menstrual blood to depict the instruction the Church gave as a maternal outpouring of love.[111]

The allure of the missions for Indian women is difficult to chronicle, because the friars, as men, focused their attention on the people they deemed all-powerful in Pueblo society, the men. As men, too, the friars were excluded from female rituals—rituals they surmised amounted to nothing more than domestic chores. In the documented cases that do exist, the padres won female allies by protecting women's rights, by respecting some of the spatial loci of their power, by instructing them that men and women were equal before God, and by allowing them to continue their worship of the Corn Mother, albeit transmogrified as the Blessed Virgin Mary. Throughout the colonial period, when men—Indian or Spanish—engaged in extramarital sex with native women and failed to reciprocate with gifts, it was the friars who protected women's rights, demanding redress from the culprits. Pueblo women, much like their European counterparts, retained control of the household and over the rearing of children, particularly of the girls who were of little import to the friars. Pueblo women were barred from active participation in male rites. So it was also under Christian rule: women served the priests as auxiliaries, cleaned the church and its altar linens, baked the communion bread, prepared food for feasting, and witnessed men's power to communicate with the gods.[112]

The friars posed not only as fathers to their Indian parishioners, but also as mothers, offering them all the religious, social, and economic benefits of maternity. Among the matrilineal Puebloans, the mother provided one's clan name, totemically named household fetishes, care and sustenance through adolescence, and the use of seeds and land on which to cultivate them. The friar as *mater* offered the young very similar gifts, thereby indebting the children to him. At baptism they were given Christian names by the priest. He was the keeper of the Christian fetishes (religious statuary, devotional pictures, relics, and so on). Daily he called them for instruction in the Gospel and the mores of civilization. At the mission boys received wheat and vegetable seeds, fruit trees, plows and hoes to work the land more efficiently, beasts of burden to expand their cultivation, and most important of all, the recognition of land rights vested in men. Pueblo boys had little contact with their fathers before their adolescent katsina initiation into a kiva. The missions presented the children a radically different model of adult male behavior. Here were grown men caring for children. In church the youths saw images of St. Anthony of Padua fondling the infant Christ, of St. Christopher carrying the Christ child on his shoulders, and of St. Joseph holding his foster son in his arms. That the Franciscans poured so much energy into the care and rearing of juveniles must have reinforced the perception that the friars were also mothers, much as Pueblo town chiefs were regarded as the father and mother of all people.[113]

The gifts Indian children obtained from their Franciscan "mothers" were experienced as losses by their natal mothers. Assessing the erosion of power Pueblo women experienced as a result of the Spanish conquest, we see the contours of what Friedrich Engels described in *The Origins of Family, Private Property and the State*, as the "historic overthrow of Mother Right." Conquest by a patriarchal society meant that Pueblo women lost to men their exclusive rights to land, to child labor, to seeds, and even to children. A thorough discussion of this process is beyond our scope. Here, suffice it to say that all of the Puebloans were matrilineal at the time of the conquest, and that those Puebloans who were in closest contact with Spanish towns became patrilineal or bilateral. Those Puebloans who most resisted Christianization—the Hopi, the Zuñi, and the Keres at Acoma—remained matrilineal. Among these people we still find a vibrant array of women's fertility societies, spirited ceremonials to vivify the earth, and a host of descendant earth-bound symbols that celebrate femininity. Among the Puebloans who became most acculturated to European ways—the Tewa and the Keres (except Acoma)—women's fertility societies were suppressed, their dances to awaken men's germinative powers were outlawed as too sinful, and, given the explicit phallic symbolism of the Snake Dance and the "demonic" character of the katsina dances, these elements of Pueblo ceremonialism largely disappeared. The native symbolism that remained was almost totally ascendant and masculine (sun, fire, arrows, and eagles)—symbols that meshed well with those of European patriarchal religion.[114]

Given the many gifts the friars dispensed and their enormous magical powers, one can only surmise what contradictory emotions the children must have felt on seeing their fathers humiliated and their native gods blasphemed. One vivid example comes to us from a 1626 confrontation between Fray Martín de Arvide and a Zuñi medicine man. Angry that his son was succumbing to the friar's enticements, the Zuñi tried to win back his son. When Arvide heard of this, he angrily accosted the medicine man saying: "Is it not sufficient that you yourself want to go to hell without desiring to take your son also?" Then, turning to the boy the friar said:

"Son, I am more your father and I love you more than he, for he wants to take you with him to the suffering of hell, while I wish you to enjoy the blessings of being a Christian." Father Arvide won that round, and the medicine man retreated. But Arvide's previous bouts with other men had not ended quite as well. In 1621 he publicly scolded a Picuris Pueblo elder for opposing his son's baptism. For meddling in familial government the Indians pummeled and dragged the friar around the plaza, leaving him for dead.[115]

The protracted struggle the Sons of St. Francis waged to become father and mother to the Indian children and to turn juveniles against their parents eventually bore fruit. By injecting themselves and their gifts into a system of calculated exchanges by which seniors gained the labor, respect, and obedience of juniors, the padres forged a cadre of youths who stood ready to denounce the sins of their parents. Blas, a young Isleta boy, behaved just as the Franciscans wanted. On a January night in 1661, Blas entered Isleta's main kiva where he found the elders "invoking the devil" in indigenous ceremonial garb. "You better be careful," Blas told them, "that is what the padres abhor and have forbidden." The men admonished Blas not to tell the friars, but the boy broke his vow as soon as he left the kiva. When the fathers heard of these clandestine incantations, they had the men rounded up and publicly flogged for planting the pernicious seeds of idolatry. The sting of those whips was not soon forgotten by Isleta's men. In 1680 they would have their revenge.[116]

The disruption of Pueblo social life at the missions, be it through the infusion of European gifts into the native economy, the relocation and reaggregation of villages, or the imposition of sexual repression, was coupled with a reorganization of Pueblo notions of time. In fact, Fray Alonso de Benavides in 1634 likened the work of the missions to a clock. "All the wheels of this clock must be kept in good order . . . without neglecting any detail, otherwise all would be lost." Imbuing the Indians with a Christian sense of time required the disruption of their daily routines and their cyclic ritual calendar. The focal point for both of these processes was the mission church.[117]

Every morning at dawn a bell summoned Indian children to church. A lesson in tidiness began the day. The edifice was swept and cleaned, and when it passed inspection, the children took up the "ways of civilization . . . reading, writing, and singing, as well as playing all kinds of musical instruments." Men like Fray Roque de Figueredo who "was proficient in the ecclesiastical chant, harmony, and plain music as well, expert in the playing of instruments for the choir, such as the organ, bassoon, and cornet" led his children in song, hoping thus to lift their spirits. The morning was punctuated by another bell calling all the villagers to Mass. After Mass, the parish census was reviewed to insure that all except those with valid excuses attended instruction. When the day's lesson was complete the Indians went home and returned at dusk for vespers. The neophytes' day ended with singing the praises of God.[118]

The formal education the Indians received at the missions was based largely on Fray Alonso de Molina's *Doctrina Christana*, a 1546 catechism. The pedagogy elaborated therein relied heavily on rote memorization, repeating numerous times the sign of the cross, the *Credo*, the *Pater Noster*, the *Ave Regina*, and the *Salve Regina*. Converts had to commit to memory the fourteen articles of the faith, the commandments of God and of the Church, the mortal and venial sins, the cardinal virtues, the works of mercy, and the powers of the soul and its enemies—the world, the Devil, and the flesh.[119]

Indispensable for the missions' educational goals were the *policía espiritual*, native assistants who served the friars as "spiritual police." Each parish had several *fiscales* (church wardens), disciplinarians who maintained order during services, punished the morally lax, and supervised ecclesiastical building projects. *Fiscales* freely administered half a dozen lashes to anyone found negligent in their Christian duties, prompting many Indians to regard the whip as the Christian symbol of authority. Equally important were the *temastianos* (Indian catechists), who led converts in prayer and memorization of the catechism. After them, a coterie of cantors, sacristans, and bell-ringers were at the friars' service.[120]

"Since not one religious knows any of the languages," said Ginés Herrera de Horta in 1601, by necessity the friars were forced to employ paraliturgies such as dances and edifying plays as their pedagogical tools to indoctrinate the Indians. The friars believed that if the Puebloans were to embrace Christianity and be kept from reverting to idolatry, magnificent ceremonies rivaling native rituals would have to be staged for them. Incense, candles, vestments, and music were essential to "uplift the souls of the Indians and move them toward the things of God," advised Fray Alonso de Molina, "because they are by nature lukewarm and forgetful of internal matters and must be helped by means of external displays."[121]

The Franciscans' focus on paraliturgies rather than on sacramentalism as an evangelization strategy was due not only to their linguistic shortcomings, which many eventually overcame, but also to the Church's fear of inadvertently nurturing heretical beliefs. In the wake of Spanish intolerance toward Islam, Judaism, and Protestantism, the post-Tridentine fathers were hesitant to develop devotions around the sacraments that might be misinterpreted by the natives. Given the Franciscan Order's emphasis on externality (the Christ St. Francis carried in his heart was available to others through the Christ he wore on his body in the form of the stigmata) New Mexico's friars chose to celebrate among the Pueblos rituals that paralleled, or at least on the surface appeared to mimic native dances and rites of passage, regardless of their deeper meanings. For example, the katsina cult was conflated with the Christian cult of the saints. Christian sanctuaries were built atop Indian shrines. Dances for seed life and game were sanitized and allowed to occur in conjunction with devotions to saints associated with horticultural activities. How this process of superimposition and replacement developed is well illustrated in the confabulation of Pueblo prayer-sticks with the cross.[122]

The cross, perhaps more than any other symbol, dominated Christian ritual in seventeenth-century New Mexico. In the daily lives of the Spanish, the cross was a powerful talisman against evil. One crossed oneself before a church, before and after prayers, and in moments of utter terror. Many a pious Christian, heeding St. Francis' injunction that one wear the crucified Christ on one's body, had a cruciform tattoo or cicatrix placed on their forehead. Men and women of every class wore pectoral crosses similar to those they placed over the windows and doors of their homes to mark the sacred from the profane. Helmets, armor, and parade banners bore the cross as a national symbol. Territorial acquisitions were marked with a cross, the symbol of Spanish sovereignty and emblem of the European God's power.[123]

The Indians apparently believed that the cross was a prayer-stick, and the Spaniards thought prayer-sticks were crosses. Whenever the Puebloans called the katsina they offered them prayer-sticks—prayer-sticks that the gods always reciprocated, announcing that they would arrive in a short time. Pedro de Castañeda saw some prayer-sticks near Acoma in 1540 and concluded that the Indians worshiped "a cross . . . [which had at its base] many small sticks adorned with plumes and many withered flowers." Whenever the Spaniards approached an unknown village, they dispatched a cross-bearing emissary to announce their impending arrival. Understandably, the Indians interpreted this act as an announcement that katsina would shortly visit. The Indians greeted Espejo's 1582 expedition "with crosses painted on their heads" and "crosses of colored sticks." The Indians of Pecos Pueblo similarly welcomed Gaspar Castaño de Sosa's 1590 expedition, "making the [sign of the] cross with their hands, saying 'amigos, amigos, amigos.'"[124]

Once the Indians recognized the power of the men who brandished crosses, it took little to convince them to worship the cross. Fray Francisco López began converting the Mansos by constructing a cross in their settlement, explaining that if they worshiped it "they would find aid for all their needs." Teaching through example, López fell to his knees, kissed the cross, and ordered the neophytes do likewise. Then "there came an Indian woman with a toothache; with much devotion she held open her mouth with her hands and put her teeth close to the holy cross. Another, in the pains of childbirth, touched the holy tree with her body." Both women felt great "comfort and joy," the fathers tell us, and presented cornmeal offerings to the cross. One will never really know how deeply the Indians understood the meaning of the cross, considering that from the very start of the conquest they defined it in native terms. According to Barbara Tedlock, the Puebloans today believe that prayer-sticks symbolize human sacrifice. If such a meaning existed in the seventeenth century, then the idea that the cross represented Christ's sacrifice for humanity's sins must have resonated at least partially in their imaginations.[125]

The reorganization of Puebloan temporal rhythms was also undertaken by establishing a rival ritual calendar that was incarnational and Christocentric—focused on Christ's birth and death rather than on cosmological events. For this the friars depended primarily on the *autos sacramentales*, didactic religious plays based on New and Old Testament narratives, popular Christian traditions, and episodes from the history of Mexico and New Mexico's conquest. Historians and literary critics for some time have regarded these plays as quaint folkloric curiosities, ignoring their powerful political content and the values their rhetorical gestures were intended to communicate. The text of every *auto* had a subtext concealed in the costumes, generational casting, and dramatic actions. Every text had its context. Drama was not pure entertainment but a moving, pedagogical instrument. The explicit purpose of the *auto* was to inculcate the Indians with a highly ideological view of the conquest, simultaneously forging in their minds a historical consciousness of their own vanquishment and subordination as the Spaniards wanted it remembered.[126]

Memory of the Spanish conquest was kept vivid in the Indian mind through a tripartite ritual formula—greeting, battle, and submission—articulated by Fray Estevan de Perea in 1633. First the Indians greeted their Spanish overlords with varying degrees of pomp and pageantry as they had in 1598—if a priest, by kissing his feet; if a civilian, by kissing his hand. Next came a battle. In 1599 the Spanish unleashed their fury against Acoma Pueblo, but to teach the Indians the ideal social order under Christian rule, plays such as "The Christians and the Moors" were often enacted. Seventeenth-century performances of "The Christians and the Moors" were marked by "loud acclamations from the soldiers, with a salvo of harquebuses, and by skirmishes and horse races." The *farolitos* and *luminarias* used today as decorative lanterns announcing a major feast were then fires evocative of warfare. One Taos Indian woman recently explained that the gunfire still heard during Pueblo fiestas symbolized "the brute force the Spanish used." The didactic *autos*, whatever their themes, always ended on a common note: the Indians' defeat and their acceptance of Christian rule. Greeting, battle, and submission marked the founding of Our Lady of Guadalupe Mission near El Paso in 1668. After the friars had been welcomed, "twelve dozen firecrackers, a beautiful castle, two mounted horsemen, rockets, bombs and bombards were fired." Then the Manso Indians bowed their heads in submission to receive the waters of baptism.[127]

Christianity's early fusions with European cosmological religions prepared it for its contact with the Indians. The preconquest Puebloan ritual year consisted of two six-month halves. A winter cycle devoted to the celebration of animal life began with the solstice on December 21 and ended with the summer solstice on June 21, initiating a summer cycle devoted to plant life. In Pueblo thought, winter was male because life was sustained during those months primarily through men's hunting. Summer was female because seeds, plant life, and the earth on which they grew belonged to women.

The Franciscans fused the calendric rhythms of Pueblo ceremonialism with Christ's life-cycle. Under Christian rule, the preparations to commemorate Christ's birth began on December 16, coinciding exactly with those four preparatory days the Indians observed before celebrating the winter solstice. During the winter solstice each town's clans and esoteric societies celebrated their unity by performing prescribed dances. Now, during roughly the same period, the friars staged a sequence of *autos* and European dance dramas. First there was a performance of *El Coloquio de San José*, telling of St. Joseph's selection as Mary's husband. *Las Posadas*, Mary and Joseph's search for hospice, was also staged on that night and on the eight that followed. Christmas eve began with the *auto* of *Los Pastores*, a play about the shepherds who traveled to Bethlehem to honor and gift the newborn Christ child. The *Misa del Gallo* (Cockcrow Mass) followed, and the night ended with a kissing of Christ's feet at the Nativity crèche. On Christmas day *Los Matachines*, a pantomime dance drama recounting the defeat of the Aztec Emperor Montezuma, his acceptance of Christianity, and obeisance before the mendicants was performed. And finally, on January 6, the feast of the Epiphany, the Christmas cycle ended with the *Auto de los Reyes Magos*, or Christ's adoration by the Three Magi.[128]

It is probably safe to say that the Pueblo audiences did not understand many of the words they heard and had to rely on what they saw— dramatic actions, staging props, and generational casting in which Christianized junior men mocked and subordinated senior men—to make sense of the Christmas plays. So seen, the nativity cycle was a war epic that announced the epiphany of a new warlord, Christ, before whom even mighty kings humbled themselves and offered gifts. The parallels between the mythology surrounding Christ's birth and that of the Twin War Boys, the sons of Father Sun conceived miraculously when a virgin ate two pine nuts, are striking. The War Twins were rowdy and troublesome boys, equated with the forces of nature (lightning and thunder) and always depicted astronomically as comets or the Morning Star. Christ too was the son of God the Father, miraculously conceived by a virgin. The Star of Bethlehem announced his birth. His warriors possessed lightning (gunpowder) and monsters (horses) ready to kill those who did not submit to Christ as their new lord. This undoubtedly explains why at Santo Domingo Pueblo the Ahyana War Dance and at Jémez Pueblo the Bow War Dance are still performed on Christmas morning to honor the newly born war god, Jesus Christ.[129]

The timing of the Christmas liturgies and the winter solstice celebrations were so close that the two became conflated in the Indian mind. Winter was a masculine period when Pueblo hunters and warriors sustained their villages through hunting magic and knowledge of the animal world. The portrayal of Christ as a war god (recall the conceptual relation in Pueblo culture between warfare and hunting) and the prominence of farm animals in the Nativity plays, particularly around the manger, reinforced these links.

Christ's incarnation and birth was but a necessary prelude to the fugue of his crucifixion and death. Joyful as the *glorias* of Christmas Mass were, paradoxically they had a sad, eerie tone to them. Foreshadowing events to come, many pictorial representations of Christ in the manger had on the remote horizon a cross, spikes, and a crown of thorns. Christ's death was the highest drama of the Christian year. And for the Franciscans who carried the crucified Christ in their hearts, Holy Week was the time they imprinted the crucified Christ on their bodies.[130]

The ritual surrounding Christ's crucifixion and death was, like the Nativity, organized around a sequence of didactic plays staged between Palm and Easter Sundays, the last week of Lent. The Stations of the Cross, fourteen episodes in Christ's final days—his condemnation to death, his carrying of the cross (John 19: 17), his assistance by Simon of Cyrene (Mark 15: 21), his meetings with the holy women of Jerusalem

(Luke 23: 27–31), with his mother (John 19: 25), and with Veronica, his three falls en route to Calvary, the stripping and nailing to the cross, his death, deposition, and burial—these were the basic themes of these Holy Week *autos.*

The formal initiation of the ritual of Christ's passion began with the celebration of Mass on Holy Thursday night, commemorating Christ's last supper with his apostles. Like Christ, stripped by his accusers, when Mass ended that night, the mission's main altar was stripped of its linens and ornaments. That night, the night Christ reflected on his own death in the Garden of Gethsemane, was a night of great solemnity. The mission bells were silent that night and only the raucous noise of *matracas* (hand clackers), the doleful laments of *pitos* (flutes), and the swish of whips beating on human flesh pierced the silence of the night. Gaspar Pérez de Villagrá wrote that Holy Thursday night, 1598, "was one of prayer and penance for all." The kingdom's colonists meditated on Christ's passion

with tears in their eyes, and begged forgiveness for their sins. . . . The women and children came barefoot to pray at the holy shrine. The soldiers, with cruel scourges, beat their backs unmercifully until the camp ran crimson with their blood. The humble Franciscan friars, barefoot and clothed in cruel thorny girdles, devoutly chanted their doleful hymns, praying forgiveness for their sins.[131]

At noon on Good Friday the congregation gathered at church and in procession carried statues of the crucified Christ and his mother through a village circuit that led to a symbolic Mount Calvary. The way was agonizingly long for those who staggered under the weight of enormous crosses. Imagine the spectacle of 600 Curac and Tajique Indians carrying "large and small crosses on their shoulders" during their 1655 Good Friday procession. Or the Hopi who that year for their procession dressed "like penitent hermits walking about praying in penitence, carrying crosses, large beads, and wearing haircloth shirts."[132]

Periodically the procession stopped to view tableaux of the Stations of the Cross. When each station ended, active penitents resumed their self-flagellation with *disciplinas* (sisal scourges), which sent bolts of pain through their bodies. Some penitents beat themselves to a pulp with wire-studded whips, which tore tiny morsels of flesh from their backs. Others bound themselves in buckhorn cholla and prickly pear cacti and focused the long, piercing spines on their genitals. Self-inflicted blows with nail-encrusted boards helped others expiate their sins.[133]

When the procession reached Golgotha, St. John's passion was read before a statue of the Crucified. The crowd retired for a few hours, and at day's end, reassembled for the *Santo Entierro,* the deposition and burial of Christ. Christ was taken off the cross, his crown of thorns and the nails were removed, his hinged arms were lowered to his sides, and the image was laid in an open coffin. In a torchlight procession the coffin was carried back to the village church and placed in the niche where it rested throughout the year. With this, the commemoration of Christ's death ended.[134]

How much of the mystery of Christ's crucifixion the Indians understood is open to speculation. As noted earlier, those chiefs and household heads who allied themselves with the Warriors of Christ also must have tried to understand the central tenets of their faith. The esoteric religious knowledge that kept the Pueblo cosmos properly balanced was secret, controlled by seniors, and only slowly and sparingly divulged to young aspirants for gifts. The friars freely preached the word of God for everyone to hear, but the relative ease with which that word was dispensed to men and women regardless of age must have made it banal. Perhaps the caciques and medicine men listened some, eager to learn what gave Christians their power. For only by admitting a superficial understanding of Christianity by the medicine men can we make sense of the calculated profanations of Christian icons that occurred during the 1680 Pueblo Revolt. Whatever their understanding of the sacrifice of Christ, the God-made-man, what was readily apparent from the pomp and solemnity of Good Friday ritual was Jesus's power and the might and sanctity of his earthly representatives, the Franciscans.[135]

On the other hand, quite early in New Mexico's colonization the Spaniards observed the extensive flagellation and bloodletting that accompanied Pueblo male war and rain rituals, and equated them with Christian piety and penitential practice. Hernán Gallegos noted in 1582 that the rain chief looked "like a flagellant." Juan de Ortega in 1601 observed that when the Indians called their gods, they flayed a robust man with reeds. This "penitent," Ortega wrote, "neither groans nor flinches in the least; on the contrary, he undergoes the penance gladly." But it was Fray Alonso de Benavides, who in the 1620s witnessed the ritual of accession for a Pueblo war chief, who most understood the ritual parallel between the war chief's ordeal floggings, which legitimated his use of force as son of Father Sun, and Christ's scourging at the pillar. Benavides writes:

They tied the naked candidate to a pillar, and all flogged him with some cruel thistles; afterward they entertained him with farces and other games, making a thousand gestures to induce him to laugh. If with all this he remained serene and did not cry out or make any movement at the one or laugh at the other, they confirmed him as a very valiant captain and performed great dances in his honor.

Benavides and his brothers, ever so eager to appropriate for their own ends ideas from the Indians' ritual repertoires, made every attempt to present Christ's flaying and death as a ritual that legitimated Christian political authority.[136]

Call it piety or purely political ploy, but on Good Friday eve in 1598, the man who commanded the instruments of force in the colony, Governor Juan de Oñate, "cruelly scourged himself, mingling bitter tears with the blood flowing from his many wounds." The padres did likewise, called themselves "sons of the Sun," insinuated rain gods, and mobilized deadly force. The friars did all of this for Christ the King, the War God of war gods, and to establish their charismatic domination over the native community.[137]

The ritualization of Christ's crucifixion and the penitential flagellation, especially the bloodletting associated with it, seems to have been interpreted by the Indians just as the friars meant it to be, as a rite of political authority. How else can one interpret the following confrontation that took place at Isleta Pueblo in 1660? Fray Salvador de Guerra emerged from his convent one day to find the Indians performing the katsina dance, which he had strictly prohibited. When his repeated exhortations to cease dancing were ignored, the friar stripped himself naked before them, began violently beating himself with a whip, placed a rope around his neck, a crown of thorns on his head, and then crisscrossed the pueblo carrying an enormous cross. When the Indians saw this they immediately stopped their dance, and some, moved to tears by the sight, asked the friar's forgiveness. The others retreated to the safety of their homes, fearing that the Christian soldiers might soon arrive.[138]

Admittedly, there is very little evidence with which to chart the slow symbiosis between the native rituals of authority and the Christian rituals around Christ's crucifixion. Mission inventories repeatedly list paintings of Christ's scourging at the pillar. The fusion of native and Christian symbols seems complete when we hear in a nineteenth-century New Mexican penitential song:

> Upon a column bound
> Thou'lt find the King of Heaven,
> Wounded and red with blood
> And dragged along the ground.

Here a bloody Christ is not scourged at the pillar but bound to a column, just as a native war chief would have been in order to prove his majesty over the cosmic forces of the sky.[139]

The liturgy of Christ's crucifixion became an intense rhetorical contest between the friars and native chiefs for the obedience and respect of the Indians. If the Franciscans proselytized like "madmen to the world," flogged their bodies to a crimson pulp, and dragged enormous crosses through the streets, it was to impress their opponents and to overwhelmingly convince their audiences that the extreme physical ordeals they were capable of enduring were signs of their immense sanctity and superior magical powers. The 1630 shouting match between Fray Alonso de Benavides and a Chililí medicine man illustrates both how familiar and appealing the Good Friday ritual was to the Pueblo Indians, and how the native priests saw in it a competing rite that was eroding their own religious (political) authority. The medicine man jeered at the friar saying: "You Christians are crazy; you desire and pretend that this pueblo shall also be crazy." He was apparently disquieted by how attentively the Indians observed Benavides, and by the fact that bloodletting was being practiced by Christianized Indians where formerly only chiefs had engaged in such communion with the gods. Benavides asked the man to tell him how the Christians were crazy. He responded: "You go through the streets in groups, flagellating yourselves, and it is not well that the people of this pueblo should commit such madness as spilling their own blood by scourging themselves." Benavides tried to explain the meaning of Good Friday to the medicine man, but he refused to listen and retreated muttering that he did not want to be afflicted by Christian madness.[140]

It is only by viewing the confrontation between the Franciscans and the Pueblo chiefs as an intense contest between two theologies for the hearts and minds of the Indian masses that we can begin to understand colonial New Mexican crucifixes with blood streaming from beneath Christ's loincloth, a symbolic wound that has no place in Catholic dogma. We saw earlier how members of Indian war, curing, and rain societies flagellated themselves with cacti to purify their bodies for contact with the holy. We saw the importance of the rain chiefs to Pueblo life and the fact that when the katsina were called or when the Snake Dance was performed, these rites began with purificatory ordeals such as flagellation and bloodletting (including penis laceration) to summon and feed the gods. If we view the flagellations and mortifications the friars routinely practiced as the other side of a polemic in which they were engaged with the rain chiefs over who had the most powerful rain magic and over which religion and which priesthood and magic was superior, we can begin to understand why the Franciscans mutilated their genitals, as the crucifixes seem to indicate. The blood that falls from beneath Christ's loincloth resembles rain drops falling from a cloud.[141]

The Indians may have interpreted Christ's loin blood as rain fructifying the earth because blood had always been seen by them as a male nu-trient of extraordinary fertilizing power. There was an equally long tradi-tion in Christian worship of viewing Christ's blood as a nutrient (for example, the devotion to the Precious Blood of Jesus and to the Sacred Heart). The friars often said that the blood of New Mexico's Franciscan martyrs had been spilt to nurture Christian souls so that a bountiful har-vest might be reaped.[142]

Sexuality and the sacred were closely linked in Pueblo thought but antithetical to Christianity. Many saints had won their places in heaven by denying the flesh, dying as virgins. Thus it would appear that cru-cifixes with bleeding genitals were vivid artifacts of tormented states of mind. Of the misogyny in Franciscan culture we amply know. "Naked," "promiscuous," and "lascivious" Pueblo women provoked deep sexual guilt in some friars, as did the sight of ritual fellatio performed by the rain chief during the Snake Dance. If, as the talion principle holds, one takes an eye for an eye and punishes the organ that causes sin, crucifixes with bleeding genitals tell us much about what the friars thought was the source of sinfulness. Understandably, the friars displaced their sexual de-sires by singing the praises of the Blessed Virgin Mary, a woman un-blemished by her sexuality, and berating those heinous females, those wells of the devil, who celebrated the pleasures of the flesh.[143]

Reviewing the impact of Christianization on the Pueblo ceremonial calendar we see the conflation of Christmas and the winter solstice. Such a fusion did not occur between Holy Week and the summer solstice, which were separated by several months and clashed in terms of seasonal gender concepts. Seeds, germination, and plant growth were the themes of summer Indian ceremonials. Certainly one finds parallel ideas in the liturgy of the resurrection, but for the Franciscans it was Christ's crucifix-ion, not his resurrection, that was the focus of Holy Week ritual. The cru-cifixion was a celebration of male power. The summer solstice celebrated Mother Earth's fecundity and the secret of life the Corn Mothers had given humanity. The prominence of the Mater Dolorosa in the passion plays and the Way of the Cross was certainly one attempt to gloss this seasonal gender disparity, for throughout the Old World and the New, the Blessed Virgin Mary was frequently presented to neophytes as a meta-morphosed grain goddess. To accommodate the Indians' summer fertility rituals, Holy Week was followed closely by a time dedicated to Mary, the month of May. By the eighteenth century, Mary and the Corn Mothers had been merged in religious iconography and myth. The Virgin now ap-peared cloaked in garb decorated with corn ears and stalks with the moon at her feet, surrounded by flowers and butterflies, Indian symbols of fertility.[144]

The feast of Corpus Christi, devoted to the living presence of Christ in the Eucharist, was another focal point of the Christian liturgical year. Corpus Christi was a moveable feast that fell anywhere from May 21 to June 24. The Catholic Church established this feast in 1264 primarily to rival pagan summer solstice rites. The main symbol of the feast of Corpus Christi was the Eucharist displayed in a solar-shaped monstrance. Little evidence exists on how Corpus Christi was celebrated in seventeenth-century New Mexico, but that it was observed is attested by the existence of Blessed Sacrament confraternities and of church inventories that list ritual paraphernalia used specifically for this feast. Moreover, Governor Bernardo López de Mendizábal in 1660 demanded that he be greeted by New Mexico's Indians with the same pomp with which they greeted the Blessed Sacrament on the feast of Corpus Christi (a desire that resulted in his prosecution before the Inquisition). If the feast was observed in New Mexico as it was elsewhere in Spain and New Spain, a solemn High Mass and a procession through the town's streets with a consecrated host were the major events of the day. The ritual function of the Mass was to create communal peace. When the Eucharist was carried in a procession through the streets, the town was integrated as one, temporarily obliterating the ranks and statuses that differentiated its various parts.[145]

Corpus Christi ended the liturgical celebrations commemorating the major events of Christ's life, nicely rounding out the six-month period between the winter and summer solstices. No major Christian feasts were celebrated between June and December, and this relatively dead period in the liturgical calendar may have been fashioned by the early Christian fathers to accommodate pagan first-fruits, harvest, and winter hunting rituals. The anthropologist Alfonzo Ortiz noted some years ago that among the present-day Tewa a clear divison exists between Catholic and ancestral rites, a religious compartmentalization that developed after the conquest. If one recalls that the Puebloans conceived of the year as two gendered six-month cycles, then the period from June to December would have left the Puebloans one cycle, the feminine cycle, intact and uncontaminated by contact with Christian ritual. One suspects that the friars may have had gender symbolism in mind here. Christian rites celebrated masculine power; the Pueblo feminine cycle was devoted to seed life and germination. Thus the Christian liturgical calendar would have reflected the gender representation of the conquest: virile Spanish victors had vanquished effeminate Puebloans.[146]

TABLE 2.1

The Kingdom of New Mexico's Population in the Seventeenth Century

Year	Pueblo Indians		Friars		Spaniards in Santa Fe		Persons Living in Spanish Households	
1598	80,000	(a)	10	(b)				
1601							200	(c)
1609			3	(b)	60	(d)		
1617			23	(p)	90	(e)		
1620	17,000	(f)	16	(f)	100	(g)		
1624	20,181	(h)						
1626	34,650	(i)	43	(i)				
1629			46	(p)				
1630	60,000	(j)			250	(k)	1,000	(k)
1631			66	(m)				
1638	40,000	(l)			200	(l)		
1656			47	(m)				
1657			70	(m)				
1679	17,000	(n)						
1680			32	(o)			2,347	(o)

SOURCES: (a) RBM, 34; (b) France V. Scholes and Lansing B. Bloom, "Friar Personnel and Mission Chronology, 1598-1629," NMHR 19 (1944): 320, 330; (c) Estimate based on Herrera Horta Testimony, Ibid.; (d) Viceregal Decree, January 29, 1609, OD, 1077; (e) Estimate based on presence of "48 soldiers" in Santa Fe reported by Donald E. Worcester, "The Beginnings of the Apache Menace in the Southwest," NMHR 16(1941): 6; (f) Viceroy to King, May 27, 1620, OD, 1140; (g) Estimate based on "50 residents" living in Santa Fe, Ibid.; (h) Fray Gerónimo de Zárate Salmerón's mission census, "Documents for the History of the New Mexican Missions in the Seventeenth Century," NMHR 4(1929):46-51; (i) Fray Gerónimo de Zárate Salmerón, Relaciones. 35; (j) RBM, 34; (k) BM, 22; (l) Petition of Fray Juan de Prada, 1638, HD, 108; (m) Scholes, Troublous Times in New Mexico, 10; (n) Petition of Fray Francisco de Ayeta, 1679, HD, 296-305; (o) Scholes, "Civil Government and Society in New Mexico in the Seventeenth Century," NMHR 10 (1935), 96; (p) Scholes and Bloom, "Friar Personnel and Mission Chronology, 1598-1629: Part II," NMHR, 20(1945): 58, 71.

Assessing the progress of Christianization among the Puebloans, we are left with clerical words that diverge from Indian actions. Dismissing, as the friars did, those Franciscan martyrs whose blood had been shed to nurture the Christian vine, and those "stupid" apostates ensnared by the devil into revolt, the picture the friars painted of their labor in New Mexico was always in rosy colors. Fray Alonso de Benavides, in a moment of exuberance, claimed that his brothers had encountered 500,000 souls in New Mexico in 1598. He later revised the figure downward to 80,000—the number generally accepted today as a fair approximation of the size of the Pueblo population at conquest (see Table 2.1). The first decade of colonization produced few Indian conversions, but in 1607, 7,000 Indians were quickly baptized in order to assure the continuation of New Mexico as a mission field. Christianization apparently progressed rapidly between 1607 and 1640. In 1620 the mission population was 17,000. With the arrival of additional Franciscans (66 by 1631) the neophyte population tripled by 1631 to about 60,000, growing at an annual rate of 11.1 percent.[147]

How genuine were these conversions? Conversion is here defined as a fundamental change in beliefs whereby a person accepted the reality and omnipotence of the Spanish God and vowed to obey Him and his ministers. By this standard the number of true Christian souls was vastly inflated—an inflation born of clerical misinterpretation. There can be no doubt that there were some true conversions. There were the Christianized boys painstakingly educated by the friars who, on their instruction, ransacked pueblos extirpating idolatry. The friars tell us, too, that preconquest fissures in the organization of pueblos were further exacerbated by newborn distinctions between Christianized Indians and "pagans," between Hispanicized converts and traditionalists who clung tenaciously, if clandestinely, to ancestral ways.[148]

The problem remaining is to assess how deeply or shallowly, how warmly or lukewarmly, "wet-heads" (baptized Indians) understood the belief they had embraced. And this is fundamentally a problem of translation. Leaving aside the fact that few of the friars spoke or understood the Indian languages, we must ask whether Catholicism, with its monotheistic emphasis on one God and its moral vision of good and evil, heaven and hell, could have been translated into terms the Puebloans fully understood, given their animistic beliefs and monistic cosmological mental universe lacking either sin or hell. I think it could not have been done too effectively, no matter how great the effort. The simple reason is that the Franciscan model of personal re-formation and evangelism, with its pronounced emphasis on externality—transforming the "outer person" (behavior) to change the "inner person" (the soul)—predisposed the friars to believe that Pueblo dissimulations were true conversions. An evangelization strategy of eradicating native rites and substituting Christian ones that mimicked indigenous gestures and paraphernalia, no matter how divergent their respective meanings, also led the friars to misinterpret the apparent piety with which the Indians worshipped God. Thus whether the Puebloans offered feathers and corn meal to the cross as they had to their prayer-sticks, honored the Christ child on Christmas as they had the Twin War Gods during the winter solstice, or flogged themselves on Good Friday as they had called the rain gods, the meanings attached to these acts were fundamentally rooted in Pueblo concepts.

Those Puebloans who nominally pledged allegiance to Christianity and at least superficially forsook their native ways did so in part out of fear and in part to reap the technological and cultural innovations offered by the friars. For Indian residents of small New Mexican pueblos constantly under attack, despoiled of their food, and forced to abandon well-watered spots, the mission fathers offered the semblance of protection. In numbers there was strength, and behind the massive wall of the mission compound there was security. Christianization to these persons mean a reliable meat supply, iron implements of various sorts, and European foods: wheat, legumes, green vegetables, melons, grapes, and a variety of orchard fruits. It does not strain the imagination to envision why such persons, understandably nervous and ambivalent at the arrival of the "Children of the Sun," might have allied themselves as Christians with the new social order.[149]

Seventeenth-Century Politics

Two diametrically opposed theories of government existed in colonial New Mexico. The first theory, a theocratic one, inspired by the scriptures and formulated by clerics and canon lawyers, described power as emanating from God down through the hierarchy of beings. "There is no authority except from God," stated Romans 13 : 1, the oft-quoted scriptural basis for this theory, "and those [authorities] that exist have been instituted by God." A second theory, best characterized as secular, was rooted in pagan sources, in Aristotle, and in medieval law and custom. Here power and authority were described as ascendant, rising from the populace to the sovereign. In this chapter we examine these theories of government, which shaped political discourse among New Mexico's Franciscans, bureaucrats, and colonists during the seventeenth century. Particular attention is given to those sociopolitical developments that led to the 1680 Pueblo Revolt.[1]

Roman Catholicism was the official state religion in Spain and its colonial empire in the 1600s. This particular Church-state relationship, known collectively as the *real patronato*, or the concessions of royal patronage codified in a series of papal bulls, had been forged during the centuries of the *reconquista* when Spain's monarchs had triumphed over the Moors on the Iberian Peninsula. For proclaiming and defending Catholicism as the one and only true religion, and for promising to convert the infidel in newly conquered territories, the pope had reciprocated, granting Spain's kings the right to establish all ecclesiastical institutions in the realm, to present the Holy See nominations for all ecclesiastical appointments and benefices, to establish diocesan boundaries, to collect and reapportion church revenues, and to review (and even veto) all communications between the pope or the generals of the religious orders and clerics.[2]

With the conquest of America the *real patronato* was extended to the Indies, adding administration of the Catholic Church as the vicar of Christ to the king's jurisdiction over military, judicial, legislative, and commercial matters. The favorite metaphor of the period for the dual functions of the monarch as king and vicar of the church was that of a warrior wielding two swords, one temporal and one spiritual.[3]

The crown's power in the colonies was exercised throughout the colonial empire by three bureaucracies. First was the office of the viceroy, who administered all civil and military matters through a number of provincial governors. Next was the *audiencia*, the district court of appeal. And third was the episcopate, charged with ecclesiastical administration. In his now classic article "Authority and Flexibility in the Spanish Imperial Bureaucracy," John L. Phelan argued that the crown intentionally established each of these bureaucracies as relatively independent but nonetheless interdependent, primarily because it distrusted its overseas officers. Ill-defined and overlapping jurisdictional boundaries provoked endless litigation among the viceroys, *audiencias*, and bishops, effectively checking the power of each group and keeping the crown well informed of its affairs even in the most remote corners of its empire.[4]

Political conflict in New Mexico was rooted in these same institutional rivalries with their ambiguous jurisdictional boundaries. Here the main irritant to harmonious government was the theoretical place of the Indian in the colonial scheme, a topic that dominated most of the dispatches that reached the king. Usually basing their assertions of dominance over the Indians and all provincial matters on the same documents, the Franciscans and New Mexico's governors vigorously contested the lineages of authority spelled out in the *patronato* and the declarations of submission by the Pueblo Indians.

The ecclesiastical theory of government advanced by one party to the political discourse in seventeenth-century New Mexico was Franciscan in inspiration, based largely (though not exclusively) on Fray Juan Focher's *Itinerario del Misionero en América* (1574), and Fray Gerónimo de Mendieta's *Historia Eclesiastica Indiana* (1596). Focher and Mendieta envisioned a theocracy in New Spain in which ecclesiastical authority reigned supreme. Their positions were based on an interpretation of the pastoral functions assigned to the papacy in St. John's Gospel. When Christ said to Peter, "Feed my sheep" (John 21: 15–17), Peter became vicar of all sheep, whether they had heard his voice and entered into the fold (John 10: 1–20) or not. The pope as Peter's successor enjoyed the "same authority held by the Blessed Peter as Vicar of Christ on earth," wrote Focher. His was the exclusive right to appoint the shepherds who would lead faithful and infidel alike. But given the enormity of the task, the pope had delegated some of his authority over the flock in America to the crown in the *real patronato*. Nevertheless, those priests sent directly by the pope to the New World, as the Franciscans in New Spain had been, exercised sacerdotal powers as vicars of Christ. The powers the king enjoyed over the Church in America were his as a vicar of the pope, and not as a vicar of Christ.[5]

Focher and Mendieta maintained that when the first twelve Franciscan "apostles" departed for New Spain in 1523 to begin the conversion of the Indians, they had been dispatched by Fray Francisco de Los Angeles Quiñones, the Minister General of their Order, as "vicars of Christ." Indeed, these friars had been granted quasi-episcopal powers by Pope Leo X (reiterated by Pope Adrian VI in the 1522 bull *Omnimoda*) in those areas where there was no see or where it was two days distant. This included the right to administer all the sacraments except those requiring episcopal ordination, to act as ecclesiastical judges, to bless chalices, altars, and churches, and to impose and absolve excommunications.[6]

From this Franciscan theory of ecclesio-political authority flowed several religiously inspired representations of the polity. The most perfect model for the terrestrial order was the Trinity. The relationships of deference and authority among Father, Son, and Holy Ghost, each with their own roles, but subordinate to the Father, was what the friars wanted humanity to aspire to. The "Act of Possession and Submission" read to the Indian lords of New Mexico in 1598 described such a political order.

In the name of the most holy trinity and the indivisible eternal unity, deity, and majesty, Father, Son, and Holy Spirit, three persons in one, the one and only true God, who, with His eternal love, omnipotent power, and infinite wisdom, rules, governs, and orders . . . in whose hands rest the eternal pontificate and royal priesthood, the empires, kingdoms, principalities, governments and states, large and small, families and individuals . . . Jesus Christ, son of the living God, universal head of the church . . . because of His sorrowful and painful death and triumphant and glorious resurrection [was] . . . granted omnipotent power, authority, and jurisdiction, in civil and criminal cases, over high and low, and power of life and death, both in the kingdoms of heaven and on earth. . . . He left as His earthly vicar and substitute Saint Peter, the prince of the apostles, and his legitimately elected successors. To them He entrusted the Kingdom, power, and empire, and the keys of heaven, in the same manner as Christ God himself had received them from His eternal Father as the head and master of the universe.[7]

Echoing the trinitarian model of hierarchy, and emanating directly from the role ascribed to the Church therein, was an anthropomorphic image of Christian society as a *corpus mysticum*, a mystical body with

Christ as its head. For New Mexico's Franciscans this body was triune—consisting of head, arms, and feet—reflecting the structure of the Trinity. The head governed the body and singularly regulated its various parts. In Christian society the pope was the social head. Since authority over the Church flowed from Christ to Peter to the popes, and from them to the Franciscans, New Mexico's prelates continuously asserted that as vicars of Christ they were the head of the body politic and therefore reigned supreme over all provincial matters.[8]

Imagining the body politic in this way led Fray Antonio de Artega, one of New Mexico's early Franciscan prelates, to assert that the role of the provincial governor and the soldier-settlers was to serve as the Church's "arms and hands that defended and protected it from heretics and other enemies." New Mexico's Indians were "the feet which sustain and carry the weight of the entire body." They paid the Spanish *encomenderos* tribute in return for protection and indoctrination in Christian culture. Fray Martín de Ojacastro carried this body metaphor further, describing the soldiers as "the bones or the fortitude [of the body] and the Indians the flaccid flesh." He urged Spaniards and Indians to become one people through faith and love, otherwise "the bones would tear its own flesh into bits and the flesh would separate itself from the bones."[9]

Throughout the seventeenth century New Mexico's Franciscans asserted their claim to headship over the body politic as vicars of Christ and tried to impose their will through three ecclesio-political institutions: the prelacy, the Holy Office of the Inquisition, and the Office of the Holy Crusade. The Franciscan superior in New Mexico, known as a *custos* or custodian, exercised quasi-episcopal powers as prelate and ecclesiastical judge ordinary for the kingdom, settling everything from domestic discord to ecclesiastical censures. The "final and surest authority," said some, was the Holy Office of the Inquisition established in New Mexico in 1626 to eradicate heresy and impose religious orthodoxy. Widely feared was the Inquisition's warrant to impound the property of its accused, to demand public penitence, and to relegate to oblivion in its secret prisons those who were deemed incorrigible. Least forbidding of the three tribunals was the Office of the Holy Crusade (Santa Cruzada), which collected and administered a tax, the *Cruzada*, conceived initially to benefit the participants of the crusades to Jerusalem. The *Cruzada* evolved in Spain into a tax earmarked for the propagation of Catholicism, and it reached New Mexico in 1633, where despite repeated complaints from the settlers that they too were waging a crusade against the infidels and should be exempt, the officers of the Holy Crusade continually levied the tax and seized intestate properties.[10]

In most areas of Spanish America these three institutions were administered by different segments of the clergy, secular and regular, who were often at odds with each other over ends and means. But in New Mexico all three were controlled by the Franciscans, and under the terms of the *real patronato* both they and their assistants were theoretically immune from civil jurisdiction and impingement by viceregal functionaries. The concentration of ecclesiastical roles in the hands of a small group of friars gave them enormous power to fashion the religious commonwealth they envisioned; and their vision, as we will see, was vigorously contested by the provincial governors as the king's representatives, and by some of the colonists as well.[11]

As Christ's vicars, New Mexico Franciscans regaled themselves with the insignias and trappings of divinity, confident that the theocratic model of government they espoused had been ordained by God. Their symbol of authority in every mission, said Fray Estevan de Perea in 1632, was "the scepter [transformed] into the caduceus of Mercury, a true shepherd's staff studded with eyes—and also a rod of peace and justice—to watch over the preservation of these conversions." Whenever a Franciscan prelate entered Santa Fe for the first time, or visited the missions in his province, he expected to be greeted with the *adventus*, that antique ritual welcome which had honored Roman emperors as divine saviors and benefactors. True to ancient formulas, when Fray Alonso de Benavides, the newly elected prelate, approached Santa Fe on January 24, 1626, "at the outskirts of the city there came to welcome him the governor, alcaldes, cabildo, all the other people, properly arranged on horseback in war array." They accompanied Benavides into Santa Fe in procession, "firing great salvos with their harquebuses and artillery, placing him in the position of honor." Though simple friars expected less ceremonious welcomes when they entered Indian villages, the Indians nonetheless had been taught that when the friars approached their towns, they should "receive them in procession, carrying a large cross, garlands of flowers," and lighted candles, and singing libations of praise and benediction akin to those with which they greeted the Blessed Sacrament on the feast of Corpus Christi. As we saw in Chapter 2, such greetings would keep fresh in Indian minds their defeat and humiliation before their Christian lords.[12]

Baroque as the theoretical justifications of Franciscan authority in New Spain were, the legal reality was that Spain's sovereign was both *rex et sacerdos*, king and high priest over the Indies. Inspired by medieval theories of divine kingship, since the Iberian reconquest Spain's monarchs had insisted on episcopal consecration and anointment to authenticate their authority as divinely derived. When a bishop representing Christ anointed the king's body with chrism, that body was imbued with divinity, conjoining the human and divine, thus reflecting on earth that kingdom the *pater noster* said existed in heaven.[13]

Fundamental to the exercise of divine kingship were the legal rights over the Church that the papacy had conceded to Spain's monarchs in the *real patronato*. Royal jurists maintained that by virtue of the bulls of royal patronage the king was the Vicar of Christ. As vicar he administered the Church and guaranteed Indian instruction. As king he governed and upheld justice. We have to look no further than the already cited 1598 "Act of Possession and Submission," read by Don Juan de Oñate to the Pueblo Indians, to see how the same document could be read as a writ for royal authority. Therein Christ is described as "eternal holy pontiff and king . . . son of the living god, universal head of the church . . . omnipotent power, authority and jurisdiction, in civil and criminal cases . . . not only king and judge, but also universal shepherd of believers and unbelievers." Understandably, such formulations of royal authority angered the Franciscans, who claimed that learned disquisitions on divine kingship were nothing but apologias for the extension of royal absolutism at the expense of the Church's universalist claims.[14]

The instrument through which kingship was exercised at the local level was the office of the governor. Theoretically governors were the instantiation of the king's secular authority as ruler, warrior, and judge, who stood in structural opposition to the clerics who administered the monarch's sacerdotal functions through the prelacy, Inquisition, and Holy Crusade. The governor's power and prestige were rooted in the prerogatives of office: the right to assign *encomiendas*, to grant land to settlers, to exploit the area's resources (often for personal profit), to administer justice to the entire population in civil and criminal cases, to legislate as needed, and to organize the province's defenses.

Governors technically answered to the viceroy at whose favor and command they served. But as Santa Fe was 2,000 miles from Mexico City, a distance that took the fastest horseman several weeks to traverse, communication was always slow, effectively placing New Mexican affairs beyond close supervision. Many a governor imposed his will as law, silencing opposition by prohibiting travel and censoring mail.[15]

The governor's civil authority was diffused throughout the kingdom of New Mexico in six and later eight administrative jurisdictions (*jurisdicciones*), each officiated over by chief constables (*alcaldes mayores*) who were themselves gubernatorial appointees. Whether it be in the organization of the kingdom's defenses or in civil and criminal cases, the alcaldes acted as authorities of first instance, the governor as the authority of second instance. Substantive cases were always forwarded to Mexico City for final resolution and appeals. The governor also heard all cases involving Indians and was obliged to provide them with legal counsel in the form of the *protector de Indios* (the protector of the Indians).[16]

The king's authority as patron of the Catholic Church at the local level was claimed both by governors and by bishops; in areas where there was no bishop, such as New Mexico, the authority belonged to the prelates. The viceroy was technically the vice-patron of the Church and it was through his authority that New Mexico's governors asserted their primacy over ecclesiastical affairs. Command over the Church and its clergy was complicated by the fact that matters of faith, morals, and clerical behavior were exclusively the purview of episcopal sees that reported directly to the pope. The king and his subordinates never questioned these papal rights over dogma and doctrine. What became an endless source of controversy were the precise jurisdictional boundaries that Church and state functionaries could legitimately claim as their own. We will see shortly that this very tension was at the root of most Church-state controversy in New Mexico during the seventeenth century. But before we turn to the intricacies of that story, let us take an extended look at the soldier-settler population of the province. For after all, their role was crucial in determining whose view of the polity would be upheld through the force of arms—a fact neither the friars nor the governors could ignore.[17]

The Spanish Soldier-Settlers

At the colony's inception in 1598, New Mexico's settlers consisted of three groups. First were the "people of distinction," said Marcelo de Espinosa, a captain in Oñate's colonizing party, who were "eager to make new discoveries from which they might derive greater profit." When New Mexico was found to be minerally impoverished these men deserted the province and returned to New Spain. Beating a track south with these men was a second group—the shiftless, unattached young men who had gone to New Mexico also seeking fortune but who had found life on the frontier too rigorous. The third group, those who decided to cast their fate with the budding colony, were rugged soldiers—a few brought their families and children—who quickly adapted to their new environment. By despoiling the Indians of food and clothing, these colonists "eat and drink and are happy and have no desire to abandon the said land; on the contrary, they want to . . . remain there for the rest of their lives," said

Espinosa. Why these conquistadores wanted to spend, and indeed did spend, the rest of their lives in New Mexico was because of the privilege they enjoyed there.[18]

The soldiers who entered New Mexico in 1598 became lords of the land by virtue of their subjugation of the Pueblo Indians. As conquerors they became a dominating class rewarded with (1) aristocratic titles as "hidalgos of an established lineage," so that they might enjoy the same honors and privileges of hidalgos and caballeros in the kingdom of Castile; (2) Indian vassalage in the form of *encomiendas* inheritable as patrimony for two generations; and (3) "building lots, pasture and farming lands, and ranches," also inheritable by their children and descendants. These benefits and honors were granted, stated the Crown, so "that a glorious memory may remain of them as the original settlers."[19]

The aristocracy New Mexicans enjoyed as hidalgos was based on military service. Most of those who entered the lower nobility as hidalgos were men of humble origin who reaped great material and symbolic benefits by virtue of their bravery, equestrian skill, and mastery of the martial arts. They were warriors par excellence who lived to protect and expand the realm, to escort the friars into pagan lands, to lead forays against hostile Indians, and by so doing, memorialize their chivalric feats and prowess, both real and imagined, as the source of their social superiority. Technically New Mexico's hidalgos were on a par with the nobles of Castile, or so the king promised in Oñate's charter. In reality the monarchy sharply circumscribed the influence of America's nobility so that their overlordship and prestige was at best a local matter.[20]

Nobility and wealth were not perfectly correlated in seventeenth-century New Mexico. Settlers with established households, known as *vecinos*, consisted of *encomenderos*, persons with rights to Indian tribute, and *moradores*, individuals who did not enjoy such rights. This distinction resembled the Iberian medieval differentiation between *caballeros* (horsemen) and *peones* (foot soldiers). The *encomenderos* jealously seized for their patrimonies New Mexico's best-watered lands, the tribute of the most prosperous Indian villages, access to trading activities, and the spoils of administrative posts. From father to son to grandson this differential access to the means and instruments of production passed, and as it did, memory of its origins in warfare was obscured. Several generations later the descendants of those first settlers would delude themselves, proclaiming that the nobility they enjoyed was really rooted in a metaphysical quality of their blood.[21]

Given the rude conditions of life on the frontier, one surmises that New Mexico's *moradores* lived from hand to mouth. Nonetheless, they cherished their aristocratic status as a mark of distinction, content with their rights to Indian service and lordship over land. Elsewhere in the empire economic success was a sure road to nobility. In New Mexico, "that miserable kingdom," as many viceregal bureaucrats cursed it, while this was theoretically true, in the seventeenth century this rarely happened. Isolated amid a sea of barbarism, in a country devoid of any mineral wealth except salt, even the most enterprising man had little from which he could profit except land and Indian labor, and the best of these had already been appropriated by the first colonizers. It was thus much easier for an old man to gain that noble title "Don" before his name, in recognition of his venerable age, than for an upstart to acquire nobility through personal enterprise. Enterprise on the marriage market was a much surer route. The third section of this book examines the factors that fostered marriages made to gain entry into the provincial nobility.

Because children inherited the blood and physical substance of their parents, New Mexico's dons uttered a shred of truth when they said that their aristocracy was based on blood. But was it pure Spanish blood, as some still claim? Those who called themselves Spaniards in seventeenth-century New Mexico were biologically a motley group. At the time of the colony's conquest, the soldier-settlers were almost equally of peninsular and creole origin. With the exception of a few foreigners, and one "mulatto" named Cristóbal López, the rest of Oñate's company proclaimed themselves *españoles*. They did so primarily to differentiate themselves ethnically as conquerors from the *indios*, and not as statements of pedigree.[22]

Since only thirteen soldiers in the initial 1598 colonizing party brought their wives, the others by necessity turned to Indian women, to black slaves, and to Apache captives for concubines, mistresses, and occasionally for legal brides. Diego de Moraga, for example, was "a man who has lived for much time scandalously with many women." Juan de la Cruz, known as "El Catalán," came to New Mexico in 1598 and shortly thereafter married Beatriz de los Angeles, "a Mexican Indian fluent in Spanish and Hispanicized [*españolada*]," who was a servant in Cristóbal de Brito's household. Given the scarcity of Spanish women and the abundance of native ones, miscegenation progressed rapidly, prompting Fray Estevan de Perea to characterize New Mexico's colonists in 1631 as a group of "mestizos, mulattos, and zambohijos"—a characterization reiterated by other officials.[23]

Migration into New Mexico was never more than a trickle during the 1600s. By 1680 nearly 90 percent of the Hispanic populace were natives of the province. In such a closed and isolated population pool, few Spaniards, whatever their pretense, could have demonstrated racially pure ancestry, and most had undoubtedly become mestizos. Those families that cleaved to the biological fiction that their blood lines were of Old Spanish origin, free of Indian, heretic, gentile, or Jewish stain, did so primarily to legitimate their privileges as a dominant class.[24]

The Spanish lords of New Mexico were "enemies of all kinds of work," said Fray Gerónimo de Zárate Salmerón in the mid-1620s. In this they were not unlike their compatriots in other areas of New Spain, for as Viceroy Luis Velasco stated in 1608, "no one comes to the Indies to plow and to sow, but only to eat and loaf."[25]

For New Mexico's *españoles*, military ambition, status, and honor were of primary concern, and to subordinates fell the tasks of industry, commerce, and physical labor. Men such as Francisco de Sosa Peñalosa entered the kingdom in 1598 with "three female negro slaves, one mulatto slave, and other men and women servants" to meet his every need. Of the numerous possessions Alonso de Quesada brought to New Mexico, "two male servants and a woman servant" were listed among the horses, saddles, and armaments. Since only 6 out of 129 soldiers brought servants to New Mexico, the scramble to enslave the natives began immediately. The 1599 assault on Acoma Pueblo and another in 1601 against the Tompiro pueblos in the region east of the Sandía-Manzano Mountains temporarily alleviated this need. Some 600 Indians were taken from Acoma as slaves; from the Tompiro pueblos every soldier obtained at least one thrall.[26]

From the colony's very start, New Mexicans became dependent on Indian slaves for most of their basic needs and as a form of capital. In 1630 Santa Fe counted a Spanish population of 250, served by 700 Indian and mestizo servants and slaves. As early as 1633, Fray Estevan de Perea complained that Indian children were being snatched from their parents "as if they were yearling calfs or colts . . . and placed in permanent slavery." By 1680 half of all domestic units had at least one Indian slave, and some households counted as many as 30. Even the ascetic friars kept household slaves. Few were the convents that did not list a number of Indian boys who attended to the fathers' needs.[27]

The timocratic ideals of seventeenth-century New Mexican society were reproduced through constant forays into Indian territory, ostensibly to wage "just war," but in reality to obtain slave labor. The constant bickering among the provincial governors, the colonists, and the friars over the appropriation of Indian slave labor was a major political theme. The reason for this was stated by one settler in 1599: New Mexico "promises excellent returns because the native Indians are excellent and intelligent farmers; they are much given to commerce, taking from one province to another the fruits of their lands and the products of their labor." For the Spaniards who so relished warfare, eschewed labor, and disdained the thought of commerce, Indian slavery was the only way they would realize dreams of lordship and leisure on the banks of the Rio Grande.[28]

In addition to Indian slavery, some soldier-settlers held *encomiendas*, grants of Indian tribute which they received for providing the Franciscans with armed escorts into new missionary fields and for assisting them in the conversion of the Indians. Don Juan de Oñate was granted the right to distribute the area's Indians in *encomiendas* in his 1595 charter (*capitulación*) for the conquest of New Mexico, and this was a right all subsequent governors up to 1680 enjoyed. The *encomienda*, or unit of "entrustment," was theoretically the Indian town, but to accommodate the needs of approximately 60 men who held *encomiendas* during the first half of the seventeenth century, some pueblos were divided among several soldiers.[29]

Encomienda tribute was assessed by household irrespective of size. Yearly each Indian household paid their *encomendero* "one *fanega* [approximately 2.6 bushels] of maize . . . valued at four *reales* and also a piece of cotton cloth six palms square [about 5.6 feet square] which is reckoned in price at six *reales*." (A hide of the same value could be substituted for the cloth.) Tribute was collected twice a year, with the May contribution usually consisting of cloth and skins, and that in October, coming shortly after the harvest, usually consisting of corn.[30]

Legal right to Indian tribute was a major determinant of wealth and status in colonial New Mexico. *Encomenderos* not only forcibly extracted payments in foodstuffs and clothing from their subject populations but also illegally appropriated Indian labor and use of native lands. This differential access to the toil of tributary Indians differentiated *encomenderos* from the non-*encomenderos* as a dominant class that exercised its hegemony in economics and politics. The modes and mechanisms by which this was accomplished in seventeenth-century New Mexico lamentably will remain a mystery because of the almost total destruction of documentary evidence during the 1680 Pueblo Revolt.

Lordship over the Pueblo Indians went hand in hand with lordship over the land. So that the "land becomes their mother and as sons they love, honor, and defend her," the crown ceded *mercedes*, grants of land, to the colonists. *Mercedes* usually encompassed terrain of various sorts: a well-watered plot for crops and household gardening, wooded areas for building posts and firewood, and meadows for livestock grazing.

Seventeenth-century *mercedes* were primarily given to individuals, but as time passed (particularly during the eighteenth and early nineteenth centuries) grants to communities and groups of landless and land-poor households became more common. As with the other spoils of conquest, what dictated the amount of land one gained as a *merced* was based on the laws of distributive justice that regulated the social body. Since society was constituted of upper, middle, and lower status persons, "it is not suitable that everyone should be an equal [in the acquisition of land]," wrote Fray Martín de Ojacastro. "Rather, as in the human body, there must be differences in members." [31]

At first glance New Mexico's productive lands may have appeared boundless, but in fact they were quite limited. Irrigation farming could only be undertaken near water, and livestock production was dependent on a settled population with adequate defenses to thwart Indian raids. The Indian pueblos that had grown most prosperous over time were those that had maintained control over well-watered plots. The crown recognized the antecedence of these claims and as protector of the Indians nominally opposed the colonists' encroachments. To circumvent the law, *encomenderos* often obtained land grants adjacent to their tributary Indians, ostensibly to facilitate the collection of their dues, but all too often to illegally obtain Indian labor and encroach upon their lands. [32]

So long as the Spanish population was small and the Pueblo Indian population was stable, few land conflicts occurred, but by the middle of the seventeenth century these conditions no longer existed. Lower tribute collections due to the sharp drop in the Indian population forced increasing numbers of settlers to turn to farming and ranching. From then on, land conflict became a major theme in Indian-white relations. [33]

The Kingdom of New Mexico was established in 1598 with 129 soldiers and their dependents. In 1600 another 80 soldiers arrived, bringing the Hispanic population (soldiers, their dependents, and their servants) to roughly 700. Quarrels, casualties, mutinies, and desertions took their toll in the following years, and by 1609 about 60 persons were left, of whom only 30 could bear arms. Additional settlers entered the kingdom and by 1620 the provincial capital in Santa Fe counted 50 households with approximately 200 residents. Ten years later Fray Alonso de Benavides reported that Santa Fe had 250 *vecinos* (landed citizens with full civic rights), and "about seven hundred persons in service; so that, counting Spaniards, mestizos, and Indians, the total is about a thousand." [34]

Pestilence swept the land between 1636 and 1640, and its effect was soon felt. Fray Juan de la Prada placed Santa Fe's population in 1638 at "something like fifty [households]—although there must be about two hundred persons." This represented a gross population decline of 50 *vecinos*, or a decline of 20 percent in eight years. Only 50 men bore arms in Santa Fe in 1638; only 200 did so in the entire province. Using the household to total population ratio of one to four reported by Father de la Prada, New Mexico's nonaboriginal population in 1638 probably totaled 800.[35]

From 1640 on, the Hispanic population grew slowly. Santa Fe remained the kingdom's only town and was soon rivaled in sheer numbers by the populace residing on the haciendas that developed in the lower Rio Grande Valley between Isleta and Senecú in the 1650s. In 1677 a convoy of 47 convicts from Mexico City was dispatched to New Mexico to buttress the area's defenses. Only 41 men arrived. The others escaped, thinking exile in New Mexico a fate worse than death. Two years later, Fray Francisco de Ayeta assessed the province's defenses and concluded that the colonists were dangerously outnumbered. Only 170 men were capable of bearing arms against an Indian population numbering 17,000 with roughly 6,000 warriors. A census conducted after the 1680 Pueblo Revolt listed 422 persons dead or missing and 1,946 survivors, of whom 474 were Indian servants. Thus one can surmise that in 1680 the population residing in Spanish households totaled approximately 2,347.[36]

New Mexico's soldier-settlers played an important role in the political life of the colony. They were, after all, the ultimate guarantors of the missions. Strong as the shield of faith and the lance of perseverance were, the Franciscans readily admitted that had it not been for the soldiers, "the barbarians would have eaten us alive." No matter how many blandishments the fathers showered on the Indians, no matter how sweet the Gospel or how melodious the Christian hymns, conversion succeeded, said Fray Antonio Margill de Jesús, only when "reinforced by the fear and respect which the Indians have for the Spaniards." Fear of Spanish horses and firearms, and of the wars of blood and fire the conquistadores waged ultimately forced the Indians to submit.[37]

But the colonists also owed allegiance to the king and his duly appointed officers. Whatever status and material reward they had won during the conquest had been granted to them by the king. Unlike the Franciscans, who saw their lives as critiques of the vainglories of the world and of the spoils of human domination, the colonists shared a culture of war with the governors. The colonists, then, stood as a pivotal group in upholding those claims of dominance over provincial affairs that the Franciscans and the governors asserted. If a settler had a highly developed eschatological sense and entrenched interests in the status quo, he might have sided with the friars against the comparatively transient governors. If, on the other hand, he were godless, anticlerical, or disgruntled, he might have allied with a recently arrived governor, hoping to obtain satisfaction or redress for past oppressions and slights.

The balance of force was in the hands of the colonists. Without them neither the governors nor the friars could effectively have their way in local politics. The problem any historian of this period faces, however, is to ascertain with any precision what exactly the colonists thought and did, given the preponderance of extant clerical documents and the relative paucity of those produced by civilians. The unavoidable result is a highly partisan view—the Franciscans' view—of New Mexican politics between 1600 and 1680. To incorporate as fully as possible the secular view of government, I have chosen 3 out of 26 governorships—those of Governor Pedro de Peralta (1610–14), Governor Luís de Rosas (1637–41), and Governor Bernardo López de Mendizábal (1659–61)—for extensive discussion primarily because the documentation for each is not one-sided. Extensive litigation over Church-state jurisdiction occurred during each of these governorships, allowing us to see in action the various social groups in the colony.

Three New Mexican Governors

We left the narrative thread of New Mexico's history with the arrival in 1610 of Governor Pedro de Peralta, with the establishment of Santa Fe as the kingdom's capital, and with some 7,000 Pueblo Indian converts. The kingdom's first Franciscan prelate, Fray Isidro Ordóñez, arrived in 1612 and promptly proceeded to lay the groundwork for his order's dream of creating a theocracy among the Indians. To realize this Ordóñez ordered that any colonist who wished to leave New Mexico could. The Spanish population, which hovered around 200, was reduced by half. Governor Pedro de Peralta warned Ordóñez that the kingdom's defenses would be seriously weakened by this flight—precisely the prelate's goal. He reasoned that the fewer civilians in New Mexico, the less would be their corrupting influence over the Indians. Ordóñez hoped that without secular distractions, conversion would proceed rapidly.

In the months that followed, the prelate and governor sparred numerous times. Ordóñez denounced Peralta's extensive but indispensable use of unpaid Indian labor to construct Santa Fe's governmental buildings. He complained that excessive tribute had been levied from the Indians to feed what were apparently starving colonists and that several soldiers had sexually abused native women. Ordóñez ordered the governor to correct these excesses or else, as a commissary of the Inquisition, he, Ordóñez, would excommunicate the governor. Governor Peralta was startled by the threat. When Ordóñez had presented his patent of office as prelate to the governor in 1612, as all ecclesiastical officials were legally required to do, his documents had not included an Inquisitorial writ. Peralta demanded to see it. Ordóñez had lied, suffered his humiliation poorly, and retorted by excommunicating Peralta, promising similar pain to "anyone who spoke or even doffed his hat to greet the governor." The prelate's antipathy toward Governor Peralta was so intense that at one point he asked Fray Luís Tirado, Santa Fe's curate, to solicit the aid of Santa Fe's citizens to kill the governor, threatening to consume the Holy Eucharist, the symbol of Christian community, and to abandon the town if they did not comply.[38]

Relations between Ordóñez and Peralta further deteriorated over the next year until the two met in violent confrontation on July 7, 1613. Peralta, in open defiance of his excommunication and in assertion of his rights as governor to stewardship over church matters, arrived to hear Mass that Sunday only to find that his chair had been removed from the front of the church and thrown into the street. Peralta carried his chair into the back of the church and from there heard Ordóñez issue an edict prohibiting, under pain of excommunication, anyone from sending dispatches to Mexico without the prelate's consent. Ordóñez boasted in his sermon:

Let no one argue with vain words that I do not have the same power and authority that the Pope in Rome has, or that if his Holiness were [here] in New Mexico he could do more than I. Believe that I can arrest, cast into irons, and punish as seems fit to me any person without any exception who is not obedient to the commandments of the Church and to mine.[39]

At the end of the Mass Peralta confronted Ordóñez and ordered him to return to his convent at Santo Domingo Pueblo, the ecclesiastical capital of the kingdom. Bitter words were exchanged. A scuffle ensued. Gunfire, bloodshed, and a string of excommunications followed. At day's end the prelate left for Santo Domingo to plan his riposte. On July 23, Ordóñez dispatched messengers to Mexico City describing the godlessness that existed in New Mexico, the governor's hostility toward ecclesiastical authority, and the endless exploitation of the Indians, and asking for the viceroy's permission to arrest Peralta. Peralta, unwilling to let the friar's version of events go unchallenged in Mexico City, but unable to obtain messengers because they feared excommunication, embarked on the trip by himself on August 10. Ordóñez and a group of allies ambushed the governor near Isleta Pueblo on August 12, arrested him in the name of the Inquisition, and held him prisoner at Sandía Pueblo's convent for the next nine months.

Those months of Ordóñez's iron-fisted rule "were a hell," recalled Fray Francisco Pérez Guerta. From the pulpit Ordóñez constantly fumed to Santa Fe's faithful "that he expected for [this] act of imprisonment to be rewarded with a miter." Anyone who showed sympathy for the governor was excommunicated. And when Fray Andrés Juárez and Fray Francisco Pérez Guerta complained of their prelate's abusive behavior, they too were imprisoned.[40]

Peralta escaped from Sandía on March 18, 1614, but was quickly apprehended. He was taken in irons, "half naked . . . like an Indian . . . seated on a horse like a woman," to Santo Domingo. There Ordóñez gathered the Indians so that they could see how their governor had been humiliated by the Franciscan prelate and to show them vividly whose power and authority was supreme. From August of 1613 until May of 1614, when a new governor, Bernardino de Ceballos, arrived in Santa Fe, Ordóñez was in total command in the kingdom, exercising secular as well as ecclesiastical powers. In November 1614 Peralta finally departed for Mexico City, where in 1617 he was exonerated of any wrongdoing in New Mexico.[41]

In the 23 years that followed Peralta's administration, practically every governor became embroiled in similar controversies with the prelates. The Franciscans, harboring an exalted sense of ecclesiastical authority, repeatedly claimed exclusive right over Indian administration and mired in endless litigation anyone who questioned this right or its purview. Governor Juan de Eulate, for example, arrived in New Mexico in December 1618, announcing that "the King was his ruler [*el Rey es su gallo*] and that he [Eulate] did not have to acknowledge the authority of the pope or of the Church, particularly in matters of ecclesiastical authority." When he forbade *encomenderos* from offering armed escort to the friars, and told the Indians that they could retain their katsina dolls and masks and could continue to live in concubinage, the Franciscans charged him with lack of respect for ecclesiastical authority, fomenting liberty of conscience among the Indians, and heresy. Eulate's rebuttal to these charges does not survive, but we do know that the Franciscans continually triumphed against the governors and successfully upheld their claims to primacy over Indian affairs. They had embroiled New Mexico's first governor, Don Juan de Oñate, in controversy until he was forced to resign his post. They had imprisoned and publicly humiliated Governor Peralta. Both Governors Peralta and Bernardino de Ceballos had been excommunicated and forced to do public penance. And even a number of

Santa Fe's citizens had humbled themselves before the friars. Indeed, it appeared that ecclesiastical rule was supreme in New Mexico.[42]

All of this changed with the arrival of Governor Luís de Rosas in the spring of 1637. In Rosas the Franciscans had their first truly formidable opponent. A fearless soldier, ruthless in his methods, and avowedly anticlerical, Rosas entered New Mexico with two objectives: to place civil government and secular authority on a superior footing, and to profit from his governorship. Both of these goals rested on the administration of the Indians, and it was about them that Rosas and the friars fought most bitterly over jurisdictional matters.

Rosas, like most of the governors who served before and after him, saw public office as an opportunity for personal gain. Governorships carried a pittance of a salary, 2,000 pesos—hardly enough to cover the cost of transporting a household to New Mexico and supporting it in appropriate style. If one purchased the post, paying as much as 9,000 pesos, as Governor Fernando de Argüello Caravajal did in 1644, economics dictated that a profit had to be reaped. The crown and the viceroy understood this and were prepared to tolerate its consequences in order to attract loyal bureaucrats to the frontier. But to men vowed to poverty, the governors seemed to be true worshipers of Mammon. Undoubtedly some of the governors were as "insatiably greedy" as the friars claimed. But that men who entered New Mexico poor "have gone out rich, and if they have entered rich they have gone out powerful," as Fray Pedro Serrano averred, was more hyperbole than fact.[43]

If bureaucratic advancement can be taken as the measure of profit, then the men who truly profited from their service in New Mexico were the friars. Fray Alonso de Benavides went on to become Bishop of Goa. Fray Tomás Manso became Bishop of Nicaragua. Fray Roque de Figueredo was repeatedly recommended for elevation to bishop. No seventeenth-century New Mexican governor experienced such upward mobility. To the contrary, most of them were tangled in the endless legal webs the Franciscans spun around them. What profit they made was exhausted defending themselves. They died as impecunious as their Christian brothers who were vowed to poverty.[44]

The only way to amass wealth in mineral-poor New Mexico was to exploit Indian labor. Rosas's legacy (his heresy to some) was to monopolize indigenous labor for his own ends, thereby depriving the friars and colonists of those services, legal and illegal, that they had long appropriated. The Franciscans allowed the settlers to extract "just" amounts of Indian tribute and labor in return for protection, escort, and deference; together they intimidated the Indians into submission through threats of force. So long as this understanding prevailed, the men who arrived every third year or so to assume governorships, as outsiders with virtually no ties to the kingdom's Spanish community, were all but powerless against the friars. Rosas must have understood the dynamics of this friar-colonist alliance against outsiders, for his aim seems to have been to splinter it in order to rule. Rosas's Apache Indian policy demonstrates how he proceeded.

Since about 1525 trade relations had been established between the Pueblo Indians and the Apaches who roamed the terrain bordering the Rio Grande. Every summer at the pueblos of Taos, Pecos, and Picuris, the Apaches arrived with their dog-laden trains to exchange hides, meat, tallow, and salt for cotton blankets, pottery, maize, turquoise, and bread-stuffs. After 1598 Spanish agricultural products (grains, fruit, and live-stock) and manufactured items (axes, spears, and firearms) were added to this trade, which in general proceeded peacefully through the mid-1630s.[45]

Rosas saw in these trade fairs the perfect opportunity to advance his aims. He took a large cache of knives to Pecos Pueblo, gave the pueblo's warriors some as gifts and asked them to barter the excess with the Apaches for pelts. The governor promised that if the braves did as he commanded, he would allow them to choose their own war captains as they had before the arrival of the Franciscans. Rosas hoped that by offer-ing the displaced warriors gifts, they would reciprocate with loyalty and labor, thereby factionalizing the pueblo and ultimately eroding the friars' authority. The scheme failed, and in reaction Rosas contended that the Franciscans at Pecos Mission had subverted his plans. He had one of the friars arrested and placed under guard; another he verbally abused. Angered by how attentively the Indians obeyed the friars, he ordered that the Indians always greet him with the words "Here stands the person of the King."[46]

From barter, Rosas turned to the next-best get-rich-quick strategy— Indian slavery. He moved forcefully to enslave the Apaches, pressing many of them into service in his recently established Santa Fe textile workshop (obraje) and selling others to miners in northern New Spain. In 1638 he attacked the Apaches on the Great Plains, killing over a hun-dred and enslaving a comparable number. The following year 80 Utes were enslaved in a similar manner. Rosas carried out his campaigns under the rubric of "just war," a claim that weighed heavily on friars' consciences.[47]

Rosas's slave raids had immediate repercussions. Every foray into Apache country brought fierce retaliation which invariably ended in a trail of ashes, trampled fields, depleted herds, and death. In 1639–40 alone, 52,000 bushels of Pueblo corn were burned during Apache raids, leaving the population hungry and distraught. Warfare equally disrupted the trade relations Taos, Picuris, and Pecos pueblos had with the Apaches and the exchange mechanism by which the Indians at these pueblos had "clothed themselves and paid their tribute." Lacking hides with which to pay their tribute, the Indians had to surrender more of their maize. They complained, as did the colonists and friars, that Rosas's schemes were exposing them to attack.[48]

The burden of increased tribute that resulted from Rosas's policies coincided with a period of massive population decline among the Puebloans. A smallpox epidemic killed 20,000 Indians in 1636, reducing their numbers by roughly one third, from 60,000 to 40,000 (see Table 2.1). In 1640 a pestilence swept the land, taking with it 3,000 souls. Faced with tribute assessments that were fixed for each pueblo despite their sharp population decline, and the loss of the Apache trade that had assured peace, many Pueblo Indians at last began to challenge the colonial regime through open defiance and apostasy. Fray Juan de Prada reported in 1638 that many neophytes had deserted their missions and "gone over to the heathen, believing that they enjoy greater happiness with them, since they live according to their whims, and in complete freedom." Flight and a demographic decline in the Puebloan population had also forced the friars to curtail Indian resettlement into *congregaciones*. Where perhaps 150 pueblos once stood in 1598, by 1640 only 43 remained—a number that remained stable for the next 40 years. Shattered too by increased competition over shrinking native resources were the mutual interests that had bound the Franciscans and colonists against outside interlopers. Therein lay Governor Rosas's ability to rule.[49]

By 1640 the political configuration of the colony had changed radically. Among the Indians there was a widespread belief that the friars' charisma had dimmed, which by native standards signified the loss of supernatural sanction. The padres' curing magic had failed to keep their pestilence-ridden kinsmen alive. The rain spirits had not visited the people, nor had the friars conjured rain. Paradoxically, the immense powers over domesticated animals, which had been so instrumental in establishing the charismatic authority of the Franciscans at the time of the conquest, had become a curse. By the mid-1630s the Apaches had obtained horses and become mounted nomads. Faced with pestilence and drought, they began preying on Pueblo granaries and livestock. Against these mounted and increasingly armed Apaches, the Franciscans had little to offer the Indians in the way of protection at the mission. The small contingent of armed soldiers scattered throughout the kingdom was no match for the Apaches.[50]

These catastrophes indicated to the Indians that the native gods were angry. Traditionally the Inside Chief and medicine men would have restored cosmic harmony through communal offerings, dances, and cures. If these failed, in all likelihood, the town would have dispersed. The Franciscans as Inside Chiefs had shown themselves impotent before the gods, but would not let the people disperse. And so the Pueblo Indians did the only thing they could. They began celebrating their ancient rites anew. They danced on Mother Earth and begged the Corn Mothers to return from the underworld with blessings. They offered sacred corn meal to Father Sun and asked the katsina to visit them with food, prosperity, and good life.[51]

The friars responded angrily to the resurgence of Pueblo ceremonialism and did everything they could to suppress it. They mercilessly flayed the most notorious backsliders, some even to the point of death, hoping to purge the Indians of their idolatrous ways. The Indians of Taos Pueblo complained to the governor in 1637, and again in 1638, of the brutal punishments they received from Fray Nicolás Hidalgo, who punished his insolent children by castration and acts of sodomy. In addition, there was a host of rapes, and many children who claimed Hidalgo as their biological father. He was finally relieved of his duties in 1639. Taos's new pastor, Fray Pedro de Miranda, scolded his congregation for calumniating Father Hidalgo. They resented the admonitions and bolted. On December 28, 1639, Taos Indians killed Fray Pedro de Miranda and two soldier-settlers, demolished their church and convent, and maculated and profaned the Holy Eucharist. They then swooped down on Picuris Pueblo and would have murdered the resident friar had he been present. Such boldness was repeated a few days later at Jémez. There, Fray Diego de San Lucas was killed clinging to a cross. At both places the Indians rejected the Franciscan theocracy and colonial regime. They killed the friars and their armed escorts, abandoned the towns into which they had been congregated, and reverted to a nomadic life.[52]

The rebellions at Taos and Jémez and the open celebration of Pueblo rituals shook the very foundations of the colony and unleashed a storm of recriminations among Governor Rosas, the Franciscans, and the colonists. The friars charged that Rosas's greed, his slave raids, and excessive extraction of labor and tribute had precipitated the revolts and driven the Indians to apostasy. Some colonists complained that Rosas had seized control of all local commerce, had expropriated their looms to monopolize the province's textile production, and had slaughtered a third of their cattle to feed his slaves. Other citizens were angered by the fact that in

1638 Rosas had stacked Santa Fe's town council (*cabildo*) with his cronies, thereby controlling the use of communal land, water, and pasturage.[53]

Rosas and his anticlerical allies on Santa Fe's *cabildo* countered that for 40 years the Franciscans had tyrannized the kingdom, controlling Indian labor, lands, and livestock. Writing the viceroy in 1639, the *cabildo* members charged that the religious prohibited them from keeping livestock, claiming that the cattle would destroy Indian cornfields. This prohibition was unjust because the friars themselves kept flocks "of one or two thousand sheep" within each pueblo, while few colonists had more than a hundred sheep. Furthermore, despite their vow of poverty, the friars had numerous horses and firearms and an excessive number of Indian porters, cooks, woodchoppers, and millers.[54]

More insidious still, the *cabildo* continued, was the Franciscans' arbitrary use of ecclesiastical power through the Inquisition, the *Santa Cruzada*, and the prelacy. The Franciscans seemed determined to subordinate royal authority in New Mexico, using their prerogatives—censures, interdicts, excommunications, and threats of Inquisitorial prosecutions—to humiliate the governor and to intimidate the citizens into siding with the Church against him. In February of 1639, for example, Prelate Juan de Salas had refused to grant confessional absolution to anyone who did not "sign a paper in their [Franciscan] favor against the honor of the government and its justices and superiors." Several times the friars threatened that if the colonists obeyed Governor Rosas, they would consume the Eucharist, close down Santa Fe's church, and leave the Christian community godless and without a priest. This was done, the Santa Fe *cabildo* insisted, for "no other reason than their pleasure so that by keeping the land oppressed and afflicted they can control it with such a powerful and superior hand."[55]

Governor Rosas and his supporters were hardly the innocent lambs they wanted the viceroy to think they were. Franciscan challenges to the governor's authority always drew an assault on ecclesiastical privileges. According to the friars, during the first year of Rosas's governorship, Prelate Antonio de Artega preached a sermon on the feast day of St. Mark explaining that the authority of the Church and of the pope were supreme. Since the Catholic monarchs were children of the Church, before all else they were subject to ecclesiastical laws. Anyone who challenged those laws was a heretic. On hearing this Rosas became very angry. He stood up in church, turned his back on the high altar and shouted: "Shut up, Father, what you say is a lie!" He stormed out of the church flanked by a band of armed soldiers saying that "he [Rosas] represented the king and

He [the king] was everything." When the Indians saw this open breach between the governor and the prelate they became disheartened, said Fray Juan de Salas. They "walked about as if dazed, and they withdrew to their cornfields." The relationship between the sacred and secular force enshrined in the structure of authority since the conquest had crumbled before its Indian audience.[56]

The Franciscans' pleas to the viceroy asking that Governor Rosas be censured for impinging on their legal rights were well founded. Rosas had violated ecclesiastical immunities by arresting Pecos's ministers when his knife-exchange scheme failed. He again violated those privileges when, at the Indians' behest, he investigated Fray Nicolás Hidalgo's actions at Taos. Matters reached the breaking point when, in January 1639, Governor Rosas banished Fray Juan de Góngora, the *Cruzada*'s representative, from the province owing to a dispute over the legal immunities that employees of the *Cruzada* enjoyed.[57]

With Góngora's departure, the *Cruzada* was left without a leader. The death of Fray Esteban de Perea in 1639 left the Inquisition in similar straits. Without these two tribunals to constrain him, Rosas moved aggressively against prelate Juan de Salas, claiming that his censures and excommunications were invalid because he had never presented his patent of office. Father Salas refused to submit to the governor's review, gathered the friars serving Santa Fe, closed down its church, and withdrew to Santo Domingo Pueblo, where by early 1640 they were joined by the rest of the kingdom's friars. Together with 73 of New Mexico's 120 citizens, the friars plotted against Rosas, repeatedly proclaiming that the only authority they recognized in New Mexico was the pope and his legate Prelate Salas. With the friars and citizens barricaded at Santo Domingo for more than a year, Rosas moved aggressively to dismantle the structure of rule the friars had established in the pueblos. He ordered the Indians not to obey the fathers and staged for them caricatures of Christian ritual that mocked clerical authority.[58]

The standoff between Governor Rosas and his forces in Santa Fe and Custos Salas, and the friars and their supporters at Santo Domingo Pueblo, ended in the spring of 1641 with the arrival of a new governor, Juan Flores de Sierra y Valdez, and a new prelate, Fray Hernando Covarrubias. Governor Flores began the mandatory review of Rosas's administration (*residencia*) but died before it was completed. In the meantime, Rosas's opponents regained control of Santa Fe's *cabildo* and found in the governor's death the perfect opportunity to imprison Rosas and sequester his property. Rosas himself was killed on January 25, 1642, by Nicolás Ortiz, a soldier who had been absent in Mexico City during most of Rosas's administration. Returning to Santa Fe on January 9, Ortiz uncovered an allegedly adulterous liaison by finding his wife, Doña María de Bustillas, in the house where Rosas was being held. With Rosas dead, the Franciscans were once again the undisputed fathers in the land.[59]

Late in 1641 Alonso Pacheco y Heredia arrived to assume the governorship vacated by Juan Flores de Sierra y Valdez's death, carrying orders to restore respect for civil authority in New Mexico and to investigate Governor Rosas's death. Entering Santa Fe in November 1642, Governor Pacheco was respectfully received by the Franciscans and the town's citizens. In a gesture calculated to reflect their conciliatory mood, the friars agreed to exhume Governor Rosas's bones from the corn patch in which they rested, to grant him absolution, and to give him a Christian burial in Santa Fe's church.[60]

In the months that followed, Pacheco pieced together the facts of Governor Rosas's death and concluded that eight soldiers were guilty of cold-blooded murder and sedition. On the morning of July 21, 1643, the eight were summarily beheaded. According to Fray Hernando Covarrubias, after Francisco Salazar's head was severed, much to everyone's amazement, he miraculously recited the Apostles' Creed from start to finish. Later that day Pacheco summoned the town's citizens, pardoned their crimes as accomplices, and ordered them to affirm their allegiance to the king. This they did before the head of Antonio Baca, the apparent ringleader in the plot against Rosas, which had been nailed to the gibbet. On July 30, Spanish and Indian representatives from the entire province gathered in Santa Fe for a solemn high Mass at which the Franciscan prelate and the governor pronounced their loyalty and obedience to the king and his appointed representatives. At last Church-state relations were calm.[61]

But the seeds of discontent were germinating in the pueblos. By the 1640s there were a significant number of Christianized youths who had reached adulthood as loyal allies of the friars. Despite the friars' weakened authority in the pueblos, these Christians openly struggled with those villagers who clung to their Puebloan religious beliefs. All of this led to increased factionalism in the pueblos—a factionalism further compounded by the ever-growing parasitic demands of the colonists. In 1643, owing to the decline in the Pueblo population, the onus of *encomienda* tribute was shifted from households to individuals, so that each Indian was required to provide one cotton blanket and one *fanega* of corn quarterly. To escape this assessment, many Indians fled their towns for life among the Apaches. So allied, Apaches and Pueblo refugees increasingly preyed on Spanish granaries and supply trains, keeping the colonists constantly on guard. Between 1644 and 1650 news reached the Pueblos that medicine men had incited the Conchos, Tobosos, Cabezas, Salineros, Tarahumaras, Opatas, and Sumas to revolt in Nueva Vizcaya (modern-day Chihuahua and Durango). Now, too, the Puebloans plotted to over-throw their lords.[62]

Starting in 1644, Governor Fernando de Argüello moved aggressively to crush Indian dissent. At the beginning of his administration (1644–47), over 40 Indians were "hanged and lashed and imprisoned for sedition." Argüello later discovered an Apache-Jémez Indian plot to attack the settlers. This he also nipped in the bud, hanging 29 men. In 1649 Gover-nor Hernando de Ugarte y la Concha unearthed a pact among the Apaches and the Indians of Isleta, Alameda, San Felipe, Cochiti, and Jémez, and repressed it by executing nine men and selling numerous others into slavery. Pedro Naranjo, a San Felipe Indian, would later de-clare that Ugarte's brutality created such resentment among the Indians that from that point on war calls were constantly raised and they "always kept in their hearts the desire to carry [them] out."[63]

The Indians' challenge to colonial rule between 1644 and the mid-1650s temporarily united the colonists, friars, and governors against their common enemy. By 1656 the Franciscans seem once again to have emerged as the dominant estate in provincial politics. Stronger in number (70 friars by 1657) and ever more confident that ecclesiastical power reigned supreme in New Mexico, the warriors of Christ stood ready for battle with any anti-Christ that might stand in their way. Such a man ar-rived in 1659: Governor Bernardo López de Mendizábal. When Men-dizábal tried to exercise the rudimentary functions of civil government, the Franciscans lashed out with their ultimate weapon—the Inquisitorial inquest. The effect of Inquisitorial prosecution, whatever its ultimate ver-dict, was to mire a governor in endless litigation in Mexico City, effec-tively leaving New Mexico without a secular head. A new governor would eventually arrive but he was unlikely to proceed aggressively against the Church, at least at first. The Franciscans knew this; they knew that their tenure in New Mexico was stable while governors came and went. God and time was on their side in conflicts with the governors, and, as we saw earlier, if the settlers could be cajoled to support their cause, the friars were invincible.

According to the friars, the intense animus that developed between Governor Mendizábal and the Franciscans, which led to an Inquisitorial inquest, had its origin in 1658 as Mendizábal traveled to New Mexico with the mission supply caravan to assume his governorship. One day during the trip two soldiers began fighting. The friars intervened to stop them. Mendizábal allegedly became very angry at the friars and rebuked them, saying "admit that I am captain general, that they are soldiers paid by the king, and that you must recognize me as universal head." According to Fray Nicolás de Freitas the friars retorted: "We do not recognize nor will we ever recognize any universal head except the Roman Pontiff and in temporal matters the king." [64]

From this point on, Mendizábal is said to have become openly contemptuous of the Franciscans. The forty-year-old governor knew well the intricacies of the laws by which he would govern. Trained by Jesuits in the arts and canon law, the hard-hitting Mendizábal had made himself a soldier par excellence. Irreverent in word and deed, aggressively anticlerical, he had served the crown well in various administrative posts.

Upon entering New Mexico, Mendizábal took offense that the greeting he received from the friars at Socorro had not befitted his honor. Fray Benito de la Natividad had constructed several rude arches, rung the mission bells as the governor's carriage approached, and welcomed him at the cemetery gate. Apparently that was not enough. Mendizábal wanted to be received like "the Blessed Sacrament on the Feast of Corpus Christi," with pallium, triumphal arches, singing and dancing Indians, mock battles, and a solemn high Mass. Mendizábal repaid the insult on reaching Santa Fe. He refused to greet the new custodian, Fray Juan Ramírez, thereby implying that he would not acknowledge his writ as prelate and ecclesiastical judge, or for that matter the primacy of ecclesiastical authority. Throughout Mendizábal's governorship he and the Franciscans would spar over Indian administration and the rights of the Church as a privileged institution. [65]

When Mendizábal began his administration in the summer of 1659, the province was in the midst of a severe famine. Food shortages existed, livestock production had faltered, and the Indians were sustaining themselves "on grass seeds . . . and very injurious herbs, and the Spaniards on bran, spinach, green barley and other herbs." To remedy the situation Mendizábal prohibited the export of livestock from the province and ordered that the wage paid to Indian laborers be increased from one-half *real* per day to one *real* plus rations. Mendizábal reasoned that if the settlers paid the Indians a "just wage," Spanish demand for native labor would decrease, thus freeing the Indians to raise their own crops. Indian agricultural surplus would eventually enter the Spanish economy through barter and tribute, hopefully relieving food shortages. [66]

Had the governor not immediately employed the Indians freed by his decree for personal use, his actions might not have created such bitterness. Instead, Mendizábal enlisted 800 of the province's Indians for a retaliatory raid against the Apaches in September 1659, a thinly disguised slaving expedition in which he captured 70 people. Numerous Indians were also put to work by the governor harvesting salt and pine nuts, weaving blankets, tanning hides and manufacturing them into shoes and leather doublets, and constructing wagons for the transport of these items to Parral, all for his personal profit. In less than a year, Mendizábal accumulated enough goods to dispatch two caravans to Parral. The cargo of one was valued at 12,000 pesos, six times his yearly salary. It consisted of 1,350 deerskins, 600 pairs of woolen stockings, 300 bushels of pine nuts, and large quantities of leather jackets, shirts, breeches, buffalo skins, and salt.[67]

The *vecinos* and friars were livid that they had been deprived of the unpaid Indian labor they had always enjoyed, albeit illegally. The settlers complained that their corn crop had been lost in 1659 for lack of field hands. The friars put their losses at 8,713 head of livestock and "numerous fields of corn." The padres were galled too that Mendizábal had deprived them of their personal servants and would only allow them to employ without pay a sacristan, a cantor, and an organist. The governor threatened that anyone who assisted the friars, be it weaving sackcloth, baking their bread, or showing them hospitality, would be punished with 200 lashes. Nicolás Aguilar, chief constable of Salinas jurisdiction, faithfully executed the governor's orders, deprived the friars of Indian labor, and was apparently amused to see Fray Nicolás de Freitas haul firewood and Fray Diego de Parraga "cook his own meals, though badly, not knowing how." When Aguilar saw how Fray Fernando Velasco struggled with a load of firewood, he allegedly quipped, "for once the good padre had sweaty balls [*cojones sudados*]."[68]

The Franciscans also fumed that Mendizábal was fomenting "liberty of conscience" among the Indians, thereby undermining mission government. The reality of the matter was that the Franciscans and New Mexico's governors quarreled most intensely about this issue whenever the Indians openly challenged the mission regime by practicing concubinage and polygamy and by celebrating their indigenous rites. Native resistance to Christianity was the work of Satan, thought the Franciscans. In worldly terms this meant that anyone who questioned ecclesiastical authority or the route the friars had laid out for the Indians to utopia was immediately branded an anti-Christ.

Mendizábal was aware of Indian grievances against the missionaries and tried to alleviate them as the kingdom's "universal head," hoping thus to win the Indians as his allies. The Indians were told that "only he [Mendizábal] and God were to be obeyed . . . [and that] no one was to punish the Indians nor should the Indians allow themselves to be punished." To this Fray Nicolás de Freitas thundered that Mendizábal's true intent was to "destroy . . . tender children of the Church" and to "hold the Indians for his particular ends by gratitude."[69]

Mendizábal's Indian policy seemed a frontal attack on the authority by which the Franciscans maintained mission discipline. Because of the governor's orders prohibiting Indian corporal punishment, "no longer do we have it in our power to correct, teach, or preach," lamented Fray Miguel de Sacristan. As a result Zuñi's residents refused to attend services, would not ring the "Ave Maria or sunset bells and did not attend choir." When Captain Diego de Trujillo tried to correct their laxity with the whip, the governor removed him from his post. When Cuarac's church warden flayed several Indian girls who refused to attend Mass and catechism, the governor had him flayed.[70]

But the most bitter denunciations of Mendizábal for fomenting liberty of conscience stemmed from his toleration of native religious rites. The Puebloans, who had suffered famine, hunger, Apache attacks, and violent repression, increasingly turned to their ancient gods for power and solace. Despite the Franciscans' punishments, the Indians continued to openly worship their ancestral gods. Mendizábal condoned all of this and even allowed the Indians to perform the katsina dance. The friars especially loathed this dance because the natives "openly invoked the devil" with horrendous "costumes, masks and infernal singing," culminating in orgy. For Mendizábal the katsina dance was simply pleasurable entertainment, "Indian nonsense (*bobería de Indios*) . . . that signified nothing." Tesuque's Indians danced it for him in Santa Fe and on seeing it he concluded: "Look there, this dance contains nothing more than this 'Hu-hu-hu,' and these thieving friars say that it is superstitious." Mendizábal contended that for decades the friars had allowed the dance "whenever it suited their own convenience," or if they wanted to mobilize an entire pueblo for sowing or other "tasks connected with their gainful occupations." He saw no reason to prohibit the dance.[71]

The Indians performed the katsina dance whenever they wanted food, rain, prosperity, and communal harmony. With puffs of smoke and feather-adorned prayer-sticks they summoned the Cloud-Spirits from the underworld. They danced, their feet pounding on Mother Earth, so that the gods below would hear them dancing and ascend to bring them happiness. Esteban Clemente, a Tano Indian, declared that in 1660 their prayers were finally answered. The katsina "came from the other life to speak." Cuarac's Indians were overjoyed in 1661 because the katsina had visited them too and "went throughout the pueblo shouting loudly to the people that he had been exiled a long time, but that now they would be happy, for they were coming to stay with them." The katsina promised good fortune and bravery, and "corn, or any other thing they requested." [72]

The return of the katsina was a fact whose full significance perhaps only the friars were prepared to understand, given their long contact with the Indians. We saw in Chapter 1 how the Puebloans conceptualized the relationship of respect and obligation that existed between the living and the dead, between a lineage and its katsina, as a model for the relationship between juniors and seniors. The katsina always visited the people bearing the gifts of happiness, prosperity, and life, just as seniors always gave juniors the gifts, esoteric knowledge, and socially necessary goods they needed in return for respect, labor, and obedience. The friars had tried to eradicate katsina worship because of its political significance—it affirmed the ties of reciprocity and obligation that structured inequality between juniors and seniors. As we saw, by boldly humiliating seniors, by depriving elders of the labor and obedience juniors had provided them, and by injecting new socially necessary goods, rites, and esoteric knowledge that only the friars could offer the children, the Franciscans had altered fundamentally the material foundation of authority in Pueblo society.

Mendizábal's attempt to win the Indians' loyalty away from the friars by tolerating native rites simply afforded the town chiefs and medicine men the opportunity to perform publicly those ceremonials they had been conducting clandestinely, thereby legitimating their moral and political authority. The division that had developed in each pueblo between Christians and non-Christians (or nominal Christians), between Hispanicized Indians and "traditionalists," widened as a result of Mendizábal's political jockeying. By 1660 the tension between these groups had grown so pronounced, said Fray Nicolás de Chávez, that "the heathen Indians ridicule and have become scornful of the Christian Indians because the devil does not appear to them as he does to the heathen, because they do not dance the katsina." [73]

Lost to Mendizábal's leniency, claimed the friars, were the years they had spent taming the monster of Indian sensuality. Friars strictly prohibited polygamy, concubinage, and promiscuity, yet the governor allowed the Indians to live "according to their appetites and unrestrained desires." He would not allow those women found living in concubinage at Cuarac, Abó, and Taos to be whipped. Allegedly Mendizábal had told the Indians that if the priests tried to correct them for these faults "they could leave their pueblos and go to live wherever they wished . . . with as many women as they did in the day of their heathenism." [74]

Had Mendizábal's conflict with the Franciscans been limited to issues of Indian administration, he might have been spared the Inquisition's wrath, for his behavior was not out of line with viceregal policies. His principle heresy was to publicly accuse the friars of failing to observe the rule of their own order regarding chastity, poverty, and obedience.

Mendizábal undoubtedly was right on the first count. During the initial years of the conquest, the Christian fathers' vow of chastity truly had impressed the Indians as a mark of divinity. But as time passed and isolation increased, the flesh became weak and concupiscence triumphed even among some friars. It would have been amazing if lapses of chastity had not occurred among the Franciscans, given their ministry to a culture that glorified sexuality, given that Pueblo women offered their bodies to men they deemed holy, and given that the mystical marriage and union with God the friars so desired were likened to human intercourse. Evidence of the clerical peccadillos that were occurring in New Mexico can be found in a 1638 Inquisition document detailing the behavior of Fray Nicolás Hidalgo at Taos Pueblo. Isabel Yantula appeared that year with a four-year-old half-breed child whom she said Fray Nicolás had fathered and kept with him in the convent. Isabel alleged that Father Hidalgo had strangled her husband and then freely enjoyed her as a woman. Margita Tultamu described similar behavior. As evidence of what she said, Margita presented a one-year-old half-breed child who the friar also kept living in the convent dressed as a Spaniard.[75]

By 1660 it was evident that some friars were not practicing chastity. Vows of sexual purity were part of the Franciscans' public ideology, but behind the convent walls private behavior had its liberties—so much so that Fray Nicolás de Freitas reported matter of factly that "all the pueblos are full of friars' children" and that many of his brothers had concubines. That this was so startled neither the friars nor the Indians, for as we saw in Chapter 1, successful men who became caciques, as the friars in essence had done, were surrounded by secondary wives and concubines who offered their love and bodies in return for gifts and benefits for their children. For centuries it had been customary that when a foreign war chief conquered a pueblo he immediately took a native wife, for by bearing children the foreign and the native were combined as one. The Puebloans always transformed that which they deemed potently dangerous and malevolent into a beneficial force by offering it food and sexual intercourse. Just as the Spanish soldiers had fallen into the loving arms of Indian women, so too eventually did the friars, though undoubtedly nagged by pangs of guilt.[76]

As a result of all the profanations and humiliations they had endured, by the 1660s the Pueblo Indians were seething with discontent. As the gulf between Christianized Indians and "traditionalists" grew deeper in every town, the discontent of the "traditionalists" was vented on the half-breed children fathered by the Franciscans, who were living symbols of the union between the foreign and the native, between the Spanish and the Puebloans, that they wanted to destroy. Fray Salvador de Guerra, in a December 1, 1660, letter to his superiors in Mexico City, reported that the Indians at Isleta continually defied his authority and had staged a katsina dance, saying that Governor Mendizábal permitted it. During this dance the Indians in native costumes had seized a child and beaten it with whips and blows until it was lifeless. Fray Salvador does not mention if he was the father of the child, only that his admonitions to the Indians that they stop were ignored. Bathed in tears, Fray Salvador stripped himself naked, placed a crown of thorns on his head and a rope around his neck, flagellated himself, and then crisscrossed the pueblo carrying a large cross on his shoulders. The Indians immediately stopped the dance and dispersed, said the friar, because the sight of "the Holy Cross caused them horror." It was probably the force that the cross represented that frightened the Indians. For as Fray Nicolás de Chávez declared in 1661, by that year the friars so feared for their lives that they "ordinarily carried harquebuses." [77]

Mendizábal stepped into this tense political environment in which village "traditionalists" were openly challenging the friars' authority. According to the friars, the governor delighted in visiting the missions to interrogate the Indians regarding their priests' sexual conduct. At Galisteo several women came forward to denounce the sexual liberties of Friars Nicolás de Villar, Miguel de Guevara, and Pedro Moreno. Mendizábal judged their claims valid and ordered the priests to compensate the women. When the clerics refused, claiming the women lied, Mendizábal rebuked them saying: "Indians were not capable of deceiving, and that he knew that there was not an Indian who would tell a lie." Twenty-two of Tajique's women raised similar cries against their pastor, Fray Diego de Parraga. Francisco Mutra added that the friar "kept taking his wife away from him at night to sleep with her, and that he had had a daughter by her, and that this had been going on for three years." Father Diego admitted his crime: "the daughter was his . . . and . . . as a man, he had enjoyed" her mother. The facts were undeniable. What riled the Franciscans most in these cases of priestly impropriety was that the governor and his constables had impinged upon ecclesiastical prerogatives through their investigations. Clerics were immune from civil prosecution. The governor clearly had exceeded his jurisdictional powers. [78]

When questioned by the Inquisition regarding these issues, Mendizábal denied ever impinging on ecclesiastical privileges. The Indians had complained to him about their friars. He simply had relayed the information to the custodian. The Indians came to him because they trusted him and hoped that through his office they would receive justice. The Indians knew that the Franciscans rarely disciplined their own. Mendizábal argued that had he wanted to subvert clerical privileges, he could have proceeded more aggressively against the Franciscans on several occasions. Fray Luís Martínez, for example, should have been severely punished for "forceably [raping] a woman, splitting her throat, and burying her in his cell." Instead, he obeyed the law and referred the matter to the Franciscan superior. Martínez admitted his crime and begged the governor to "confuse" the Indians lest they rebel. In this Mendizábal obliged him, but in nothing else.[79]

Mendizábal's claim that the Franciscans were not observing their vow of poverty was also a difficult pill to swallow. Many of the friars led lives of extreme austerity devoid of material luxuries and human comforts. What energy they did not pour into evangelization they spent working the land to accumulate agricultural goods for the purchase of church furnishings. In fact, an inverse relationship existed between the padres' religious successes and their desire to purchase ornate ritual objects. The friars believed that the psychological appeal of Pueblo religion was in its gay externalities. As Christianity began to falter they spent increasing amounts on more dazzling ornaments to impress the Indians. Such expenditures put the Franciscans and the kingdom's various governors on a collision course over how the profit of Indian toil would be spent. Mendizábal found it incomprehensible that men who imitated St. Francis and had vowed themselves to lives of poverty should need sumptuous church inventories. He reminded them that when the Gospel was first preached in New Mexico, it had been in "a few huts of straw and some cloth ornaments." Had the friars forgotten their apostolic model? Apparently they had, and Mendizábal's reminder was nettlesome, given that the Church had accumulated large tracts of land, stocked granaries, built up immense herds, and constructed an extensive collection of buildings, while the kingdom as a whole bordered on economic disaster. Mendizábal warned that if the Indians spent their entire time building convents and laboring on Church farms, the area would be submerged in oblivion.[80]

Mendizábal's final charge, that the Franciscans did not observe their vow of obedience, stemmed from his controversies with the friars over whose authority was supreme in New Mexico. The germ of the problem was that Mendizábal claimed to be "universal head" of the province. Recall the "Act of Possession and Submission" read to the Pueblo Indians in 1598. Therein Jesus Christ was proclaimed lord and universal head of the

Church. Well versed in canon law, Mendizábal legitimately claimed by right of the papal concessions granted in the *patronato* that as the king's legate he was both temporal and spiritual lord. Since the Franciscans had never really accepted the vicarial theory of kingship, they did their very best to silence anyone who vigorously advanced such ideas. Thus the murder of Governor Rosas in 1641 and the trumped up Inquisition case against Mendizábal.

The settlers were the pivotal group in provincial politics. When they judged governors excessively exploitative and abusive, they allied with the friars to rid themselves of such men. If instead the settlers thought the Franciscans were being tyrannical and monopolizing the area's resources, and if the governor managed to harness this discontent, there was little the friars could do to restrain the governor short of murder. Had Mendizábal simply insulted the Franciscans, it would not have affected his tenure. But instead, on entering New Mexico he seized long-standing *encomiendas* and awarded them to retainers, as was his prerogative. Other *vecinos* became disgruntled because he deprived them of their offices as *alcaldes mayores*, highly desired posts because of their political power and control over Indian labor. Mendizábal also thoughtlessly staged slave raids into Apache territory, which the Apaches always reacted to with retaliatory depredations, and charged the colonists inflated prices for luxury goods he sold out of his home. Thus when the Franciscans had Governor Mendizábal shackled and carted off to Mexico City to answer to the Inquisition for his alleged crimes, the settlers did not heed his cries for help. "Gentlemen, look at your governor," Mendizábal pleaded, "Regard my fate and see what the Fathers do. Do you not see that the Custodian holds me a prisoner? . . . Such a thing has never happened except to a God Man and now to me. I swear to Christ that I am a better Christian than all the men in the world. Look, gentlemen, there is no longer God or King, since such a thing could happen to a man like me. No! No! There is no longer God or King," he cried, as the cart carrying him disappeared on the horizon. To the very moment of his death in the Inquisition's prison, Mendizábal denied all the charges against him—heresy, blasphemy, propositions contrary to the cult of the Church, destruction of the Church's authority, and Judaism. The Inquisition exonerated him posthumously.[81]

Little is known about the governors of New Mexico in the years that followed, except about Mendizábal's successor, Governor Diego Dionisio de Peñalosa Briceño y Berdugo (1661–64), who was ensnared in similar disputes with the friars. The Inquisition found Peñalosa guilty of having encroached on ecclesiastical privileges, of having uttered "evil-sounding doctrines, erroneous dogmas, and blasphemous locutions," of having spoken ill of the pope, and of having shown seditious attitudes toward the power of the Holy Office. The Inquisition sentenced Peñalosa to a heavy fine, forced him to publicly abjure his errors, barred him from public office, and exiled him from New Spain and the West Indies. Broken and penniless, he died in France in 1687.[82]

As we review the period from 1598 to 1680, it is apparent that through alliances, censures, excommunications, and physical force the Franciscans had realized, if only imperfectly, the theocracy of which they so dreamed. During those years they virtually reigned supreme over the land and silenced all their opponents. They succeeded because they held sway over the colonists through various exchanges and psychological ploys, and retained their leadership in the Indian pueblos through gifts, magic, converts, and force. But if the Inquisition cases against Mendizábal and Peñalosa reveal anything, it is that by the 1660s things were not well in the Indian utopia. The pueblos were like tinder ready for the slightest spark to ignite them into revolt. To the Franciscan fire of mystical love that enflamed the province in rebellion in 1680 we now turn.

Franciscan Theocracy

By the mid-1640s it had become clear to many Indians that the Franciscans were no longer the supermen they had once seemed. The novelty of their gifts had worn off and their magic had proven ineffectual in producing rain, health, prosperity, and peace. As some of the original mission personnel died and younger, less experienced friars replaced them, the charisma with which the initial friars had established their authority as town chiefs did not easily transfer over and only fed village factionalism. Given that native hunting and warfare had been supplanted with the arrival of European herds and armaments, it fell to the medicine men to reestablish harmony in the cosmos, to call the ancient gods anew, and to rid the area of the witches (that is, the friars) who had stolen their hearts.

It did not take the fathers long to discover that their children had reverted to idolatry, were invoking the devil, and were clandestinely wallowing in the forbidden pleasures of the flesh. They responded as any father would have with disobedient children—punishments began. None of the backsliders was spared the whip, and some even were beaten to death out of fatherly love. In 1655, for example, Fray Salvador de Guerra discovered that a Hopi Indian named Juan Cuna had been worshipping idols. Guerra viciously whipped Juan until "he was bathed in blood." A second beating was inflicted later that day inside the church. Juan Cuna died in flames that surely resembled those of hell, for when the beating was done, the friar drenched him from head to foot with burning turpentine. Father Guerra justified this sort of punishment to ecclesiastical authorities as necessary to abolish idolatry. He stated that several other Indians had received similar treatment, a statement corroborated in 1663 by Nicolás de Aguilar, and by those survivors who were permanently "marked by the burns."[83]

As the Franciscans lost their grip over the Indians and their punishments only bred more hatred, they found themselves isolated and increasingly turned within themselves to find comfort in God, yearning for his tender kisses, wishing that his love would pierce their hearts. Through preaching they had begotten many spiritual children, but only prayer and meditation would nurture their own souls. "Spiritual children . . . are dear and precious," St. Bernard had said, "but the kisses of the spouse are infinitely more agreeable. It is a good thing to save several souls, but it is much sweeter to be with the Word."[84]

The Franciscans had spent years preaching to the Indians, but their labor largely had been for naught. Now, to prove how much they really loved the Indians, they prepared themselves to offer the perfect example of that love, their own deaths through martyrdom. The desire for martyrdom had been a burning drive among many of the friars who entered New Mexico. In fact, 49 of the hundred or so friars who served in New Mexico during the seventeenth century died as martyrs, suffering pains not unlike those they meted out to the Indians. Fray Juan de Escalona traveled to New Mexico in the early 1600s because in a vision he had seen his martyr's crown there. Escalona's confessor tells us that one afternoon while the friar was enraptured praying the Ave Maria, he suddenly shouted out, "Beati primi, beati primi" ("blessed are the first"). Asked what he had seen, Escalona explained:

Yesterday afternoon, when we were praying the Ave Maria, God our Lord revealed . . . to me that some religious of my father, Saint Francis . . . are to be martyred [in New Mexico]. These religious appeared before me and I saw them being martyred in spirit, and because I was joyful to see them suffer martyrdom with so much spirit and courage, I said: Beati primi, Beati primi.

Escalona reached New Mexico but despite his tireless efforts to convert Indians, reports of his prayer-induced levitations, and frequent visitations by Saint Francis, he died of natural causes and was buried at Santo Domingo Pueblo.[85]

Mother María de Jesús Coronel (1602–65), abbess of the Franciscan convent at Agreda, Burgos, spiritual confidant to King Philip IV, and an avid patroness of New Mexico's missions, inspired several of her devotees to travel to New Mexico in search of martyrdom, claiming that she had led several Franciscans to their deaths there. Mother María said that between 1620 and 1631, she had traveled to New Mexico "three and four times" a day with Saint Michael and Saint Francis as her wings. And because of the many wounds she received from the Pueblo Indians, the "heavenly angels crowned her, wherefore she attained martyrdom from our Lord."[86]

In 1670 Fray José Trujillo arrived in New Mexico, culminating a lifelong quest for martyrdom that had begun in Spain in 1634. Father Trujillo had traveled to the Philippines, to Japan, to Mexico, and finally to New Mexico. It was in Manila in 1649, while conferring with Mother Juana de San Antonio, a nun widely renowned for her holiness and mystical flights, that he learned the location of his martyr's crown. The venerable mother asked Trujillo if he sought martyrdom. "Yes," he said. "Know that it is not here but in New Mexico that God our Lord will satisfy your desires." A decade after Trujillo reached the Rio Grande Valley he was clubbed to death by the Zuñi Indians. Finally he got the mystical marriage he so desired.[87]

Like innocent lambs being led to the slaughter, the Franciscans were "anxious to suffer martyrdom for God," and frequently fantasized about their impending deaths. Friars Juan de Padilla, Luís de Ubeda, and Juan de la Cruz, to name but a few, rushed into adversity hoping to die as fools for Christ. The hagiographers tell us that these men "did not fear turning their backs to hazards . . . or baring their chests to risks, but rather endangered their lives for the salvation of souls." When these martyrdoms became known, said Fray Alonso de Benavides in 1630, "it caused very fervent desires in many to imitate them." Fearlessly the friars exposed themselves to danger knowing that the pains of torture were momentary while those of hell were eternal. Faithful unto death, they uttered the words of their redeemer: "whoever loses his life for my sake and the gospel's will preserve it" (Mark 8:35). Fray Francisco de Porras was killed by the Hopi on June 28, 1633, "to the great sorrow of all," says his biographer, "but to his own great joy because he had attained the goal he sought." Fray Roque de Figueredo too "found life in Christ which he [was] determined to lose in love for him." Though Zuñi's warriors heaped all sorts of insults on him, he did not cower, for "his desire to die triumphantly was greater than his fear of the fatal blow at the hands of the barbarous Indians." Fray Francisco Letrado likewise awaited his persecutors joyfully. With crucifix in hand, as the manuals on martyrdom instructed, Letrado uttered words that "would benefit the souls of bystanders." As the Indians' treacherous arrows pierced his body, he must have thought those things that he was taught to visualize at the moment of death: the Passion of Christ, and Mary and many angels awaiting his soul with a crown in their hands. Bear in mind that though the martyrdoms of these Franciscans may appear like supreme acts of pacifism, they were, quite the contrary, supreme acts of aggression. The Indians were provoked to murder only when they were pushed beyond their human limits. More to the point, the Spanish soldiers always retaliated with brute force whenever the Indians killed their friars. For the friars, then, the means justified their ends.[88]

The Pueblo Revolt and Its Aftermath

The years 1666 to 1670 were marked by drought and meager maize production. Famine swept the land in 1670, and a decade of pestilence and death followed. The Indian population, which in 1638 had totaled roughly 40,000, by 1670 had fallen to 17,000. To complicate matters, in 1672 hordes of hungry Apaches and Navajos in similarly desperate straits began attacking the kingdom's settlements with unprecedented regularity, killing and stealing, and carrying off whatever food they found. The Puebloans' discontent hardly needed stoking. For years they had resented the Spanish, and now they spoke openly of rebellion. The medicine men told their tribesmen that the reason they suffered so was because their ancient gods were angry. If they offered the katsina gifts and respect, they would surely bless them with rainfall, fertility, and happiness. The first group to openly defy colonial rule were the Tewa, the Indians who had had the closest contact with the Spaniards during the seventeenth century. In 1673 they publicly performed prohibited dances, making offerings to their gods and begging them to return. The medicine men worked feverishly, placing hexes on the Christians and stealing their hearts. Apparently their magic worked. In 1675 alone, Indian witchcraft was blamed for sending seven friars and three settlers to their graves.[89]

Ominous forebodings of events to come were everywhere. In 1672, the Jumano Indians of Abó Pueblo revolted, burning their church and murdering Fray Pedro de Avila y Ayala. Before killing Father Pedro with blows from their tomahawks, the Indians stripped him, placed a rope around his neck, and cruelly flogged him. His naked body was found hugging a cross and an image of the Blessed Virgin Mary. In an act symbolic of the death-blow the Indians believed they had given Christ and the Trinity, three lambs whose throats had been slashed were placed at the martyr's feet. The message was unequivocal. Yet one friar read it as saying that the Franciscans were "like lambs among wolves, and these three lambs gave testimony that the dead father was a lamb." Three years later, in 1675, the Virgin Mary of Toledo appeared to a sickly New Mexican girl, cured her illness, and ordered her to "arise and announce to this custody that it will soon be destroyed for the lack of reverence that it shows its priests." The Virgin's apparition sparked a flurry of high Masses throughout the province and prompted Fray Juan de Jesús to urge his brother at San Diego de Jémez Mission to cease construction on the colaterals he was building on the church's nave. Time would be spent best "uniting ourselves with God and preparing to die for our Holy Faith," Fray Juan de Jesús advised, "for the colaterals will soon end in the ashes and many of us in death." [90]

Governor Juan Francisco Treviño, who had arrived in the province in 1675, dealt with the widespread Indian sedition by launching a campaign against idolatry. At Nambé, San Felipe, and Jémez he had known "sorcerers" hung. Forty-seven medicine men who admitted practicing witchcraft were arrested, flogged, and sold into slavery. Before these men could be taken out of the kingdom, the Tewa, armed with clubs and shields, descended on Santa Fe demanding that Treviño release them, threatening to kill him and all the colonists if he refused. The governor pleaded: "Wait a while, children, I will give them to you and pardon them on condition that you forsake idolatry and iniquity." The Indians stood firm. Treviño capitulated. [91]

The confrontation between Treviño and the Tewa over the medicine men indicated how radicalized and defiant the Puebloans had become. One of the men who felt the sting of Treviño's whip was Popé, a San Juan medicine man. Convinced that the yoke of subjugation could no longer be tolerated, Popé moved from San Juan to Taos, the northernmost pueblo, to escape the governor's watchful eye and to plot a provincewide revolt. At Taos, Popé conferred with the caciques of the surrounding pueblos, with the war chiefs who had been marginalized by the superior force of the Spaniards, and with Pueblo dissidents who had escaped the missions' tyranny and taken refuge among the Apaches.

Popé's genius lay in his brilliant organizational skills and his ability to inflame the popular imagination through the millenarianism he articulated. He told the disaffected, the hungry, and the displaced that their ancient gods would not return bearing gifts of happiness and prosperity until the Christians and their God were dead. Then their sadness and misery would end, for they would be as they had been at the time of emergence from the underworld. "They would gather large crops of grain, maize with large and thick ears, many bundles of cotton, many calabashes and watermelons," and would enjoy abundant health and leisure. To those elders and chiefs who had been flayed by the friars for their polygamous marriages, or sheared of their hair as fornicators, Popé promised that "who shall kill a Spaniard will get an Indian woman for a wife, and he who kills four will get four women, and he who kills ten or more will have a like number of women." To a people who had seen their agricultural lands usurped and their tribute payments grow onerous over time, Popé offered liberation. When the Spaniards were all dead, he promised, they would "break the lands and enlarge their cultivated fields . . . free from the labor they performed for the religious and the Spaniards."[92]

From Taos Pueblo, Popé sent messengers throughout the kingdom announcing that if the people respected the katsina and called them properly, they would return to usher in a new age. Popé himself regularly called Caudi, Tilini, and Tleume, the katsina who lived in the kiva of the Taos medicine society but "never came out." Finally, after many prayers and offerings, the katsina came out "emit[ting] fire from all the extremities of their bodies." They told Popé that "they were going underground to the lake of Copala" and would return after the Spaniards were gone. The katsina showed Popé how to defeat the Christians and gave him a knotted cord, which he was to circulate to all the pueblos. Those villages that wished to join the rebellion were to untie one knot as a sign of obedience, and by the others would count the days to revolt.[93]

Popé enlisted the caciques of Taos, Picuris, San Lorenzo, Santo Domingo, Jémez, and Pecos, as well as a number of prominent mixedbloods: Domingo Naranjo from Santa Clara, Nicolás Jonva from San Ildefonso, and Domingo Romero from Tesuque. They met secretly each time a village celebrated its saint's feast day so that their travel to and fro would not provoke suspicion. August 11, 1680, the first night of the new moon, was chosen as the date for the revolt. They knew the settlers would be most vulnerable to attack right before the triennial supply caravan arrived from Mexico City in mid-September with ammunition and horses.[94]

On August 9, 1680, Popé dispatched two messengers to all the pueblos with knotted cords indicating that only two days remained. They told the caciques that a letter from Po-he-yemu, "the father of all the Indians, their great captain, who had been such since the world had been inundated," had arrived from the north informing that "all of them . . . should rebel, and that any pueblo that would not agree to it they would destroy, killing all the people."[95]

The caciques of Tanos, San Marcos, and La Cienega opposed the rebellion, and on August 9 informed Governor Antonio de Otermín of its impending approach. Otermín had Popé's messengers arrested and tortured until they revealed what the knotted cords meant. Tesuque's Indians learned of this, and fearing that all might be lost immediately dispatched runners to the confederated pueblos informing them that they should rebel the next day.[96]

August 10, 1680, began for Fray Juan Pío like any Sunday morning. He left Santa Fe on foot to say Mass at Tesuque, accompanied by his armed escort, Pedro Hidalgo. But on this day the pueblo was totally deserted. The friar searched everywhere for the Indians and finally found them a few miles outside the village armed and wearing war paints. "What is this, children, are you mad?," the friar asked. "Do not disturb yourselves; I will help you and will die a thousand deaths for you." Before he could say anything else, a shower of arrows pierced his breast. Pedro Hidalgo would have been killed too had he not been on his horse. He barely escaped, and by ten that morning was back in Santa Fe reporting to the governor. All day emissaries from every part of the kingdom arrived in Santa Fe telling of the massacres they had seen. The Indians' fury had struck the entire province like a bolt of lightning. In one moment a century's work seemed destroyed.[97]

The revolt proceeded as Popé had instructed. First the Indians stole or killed "the principal nerve of warfare," the horses and mules, which the Spaniards had introduced into the province and which had been so instrumental in the conquest and subordination of the Puebloans. Without these beasts of burden, the Spaniards were helpless against mounted Pueblo and Apache warriors. Without horses the Spanish could not communicate rapidly with the centers of authority in New Spain. Indian runners could outrun and outstalk any settler. Whatever technological advantages the Spaniards had on account of their armaments, the Indians offset in numbers. Against roughly 170 colonists capable of bearing arms stood 8,000 or more Indian warriors; a ratio of approximately 1 to 50.[98]

Once the horses were in Indian hands, Popé's forces isolated the settlements in the northern half of the kingdom (the Rio Arriba) from those in the southern half (the Rio Abajo). In the north, all roads to Santa Fe were blocked, and one by one the Spanish settlements were pillaged and razed by the Indians, who scavenged whatever armaments they could. In a few hours 401 settlers and 21 friars were killed. Those who survived gathered at the governor's residence in Santa Fe. The colonists of the Rio Abajo gathered at Isleta.[99]

By August 13, all of the villages in the Rio Arriba had been destroyed and only Santa Fe stood, surrounded by Pueblo and Apache warriors who were ready for a final assault. Grossly outnumbered but stubbornly refusing to admit defeat, Otermín made one last peace overture. Through Juan, a Tano Indian servant turned rebel leader, Otermín implored the caciques "that even though they had committed so many atrocities, still there was a remedy, for if they would return to obedience to his Majesty they would be pardoned." The chiefs jeered and demanded through Juan that

all classes of Indians who were in our power be given up to them, both those in the service of the Spaniards and those of the Mexican nation of that suburb of Analco. He demanded also that his wife and children be given up to him, and likewise that all the Apache men and women whom the Spaniards had captured in war be turned over to them, inasmuch as some Apaches who were among them were asking for them.

Otermín refused, and the battle for Santa Fe began.[100]

For nine days Santa Fe lay under siege. To hasten the colonists' surrender, the rebels cut off their food and water. By August 20th the Indians sensed victory. That night they were heard shouting gleefully: "Now the God of the Spaniards, who was their father, is dead, and Santa María, who was their mother, and the saints . . . were pieces of rotten wood" and that "their own God whom they obeyed [had] never died." Determined that it was better "to die fighting than of hunger and thirst," the colonists at Santa Fe marshalled all their firepower for a final assault on the morning of August 21. The strategy worked. Popé's forces quickly lost 350 men and temporarily were set to flight. At day's end, Otermín and the settlers decided to abandon Santa Fe before the Indians recouped their losses and returned to rout them. Otermín hoped that he would be able to join forces with the settlers of the Rio Abajo, whom he thought were still gathered at Isleta, and return north with them to subdue the apostates. But unbeknownst to him, the refugees at Isleta had already fled south toward El Paso.[101]

The colonists' retreat south from Santa Fe was filled with horrors. In every village they found piles of mutilated bodies strewn amid ashes of still smoldering fires. At Sandía Pueblo the mission's statues were covered with excrement. Two chalices had been discarded in a basket of manure, and the paint on the altar's crucifix had been stripped off with a whip. Feces covered the holy communion table and the arms of a statue of Saint Francis had been hacked off with an ax. At every mission along their route they reported the most unspeakable profanations of Christian *sacra*.[102]

The Christians felt equal revulsion on seeing and hearing of how the friars had died. On that August night of rebellion, the Jémez Indians apprehended Fray Juan de Jesús, bound him naked onto a pig's back and paraded him through the town, heaping all sorts of jeers and blows on him. Then they removed him from the pig, forced him onto his hands and knees and took turns riding atop his back, repeatedly spurring his haunches to prod him forward. When the warriors were ready to kill him, some dissension erupted in their ranks. But showing a fidelity to death and a love for his persecutors that the manuals of martyrdom assured him would win a crown in heaven, Father Juan allegedly said: "Children, I am a poor old man, do not fight, do not kill each other in order to protect me; do what God permits." And so they shoved a sword through his heart and gave him numerous blows. His body was discovered by the Spaniards in some woods near the pueblo.[103]

Though the Christians were aghast at how the Pueblo Indians had manifested their anger, one only has to recall the massive desecration of katsina masks, kivas, and other native sacra that occurred during the Spanish conquest to understand why the Indians retaliated so exactly during the Pueblo Revolt. The tables were now turned in this contest of cultures. The Indians had learned well from their overlords the functions of iconoclasm in political spectacle.

When Otermín's forces finally reached Isleta, the pueblo was deserted. A week earlier, on August 14, news had reached Isleta that all the Spaniards of the Rio Arriba had been killed, and acting on this information, the settlers, under the leadership of Alonso García, had abandoned Isleta and retreated south. The reconquest of New Mexico would have to wait. For the moment, the only succor either refugee group could expect was from the mission supply train they knew was advancing toward New Mexico. News of the revolt reached Fray Francisco de Ayeta's supply caravan on August 25, just south of El Paso. He promptly advanced toward Socorro, and it was near there on September 6 that the Isleta and Santa Fe survivors of the rebellion were finally united. Together they numbered 1,946, of whom approximately 500 were Pueblo and Apache slaves.[104]

The Christians' defeat and departure were cause for great celebration among the Pueblos. Popé and his two captains, Alonso Catiti of Santo Domingo and Luís Tupatu of Picuris, traveled throughout the province ordering everyone to return "to the state of their antiquity, as when they came from the lake of Copola; that this was the better life and the one they desired, because the God of the Spaniards was worth nothing and theirs was very strong." Popé promised that if they lived in accordance with their ancestral laws, there would be endless peace, prosperity, and harmony.[105]

But none of this would be possible so long as there were vestiges of Christianity. Crosses and images of Christ, of the Virgin Mary, and of the saints had to be destroyed. Churches had to be razed and their bells shattered. Men and women were to forget their Christian names and use only native ones. They were to purify themselves by plunging "into the rivers and wash[ing] themselves with amole [a soap-root] . . . washing even their clothing, with the understanding that there would thus be taken from them the character of the holy sacraments." Anyone who spoke Spanish or uttered the name of Jesus or Mary would be punished severely. Men were to abandon the wife they had taken in matrimony "for any one whom they might wish." Everyone was "to burn the seeds which the Spaniards sowed and to plant only maize and beans, which were the crops of their ancestors." All of this was to be done in the presence of the children so that they would learn the ways of the ancients and the meaning of respect.[106]

Within weeks of the Spaniards' defeat, the indigenous sacral topography was restored. "Flour, feathers, and the seed of maguey, maize, and tobacco" were offered to the spirits at pre-conquest shrines. Kivas that had been desecrated and filled with sand were emptied and resacralized. At last the gods who had abandoned their people and allowed them to perish from hunger and sickness returned from the underworld.[107]

The Spanish survivors of the Pueblo Revolt were genuinely confused by what had happened. They thought themselves blameless and self-righteously pinned the entire disaster on the Indians. A visibly shaken Governor Otermín bristled that the devil had ensnared the Indians with idolatries and superstitions to which "their stupid ignorance predisposes them, for they live blindly in their freedom and stupid vices." In the months that followed, Otermín gleaned the whys of the revolt. Answers came from five Indians he captured. From Pedro Nanboa, an 80-year-old Indian, Governor Otermín learned that for more than 70 years the Indians had resented Spanish rule because the Christians had destroyed their religious objects, had prohibited their ceremonials, and had humiliated and punished their old men. For this reason the Indians "had been plotting to rebel and to kill the Spaniards and the religious . . . planning constantly to carry it out down to the present occasion."[108]

Two Queres Indians voiced more specific complaints. They objected to the "ill treatment and injuries" they had received from Otermín's constables who "would not leave them alone, [had] burned their estufas [kivas]," and constantly beat them. The Queres had wanted to be "free from the labor they had performed for the religious and the Spaniards." They had grown "weary of putting in order, sweeping, heating, and adorning the church." The Tano Indians agreed. They too had "tired of the work they had to do for the Spaniards and the religious, because they did not allow them to plant or do other things for their own needs." Had the Christians shown them respect there might not have been a rebellion, explained Joseph. Instead, "they beat [us], took away what [we] had, and made [us] work without pay."[109]

The Franciscans pondered the Pueblo Revolt and concluded that the only thing they were guilty of was selfless love for the Indians. Fray Antonio de Sierra wondered why it was that "the Indians who have done the greatest harm are those who have been most favored by the religious and who are most intelligent." What seemed to preoccupy the friars most were the martyrdoms their brothers had suffered. These were not a cause for sadness and tears, but a cause for joy. "We do not mourn the blood shed by twenty-one of our brothers," wrote Fray Juan Alvarez, "for from them there comes to our sacred religion such an access of faith and such honor and glory to God and His church." Fray Francisco de Ayeta was similarly philosophical; that "which the world calls losses, they [are] really the richest treasure of the church."[110]

The viceroy, dignitaries of the Franciscan Order in New Spain, and a few survivors of the Pueblo Revolt gathered at the Cathedral of Mexico City on March 1, 1681, to eulogize New Mexico's martyrs. In his sermon, Doctor Ysidro Sariñana y Cuenca, the cathedral's canon, reflected on how a century's work among "wild beasts," teaching them how to cultivate the soil, clothing their nakedness, and showing them how to live in houses, had ended. The arrows that had sapped the lives of the friars were like a "womb pregnant with darts." Their suffering was "the sure road to life; because the better title corresponding to such deaths is to call them lives," said Sariñana. New Mexico's martyrs had perfectly imitated Christ. Like Christ, they had died because of their Father's love for humanity and because of man's hatred and ingratitude. God did not love the sins of the persecutors, but he loved the patience of the persecuted. He did not love the evil hand that wounded, but he loved the suffering of the wounds. When the arrows of treachery had pierced the martyrs' breasts, when tomahawks had crushed their skulls, and when flames had consumed their bodies, they had been united in mystical marriage with God, a true sign of their perfection. No words captured the mood of that day better than those of St. Ignatius of Antioch: "I am yearning for death with all the passion of a lover. Earthly longings have been crucified; in me there is left no spark of desire for mundane things, but only a murmur of living water that whispers within me, 'Come to Father.'"[111]

The New Mexican survivors of the revolt settled near the Franciscan mission of Our Lady of Guadalupe, which had been established in 1659 near the present-day site of Ciudad Juárez. There the colonists nursed their wounds and sustained themselves on what little food Father Ayeta had procured for the friars and on what could be extracted from the local Indians. For almost a year they waited for orders and reinforcements to arrive from Mexico City. Finally, in the autumn of 1681, Otermín was ready to punish the apostates. His compatriots were not. Many of them had fled further south. Those who had remained wanted no part in the reconquest. Even the friars were cool to the idea. Otermín, aware that news of the Pueblos' victory had spread like an "infection" throughout northern New Spain, knew that if El Paso and New Mexico were abandoned, the entire area north of Parral would be lost. Already the Indians of Nueva Vizcaya were in revolt. Those around El Paso were seething with discontent because of their exploitation by New Mexico's refugees. All across the north, from Sonora to Coahuila, the drums of war could be heard. On the viceroy's orders, Otermín gathered his troops at El Paso (which had been founded earlier that year), forbade the colonists to desert the area, and departed north on November 5, 1681, with 146 soldiers and 112 Indian allies, many of them "mere boys and raw recruits."[112]

Between November 26 and December 4, Otermín's troops marched north, visiting the abandoned villages of Senecu, San Pascual, Socorro, Alamillo, and Sevilleta. On December 5 they reached Isleta Pueblo and conquered its inhabitants with little effort. Otermín gathered the Indians in the plaza, chastized them for their apostasy, and ordered them to erect large crosses for their houses and little ones to wear around their necks. Fray Francisco de Ayeta arrived the next day. He was triumphantly greeted outside the town by Otermín and the Indians, shouting: "Praised be the most holy sacrament and the purity of our Lady, the Virgin Mary, conceived without stain of sin." Ayeta celebrated Mass the next day. He absolved the Indians' apostasy, baptized their infants, and ordered men to take those wives they had been given in matrimony and to burn all their idols. Before the royal standard, the Indians swore vassalage to the King anew, exclaiming: "Long live the king, our Lord Charles II, God Save Him!" Three volleys of musketry were fired, bugles were sounded, and church bells were rung.[113]

Otermín dispatched emissaries from Isleta to the northern pueblos to announce his arrival and peaceful intent. He expected the Indians to hail his return as repentant apostates, weary of their Apache enemies and of their caciques. Nowhere was such a greeting forthcoming. Alameda, Puaray, Sandía, San Felipe, Santo Domingo, and Cochiti were all abandoned before Otermín's troops entered them. The maize bins at each pueblo were well stocked and what corn there was Otermín had destroyed. By Christmas eve Indian hostilities were growing, and knowing that his troops were ill-prepared and poorly provisioned for a major attack, Otermín retreated to Isleta. By the beginning of 1681, the Spaniards were back in El Paso. The expedition had been a resounding failure. Only the southern pueblos had been penetrated. The Tewa Pueblos and those at Taos, Picuris, and Jémez had not been molested. Substantial force would be necessary to reconquer New Mexico.

The jubilation that swept the pueblos at the defeat of the Spaniards was short-lived. According to Juan, a captured Tiwa Indian, by late 1681, people were muttering that Popé had deceived them. They had had "very small harvests, there [had] been no rain, and everyone [was] perishing." Popé's alliance splintered. Civil war erupted at many pueblos among the caciques, the medicine men, and the warriors, each claiming precedence and superior magical powers. In the midst of this chaos, ill-provisioned pueblos began to prey on the granaries of their neighbors. The Queres and the inhabitants of Taos and Pecos waged war against the Tewa and the Tanos. Then the Queres alliance disintegrated and each pueblo declared itself independent. The Tewa and Tanos deposed Popé as their leader because of his excessive demands for women, grain, and livestock. Luís Tupatu replaced him. Around 1683 the Yutes (modern-day Utes) and Apaches waged what must have seemed an endless war against Jémez, Taos, Picuris, and the Tewa.[114]

Widespread hunger and pestilence were followed by another nine years of drought. Legend holds that even the Rio Grande dried up during those years and did not carry water again until a virgin was sacrificed to Horned Water Serpent. Taking the decade of drought that preceded and followed the Pueblo Revolt, we can understand the ecological factors that fueled village factionalism and internecine warfare. Pueblo mythology says that such struggles were endemic to their lifeway and always forced them to migrate until they found a safe place to call home.[115]

Between 1682 and 1692, the 50-soldier presidio established in El Paso in 1683 provided the main force for attempts by the Spanish colonists to reconquer New Mexico. It was not until news reached the Spanish crown that French exploratory teams had made incursions into the Mississippi Valley and Texas that efforts were intensified to reestablish Spanish authority over New Mexico and to colonize Texas as a defensive buffer for the silver mines of northern New Spain. The man chosen for the former task was Don Diego de Vargas Zapata Luján Ponce de León, who assumed New Mexico's governorship in 1691. Scion of one of Spain's noblest families, the 48-year-old governor was soon to enter Pueblo country to subdue the infidel and make a world safe for Hispanicism, much as his ancestors had done during the reconquest of Spain.[116]

With the Pueblo Revolt, a century of Christian rule came to an abrupt end. Perhaps in the Kingdom of New Mexico, more perfectly than anywhere else in the New World, the Franciscans had created the semblance of that terrestrial theocracy for which they so worked and prayed. Had the pope rather than the king of Spain been the vicar of Christ in the Indies, as the Franciscans steadfastly maintained, the Antichrists of the colony (the governors) would not have polluted the minds and bodies of innocent Indian babes. Unbeknownst to the martyred friars, who believed that their blood would fructify the soil for an abundant harvest of souls, if anything, their deaths thoroughly repudiated clerical rule. We will see in the next chapter that when New Mexico's reconquest was achieved, the zeal, the will, and the way for clerics to successfully challenge the primacy of secular rule were gone.

PART III

 The Eighteenth Century

4

The Reconquest of
New Mexico

After the Corn Mothers, Iatiku and Nautsiti, had lived on the earth together for a while they began to quarrel because Nautsiti was selfish and
hoarded the things in her basket, say the Acoma Indians, explaining how
it was that their Corn Mothers first separated and how they were reunited
after many years. Because the sisters constantly argued, Nautsiti decided
to leave her sister, taking with her the child she loved and her basket,
which contained sheep and cattle fetishes, wheat and vegetable seeds,
many metal things, and something written. Nautsiti offered to share these
things with her sister, but Iatiku refused to accept them, saying that she
"did not want her children to have them." Nautsiti departed to the east
and promised Iatiku that "in a long time to come we shall meet again and
then you will be wearing clothes." [1]

A woman bearing a likeness to Nautsiti returned to the Pueblos in
1692, just as she said she would. Her name was Nuestra Señora del
Rosario, La Conquistadora, Mary, Our Lady of the Rosary, Virgin of the
Conquest. In one arm she carried her infant son, Jesus Christ, and in the
other she clasped a rosary. Around her were the things she had brought to
life: cattle, sheep, vegetables, metal tools, armaments, and writings. Our
Lady of the Conquest returned to New Mexico on August 21, 1692, carried by 60 Spanish soldiers and 100 Indian auxiliaries. Heading the
troops who would restore her terrestrial kingdom among the Pueblos was
Don Diego de Vargas, the reconquerer of New Mexico. Marching to clar-
ions and to the beat of war drums, the troops of the reconquest advanced
north, reaching the walled city of Santa Fe on September 13, 1692. [2]

"Praised be the Blessed Sacrament and Our Lady of the Ransom,"
Vargas shouted at Santa Fe's gates that September day, bidding the In-

dians to let him enter. The Indians refused and instead recited all their grievances against the Spanish, asking why they should submit. They should submit, Vargas explained, so that they could repudiate the devil and become Christians anew. No one listened. At day's end Vargas and his forces prepared to storm Santa Fe. "I again exhorted, persuaded, and pleaded with them in a loud voice," said Don Diego, "telling them that it was necessary that they answer me with a decision as to whether or not they wished to be Christians and to render the obedience and submission which they owed to our holy faith and the king." The Indians agreed to accept the peace Don Diego offered only if the soldiers disarmed before entering the city.[3]

Vargas and several friars finally entered Santa Fe on Sunday, September 14, the feast day of the exaltation of the Holy Cross. The Indians erected a life-size cross in the plaza for them. Vargas approached the cross, knelt, kissed it, and then turned to the crowd, pardoned their rebelliousness, and demanded that they proclaim the king as their rightful lord. "Long live the king!" the Indians shouted thrice. The friars then sang the *Te Deum Laudamus*, pardoned the Indians' apostasy, baptized newly born infants, and distributed rosaries and crosses.[4]

In the days that followed, Don Luís Tupatu, the man who had replaced Popé as the Tewa leader, visited Vargas at Santa Fe. Dressed as a Spaniard, Don Luís made three genuflections before Vargas, "each time falling to one knee." Wearing a silver cross around his neck, and carrying an image of Our Lady of Guadalupe, a purse of relics containing an *Agnus Dei*, and a rosary Vargas had sent him for safe passage, Don Luís submitted to Christian rule, promising fidelity to God and king.[5]

Vargas visited all the pueblos in the months that followed, largely to ceremoniously display the royal standard and to resacralize the topography the infidels had profaned. Since the Indians outnumbered Vargas ten to one, he had no desire to engage them in battle. His purpose was to survey New Mexico's post-revolt political geography to plan the recolonization of the province. Vargas was back in El Paso with news of the reconquest by Christmas of 1692. Finally a new Cid had subdued the rebellious apostates.

Throughout 1693, Vargas gathered the manpower and provisions to resettle New Mexico, promising land, honors, nobility, and slaves to those who would come along. On October 13, 1693, a party of 100 soldiers, 70 families, and 18 friars—some 800 persons in all—departed El Paso for Santa Fe.[6]

All along the road north, the expedition's members were greeted as gods with rude arches, dances, hymns of praise to the Blessed Sacrament and Our Lady of the Conquest, and gifts of corn. Not in Santa Fe, however. There, rumors had circulated that Vargas intended to behead everyone who had revolted in 1680. Understandably, when the troops reached Santa Fe on December 16, 1693, there were no acclamations of joy. Vargas asked why he had not been greeted outside the city's walls as was customary when a Spanish governor or Franciscan prelate arrived. The snow was too high, the Indians responded. But now, assembled before a cross in the city's plaza, when Vargas shouted "Praised be the Blessed Sacrament!" the Indians responded "forever." On their knees they vowed allegiance to the king, recited a litany to the Virgin Mary, and sang the *Te Deum*.[7]

The colonists pitched their camp outside the city's walls that night, because they suspected that their presence might provoke an attack. The next morning corn and labor were demanded of Santa Fe's Indians, but they would not surrender either. Instead, hoping to divide and scatter the Spanish forces, various pueblos feigned concern for their spiritual welfare and asked that a friar be sent to minister to them. If soldiers escorted the friars, as they always had, Santa Fe would be left vulnerable to attack. The friars refused to go. Though willing to work among the Indians, these men were not the zealous ascetics of the previous century. They had no desire to suffer martyrdom and would not budge from the security of their camp.[8]

For weeks the colonists suffered privations and bitter cold while camped on the outskirts of Santa Fe. Then they began to grumble and to demand that Vargas evict the Indians from the city. Santa Fe's dwellings were rightfully theirs. Vargas agreed and told the Indians to disperse, but they responded by closing the city's gates on December 28 and digging in for a fight. Don Diego de Vargas rallied his troops and approached the city's gates, imploring the Indians in the name of the Blessed Sacrament and Our Lady of the Conquest to surrender. The Indians retorted blasphemously, writes Vargas, saying that "the devil was stronger than god or Mary." Sounding the trumpet and war drum, the Spanish opened fire crying, "Santiago! Santiago! Death to the rebels!" The Indians responded with a volley of arrows, stones, and jars of boiling water. Santa Fe was under siege for three days until finally, on December 30, 1693, the Indian warriors surrendered. All 70 of them were executed; the Indian women and children, approximately 400 in all, were distributed to the colonists as slaves. At last the kingdom's capital was secure and a base for the reconquest of the rest of New Mexico had been established.[9]

By the end of the decade that followed, though the struggling colony was rocked by smaller revolts, for all practical purposes Spanish authority had been firmly planted. A presidio with an armed garrison of 100 soldiers was established in Santa Fe in late 1693. On April 21, 1695, 44 families left Santa Fe to found the kingdom's second town, Santa Cruz. And by 1706 the kingdom's third town had been established at Albuquerque.[10]

The Eighteenth-Century Colony

During the seventeenth century, New Mexico had been kept in the Spanish empire as a frontier outpost primarily as a Franciscan mission field and as a supply colony for the silver mines of northern Mexico. As we saw, the friars failed to establish the kingdom of God on earth, at least among the Pueblo Indians. With the loss of New Mexico in 1680, the mystical impulse that had given rise to these missions a century earlier had definitively been spent. The crown's motives for reconquering and recolonizing New Mexico in the eighteenth century were very different: foreign encroachments on Spain's American territories and a rise in nomadic Indian attacks necessitated the creation of a defensive frontier. New Mexico would play a vital role in the protection of northern Mexico, as would the colonies established in Texas and California.

While the Spanish were still smarting from the Pueblo rebels' victory and defeats farther south in the Tarahumara and the Altar Valley of Sonora, the French and English had begun to encroach on Spain's North American territory. In 1682, Robert Cavelier, sieur de La Salle, led a French expedition out of the Great Lakes down the Mississippi River to its mouth. On April 9, La Salle proclaimed the river, its delta, and adjacent lands possessions of King Louis XIV, or Louisiana, effectively dividing the Spanish frontier in half, into western and eastern parts.[11]

On the eastern seaboard the Spanish missions that had begun with the founding of San Agustín in Florida in 1565 and had expanded to the area just north of the Savannah River also came under attack. English colonists moving south from Virginia into the South Carolina and Georgia backcountry sparred with the Spanish during the second half of the seventeenth century. By the beginning of the eighteenth century, the Spanish had been pushed back into a weak defensive posture in Florida.[12]

The movement of the French into the trans-Mississippi west had an immediate impact on New Mexico. The growing presence of French colonists in Illinois and on the eastern edges of the Great Plains pushed the Comanche, Pawnee, Kansas, Wichita, and Osage Indians in a south-western direction, into Apache and Navajo hunting grounds. Enmities had existed between the Apaches and the Comanches for some time. But now, forced to compete for hunting grounds, pushed even farther south by the southwestern migration of various Plains tribes, and hemmed in on the west by the Spanish towns and pueblos in New Mexico, the Apaches began to raid the Rio Grande's settlements with increasing regularity.

From the beginning of New Mexico's colonization, the settlers knew that large bands of nomadic Apaches roamed the peripheries of the king-dom, hunting, gathering, seasonally practicing agriculture, and regularly entering the Pueblos to trade hides and meat for corn, pottery, and blan-kets. Initially the colonists paid these Indians little heed and could not even differentiate them ethnically. But by the 1640s, when the Spanish realized that New Mexico lacked precious mineral wealth, they turned to these Indians for their personal enrichment, pressing many of them into slavery. Apaches were prized as laborers in New Spain's silver mines, on henequen plantations in the Yucatán, on Cuban tobacco farms, and in New Mexican households. Had the Apaches remained on foot, running in all directions when hunted by mounted horsemen, the Spanish would have kept the upper hand. But by 1650 that too had changed. The In-dians quickly understood that the horse was the principal nerve of war and by the 1650s had acquired them through raids and barter.[13]

Horses gave the Apaches greater mobility and range. Their equestrian skills became legendary and their hunting grounds expanded. By the 1670s the settled towns of the Rio Grande Valley, Pueblo and Spanish alike, became their targets, and against such swift and crafty enemies the beleaguered colonists could do little to repel attacks—attacks that only grew in intensity as disgruntled Pueblo apostates took refuge among the Apaches.

During most of the seventeenth century the Navajos had been thought of by the Spanish as one of the many Apache bands; they were simply *apaches navaju*. The Navajos emerged as a distinct ethnic group in Euro-pean consciousness as a result of the cultural amalgamation that took place on the margins of New Mexico before and after the Pueblo Revolt. Between 1670 and 1700, the Navajos, like the Apaches, harbored Pueblo refugees. As a result of this contact a close relationship developed be-tween them and the Indians who had been resettled in the Jémez *con-gregaciones*. The Navajos assisted the Jémez Indians during the Pueblo Revolt, and together they formed one of the last strongholds of resistance during the reconquest. Through this contact and intermarriage, Navajo culture was profoundly altered. From the Puebloans the Navajos acquired weaving, pottery making, and building arts. With the introduction of superior agricultural techniques and animal husbandry the Navajos' dependence on hunting and gathering slowly gave way to light farming and herding, eventually producing a more settled way of life during the eighteenth century.[14]

The increasing level of Apache warfare that New Mexico experienced after 1700, due to Spanish slave raiding and French-Spanish territorial rivalries fought through Indian intermediaries, was aggravated further by the French decision to sell guns to the Comanches and the Pawnees. Though neither group ever secured enough guns or ammunition to seriously menace the Spanish, they had enough firepower to frighten the Apaches and to harass the Rio Grande towns. In consequence, the Apaches raided the closest towns to secure horses, arms, and food. The end result was a weakened colony in a constant state of war—precisely what the French had hoped to achieve in arming the Plains Indians in the first place.

The Spanish responded to the French and English interlopers and to the Indian menace by fortifying frontier defenses. New Mexico's complete reconquest became essential. Colonizing parties were dispatched into west Texas to check French expansion there. Additional troops were sent to Florida. A string of presidios, garrisons of armed and mounted soldiers, was constructed across northern New Spain to better protect the region from Indian attacks. This arc-shaped string of forts ran from the top of the Gulf of California across southern Arizona, through El Paso, Texas, and finally over to San Antonio. Obviously, New Mexico's settlements were located several hundred miles beyond the line of presidios and were, as colonial bureaucrats often put it, "an island in a sea of barbarism," completely surrounded by enemies. Against such opponents, Santa Fe's presidio with 100 soldiers never really had enough manpower to insure the kingdom's security.[15]

The Kingdom of New Mexico's settled population in the eighteenth century consisted of four major population groups. Three of these groups, what broadly constituted Spanish society, lived in Santa Fe, Albuquerque, and Santa Cruz, the province's three major towns, and in the farming hamlets that hugged the banks of the Rio Grande between the pueblos of Taos and Isleta. Fray José de Vera described this society as consisting of "three classes of people . . . superior, middle, and infamous." The dominant class was the nobility. Below them, landed peasants, who were primarily of mestizo origin but who considered themselves *españoles* to differentiate themselves from the Indians, were by far the most numerous "middle" group. At the bottom of the social hierarchy were the "infamous" *genízaro* slaves, detribalized Indians, primarily of Apache and Navajo origin, who had been captured by the Spanish and pressed into domestic service. The Pueblo Indians were the fourth major population group. They lived in their own economically independent and politically autonomous towns. As a vanquished class they paid tribute and labor to the nobility, but because the crown protected their legal rights and the integrity of their villages and of their lands, they fared far better under colonial rule than did the *genízaros*, who were deemed sociocultural outsiders forced to live in Spanish towns. The Pueblo Indians were considered outsiders to Spanish society too, but theirs was a self-imposed insulation that protected their corporate rights to land and assured the preservation of their native ways.[16]

New Mexico's nobility consisted of fifteen to twenty families who intermarried to assure their continued dominance. Their sense of aristocracy was rooted in the legally defined honor granted to the kingdom's colonizers by King Phillip II in their 1595 charter of incorporation. After New Mexico's *reconquista* in 1693, ennoblement continued to be gained through exemplary military service, and as a consequence, bravery and physical prowess were hallmarks of aristocratic status. The economic basis of the nobility's power was land. Whatever fortunes they amassed were based on agriculture. By comparison with the titled peerage of central Mexico, New Mexico's nobility at best sported the life of a comfortable gentry. Yet perhaps because of their isolation—and the attendant belief that they were a cultural oasis in a sea of barbarism—New Mexico's aristocracy fashioned a style for itself that was second to none.[17]

Being of gentle birth was first among the nobility's claims to precedence and leadership in society. They all boasted of Spanish peninsular origins and of the pure blood that ran through their veins. For some the claim was justified; for others it was not. When Don Diego de Vargas set out to reconquer New Mexico, he was ordered to do so "with a hundred gentlemen soldiers from Spain." If indeed he was able to recruit them—there is no record of it—then New Mexico's aristocracy had cause to gloat. What makes their claim suspect is that, of the 13,204 persons who married legally between 1693 and 1846, only 76 individuals said that their parents were from places other than New Mexico, and of these only 10 said they were from Spain. The 1790 census of the kingdom revealed a very similar pattern. Only 68 out of roughly 16,000 persons had been born elsewhere; 2 had been born in Spain.[18]

Whatever the fact or fiction regarding the nobility's ancestry, their superiority before the law was real and promoted a value system in which honor was all. Men of honor owned slaves. They rode horses and carried arms while their inferiors needed special license to do so. They trampled the fields of the peasants without fear while out for an afternoon of sport. They cursed and they gambled and they staged their fandangos. They eschewed physical labor, instead reveling in their rituals of precedence, in ostentatious displays of lavish clothing and consumption of luxury goods, and in respectful forms of address and titles. Their sense of noblesse oblige was great, for after all, it was their superior birth, blood, and honor that defined what society was all about. Needless to say, such values were buttressed by force of arms, wealth, and a legal superstructure based on a belief that the nobility's worth gave them the right to rule.

Landed peasants, primarily of mestizo origin, were next in the hierarchy of honor. They had been recruited for the colonization of New Mexico with promises of land, and in 1700 all enjoyed rights to *merced*. Though humble in origin, they nonetheless participated in Spanish society. They too had a personal sense of worth not easily trampled. They too fashioned themselves into *españoles* lest they be confused with infamous Indians and half-breeds. They too were men of honor who protected family and home as believers in the one true God.

Lowest in prestige and status were the *genízaros*, a diverse group of detribalized Indians who resided in Spanish towns and performed the community's most menial and degrading tasks. Because the *genízaros* were primarily slaves, they were considered dishonored and infamous. Culturally, their presence in Spanish towns was represented in two ways: as intruders in Spanish society and as outcasts from the Pueblos.

The representation of the *genízaro* as an intruder in Spanish society stemmed from their status as slaves. Theoretically, Indian slavery had been outlawed in all of Spain's possessions with the 1542 publication of the New Laws, a prohibition reiterated in the 1680 Recompilation of the Laws of the Indies. But on the remote margins of the Spanish empire, in places such as Chile, the Amazon, and New Mexico, Indian slavery was tolerated as a way of compensating the men who colonized these regions. Accordingly, Indians who refused to submit to Spanish rule and who resisted the word of God could be captured as slaves in just war and kept in bondage for ten to twenty years. This was the justification Governor Juan de Oñate invoked in 1599 when he razed Acoma Pueblo and enslaved all of its inhabitants. The Indians of the Tompiro Pueblos similarly defied Spanish authority and were pressed into domestic slavery among New

Mexico's colonists in 1600. Spanish raids into Indian territory, ostensibly to punish heathen insubordination, but in reality to capture slaves, were, as we saw in Chapter 3, constant throughout the 1600s. For these slaves, treated like "yearling calves or colts," said Fray Estevan de Perea in 1633, bondage was not a temporary state. It was permanent. For this reason the Indians showed great hatred "for our holy faith and our Christian name," continued Perea, "and our holy law is taken to be a law of slavery."[19]

The Pueblo Revolt tempered the level of Indian enslavement in New Mexico and forced a redefinition of the infidel. Admittedly, when the troops of Don Diego de Vargas reoccupied Santa Fe in 1693, the city's Tano Indian residents were given to the colonists as slaves. New Spain's viceroy sanctioned this policy. Apostate Indians could be punished with ten years of enslavement, and were. But increasingly after 1693, faced with the realization that there were limits to the exploitation the Pueblo Indians would tolerate, the colonists focused their hatred on a new enemy, the Apaches. "Just war" was waged against the Apaches because they were infidels. As a result of this status, scores of men, women, and particularly children were brought into Spanish towns enslaved as prisoners of war.

As defeated enemies living in Spanish towns, they were considered permanent outsiders who had to submit to the moral and cultural superiority of their conquerors. The term *genízaro*, (from the Turkish *Yeni*, "new," and *Cheri*, "troops") reflected this fact. The janissaries of the Ottoman Empire were slaves, primarily children, who had been seized from subject Christians for use as shock troops in the sultan's wars.[20]

In addition to the slaves Spaniards captured in warfare, throughout the eighteenth and early nineteenth centuries New Mexico's slave population was augmented through the purchase of Indian slaves from the Apaches and Comanches. These were captives the tribes had seized from one another in war. Beginning in the 1700s the Apaches and Comanches regularly entered Pecos, Taos, and Picuris pueblos to trade meat, hides, and captives for Pueblo blankets, pottery, corn, and turquoise. The Spanish colonists encouraged this trade, offering the Indians manufactured products (glass beads, trinkets, and cloth), agricultural implements (axes, hoes, wedges, and knives), and horses for what they most desired—slaves.[21]

The Christians justified the purchase of these *indios de rescate*, or bartered Indian captives, because they had been enslaved through intertribal warfare. Governor Vélez Cachupín encouraged the trade in 1752, fearing that if it were curtailed, endless bloodshed would result. The Indians would kill their captives rather than allow them to be "ransomed" by the

Spanish and "redeemed" through baptism. The 1680 Recompilation of the Laws of the Indies stated that such ransomed Indians incurred debts that had to be repaid to their masters through work for an unspecified period. Masters were to treat their captives well and to Hispanicize and Christianize them. The crown repeatedly ordered that these captives not be "marketed as slaves," but no one paid these decrees much heed. As Fray Pedro Serrano noted in 1761, "When these barbarians bring a certain number of Indian women to sell, among them many young maidens and girls . . . before delivering them to the Christians who buy them, if they are ten years old or over, they deflower and corrupt them in the sight of innumerable assemblies of barbarians and Catholics . . . without considering anything but their unbridled lust and brutal shamelessness, and saying to those who buy them, with heathen impudence: 'Now you can take her—now she is good.'"[22]

Peaceful barter tended to degenerate into endless war. The Hispanic settlers took advantage of the Indians' lack of familiarity with the value of manufactured goods and played "infamous tricks on them," said Fray Atanasio Domínguez in 1776. The greed displayed at these markets reached such extremes, lamented Fray Pedro Serrano, "that heedless of the trading, or of God, or the king, or the law, or the kingdom, or even of themselves, these men with their wrongs and injustices stir up the barbarous nations, and lead them to conspire." The Plains Indians responded the only way they could, said Domínguez, "always carry[ing] off all they want."[23]

Sparked by such injustices, Indian depredations on Spanish settlements bred a vicious cycle of retaliatory raids. Though reasons could always be fabricated to punish the *indios bárbaros*, a simple tally of the booty colonists seized in their raids unmasked their true intent. Whether during the seventeenth century or the eighteenth, the ledger's bottom line was always the same; the Indian debit column was in the red. Governor Manuel Armijo in 1838, for example, entered Navajo territory ostensibly to free a New Mexican settler captured in a raid. Armijo accomplished his task and did quite a bit more. His journal listed that 76 Indians had been enslaved, and that 226 horses, 2,060 sheep, 6 serapes, and 160 buckskins had been seized.[24]

In mineral-poor New Mexico, slaving was an easy way to obtain domestic service and chattels that could be exchanged for luxury goods. Slaves were a medium of exchange and were pieces of moveable wealth. "I owe Felipe Saíz, a resident of Parral, a few pesos, which I agreed to pay with a little Indian girl," stated a 1718 will. Don Joseph Reaño paid for his purchases in Chihuahua in 1761 with *inditos* (little Indians), as did Juan Miguel Alvarez del Castillo that same year. Bureaucrats realized the spoils of political office through the capture and sale of slaves. Slaves were the kingdom's "gold and silver and the richest treasure," claimed one friar in 1761. When tangible symbols of status and wealth were few, slaves were a mark of distinction. The aristocracy found in a slave's infamy the meaning of their own honor. Many a young aristocratic bride was dowered with slaves to begin married life as a testament that she had indeed secured an honorable husband. The friars knew human bondage for what it was, brutal human degradation. Many of them denounced the institution, but found life too taxing without the sexual comforts and labor it provided. The losers in all of this were the Indians and the Royal Treasury. The latter was forced to provide soldiers and arms for a state of war that New Mexico's elite had no real interest in ending.[25]

From the early 1640s to the 1850s, New Mexico's Spanish settlements were constantly under siege by the mounted nomadic Indians surrounding them. One way to gauge the extent of this warfare and its effects is through the burial records of Hispanos killed during Indian raids and the baptismal records of nomadic Indians. Such baptisms are a fair index of Indian enslavement, because captives were always baptized before incorporation into a Christian home. Since slaves bound for labor elsewhere were seldom christened, baptismal records underestimated the true levels of slave hunting in New Mexico.

A positive statistical association exists between the number of white settlers killed by nomadic Indians and the number of nomadic Indian baptisms. Between 1700 and 1849, nomadic Indians killed 820 whites, and 3,294 nomadic Indians were baptized (Kendall Tau B = 0.39, $p < .05$; see Table 4.1). As the number of Indian captives rose, so did the number of Spanish deaths. The strength of this pattern increased over time. A positive statistical association exists between the decade in which white deaths occurred and the number of Indian baptisms (Kendall Tau B = 0.4, $p < .03$). Disaggregating these data by tribe, time becomes the major source of variation. The association between decade and the number of baptisms was negative for Apaches (Tau B = −0.52, $p < .01$) and Pawnees (Tau B = −0.53, $p < .01$) because 84 percent of all Apache (N = 938) and 83 percent of all Pawnee (N = 24) baptisms occurred during a very short period, between 1700 and 1759. Ninety-four percent of all Ute baptisms occurred between 1780 and 1849 (N = 625) resulting in a positive association between decade and number of baptisms (Tau B = 0.81, $p < .001$). Comanche, Kiowa, and Navajo christenings were rather

TABLE 4.1

Number of Whites Killed in New Mexico by Nomadic Indians, and Number of
Nomadic Indian Baptisms Between 1700 and 1849

Decade	Whites Killed by Nomadic Indians	Nomadic Indian Baptisms
1700	52	74
1710	4	40
1720	16	109
1730	15	180
1740	58	752
1750	30	260
1760	11	81
1770	211	163
1780	66	200
1790	23	119
1800	63	269
1810	35	181
1820	91	363
1830	88	166
1840	57	57
TOTAL	820	3,294

Kendall $\tau B = 0.39$; $p < .05$ for death $\times$ baptism
Kendall $\tau B = 0.41$; $p < .05$ for baptism $\times$ decade

Raw data are from Brugge, *Navajos in the Catholic Church Records of New
Mexico, 1694-1875* (Window Rock, 1968), 30-31.

evenly distributed throughout the 1700 to 1849 period, thus no association was found (Comanche Tau B = 0.17, p < .4; Kiowa Tau B = 0.27, p
< .16; Navajo Tau B = 0.19, p < .33).

Of the 3,294 nomadic Indians who were baptized and entered Hispano households between 1700 and 1849, the largest group was Navajos, representing 37.5 percent of the total. Apaches followed at 24 percent, Utes at 16 percent, and Comanches at 5 percent. Approximately
two out of every five nomadic Indians baptized in New Mexico were
identified explicitly as slaves. They were "in the power of," "in the dominion of," or "a captive of" a particular person. Baptism afforded one
the possibility of spiritual salvation, and it was to this that the friars al-
luded when they occasionally penned in the baptismal registers that an
Indian had been "redeemed" from the gentiles. Thirty-three percent were
referred to as "adopted," an expression of the officiating friar's hope that

the master-slave relation would be a quasi-filial one. One out of every eight was an *indio de rescate*, a slave purchased during the Indian trade fairs. One out of every five Indians baptized was a *criado* (from the verb *criar*, meaning to rear). Fray Juan Agustín Morfi in 1776 said these Indians were "called *genízaros*; they are Comanche and Apache captives obtained as children [by the Spaniards] and reared (*criados*) among us." "The *indios genízaros* are those which New Mexicans purchase from the Comanches," stated another official in 1774. In an 1820 petition the residents of Abiquiu referred to themselves as "*genízaros criados.*" Marc Simmons has argued that New Mexicans skirted the laws against Indian slavery and "avoided calling the captives slaves, and instead used the euphemism of *criado.*"[26]

Over time, the words *genízaro* and *criado* came to be used interchangeably to refer to all detribalized Indians residing in Spanish towns. Of course, not all Indians of nomadic origin in Hispano towns entered as slaves. Some Plains Indians willingly left their lives of warfare for the security of a Spanish town. The high point of Apache baptisms, 1730 to 1760, was the period of greatest hostility between the Comanches and the Apaches. Outbreaks of smallpox among the Plains Indians in 1710, 1780, and 1803 resulted in numerous conversions followed shortly by last rites: infected with the pox, some Indians desperately sought baptism, believing that its waters might cure them.[27]

The representation of *genízaros* as intruders in Spanish society existed alongside an image of them as outcasts from their natal group. The intruder-outcast representations correlated closely with tribal origin. The nomadic Indians were largely vanquished prisoners of war. The outcasts were predominantly marginalized Pueblo Indians who had been shunned by their kinsmen, who were exiled from their towns because of some transgression, or who simply thought life in Hispanic towns was more appealing. In Spanish society these "fallen" Pueblo Indians fared poorly. Displaced and caught between two cultures, they entered Hispano households as domestic slaves and were also generally referred to as *genízaros*.

The expulsion of "fallen" Pueblo Indians from their own villages was largely the by-product of Spanish labor demands. Though tribute payment had ceased with the abolishment of the *encomienda* after New Mexico's reconquest in 1693, the settlers continued to demand labor and raw materials from the Pueblo Indians through the *repartimiento*, a rotational labor draft. The entry of Pueblo women into Spanish towns to perform *repartimiento* labor was a perfect occasion for their sexual abuse by Spanish men. The governors of fourteen pueblos complained to the viceroy in 1707 that many of their women had been raped while performing their weekly labor. "When Indian women enter Santa Fe to mill wheat and spin wool they return to their pueblos deflowered and crying over their dishonor or pregnant," attested Fray Pedro Serrano in 1761. Miguelillo, a sixty-year-old Zuñi bachelor, in 1792 told of one strategy men used to protect their women from the Spanish. Miguelillo said that he had never married "because of the tribute service, it has often resulted that an Indian woman gave birth to a light skinned child, and then she tried like the devil to convince her husband that the child was his. And so there is extreme suspicion, and I have seen some poor Indians pay someone else to perform their service so that their wives do not have to." Fray Carlos Delgado observed in 1750 that when Pueblo men discovered the defilement of their wives or daughters, they banished them from the pueblo. In many cases these victims of Spanish sexual abuse were permanently stigmatized as outcasts. The only options such marginalized women had were to become servants in Spanish households or to join a nomadic tribe.[28]

If somehow a woman concealed her disgrace but later gave birth to a fair-skinned child or one who displayed visible signs of mixed ancestry, the child was abandoned at the doorsteps of the local mission. The baptismal registers record the discovery of these babies as *hijos de la iglesia* or children of the church. *Hijos de la iglesia* were baptized and placed in Christian homes, and subsequently referred to as *criados* or fosterlings. Approximately 10 percent of all persons living in Spanish towns during the eighteenth century were "children of the church."[29]

Since I described in Chapter 1 the positive value the Pueblo Indians attached to sexuality and their general sexual openness, the reader may find the shunning of such women and children odd. It reflects in part the impact on the Puebloans of two centuries of a repressive Christian sexual morality. Too, by the eighteenth century Indian women were less willing to give their bodies to Spanish men because they knew that they would receive nothing in return. And given the concern of the Pueblo Indians to protect their culture from further destruction after the Pueblo Revolt, it is easy to see why, as Adolph Bandelier states of Pueblo sexual morality in the eighteenth century, "toward outsiders the strictest abstinence was observed." This also explains why, as one friar noted, Indian men who enjoyed sexual rights to a particular female "cut off the nose and ears of the woman taken in adultery."[30]

Pueblo Social and Cultural Changes

In the years immediately following the Pueblo Revolt and reconquest, Pueblo geography was again transformed through a series of town abandonments and population reaggregations. This process was particularly pronounced in the southern half of New Mexico where whole linguistic groups were absorbed into others. Gone were the Piro, the Tompiro, the Southern Tiwa (Alameda, Isleta, Puaray, Chililí, Tajique, Quarai, Abó, Gran Quivira), and the Southern Tewa (San Marcos, San Cristóbal, Galisteo, San Lorenzo) pueblos. The Northern Tiwa, the Northern Tewa, the Towa, the Keres, and the Hopi pueblos remained relatively stable, although their populations were swelled by refugees from abandoned villages. The six Zuñi pueblos became one, known simply as Zuñi. Southern Tewa refugees established Hano Pueblo in the Hopi region in 1696 and reoccupied Galisteo in 1706. Displaced Keres lineages founded Laguna Pueblo in 1698. And those Tiwas who had taken refuge among the Hopi after the Pueblo Revolt returned to the Rio Grande Basin in 1740 to establish Sandia Pueblo.[31]

In 1693 the Franciscans returned to New Mexico to care for the spiritual welfare of the Puebloans. The Indians were not particularly eager to see them, but admitted them into their towns for fear of Spanish force of arms. Nevertheless, at many pueblos the caciques ordered their people not to listen to the friars or to accept any of their gifts. As one Hopi chief explained, "the father wants to deceive us by bringing us gifts, and therefore let no one accept anything."[32]

The coolness with which the Indians received the friars was characteristic of relations that would exist during the 1700s. In the previous century the friars had been the principal intermediaries between the pueblos and Spanish institutions. As men who enjoyed great political authority in the pueblos, the Franciscans had supervised mission life, had interpreted Spanish secular demands for the Indians, and as much as possible had kept the outside world at bay. The crown, however, had always thought of the missions as temporary acculturating institutions that would transform the Indians into model citizens, giving them the rudiments of town life and an economy oriented to Spanish needs and self-government.

Town government had been established at all the pueblos in 1621. Under the close supervision of the friars each Indian village was allowed to elect a *gobernadorcillo* (petty governor), an *alguacil* (sheriff), and several *mayordomos* (ditch bosses), sacristans, and *fiscales* (church wardens). During the seventeenth century these officers were, more often than not, allies of the local friar, instruments for the execution of his will, and, at times, mere pawns in political conflicts with the provincial governors.

After the *reconquista* this structure of town government was reestablished in the pueblos, albeit with some fundamental changes. The role of intermediary between the pueblos and Spanish society shifted from the friars to the Indian officers. No longer would the Indians answer primarily to the friars, nor would they depend on them for election to these posts. Rather, the group that emerged as most powerful in the selection of these officials were the caciques and the medicine men who controlled the "traditional" or native religious (political) order. They chose the men who would represent the pueblo before Spanish authorities and who would translate Spanish demands. The main qualification men for these posts needed was to "know the Spanish language and Spanish institutions." Fray Juan Agustín de Morfi noted in 1778 that even though only Indians were supposed to serve as their own petty governors, some *coyotes* and *mulatos* who were living in the pueblos had managed to get themselves appointed to the post. These men had been selected because they were highly acculturated Christians. In addition, whereas in the seventeenth century the Indian town officials had been under the immediate control of the friars, in the eighteenth and nineteenth centuries they were placed under the direct supervision of the Spanish chief constable in their administrative jurisdiction (*alcaldía*), thus fundamentally shifting control over Pueblo government from clerics to civilians. The result of these changes was to relegate the friars to the role of ritual specialists in the pueblos and occasionally to Indian advocates before the civil courts.[33]

To appreciate how Pueblo-Spanish relations evolved in the period after 1693, let us examine how the Indians conceptualized their town officials. We saw in Chapter 1 that the relationship between law and force, between peace and violence, was expressed in the Inside Chief–Outside Chiefs dichotomy. The Inside Chief maintained peace and harmony in the pueblo among the various lineages and esoteric societies; the Outside Chiefs or warriors defended the village against all sources of malevolence outside the town. In Chapter 2 we also noted that as part of their conquest theater, the friars had presented themselves as Inside Chiefs and the Spanish governor and soldiers as Outside Chiefs. Pueblo warriors were defeated and subordinated to the latter. In the eighteenth century the Puebloans maintained this indigenous spatial conceptualization of peace and violence, calling the Indian civil officials Outside Chiefs. What made this spatial conceptualization particularly appropriate for post-1700 political developments was that in this period the pueblos truly emerged as the isolated politically autonomous towns we now know, actively protecting their culture and corporate rights against outsiders.

The rise of nomadic Indian warfare in the Rio Grande Basin was equally important in reinforcing the cogency of the inside-outside Pueblo dichotomy. When Apaches, Navajos, and Comanches began raiding New Mexico's villages, they preyed on Puebloans and Spaniards with equal intensity. To fortify what were rather meager provincial defenses, the Spaniards armed some of the Puebloans as allies and appointed a *capitan de guerra* (war captain) for each pueblo to organize all able-bodied warriors into militia contingents to fight alongside Spanish regular troops. By the eighteenth century, Pueblo warriors were once again protecting their own towns.

The ritual installation of Indian civil officials that Alfonso Ortiz observed at the Tewa pueblo of San Juan in 1968, though contemporary, offers considerable historical insight into the Indian understanding of the functions and sanction of these Indian town officials. Every year on December 29 the moiety chiefs at San Juan nominate a man to serve as governor for the next year, "to carry on the work of our elder *Yosi Rey* (God and King)." Nominations are also advanced for *Santu tenente* (holy lieutenant) and *Santu pika mayo* (holy church warden), or "those of the entrance to the *misa teh* [mass kiva or church], so that when our elder *owha* ["katsina-like person" or Catholic priest] has need, they shall come forth." When nominations are complete, the heads of the various male esoteric societies are asked for their approval saying, "these are the children we have chosen to open the village and the plain." If all agree, on the next evening their names are announced to the outgoing officers. On December 31 the outgoing officers resign their post by telling the Summer moiety chief: "We have sat on cloud blossoms this year and dropped over our heads these duties. Now, the authority of the blue saints on Hazy Mountain, the yellow saints of *Tsikomo*, the red saints of Turtle Mountain, and the white saints of Stone Man Mountain returns to them." On January 1 the new officers are sworn in "in the name of God, the saints, and the three kings," and given Spanish metal-topped canes of authority symbolic of their offices. On the next day the officers gather and carry a basket of feathers to the moiety chiefs so that the chiefs work "to put us [the new officers] on top of cloud blossoms," or so that the chiefs give supernatural sanction to the authority of the officers. The installation is complete on January 6, the Feast of the Three Kings, when a Mass is said to invoke the blessings of God and the saints.[34]

In the decades following the *reconquista*, the world inside each pueblo was hardly a haven from the outside. As before the Pueblo Revolt, the Indians were required to perform tribute labor for the colonial population, and it was the duty of their governor to organize and deliver it. The onerous tribute burdens of the *encomienda* had been outlawed, only to be replaced by the *repartimiento*. *Repartimiento* levies were performed on a weekly basis; draftees were called *semaneros* (from the word *semana*, meaning week). The pueblos of the Rio Arriba (those Indian towns from Santa Fe north) provided service from Easter to All Saints Day (roughly

April to November); the pueblos of the Rio Abajo (the Indian towns south of Santa Fe) served the remainder of the year. Every Sunday morning, each pueblo's *semaneros* reported to the governor's palace in Santa Fe for work assignments. Males worked constructing public buildings, cleaning irrigation ditches, and cultivating the governor's fields and those of his constables. Females provided domestic labor, shucking corn, thrashing wheat, grinding both into flour, and baking bread. All Indians were required to perform service and "not even pregnant women are exempt," reported Fray Juan Sánz de Lezaún in 1760. "The major part of them abort because of the excessive work they perform and the long walk" to Santa Fe.[35]

The role the Indian governors played in the organization of labor drafts constantly exacerbated factionalism within the pueblos between "conservatives" (those who clung to traditional Indian ways) and "progressives" (those who embraced Christianity and European mores of comportment and dress). During the 1700s several pueblos complained to the Spanish authorities about the excesses and mistreatment the Indians suffered at the hands of their officers. Indian officers would likewise lament how the indigenous caciques urged their tribesmen to resist Spanish law. In 1771, for example, the governor and war captain of Isleta Pueblo denounced the cacique, whom the Indians held "as a king, whose commands they obey." The cacique told his people "not to forget their ancient language which they must always conserve for the memory of their ancestors." Though the pueblo governor and war captain were angered that the Indians did not obey them, aside from their protests before the Spanish courts there was little they could do. The village conservatives obviously had the upper hand in pueblo politics. New Mexico's governor, Pedro Fermín de Mendinueta, reviewed the case and ordered Isleta's Indians not to use the word cacique or to obey him, but nothing was really done to upset village power relations.[36]

When Popé and his conservative allies defeated the Spanish in 1680, their goal had been the complete destruction of Spanish cultural influence in the pueblos. But in the first century of sustained contact with the Spanish, Pueblo culture had witnessed profound innovations—innovations that many were not willing to surrender. Iron tools had become common currency. European seeds such as winter wheat had extended the growing season. Cattle, pigs, and chickens had become the dominant source of meat for the Indians. Horses were now essential for war. And Spanish had become the lingua franca for communication across native language groups.[37]

Pueblo population decline and village abandonments after 1680 also profoundly affected social organization. At those pueblos in closest contact with Europeans during the 1600s—the Tewa, the Tiwa, and the Queres (except Acoma)—by the 1700s a shift from matrilineal to patrilineal or bilateral forms of kinship was apparent. Household ownership and land rights previously vested in women passed to men. Newlywed women were ordered to establish households independent of their mothers. Matrilineages that had been the affiliational units of male ceremonialism gave way to dualistic moieties, a ritual organization that collapsed a complexity of lineage ritual roles into a dyadic opposition. For example, among the San Juan Tewa, where formerly ritual leadership had been won competitively, now roughly half of the pueblo that formed the Summer People moiety ruled and staged all communal rites half of the year, alternating with the other half of the population, the Winter People moiety, who ruled the rest of the year. Anthropologists believe that this change was an adaptation to the disruption of lineages due to movement, recongregation, and population decline. Given the inherent factionalism that had historically disrupted these now weakened and fragile pueblos, we find that ritual roles and town leadership became hereditary rather than competitive in order to maintain cohesiveness. At the more traditional, less acculturated Western Pueblos (Zuñi, Hopi, Acoma, and Laguna), leadership also became hereditary, but matrilineality remained intact.[38]

A century of contact with Christianity had also profoundly transformed Pueblo religious symbolism, though how profoundly beliefs were changed remains harder to ascertain. That this was so should not strike us as odd, for as was emphasized in Chapter 1, a pueblo's sacred fetishes, dances, prayers, and rituals at any one time were those of the lineages living together. When new lineages joined a town, be it through warfare, marriage, or peaceful trade, new dances and new gods were routinely incorporated into the native pantheon.

Contact with a monotheistic religion fundamentally altered the Pueblo concept of the supernatural. Admittedly, the evidence here is not ideal. But in 1681, when Governor Otermín captured a Spanish-speaking Indian named Joseph and questioned him about the causes of the Pueblo Revolt, among the many things Joseph said was that the Spanish God was dead "but that their own god lived." Joseph spoke not of gods, but of one god. A similar point emerges when the Tewa explain the Spanish conquest. They say that "when Jesús came down he took Poseyemu [the son of Father Sun] away." The oldest Pueblo traditions explain that Father

Sun had two sons, the Twin War Gods. Among the Tewa, Poseyemu, a lone son of Father Sun, is said to have been driven away by Christ, son of God the Father. The more common idea among the Pueblos was a female theory of origin, which explained that "when Padre Jesús came, the Corn Mothers went away." What we see here, then, is the matrilineal mythology of godly descent replaced by a patrilineal theory, polytheism by monotheism. The Tewa were the Indians in closest contact with the Spaniards during the seventeenth century and the group largely responsible for organizing the Pueblo Revolt. For them, the Pueblo Revolt was a contest between rival gods. If the Tewa gods were going to triumph, they had to equal the Christian gods in strength. I suspect that the intense contestation that occurred between the priests of both religions during the seventeenth century explains why the Twin War Gods were transformed into a lone Poseyemu who stood ready to challenge and defeat Christ.[19]

Exactly a century after New Mexico's reconquest, in 1793, the caciques of various Tewa pueblos were jailed by Governor Fernando de la Concha for holding "seditious" meetings. When questioned about these meetings Bentura Piche said that their leader, Asencio Peña, had told them that "it was true that the God of the Spaniards was powerful but that his [god] was his equal [parejo]." On hearing this the governor had the lot whipped, fined, and jailed for various lengths of time.[40]

In a similar vein, we must also ponder the actions of Popé, the leader of the Pueblo Revolt. When he entered the medicine society kiva to call the katsina from the underworld to learn how to defeat the Spanish, he regularly called "Caudi, Tilini, and Tleume." The Indians knew that the Christians had three persons in their god, the Trinity. To challenge that Trinity, and ultimately to kill it, Popé called on three katsina who were an equal match for the Father, Son, and Holy Ghost. It was no coincidence that at the feet of the martyred Fray Pedro de Avila y Ayala were found three lambs with their throats slashed.

Throughout the seventeenth century, the Franciscans had tried to conflate God and the Christian saints with the Pueblo katsina in liturgy and iconography. In Pueblo myth and artistic motifs, fog, snow, dew, clouds, and mist were all natural manifestations of the katsina, the Rain-Spirits or ancestor dead. We can thus still see on colonial New Mexican reredos the image of God the Father surrounded by clouds. During religious dramas the priest who impersonated God was placed "in a basket which was covered with cotton to represent a cloud," writes Charles Basil Martin, regarding the staging of religious dramas in colonial New Mexico.[41]

The first mention of martyred friars being incorporated into the native pantheon as katsina occurred in the late 1630s. In 1639 the Indians of Taos Pueblo revolted and killed their pastor, Fray Pedro de Miranda. Shortly thereafter, when the Taos Indians staged the katsina dance, a man wearing the martyred friar's vestments participated in the dance. The Jémez Indians have a legend concerning Fray Francisco Casañas de Jesús María, whom they were prepared to kill in 1694. When the warriors went to the convent to look for the friar, he was nowhere to be found. Instead, the men found footprints in newly fallen snow, which led to a nearby spring. Over the spring the men saw a dense cloud of fog, heard sweet singing, and thus concluded that the cloud was Fray Francisco. Similarly, the Acoma Indians have a category of katsina, the *kopishtaiya*, who come from the east, live there, vow perpetual sexual continence (quite an anomaly in Pueblo thought), and have potent medicine magic. Everything of Spanish origin in Acoma's cosmology—wheat, writing, legumes, livestock, and metals—is said to have come from the east. The *kopishtaiya* are the mythic equivalents of Catholic priests. Linguistic evidence from the Tewa underscores this point. The Tewa call their katsina *oxua*. A Catholic priest is *owha*, which means "cloud-like" or "katsina-like." Fray Alonso de Benavides noted in 1634 that when the Indians martyred the friars they cut off their heads. The Indians decapitated Fray Agustín Rodríguez and kept his head as a war trophy, which they regularly fed with cornmeal. The body of Fray Martín de Arvide was found without head or hands. And some of the Franciscans who died during the Pueblo Revolt lost their scalps. As we saw in Chapter 1, the head and scalp of an enemy dead was transformed into a beneficent household rain spirit through feeding and intercourse.[42]

We can also turn to architecture to see how the Franciscans wanted the Indians to think of them and of the saints as katsina. The belfry of Zía Pueblo's church, the church facades at Laguna and Santo Domingo Pueblos, and the courtyard gate at Taos Pueblo's church all reproduce architecturally the Pueblo cloud motif so prominent on antique pottery and female ceremonial headdresses. In Laguna Pueblo church the space in the transept, which in European churches is covered with the Stations of the Cross and pictures of the saints, is decorated with the Pueblo cloud symbol.[43]

It was noted earlier that the Acoma Indians believe that one of their Corn Mothers, Nautsiti, greatly transformed, returned during the reconquest as Our Lady of the Conquest. When the Zuñi Indians are asked how a statue of the Santo Niño de Atocha (the Christ Child of Our Lady of Atocha) came to sit on the same altar with their indigenous animal fetishes, they explain that one day the daughter of the Sun visited the earth and bore an infant son. She left her child at Zuñi and then moved off to Laguna Pueblo. Eventually, they both turned into wood. The Christ Child holds a basket full of items and is considered a female fertility deity. As with Pueblo fetishes, the Santo Niño is regularly fed, not sacred corn-meal but bits of cheese, a European-origin food. In this case, just as the Zuñi incorporated scalps, fetishes, and ceremonies of conquering and conquered groups, so too the Christian images of their Spanish con-querors came to rest on Pueblo altars. This is also the reason why the Indians still keep the dance costumes for such Spanish dance dramas as "Los Matachines," the "Moros y Cristianos," and "Las Posadas" in their kivas alongside their katsina masks and outfits.[44]

Despite these changes in Pueblo religion wrought by a century of Christianization, what Pueblo anthropologists have long described as the clear separation or "compartmentalization" of Christianity and native beliefs did not fully develop until the first decades of the eighteenth century. Then, particularly during the governorships of José Chacón Medina Salazar y Villaseñor (1707–12) and Juan Ignacio Flores Mo-gollón (1712–15), virulent campaigns to eradicate the visible form of Pueblo idolatry were waged yet again. Governor Chacón found it par-ticularly repugnant that the Pueblos, "keep the scalps from their enemies, the unfaithful enemies who they kill in battle, bring them and dance pub-licly, introducing many superstitions and scandalous acts in these dances, and they use . . . *estufas* [kivas] in which they invoke the devil, and in his company and with his advice and suggestion they exhort one thousand errors." Chacón demanded that these practices cease, promising stern punishment if they did not. Governor Flores responded more forcefully when he heard that at Pecos and other pueblos kivas had been con-structed "under the pretext of the women getting together to spin." Early in 1714 Flores dispatched soldiers to the pueblos to destroy such rooms, admonishing the Indians that if they wished to build rooms for the women to congregate, they had to have a "door onto the street so that those who enter and leave, and what they do inside, may be known."[45]

During Flores's administration there were several attempts to define what was proper behavior for Christianized Indians. In 1713, for example, Jerónimo Dirucaca, the ex-governor of Picuris Pueblo, was charged with sorcery, idolatry, and concubinage. Allegedly, when the friar at Picuris preached to the Indians telling them to "live as Christians, fearing God," Dirucaca had told them "not to listen to what the friar told them, but only to what they had been taught by their ancestors." Dirucaca admitted living in concubinage with two women, a mother and her daughter, and fathering children with both. He was also accused of killing four women with hexes because they would not submit to his sexual advances, but of this there was little tangible proof. Despite the seriousness of his offenses, he managed to get out of his predicament by showing the governor several small silver veins.[46]

In 1714 Governor Flores also initiated discussions among the colonists as to what was and was not proper Indian behavior. How should the Christianized Indians dress, particularly while serving as Spanish allies on Apache campaigns? Many of the colonists were opposed to the Indians wearing war paints and feathers for the simple reason that in such attire they were indistinguishable from the enemy. Equally anxiety-provoking were the firearms the Puebloans had been given to help defend the province. With still vivid memories of the Pueblo Revolt, several colonists feared that the firearms might be used against them and thus wanted the Puebloans disarmed. In the end the Puebloans were allowed to dress as they pleased and to keep their arms. The net effect of these discussions and campaigns against native religious practices was to drive Pueblo religious rites underground and to shroud them in a thick veil of secrecy from outsiders. If Pueblo religion was to survive on equal footing with Christianity under such repressive conditions, there simply was no other choice.[47]

The friars labored among the Pueblos during the eighteenth century believing, some perhaps more naively than others, that idolatry had been nipped in the bud and that a syncretic Catholicism that incorporated native and Christian concepts and symbols, regardless of their disparate meanings, would satisfy the Indians' psychological needs. As was seen earlier, the Franciscan strategy of Christianization called for the open eradication of native ceremonialism and the substitution of parallel Christian rites such as aspersion, the use of incense, fasting, sexual continence, purificatory flagellation, head washing, naming, and offering food. After 1693 the friars also actively tried to fuse the Indian notion of a sacred natural world with the Christian supernatural. This is particularly vivid in ecclesiastical iconography. When God the Father was depicted, says Father Thomas J. Steele of eighteenth-century New Mexican religious art, he held a "power symbol in his left hand—lightning or arrows, and occasionally a heart." Lightning and arrows were the Pueblo weapons for war; the heart of anything was the source of its life and breath. God the Father holding a heart symbolized his control over men. I have already discussed at some length the fusion of symbols in those crucifixes with bloody loincloths.[48]

This union of the Indian natural and Christian supernatural was particularly pronounced in the cult of the saints. When ordinary saints were depicted, powerful animals were placed next to them. St. James rode atop a horse crushing the head of a serpent, oxen pulled the plow of St. Isidro, and St. Francis was surrounded by birds and beasts. The evangelists were represented not as four men, but as an eagle, a lion, an owl, and a bird (angel). Of course one could argue that these were ancient Christian motifs that were particularly pronounced in Franciscan mystical thought. Why, then, does St. Raphael hold a native fish? Why is San Procopio leading a New Mexican deer up a mystical ladder? Why is Our Lady of Guadalupe crushing the head of a native turkey that holds arrows in its claws? These images have no apparent European origin.

All the blood, sweat, and tears the Franciscans shed nurturing their congregations with the "sweet milk of the Gospel" failed to weld the two religions as one because the friars never believed that the Indians were capable of serving as Catholic priests. The Puebloans routinely incorporated the other into their social world through feeding and intercourse, but the Franciscan Order would not ordain Indians and steadfastly refused to do so. The casuistry the Franciscans invoked to keep their priestly ranks pure was entirely paternalistic. After all, Indians were an inferior race of ill repute, easily given to heresy. They were "weak and frail" children of low intelligence who would remain perpetually minors in need of a father's guidance. The Indian's innate humility, said Fray Gerónimo de Mendieta, made him ineligible for the priesthood, because "the majority of them are not fitted to command or to rule, but to be commanded and ruled. . . . They are not fitted for masters but for pupils, not for prelates but for subjects, and as such they are the best in the world." Such discriminatory arguments were not new. Black, Jewish, and Muslim converts had been denied ordination on similar grounds, as Asians and Goans would be later on.[49]

Franciscan mystical thought was narcissistic and self-indulgent. The friars could reach mystical marriage and union with God. Indian neophytes could be purged, illuminated, but never really enjoy perfect union; that was solely a European privilege. In mystical marriage one fully participated in the sacred and was merged with the godhead. "Children" and neophytes were ill-prepared for such profound experiences.[50]

Eighteenth-Century Demography

Throughout the eighteenth century, numerous censuses of New Mexico's population were conducted to chart the number of souls in the Christian fold and the growth in the ranks of the king's subjects. Given the various purposes these censuses played in imperial politics, extant documents do not always list those facts that modern demographers would deem pertinent and indispensable. No full and accurate count of New Mexico's total population exists before 1749. With the establishment of El Paso in 1683, those Indian pueblos south of Isleta del Sur that were still inhabited were aggregated with El Paso and no longer listed with New Mexico. Repeated efforts during the 1700s to reestablish Christianity among the Hopis failed, and for this reason they too were not reported on New Mexican census rolls. Given these caveats, New Mexico's population in 1693 may have numbered around 14,000, with approximately 3,000 nominally white persons and roughly 9,000 Pueblo Indians. Over the next 150 years this population more than tripled, reaching 63,498 persons by 1842 (see Table 4.2). Disregarding the 1746 census of New Mexico, which had extremely poor data, between 1749 and 1842 the average annual population growth rate was 1.05 percent. To smooth out the erratic fluctuations in the "Total Population—Growth Rate" reported in Table 4.2, geometric growth rates were calculated for these data. These rates were then subjected to regression analysis to derive the best linear fit of observed population by year. The geometric an-

TABLE 4.2

New Mexico's Population, 1746-1850

Year	Total Population	Growth Rate (Pct.)	Spanish Population	Growth Rate (Pct.)	Indian Population	Growth Rate (Pct.)
1746	9,722		4,143		5,579	
1749	15,921	17.87%	4,353	1.66%	11,568	27.52%
1750	14,377	−9.70	3,809	−12.50	10,568	−8.64
1760	16,449	1.36	7,666	7.24	8,783	−1.83
1765	15,354	−1.37	6,329	−3.76	9,025	0.55
1776	18,344	1.63	9,742	4.00	8,602	−0.44
1790	24,998	2.24	16,358	3.77	8,640	0.03
1792	28,177	6.17	18,799	7.20	9,378	4.18
1793	29,041	3.07	19,394	3.17	9,647	2.87
1800	29,008	−0.02	19,276	−0.09	9,732	0.13
1810	35,400	2.01	25,770	2.95	9,630	−0.11
1811	36,654	3.54	26,907	4.41	9,747	1.21
1817	36,597	−0.03	27,175	0.17	9,422	−0.56
1820	38,359	1.58	28,436	1.52	9,923	1.74
1829	42,050	1.03	31,117	1.01	10,933	1.08
1842	63,498	3.22	46,988	3.22	16,510	3.22
1850			58,415	2.76		

SOURCES: Same as for Table 4.1.

TABLE 4.3

Geometric Growth Rates for New Mexico by Jurisdictions, 1707-1842

	Spanish (Pct.)	Indian (Pct.)	Total (Pct.)
Santa Fe Jurisdiction:			
Santa Fe, Pecos, Galisteo	2.54%	–2.32%	1.50%
Keres Jurisdiction:			
Jémez, Zía, Santa Ana, San Felipe, Santo Domingo, Cochiti	5.02	0[a]	0.935
Santa Cruz Jurisdiction:			
Santa Cruz, Pojoaque, Nambé, Santa Clara, Abiquiu, San Juan, San Ildefonso	2.24	0[a]	1.69
Taos Jurisdiction:			
Taos, Picuris	3.76	0.345	1.81
Albuquerque Jurisdiction:			
Albuquerque, Atrisco, Belén, Tomé, Isleta, Alameda, Sandía, Bernalillo	2.50	0.898*	1.95
Zuñi Jurisdiction:			
Zuñi, Acoma, Laguna	—[b]	—[b]	—[b]
TOTAL POPULATION	2.66%	0.382%	1.61%

* The earliest census (1750) was an extreme outlier and was dropped from the analysis presented here.
[a] Reported as zero because fitted regression slope was not significantly different from zero.
[b] Zuñi had too few reported points for a meaningful regression analysis.

REGRESSION EQUATIONS:

Santa Fe:	Spanish, $Y = -36.95 + .02512X$; Indian, $Y = 47.03 - .02295X$; Total, $Y = -18.49 + .01492X$
Keres:	Spanish, $Y = -81.11 + .04902X$; Indian, $Y = 7.84 - .0000096X$; Total, $Y = -8.50 + .00931X$
Santa Cruz:	Spanish, $Y = -31.25 + .02220X$; Indian, $Y = 10.35 - .00180X$; Total, $Y = -21.19 + .01672X$
Taos:	Spanish, $Y = -59.34 + .03693X$; Indian, $Y = .52 + .00345X$; Total, $Y = -24.67 + .01796X$
Albuquerque:	Spanish, $Y = -35.82 + .02466X$; Indian, $Y = -9.31 + .00894X$; Total, $Y = -26.10 + .01936X$
Zuñi:	Spanish, $Y = -69.60 + .04147X$; Indian, $Y = -11.60 - .00201X$; Total, $Y = 7.36 + .00039X$
Total:	Spanish, $Y = -37.39 + .02622X$; Indian, $Y = 2.35 + .00381X$; Total, $Y = -18.55 + .01602X$

nual growth rate for New Mexico between 1749 and 1842 was 1.61 percent (see Table 4.3). Figure 4.1 depicts the geometric growth rate for the total population on a logarithmic scale.

New Mexico's nobility and landed peasantry, referred to here as the Spanish population, numbered roughly 800 in 1693. By 1749 it had grown fivefold, to 4,353 individuals (see Table 4.2). In the next 25 years this population doubled, to 9,742 by 1776. The rate of growth accelerated after 1776, the population again doubling, this time in only fourteen years. By 1790 there were 16,358 so-called Spaniards in New Mexico. It was a good 40 years before the population reached 32,000; by 1850 it stood at 58,415. Given the fluctuations in the average annual growth rates reported for Spaniards in Table 4.2, a geometric growth rate for these data was also calculated. As Table 4.3 indicates, New Mexico's Spanish population grew at a geometric rate of 2.66 percent annually. Figure 4.1 illustrates this result in comparison to the total population in the province, which grew at a geometric rate of 1.61 percent per year.

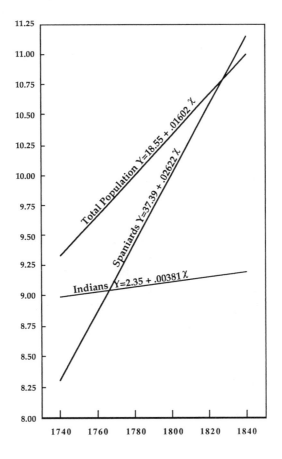

Figure 4.1.   Geometric Growth Rates for New Mexico's
              Spanish, Indian, and Total Population, 1700-
              1860. (Plotted on a logarithmic scale.)

TABLE 4 4

Spanish Population in New Mexico Towns, 1749–1820

	Santa Fe		Santa Cruz		Albuquerque	
Year	Spanish Population	Growth Rate (Pct.)	Spanish Population	Growth Rate (Pct.)	Spanish Population	Growth Rate (Pct.)
1749	965					
1750			1,303		700	
1760	1,285	2.64%	1,515	1.52%		
1765			1,306	−2.93		
1776					2,416	4.88%
1779	1,915	2.12	1,821	2.40		
1782	2,419	2.92	1,610	−4.02		
1790					5,955	6.66
1792	3,662	5.11	3,116	6.38	6,153	1.65
1793					6,225	1.66
1794	3,035	−8.96	2,617	−8.36	6,335	1.28
1795	3,253	7.18	2,699	3.13		
1800	3,698	2.60	2,594	−0.79		
1805			2,241	−2.88		
1811	5,024	2.82	2,521	1.98		
1820	6,038	2.06	2,523	0.01		

Examining in closer detail the Spanish population residing in New Mexico's towns (*villas*) one finds that growth was most pronounced at Albuquerque (see Table 4.4). There, the population grew at an average annual rate of 3.22 percent, rising from 700 Spaniards in 1750 to 6,335 by 1794. Santa Fe's Spanish population of 965 in 1749 grew to 6,038 by 1820, increasing at an average annual rate of 2.05 percent. Santa Cruz, with 1,303 Spaniards, was the most densely populated Spanish town in 1750; it took 70 years for this population to nearly double to 2,523 in 1820. In fact, between 1750 and 1820, the average annual rate of growth for the Spanish population at Santa Cruz was negative, at −0.323 percent.

Again, primarily to correct for sharp population discrepancies from date to date, geometric growth rates for the Spanish population were calculated by administrative jurisdictions. So analyzed, the highest percentage rate of geometric growth occurred in Keres Jurisdiction. (See Table 4.3, which lists geometric growth rates for New Mexico's various jurisdictions and the villages in each jurisdiction.) The Spanish annual rate of geometric growth for Keres Jurisdiction was 5.02 percent, followed by Taos Jurisdiction with 3.76 percent, Santa Fe Jurisdiction with 2.54 percent, Albuquerque Jurisdiction with 2.50 percent, and finally Santa Cruz Jurisdiction with 2.24 percent.

The number of *genízaros* one finds in eighteenth-century New Mexico greatly depends on who is included in the category. If one counts only persons explicitly identified as *genízaros*, the number is a small fraction of the total population. There were 677 *genízaros* reported in a 1765 census. Fray Atanasio Domínguez counted 650 in 1776. If one includes slaves and *criados* in the category, then the numbers are more substantial. Fray Andrés Varo said that there were 1,310 slaves in the kingdom in 1749. The American merchant Josiah Gregg found more than 1,000 slaves in the 1840s, prompting the archaeologist Albert H. Schroeder to estimate that "about one-third of the population of New Mexico by the late 1700s was *genízaro*." In 1793 New Mexico's total population was 29,041; *genízaros* may have numbered as many as 9,680.[51]

How were *genízaro* slaves and servants distributed in Hispano households? The earliest household enumeration was a 1680 muster of the Pueblo Revolt's survivors. There were 426 slaves and servants among New Mexico's refugees. Forty-five percent of all households contained no slaves (see Table 4.5). The twelve largest households contained 256 slaves. Put another way, 21 percent of the slave-holding households contained 60 percent of the slaves; the other 79 percent of the households

TABLE 4.5

Number of Slaves in New Mexican Households, 1680-1845

Number of Slaves per Household	1680		1790		1818		1823		1845	
	No.	Pct.	No.	Pct.	No.	Pct.	No.	Pct.	No.	Pct.
0	56	44.8%	918	93.2%	620	95.5%	266	94.0%	1081	96.8%
1	15	12.0	29	2.9	17	2.6	6	2.1	19	1.7
2	19	15.2	23	2.3	4	.6	6	2.1	6	.5
3	4	3.2	9	.9	6	.9	4	1.4	3	.3
4	8	6.4	3	.3	2	.3	0	.0	4	.4
5	3	2.4	0	.0	0	.0	0	.0	1	.1
6	2	1.6	3	.3	0	.0	1	.4	0	.0
7-9	6	4.8	0	.0	0	.0	0	.0	7	1.0
10-33	12	9.6	0	.0	0	.0	0	.0	0	.0
Total	426		132		51		36		184	

SOURCES: 1680 Muster of Pueblo Revolt Survivors, RPI, I, 136-153; 1790 Census of New Mexico, SA 12:319-502; 1818 Census of Santa Cruz, AASF-LD 54:543-563; 1823 Census of Santa Fe, MA 3:2-285; 1845 Census of Santa Cruz and Jémez, MA 40:361-556.

held 40 percent. The 1790 census of New Mexico reported a total of 248 *sirvientes* (servants) and *criados*. A statistical analysis of a 33 percent random sample of the household records for this census showed that 93 percent of all households held no servants or slaves; slightly less than 1 in 10 households did (see Table 4.5). Similar analyses of an 1818 census of Santa Cruz, an 1823 census of Santa Fe, and an 1845 census of Santa Cruz and Jémez indicated that only one in twenty households had residents explicitly identified as slaves or servants, a slight drop from 1790 when one in ten households held such. Interestingly, between 1818 and 1845, the average number of servants per household in Santa Cruz more than doubled, from 0.07 to 0.16. This result confirms other observations regarding the rise of debt peonage there after Mexican Independence in 1821.[52]

The Pueblo Indian population in 1679 was estimated at 17,000 (see Table 2.1). By 1693 it had dropped to approximately 14,000, a loss of roughly 18 percent. Between 1706 and 1860 Pueblo population grew slowly when compared with Spanish population growth. Table 4.6 presents the population of New Mexican Pueblos between 1706 and 1860. Throughout the eighteenth century the Pueblo population hovered between 8,000 and 9,000. The pueblos that experienced a positive average annual percentage growth rate between 1706 and 1821 were Taos, 0.442 percent; Picuris, 0.087 percent; San Ildefonso, 0.886 percent; Pojoaque, 3.712 percent; Tesuque, 0.320 percent; Acoma, 0.221 percent; and Zuñi, 5.472 percent. Population decline or negative growth rates occurred at Sandía, −0.878 percent; Isleta, −0.033 percent; Santa Clara, −1.04 percent; Nambé, −0.5 percent; Galisteo, −0.446 percent; Pecos, −2.466 percent; Cochiti, −3.460 percent; Santo Domingo, −0.523 percent; San Felipe, −2.134 percent; Santa Ana, −0.049 percent; Zía, −3.46 percent; Jémez, −2.106 percent; and Laguna, −1.112 percent. Clearly the pueblos that grew fastest during the 1700s were Zuñi and Pojoaque. The sharpest decline occurred at Cochiti, Pecos (eventually joined with Jémez in 1838), Zía, San Felipe, and Jémez.

To study broader demographic trends and to correct for sharp census reporting discrepancies, town-level data were aggregated by administrative jurisdictions. A geometric growth rate subjected to regression analysis and plotted on a logarithmic scale was then undertaken. The results, presented in Table 4.3 and graphically depicted in Figure 4.1, show that New Mexico's total population grew at a geometric rate of 1.61 percent per year. The population classified as Spanish grew at 2.66 percent per year, almost seven times faster than the Indian population, which experienced a 0.382 percent growth rate. The Indian population in Albuquer-

TABLE 4.6

New Mexico's Pueblo Indian Population, 1706-1860

	1706	1730	1750	1752	1760	1765	1776	1782	1785	1789	1792	1794	1795	1800	1805	1811	1820	1821	1860
Acoma	760	600	960	890	1,502	1,184	530	820	458	783		667	791	757	722	824	825		523
Cochiti	500	372	521	309	450		486	720		527	556		518	505		697	331	339	172
Galisteo	150	188	220	195	225	235	152												
Isleta			421	318		375	454	410		383				479		505	513	511	440
Jémez	300	307	378	207	373	309	345	485	277	265		298	277	270		287	321	330	650
Laguna	330	400	528	415	600	534	699	668		653		793	753	802	782	968	950	779	927
Nambé	300	400	199	144	204	223	183	155	153				215	178	183	86	224	231	103
Pecos	1,000	521	300	318	433	532	269	152	179	138	186	180	165	159		131	58	54	
Picuris	300		247	238	328	288	223	254	154	213		228	223	251		282	326		143
Pojoaque	136		130	79	99		98	63		77		54	78	79	82		91	93	37
Sandia			440	219	291	205	275	304		252		296	279	236		388	397	405	217
San Felipe	530	234	400	224	458	411	406	532	256	260	381	185	261	289		466	473	310	360
San Ildefonso	300	296	371	262	484	309	387	240	229	317	548	253	194	251	262	278	304	527	154
San Juan	340	300	500	217	316	259	201	260	166	205		198		202	210	208	236	232	341
Santa Ana	340	209	353	211	404	408	384	356	346	399		465	486	634	620	518	527	471	316
Santa Clara	200	279	188	163	257	252	229	134	199	201		186	188	193	183	241	244	180	179
Santo Domingo	240	281	300	214	424	267	528	650	351	493	722	527	496	483		718	711	726	261
Taos	700	730	456	451	505	506	427	518		479		514	505	531		630	751	753	363
Tesuque	500		171	147	232		194	138	151	152		148	161	155		158	181	187	97
Zia	500	318	481		568	479	416	275	307	222	461	273	289	262	347	269	307	196	117
Zuñi	1,500		824	745	664	1,593	1,617	1,935		2,437	1,814	2,716	2,552	2,716		1,610	1,064	1,597	1,150
TOTAL	8,926	5,435	8,388	5,966	8,817	8,369	8,503	9,069	3,226	8,456	4,668	7,981	8,431	9,437	3,391	9,264	8,834	7,921	6,550

Sources for TABLE 4.1.

(1706) "Report of Fray Juan Alvarez on the Missions of New Mexico," AGN-PI 36-2:43-45; (1730) "Letter of Bishop Benito Crespo to Viceroy Juan Vásquez de Acuña," AGN-ARZO 7:1-6; (1750) "Report of Fray Juan José Toledo on New Mexico's Missions," BN 8-81; (1752) "General Census of the Kingdom of New Mexico," AGN-PI 102:3; (1760) Eleanor B. Adams, ed., *Bishop Tamarón's Visitation of New Mexico, 1760* (Albuquerque, 1954); (1765) Donald C. Cutter, trans., "An Anonymous Statistical Report of New Mexico in 1765," NMHR 50 (1975):347-52; Fray Atanasio Domínguez, *The Missions of New Mexico, 1776*, Eleanor B. Adams and Fray Angélico Chávez, trans. (Albuquerque, 1956); (1782) "Report on New Mexico's Missions," AGN-PI 161-5:88; (1785) "The State of Christianity in the Missions in New Mexico," AGN-CALIF 29:3:197-209; (1789) "Census of Governor Fernando de la Concha," Ritch Papers, Huntington Library, San Marino, California; (1792) "State of New Mexico's Missions," AGN-PI 161-5:147; (1794) "State of New Mexico's Missions," AASF 53:108-114; (1795) "Missions of New Mexico," AASF 53:153-156; (1800) "General State of the Kingdom of New Mexico," SA 14:651; (1805) "Census of the Citizens and Persons in the Province," SA 15:608; (1811) "Census of the Province of New Mexico," AASF 53:743-44; (1820) "State of the Missions in the Province of New Mexico," SA 20:498-99; (1821) "Census of New Mexico's Missions," SA 20:1077; (1860) F. W. Hodge, ed., *Handbook of American Indians North of Mexico* (Washington, D.C., 1912, Part 2), 325.

que Jurisdiction showed the highest geometric rate of growth—0.898 percent. Keres Jurisdiction had the fastest growing Spanish population in the kingdom, an annual geometric rate of 5.02 percent. A comparison of the fastest growing Spanish and Indian areas indicates that pueblos were growing at approximately one-sixth the pace of the Spanish towns.

Particularly noteworthy is that the Indian population in Santa Fe Jurisdiction declined almost at the same geometric rate that its Spanish population grew—at −2.32 percent per year. Indeed, a cursory comparison of the Spanish and Pueblo population in New Mexico between 1750 and 1820 clearly indicates that this depopulation of the Pueblos was a broader demographic pattern (see Table 4.2). In 1750 there were 3,809 Spaniards and 10,568 Pueblo Indians; in 1776, 9,742 Spaniards and 8,602 Puebloans; in 1800, 19,276 Spaniards and 9,732 Puebloans; and, in 1820, 28,436 Spaniards and 9,923 Puebloans. Migration into New Mexico from points farther south did not begin to occur until the 1790s, so the rapid rise in the population classified as Spanish was due in part to the migration of Pueblo Indians into Spanish towns.[53]

The depopulation of some pueblos and the extremely slow growth witnessed in others was due to several factors. First, I have already mentioned the excessive *repartimiento* labor that the Spanish governors demanded of the Pueblos. The labor they performed on Spanish farms during planting and harvesting seasons regularly robbed the Indian community of the labor it needed for the cultivation of its own crops. Undercultivated Indian fields meant food shortages, malnutrition, and, ultimately, higher mortality rates. Tribute paid in agricultural products further depleted native food reserves, and when drought, pestilence, or low crop yield followed on years of excessive Spanish demands, the hungry and helpless were forced to forsake their pueblos for life in Spanish households. Such economic marginalization explains one representation of the *genízaro* as an outcast.[54]

The sexual marginalization of Pueblo Indian women and the expulsion and abandonment of their mixed-blood progeny was another source of Pueblo depopulation. I noted earlier that *genízaros* were also deemed outcasts from Pueblo society and that Pueblo women who had been violated by Spaniards and shunned by their kin had no option but to migrate into Spanish towns. Recall, too, that their children, those *hijos de la iglesia* or foundlings, constituted 10 percent of all New Mexicans who legally married between 1700 and 1846. If one considers that lower status persons were less likely to have the wherewithal to marry legally and that infant mortality was quite high, we can begin to see why Albert

Schroeder's estimate that *genízaros* made up one-third of New Mexico's population is probably correct.

Finally, the limited land base that every pueblo had for its food needs also influenced the extent to which Indian population could grow and successfully sustain itself. Pueblo women were known to control their number of children to no more than four by using herbal uterine irritants that caused them to spontaneously abort. Excessive population growth not otherwise controlled was probably siphoned off to Spanish towns.[55]

5

Honor and Social Status

There is a Spanish folktale of the seventeenth century that Hispanos in New Mexico still tell their children whenever the family gathers to listen to stories of bygone days. "La Constancia" (which means constancy or sexual fidelity), as the tale is known, describes the values that most pre-occupied New Mexico's Spanish colonists. Set in New Mexico and in Re-conquest Spain, the story tells of seduction and intrigue, of malevolence, rivalries, and a pact with a witch, of how one man took the honor of an-other, and most importantly, of how honor was won and lost honor avenged. The focus of this chapter and of the next is the value of honor the Spanish colonists placed at the very center of their moral system. Be-cause honor could be won, its loss—or dishonor—will concern us here too. The story of "La Constancia" vividly illustrates all of this, so let us begin by reading of her travails.

La Constancia was a beautiful woman who lived happily with her hus-band, José María, in New Mexico. Because of her great beauty, Constancia constantly gained the attentions of men. One day a wicked vagabond laid eyes upon her and immediately tried to seduce her. He failed and his fail-ure was so humiliating that he decided to ruin Constancia's marriage and reputation. With the help of a witch, the vagabond stole a necklace from Constancia that her husband had given her as a wedding present. The vagabond presented the necklace to José María as evidence that his wife had committed adultery. José María believed the scheme and surrendered his public honor and wealth because of his wife's alleged acts. To punish Constancia, José María locked her in a box and threw her into the sea. After many days the box landed on the coast of Spain, where Constancia emerged amid a fierce battle between the Christians and the Moors. Not knowing what to do, Constancia prayed to the Virgin Mary. In an apparition the Virgin told Constancia to become a man, to put on armor and to kill every infidel Moor possible. Constancia did as she was told and managed to secure the city and to force out the attackers singlehandedly. The Catholic monarch was so grateful that he bestowed honor, wealth, and the crown of the kingdom on Constancia, whom everyone thought was a man. She returned home, avenged her reputation, restored her husband's honor, and finally placed her crown upon his head. She removed her armor and became a woman again.[1]

The Importance of Honor

The feats of La Constancia reveal the origin of honor as a reward for valor in war and its intimate connection to the sexual spoils of conquest—women. Honor to the men who colonized New Mexico and forced the Indians to submit was one of the core values of the moral system they were to establish. Honor mediated social relationships between individuals and groups on the basis of ethical choices. Spanish New Mexicans were particularly concerned about their honor from the seventeenth to the early nineteenth centuries, a concern they brought from Spain as part of their cultural baggage. The value originated in the Mediterranean, where it had long been the idiom for competition over scarce resources.

Honor was first a value judgment concerning one's social personality, a reflection. It was not only the value of a person in his or her own eyes, but also the recognition of that worth in the eyes of others. It was a belief that the image of self, one's reputation, was the basis for pride and precedence. But before honor could become a right to pride, it had to be acknowledged by others. Honor materialized when deference was paid or when preferential access to scarce resources was gained because of it. Because public recognition of honor was essential to its value, the number of persons paying one honor depended on their familiarity with the claim and their willingness to pay it.[2]

Honor ultimately depended on brute force. "Honour consisteth only in the opinion of Power," wrote Thomas Hobbes in *Leviathan*. "To obey, is to Honour; because no man obeys them, whom they think have no power to help or hurt them. And consequently to disobey is to Dishonour." The claim to honor, says Julian Pitt-Rivers, was an assertion of power. "Might is the basis of right to precedence, which goes to the man who is bold enough to enforce his claim."[3]

Honor was a polysemic word embodying meaning at two different but intrinsically interrelated levels, one of status and one of virtue. When José

María thought that La Constancia had lost her sexual purity, the honor that concerned him was honor as a social virtue. When La Constancia defeated the Moors, the honor she won was honor as social status. Chapter 6 of this book is devoted entirely to a discussion of honor-virtue as a code for personal ethical conduct. Our focus here is on honor-status, which was a measure of social standing, ordering along a single vertical continuum those persons with much honor and differentiating them from those with none. In the Spanish body politic, first of all was the honor of God. The honor of the king was next, for his sanction to temporal power was divinely imbued. The honor of the corporate Church followed, then that of the religious orders, the aristocracy, the landed peasantry, on down the line to those persons who had no honor, Indians and *genízaro* slaves.

For honor-status to arise, there had to be a bestower of honor, a possessor, and observers. During the reconquest of the Iberian Peninsula from the Moors between 711 and 1492, the Catholic monarchs of León-Castile, Aragón, and Portugal defined honor as an award of status for those who helped win back the realm. The Catholic kings lacked the wherewithal to wage a religious war against Islam, and so it fell to small groups of privately financed soldiers to accomplish this goal. As the Moorish frontier was pushed back, those men who conquered and defended new territory were compensated for their labors with titles to land and to nobility (*hidalguía*). Nobles were exempted from paying personal taxes, from having liens placed on their property, or from being subjected to base forms of punishment. The honor-status obtained through such excellence did not depend on an intrinsic concept of honor, only the specific definition the bestower gave it at any one time.[4]

In New Mexico, as on the Islamic frontier, to Don Juan de Oñate, to the notables of the conquest, and to their descendants, King Philip II bestowed all the honors and privileges of Castilian noblemen for showing prowess and courage in forcing the infidel Indians to submit. The honor of the men so ennobled, particularly after the reconquest, was based on their power and might, on their lands and wealth, on their ancestry and gentle births, on their religion and Christian names, and on their personal elegance and pomp. Such honor, socially validated as fame and glory, existed in Spanish New Mexican society only because of the presence of Indians who were dishonored and infamous.[5]

Dishonor was the negation of honor; infamy and ill repute were its social corollaries. The Siete Partidas, the thirteenth-century Castilian legal code, which was the foundation of seventeenth-century Spanish law in America, equated the loss of honor with death. "Two crimes are equal, to kill a man or to accuse him of wrong-doing; for a man once he is defamed, although he be innocent, is dead to the good and honor of the world; and besides, the slander may be such that death would be better for him than life." The infamy of dishonored men was likened to social death in the Partidas, hence the legal maxim, death before dishonor. Gaspar Pérez de Villagrá expressed this idea well in his 1610 *History of New Mexico*. Writing about the defeat of Acoma Pueblo in 1599, he asked rhetorically: "Acomans! Did you not solemnly promise that if victory were denied us, you would all sooner perish than surrender your honor? Death is a thousand times more welcome than a life of infamy and disgrace."[6]

A person without honor was worse than dead in colonial New Mexico. Honor was born of victory and dominion, dishonor of vanquishment and domination. The conquest and reconquest of the Pueblo Indians had defined them as infamous and dishonored. Indeed, much of Pueblo public ceremonialism from the eighteenth century on consisted of dance dramas—"Los Moros y los Cristianos," "Los Matachines," "Los Pastores"—that retold their defeat and submission to Christian rule. As we saw, these dramas were highly charged ideological projections of Pueblo history as the conquerors wanted it remembered. Regularly throughout the course of the year the Puebloans were forced to publicly mock themselves and to relive the humiliation of their defeat at Spanish hands. Partially as a result of this humiliation, partially as a way to preserve their culture, during the eighteenth century the Puebloans isolated themselves from Spanish towns. Obviously, they continued to enter Spanish towns to perform their labor duties, to trade some of their excess products for manufactured goods, and to help defend the province from Apache attacks. But when these tasks were done, they retired to a world apart.

The enemy within, that is, the *genízaro* Indians residing in Spanish households and towns, became convenient targets for Spanish racial hatred during the eighteenth century. The *genízaros'* status as slaves taken as captives in war and as outcasts from their pueblos defined their infamy and dishonor. Since at least the time of St. Augustine, Christian theology had sanctioned the enslavement of prisoners of war in lieu of death. Through the victor's generosity his prisoner's physical death was commuted into slavery and symbolic death; a death which, as Orlando Patterson points out, has been historically a universal feature of slavery. In all those places where the existence of human bondage is recorded, argues Patterson, slaves were individuals devoid of genealogical ties to the community they served, what he calls "natal alienation"; they were dishonored by their status as slaves and by the degrading forms of work they performed, and were dead to the community that cherished honor.[7]

The presence of Indian slaves in New Mexican society gave meaning to honor-status. Much of what was considered Spanish culture on this northern frontier of New Spain gained its meaning in opposition to and as an exaggeration of what it meant to be an Indian or a *genízaro*. What the Puebloans and *genízaros* were, the Spanish were not. What the Spanish were, the Puebloans and *genízaros* were not. Negative stereotypes of the other, that is, of the defeated and fallen Indian within Hispano society and outside of it, defined the boundaries between "them" and "us," between the dishonored and the honored.

The timocratic values of society were premised fundamentally on slavery, and so it is to this topic that we now turn to explain how avoidance of the *genízaro* worked itself out in law and in the generation of religious, ethnic, racial, lineage, and land-owning distinctions that constituted the operative status hierarchy.

Slavery

As was noted in Chapter 4, 3,294 nomadic Indians entered Spanish households as slaves between 1693 and 1846. By 1800 they numbered perhaps as many as 7,000 out of a total Spanish population of 19,276. Bondage was primarily a domestic household institution and so its meaning, particularly to the slave, was found at the interpersonal level. How one was treated by the master of the household, by the master's kin, and by the larger community was what mattered most to slaves.[8]

Before slaves entered a Hispano household they were stripped of their former names, baptized, and given Christian names. "On arriving home (after a slaving expedition)," wrote Manuel A. Chávez in the early 1800s, "the first thing to do was to take the children to the priest to baptize them and give them a name. They would naturally take your name." Mary of the Trinity, Francis of the Holy Spirit, Ann of the Incarnation, and John of the Angels were favorite slave names. Names were marks of social status. The addition of a "Don" or "Doña" to one's name was a sign of noble ancestry. *Capitán* or *alcalde* (constable) signified an honorific post. A Fray before one's name meant that one's life had been devoted to Christ. Don Diego de Vargas Zapata Luján Ponce de León, the man who reconquered New Mexico, was the descendant of a long line of warriors. His name indicated that, so that it might be known and remembered by all. And so those lofty compound slave names denoting spiritual origin through the Trinity, the Holy Spirit, and the Angels, far from a trivial act or a simple legal formalism, indicated a natal origin in slavery and incorporation into the Christian community through baptism. Children born in wedlock carried a patronym. Slaves did not and everyone knew that.⁹

Kinship was the dominant mode of affiliation in colonial New Mexico; everyone was enmeshed in its web. Lacking genealogical ties to the community slaves entered their owner's household as part of his or her symbolic capital by which their eminence in the community was known. The enmeshment of Indian servitude in the language of kinship has led some historians of New Mexico to erroneously conclude that slavery was a "benevolent" institution. This claim is based primarily on declarations before the courts in which slaves spoke of their masters and mistresses as "father" and "mother," and were referred to by them as "son" and "daughter." Sebastiana de Jesús declared in 1715 that her duenna, Lucía Ortiz, was "the mother who raised me." Soledad Chávez said of her Indian slave María in 1819, "the girl is family." ¹⁰

The filial and kinship terms used to refer to slaves in legal documents tell us little about the nature of slavery or whether it was benevolent or not. Rather, they were statements concerning authority relationships within the household, particularly a father's right to rule over wife, family, and thralls. The crown tolerated slavery in New Mexico as a way of "civilizing" the Indians. When slave owners came before the courts to answer to charges of slave mistreatment, it was in their interest to portray slave relations as governed by the same rules that regulated family. Fathers were ideally loving, stern, and guiding. To have said otherwise would have been to expose oneself to the loss of mastership over another.

The language of ownership used in court documents to refer to slaves is more frequent and more revealing than the fictive kinship terminology. To Don Francisco Guerrero, Santa Fe's chief constable, the escapee from the town's guardhouse in 1757 was "the *genízaro* Indian servant of Doña Feliciana Coco." "Manuela, the servant of Isabel Chávez," complained of mistreatment in 1763. And the words with which "the boy servant of Francisco Apodaca" was returned to his owner after a flaying for petty larceny revealed his legal status. The youth was entrusted to Apodaca in 1765 "with total power over his person." In each of these instances, and in many others like them, the Spanish preposition *de*, denoting ownership and possession, was used to refer to the slaves. As persons who had no honor, slaves had social and legal personalities primarily through their masters.¹¹

Those who maintain that slavery in New Mexico was benevolent will be startled to find that none of its participants saw it so. The meaning of slavery to masters, slaves, and priests was revealed in the selection of a slave's baptismal godparents (*padrinos*). Between 1693 and 1849, 3,294 Indian slaves were baptized. In 280 of these cases the officiating priest recorded the names of the godparents and their relationship to the slave. Fourteen percent (N = 39) listed the owners as the godparents. A combination of owner and nonowner served as *padrinos* in 20 percent of these christenings (N = 57). But in the majority of cases (65 percent, N = 184), no apparent relationship existed between the slave's godparents and the master. A more striking pattern emerges in the godparenthood information on the children born to slaves in captivity. Only in one out of 113 baptisms was the child's godparent also its parent's master. Seven owner-nonowner combinations acted as godparents. In 92 percent of these cases (N = 105) the child's *padrinos* were totally unrelated to the slave's master.[12]

Why were masters not preferred as baptismal godparents? Stephen Gudeman and Stuart B. Schwartz have proposed that the answer lies in the ideological clash between baptism and slavery. In Christian theology a person was made of body and soul. Baptismal sponsorship created a spiritual bond between the baptized person and his or her godparents, which entailed obligations of protection, instruction, and succor to help the person save his or her soul. Unlike slavery, which is a bond of domination over human volition expressed as control over another person's body and signified through servility, baptism is an expression of equality born of participation in the mystical body of Christ. Two rather incompatible states, spiritual freedom and physical bondage, were brought together when the Church insisted that captives be baptized. The contradiction was resolved by selecting a sponsor other than the slave master for the baptized person's liberation from original sin and rebirth into Christ's salvation. Masters may have refused to serve as godparents out of fear that by so doing they abrogated some of their temporal powers over the slave. And certainly when slaves chose *padrinos* for their children they invariably avoided choosing their owner for their children's spiritual salvation.[13]

Within New Mexican households slave treatment ran the gamut from the kind neglect of some to the utter sadism of others. To be a slave or *criado* in a Hispano household was to be a marginal and stigmatized person. At the crack of dawn they were the first to rise to perform their duties. They got the hearth's fire going, braved the morning cold to chop wood and to haul in water for the day's needs. If chamber pots had to be emptied, if a family member was sick and had to be cared for, if the master's toe nails had to be clipped, it was the *genízaro* slave who did it. When Fray Diego Martínez called at the Santa Cruz home of Ana María Velásquez at midnight on March 26, 1809, it was Gerónima, María's In-

.Iian slave, who rose to answer the door and in so doing was kicked and beaten by the angry priest.[14]

Both inside the household and outside of it, *genízaros* were addressed as children, in the second person Spanish informal and personal *tu* (you), but had to address their masters and local citizens with the formal *usted*. In Indian society increasing age brought increasing respect, but not for New Mexico's slaves. They were permanently infantilized, even by the master's own children. An Indian slave named Bárbara, described in 1762 as old, sickly, and no longer capable of working, expected that when her master died his son, Joseph Gallego, whom she had suckled with her own breast milk, would free her. Gallego refused Bárbara's request and beat her every time she raised the issue. Bárbara's children, who were not allowed to see their mother, sought the governor's intercession. Arrogantly Joseph Gallego explained to Governor Vélez Cachupín that he had taken Bárbara to his house "not because of her service but because my deceased father bought her." His behavior could not be deemed cruel, explained Gallegos, because he was simply preserving his father's patrimony. The governor sided with Gallegos, Bárbara had "no basis" for demanding freedom.[15]

In the presence of honorable men, *genízaros* stood, bowed their heads, and took off their hats. Don Tomás de Albear of Santa Fe severely chastised Cayetano Pasote in 1751 "for lacking the urbanity of removing his hat" in Don Tomás' presence. And when the nobility staged their feasts and dances, the slaves served and looked on vicariously from the margins, not knowing the steps of genteel courtly dance, and lacking the velvet brocade gowns of the Doñas, or the dandified clothes of the Dons.[16]

That slaves lacked genealogical ties to the Spanish community and had been torn from their history through violence was humiliation enough in a society that prided itself on ancestry. Some masters compounded the hurt by refusing to allow their slaves to marry, establish families, or retain their own progeny. When slave women bore children while in captivity, the children were sometimes sold or given to another household as gifts. Petrona, Gabriel Quintana's *criada*, begged the ecclesiastical court in 1777 that her master not be allowed to give her child away. "For the love of Holiest Mary, do not take away my daughter, I promise to give her a Christian education," pleaded Petrona. But her pleas fell on deaf ears and Quintana had his way.[17]

Numerous decrees on the ideal treatment of slaves were regularly pronounced by officials of the Church and state. Had slaves and *criados* been treated all that well, perhaps such repeated pronouncements would have been unnecessary. The only picture of ideal slave treatment in New Mexico is a rather late one, offered by Pedro León, an Indian trader from Abiquiu, as he stood accused of illegal slave trafficking in 1852. Begging clemency of the court, and thus coloring what he had to say about slavery, León stated:

[Slaves] are adopted into the family of those who get them, are baptized and remain [and are] trusted as one of the family—The head of the house standing as Godfather—The Prefect has the right to free them whenever maltreated—The Indian has a right to choose a guardian—Women are freed whenever married—say from 14 to 16—Men ditto from 18 to 20—At the death of Godfather never sold—always freed—The Godfathers provide husbands and wives for them the same as their children—When the Godfather dies they are free—As soon as they are baptized they cannot be sold any more. . . . It would be contrary to the laws of the Church.

In some households slaves were undoubtedly treated as warmly as León suggests. For when a slave was obtained in infancy, close emotional attachments developed with the master. Slaves after all resided in the same house with their owner; they worked serving the master and his children; they ate the same food the female servants prepared for everyone else; and they slept in their master's house, sometimes in his bed for his pleasure and frequently at his feet. Some slave women even offered their breasts to the master's children, suckling them with their milk.[18]

Masters enjoyed enough access and time with their female slaves for sexual intimacies, whether won through seductive ploys or taken through force. One Santa Fe don admitted on his deathbed that he owed his Indian slave her virginity. He bequeathed the girl 200 pesos so that a prospective husband might overlook this loss. When Joseph Manuel married Elena de la Cruz in 1720, he declared that he was the illegitimate son of Don Antonio de Reynosa and that his mother, María de la Encarnación, was Reynosa's slave. Manuel Martín admitted that Melchora, the girl servant he kept in his house, was actually his daughter. Melchora had been conceived by "a pure *genízara* Indian slave" whom he had purchased. And Alejandro Mora was no fool. In 1751 he raped his slave Juana "to determine if she was a virgin." Because she had resisted, said Juana, "he hung me from a roof-beam and beat me."[19]

The sheer proximity between slave and master, their outsider status and their lack of honor, regularly made them scapegoats. Frustrations precipitated by a poor harvest, by the low price one's livestock brought at market, by a wife's infidelities, or by an affront to one's honor could be and often were vented on slaves. Trivial insubordination or impertinences, real or imagined, were paid for by slaves with a wallop.

A patriarch's natural law authority over his family gave him the right to correct and punish an erring wife, child, or slave. The whipping Don Francisco Armijo gave his wife, Doña María Rosalía Maestas, in 1816 for her public lack of modesty, was mild compared to those Alejandro Mora regularly gave his slave Juana. In the annals of New Mexican slavery Mora's sadism knows no rivals. In 1751 Mora's wife complained to the authorities that Juana, a slave she had brought to the marriage, was being treated inhumanely. Bernalillo's constable investigated and found Juana's body totally covered with bruises. Her neck and body had burns from the application of live coals. Her ankles were scabbed from restraining manacles. Her knees had festering ulcers. Mora had initially broken Juana's knees to keep her from fleeing. The knee wounds never healed because Mora periodically reopened them, mincing the flesh with a sharp flintstone. Juana's description of her life was particularly poignant:

I have served my master for eight or nine years now but they have seemed more like 9,000 because I have not had one moment's rest. He has martyred me with sticks, stones, whip, hunger, thirst, and burns all over my body. . . . He inflicted them saying that it was what the devil would do to me in hell, that he was simply doing what God had ordered him to do.

Women in Bernalillo were too sexually lax, said Mora in his own defense. He had punished Juana only to assure that she did not follow in their ugly steps. Juana was removed from Mora's household and there the matter ended, without even a reprimand.[20]

Admittedly, the Mora case is an extreme one. Yet one wonders what fate befell Pedro García's female Indian slave. Her badly beaten body was discovered in 1745, apparently murdered. Then there was the dismembered body of Domingo, Doña Josefa Bustamante's Indian servant, which was discovered in the cow patch behind her Santa Fe home in 1774. In neither case was culpability established, or for that matter investigated. Contemporaries seemed to regard slave and servant deaths as matters of minor importance, which deserved little comment.[21]

Slavery was an uplifting privilege, or so some owners convinced themselves. Governor Vélez Cachupín reminded colonists in 1752 that Indian slavery was illegal but was tolerated in New Mexico "so that they [captives] can be instructed in Our Holy Catholic Faith and made cognizant of the Divine Precepts, so that they may win their own salvation in honor and glory of God, our Lord." Slavery "civilized" Indians by giving them the requisites of culture: clothes, life in a European styled home, and knowledge of the one true God. At the baptismal font every friar reminded owners that these were things they had to provide their slaves.

Slaves silently endured assaults, humiliations, and cruelties, but were quick to seek legal redress when deprived of their minimal needs. A good master clothed them, housed them, and taught them how to pray. Justifiably, the "*genízara* Indian" of María Sánchez complained that her mistress "fed her poorly, dressed her so badly that she went about almost naked, and that her body was covered with welts from the beatings she received." "Not even gentiles treat slaves with such inhumanity," the girl protested. María Sánchez was ordered to properly dress and treat the girl. The servant of María Soledad Chávez in 1819 begged the chief constable of Jémez to intervene on her behalf because she was forced to go about "half-naked except for some tattered skins." The girl was returned home with the promise that she would be properly dressed.[22]

New Mexico's authorities listened to slave complaints, albeit with feigned concern, because they feared apostasy. When slaves believed that masters had exceeded "normal" punishment, they appeared before the courts, sometimes with priests as their advocates, other times alone, to demand their freedom, and if not that, the right to serve a new lord. The slaves of Tomás Chávez and those of Isabel Chávez launched such complaints in 1763, as did the thralls of Gregoria Baca in 1766, to name but a few. They all said that they had endured the pains of hell serving cruel masters. In justice they deserved freedom. Not one was granted her or his wish. Service to a new master was more in line with the timocratic ideals of frontier society, in which everyone had a place and knew it.[23]

New Mexico's settlers valued female slaves more highly than males and paid twice as much to acquire them. At the 1776 Taos fair, girls between the ages of twelve and twenty sold for two horses and some trifles— roughly 60 to 80 pesos (T)—while men in the same age group cost half as much. Don Clemente Gutiérrez, a New Mexican merchant, had six female slaves for sale in 1762; the asking price was 70 pesos (T) each.[24]

The preference for female slaves is easy to understand. In a province where only one out of every three children born was likely to reach the age of twenty, female slaves were essential for social and biological reproduction. The pretensions of aristocratic households were hollow without slaves. Who would perform the menial household chores? Corn had to be shucked and wheat threshed, ground into flour, and baked into bread. Chili peppers had to be tied into *riestras* and hung out to dry. Any meat that was not immediately consumed after a slaughter had to be salted and dried into jerky. There were buildings to construct and to plaster—all women's work. When not otherwise caring for household needs female slaves undertook production for the market. Animal pelts had to be tanned and sewn into shoes and saddles. Cotton and wool were spun and knit into socks, gloves, and caps, or woven into blankets and rugs, all of which would be sold in Chihuahua for manufactured goods and luxury items. And the illegitimate children slave women bore often remained in the household as additional working hands.[25]

Male slaves, particularly those between the ages of 15 and 30, were a troublesome lot and posed serious threats to the tranquility of the province. These men were brought before the civil courts for not knowing or respecting their state in society, for failing to respect the property of others, and for their unbridled lust. As nomads who had formerly obtained their livelihood through hunting, Indian slaves thought nothing of slaughtering animals they found roaming loose. Brand marks meant little to them. To teach the meaning of such marks, Governor Gaspar de Mendoza in 1741 had Antonio, Diego Martín's thrall, given 200 lashes for killing a citizen's mules. Mendoza hoped that the beating would tame Antonio's rebelliousness and lack of respect for Spanish law, but instead it only strengthened his will. Antonio escaped to the land of the Apaches, was recaptured, and for years continued to irritate both his master and the law. Juan de la Cruz likewise was given 50 lashes and sentenced to four years of penal servitude in a sweatshop in northern Mexico for selling a branded horse, which he said he found in a ravine near San Juan. Such a stern punishment Governor Vélez Cachupín hoped would serve "as a good example and concept of our justice."[26]

Numerous cries were raised about the Indian slaves who escaped from their masters' homes at night to seduce (*enamorar*) slave and lower-class women. The crux of the problem was that for slave men Christianity meant celibacy. Given the sexual freedom of their native cultures and the fact that the Spaniards would not allow captive men to express their sexual desires, the authorities were constantly plagued with disciplinary problems born of lust. Such was the case in 1794 when Francisco, the slave of Francisco Chávez, escaped to be with Teresa del Valle. The two had been separated several times by their owners, and had once taken flight among the Apaches and had been recaptured. Despite all the obstacles, their "desires" always brought them together. Fearing that they might become apostates, the governor ordered them separated once again.[27]

The slave regime was more of an encumbrance on Indian men than on women. Thus it was common to find that men escaped as soon and as often as possible. Joseph Velásquez's slave fled in 1713 after only eight days of captivity. Bentura, the thrall of Diego Torres, the Ute slave of

Pedro Salazar, and Miguel Tafoya were but a few of those slaves who escaped during the eighteenth century. The authorities were always distressed when slaves fled "from the kingdom or dismembered themselves from Christianity," because as one apostate, Pedro de la Cruz, put it in 1747: "I will return within a short time with the Comanches and will expel the Spaniards by the hairs (*greñas*)." When Pedro was reunited with his tribe he indeed returned to avenge his enslavement. Runaway slaves were particularly dangerous because they knew the layout of their master's household, where arms and livestock were kept, and how much resistance an attack might face. On such raids they took what they wanted and if possible repaid the loss of their Indian wives and children through the capture of Hispanos. María Rita Peralta, a Spanish woman, was captured by the Comanches at Tomé sometime in the early 1770s. In 1780 Don Antonio Gil Ibaro found her at a slave auction in Texas, purchased her for 2 hides and 50 pesos, and returned her to her parents. Governor Fermín de Mendinueta in 1768 stated succinctly the consequences of fugitivism on Hispanic settlements: "Once the idea germinates in the hearts of these Barbarians of scorn for our armaments and for the value of the king's vassals, their natural cowardice may be inspired, loosing that ancient respect and fear that has kept them at peace." [28]

So that scorn might not take root in heathen hearts, the number of male slaves in the province was kept low. That is why they fetched a lower price at market than females. Indian captives regularly were marched south to work in the Parral silver mines. Some went on to plantations in Veracruz, and after 1800 many were shipped off to Havana and to Yucatán. Don Mariano Varela's 1788 accounts book noted that he had delivered 108 Apache slaves to Chihuahua. He started the trip with several hundred slaves, but ten died en route and many others escaped and returned to New Mexico, blazing a trail of murders and robberies, which was precisely what everyone feared. [29]

The presence of significant numbers of *genízaro* slaves and *criados* in Spanish towns and villages who had no genealogical ties to the Hispano community, who were dishonored by their status as thralls, and who were deemed socially dead amid men and women of honor generated negative stereotypes of what it meant to be an Indian. It was by contrasting themselves with the other that Spaniards—aristocrats and landed peasants alike—defined themselves and their honor. *Genízaros* were first and foremost prisoners of war captured by the Spanish, or, as Fray Atanasio Domínguez put it in 1776, "ransomed from the pagans by our people, are then emancipated to work out their account." Because Spaniards "only as a last resort . . . serve themselves," said Domínguez, *genízaros* "are servants among our people." Writing in 1778 on the state of affairs in New Mexico, Fray Juan Agustín de Morfi said that *genízaros* were

captive Comanches, Apaches, etc., who were taken as youngsters and raised among us. . . . Since they are the offspring of enemy tribes, the natives of this province, who bear long grudges, never admit them to their pueblos. Thus [the *genízaros*] are forced to live among Spaniards, without lands, or other means to subsist . . . they desire sites for villages but fail to obtain any, either because no one wants to provide them or because most lands have been occupied . . . on account of their poverty, which leaves them afoot and without arms . . . they bewail their neglect and they live like animals.[30]

Domínguez also observed that New Mexico's residents spoke Castilian of various sorts. The European-origin Spaniards spoke "with courtly polish," the landed peasants spoke "simply and naturally among themselves," but the *genízaros* did "not wholly understand it [Spanish] or speak it without twisting it somewhat." Domínguez offered several assessments of the *genízaro* character. They were "weak, gamblers, liars, cheats, and petty thieves." They were "examples of what happens when idleness becomes the den of evils." Belén's *genízaros* had no way of supporting themselves, he added, and lived by their luck, "only they and God know whether they have managed to get their hands on what belongs to their neighbors."[31]

The caricatures Domínguez and Morfi drew portrayed the *genízaros* as Indians of pagan ancestry who owned no land, lacked the means to earn a subsistence, owned no horses, carried no firearms, lived like animals, spoke a twisted form of Spanish, and were characterized by their depraved habits. Salvador Martínez, a Spaniard from Albuquerque, summarized the popular stereotype of the *genízaros* when he complained in the early 1800s that those living in the vicinity of Belén "were fugitives from their masters, odious people, vagabonds, gamblers, and thieves without the political or economic organization of a Republic." These ideas remained ingrained in the popular memory, for to this day mischievous and unruly children are taunted with the saying: "*genízaro, genízaro, puro indio de rescate,*" (*genízaro, genízaro,* pure bartered Indian). When New Mexicans say today "*no seas genízaro,*" or "don't be a *genízaro,*" they mean "don't be a liar." Frances Swadesh recently discovered that in northern New Mexico, when someone was referred to as a *genízaro,* it meant crude, low class, or "*indiado*" (Indian-like). Florence Hawley Ellis was told similar things in the 1950s about Belén's *genízaros* by the settlers who lived across the river from them in Tomé. Belén's *genízaros* were "semi-slave, low class, and without ability."[32]

If Indianness, slave and ex-slave pagan origin, dishonor, crude character, bad habits, and twisted language defined the *genízaros*, a list of an-
tonyms defined what it was to be a Spaniard. The differences between
aristocrats and landed peasants were of degree rather than kind. Spaniards, whatever their estate, were men of honor in comparison to the vanquished Indians. Even the lowliest Spaniard felt a sense of honor around
slaves. Landed peasants shared fully in the benefits of a timocratic culture
because, unlike *genízaro* slaves, they were long-time members of the
Christian community and as such had been given land by the king. Landowners were *vecinos* or citizens with full voting rights in town councils
(*cabildos*). By owning land Spaniards could earn their own subsistence
and were not dependent on others for their livelihood, as were slaves.
Spaniards owned horses and firearms and spoke Castilian well. When
men of honor said that *genízaros* "lived like animals," they meant that
they dressed poorly or scantily and showed little modesty or restraint in
their sexual comportment. As we will see in the next chapter, because
slave women bore illegitimate children, failed to establish stable unions,
were frequently sexually assaulted, and reputedly licentious, to be a Spanish woman, regardless of one's class, was to be concerned for one's sexual
purity and reputation, to guard one's virginity, to marry, and to be continent in matrimony. Finally, men of honor were men of their word—words
which carried force and were as binding as our modern contracts. Quite
appropriately, *genízaros* and ex-slaves were considered liars.

To protect their honor-status as Spaniards and lords over the Indian
slaves that resided among them, an elaborate legal structure was established in colonial New Mexico. The frontier of barbarism was populated
by a complex mix of hostile Indians, pagans, aristocrats, upstarts, va-
grants, and convicts. It was through the law, civil and ecclesiastical, and its
instruments of force that the Spaniards who considered themselves noble
and honored maintained their positions of privilege and their control over
the means and instruments of production. To see how Spaniards perpetuated the luster of their own honor and the dishonor and infamy of the
Indians, both *genízaros* and Puebloans, we turn now to a discussion of the
legal and social categories by which "them" and "us" were differentiated.

Honor and the Law

The Spanish conquistadores throughout the Americas were granted
titles of nobility and guaranteed special privileges for their labors in the
expansion of the realm. To assure that these privileges were protected,
whenever a person stood before a court of law one of the first things re-

corded in the docket was the person's *calidad*, his or her social status. The *Primer Diccionario General Etimológico de la Lengua Española* defined *calidad* as "the various qualities which constitute the essence of a person or thing, that which constitutes the status of a person, his nature, his age and other circumstances and conditions." *Calidad* and *nobleza* (nobility) were synonyms, the dictionary stated. Both referred to the character of a person deemed privileged by the state. "*Calidad* evaluates the person solely . . . in relation to his rights and privileges; *nobleza*, in relation to the honor and virtue which is assumed to accompany it."[33]

When a person's *calidad* was requested in a legal proceeding, the response was usually the individual's age, sex, place of residence, race, legitimacy or illegitimacy, civic status (i.e., whether a landowner or not), occupation, or any combination of these. The amount and type of punishment one received depended on this information. Spaniards by virtue of their honor could not be publicly flogged. For half-breeds and erring Indians, the whip was the only sure teacher. Governor Fermín de Mendinueta pronounced in 1768 that in robbery cases, "if the person is of *color quebrado* [a half-breed] they will receive twenty-five lashes at the pillory; if white they will be tied to the pillory and shamed publicly with the item they stole hanging from their neck." Cayetano Pasote of Santa Fe, a "*lobo* by *calidad*" was found guilty of assaulting Don Tomás Albear in 1752 and of "lacking in the respect and reverence owed [Don Tomás] because of his superiority in *calidad*." Cayetano was given 200 lashes and exiled to Tomé for ten years. María Josefa and her daughter María Francisca were found guilty of murdering Agustín Jirón in 1773. María Josefa, an Indian, "owing to her *calidad*" was punished with 200 lashes. Since the daughter was not yet 17, she received only 20 lashes because "the law provides that when a person is between 17 and 25, a judge can make full or partial exception due to the lack of full understanding a person has at those ages." Minors received less severe punishments, as did *indios sin razón*, Indians who lacked rational faculties to understand the full significance of their crimes.[34]

The only documentary body in which *calidad* declarations were continuously reported between 1693 and 1846 were the marriage investigations of the Catholic Church. Although baptismal registers recorded a person's social status as often as they ignored it, when people married, scrupulous attention was paid to their *calidad*. The anthropologist Edmund Leach proposed why this was so. Every culture determines if a person is a compatible equal by asking: "Do we intermarry with them?" New Mexicans asked themselves this question, too, because for most of them their social standing was dependent on it. Only the first generation

TABLE 5.1

Calidad of Marital Candidates in New Mexico, 1694-1846

	1690-99		1700-1719		1720-39		1740-59		1760-79		1780-99		1800-1819		1820-39		1840-46	
	No.	Pct.	No.	Pct.	No.	Pct.	No.	Pct.	No.	Pct.	No.	Pct.	No.	Pct.	No.	Pct.	No.	Pct.
Race																		
Español	1		29		5		—		484		738		603		678		—	
Mestizo	2		6		2		—		36		7		—		—		—	
Mulato	1		4		—		—		11		1		—		—		—	
Coyote	2		1		1		—		64		8		3		—		—	
Genizaro	—		—		—		—		24		37		—		—		—	
Negro	1		5		1		—		—		—		—		—		—	
Indio	1		1		—		—		84		25		36		72		—	
Subtotal	8	7.4%	46	9.2%	9	4.5%	—		703	77.9%	816	52.2%	642	37.8%	750	11.6%	—	
Occupation																		
Soldado	14		57		11		—		1		7		3		10		—	
Esclavo/Criada	—		2		1		—		—		—		—		—		—	
Subtotal	14	13.0	59	11.8	12	6.0	—		1	0.1	7	0.5	3	0.2	10	0.2	—	
Civic status																		
Vecino	71		301		176		2		179		520		436		2,510		1,679	
Residente	9		44		1		—		3		9		7		384		—	
Natural	—		21		—		—		—		—		—		—		—	
Subtotal	80	74.0	366	73.2	177	88.0	2	100.0	182	20.2	529	33.8	443	26.1	2,894	45.0	1,679	90.1
Nationality																		
Ciudadano	—		—		—		—		—		—		—		728		111	
Mexicano	—		—		—		—		—		—		—		504		9	
Subtotal	—		—		—		—		—		—		—		1,232	19.1	120	6.4
No mention	6	5.6	29	5.8	3	1.5	—		16	1.8	212	13.5	609	35.9	1,553	24.1	64	3.5
TOTAL	108	100.0%	500	100.0%	201	100.0%	2	100.0%	902	100.0%	1,564	100.0%	1,697	100.0%	6,439	100.0%	1,863	100.0%

SOURCE: AASF-DM Reels 60-79.

of conquistadores won their honor and privileges through achievement. For this fame and familial worth to live on through ascription in their children and grandchildren, and continue as the basis for their preferment in society, attention had to be given to marrying an equal or better. Honor could be squandered through a misalliance. Careful control over marriage guaranteed the maintenance of social boundaries between dominant and subordinate groups.[35]

The *calidad* labels recorded in the 1693–1846 matrimonial investigations (*diligencias matrimoniales*) reveal how social status was defined in colonial New Mexico, and how these definitions changed over time. The declarations of marriage candidates regarding their status fall into four general categories: racial, occupational, civic, and nationality (see Table 5.1). Between 1693 and 1759, the vast majority of individuals, approximately eight out of every ten, were categorized by a civic status. They were listed as *vecinos* (landowners), *residentes* (residents), or *naturales* (natives) of a particular town or settlement. Social status was equated with occupation for approximately 10 percent of all marriage candidates between 1693 and 1759. These were primarily soldiers who enjoyed special legal privileges (*fueros*), and slaves and *criados* who lacked full community membership.

Race was very infrequently mentioned as the basis of a person's status before 1760 and represented only 4.5 to 9.2 percent of declarations. The "no mention" category, that is, when the officiating priest failed to record the nuptial candidate's *calidad* either because it appeared unimportant or was so obvious, accounted for about one in twenty records between 1693 and 1759.

Beginning in 1760, a shift in the general distribution of *calidad* labels occurred. Whereas before 1760 racial labels accounted for less than 10 percent of total observations, after 1760 and into the beginning of the nineteenth century, race became the dominant way of defining social status. In the 1760–79 period, for example, race was equated with social standing for 78 percent of all marriage candidates. More than half of the persons who married were listed by race in the 1780–99 period. Beginning in 1800 the proportion of racial status labels declined both in absolute terms and in relation to civic status, nationality, and "no mentions." Of importance too was the progressive polarization of racial labels between 1760 and 1846 into just two: *español* and *indio*. The intermediate hues of race, so important between 1760 and 1799, had begun to disappear from the records by 1800.

The equation of *calidad* with civic status likewise decreased dramatically after 1760. In the 1760–79 period civic standing accounted for

20.2 percent of all *calidad* assignations, 33.8 percent between 1780 and 1799, and 26.1 percent between 1800 and 1819. After 1820 the percentage of civic status labels increased again, just as race started to disappear. Between 1820 and 1839, for 45 percent of all marriage candidates, *calidad* meant civic status, and between 1840 and 1846, it was so for 90.1 percent of all individuals. Note that the category that comprised the most civic status declarations was *vecino*, landowners with full civic rights.

With Mexican Independence in 1821 racial distinctions were legally abolished. This explains the emergence of the status category I have termed "nationality." Individuals formerly classified by their race, or presumed socio-racial standing, after 1820 were listed either by a nationality label such as *ciudadano* (citizen), *mexicano* (Mexican), or "no mention."

Examining the period from 1693 to 1846 as a whole, one sees major shifts in *calidad* classifications. As Table 5.1 shows, civil status dominated between 1693 and 1759, representing 70 to 90 percent of the total observations. Racial status became most important between 1760 and 1799, reaching its highest level at 78 percent during the 1760–79 period, and then tapering off. Between 1800 and 1819, race and "no mention" each accounted for about one-third of all *calidad* assignations. Finally, after 1820 civic status was again the dominant meaning given to *calidad*.

Why race became a major concern for those individuals who married between 1760 and 1799, as well as for those priests who officiated at matrimonial investigations, begs exploration. To the relationship between race and honor we turn.

Race and Honor

From the early days of the New Mexican colony the Spanish thought of society as composed of conquerors and conquered. The Indians were vanquished heathens engulfed in satanic darkness. It was only because of the Christians that the Indians came to see the light and gain knowledge of the One True God. Throughout the seventeenth and the first half of the eighteenth century the "us-them" distinction the conquistadores drew was primarily religious, but thoroughly imbued with notions of race and nationality. The conquerors were honorable because they were Christians, Spaniards, "civilized," and white. The vanquished Indians were dishonored because they were everything their victors were not: heathens, Amerindians, "uncivilized," and dark. Indeed, much of the terminology for this religious and racial distinction was drawn from the Iberian reconquest from the Moors between 711 and 1492.

There were no Moors in New Mexico, yet some of the colonists spoke of the Indians as Moors. The Indians carried "Moorish bows" (bows and arrows), they worshiped in "mosques" (kivas), and according to Santa Fe's resident, Joseph de Armijo, who suffered from insomnia, his sleeplessness in 1749 was due to a fear that "the Moors might attack unexpectedly." Alejandro Mora of Bernalillo did not dream of Moors. But in 1751 he justified beating his Indian slave with words evocative of religious hatreds in the Old World. "God has given me life," said Mora, "so that I might do to these Jews what they did to Our Holiest Lord."[36]

During Spain's reconquest, Muslims and Jews residing in conquered territory were forced to convert to Christianity. These converts became known as *conversos* or New Christians, and were differentiated from the true standard-bearers of the faith, the Old Christians, to whom Spain belonged and to whom all honor and distinction flowed. In New Mexico Old and New Christians were to exist as well. The Puebloans and *genízaros* who bowed their heads in submission to accept the waters of baptism were New Christians, and the Spaniards the Old. Don Joseph Romo de Vera and Doña Angela Valdez of Santa Fe proudly boasted in 1745 that "our families are Old Christian Spaniards, descendants of such, and pure of taint with the bad races—Moors, Jews, and those newly admitted to the flock of Holy Mother Church." Francisca Rodríguez affirmed in 1778 that she too was an Old Christian, as did Francisca Pacheco in 1801. Both women sought admission to religious orders that were open only to those firm in their faith.[37]

Another socio-legal distinction of peninsular religious origin widely used during the colonial period, not only in New Mexico but in the entire Southwestern Borderlands, was the category *gente de razón*, which meant literally "people of reason," or rational beings. There is a great deal of confusion among contemporary scholars over precisely what this label meant and to whom it applied. The category is best understood through its opposite, that is, *gente sin razón*, "people lacking reason," or irrational persons. The Holy Office of the Inquisition developed this legal distinction to protect neophyte Indians from prosecution for heretical ideas. Since Indians were *gente sin razón*, mere children lacking the rational faculties to understand the complexities of the faith, they could not be punished like *gente de razón*, rational individuals who fully understood the implications of their behavior. In time these two categories, rational and irrational, entered common parlance as ethnic signifiers, differentiating Spaniards from Indians.[38]

Spanish towns and Indian Pueblos during the 1600s were, by royal and ecclesiastical design, clearly distinct and spatially separated entities. With the entry into Spanish towns during the 1700s of *genízaros* as prisoners of war and Pueblo outcasts, the enemy was now within. This closer contact with Indians, which often took the form of illicit sexual liaisons, gave rise to increasing numbers of half-breeds. This in turn precipitated racial fears, particularly among New Mexico's aristocrats, who expressed concern over the pollution of their blood lines and the loss of honor. It was to make sense of these racial changes that legal color categories were increasingly used after the 1750s. By saying this, I do not mean to imply that racial concerns did not exist before. They did. It was just that in the 1600s the ethnic divisions in New Mexico were rather simple: One was either a Spaniard or an Indian, there being few intermediate hues. But as the Pueblo Indians were Christianized and miscegenation gave rise to individuals of mixed ancestry, the former religious foundation to definitions of race was no longer adequate to describe the changes under way. For this New Mexicans turned to central New Spain, whence they drew the legal color categories they were to recognize.

Before we examine what these categories were, bear in mind that they pose some rather complex interpretive problems. Sometimes a person's racial classification was the result of a personal declaration, at other times it was the subjective assessment of, say, a census taker. Priests and bureaucrats gave race differing amounts of significance and thus could classify the same person quite differently. The use of certain racial categories fluctuated enormously over time and from place to place. Aside from their legal definitions, we have little information concerning what racial classifications may or may not have meant in the routine of daily life. The racial labels introduced in New Mexico in 1598 remained fixed for several centuries though the meanings attached to them changed, as did the people who were classified as such. One only has to look at the word *mulato* to see this.

Professor John Nitti of the University of Wisconsin's Medieval Spanish Dictionary Project informs me that the word *mulato* initially meant a racial mixture of any sort. Offspring of Spaniards and Moors were known as *mulatos* in medieval Iberia, as were later mixtures between blacks and Indians, and between Frenchmen and Indians. Eventually *mulato* came to mean specifically a mixture between a black and a white. *Mulato* appears in New Mexican church records, though there is no evidence that the individuals classed as such had any black African ancestry. From 1700 to 1744, Fathers Junco and Maulanda listed all the baptisms at Cañada de Cochiti as Indians. After 1744 the same priests listed all Spanish baptisms as *mulatos*. *Mulato* in New Mexico simply meant an individual of mixed Spanish-Indian ancestry. Father Prada of Abiquiu gave the word this meaning in 1802 when he referred to his parishioners as "*indios mulatos.*"[39]

As we saw earlier, the two main cultural groups in New Mexico were

Spaniards and Pueblo Indians. Spaniards were classified by national origin as *español europeo, español,* or *español mexicano*. Indians were simply *indios*, though sometimes Indians of a particular nation were identified by language group. If an Indian spoke Spanish, he or she was an *indio ladino*. The term *genízaro* differentiated Pueblo Indians, referred to simply as "Indians," from detribalized Indian slaves living in Hispanic towns. The progeny of unions between Spaniards and Indians were known as *mestizos* or *mulatos*. Broader still, without specifying the nature or extent of racial mixture, was the label *color quebrado*, literally "broken color" or half-breed.

Two zoomorphic racial categories were used widely in colonial New Mexico to refer to the half-breed children of Indian slave women born in captivity—*coyote* and *lobo*. In many cases the slave's master was the child's father, a fact rarely admitted but suggested in baptismal registers as "father unknown." María Juliana, a servant in the household of María Soledad Chávez, was described as "one of those girls they call *coyotas*, the daughter of a Zuñi Indian woman." Pueblo, Apache, and Navajo animal myths portray the coyote and lobo as marginal animals, misfits obsessed by uncontrollable sexual desires and wanderlust. "Coyote is a death figure, probably for the simple reason that he feeds on dead things," writes Hamilton Tyler of Pueblo animal beliefs. Indian slaves were considered socially dead and marginal to both Pueblo and Spanish society. I suspect this is why the children of slaves were known as *coyotes*. This canine association probably also arose from the sexual aggressiveness of Indian women. The friars complained that Indian women preferred sexual intercourse in a "bestial fashion," in *more canino*, or in the way of dogs. Dogs were the only beasts of burden the Indians knew before the arrival of European livestock. One common way for Spaniards to dehumanize Indians and half-breeds was to hurl the epithet "dog" in combination with some other expletive: dirty dog, Indian dog, half-breed dog. The caciques of fourteen pueblos complained to the viceroy in 1707 that New Mexico's citizens were referring to them as dogs and demanding labor of them as such. When Diego Velásquez called the Indian slave Juan Trujillo an "Indian dog" in 1769, Juan retorted "you will pay for that you Spanish son-of-a-bitch." And he did. Juan drew his bow and shot an arrow into Velásquez's chest, nearly taking his life.[40]

Don Pedro Pino, New Mexico's representative to the 1812 Cortes at Cádiz, reported to that assembly that "In New Mexico there has never been known any caste of people of African origin. My province is probably the only one in Spanish America to enjoy such distinction." Don Pedro was patently wrong, but advanced the claim to validate a myth he wished to perpetuate, namely that New Mexico's nobility had preserved their honor and racial purity over the centuries. Had Don Pedro investigated the matter he would have discovered that Sebastián Rodríguez, "a Black from San Pablo de Luanda" in Angola, was Don Diego de Vargas's drummer during the 1692 reconquest of the kingdom. Francisco Rico, "a native Black from the Congo," was married in Santa Fe in 1697, as was Dominga de la Concepción, "a black slave," in 1705. The number of blacks in colonial New Mexico probably never totaled more than a dozen. By 1800 they had so interbred with the Indian and European-origin population that their former distinctiveness was no longer even remembered, or at least not by Don Pedro Pino and his clan.[41]

Theoretically, the children of interracial unions and liaisons were ranked hierarchically according to the degree of mixing between the races. A Spanish father and an Amerindian mother engendered a *mestizo* child. A Spaniard and a black woman begat a *mulato*. A *mestizo* and a Spanish woman produced a *castizo*, and so on. Although there were defined categories for every possible combination between Spaniard, Amerindian, and Black, only the most pronounced degrees of mixture were acknowledged.[42]

The racial labels recorded in New Mexico's legal dockets were perhaps as precise as frontier conditions marked by social fluidity permitted. There was no direct correspondence, except perhaps at the extreme ends of the classification scale, between race and actual physical color. A 1677 roster of colonists bound for New Mexico listed several as Spaniards who all looked very different. The *españoles* Juan Blanco and José López were described as having "fair skin," while José Cortez, Phelipe López García, and José de Alvarado had "dark complexions." Gaspar Luís and Juan González were listed as *mestizos*, yet in appearance they were identical to most of the *españoles*—they were "dark." In a 1766 document Juan Sandoval was listed as being "by appearance of white racial status." Julian Vigil's racial status was "*mestizo*, according to reputation." Joseph Baca was appointed militia lieutenant at Ojo Caliente in 1766 because "he is known as a white man." Racial categories (*español, mestizo, mulato*) were sometimes used interchangeably with descriptions of physical color (*blanco, pardo, prieto*), though the latter had no real definition in law. Comments that a person "appeared to be," "was reputed to be," or "was known to be" of a certain race indicated the degree to which racial mixing and passing existed on this remote fringe of northern New Spain and complicated the classification system.[43]

The Chilean sociologist, Alejandro Lipschütz, called the racial system that developed in Spanish America a "pigmentocracy," because honor, status, and prestige were judged by skin color and phenotype. The whiter one's skin, the greater was one's claim to the honor and precedence Spaniards expected and received. The darker a person's skin, the closer one was presumed to be to the physical labor of slaves and tributary Indians, and the closer the visual association with the infamy of the conquered. In Spain families guarded their *limpieza de sangre* or blood purity through avoidance of Moors and Jews. In New Mexico, families of aristocratic pretension feared that their bloodlines might be metaphysically polluted by Indians, *mulatos*, and, as one man put it, "castes which are held or reputed as despicable in this kingdom."[44]

The nobility and landed peasantry thought of half-breeds as despicable because of the presumption that they were of illegitimate birth. Indeed, many of them were. Throughout the eighteenth century high levels of illegitimacy occurred in Hispanic settlements because of the sexual exploitation of female slaves and *criados*. One New Mexican friar complained in the 1730s that it was not uncommon for slave owners to boast that "fornicating with servants is good so that they do not seek men." Fray Joseph Manuel de Equía y Leronbe, Nambé's pastor, wondered whether it was not total hypocrisy for him to "free the Indians from their heathen existence" only to enslave them with the stigma of illegitimacy. He wrote in 1734:

They claim that by selling Apache Indians into slavery they will be redeemed from their lives as infidels. What benefit is it to condemn them so that they do not live as infidels? Enslave them so that they do not have freedom? I said condemn them and I can prove it. I have not baptized the child of an Indian woman servant who was not a *coyote* with father unknown, as the registers will certify. The masters of these Indian women are constantly vigilant so that they do not escape and so that they do not marry.[45]

The baptismal registers bore the friar out. Between 1693 and 1848, 176 infants were recorded as born to Indian slaves and baptized. Of these, 144, or 82 percent, were illegitimate. Similar results were found in marriage heredity declarations. Of the 7,128 persons who declared their birth status, 3,349 said that they were illegitimate—a number that accounts for approximately 25 percent of all persons officially married. Admittedly, heredity declarations at marriage underrepresent the true level of illegitimacy. Individuals could, and often did, lie about their ancestry because illegitimacy was a mark of dishonor. The level of reported bastardy was highest among *genízaros* who did not marry and lived in concubinage. Aristocrats maintained mistresses and/or sexually exploited their slaves but rarely admitted fathering illegitimate children. As Fray Equía y Leronbe noted, such children were listed in baptismal registers as "father unknown."[46]

A strong statistical association was found between the number of

TABLE 5.2

Numbers of Slave Baptisms and of Illegitimate Children, by Place, 1700-1849

Place	1700-1749		1750-74		1775-99		1800-1824		1825-49	
	Slave baptisms	Illegitimate children	Slave baptisms	Illegitimate children	Slave baptisms	Illegitimate children	Slave baptisms	Illegitimate children	Slave baptisms	Illegitimate children
Spanish settlements north of Santa Fe	331	83	68	138	209	174	274	527	289	154
Santa Fe	6	81	41	25	142	14	140	4	48	—
Spanish settlements east of Santa Fe	32	—	10	—	15	—	40	—	21	—
Spanish settlements between Santa Fe and Albuquerque	97	15	67	17	61	22	109	30	45	16
Albuquerque	145	14	9	4	48	—	29	—	57	—
Spanish settlements west of Albuquerque	44	—	136	—	86	—	69	—	32	—
Spanish settlements south of Albuquerque	115	158	20	125	97	345	161	1076	144	280

SOURCE: AASF-*DM* Reels 60-79; Brugge, *Navajos.*

slave baptisms in New Mexico between 1700 and 1849 and the number of illegitimate children born during these years (Spearman's correlation coefficient 0.86, significant to the .01 level; see Table 5.2). Spearman's correlation coefficient ranges from 0, meaning no statistical association, to 1, a perfect association. Spearman's correlation coefficient was 0.41 between 1700 and 1749, 0.16 between 1750 and 1774, 0.66 between 1775 and 1799, 0.88 between 1800 and 1824, and 0.66 between 1825 and 1849. The years when slave raiding was highest, 1775 to 1824, were also years during which the number of Indian slaves entering Hispanic settlements was closely associated with high levels of illegitimacy. These results are explained by the fact that bondage made it difficult for slaves to establish stable unions. Since Indian slaves owned little moveable property, there was no legal or social reason for them to be concerned for the legitimation of their progeny. Sacramental marriage was itself a symbol of social status, a sign of honor that was unavailable to slaves.

One only has to examine the sexual history of an Indian slave named Melchora Martín to see how the generative capacities of thralls reproduced the labor force and swelled the ranks of the illegitimate. Melchora's story begins in 1731 when Manuel Martín married Elena Roybal and established a household near the Spanish settlement of San Juan. Shortly after his marriage Martín purchased an Indian slave, and three years later she bore Martín's child, named Melchora. Melchora was reared in Martín's home and sometime around 1761 herself gave birth to an illegitimate baby girl, "father unknown." Manuel Martín may have impregnated Melchora; she would not say, although she did not hesitate to name the fathers of her other children. Around 1763 María Martín, Manuel's legitimate daughter, married Salvador García. Melchora and her daughter were given to the newlyweds as a wedding present. In the García household Melchora bore two more illegitimate children, a daughter and a son. Joseph Antonio García, Salvador García's brother, fathered the daughter. Joseph Luján, himself the bastard servant of San Juan's chief constable, Don Manuel Parejas, fathered Melchora's son.

María Martín fell ill and died, and when Salvador García remarried, Manuel Martín demanded Melchora's return. A few days after Melchora and her children were reinstated in Martín's home, Juan Sandoval asked for her hand in marriage. Melchora wanted to marry Juan, with whom she had become intimate while both were servants of Salvador García. Sandoval's father opposed the marriage, and shortly thereafter Melchora bore her fourth illegitimate child.

Manuel Martín was furious that Juan Sandoval had broken his promise of marriage to Melchora, and ordered his former son-in-law, Salvador, to rid himself of Sandoval's services. Julian Vigil became Salvador García's new servant, and hardly a year had gone by before Melchora gave birth again; the father was Julian Vigil. Manuel Martín was so angry with Melchora over this last birth that he severely beat her. Melchora sought succor from the ecclesiastical judge, and the complaint she launched against her master for mistreatment in 1766 brought this story to light. Manuel Martín admitted that he had repeatedly chastised Melchora, but "because of her perverse untamable inclination the whippings were not enough to contain or to correct her." Melchora was placed in a good Christian home "so that she can be subjected and contained." Her children were left in Manuel Martín's custody, and one can only wonder whether they fell prey to the same misfortunes that characterized their mother's life.[47]

Church and state officials saw concubinage as the standard form that interracial sexual relations took. Consequently, persons of mixed origin were automatically presumed to be illegitimate. The Spanish legal theorist Juan de Solórzano Pereira, writing about mestizos and mulattos, noted that "generally they are born in adultery and other ugly and illicit unions, because there are few Spaniards of honor who marry Indians or Negroes. This defect of their birth makes them infamous, to which are added the stain of different color and other vices." For Solórzano, illegitimacy, racial mixture, and infamy were synonymous. The first edition of the *Diccionario de la Academia Española*, published in 1737, reached a similar conclusion. "*Raza*" (race) meant "caste or racial status of origin. When speaking of persons, it usually means illegitimacy. Also, stain or dishonor of the lineage."[48]

Mixed physical color was a sign of illegitimate birth associated with illicit sexual unions. The racially mixed progeny who resulted from concubinage and adultery ultimately led to the blurring of phenotypic characteristics in the population, and this, particularly after the 1760s, necessitated a stricter racial classification of the population. Without such categories, the aristocracy's claims of racial purity and honor had no significance.

Throughout colonial Spanish America, race functioned as a metalanguage: with few exceptions, a person's occupation and status were often quickly deduced by simple appearance. For such visual evaluations of race to be correct, a close correlation had to exist between all the constituting elements of racial definition: legal color, actual physical color, and phenotype. When such a correspondence existed, it meant that in the daily life of a face-to-face community, race was a visual metonymic sign of a person's position in the social division of labor, symbolic of a propinquity to the infidel, or in the case of slaves, their dishonor and social death.

Only one documentary source on the relationship between race and occupation in colonial New Mexico exists, the 1790 census of the kingdom. Table 5.3 presents an analysis of this relationship. Heads of households were classified by occupation only at Albuquerque, Santa Fe, and Santa Cruz. Persons classified as Spaniards were predominately farmers. Forty percent of all *mestizos* were day laborers, 33 percent were farmers, and 23 percent were artisans. *Color quebrados* were primarily farmers. One half-breed was listed as a rancher owing to the large amount of land he owned. He was an exception, for 95 percent of all ranchers were Spanish. Among mixed-blood men (i.e., *mestizos, castizos, color quebrados*), *mestizos* showed the greatest occupational variability, with sizeable proportions working as day laborers, farmers, and artisans.

Genízaros were primarily artisans (blacksmiths, silversmiths, masons, carders, spinners, weavers). Some *genízaro* ex-slaves had acquired land by 1790, and thus 21 percent of them were listed as farmers. Similarly, because of their knowledge both of the local terrain and of the languages of the hostile Indians who surrounded the Rio Grande Valley, *genízaros* were increasingly employed as interpreters, guides, and muleteers. Muleteers were petty entrepreneurs who owned the mules on which they transported goods. If a person did not own his mules and simply drove someone else's, the mule driver was listed as a day laborer. Indians residing in Albuquerque, Santa Fe, and Santa Cruz were primarily artisans (weavers); three out of ten were day laborers, and a couple were listed as farmers.

A statistical analysis of the relationship between race and occupation in the 1790 census revealed that at Albuquerque and Santa Cruz the occupations Spaniards held were significantly different from those of mixed-blood men (Albuquerque, chi-squared 57.5 with 4 degrees of freedom, probability .0001; Santa Cruz, chi-squared 79.8 with 1 degree of freedom, probability .0001). Spanish men were primarily ranchers and farmers while mixed-blood men and *genízaros* were farmers, day laborers, and servants. In Santa Fe no relationship was found between race and occupation in 1790 (chi-squared 3.6 with 2 degrees of freedom, probability 0.164).

Aside from somatic evaluations of race, clothing and hair styles were also rather pronounced signs of one's position in the social structure. In a kingdom where Indians were easily identified by the loincloths and shawls that barely concealed their nakedness, dress revealed one's status and

TABLE 5.3

Racial Composition of Occupational Groups in New Mexico, 1790

Occupational Group	Spanish		Mestizo		Castizo		Color Quebrado		Genízaro		Indian		Total	
	No.	Pct.	No.	Pct.	No.	Pct.	No.	Pct.	No.	Pct.	No.	Pct.	No.	Pct.
Rancher	21	3.1%	—	—	—	—	1	1.9%	—	—	—	—	22	2.1%
Farmer	467	69.6	86	33.2	1	7.1	35	64.8	8	21.1	2	15.4	599	57.1
Merchant	1	0.2	—	—	—	—	—	—	—	—	—	—	1	0.1
Artisan	84	12.5	61	23.6	7	50.0	13	24.0	14	36.8	7	53.8	186	17.7
Muleteer	—	—	2	0.8	—	—	2	3.7	3	7.9	—	—	7	0.6
Shepherd	1	0.2	5	1.9	2	14.3	—	—	2	5.3	—	—	10	1.0
Day laborer	94	14.0	104	40.1	4	28.6	3	5.6	11	28.9	4	30.8	220	21.0
Servant	—	—	1	0.4	—	—	—	—	—	—	—	—	1	0.1
Other	3	0.4	—	—	—	—	—	—	—	—	—	—	3	0.3
Total	671	100.0%	259	100.0%	14	100.0%	54	100.0%	38	100.0%	13	100.0%	1049	100.0%

SOURCE: SA, Reel 12: 319-502.

one's honor. Governor Pedro Fermín de Mendinueta, a cosmopolitan and well-traveled man, marvelled that nowhere had he seen a people more preoccupied with external appearances, trappings of honor, and clothes than in New Mexico. "These people are so materialistic," wrote Mendinueta in 1768, "that only outward appearances impress them." As residents in Spanish towns, Indian slaves often appeared before the civil courts demanding proper clothes. María Francesca, a Cochiti Indian, killed her husband Agustín de Jirón because he had failed to fulfill his marriage promise that he would clothe María as a Spaniard for her life off the pueblo. The lack of a proper "Spanish" dress, shoes, and shawl was so humiliating that she finally took justice into her own hands. Agustín's end came one warm afternoon in 1773 as he dozed on his wife's lap while being deloused. María Francesca tied her belt around Agustín's neck and strangled him. As Agustín struggled and gasped for air, María's mother repeatedly thrust a knife into his chest.[49]

Hair style, too, particularly among women, was a sign of social status and ethnic identity. The Piro Indians wore their hair in a braid that hung down the back of the neck. The Southern Tiwa had skullcap hairdos. The Queres plaited their hair and cut it in front, and Hopi maidens wore it in large puffs. Spanish maidens also wore their hair in braids. When Camilia Montaño decided to leave her parents and home in Placitas in 1830 for life in bustling Bernalillo, she forsook her braids for something more stylish and becoming. Gone too were the drab black dresses the women in her village wore. She dressed herself in brightly colored clothes and started to accentuate her figure by fastening sashes around her waist. Camilia's husband did not take kindly to all of this and one day killed her, laying her head open with a stone machete. And perhaps one of the most potent symbols of social dishonor, because of its sexual connotations, was to be scalped or deprived of head hair. When Don Francisco Armijo felt his wife had dishonored him in 1816 by lacking sexual restraint, he cut off her braids and hurled them at his mother-in-law.[50]

Both at the level of official ideology as articulated in legal dictionaries and statutes, and in the declarations of aristocrats concerning the basis of their nobility, a person's social status—*calidad*—was a summation of various measures of social worth within the community: religion, race, ethnicity, legitimacy, occupation, and ownership of land. How these various statuses interacted, at least at the level of action, was poignantly revealed when men uttered indecorous words and verbally abused each other.

The fiercest fighting words one could utter were slurs impugning a person's total social personality—one's race, ancestry, and position in the division of labor. On June 3, 1765, for example, Eusebio Chávez beat his father-in-law, Andrés Martín, with a large stick and dragged him by his hair, leaving Andrés's arm badly bruised, his chest covered with welts, his scalp swollen, and his hair completely tangled and caked in blood. The reason was that Martín had called Chávez a "*perro mulato hijo de puta*" ("mixed-blood dog son of a whore"). Chávez claimed that the fight and insults occurred because Martín had flooded his fields on four different occasions, preventing him from completing his spring planting. When Chávez confronted his father-in-law, asking why he had again flooded his fields, Martín verbally abused him and lunged at him with a stick. The two fought, but Martín was no match for his young son-in-law. The two eventually were reconciled and all charges were dropped. Nonetheless, the governor ordered Chávez to kneel at the feet of his father-in-law and, before an assembly of Albuquerque's citizens, beg his public forgiveness "for having lacked in the respect owed [Andrés Martín] due to his age and the dignity of being his father-in-law." [51]

In another case, Manuel Valerio of Santa Cruz struck Juan Antonio Salazar on the head with a shovel, creating a wound that was "three fingers long and one finger wide." The 1745 fracas began because, claimed Salazar, "Valerio injured my fame with indecorous words calling me a cuckold, *mulato*, and other things." Before the chief constable Valerio admitted that his insulting words had indeed precipitated the fight with Salazar. The two eventually were reconciled when Valerio apologized to Salazar for wounding him and for having defamed him with such foul words. The constable ordered them to live in peace, and there apparently the matter ended. [52]

In this chapter we have seen how the Spanish colonists in New Mexico defined their social status and basis for preferment in society through the concept of honor. Honor was a complex measure of social status based on one's religion, ethnicity, race, occupation, ancestry, and authority over land. Spaniards reveled in their honor only because they lived among *genízaros* who were dishonored by their enslavement, and among the Pueblo Indians who had been vanquished in defeat. Thus much of what it meant to be honorable was a projection of what it meant to be a free, landholding citizen of white legitimate ancestry, and by contrast what it meant not to be a slave, an outcast, or an Indian.

We began this chapter with the story of La Constancia, and of how she lost her honor-virtue through an alleged sexual infidelity, and how she won honor-status through military defeats. It is to the topic of honor-virtue that we now turn.

6

Honor and Virtue

On a cold November night in 1726, Catharina de los Ríos of Santa Fe lay sick in bed, feverish, delirious, her body totally covered with a pox-like rash. Fearing that death was near, and wishing to die with a clear conscience, she summoned Fray Francisco Romero, the local representative of the Inquisition, to confess her sins and to denounce herself and her paramour, Francisco Montes Vigil, for the sins of heresy, blasphemy, and the desecration of sacred images. Catharina thought that her sickness was God's punishment for her *desvergonzada conducta*, her shameless conduct. The priest arrived and Catharina recounted the following story. On several nights, some ten years earlier, she and Francisco had consumed large amounts of corn brandy and under its influence had undressed and engaged in the carnal act. At the point of ecstasy Francisco had blasphemed the name of the Almighty, uttering heretical words by shouting: "I am God and my pleasure is even better than if I were in heavenly glory." The desecration of the sacred images occurred after coitus, when Francisco asked Catharina to remove the rosary and medals she wore around her neck and placed them in her *partes vergonzosas* (shameful parts). Catharina had never confessed this *deshonor* (dishonor) because she feared reprisals from Francisco. He had told her that their acts were not a sin, and if she confessed them he would have her exiled from New Mexico. Fearing him, Catharina never complained until the day she thought eternity was at hand.[1]

   Don Francisco Armijo arrived at the Albuquerque home of his mother-in-law. Doña María Antonia Durán, in a very agitated mood at about nine in the evening of March 12, 1816. In one hand he had his whip, in the other a knife. He demanded to see his wife, Doña María Rosalía Maestas, who had been staying with her mother while he was out of town. When his wife entered the room Don Francisco began whipping her violently. He threw her to the floor, put his foot on her throat, and with the knife cut off her braids and hair. Don Francisco hurled the braids at his mother-in-law and dragged his wife out of the house. Why such violent treatment? Don Francisco said that it was "to protect my honor." He had heard that during his absence Juan García had propositioned his wife to adultery, giving her two sheep as a present, and had taken her in his carriage to the fiesta at Los Ranchos. For this Doña María Rosalía had brought scandal to his reputation "because she will not live in seclusion . . . she is shameless." [2]

What do these two examples have in common? The language employed to express the most intimate violations of self-integrity is what is important here. When Catharina de los Ríos wanted to repent for the shameless conduct that had dishonored her, when Francisco Montes Vigil desecrated the Christian images by placing them in Catharina's shameful parts, when Don Francisco Armijo complained that his wife was shameless and whipped her and cut off her hair to guard her honor, they were expressing the basic tenets of what Spaniards said constituted a virtuous life. The nexus between personal public behavior and a social structure predicated on conquest and force was provided by honor and shame, the values that most fundamentally defined virtue in colonial New Mexico. In the last chapter we explored the meaning of honor-status. Here we will examine honor-virtue, focusing on what it meant in ideal terms and how individuals reconciled that ideal with behavior when honor had been lost through seduction.

The Boundaries of Virtue

If honor-status was an award for valorous conduct, its maintenance over time, especially if it had been inherited from one's father through ascription, depended on honor-virtue. Honor-virtue divided society horizontally by status groups, and within each group it determined the pecking order of persons in the status hierarchy according to reputation, that is, their reproduction of ideals of proper social conduct. The order of precedence to which peers submitted and their willingness to validate a claim to pride depended totally on their evaluation of the person's behavior according to established community norms. Since precedence at the upper levels of the social order guaranteed control over more resources and power, it was usually among the aristocracy and elites that the most intense conflicts over honor-virtue occurred. The vendetta and lineage feuds were typical of the fights in which men engaged to avenge sullied reputations and claims to virtue.

Honor as virtue was an attribute of individuals and of corporate groups. When speaking of personal honor, it was considered a state of conscience that elevated the person's actions above reproach. If a person's intentions were honorable, it was irrelevant what others might think. This focus on intentions gave honor an aspect of personal autonomy that was displayed particularly in the desire to preside over others.[3]

Honor also belonged collectively to one's family and to one's kindred as a group. *Dime con quien andas y te dire quien eres*, the Spanish proverb held: tell me with whom you walk and I will tell you who you are. The patriarch of a family or household was responsible for the actions of all of his dependents. The conduct of children reflected on the father. Transgressions were perceived by others as signs of poor familial socialization. The honor of one reflected on all, just as the dishonor of one tarnished all.

Honor-virtue prescribed gender-specific rules of proper social comportment. Honor (*honor*) was strictly a male attribute while shame (*vergüenza*) was intrinsic to females. Infractions of behavioral norms by males were dishonoring, in females they were a sign of shamelessness. The shamelessness of a female reflected on the male head of the household and dishonored him and the family as a group. Honor and shame were synonymous at certain levels of definition. Men were honorable if they esteemed honesty and loyalty and were concerned for their reputation and that of their family. Women embodied the sentiment of shame and were considered honorable if they cherished these same values.[4]

Honor and *vergüenza* promoted conduct among men and women that was believed to spring from intrinsic natural qualities. Women displayed *vergüenza* when they were sexually pure and displayed the utmost discretion around men. *Vergüenza* brought a blush to a woman's face when lewd matters were discussed and called for timidity around men. Nature too was the source of a man's *honor*. Men were honorable if they acted with *hombría* (manliness) and exerted authority over their family. Both in males and females these ethically valued qualities were rooted in sexual physiology.

The *miembro*, the virile member or penis, produced masculinity and *hombría*. Men were legally impotent without it. In 1781 Jacinta Trujillo of Abiquiu demanded an annulment to her eight-day-old marriage with Antonio Choño, because he was like a woman, "totally lacking a member." An emasculated man was referred to as *manso*, meaning meek, gentle, humble, and lamblike. *Manso* was also the word used to signify a castrated animal or person. New Mexico's Indians were conquered and made *mansos* by a technique for which Fray Nicolás Hidalgo was renowned. In 1638 the friar beat Pedro Acomilla of Taos Pueblo and grabbed him "by the member and twisted it so much that it broke in half." Asensio, a Nambé Indian, did not lose his penis in his confrontation with Baltasar Baca, but his humiliation was just as emasculating. Asensio found Baca stealing four of his watermelons one day in 1743, and because he tried to stop him, Baca grabbed Asensio by the virile member and twisted it until he fainted from the pain.[5]

Some Spanish men even equated penis size with virility and manliness. In 1606, Gaspar Reyes found himself sick and destitute. Hoping to secure charity from the local Franciscan friars, he begged for food at their residence. A certain Fray Pedro took him in and fed him lavishly with a meal, which even included wine. When Gaspar was finished eating, the friar "stuck his hand in my pants, took my virile member and wriggled it . . . and said to me, yours is small, mine is bigger." The priest then took Gaspar to his cell where he tried to use his posterior for a nefarious end. To be buggered was a symbolic sign of defeat equated with femininity; to bugger was an assertion of dominance and masculinity. It was thus not insignificant that it was a priest who was concerned about penis size and actively tried to sodomize Gaspar. Any man who did not assert his sexuality and preferred abstinence or sexual purity ran the risk of being labeled tame, assumed castrated, and thereby lacking the necessary appendage of honor.[6]

If masculinity and honor were dependent on the virile member, femininity and shame were located in the *partes vergonzozas*, the shameful parts. Antonia García of Santa Fe complained to the Inquisition in 1725 that Fray Francisco Romero had solicited sex from her in the confessional "with evil caresses to my shameful parts." Marcos Sánchez of Tomé savagely beat his concubine Manuela Carrillo in 1793 because he had heard that she was sleeping with another man. Marcos confronted Manuela about this one night and tried to force himself on her. Manuela resisted, and because she did, testified Manuela's mother, "he threw her to the floor, spread open her legs and scratched her shameful parts, and then he took his pouch of tobacco and emptied it on her parts and then rubbed them with dirt."[7]

The ultimate sign of female physiological purity was the intact maidenhead, an ideal perhaps only maintained by nuns, the symbolic brides of Christ, and Mary, the Mother of Christ, who conceived without the loss of her virginity. One incredulous New Mexican who dared to question Mary's purity was pursued by the Inquisition for propositions contrary to the Catholic Faith. Don Francisco Paris of Santa Fe was reputed to have said of the Virgin Mary in 1804: "a virgin! How can she be a virgin? A woman once she conceives cannot be a virgin."[8]

If a woman lost her maidenhood, she also lost the natural and ethical qualities that stemmed from it. In 1725, Manuela Armijo of Santa Fe protested to the ecclesiastical judge that Juan Lovato "took my virginity and cleanliness with a promise of marriage." Lovato admitted, "It is true that I violated the virginity, purity and honesty of Manuela Armijo, but it was not with a promise of marriage."[9]

Because honor and shame were so closely tied to self-conceptions, concern over honor-virtue was often represented through body symbolism. The head, the heart, the blood, and the genitalia figured prominently when honor was discussed. A person's head was the symbol of personal and collective honor. The king's honor was exhibited through a crowned head, the honor of the bishop through his miter. Honor and precedence were paid by bowing one's head, by taking off one's hat, or (for women) by covering their heads. Decapitation was a particularly dishonorable punishment because it was believed that honor surrounded the head. Honor challenges were frequently initiated through a slap to the face. Manuel Martín of San Juan punished his daughter for bearing an illegitimate child in 1766 by cutting off all her hair. A bald head signified her shamelessness to the community. Catholic priests cut a tonsure in their hair as a sign of their vow of chastity and pledge to sexual purity.[10]

The heart was the organ through which personal desires and conscience were experienced. "I wish to marry for no other reason than to serve God and because it comes forth from my heart, without it being the result of any other motivation," said Sebastiana de la Serna of her 1715 marriage bid. Concupiscence sprang from the heart, said Fray José de la Prada. Writing the governor of New Mexico concerning the sexual laxity of his congregation, Prada complained that "their customs and heathen wantonness have sunk very deep roots into their hearts." In a sermon on lust another friar warned his congregation of the metabolic repercussions of an unregulated heart. "It is from the heart that we must displace this monster of sensuality . . . it is the cause of so many sudden deaths, infectious disease, and numerous maladies of the liver." It was through the heart too that one experienced the operations of conscience. When one's word of honor was given to another, the word was deemed sealed in the heart.[11]

Blood was the essence of life and the vehicle through which honor was perpetuated. "Stains of honor are only cleansed by blood," a Spanish aristocratic motto asserted. "Blood is the soap of honor," another proverb held. In colonial New Mexico, the racial preoccupations of the nobility were expressed through their concern for their purity of blood. To assure that their blood was not metaphysically polluted they guarded against marriage with dishonored and infamous persons—Indians and slaves. Don Andrés Luján and Doña Juana Vigil of Valencia, New Mexico, as late as 1837 expressed the belief that freedom from blood contamination was the basis of their honor. Seeking an episcopal dispensation for their proposed incestuous marriage, they argued: "Our families have always maintained themselves clean and with honor, not mixing with castes their purity of blood."[12]

Earlier, when we explored Pueblo gender concepts, we saw that the process of plant germination was symbolically equated with human generation. The sky fructified the earth with rain as men their wives with semen. Sky and earth were relatively equal and fundamentally dependent on each other. New Mexico's Spaniards also likened the earth to females and furrows to their genitals. The germination process in which men engaged through plowing and planting was similar to the penis's function in insemination. The Latin etymology of the verb "to sow" and the noun "season" was the verb *serere*, which as a noun also meant "semen." Sexual intercourse was a fertility ritual. The phallus was like a plowshare creating furrows in the female earth. The woman below on her back spread open her legs, the man from above inserted the penis as he would the plow into the ground for the implantation of seeds. Tomás Sánchez, the seventeenth-century Spanish theologian, in his *De sancto matrimonii sacramento*, proposed that nature itself prescribed this sexual position. "We must first of all establish what is the natural manner of intercourse as far as position is concerned. . . . The man must lie on top and the woman on her back beneath. Because this manner is more appropriate for the effusion of the male seed, for its reception into the female vessel." The different gender roles that Spanish and Pueblo women were allowed was poignantly revealed when Sánchez railed about the *mulier supra virum* (woman above man) coital position. "This method [of intercourse] is absolutely contrary to the order of nature," wrote Sánchez:

It is natural for the man to act and for the woman to be passive; and if the man is beneath, he becomes submissive by the very fact of his position, and the woman being above is active; and who cannot see how much nature herself abhors this mutation? Because in scholastic history it is said that the cause of the flood was that women, carried away by madness, used men improperly, the latter being beneath and the former above.[13]

Every society prescribes the scope of behavior appropriate for each gender. Colonial New Mexican society was no different. There, the values of honor and shame defined the acceptable acts men and women could undertake. The sentiment of shame that prescribed female sexual purity was appropriate only to women. Men of honor enforced female purity in mother, wife, daughters, and sisters, and protected it from assault. Concurrently, though, men enhanced their honor through the conquest of another man's woman. It was precisely in this contradiction that positioning in the virtue hierarchy occurred. Precedence was determined by how these two imperatives, female sexual protection within the family and sexual conquest over other women, were reconciled.

Because God had created woman as the weaker of the sexes and rendered her helpless before the desires of men, male authority enforced through seclusion was one way to guarantee female virtue and maintenance of the family's honor. Doña María Luisa de Aragón of Tomé expressed a correlate of this conception of the female when she lamented in 1766 that her married daughter had conceived a child from an adulterous liaison while her husband was absent in Mexico City. Doña María stated, "My daughter had that unfortunate frailty to which all of the feminine sex are exposed." Frailty to the ploys of men and the desires of the flesh meant that it was necessary to seclude women to protect their virtue. Men could win and enhance their honor through action, but a woman's virtue was something that could not be won, only maintained or lost. For this reason Juana Trujillo's parents kept her public contacts to a minimum. In 1705 she refused to talk to a friend she encountered in Santa Fe's plaza while running errands with her brother because "I feared that they would beat me at home particularly if my brother told my parents that he left me talking." Governor Bernardo López de Mendizábal in 1663 said that he cared for the purity of his female servants by keeping them in a bedroom adjacent to his, with access only through his room. The women entered the governor's bedroom as they wished, even when Mendizábal and his wife were in bed. The male servants had strict orders that when they came to the room they should speak from the door but not enter. A friend advised Francisca de Salazar in 1702 that if she wanted to protect her daughter Juana's virginity she should keep her always behind locked doors.[14]

A double standard existed with regard to social behavior. Don Agustín Durán of Santa Fe cogently expressed these different expectations in male and female conduct. In a note to the vicar of the province on December 20, 1845, opposing the marriage of a son José to his sister-in-law, Doña María Solomé Ortiz, on the grounds of incest, Durán wrote:

The intimate relations between the two houses, the great physical difficulties which deter the father from watching over his daughters [the father of Doña María was described as a very old and blind widower], and the familiarity between my son and Doña María, may be the cause of unfortunate consequences. Were it up to me I would put an end to this so as not to cause damage, but I am forced to accept the natural facts: my son is a man and it is not possible to keep him in seclusion like a woman. This being the case, what am I to do?

Men could not be secluded because domination and conquest were essential qualities of masculinity necessary to safeguard family honor.[15]

A sexually shameless woman who had dishonored her husband or her father could in no way restore or avenge her honor. Only a man could do that. The folktale "La Constancia," with which we began our discussion of honor-status in the last chapter, splendidly makes this point. Recall that after Constancia lost her honor because of an alleged act of adultery, she had to transform herself into a man, donning armor and killing all the infidel Moors possible in order to restore that honor. The story of "La Constancia" also vividly illustrates the relationship between honor-status and honor-virtue. When José María believed that his wife's virtue had been taken, he forfeited his own honor. That honor was avenged and restored only after displays of military prowess had been rewarded anew by the king with honor-status.

Honor-virtue was militantly protected, fiercely contested, and rather scandalously lost. An exaggerated moral code for personal public behavior based on honor developed among New Mexico's Spanish colonists because the social and legal institutions that would have provided society an orderly tenor were absent on this remote frontier where might was right. Given the exploitative nature of class relations in the colony, the assorted amalgam that constituted society, and the absence of law and order, it was through principles of familial government, through ideas of personal and familial worth and good conduct, that a semblance of hierarchy and cohesiveness was maintained.

Understandably, then, consensus existed among New Mexico's colonists regarding what sort of behavior was virtuous and worthy of honor. Men of the nobility and landed peasantry alike were concerned for their personal and familial repute. They judged honor by how well they resolved the contradictory imperatives of domination (protection of one's womenfolk from assault) and conquest (prowess gained through sullying the purity of other men's women), and how they minimized affronts to their own virtue, so as to maintain their own honor-status intact. Female seclusion and a high symbolic value placed on virginity and marital fidelity were essential for this aim.

Yet only in aristocratic households, where servants and retainers abounded, could resources be expended to assure that females were being properly restrained. The maintenance of virtue among aristocratic fe-males was possible only because Indian and *genízaro* women could be forced or persuaded to offer sexual service. Slaves were dishonored by their bondage, lacked familial ties to the community, and could therefore be abused without fear of retaliation. For as one friar lamented in his 1734 report to the viceroy, Spanish New Mexicans justified raping such women by saying: "an Indian does not care if you fornicate with his woman because she has no shame." [16]

The landed peasantry prized honor-virtue just as much as the nobility because it signified participation in the values and ideals of Spanish so-ciety. No matter how lowly the peasant, he prided himself on being a Spaniard and thereby a player in the game of honor. Like men of the no-bility, his sport was the conquest of Indian and *genízaro* women, his boast, the capacity to maintain the purity of his own women intact. Manuel Alvarez, the United States Consul in Santa Fe, astutely observed this phenomenon in 1834 when he wrote, "the honorable man (if it is possible for a poor man to be honorable) has a jewel in having an honor-able wife." [17]

The peasantry undoubtedly had to reconcile gender prescriptions with the exigencies of production and reproduction. The required partici-pation of all able-bodied household members at planting and harvest meant that there were periods when constraints on females of this class were less rigorously enforced. Juana Carrillo of Santa Fe admitted as much in 1712, when she confessed enjoying the affections of two men her father had hired for the spring planting. In households where men were frequently absent, such as those of soldiers, muleteers, shepherds, and hunters, cultural ideals were necessarily less rigid. The fact that females married to such men had to supervise family and home by themselves for large parts of the year, stave off Indian attacks, and care for the group's public rights meant that it was difficult for them to lead sheltered and secluded lives. Indeed, it was not uncommon to hear these women lament that they had been assaulted, raped, or seduced while their husbands or fathers were away from home. [18]

Seduction: The Conflict Between Status and Virtue

The preceding discussion of what honor and shame meant to men and women was culled largely from civil and ecclesiastical court cases. Such conflictive situations established the definition of the ideal, and just how far it could be pushed before the authorities responded. To see how the honor code functioned in action, let us turn to seductions to illustrate how honor was won and lost through access to female sexuality.

Seductions in colonial New Mexico followed a rather standard pattern. A young man would begin courtship by gaining the attention of a girl, sending her flowers or love notes, serenading her, or simply giving her affectionate glances from a distance, a wink and a smile at a dance. After she was sufficiently knowledgeable of his attractions and had reciprocated with trust, he would usually take advantage of the confidence, and by promising marriage would satisfy his desires. The discovery of the illicit sexual act was likely only if pregnancy resulted, or if the man reneged on his promise and tried to marry someone else. Then a whole range of actions was possible, depending on the particular circumstances and the status of the individuals involved. The seducer, the seduced woman, and the parents and families of both had differing and sometimes contradictory interests to protect. Let us see how each acted to preserve, enhance, or recoup their honor.

When a man's daughter was seduced she was considered shameless. Her shamelessness dishonored her father and family as a whole. The verdict of public opinion or the family's reputation and honor depended on the father's riposte. The absence of a response to an affront was dishonorable and socially negative. If a man admitted his weakness and humiliation and did not contest the defilement of his property and of his honor, he became a cuckold in the community's eyes.

The most desirable way for a father to restore his honor and that of his sullied daughter was to demand marriage. If the seducer kept his word of honor and married the woman, the honor-virtue that she left exposed through seduction was thereby restored. If no one publicized the matter, the reputation of the woman and the honor-status of her family would not be decreased. For example, María del Rosario Martín of San Juan in 1785 discovered that she had been impregnated by her lover Mariano Sánchez. María pleaded passionately before the ecclesiastical judge—for her parents were dead—that in justice Mariano should fulfill his promise of marriage. She recounted how one of Mariano's brothers had also seduced, impregnated, and under parental counsels abandoned a woman. María rightfully feared that "it can be presumed that his father wants to do with me as he did with the already mentioned daughter-in-law, and seeing that I must protect my honor and that of my family, and if this matter is not resolved not only will I remain dishonored, but it is also possible that my brothers will take my life, an attempt they have already made." Bowing to familial pressure, Mariano finally married María.[19]

When the social distance between a male and his pregnant lover was too great, the maintenance of family honor-status was deemed to be more important than restoring the honor-virtue of the woman through marriage. The marriage of an aristocrat and a peasant woman could only bring dishonor upon his family, for ideally marriage was a sign of equality. Mexican clerics inquired of the Crown in 1752 what their policy should be when seduction occurred between partners of widely disparate status. The response came in an order stating the following:

> If the maiden seduced under promise of marriage is inferior in status, so that she would cause greater dishonor to his lineage if he married her than the one that would fall on her by remaining seduced (as when for instance a Duke, Count, Marquis, or Gentleman of known nobility seduces a mulatto girl, a *china*, a *coyota*, or the daughter of a hangman, a butcher, a tanner), he must [not] marry her because the injury to himself and his entire lineage would be greater than that incurred by the maiden by remaining unredeemed, and at any rate one must choose the lesser evil . . . for the latter is an offense of an individual and does no harm to the Republic, while the former is an offence of such gravity that it will denigrate an entire family, dishonor a person of pre-eminence, defame and stain an entire noble lineage, and destroy a thing which gives splendor and honor to the Republic. But if the seduced maiden is of only slightly inferior status, or not very marked inequality, so that her inferiority does not cause marked dishonor to the family, then, if the seducer does not wish to endow her, or she justly rejects compensation in the form of endowment, he must be compelled to marry her; because in this case her injury would prevail over the offence inflicted upon the seducer's family for they would not suffer grave damage through the marriage whereas she would were she not to marry.[20]

Competition for honor-virtue was limited to persons of equal status. Thus the refusal to challenge someone of a much higher or much lower state was honorable because of the recognition of these disparities. Such opponents often had their day in court. An affronted father recognized his powerlessness to respond to the pique of a more formidable adversary, or admitted his frustration in dealing with a *genízaro* pleb who showed utter disregard for honor. The only hope for redress in such cases was through the legal system. Differences in status and power were obvious when in 1775 the chief constable of Santa Cruz, militia captain Don Salvador García, as legal representative for his son Esteban, appeared to arbitrate an agreement with a lowly farmer, Gregorio Martín, who represented his daughter Josepha. Esteban had tarnished the honor and reputation of Josepha and now refused to marry her. Martín demanded of García some sort of compensation to restore the honor of the family and of his daughter. After considerable jockeying, García agreed to pay Martín

150 pesos (T), provided that Josepha place no obstacle to any marriage that Esteban might later contract. The parties were satisfied. An agreement was signed. In a very similar 1725 Santa Fe case, Juan Lovato paid Manuela Armijo 200 pesos (T) to help restore her honor, lest she appear a dissolute woman.[21]

The honor of the male seducer was quite a different matter. He could and often did marry the woman he defiled to make good on his word and to restore honor. But men who had no intention of marrying the women they seduced contested their virtue. One ploy was to admit the obvious: that a pregnancy had resulted from illicit sexual activity, but that no promise of marriage had been given. Inés García of Santa Cruz in 1736 claimed that Marcial Martínez had snatched the flower of her virginity with a matrimonial bid. Martínez denied ever promising anything and demanded proof of his word and deed. This Inés did by summoning several witnesses. Juan Tomás Martín testified that he had heard Antonia Maese, Inés' mother, say that Marcial had given her daughter a promise of marriage. Juan also remembered that on Holy Wednesday, as he passed by the García residence, he peered through a window, knowing that the family was out of town, and "saw the said Marcial Martínez inside with the said Inés and they were engaged in the carnal act." Antonio Montoya related how Antonia Maese had asked him to look after her daughter while she attended Holy Week services in Santa Fe. On Holy Wednesday Montoya briefly left his home and when he returned was informed by his wife that Inés had gone to the house of Francisco Martínez, the father of Marcial, to mill some wheat. Montoya went in search of Inés and when he reached the Martínez house found that the door was bolted from within. He waited outside from ten in the morning until four in the afternoon when at last the door was opened and Marcial emerged. Inés followed, carrying the jar of wheat, said Montoya, which was "only cracked but not milled." No concrete evidence existed that Marcial had given Inés a promise of marriage, and therefore he was not forced to marry her. But because Inés was pregnant, she demanded 70 pesos (T) to absolve Marcial of his wrongdoing. By claiming poverty, Marcial managed to get the sum reduced to 35 pesos (T), which he paid with ten sheep, a white cotton bedspread with black and yellow fringe, one string of chiles, and four bushels of corn.[22]

The burden of proof in seduction cases was always upon the woman and her family. She had to produce witnesses who would testify to her betrothal, to her good conduct, and to her virginity. If witnesses to the betrothal did not exist, the woman at the very least had to produce the prenda, the gift ritually exchanged between lovers as an outward sign of their intention to marry. The *prenda*, often a rosary, a religious medallion, or small piece of jewelry, was given great importance by the courts because after such a gift had been presented, a maiden felt secure in submitting to the sexual desires of her husband-to-be. Then, even if she became pregnant from premarital intercourse, the impending marriage would save her from any public dishonor or scandal. The exchange of *prendas* made it more difficult for the male to renege on his word—though as the evidence indicates, not impossible.

Juana Luján of Santa Fe complained to Fray Manuel Moreno in 1702 that Bentura de Esquibel had taken her honesty and virginity. She wailed over the loss of honor and recounted the events of her seduction. Asked for concrete proof of a word of marriage, Juana presented the *prenda*, a silver image of Our Lady of Guadalupe, that Bentura had given her. When Juana Padilla discovered that she was with child in 1777, she too told the local priest how she had allowed herself to be conquered by the carnal appetite of Gregorio of Isleta Pueblo. She demanded that he keep his promise of matrimony assured with the exchange of a rosary. Gregorio denied all and explained, "it is true that she gave me a rosary but it was not given as a *prenda*, she gave it to me because I did not have one, and she told me, take this rosary so that the devil does not take you, but she did not say it was a *prenda*." Gregorio vowed that he had no desire of making Juana his wife. He was a footloose man with no intention of settling down. Neither woman ever got the marriage she wanted. Juana Luján was awarded 200 pesos (T) "because Bentura Esquibel tarnished her honor." Gregorio was forced to pay Juana Padilla two black shawls for her dishonor.[23]

A second strategy available to men to avoid responsibility for a seduction was to impugn the girl's reputation. Here the male admitted his promise and sexual contact, but claimed that his refusal to marry was based on the fact that he had not found the girl a virgin. The contradictory aspects of honor surfaced in these instances. On the one hand, a father and sons exhibited honorable conduct by aggressively protecting the sexual virtue of their womenfolk, placing great value on premarital virginity and marital fidelity. On the other hand, male honor was also secured and enhanced through displays of virility, notably the corruption of other men's women. So the logical ploy in such seduction cases was for a man to argue that he wanted to marry a bride of virtue and good repute, that the woman had been easily seduced, evidence of her sexual laxity, and that she was already lacking the flower of her body when they copulated. The law only punished the seduction of a virgin, while others, particularly widows, abandoned women, and *genízaros*, were considered sport for the prowess of men. Thus, if the seducer could produce witnesses to testify to the female's promiscuity, he most certainly would avoid punishment for his conduct.

"Human frailty was the cause of my dishonor," explained Juana Rodríguez in 1705, in response to Sebastian Luján's accusation that she was "a woman of the world who had no honor." Sebastian had proposed marriage to another woman. When Juana heard of this she quickly asked the local priest to impede it, claiming that she had a previous promise. Juana sobbingly told Santa Fe's ecclesiastical judge how on the September feast of the Virgin Mary, while she was home alone, Luján conquered her.

When I entered the house to put away some hides, he followed after me . . . and [when I wanted] to exit, he would not let me, and three times he solicited my flower with a promise of marriage, and just as we frequently played together, he began to play with me on this occasion, and he solicited his pleasure, but as a woman I resisted, and he told me that my resistance was a sign that I was not a virgin, finally I admonished him not to leave me dissolute and then consented freely to his pleasure and let him deflower me.

María de las Nieves watched all this through a crack in the door and later found Juana weeping and cleaning her genitals with a blood-soaked cloth. Asking her what had happened, Juana explained how Sebastian had taken her virginity and pleaded "for the love of God do not tell my mother or any other person."

Sebastian Luján on his behalf presented Calletano Fajardo who testified that he personally had had "dry loves" (anal sex) with Juana and had heard her say that Francisco Perea had deflowered her with a promise of marriage. Luján responded to the charges against him saying:

That I violated the said Juana Rodríguez with a promise of marriage is false. I did not lie to her nor will I deny that as . . . a man I wooed her, she consented to my pleasure, and she could easily have asked me for a *prenda* as a sign of any promise. When I had the act with her I found that she no longer had the flower of her body. And the testimony by the witness on Juana's behalf that she saw us copulate and later found Juana crying and cleaning herself could have been done to solace her evil. For if she had the audacity to embrace a single man she most certainly could have reached similar extremes with others. . . . She is at fault in this case for she roams the streets alone at night, going from house to house.

Luján presented enough evidence to impugn Juana Rodríguez's sexual purity. Luján was allowed to marry Juana Trujillo, leaving Juana Rodríguez destitute and dishonored.[24]

The reputations of other New Mexican women were similarly scrutinized by the authorities to determine whether they were virgins at the time of their seduction. Margarita García Jurado of Bernalillo in 1750, Gerónima Chávez of Isleta jurisdiction in 1775, and María Guadalupe Ortiz of San Isidro in 1805 all complained of their betrayal by men with whom they had consented to intercourse only after obtaining a promise of marriage. The men all acknowledged their acts but claimed that they were not the first to enjoy intimacy with these women. The virginity of each was slurred by persons familiar with the village gossip. None of the women got the marriage she demanded. There was insufficient evidence in the case of Thomas Lovato and Margarita García Jurado. He was sternly warned that his sinful acts and rebellious obstinacy would be more severely punished in the future. Lorenzo Romero and Thomás Maese each paid a small sum of money as indemnification to Gerónima Chávez and María Guadalupe Ortiz. All three women were of low social status, referred to by the men as *común*, meaning both common and communal. Marriage to women so commonly frequented by others was totally out of the question and had never even been considered when the illicit commerce began, or so the men claimed.[25]

For males, seduction, aside from fulfilling sexual urges, was an opportunity to exhibit their virility. Since women were pawns in the honor system, their spoliation afforded men boasting material to enhance their own reputation. Preeminence in this value schema was achieved not only through the accomplishment of an act, but through public recognition of that act as a feat. An affront, if not personally or publicly perceived as such, could hardly bring insult or elevate one's status. So gloating publicly of a power to use and manipulate women was common. José Salazar of Albuquerque displayed great braggadocio in 1766, explaining to his friends how he had had 15 illicit acts of intercourse with María Rosa Chávez:

When a table is placed before you, who will not eat. It is true that as a man I solicited her, she admitted me and I ruined her, but not now or ever will I marry her even though they may quarter me; my spirit has been very deeply chilled by the fact that they have demanded that I marry her, and even though they may put me in the stocks up to my neck, I will never marry her.

Proof of betrothal was not produced, so José never married María.[26]

When Juana de Guadalupe in 1705 tried to impede the marriage of Antonio de Belásquez to Juana Rodríguez because of a prior promise to her, Belásquez responded:

I made love to the said Juana de Guadalupe after having known that she treated illicitly with Juan Antonio Ramos, the Indian Mariquite, Zhacambe, and many others who I will not mention so as not to become a bother. This being the case, I entered into the ranks just like the rest of them without having given her a promise of marriage as she alleges. It would be of very grave consequence to wish to enter into the state of matrimony with a person who roams in the fashion I have just described. And besides that, if she gives me legitimate proof that I deflowered her and gave her a promise of marriage, I will immediately do whatever you, reverend father, decide. For if the said Juana de Guadalupe had shame and respect for the ecclesiastical tribunal, she would not have the audacity to expose her honor to public scrutiny only to remain totally defamed. If I owed her anything, I am a Christian and as such would act according to the laws of conscience . . . but in this matter she appears to be acting more under the influence of her mother than of her free will, and as such, I am convinced that this appears to me more dementia than justice.

Juana dropped her opposition to the marriage when confronted with her less-than-proper past. She said that she no longer wished to marry Belásquez "because I fear a bad life with him, because of his threats, and because of the mistreatments I have already experienced . . . and I fear, as he has already warned me, that he will treat me not as his wife but as his slave." Instead, Juana demanded that her honor be indemnified. Belásquez refused. He had not taken Juana's honor and felt that alms were inappropriate in the case. "As a man I had her single and free by the same luck that others have had her," he explained.[27]

Reputation was a public evaluation of how well someone personified the ideals of the honor code. Just as it was in the self-interest of men to have their sexual feats and prowess proclaimed, it was also to the benefit of women and particularly of their fathers and brothers to keep the knowledge of any frailty that might occur as secret as possible. In this task they often had the help of parish priests, who felt a primary responsibility for protecting the virtue of women and attenuating public scandal. To have it known that a daughter had been seduced and lost her virginity was to significantly alter her symbolic value on the marriage market. Familial resources could be severely taxed by marrying such a woman. If a father was going to secure her an honorable husband, a significant dowry would have to be offered, one that adequately remunerated the male for the acceptance of a spoiled woman. If the economic means to counterbalance the loss of virtue did not exist, parents might have to consent to someone of a lower status becoming their son-in-law, or face the possibility of never marrying off their daughter.

For this reason village gossip was a significant force to contend with when attempting to minimize the impact of affronts to one's honor. Alameda's constable, Don Cleto de Miera, understood this when in 1805 he wrote Governor Real Alencaster, relating the details of the seduction of his daughter María de las Nievas Miera y Pacheco by Josef Trujillo. Don Cleto protested that Josef "denigrates my person by the mere act of saying, [as he has] repeated on two occasions, that my daughter has become pregnant because of her unruly habits. [This] young man talks too much and without restraint, causing prejudice to my honor." Several persons had urged Josef to marry María, but he refused. When María bore his child, the parish priest summoned Josef so that the illegitimacy could be resolved prudently. Josef stood firm in his resolve. When the ecclesiastical judge ordered María and Josef punished for their behavior, Josef fled to seek the governor's aid. María was placed in isolation in a good Christian home as a punishment and warning to other girls lest they fall prey to the weaknesses of the flesh. Trujillo was finally apprehended and charged with ravishment in the civil courts.

This is what María had to say about her defilement:

Trujillo, availing himself more of absolute force than of promises or gifts, deflowered my virginity without even the least bit of my consent, adding to this the countless pleas which I made of him, but which were finally useless and had no other result than to quiet the fact of my ravishment, not so much because he was concerned for my honor, but so that his crime would not be discovered. I was effectively silenced because on no occasion are women who enjoy the state of virginity permitted scandal or involvements. Trujillo took my virginity and now states in his affidavit that I have bad and unruly habits. I was silenced and would have remained silent to protect my honor and that of my parents, but time finally displayed my disgrace with a pregnancy from the said rape, and because of this my parents finally charged me to declare, not without substantial shame, that: the said Josef Trujillo (and none other) raped me in the manner I have described. My father reproached the young man shortly after my declaration, without scandal, the parish priest did the same, without publicizing it; and because Trujillo's conscience bothered him because of this crime, and he realized that he could suffer some prejudice for his infamy, or better, he realized that he was going to be apprehended, he fled.

María had soured on the idea of marriage to Josef and only wanted proof of Trujillo's allegation that she was a woman of bad habits. If he could not prove this, he deserved the sternest punishment possible. Trujillo's defense was pointless and rambling. His most damning comment was that he had seen María outside her father's home alone at night. He proved nothing. Although Trujillo was apparently guilty, the final pages of this court docket are missing. María de las Nievas however, appears never to have married.[28]

Village gossip was always a powerful force in the regulation of social behavior. Its circulation was quick and its repercussions wide. Just as known dishonors lowered one's status in the eyes of the community, re-puted peccadillos did too. The reader will recall the folktale "La Con-stancia." José María, Constancia's husband, was dishonored not because Constancia actually committed adultery with the vagabond, but because José María believed what he had been told about his wife's behavior. Similarly, Don Francisco Armijo whipped his wife María in 1816 because he had heard that she had been propositioned to adultery while he was out of town. In neither case was the woman asked if the charges were true. The husbands were more concerned about what everyone else thought. Thus individuals had to be constantly on guard to exhibit con-duct befitting their sex, as well as vigilant that no one maliciously tar-nished their reputations.

Concern for reputation prompted Doña María Manuela de la Luz Romero to sue Mariano Baca in 1767. Baca, a half-breed of very low status and "depraved habits," had been telling people that he had seduced Doña María, an Albuquerque aristocrat, and was intent on redeeming her through marriage. Doña María appeared before the civil court and charged Baca with slander. "I am an honest and sheltered maiden. The good upbringing and prudence with which my parents raised me is pub-licly known in Albuquerque. They have given no one cause, either be-cause of their acts or mine, to defame my honor or that of my parents." She demanded that Mariano be punished for tarnishing the virtue that honorable and well bred maidens customarily guarded with great care. To prove that Mariano's allegations were false, Doña María went to the home of Albuquerque's ecclesiastical notary, Joseph Hurtado de Men-doza, on April 21, 1767, to ask that he witness a gynecological examina-tion that would establish Doña María's virginity. She was accompanied by Bárbara Benavides, a respected midwife from Atrisco, and Gertrudis Montoya, a friend. The notary agreed to certify the proceedings in the presence of his wife, his sister, Bárbara Benavides, and Gertrudis Mon-toya. Mendoza attested:

I examined [Doña María] visually with the four women. . . . Bárbara the mid-wife, placed the second finger of her right hand in the narrow concave of her geni-tals and could penetrate no further than the tip of the said second finger, entering only as far as the middle of the nail . . . for this reason it is indisputable that she is a virgin and the slander which has been voiced is false.

When the justice in Durango, Don Antonio Lavendera, reviewed the case, he was furious at the notary's participation in the examination. "This notary has shown himself dishonest, of depraved habits and poor upbringing," Lavendera wrote. "He should be aware that such examinations and reviews are only tolerated among the most immoral; and even more amazing is the fact that a woman who claims to be so honest and sheltered would let herself be examined in such manner." For his participation in this certification Lavendera ordered Hurtado placed in the pillory for one hour. Mariano Baca's punishment was left to Governor Pedro Fermín de Mendinueta, who ordered him tied to the gibbet and given one hundred lashes, and sentenced him to one year in jail. The governor hoped that such a severe punishment would deter other low-status men from besmirching the honor of aristocratic maidens and forcing them to undergo such scandalous examinations to recover their reputations. The governor further ordered the constable of Albuquerque to publicly proclaim on the next major feast day that the rumors that Mariano Baca had circulated about Doña María were totally false.[29]

Similar gynecological examinations were performed, albeit without male supervision, to determine if other women were virgins. When Antonio Román Sánchez and Manuel Chaves, both from Isleta, claimed in 1775 to have seduced maidens, Father Junco got the local midwife to examine the girls. The maidenheads of both women were intact. The midwife certified that the men had lied. For defaming these females, Antonio and Manuel were placed in the stocks.[30]

Once a bit of information had been disseminated by word of mouth, it was often difficult to amend. A public declaration was hardly an adequate way to restore someone's honor. Once the damage was done, it could never be totally rectified. Gossip spread like wildfire, and often blazed beyond containment. María Rosalía Madrid of Santa Cruz was the victim of such pernicious innuendo. In 1813 when she called on Francisca Córdova to borrow a tub, Francisca asked her about the broken promise of marriage with which she was trying to stop the betrothal of José Fresquis. "I was extremely shamed and went home crying to tell my father Don José Ignacio Madrid," said María. The story was a total fabrication. Nonetheless, it had been circulating for six months before she heard of it. Don José Ignacio Madrid was livid over the slur to his family's honor and had Francisca Córdova, her husband Miguel Barela, Joseph Manuel Guillén, and José Fresquis jailed to determine who had been spreading such a lie. Guillén told the court that he had learned of the matter from his wife, who said the information came from Ramón Cárdenas.

Cárdenas said that it had been told to him by Simón Bernal, and Bernal said that the wife of José Manuel Guillén had told him . . . the flames of this hell then jumped to Juan Josef Esquibel, and the flames continued to rage into a burning inferno, landing next on the daughters of Josef Maestas who told the said Esquibel, and still not extinguished, this artificial fire landed on José del Carmen Fresquis who was the person who told my wife the story when we went to a wake.

The case ended when José Fresquis admitted that he had had no relation with María and that the charge of a broken promise of marriage had been launched, not by María Rosalía Madrid, but by a woman from Truchas. He vowed to correct this grave misunderstanding, but by then the damage had been done.[31]

Public reputation, a peer evaluation concerning one's reproduction of ideal values of virtuous social conduct, was ultimately the source of an individual's right to precedence. To determine a person's position on the vertical hierarchy of honor-status, aristocrats and peasants alike evaluated the honor-virtue of members of their status groups. If an aristocrat was deemed virtuous, his family and kin would gain precedence before those persons deemed dishonored. The same held for the landed peasantry. The virtuous peasant was preferred over the corrupt. Of course, it is important to remember that because honor-status was largely ascribed and honor-virtue achieved, the most vice-ridden aristocrat always enjoyed more honor-status than the most virtuous peasant. Similarly, the most corrupt peasant enjoyed more honor than the Indians and *genízaros*, who had no honor.

The status hierarchy which was established in colonial New Mexico and which regulated social relations until the beginning of the nineteenth century was a Spanish monarchical tool used to reward those groups that had expanded the realm. Honors, as well as the concept of honor as a moral code, were elements of a feudal patriarchal ideology employed by the state to bolster its own power, to legitimate the rewards it granted persons for service to the monarchy, and to sanctify the reality of unequal power relationships in society. Embedded in this ideology was the belief that God's earthly and natural design made men dominant over women and that therefore females should submit to male authority. Conquest, domination, and protection were marks of human excellence; they were qualities that maintained the patrimony and perpetuated an honored image of the self over time.

Honor and Marriage

Marriage was the most important ritual event in the course of life, and it was an occasion when it was necessary for the honor of the family to take precedence over all other considerations. The union of two properties, the joining of two households, the creation of a web of affinal alliances, and the perpetuation of a family's symbolic patrimony—its name and reputation—were of such importance to the honor-status of the group that marriage was hardly a decision to be made by minors. The norm in New Mexico was for parents to arrange nuptials for their children with little or no consideration for their wishes. Filial piety required the acceptance of any union that parents deemed appropriate or advantageous.

Arranged marriages that furthered familial honor were frequently at odds with the personal desires of the marital partners themselves, especially with the expression of their love. In this chapter we return to the central theme of this book: how marriage structured inequality. In Chapter 1 we saw how marital gifting and the debts created thereby exposed the subordination of juniors to seniors in Pueblo society. In Chapter 2 we explored the meaning of mystical marriage in Franciscan clerical culture and observed in the soul's ordered progression toward her lover, Christ, the ideal submission of inferiors to superiors. Here we focus on Spanish New Mexican society in the eighteenth and early nineteenth centuries to discuss the concerns of honor that parents expressed at marriage, the mechanisms they used to control mate selection, and the constant struggles they waged to preclude filial expressions of love.

Love in colonial New Mexico was considered a subversive sentiment, antithetical to the status concerns of a family and to authority relations within the home. Love glorified personal autonomy and portrayed sexual passion as an intrinsic desire of the species—natural, free, and egalitarian. The egalitarianism of love arose from its obliviousness of status and kinship considerations. Love pangs welled up in the individual and were true only to the self. Studying the ways in which love disrupted African village structure, Max Gluckman concluded that the expression of this sentiment and the establishment of an affective bond based on it estranged people from their kinship network. Therefore, after matrimony, kinsmen constantly tried to sabotage the cohesion of the love bond so that group solidarity could be reaffirmed. Even in marriage excessive love was distrusted because it held the potential of making people forget their social obligations.[1]

The best way to assure that familial considerations in marriage would be placed above all else and that personal likes and desires did not complicate the matter was to preclude the expression of love. Perhaps the easiest way this could be done was to arrange a marriage while the candidate was still in infancy. By the time the child reached adolescence he or she would be faced with a fait accompli. There would be little choice but to do as parents ordered, and certainly the issue of love was unlikely to surface. One New Mexico folk poet described this practice thus:

> On the day of my birth
> They christened me
> They found me a wife
> And they married me.[2]

Equally common was the use of threats, intimidation, and force to convince a child to marry a person the parents or guardians considered advantageous. Antonio de Esquibel in 1702 warned his younger brother Ventura that he, Antonio, would "shame him publicly with curses and make him bite the dust (*morder la tierra*)" if he tried to marry Juana Luján, a woman who was not his equal. Ventura retorted that he would enter the holy state of grace with whomever he chose, "for first comes my soul and I do not want the devil to take me." Unfortunately for Ventura's soul, he never married Juana Luján. His master, New Mexico's governor, would not allow him to marry and instead sent Ventura to Parral to forget his love. Similar words of warning were issued by Doña Rafaela Baca to her daughter Barbara in 1772. If Barbara tried to contract marriage with Miguel Baca, forewarned Doña Rafaela, "I will tie a stone around her neck and throw her into the Rio del Norte."[3]

Although it was technically contrary to canon law for a parent to force a marital partner on their child, the practice was not all that uncommon in colonial New Mexico. Typical was the case of Vicente Luna, a resident of the Spanish settlement near Isleta. In 1774 Vicente told his father, Don Domingo Luna, that he desired to marry Bitoria Chávez, the daughter of Don Vicente Chávez. Don Domingo thought his son's request was totally inappropriate and instead contracted a marriage with María Bárbara Chávez, the daughter of Don Francisco Chávez. Vicente accepted Don Domingo's choice "due to all the grief and threats my father expressed; I finally decided to marry María Bárbara against my will, only to please my father." Shortly after the betrothal Don Domingo died and Vicente immediately petitioned the ecclesiastical judge to invalidate his engagement. Bitoria Chávez was still the woman he truly wanted to marry and finally did.[4]

The 1786 marriage of Francisco Narpa and Juana Lorem in Sandía similarly provides a glimpse of the familial motivations involved in an arranged union. Appearing before the provincial ecclesiastical judge to explain how and why he had married, Francisco said: "Having agreed with Juana Lorem that we wished to marry, I asked her grandmother Tomasa Cibaa, and with her permission and that of her relatives, I married." Juana Lorem had a very different understanding of the events that led to her marriage to Francisco. She told the judge, "It is totally false that I agreed to marry the said Francisco. I never wanted to marry the said Francisco. But for fear of my grandmother Tomasa Cibaa I contracted the matrimony." Finally, Tomasa Cibaa explained, "I ordered my granddaughter Juana to marry the said Francisco Narpa because he is moderately wealthy, and it is true that I pressured Juana to appear before the priest [for the matrimonial investigation] and to say nothing that might provoke questioning." The details of this marriage surfaced as part of an investigation to determine if the union was incestuous. Francisco had fathered a child by María Quieypas, Juana's mother, and therefore his marriage to Juana Lorem was invalid. The matrimony was annulled, dotal and patrimonial property were confiscated, the three were publicly flogged, and Narpa was exiled from New Mexico.[5]

Of course, I do not wish to suggest that arranged marriage was an inflexible rule. The extent to which parental preference for arranged marriage could be enforced was mediated both by the person's status and by each family's particular fertility history. The number of children in a family, their birth order, and their sex dictated the options available to parents to secure their son or daughter an acceptable or advantageous spouse. These and other variables also conditioned the range of filial responses possible—whether a son or daughter would respond to duty or to sentiment, whether they resisted, or whether they attempted some solution that might appease everyone's concerns.

From a father's point of view, a round of poker is an excellent metaphor to describe the way in which limited resources (the patrimony) were manipulated to maximize the gains associated with marital alliance. Pierre Bourdieu has applied this metaphor to the marriage of a family's children. Success at enhancing and perpetuating the family's status is based not only on the hand one is dealt (whether the nuptial candidate is an only child, the eldest of several sons or the youngest of many daughters) but also the skill with which the game is played (bids, bluffs, and displays).[6]

The patrimony was the material resource a father had to apportion among his children at strategic moments to maximize their reproductive success. Although legally every legitimate child in New Mexico was entitled to an equal share of this wealth, practice varied by class. Aristocratic holders of large land estates preferred male primogeniture as a way of keeping their property intact. The eldest son, as the heir of the household head's political rights over the group and the person responsible for the name and reputation of the family, was the individual to whom a disproportionate amount of parents' pre-mortem resources was committed. As first in importance, even if preceded by older sisters, a misalliance for him would lower the entire family's public rating and diminish the possibilities of securing honorable partners for his unmarried brothers and sisters. Therefore, he was the child of whom parents expected the most and the child disciplined most severely to assure obedience, but he was allowed the greatest excesses in other matters. He was also perhaps the most predisposed to bow to familial duty over any personal desires.

If the eldest son married well and the family's position had been attended to, filial participation in the marriage selection process was more flexible in subsequent cases. Since younger sons were unlikely to fare quite as well in the acquisition of marital property and could expect only enough money and moveable goods to avoid misalliance, fathers might be more open to a son's suggestion regarding the eligible brides.

Daughters of the nobility were a potential liability on the marriage market, dissipating the material and symbolic patrimony by having their dowries absorbed into their husbands' assets. Every attempt would be made to dispose of nubile females as quickly as possible and at the most minimal expense. If a daughter experienced a prenuptial dishonor, such as the loss of her virginity, additional resources would have to be committed to secure her an appropriate mate. Thus large amounts of time and energy were spent assuring that a maiden's sexual reputation was maintained. Undoubtedly, the result was that a woman's freedom to object to a marriage, to express her desires in spouse selection, were more limited than those of her brothers.[7]

Peasants enjoying rights to communal land grants practiced partible inheritance. Sons were given their share of the family's land when they took a bride and were assigned a certain number of *vigas* ("beams"—a way of dividing the space in a house) in the parental home. If space limitations prohibited such a move, assistance was given in the addition of rooms to the house or the construction of a separate edifice in the immediate vicinity. For females, dowries usually consisted of household items and livestock. Daughters seldom received land rights at marriage because parents fully expected the husband's family to meet this need. The authority relations springing from this mode of property division meant that parental supervision over spouse selection and its timing was as rigidly exercised as among the nobility.

For landless freed *genízaros*, Christian marriage was a symbol of social status and an index of acculturation. Since many *genízaros* held no property to transmit and their alienation from kin through enslavement had made the perpetuation of family name virtually impossible, marriage meant little except to status climbers. Indeed, the baptismal records of the Catholic Church indicate that many *genízaro* children were illegitimate, that their parents lived in concubinage, and that apparently few of them sought sacramental marriage.

Wage-earners and landless peasants did not seem particularly concerned over whether or whom their children married. Once children were old enough to leave the familial hearth in search of a livelihood, parental control over their behavior all but ceased. If members of this status group chose to marry, it was primarily to demonstrate their adherence to the values of Spanish Christian society. Then, their main concern was timing. Before one married, one had to accumulate a nest egg with which to establish a conjugal residence.

Heads of noble households arranged marriages for their slaves and servants as readily as for their own children. Governor Juan de Eulate's female servant complained to Santa Fe's prelate in 1621 that the governor had forced her to marry against her will. Despite the fact that she was now married, the governor continued to demand intimate favors. Prelate Fray Estevan de Perea tried to sequester the girl and to annul her marriage, but Eulate would not let the prelate near her. Perea threatened the governor with excommunication. The governor retorted that if he tried that, he would arrest the prelate and would take him bound in a leather sack to Mexico City. Fearing such a fate, the prelate retreated and the governor had his way. Governor Luís de Rosas likewise forced his retainer Polonia Varela to marry Juan Bautista Saragosa in 1640. Juan contracted the marriage only because the governor had kept him in the stocks for several days without food and had told Juan that if he did not marry Polonia he would be whipped and gibbeted. Polonia said that she had agreed to marry Juan because she feared Governor Rosas, knowing that "he was such an absolute lord that with or without law he trampled on everyone."[8]

The details of Governor Pedro Rodríguez's meddling in the marital choice of his servant, Bentura de Esquibel, surfaced in 1702. Early in April that year, while attending Sunday Mass in Santa Fe, Juana Luján heard her pastor, Fray Manuel Moreno, announce that Bentura de Esquibel would marry Doña Bernardina Rosa Lucero de Godoy. As soon as Mass was over, Juana wrote a note to her priest: "Most Reverend Father. Would your reverence impede the marriage of Bentura Esquibel. It has come to my attention that he wants to contract matrimony with the daughter of Lucero. I have very urgent reasons for impeding the marriage. Signed: Juana Luján."

The following day Juana Luján appeared before Father Moreno and explained that Bentura could not take Doña Bernardina as his wife because he had already given her, Juana, a previous promise of marriage. Because of that promise she had allowed Bentura to snatch the flower of her body. Juana now demanded that Bentura make good on the promise by which he had enjoyed her. "As proof that Bentura de Esquibel truly gave me his word of marriage," said Juana, "I have a silver medal of Our Lady of Guadalupe, the weight of a silver coin."[9]

According to Mateo Márquez, Bentura had wanted initially to marry Juana Luján so as to free her from her "damnification." In fact, when Mateo had confided to Bentura his desire to court Juana, Bentura had told him, "do not do any such thing for I have already given her a promise of marriage and she will be my wife because of that promise." But when Bentura finally got around to asking Juana Luján's mother for her daughter's hand in marriage, she said no. "It is not my wish, nor the wish of Juana's kin," said Juana's mother, "for I want to marry my daughter to a man who knows how to work." Bentura's father also objected to the union because "Juana Luján is not Bentura's equal in honor or social status." To dull Bentura's desires for Juana, the governor, his master, sent him to Parral. The months passed and time finally exposed Juana's dishonor—her pregnancy. During this time of separation, Bentura's heart hardened and he decided that he no longer desired Juana as his bride. He wanted Doña Bernardina Lucero de Godoy instead.

Before the ecclesiastical judge who was asked to determine which woman would be allowed to marry Bentura, Bentura admitted seducing Juana with a promise of marriage and having had sex with her for three months. But Bentura cooled to the idea of marriage when he discovered that Juana's virginity was not intact. Juana was a woman who did "not guard her fidelity," attested Bentura, "who lacked honesty, and who did not conduct herself with modesty as an honorable woman . . . she had no shame." Bentura instead wanted to marry Doña Bernardina because "she is a young maiden of whom no one gossips . . . and she is my equal for she is Spanish while the other woman is not."

Juana explained to the ecclesiastical judge that Bentura's allegations were totally false. She had no proof of her virginity except God's all-knowing and:

> evident signs which demonstrated that I was a virgin, like the blood which re-mained stamped in Bentura's shirt and the blood in his handkerchief which I took the next day with a deep sense of shame, down to the river to wash it, there my cousin saw it all . . . and she asked me what blood that was, and I told her in confidence what had happened the night before, and I hurled the handkerchief into the river so that it would not remain as a constant witness to my frailty.

To Bentura's statement regarding her low social status she replied: "I can-not deny that his Lordship [Don Antonio Lucero] is very honorable, but not that she [Doña Bernardina Lucero] is my superior in social status, for in this, one is just as good as the other." In the end, Juana Luján removed her marital petition because she feared the governor who "is a powerful enemy . . . who with his violence can prove almost anything, and since I am poor and helpless, I drop my claim." The ecclesiastical judge allowed Bentura to marry Doña Bernardina because she was his equal in *calidad* and ordered that Juana Luján be endowed with 200 pesos in products of the land "because Bentura owed her her honor."

As the case of Bentura de Esquibel illustrates, New Mexico's Spanish colonists believed that there should be *igualdad de calidad* (equality in social status) between marriage partners. Parents actively objected to mat-rimonial bids when disparity, whatever its basis, was too great. Miguel Durán, a soldier at Santa Fe's presidio, for example, appeared before the ecclesiastical court in 1708 and demanded that his fiancée, María Rincón, a Spaniard of noble ancestry, be sequestered from her parents so that she could marry whomever she chose. María's mother, Doña Antonia de Valenzuela, objected to the union because of the "notorious disparity in that the said man is of *color pardo* [brown color]." Miguel Durán was also a widower whose parents were unknown. All of these facts taken together, his occupation, his race, and most likely his illegitimacy, made him an unsuitable match for the daughter of an aristocrat. In the end, the marriage was not celebrated, nor does it appear that María ever married.[10]

In February of 1705, while Sebastian Luján and Juana Trujillo were preparing to marry, Juana Rodríguez, a *mestiza* who resided in Santa Fe's Analco district, a segregated zone in which *genízaros* lived, appeared before the ecclesiastical court to oppose the marriage. The intersection of honor-status and honor-virtue, as well as the relationship between marriage and seduction are vividly illustrated in this case. Juana Rodríguez claimed that Sebastian Luján had given her a previous promise of marriage and because of that promise she had submitted to his desires and allowed herself to be deflowered. During the litigation, Juana de Valencia, Juana Rodríguez's mother, confronted Juana Trujillo and asked her if it was true that she wanted to marry Sebastian Luján. Trujillo responded, "no . . . I would rather have as my husband a pastor than a gallant gentleman." Valencia commended Trujillo saying, "you do well, for he is not your status [*calidad*] equal."

Several days later Juana Trujillo and Juana Valencia again met in a street behind Santa Fe's plaza and again Juana Valencia broached the topic of Sebastian Luján's marital bid. "I have heard that you want to marry Sebastian Luján," said Valencia. "Sebastian is not going to marry anyone, not even the queen," responded Trujillo in an angry tone. "There is no need to fight over a man for there are many with whom my daughter can be married . . . and besides, the *calidad* of Sebastian Luján is not very good, for although his father may be a Spaniard, I know that his mother was a poor *castiza*, the daughter of a *coyota* from Zuñi." "I tell you this," said Valencia to Trujillo, "only because I know that the man is not your equal in social standing." As the case progressed, Juana Trujillo admitted denying that she desired to marry Sebastian Luján "so that my reputation would not become a public matter." Fray Juan Alvarez, the ecclesiastical judge, reasoned his final determination in the case as follows:

Juana Rodríguez has lost her honor; Juana Trujillo has lost not only her honor, which the said Sebastian Luján owes her, but also her esteem, her good name and her reputation, which up to this time had been acknowledged by all . . . therefore, on all counts the person and honor of Juana Trujillo must be favored by this tribunal, for her racial status and name are notorious in this kingdom, for she is regarded as a Spaniard, which she indeed is, and the daughter of noble parents, and because she came in the company of her parents from Mexico City as a colonist to settle this kingdom, the king has conceded them special privileges as colonists . . . so, I must prefer Juana Trujillo . . . for she is the daughter of a family held in high esteem, reputation and good name, and how can she return to her parents having lost the greatest jewel of her honor . . . and so because of her status and honorific redemption, which must be attended to, I favor Juana Trujillo.

Sebastian finally married Juana Trujillo. In this instance when the honor-virtue of two women had been lost, it was the honor-status of the noble woman that established the precedence of her virtue, and therefore her honorific redemption through marriage.[11]

Female Seclusion

Every male household head had a sacred space, a physical territoriality that surrounded him and his various forms of property. The profanity of the external world was ritually set apart from the sanctity within the household by crucifixes and icons that marked door posts and windows and protected the inhabitants from evil invasions. The groom lifting his new bride over the threshold symbolized both the creation of a new household and passage into a man's sacrosanct domain. Things that promised existence over time, which provided shelter from the hostilities of the environment, had to be jealously guarded within.

Women were the things honorable men guarded most intensely in their households. Since it was through the female's childbearing capacity that the family was reproduced, and maternity was undeniable while paternity was not, males attempted to strictly supervise their females' sexuality. The seclusion of a wife, daughters, mother, and sisters, and the high symbolic value placed on premarital virginity, helped accomplish this. As a result of such premarital sexual segregation, when women finally did marry they frequently lacked the most rudimentary knowledge of their mate. The 1703 statement of María Archuleta was typical of others made by New Mexicans at the time. María had no "carnal knowledge" of her betrothed Miguel Martín and knew him "only by sight." Residence in the same village assured men familiarity with the eligible women, but if the nuptial candidates were from different towns, the chances of them having met before their engagement or marriage were slight. María Michaela Tafoya of El Paso said in 1802 that she had journeyed with her uncle, José García, to Bernalillo under the pretext of attending the festivities on St. Peter's Day. Instead of partaking of the celebrations, they called at the home of Juan Domingo Archiveque, where she met their son Juan Pablo. María later discovered the purpose of the trip "being no other . . . than to meet me so that they could ask for my hand in matrimony." The next time she saw Juan Pablo, his parents proposed the marriage. She had thus only seen Juan Pablo twice before they were joined in wedlock.[12]

The differential length of time persons knew of each other before engagement and marriage was dependent on sex. Information pertaining to this time difference is recorded in only two rather late sources: the matrimonial books of Santa Cruz Parish between 1832 and 1833 and San Miguel del Vado Parish between 1829 and 1833. These registers indicate

TABLE 7.1

Length of Time Spouses had Known of Each Other
Before Marriage in Two Parishes

Length of time he/she knew him/her	Santa Cruz de la Cañada Parish 1832-33				San Miguel del Vado Parish 1829-33			
	Males		Females		Males		Females	
	No.	Pct.	No.	Pct.	No.	Pct.	No.	Pct.
One year or less	4	30.7%	5	29.4%	16	23.8%	20	76.8%
2-3 years	2	15.4	5	29.4	15	22.3	3	11.6
4-10 years	—	—	—	—	28	41.8	3	11.6
"Many" years	7	53.9	7	41.2	8	12.1	—	—
Total	13	100.0%	17	100.0%	67	100.0%	26	100.0%

SOURCES: AASF-*DM* Reel 72:272-347, and Reel 74:26-50.

(see Table 7.1) that about half (43 out of 80) of all men marrying had known of their brides since childhood or for a large part of adolescence. When Nepomeceno Varela married María Juana Rufina Rael in 1831, he said that he had known of her "since birth." María was more realistic in her assessment and claimed she had known of Nepomeceno "since I had use of my reason." Women more frequently stated that they did not know the men they married. At San Miguel del Vado, for example, seven out of every ten men had known of their bride for two or more years, while only two out of every ten women had known of their future husbands that long. Typical of this were the 1832 statements of José Antonio Trujillo and María Estefana Pacheco. He had known her for eight years while she had known him for only one month. Seven out of every ten women married at San Miguel del Vado between 1829 and 1833 had known of their partner for one year or less. In a society that valued female chastity highly and enforced it through the seclusion of women, the fact that brides did not know their husbands long before marriage was not unusual. Personal acquaintance of the proposed couple was irrelevant when parents arranged marriages for their children.[13]

Although the social ideals of proper sexual conduct prescribed the segregation of young men and women, enough examples exist to show that some young women escaped the watchful eyes of elders. Only in aristocratic households, where servants abounded and productive activities did not consume all familial resources, could time and energy be expended to see that a daughter was properly restrained. If a parent had been widowed, if the family was particularly large or of low repute, the chances of being constantly attentive to a daughter's activities were lower.

Because many New Mexican homes provided access to bedrooms through internal courtyards, young men often gained access to females at night by scaling external walls. Parents discovered illicit romances on hearing groans in the next room, footsteps overhead, or various disturbances outside. Bentura de Esquibel boasted in 1702 that he frequently shared intimacy with his love Juana in Santa Fe, "and through the roof he would enter at night to see her." Their carnal acts were witnessed only by God Almighty, for their meetings occurred "in such solitude that even though her father and mother were in the same house, they were in a different room and could not hear, see, or note what was happening." Pedro de Montes de Oca once carried a message to Juana in which Bentura told her:

that he kissed her hands, and how was she, and that he . . . wanted to enter the holy state of matrimony with her, to let him know her thoughts and desires. . . . Juana Luján responded that I [Pedro de Montes de Oca] should tell Bentura de Esquibel that she kissed his hands, and how was he, and that she had waited for him so long, and that she wanted him to know that even if he went to Mexico City, or elsewhere, she would wait for him for four years, and if after that something happened or if there was some other mishap, that he should not blame her.[14]

Miguel Chávez of Albuquerque apprehended Joseph Antonio Salazar in 1766 "scaling my house, violating one of my daughters and due to this violation she is now pregnant." Francisco Salazar, Joseph's father, claimed that Joseph had been lured into the act. "Scaling walls is quite different from entering through the door or being given free entry to a house," Salazar stated. "And if my son went there, it was only because of the encouragement he received from Miguel Chávez who even unsaddled his horse . . . encouraging my son's visits with such great vigor, letting my son have his pleasure so that they could then demand marriage."[15]

In the early morning hours of Christmas Day 1763, Gertrudes de Armijo was awakened by footsteps she heard overhead. Quickly she summoned a soldier from the presidio and caught Blas López as he descended from the roof of her house. Earlier that evening Blas had scaled an exterior wall and entered the home, and had convinced Gregoria Tenorio, Armijo's daughter, to go with him to midnight Mass. Blas hid Gregoria under his cape throughout midnight Mass, causing considerable scandal. Gertrudes caught the two when they returned, as Blas tried to enter the house to spend the night with Gregoria. Gregoria said that she had gone with Blas because he told her "not to worry about being seen together, that he was taking me so that people would see me with him, that he wanted no other woman but me, that he wanted to marry me and not the woman from Cañada, and for these reasons I submitted, not knowing that all his promises were such lies." López denied all. He was notorious for wooing women with promises of marriage, obtaining his satisfaction and then abandoning them. For this incident López was punished with four years exile from New Mexico and a 50 peso (T) payment to Gregoria for her dishonor.[16]

The routine of daily life provided enough opportunities for expressions of desire and love. In 1763, Manuela and María Paula Chávez, both servants in Albuquerque, succumbed to the flesh "while out tending to the sheep." Juana de Guadalupe of Santa Fe experienced her "frailty" while at the house of Antonio Belásquez exchanging some goods. Juana Rodríguez had "dry loves" (amores secos or anal intercourse) with Bentura, her beau, while collecting pine nuts outside Santa Fe in 1705. Francisco Belásquez saw Calletano Fajardo and his friend "play, titillate each other amorously, and kiss (though they were only what is called dry kisses [osculos secos] . . . while going to see the cañute games in Analco." Josef Montoya became extremely suspicious of his sister-in-law, María Miranda, and her suitor, Josef Durán y Chávez, in 1771, "because they displayed behavior which led me to believe that they were having an illicit friendship." Josef told María's father about this conduct, but he seemed unalarmed. Four months later María sued Josef Durán y Chávez for the loss of her virginity. Josef admitted sharing intimacies with María one day while out horseback riding together. "But I did not impregnate her," explained Josef, to the charge that he had snatched the flower of María's body and engendered her with child. "Even if I were a cock I could not have made her bring forth a child so quickly." María gave birth in 1771, and since sex with Josef had occurred only three months earlier, he was obviously not the father.[17]

Ritual Inversions

Aside from covert attempts to gain the affections of women, enough ritual events existed in community life where the sexes could meet and intermingle with a minimum of supervision. These events usually marked major seasonal changes measuring the passage of time—rites of sowing and harvest, first fruits, religious feast days, or the celebration of a village's founding. During such rituals, when public comity prevailed and the normative constraints of the social structure were lowest, egalitarian sentiments such as those of love and passion could be expressed momentarily without public sanctions or danger to the social order. The consumption of alcohol at these events lowered inhibitions. Demure and

listless maidens became footloose and gay, and their consorts were transformed into bold and daring young men. Stolen kisses might be less ob-
jectionable at a dance, and furtive groping or moments of intimacy might
escape the notice of the merry mass. One popular proverb reminded New
Mexicans of the occasion to adultery that celebrations provided and cautioned: "Keep your eyes off the wife of the guitarist." [18]

Needless to say, many ignored the advice. Pedro Martín, for example,
was already quite tipsy when he left the October 1812 Rio Arriba fiesta
dance to fetch Juana Baca. Juana's parents were at the festival and wanted
her to join them. Pedro went for Juana and after much convincing she
finally agreed to go with him. But hardly had they rounded the hill near
her home, riding together on Pedro's horse when, said Juana, he "started
caressing my breasts, touching my private parts, and saying that he wanted
to enjoy me and I pleaded with him, asking if he was not a Christian, he
then unfastened his belt and took off his neckerchief." Fearing for her life,
Juana submitted. [19]

The night of merriment for José Antonio Lucero, for his wife, María
Manuela García, and for her mother, María Soledad Chávez, was not
really over when they left the Alameda fiesta dance in 1819. Taking hospice in the house of José Perea, the three climbed into bed together. Estanislado Trujillo and his wife, who were sharing the same room with the
three, were awakened by all the commotion. Estanislado reported that:

The mother lay down in the middle, with the daughter at one side and Lucero on
the other and such conduct made me extremely suspicious, so I remained awake
most of the night observing what might occur there. And what happened was that
shortly after they went to bed, the mother and son-in-law started caressing each
other as husband and wife, and from there they led up to the ultimate extreme. [20]

The lurid and lusty behavior that prevailed at celebrations provoked
church officials to demand restraint. One priest exhorted women in an
1800 sermon on penance to refrain from dance because of the occasion to
sin that a swivelling hip or bouncing breasts might create. These enticements were the work of the devil and tempted men to indulge in the tran-
sitory pleasures of the flesh. The priest blasted: "You women, dancers of
the devil, scandalous persons, you are the damnation of so many souls.
Oh! What horror! . . . you provocative women, dancers of the devil,
scandal, nets of the devil, basilisks of the streets and windows, you kill
with your stirrings, with your—." [21]

Fray Joaquín de Jesús Ruiz believed that the sexual excess and lascivi-
ousness displayed at fiestas would be curtailed only if constables undertook their duties seriously. Fray Ruiz also proposed the establishment of a

night patrol in 1774 to make sure that unmarried men were not roaming the streets engaging in sin. Don Bernardo Bonavía y Zapata, the Commander-General of the Western Internal Provinces, took more drastic steps to end such public licentiousness. In 1817 he outlawed all public dances because proper decorum and honesty were not being exhibited. In a letter to New Mexico's governor, Commander Bonavía y Zapata wrote:

Citizens of distinction are capable of maintaining the peace in their own homes. They do not let their guests profane or scandalize; but concerning the common people, I beg and entreat the venerable secular and regular clergy to help extirpate these diversions which are so contrary to good behavior, and I order the civil and military authorities to impede them, punishing and correcting delinquents in the same manner as is done with other scandalous public displays.

The prohibition of dances continued into the first years of the Mexican Republic and was achieved through the imposition of a heavy tax.[22]

Unconstrained unison at festivals and dances had cathartic, as well as revolutionary, potential for resolving conflict; both possibilities had to be held in check by secular and religious authorities. Every bureaucrat thus hoped that when the lights went out, the music ended, and a new day began, life would continue as before—regimented and hierarchically structured. The fiesta should only be a temporary suspension and release, necessary to dispel internal community tensions.[23]

Parents arranged marriages for their children to assure the perpetuation of their patrimonies, of their honor, and of their good family names. Although strict supervision of adolescent behavior was employed to achieve this aim, particularly among the nobility, and particularly with their women, enough occasions existed in the routine life of the community when normative constraints were weakened. At festivals, dances, and rites of passage, the rigid hierarchies of age, sex, and class were temporarily suspended, and it was then that expressions of love blossomed. Such expressions were encouraged by the clergy, who as spiritual fathers frequently aided young men and women in subverting the profane concerns of biological parents. We saw in Chapter 2 the intensity of the tug-of-war that the Franciscans waged against Indian adults for the minds and hearts of the Pueblo children during the seventeenth century. In the next chapter we will examine a similar struggle, again between spiritual and biological fathers, only this time for the children of the Spanish colonists during the eighteenth and early nineteenth centuries.

8

Marriage and the Church

Several models of marriage existed side by side in colonial New Mexico. Whether one was a priest, a marital candidate, or the parents of the bride and the groom largely dictated which model would be considered sacred and which profane. For the Catholic Church marriage was a sacrament instituted by Christ. How this sacramental theory squared with familial collectivist notions of marriage as the seal to a social alliance between two kinship groups is our concern in this chapter. But before examining the conflicts that these contradictory models of marriage provoked between clergy and laity, let us begin with a discussion of the Church's concept of dualism, which was so central to these debates.

Catholic theologians defined the human as constituted of body and soul. To engender a child, a man and woman united in intercourse, sharing physical substance, semen and an ovum. Once that child was conceived and born into the world, its rebirth into Christ and the life of the spirit was accomplished through baptism. As we saw in our discussion of Pueblo Indian baptisms in the seventeenth century, and again when we discussed slave baptisms and the selection of their baptismal godparents, the friars believed that baptism as an act of spiritual regeneration rivaled, and indeed surpassed, in importance physical generation. When a priest christened a child, said St. Thomas Aquinas in the *Summa Theologica*, that child was "born again a son of God as Father, and of the Church as Mother." The priest who lifted the child at the baptismal font stood in the place of God, Aquinas asserted. Fray Junípero Serra clearly understood the implication of this fact for kinship politics, stating of Indian neophytes: "Sir, they are our children, for none except us have engendered them in Christ. The result is we look upon them as a father looks upon his family. We shower all our love and care upon them."[1]

The primacy of the spirit over the flesh in Catholic theology meant that in the eyes of New Mexico's friars mystical marriage and union with God constituted the highest state of religious perfection one could reach. The friars had themselves rejected kith and kin and the vainglories of the world for a life of the spirit. Vowing lives of chastity and celibacy, they logically heralded virginity as the paragon of godliness and carnality as the human curse wrought by the Fall. One has to look no further than the 1563 marriage canons of the Council of Trent to see this position articulated: "Whoever shall affirm that the conjugal state is to be preferred to a life of virginity or celibacy, and that it is not better and more conducive to happiness to remain in virginity or celibacy than to be married, let them be excommunicated."[2]

The high moral value that clerics placed on virginity made them natural allies of fathers who were concerned about protecting the virtue and sexual shame of their womenfolk. When we examined how concern for honor and shame were expressed in seduction cases, we noted that priests often became advocates for the females in order to rescue their shame, and thereby restore familial honor. In the towns and villages in which they ministered, priests fostered peace and order by creating community at the local church, by celebrating Mass (the ultimate ritual of peace), by serving as exemplars of virtuous life, and by mediating the Christian community's relationship with its God. But besides promoting such relationships of identity, clerics also fostered relationships of opposition, at least in matters of the spirit and flesh. When masculine honor was concerned, especially if honor was being equated with sexual prowess, clerics clashed with men who reveled in their exploits. Adultery, to take but one example, pitted priests and men against each other where honor was concerned. The friars denounced adulterous men as sinners, yet in terms of honor it was the adulterer's conquest of another man's woman that made him the paragon of virtue.

For clerics who glorified chastity and nurtured the life of the spirit, sacramental marriage was a less desirable, albeit necessary, institution. Matrimony had been instituted by Christ as a *remedium peccati*, a remedy for the sinful fires of lust, as a means of reproducing the species and educating children, and as an indissoluble sacrament that conferred on a couple sanctifying grace so that they could endure the rigors of conjugal life. Granted, marriage was the least desirable way to know God, but as a sacrament it nonetheless enhanced one's spiritual life. Spiritual fathers had to nurture souls and lead them to Christ. It was primarily to fulfill this paternal duty that the Church regulated marriage.[3]

Until 1776, matrimony was totally under the jurisdiction of the Catholic Church. The Church determined who were and were not appropriate partners, specified the juridical form of marriage, and defined the ritual gestures that constituted the sacrament—powers it had been granted in America in the *Real Patronato*.[4]

As custodian of a person's spirituality in matrimony, the Church theoretically subordinated concerns of the body, those familial interests in honor, property, and lineal solidarity that were the essence of the popular model of marriage. To assure that such interests were not placed before spiritual salvation, the Church elaborated an expansive theory of incest, which, by prohibiting marriage between close relatives, promoted a broad concept of Christian community. Similarly, rooted in the belief that everyone had a right to choose a vocation freely and that sacramental grace was accessible to all, the Church maintained that parents could not force children to marry against their will. We now turn to how these issues worked themselves out in theory and practice, examining first the Church's theory of marital impediments, then the exercise of consent and free will, and finally the rituals that marked marriage and alliance.

Impediments to Marriage

The Church determined who were and were not appropriate marital partners. It did this through a theory of marital impediments spelled out in canon law, which defined incest and the requisites that made a person physically competent to undertake marriage. Canonic impediments fell into two categories: dire impediments, which prohibited marriage, required papal or episcopal dispensation, and annulled a nuptial if discovered after it had occurred; and preventative impediments, which were less severe, could be dispensed by the lower clergy, and infrequently undermined the validity of the sacrament. The most important dire impediments were consanguinity, affinity, religious vows, differences in religion, bigamy, polygamy, male impotence, crime, misrepresentation, and coercion.[5]

As stipulated in the marriage canons of the Council of Trent, before persons anywhere in Christendom could marry, they had to submit to a *diligencia matrimonial*, a marital investigation which established that no impediments to marriage existed. The extant *diligencias* for New Mexico between 1694 and 1846 in the Archives of the Archdiocese of Santa Fe number 6,558. They indicate that due to the area's limited population from which partners could be chosen, the most common dire impedi-

TABLE 8.1

Dispensations Granted for Consanguinity in New Mexico, 1700-1846

	1700-49	1750-99	1800-1846	Total Period
Degree of consanguinity				
2nd	3	1	4	8
3rd	3	19	49	71
4th	8	53	111	172
Total	14	73	164	251
Total marriage investigations	352	1,240	4,966	6,558
Dispensations as percent of marriage investigations	3.9%	5.8%	3.3%	3.8%

SOURCE: AASF-*DM* Reels 60-79.

ments were consanguinity and affinity. The Church prohibited marriage between persons related up to the fourth degree of consanguinity or affinity, whatever its basis. Consanguinity was a relationship based on direct blood descent. Children begotten in wedlock were *legitimate* consanguines of their parents and siblings, *natural* consanguines if conceived illicitly, and *legal* consanguines if adopted. Marriage created *legitimate* ties of affinity, illicit sex produced *illegitimate* affinity, and the relationship between godparent and godchild, between confessor and penitent, and between catechist and catechumen established bonds of *spiritual* affinity that made marriage between individuals so related inappropriate.[6]

There were 251 consanguinity impediment dispensations granted to New Mexicans between 1694 and 1846 so that they could marry close kin (see Table 8.1). No union between first degree consanguines (i.e., between siblings) occurred; all were between the second and fourth degrees. Degrees were calculated by measuring the generational distance from a common ancestor, omitting the root. A brother and sister were first degree consanguines; a nephew and niece second degree; second cousins a third degree; and so on. A transverse link was created through a common ancestor (as opposed to a direct biological relation) and contained as many degrees as there were generations in the descent of the longer line, excluding the common ancestor.[7]

Close cousin marriages occurred in New Mexico primarily among the nobility. In 160 out of 250 consanguinity dispensation requests, members of the nobility asked the Church's permission to marry close relatives in order to maintain their honor, social status, blood purity, and familial wealth. The function of such marriages was to reinforce blood lines and lineal solidarity. Property and labor, which at marriage normally would have been transferred outside the kinship group's control, were thereby kept intact. Typical of the arguments the aristocracy used before the ecclesiastical courts to obtain dispensations for the consanguinity impediments was that presented by Don Antonio Chávez of Atrisco, who in 1718 wanted to marry his second cousin Doña Antonia Baca of Bernalillo. Don Antonio said he desired her as his bride because "Antonia Baca is very poor and if her guardians were to die, she would be exposed to the danger of ruination, or at the very least having to marry someone who is not her equal, to which must be added the cause of *angustia loci* [i.e., not enough unrelated members of one's status with whom to contract marriage] here, for the lack of population in this miserable kingdom is well known." Fray Antonio Camargo granted the dispensation Don Antonio sought but as his penance ordered him to work personally on the construction of a church in Albuquerque for four months, to donate 2,000 adobe bricks, and to collect alms throughout the region once a week for sixteen weeks so that Masses could be prayed for the poor souls in purgatory.[8]

The proportion of affinity to consanguinity dispensations recorded in New Mexico was approximately 1 to 6, occurring at a rate of less than 1 per 100 (see Table 8.2). Just as matrimony between cousins had important structural implications for the functioning of the kinship system, so too did affine marriages. The Alarid and Chávez families understood this when in 1829 they maintained their marital alliance intact by having Don Joaquín Alarid marry his deceased wife's sister, Doña María de la Luz Chávez. Canonists frowned on such unions in the first degree of affinity. New Mexico's clerics seemed less troubled by them. Curate Madariaga of

TABLE 8.2

Dispensations Granted for Affinity in New Mexico, 1700-1846

	1700-49	1750-99	1800-1846	Total Period
Degree of affinity				
1st	2	1	2	5
2nd	—	3	7	10
3rd	—	3	12	15
4th	—	1	12	13
Total	2	8	33	43
Total marriage investigations	352	1,240	4,966	6,558
Dispensations as percent of marriage investigations	0.6%	0.6%	0.6%	0.6%

SOURCE: AASF–*DM* Reels 60-79.

Tomé even intervened in Don Joaquín's case, arguing before the vicar that the marriage should be allowed because "the candidates are persons of distinction, honor, and good conduct in this territory."[9]

Less frequent, though all the more irksome for the custodians of New Mexico's morals, were the cases of illegitimate affinity. Sinful liaisons not only denigrated the sacrament of matrimony, but also left illegitimate children as their product. Barbara Chávez of Belén bore a bastard in 1796 as the result of the illicit coition she had enjoyed with Luís Contreras. Luís later tried to marry Barbara's sister, Juana Chávez, with whom technically he had a first degree affinity impediment due to sex with Barbara. Both women were pregnant, and in a justifiable quandary Fray Mariano Sánchez sought episcopal counsel. The bishop ordered Luís and Juana married after they performed public penance for their sin.[10]

In addition to incest prohibitions, three other categories of dire impediments to marriage existed in canon law: religious conditions, physical inadequacies, and crime. The first of these obstacles was defined as a previous commitment to God through a clerical vocation or a commitment to a different religion or another individual. Once a solemn vow of chastity had been made, or holy orders in the Catholic Church had been conferred, sacramental conjugal life was no longer possible. Differences in the religious affiliation of nuptial candidates were also an encumbrance to such a state. Before matrimony between a Catholic and a Jew, Protestant, or Muslim could occur, the non-Catholic had to be baptized. Henry White, Joseph Portelance, and Alexander Montgomery were but three of the 90 foreigners who were baptized between 1821 and 1846 so that they could marry native New Mexican women. Though undoubtedly some of these conversions were genuine, Thomas James, a Missouri hunter and trader, in 1822 exposed Hugh Glenn's as "a sordid . . . hypocracy [sic]." Of Glenn's Santa Fe baptism James wrote, "He changed his religion more rapidly than his clothes, and made each change a profitable speculation to himself. Such pliability of conscience may serve a temporary purpose."[11]

Bigamy and polygamy were also considered impediments of previous commitment because they violated the permanence of the matrimonial bond, which could be dissolved only through death. Marrying twice or having several wives was such a heinous crime that it was under the jurisdiction of the Inquisition. In New Mexico polygamy occurred primarily among the Indian population, but two cases did surface among Hispanos. A denunciation before the Holy Office for bigamy or polygamy, whatever else it might accomplish, often helped abandoned wives locate estranged husbands. A search for José Antonio Díaz in 1743, and another in 1830 for José Antonio Gutiérrez were conducted. Individuals known by these names resided in El Paso and Isleta, but the investigations concluded that neither was a bigamist; both simply happened to have very common names.[12]

The fundamental purpose of matrimony was procreation. Anything that hindered this end, be it impotence, a disparity in genital size that made intercourse impossible, or the lack of a penis, was a dire impediment to marriage. If such an impediment was not detected before the nuptials, a spouse had up to 30 days after the ceremony to protest. In 1781, eight days was all it took Jacinta Trujillo of Abiquiu to demand her freedom from Antonio Choño. Although the impediment of impotence was usually difficult to substantiate, in Jacinta's case, it took Fray Sebastian Fernández only seconds to conclude that she had cause. "Antonio totally lacked a virile member, although the rest of his parts were intact," reported the friar. Amazed and somewhat perplexed, the friar wanted an explanation. He had known Antonio as happily married to his then deceased first wife. "A few years ago I experienced a sickness and the said member fell off in parts," said Antonio. The laws of nature and those of the Church maintained that this was an invalid matrimony. Jacinta Trujillo was thus free to remarry as she chose.[13]

Criminal activity such as killing one's spouse with the intent of marrying another was also a dire impediment to matrimony. Obviously, this too was a difficult charge to prove. A well-executed crime would always lack evidence, but eyebrows might be raised and suspicions aroused if the mourning period for one's deceased spouse was too short, indecorously observed, or too quickly followed by remarriage. "The speed with which marriage has been proposed after the death of the bride's first husband," wrote Fray José de Castro in 1812 concerning the proposed union between José Antonio Mestas and María Antonia Martín, Domingo Trujillo's widow, "leads me to suspect that a promise of matrimony was given while she was still married." In addition to the impediment of crime, the friar continued, "there is also suspicion because the husband was insane at death and could have been given some drink to bring about his end." Juan Ignacio Sandoval and Bernardo Abeyta testified that they had heard Mestas say that as soon as Domingo Trujillo died, he would marry his widow. On the basis of this evidence, the nuptial between José and María was prohibited, and the two were sternly warned to avoid the sinful state of concubinage, which the "Supreme Legislator" punished with damnation. We can only imagine what ulterior motive Fray Diego Martínez had for advising Juana Josefa Gómez of Pojoaque in 1809 to poison her husband with a weed called "el Peco." The friar promised Juana that if she killed her husband he would bury the man without charge, would forgive Juana's sin, and would support her in whatever she needed. Juana wanted to remarry and so she ignored the friar's advice, and let her husband die of "natural cause." [14]

The last category of dire impediments arose from the application of the ecclesiastical principle that a valid marriage could only be contracted if the full consent of the parties existed. Misrepresentations such that a person's name, status, or wealth was different than that specified in a marriage proposal automatically violated consent requirements. The use of force by parents to get their children to marry impinged upon free consent, as did the marriage of minors who could not legally express their true will. The discovery of coercion in most cases automatically dissolved a marriage.

The Principle of Consent

The impediment of force, based on the principle that consent was fundamental to the sacrament of matrimony, had a long history in canon law derived primarily from Roman tradition. Roman law had recognized two types of marriage defined by the power (*manus*) a husband exercised over his wife. The oldest class of marriage, *cum manus* (with power), entailed the judicial transfer of a woman from her father's to her husband's authority, her incorporation into her husband's family, and her subjugation to her husband, even though he himself might still be under the authority (*patria potestas*) of his own father. [15]

By the time of the classical Roman jurists, says Percy Corbett, the institution of *manus* had become obsolete and "a matter of legal archaeology." A freer form of marriage known as *sin manus* (without power) replaced it, governed only by the legal maxim "*consensus facit nuptias*" (consent makes the nuptial). So long as mutual consent to marry was expressed, a couple was legally united in binding contract. Open cohabitation, a female's public transfer from her father's to her husband's house, or witnesses to the consent were accepted as sufficient proof of contract. When consent no longer existed, the marriage could be dissolved by either spouse without judical recourse or prejudice. [16]

During the first eight centuries of its existence, the Catholic Church accepted the Roman legal maxim of mutual consent as the judicial form of marriage. When two individuals desired to be husband and wife, all that was technically necessary was the public expression of that desire. Sexual intercourse was considered a testament of such a vow, the presumption being that full consent had been exercised. [17]

Such marriages, which parents considered secret or clandestine because they were contracted without parental consent or even witnesses to verify the validity of the contract, created numerous problems. Individuals could, out of malice, claim that a secret marriage existed where none in fact had occurred—so too the opposite. A man and a woman might in the heat of passion express a desire to marry, then later, out of remorse or in greater control of their rational faculties, renege on the contract by publicly celebrating another. A woman who gave herself in copulation believing that she was married might rudely discover that she was not, and lack judicial recourse. Quarrels, questions over the legitimacy of children, and litigation over patrimonial rights were all inevitable consequences of these so-called clandestine marriages.[18]

A distinction between valid and legitimate marriage was introduced into canon law in order to curb some of the most notorious abuses of the principle of consent. The canonists maintained that because marriage was a bond in natural law, and since the expression of mutual consent— usually through intercourse—constituted the sacramental act, any union meeting this requisite was valid. Just as a person could be incorporated into the mystical body of Christ through a covert baptism of faith to avoid persecution, a man and a woman might similarly be joined secretly in marriage. So long as the marital bond was monogamous, fidelity prevailed, and the couple promised to live together until death, the union was valid. However, a marriage would be judged legitimate only if consent was certified by a priest.[19]

The Church's sanction of clandestine marriages was controversial primarily because of the high incidence of common law unions based solely on consent and conjugation. Many parents believed that the Church's recognition of clandestine marriages was simply a seducer's license. The matter was finally resolved at the Council of Trent (1545–63). It was there that the law on clandestine marriages in effect in colonial New Mexico was established. In November of 1563 the Council decreed that the Church would recognize as legally valid only those marriages in which the expression of consent had been witnessed by a priest and at least two competent persons, and recorded in the parish register. Consent, defined as the right to choose a partner freely, remained the essence of the sacrament. What changed was the Church's willingness to accept as valid sacramental or binding customary marital practices. Only those marriages that the Church administered, public or secret, would be recognized in canon law. The Tridentine marriage canons gave the sacrament a more precise legal definition to reduce the possibilities of contesting its validity.[20]

Arranged marriages that furthered familial honor concerns were a complex issue for the Church. Scripture and canon law were fraught with ambiguities and contradictions on the matter. Christian ideology reinforced the honor code regarding the obedience and personal subordination children owed their parents. "Honor your father and mother," ordered the fourth commandment. "Children obey your parents in the Lord . . . with fear and trembling . . . with good will doing service, as to the Lord," enjoined St. Paul in his Epistle to the Ephesians. The Church maintained that the law of nature bound parents and children in a relationship that entailed reciprocal rights and obligations. The authority of a father over his wife, children, and servants emanated from God's power over creation and therefore his was the right to guide and discipline children as necessary. Filial submission, St. Paul promised, would be reciprocated with parental love, protection, and guidance.[21]

But the vexing question a cleric was obliged to ask in the case of marriage was, When was parental guidance and filial obedience simply outright coercion? The issue was of some importance because forced marriages, or those contracted under duress, were invalid. Matrimony was the sacramental union of free wills based on mutual consent. Ideally, it was the work of God and "what God has joined together, let no man separate."

The autonomy of individual will, responsibility, and conscience in undertaking marriage was central to Christian thought. In arranged marriages, in which conflicts between obedience to parents and obedience to one's conscience existed, the will of the individual was to take precedence. The oft-quoted scriptural limitations on parental authority came from St. Matthew's gospel: "Call no man your father upon the earth: for One is your Father, which is in heaven." And again:

Think not that I am come to send peace on earth: I came not to send peace, but a sword. For I am come to set a man at variance against his father, and the daughter against her mother, and the daughter-in-law against her mother-in-law. And a man's foes shall be they of his own household. He that loveth father or mother more than me is not worthy of me: and he that loveth son or daughter more than me is not worthy of me.[22]

A mechanism for the determination that a person was marrying freely existed in canon law. When a priest suspected that a marriage was being contracted under duress or was being discouraged by parents, he was obliged to investigate the matter fully. The friar ascertained the true will of the nuptial candidates by sequestering them and placing them in deposit (*en deposito*) in a good Christian home where they would be isolated from parents and any pressures that might influence their decision. After three days of solitude, the priest would return, accompanied by a notary, and would take depositions concerning each person's desire to marry. If the priest was convinced that a person truly wished marriage, even though parents might oppose it, he was free to dispense with two of the three required banns so that the ceremony could be celebrated quickly. If the opposite was true, and the person was being coerced into a union, clerics were obliged to prohibit matrimony. Let us illustrate this point with a few examples.

Don Salvador Martínez of Albuquerque sought ecclesiastical intervention in 1761 so that he could marry Doña Simona Valdez. Don Salvador had asked Doña Simona's parents for their daughter's hand in marriage twice. His first proposal was flatly refused, his second ignored. "If she wants, she can marry," Simona's father had told his neighbors, "she can do as she pleases." Martínez responded that that was a lie, "she has not even been asked what her feelings or desires are because her parents do not like the idea that she may escape from her slavery." *En deposito* Doña Simona admitted that she truly wanted Don Salvador for her husband. The matrimony occurred despite parental objections, which may have been due to a gross age difference. Don Salvador was a 62-year-old widower. Doña Simona was only 19.[23]

Miguel Sandoval Martínez, a soldier at Santa Fe's presidio, similarly gained his pastor's assistance in 1697 to remove Lucía Gómez from the house of her widowed mother, Juana Ortiz. Miguel and Lucía secretly had given each other a promise of marriage in 1696. They had not been able to publicly celebrate it because Lucía's mother had objected. "And because of that, all of her relatives and in-laws have threatened me," said Martínez, "warning that if [Lucía] enters the state of Godly grace with me they will take her life as well as mine." In seclusion Lucía said that she had always desired to be Miguel's bride but had stifled momentarily those feelings because "my mother forbade it and threatened me." As a result of clerical intervention, the couple was finally joined in wedlock.[24]

According to canon law the essential requisite for matrimony was consent. From the outset of America's colonization the Spanish crown ordered that Indian and slave marriages also were to be regulated by the same norm. "My will is that Indians have total liberty to marry anyone of their choice, be it with another Indian or with a native of this place," ordered King Charles V in 1515. "No Indian chieftain, even if he is an infidel, can marry more than once, nor keep women locked up, nor deprive them of their freedom to join with a person of their choice," stated the royal edict of December 17, 1557. The law was notoriously abused, prompting its reiteration in 1595, 1596, 1628, and in the 1680 *Recompilation of the Laws of the Indies.*[25]

The liberty of New Mexico's Pueblo Indians to marry freely was duly documented and rigorously enforced by the missionaries. The experience of *genízaro* slaves was another matter. Responding to clerical complaints regarding slave treatment in New Mexico, Governor Francisco Antonio Marín del Valle wrote the viceroy in 1758 explaining that "slaves in the kingdom are treated well and allowed every liberty to marry freely." Contrary to what the governor asserted, the extant evidence verified the friars' complaints. Despite the fact that 3,294 *genízaro* slaves entered New Mexico between 1694 and 1848, only 20 slave marriages were recorded during these years. As we noted earlier, many of the slaves that entered New Mexican homes were children. Thus by the time they reached marriageable age they were often legally eligible for manumission. But if a master wanted to retain their services, it was in his or her interest to discourage marriage. Fray Josef Manuel de Equía y Leronbe, Nambé's pastor, in 1734 accused slave owners of extending the period of bondage and saying that it was necessary to "fornicate with one's Indians so that they do not seek husbands." The friar maintained that in most cases the prohibition of a thrall's marriage was not always blatant and often took more subtle forms. Don Ignacio Roybal created psychological conflicts in his slaves, explained the friar, by telling them that "only ingrates marry and leave their masters." The accusation Fray Josef leveled against Don Ignacio gained credence in 1741 when it was discovered that two of Don Ignacio's married children were prohibiting their slaves from marrying freely.[26]

The string of events in this case began one night in 1741, as Cipriano, Don Bernardo Roybal's Indian slave, was rounding up his master's sheep near Santa Cruz. Knowing that Don Bernardo was out of town, his brother-in-law, Manuel Martín, took the absence as an opportunity to threaten Cipriano to drop his bid to marry Isabel, Martín's servant. Though Cipriano had lived in concubinage with Antonia, another slave in Don Bernardo Roybal's household, and had sired her child, Cipriano insisted that Isabel was the woman he wanted as his bride. Despite Manuel Martín's displeasure over this prospect and his attempts to marry Isabel to his brother Josef's Indian servant, Isabel too insisted that she wanted to marry Cipriano. "I never wanted to marry [Josef Martín's] Indian," explained Isabel, "because he does not know how to pray, nor is it in my heart to marry him."

When the Martín family, deeply tied to the Roybals through affinity (three of Sebastian Martín's children—Margarita, Manuel, and Angela—were married to three of Ignacio Roybal's children—Bernardo, Elena, and Ignacio), discovered that Cipriano had beaten Antonia in an effort to get her to drop the impediment of previous promise of betrothal to his marriage with Isabel, Manuel Martín was furious. Manuel, along with his father Sebastian, and Salvador Torres apprehended Cipriano, roughed him up, and as he fled, he abandoned Don Bernardo's sheep. That night the sheep trampled Rosa Martín's wheat field. Rosa sued her brother-in-law Don Bernardo for the cost of the wheat. Don Bernardo countered with a suit against Manuel Martín for beating Cipriano and for threats. According to Don Bernardo, Martín had said that "he was going to kill me and all of my people, ignoring that I am married to one of his older sisters." After lengthy interrogation, the two Indian slaves, Cipriano and Isabel, were allowed to marry over their masters' opposition. Manuel Martín was fined 50 pesos (T) for the public disturbance he had caused and was ordered to compensate his sister for the destroyed wheat. As this case indicates, the Church had protected the right of Indians and slaves to marry freely.[27]

The freedom that the Catholic Church granted the sexes in the selection of conjugal mates formed the legal basis for the subversion of parental authority. But as experience in the Spanish empire testifies, the law and its execution were two very different matters. It was not uncommon for clerics charged with the interpretation and execution of canon law to enforce it selectively or to bend its dictates to avoid misalliances or subversion of the social order. If a friar believed an arranged marriage was a good match, he might uphold parental prerogatives, rationalizing that the natural authority of a father over his children was in full accord with the will of God.

That such irregularities occurred was attested by Josef Armijo of Santa Fe, who in 1710 complained to Fray Lucas Arebalo that María Velásquez was, against her will, being prevented from marrying him. Fray Lucas questioned María and quickly ascertained that she wanted to marry Josef. When the friar suggested that she enter into his custody so that the nuptial could be performed, María begged him not to remove her from her home. "I fear my parents, and so that they do not beat me or cause me other harm, do not tell them that I wish to marry but instead tell them that I do not wish to marry . . . that way I can escape from the house with greater safety." María fled to the convent the next morning and was placed in deposit. While there, she was visited by her gossip (*comadre*), Lucía Gómez, who asked her: "Do you really wish to hurt your parents by marrying that young man, a prospect that so displeases them that they are in total anguish? Do you think it impossible to find another good man, more to your parent's liking with whom to contract marriage?" Moved by the words and tears of her *comadre*, María agreed that she would not marry Josef, if her father promised not to subdue her as rigorously in the future. Gómez consulted María's father and returned with a note in which he told his daughter that he would marry her to anyone he chose and "in the future would be even sterner with her."

Later that day, without explanation, María's father and Fray Lucas returned María to her parents' home. Had Josef Armijo not fully understood his rights under canon law, his bid might have been stymied. Instead, he immediately appealed to the provincial ecclesiastical judge, Fray Miguel Muñoz, telling him it had already been determined that María wanted to marry "of her own free will." For Fray Lucas to have acted as he had saying that "María had had a sudden change of heart," was highly suspect. Such behavior was scandalous. It was the work of various people, blasted Armijo, "the product of bad advice which ignored the decrees of the Holy Council of Trent which prohibited this type of influence and excommunicated for such counsels" while a person was in isolation. Fray Muñoz agreed. Fray Lucas had acted illegally. A new investigation was ordered and as soon as María and Josef affirmed their desire to marry, they were. Thus the ability of parents to utilize their bonds of friendship and trust with the local friar to subvert filial desires was one strategy to thwart a marriage, one that was perhaps more common than the extant documentary evidence would have us believe.[28]

The great latitude that a priest or ecclesiastical judge could exercise in determining whether a person's free will to marry was being exercised was illustrated in another case, one reported by Fray Pedro Montaño, Albuquerque's pastor, to the viceregal court in Mexico City in 1733. Chronicling the notorious abuse of authority that Santa Fe's vicar had displayed, Montaño recounted how Manuel Armijo and Francisca Baca of Santa Fe had expressed their desire to wed, but had been kept from so doing by Francisca's father, Don Antonio Baca. Don Antonio, a great-great grandson of Don Cristobal Baca, one of New Mexico's original conquistadores, felt that Manuel Armijo, a mestizo of lowly repute, was no match for his noble and illustrious daughter, Francisca. Manuel Armijo was not easily deterred by Don Antonio's opposition, and legally petitioned Santa Fe's vicar, Don José de Bustamente y Tangle, to sequester Francisca Baca and to place her in a neutral home so that she might express her wish to marry him. The vicar, himself a partisan in the case, was deeply tied through bonds of blood and affinity to the Baca family. He placed Francisca *en deposito* but allowed several of her aunts and uncles to speak to her, and himself sent her a note saying that even if she was pregnant not to fear, all would be taken care of discreetly. Of course, all of this contact was illegal. The Baca clan got their way and Francisca proclaimed that she did not wish to marry Manuel Armijo, or so the vicar legally certified.

In the days that followed, Francisca again expressed her desire to marry Manuel. To keep that from happening, her father sent Francisca to his sister's hacienda near Albuquerque. But unbeknown to her brother, Doña Josefa Baca had a solution for her niece's love sickness. On August 10, 1733, the feast of St. Lawrence martyr, celebrated to commemorate the martyrdom of the Franciscans killed during the 1680 Pueblo Revolt, Doña Josefa and Francisca attended Mass in Albuquerque. When Mass ended and the congregation had exited to watch a performance of the play, "The Christians and the Moors," Fray Pedro Montaño remained at the altar. Doña Josefa and Francisca approached him and suddenly through a side door entered Manuel Armijo. There the priest pronounced them husband and wife. Apparently the whole plot had been orchestrated by Doña Josefa who herself was the family's black sheep because she had never married, yet had borne six illegitimate children. The Franciscan friars facilitated Manuel and Francisca's marriage primarily to embarrass the vicar before the crown and to show how arbitrarily he performed his chores. Had that not been the case, the friars probably would not have sanctioned such an unequal marriage.[29]

From the evidence in ecclesiastical archives, "absolute" legal liberty to choose a spouse freely meant, in fact, freedom to select a mate from within one's own class and ethnic group. Only one example in over 150 years, the one cited above, exists of a cleric sanctioning a cross-class marriage over parental objections. Although the Church in theory opposed forced marriages that furthered familial honor concerns and stood ready to subvert parental authority, in reality in rarely did. Had clerics constantly undermined hierarchically structured authority relations within the family, anarchy might have reigned. Catholicism, whatever potential for opposition existed in its radical concept of spiritual life, was, in the final analysis, an ideological arm of the Spanish state, which legitimated the colonial order and more often than not, preached social accommodation. To this end the Church's strictures on children honoring parents and obeying God and king served it well.[30]

Cultural Contradictions and Social Action

In describing the relationships of alliance and opposition that clerics established with children and parents to further their interests in sacramental matrimony and the maintenance of an orderly rule-bound society, my intention has not been to represent the negotiation of marriage as a stark, either-or process. Obviously, the sources used here to discuss marriage are ecclesiastical court records that always document extreme examples. The negotiation of marriage was, in reality, a much more complex and ambivalent process. According to the native cognitive model of New Mexicans, behavior was the outcome of interplay between several realms. Individual actions were the result of mediation between external forces, such as social rules, values, and chance, and internal physical drives, such as sentiments and emotions. The head and the heart were two body parts that were deemed particularly important in synthesizing beliefs about hierarchy, honor, and desires, and translating them into behavior.

External factors were comprehended through the head. Rational faculties resided in the head. Reason, probity, and the conscience were perceived to be located here. The head was the symbol of personal and collective honor. If the head was the source of reason, its antithesis, emotion, was rooted in the heart. The heart was the organ through which "natural" urges were experienced and felt. True desires sprang from the heart. When one gave one's word of honor, it too was believed to come from the heart. The heart as a natural symbol for love had been enmeshed in the popular consciousness of Western Europeans since at least the thirteenth century. The songs and poetry of courtly love diffused to the New World drew the heart as the well of sentiment. As roving troubadours performed their medieval romances in New Mexico's villages, the motifs of their repertoire—the all-consuming love that tormented the courtier, the impossible desires of an inferior man for a married lady, the discovery of an adulterous liaison that ended in death for the two lovesick individuals—resonated in the imaginations of young and old.[31]

The tensions between external forces and personal desires symbolized as conflicts between the head and the heart, between reason and sentiment, between collective responsibility and individual will, provided Hispanos with a variety of options and explanations for their behavior. One can see the equivocation over such ideals in the 1715 statements of Sebastiana de Jesús of Santa Fe. Appearing before the local priest for the matrimonial investigation necessary so that she could be joined in wedlock with Gerónimo Ortega, she was asked if she truly wanted to marry. Sebastiana said:

When the mother who raised me, whose name is Lucía Ortiz, asked me about the marriage the first time, I said no, I did not want to marry; but later, so that my mother would not be angry I said yes. But now, the desire to marry him does not spring from my heart . . . and having heard that the father of Gerónimo de Ortega has become a public ward in Santa Fe, I refuse to marry him. And if I marry him it will be only because my mother forces me to. I must do as she wishes, and

will do it only to please her. . . . I do not wish to marry, it is not of my heart. . . .
Before it was not of my heart and it is even less so now.

Fray Antonio Miranda was uncertain whether Sebastiana was being
forced into matrimony so he ordered a new declaration taken. When
asked again she said blankly that she wanted to marry Gerónimo "of my
absolute liberty."[32]

The individuals who articulated the ideals of marriage formation as
consisting of contradictory views, for example that arranged marriage
was opposed to marriage choice and hierarchy was opposed to egalitarianism, were advocates of a particular position with a vested interest in
presenting the cultural system as being rigidly circumscribed by these di-
chotomies. In reality, much behavior fell along a continuum defined only
at its extremes by such oppositions. After all, our sources of information
for these prescriptions come largely from litigation before the civil and
ecclesiastical courts, which established the outer limits of what was and
was not proper conduct. In their daily lives individuals negotiated their
behavior pragmatically in dynamic relationships with one another using
the ideals of the cultural system as anchors.[33]

The dialogue that undoubtedly occurred between the generations
while negotiating a marriage match was seldom voiced and rarely recorded. Folk songs are the only sources that give us a hint of the interaction between the generations that must have been central to the selection
process. "The Recent Bride," an early nineteenth-century song from
Taos, explores the tensions between parents and children over marriage
choice. Parents, having themselves at one time perhaps experienced the
same feelings, could articulate the child's view. But they did so negatively,
casting duty and sentiment, reason and passion, paternal love and romantic love as irreconcilable. The parental objective clearly was to subvert individualistic filial behavior. By describing the consequences of ignoring parental counsels, they hoped to have their expectations fulfilled.

> A recent bride and woe is me
> I weep the livelong day
> To think I'm wed so unhappily
> Nothing can my fate allay.
>
> Before I wed my mother dear
> Did try to turn me from my course,
> Her counsels wet with many a tear
> I now regret with great remorse.
>
> But willful was I, I paid no heed
> And God has fully punished me,

But willful was I, I paid no heed
And God has fully punished me.

For my husband I have found to be
A man who drinks and drinks and drinks,
He has already forgotten me
Of his young bride he never thinks.[34]

In "La Señora Chepita" the generational conflict was more explicit.

Oh what times these are Señora Chepita;
Oh what things are happening these days!
Laboriousness is no longer prized,
Misery engulfs us all,
Progress itself is lost.
Oh what times these are Señora Chepita!

In my time commerce bleated
And the crafts with much to do.
Lovers were always constant,
No woman was ever false.
Women in times past
Spent their time only caring
For their children, husbands and servants
And of none did they gossip.

Today it is common to see
That honor is snatched from one another
In others defects are found
While ignoring one's own, Señora Chepita.
If a young man made a conquest
He would hide it with just reason
So that none would know
The secrets of his heart.[35]

From the parents' point of view presented above, their society was portrayed as orderly and rule bound, whereas that of the new generation was chaotic and without rules. The song was not a statement of fact. If we took such comments literally, the folk songs in which the older generation laments the shortcomings of the new—a lament so common in every historical period—would lead us to believe that society was constantly in a state of breakdown. These songs were instead comments about what parents wanted their children to do. Parents refused to legitimize the norms that guided filial behavior by denying that such norms existed. These songs expressed parental displeasure. They attempted to convince sons and daughters to obey parents and to do things the way they had been done in "the good old days" when father ruled. Such appeals to tradition and authority were necessary because as we saw when discussing close kin marriages among the nobility, children had their own ploys for getting what they wanted.[36]

Parents and children negotiated their actions with different amounts of power. The dynamics of the process were clearly skewed in favor of elders both in conscious and unconscious ways. Sons and daughters were familiar with the whole range of options they could undertake in their nuptial formation and exactly what was expected to assure property transmission, to assuage a family's symbolic patrimony, and to avoid scandal and ostracism. Norms and the authority of custom buttressed parental prerogatives as did the socialization process. Personal "tastes" were learned in infancy and reinforced through avoidance of contact with certain persons. Thus a child's desire for a certain mate, what might be labelled an "individualistic" urge, was largely the result of interaction with persons of similar status, race, education, and subcultural traits.[37]

The Rituals of Betrothal and Marriage

The third realm of ecclesiastical jurisdiction over marriage was the ritual of matrimony itself. Here again the Church, as in its conflict with the laity over its definition of incest and free will, had progressively expanded the importance of the nuptial rite that it controlled, simultaneously debasing ancient, popular rituals of alliance. This conflict was most evident in the varying amounts of significance that the laity and clergy each gave to the betrothal and to the nuptial. In the popular mind the betrothal established a marital contract and alliance between two kinship groups. Thus the ritual gestures of the betrothal celebrated the creation of community between groups whose social relationships were normally marked by fear, suspicion, and enmity. Juxtaposed to this collectivist view of marriage was the Church's view of matrimony as a sacrament. Since the fourteenth century, and particularly after the promulgation of the Council of Trent's marriage reforms, canonists increasingly had stressed the individualistic implications of the sacrament in order to thwart lineal solidarity and to expand its own power. Ultimately, the Church refused to recognize rites of betrothal and proclaimed that the only ritual of juridical and sacramental significance was the nuptial it administered. As we will see, the Church simply appropriated popular rituals of alliance as its own and placed them under clerical supervision.[38]

When a father decided that it was time for his son to marry, or when a son had obliquely suggested that his family should form an alliance with another, and a prospective partner had been settled upon, local custom determined the betrothal rites that would follow. The complex process leading to marriage began with the proposed groom and his parents paying a social visit to the prospective bride's home. New Mexico's elites used this social call as the opportunity to relay a formal letter in which they asked for the hand of the bride (*pedir la mano*) in marriage and to elaborate the economic terms of the agreement—what the groom would bring to the marital community. "The letter was an ordinary business document," recalled the United States Attorney for New Mexico, William Watts Davis in 1853, "and [was] couched in about the same language as would be used in the purchase of a mule or the hire of a burro."[39]

Commoners also used the social visit between parents to publicly broach the question of marriage between their respective children. After a perfunctory conversation concerning the weather, crops, and politics, the issue of matrimony would be raised. It was not uncommon for the groom's parents to be accompanied on this call by a minstrel who would sing the proposal in verse. Some songsters boastfully advertised that the eloquence and imagery of their style would secure a bride without fail. Whether in letter or song, whether disguised or not, the object of the proposal was clear. When the hand of a woman in marriage was requested, men exchanged a proprietary right that women could not similarly claim.[40]

Once marriage had been proposed, a response was eagerly awaited. A negative decision came quickly. Failure to secure the desired bride frequently was expressed by saying *nos dieron calabazas* (they gave us pumpkins). A positive decision always came fifteen days after the initial proposal. The acceptance would be conveyed through another formal visit or through a personally delivered letter. Don Antonio José Chávez of Santa Fe, in his letter of April 20, 1820, to Don Juan Armijo of Peña Blanca, accepted the matrimonial offer thus:

With regard to your kind request for my daughter María del Carmen, so that she may enter the holy state of matrimony with your very honorable son, Antonio Timoteo Armijo, as God wills it, and it is my daughter's and also my wife's desire, the marriage should occur between my daughter and your son. My wife and I believe that this is the disposition of divine providence, and thus we accept the wedding in whatever manner you may see fit. In the interim, my wife and I pray that Our Lord may grant you good health for many years.

Once the conditions of marriage were accepted, the dates for the betrothal and nuptial would be set and preparations for the festivities would begin.[41]

The passage from adolescence to adulthood associated with the rituals of betrothal and marriage was marked by three distinct phases: separation, marginality, and reaggregation. Arnold Van Gennep, the Belgian folklorist who proposed this ritual model, believed that all rites of passage conformed to a similar spatiotemporal ordering. The ceremonial complex always began with the separation of the subjects from an old state and ended with their incorporation into a new one. The ceremonies during the period of marginality progressed by degrees, stages, and steps, repeating over and over again symbolic acts that compressed into brief moments changes that normally would have taken years to accomplish. The ritual gestures associated with a betrothal and nuptial were aimed at compensating both kinship groups for their losses and gains—be it through the forfeiture or acquisition of a productive member, the incursion of large wedding expenses, a halt in the work routine, or a change in a household's productive capacity—and simultaneously recognized the creation of a new household and elevation of the bride and groom to full community membership.[42]

The *prendorio*, as the betrothal was called (a word derived from *prenda* meaning a jewel or highly prized object), initiated the separation of the marital candidates from their single adolescent state. The rite commenced with the arrival of the groom and his immediate kin at the home of the bride's family where her relatives had gathered. After pleasantries had been exchanged, the groom's father would say, "we wish to meet the desired jewel." The bride would enter, dressed in her best clothes, walking demurely, her eyes downcast. She would take the proffered arm of her father-in-law, and would be presented to each of the groom's relatives. She would be introduced to each of her future in-laws with the words, "meet as your servant (name of person)." Before each person she would curtsy, embrace, and receive a kiss. This done, the process would be repeated with the groom, who would successively bow to and kiss each of his bride's kin.[43]

Once peace and amity between the two kinship groups had been accomplished through the embrace and kiss, the bride and groom gave each other gifts, which symbolized the marital exchange of the young woman. First the female offered her future spouse a rosary or a medallion with an image of the Virgin Mary as a sign of her virginity. He countered by presenting the *donas*, a handcrafted chest containing the wedding trousseau, which included the bridal gown, clothing, jewelry, household goods, and occasionally money. Children of New Mexico's rich often made a special trip to Chihuahua to purchase the items for the *donas*, returning with silks, brocades, linens, lace, and bolts of white satin for the bride's wedding dress. The amount of wealth conveyed by this gift varied enormously by class. To contemplate marriage without being able to present the bride with an appropriate trousseau was considered inappropriate and shameless. Consequently, lower class men often postponed their marriages, sometimes indefinitely, or opted for temporary concubinage until sufficient capital had been accumulated for the proper gifts.[44]

If dotal property was to be presented by the father of the bride, it was offered as a counter-gift after the exchange of the *donas*. The dowry functioned as a premortem accession to inheritance, which guaranteed a woman enough wealth to attract a husband of similar or higher social standing. It helped finance the initial costs of creating a household and also provided some economic security in the event of an early widowhood.

The major form of moveable wealth in New Mexico, livestock, was the item most frequently used to dower women. Don Luís Durán y Chávez received "700 pesos . . . in 200 young, healthy and sheared ewes, 14 cows, and one team of plow oxen," from Doña Eduarda Itturrieta's father at their 1747 betrothal. Doña María de la Luz Baca took to her 1765 marriage with Don Francisco Trevol Navarro "500 ewes, 6 sheep, 20 mares, 1 colt, 4 mules, 1 he-mule, and 2 horses." [45]

Only seven extant dotal letters for the period 1693–1846 exist in New Mexican archives. The dowries of six aristocratic women were each worth 1,000 to 1,500 pesos in livestock. Ursula Chávez, a woman of apparently humble ancestry, reported that the value of her dowry in 1750 was 200 pesos (T), a sum worth 100 sheep or 10 oxen. Data on dotal property in other areas of colonial New Spain indicate that although New Mexican dowries never reached the 20,000 peso value found in Mexico City and Guadalajara, they were comparable to those in other towns of northern New Spain. In Monterey, for example, approximately two-thirds of all extant dotal letters for 1640–1790 were valued at less than 1,000 pesos.[46]

Dowry was legally inalienable female property, which at her death devolved intact to her children, and lacking these, reverted to her natal family. But since the dowry was usually managed by a woman's husband, it could be used exclusively to further his economic interests. Manuel A. Otero of Tomé was alleged to have parlayed his wives' dowries into a considerable fortune. In 1851, Dun and Bradstreet Associates gave Otero a high credit rating, and noted in their report that "he has been married 3 times and is said to have made $25,000 each time." Manuel Vigil, Taos' chief constable, did not fare quite as well in his ventures. Inventorying in 1776 the dotal property of his deceased wife, Gertrudes Armijo, Vigil lamented that the 200 sheep she brought to their marriage had been killed by the Navajos. Twelve horses, 2 mules, 24 religious paintings, pewter plates, china cups, and personal clothing was all that remained of his wife's dowry.[47]

Once the dowry was formally exchanged, men of wealth would reciprocate by presenting the bride with *arras*, moveable goods that the groom's family contributed to the union. By law, the value of the *arras* was limited to 10 percent of the man's wealth at the time of his betrothal. This contribution automatically became the property of the bride and passed on to her heirs at death.[48]

The exchange of *arras* was a financial hardship for many families and thus constituted a gesture that could be omitted from the betrothal and enacted instead in a highly ritualized form during the nuptial ceremony. The fee an individual paid the local priest for a marriage often included the rental of a small pouch containing thirteen gold or silver coins, which were used during the rite to symbolize the bride's endowment with *arras*.[49]

Once the formal exchange of gifts was complete, the *prendorio* ended with salvos and toasts over wine and *bizcochitos* (sugar cookies). *Bizcochitos* sweetened and therefore neutralized the groom's potential adversaries. Sugar dulled the bitterness of losing a sibling and made the prospect of having to integrate a new person into the kinship group more palatable. Finances permitting, a night of celebration would follow.[50]

Popular custom and canon law were seriously at odds concerning the importance and significance of the betrothal. By tradition, the rituals of the *prendorio*—the exchange of *prendas*, *donas*, dowry, and *arras*—symbolized the contract and economic alliance that had been forged between two families. Much to the consternation of the Church, which maintained that the nuptial was the only binding contract, in popular belief the nuptial simply legalized and sanctified an agreement between two families.

What happened in the case of a broken betrothal? Several New Mexicans discovered that because the Church and state did not recognize the legitimacy of the betrothal as a binding contract, neither priests nor civil officials would intervene as arbiters in such disputes. Isidro Sánchez could barely control his anger over the humiliation he felt when his espoused, Feliciana Chávez, paraded through Santa Fe's streets in 1744 "boasting and shouting, firing muskets and yelling defamatory statements" at him. According to Isidro, Feliciana had gathered together with the children of the village to taunt him with accusations of being a liar and a bad soldier unfit for the service of the king. Even though Isidro had given Feliciana a promise of marriage, had exchanged *prendas* at their engagement, and had even shared intimacies with her, she now no longer wanted to marry him. To add injury to the insult, Feliciana secured an affidavit from the vicar certifying her virginity and freedom to marry as she chose. "What justice was this?" Isidro plaintively asked the governor, seeking his intercession. Governor Joachín Codallos y Robal retorted that the case was outside of his jurisdiction and that there was nothing he could do. Instead he scolded Isidro and warned him to moderate his temper when addressing dignitaries of the state.[51]

Only when a broken betrothal provoked a fracas or was complicated by property litigation could judicial recourse be expected. Otherwise, disputes had to be settled through the means Thadeo Romero and Gregorio Jaramillo employed. Thadeo stood before Fonclara's authorities in 1747, his arm broken, his head gashed open, and his clothes drenched in blood, to denounce Gregorio Jaramillo. The two had quarreled after Romero had informed Jaramillo that the agreement they had had concerning marriage with Jaramillo's daughter was off because of the gossip Romero had heard. "Go to the devil," Jaramillo responded, "I do not care if you do not marry my daughter." Romero left the Jaramillo household and as he did so shouted back at Jaramillo and his wife, "go to the devil yourself and hang that on your nose." "What?" Jaramillo replied. "You cuckold pimp," Romero retorted. Hearing this, Jaramillo chased after Romero and in a nearby canyon hurled a stick at Romero, which broke his arm and cut open his head. The governor heard the case and fined Romero fifteen pesos (T) for the verbal abuse of Jaramillo and his wife and ordered that he never return to their house again. Jaramillo was also fined 30 pesos (T) for the injuries inflicted on Romero. The injured pride that resulted from such aggressive exchanges was rarely forgotten; frequently it festered for generations and fostered vendettas.[52]

The celebration of the betrothal usually signaled the commencement of conjugal rights. To a clergy increasingly anxious over the significance of secular rituals and the importance of subordinating them to ecclesiastical jurisdiction, the onset of sex before the nuptial was particularly repugnant. It was thus to be expected that when curate Don Juan Rafael Rascón, the vicar general of New Mexico, heard of the liberties Francisco Zapata and his fiancée, Gertrudes Zuñi, of Taos, enjoyed, his rebuke was stern, albeit ineffective. During 1828–29 Rascón had Francisco and Gertrudes separated and chastized for their sin on three different occasions. Although the custodian of New Mexicans' morals claimed that his action was necessary to nip the bud of illegitimacy that cohabitation fostered, his order also was motivated by a concern to minimize the importance of the popular rite of betrothal and to replace it with the sacramental church nuptial. The free union of two wills and the mingling of one flesh was all that was technically necessary to enjoy the sacrament. Yet had the Church accepted as legitimate any liaison that met these conditions, the theory of impediments that served the post-Tridentine Church as a tool to regulate and regularize nuptial formation throughout Christendom would have been subverted. Post-betrothal cohabitation violated ecclesiastical injunctions. A marital contract was concluded without clerical verification of the volitional state of the partners, therefore the inception of sexual association was illegal. Needless to say, such concerns undoubtedly provoked more anguish in the minds of priests than in those of the populace.[53]

The period between the betrothal and the celebration of the nuptial could be as short as a few hours or separated by weeks, months, and in one case, that of María del Carmen Vigil and José Abeyta, who married in 1821, four years after their betrothal. The interval between the two ceremonies was occupied with preparations for the wedding festivities and in the careful execution of the ecclesiastical prerequisites for marriage. A *diligencia matrimonial* (matrimonial investigation) would be undertaken by the local priest to assure that no canonic impediments to the union existed. Public notice of the proposed marriage would be given to the community by reading banns at church on three successive Sundays. Persons aware of hidden impediments to the matrimony were urged to step forward and express any information that might invalidate the proposed union. And finally, the bride chose her *padrinos* (ritual godparents) for the ceremonies.[54]

The monthly distribution of Spanish marriages in New Mexico between 1693 and 1846 (see Figure 8.1) conformed to rhythms in the cycle of agricultural production and major feasts in the liturgical calendar. The greatest number of Spanish marriages occurred in September, at the end of the harvest, when the financial resources for a nuptial celebration were most readily available. Fewer marriages occurred during Advent (November-December) and Lent (February-March), with an increase in numbers shortly after Christmas and Easter. This particular monthly distribution in marriages also may have reflected the female gestation period. Infants conceived in September would be due in June, during the "dead period" between planting and harvest when minimal agricultural labor was necessary. Similarly, females impregnated in January would not give birth until October, well after the year's crops had been gathered and prepared for winter storage. New Mexicans' monthly preferences for their marriages were not significantly different from patterns in central and northern Mexico during the colonial period.[55]

Figure 8.1 also depicts the monthly distribution of Pueblo Indian Christian marriages. A statistical comparison of the Spanish and Pueblo Indian monthly distribution of marriages indicated that the patterns were very significantly different (chi-squared 230.3 with 11 df; probability .000) and could not have been due to simple random variation. Unlike

Percent

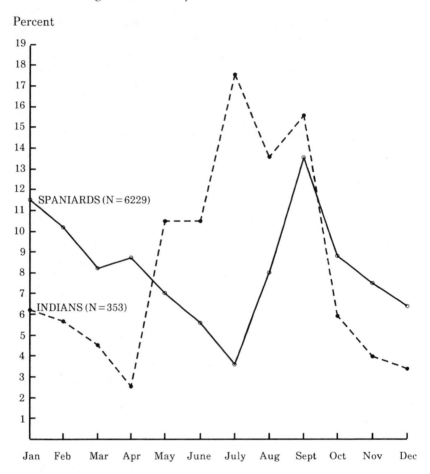

Figure 8.1. Monthly Distribution of Marriages in New Mexico, 1693-1846.

the Spaniards, the Indians who married sacramentally did so primarily in the summer months from May through September; the high point being July. Bearing in mind that the summer and winter solstices were the beginning and end points of the six-month Pueblo cycle of time, there did appear to be a preference for marriage around the summer solstice.

The rituals enacted during the wedding day proceeded through three phases: the bride's departure from her parental home in procession with her kin, the religious ceremony, and the procession from the parish church to the groom's household. This ceremonial sequence also conformed to

Van Gennep's tripartite model of separation, liminality, and reincorporation, and performed several different functions. The juridical transfer of a woman was legitimized in the eyes of the community through the public procession, the bride's change of residence was accomplished, and passage into a new social status was marked spatially and temporally.

The fanfare began with the bride's separation from her natal dwelling, traveling with her *padrinos*, bridesmaids, family, and friends to the local church. Inside the sanctuary the groom, groomsmen, and family would be waiting. The bride's retinue entered the church: first the family and guests, next the bridesmaids and the *padrinos*, and finally the veiled bride (the veil symbolized her subordination and her liminal position between two statuses) at her father's side. At the altar the bride's father literally gave the hand of his daughter to the groom, leaving aside filial status for conjugal life. Left aside too was the adolescent peer group represented by the bridesmaids and groomsmen.

The sacramental rite or nuptial was set within the celebration of Mass. After the gospel the priest would descend from the altar to explain to the marital candidates and the village community the obligations entailed by matrimony, and would end joining the couple with the words *ego vos in matrimonium conjugo*. Next the wedding ring was blessed. A gold band was customary for girls from wealthy families. A leather or wooden ring served commoners the same purpose. The groom gave the ring to his bride, placing it first on her left thumb with the words: "In the name of the Father, (then on the index finger) and of the Son, (then on the middle finger) and of the Holy Spirit, (and finally on the fourth finger) Amen." [56]

The use of a ring as a mark of a marital contract has a long history. Recorded first among the Egyptians as a sign of an eternal bond, in the hands of the Romans the ring became a token sealing the betrothal pledges, and to Christians a symbol of the indissoluble nature of matrimony and a vow to marital fidelity. The wedding ring was always placed on the fourth finger of the bride's left hand because it was believed (though an anatomical fallacy) that a vein ran from that finger directly to the heart. In medieval body symbolism one wielded power and authority with the right hand and accepted subordination with the left. Thus, asking for the hand of a woman in marriage and marking it with a ring signified the transfer of tutelary rights over a female. These rights were also sexual, for one cannot avoid noting the symbolism of thrust and penetration associated with the gesture of slipping the ring from finger to finger, passing beyond the second joint only on the fourth finger where the ring finally rests. [57]

In some parts of New Mexico, the ring presentation was followed by the binding of the couple with a large rosary, rope, or ribbon to symbolize the union that had been formed. The presentation of *arras* was saved for last, and then performed only if it had not already occurred at the betrothal. The parish priest kept a pouch containing thirteen coins, which he rented to wedding parties so that individuals of modest means could symbolically endow their bride during the nuptial. Once the marriage was solemnized, the priest resumed the Mass, stopping only after the *Pater Noster* to embrace the groom with the kiss of peace, which the groom gave to his bride. With the celebration of the Mass complete, the couple left the church, the bride now unveiled and at her husband's side.[58]

Evil spirits who might prey on the newlyweds were dispelled with gun salutes, music, and the gaiety that greeted the luminaries as they exited from church, or they were distracted with such food as rice or pinole (sweetened cornmeal). The merriment also marked a new phase in the progression of the ceremonial complex. With the juridical transfer of the female officialized and sanctified through the nuptial, the festivities to mark her physical transfer began. Striking up a tune on their violins and guitars, the musicians led the wedding guests in procession from the church to the groom's parents' home, serving notice to the community through all the commotion that a new social unit had been formed. Witnesses, either to the noise or to the ceremony, tacitly accepted the union and celebrated the bride and groom's passage into conjugal life.[59]

A sumptuous banquet awaited the newlyweds and their guests. The feast, above all else, marked the newly forged alliance between families. In colonial New Mexico, meals were only shared between trusted friends and relatives. A shared meal signified the marital affinity that now joined the groups. When the meal ended, hours of dancing followed. The first dance was always the wedding march. It began with women standing in a line behind the bride and the men behind the groom. To the music of fiddles each group promenaded in a single file. The two groups came together after a jaunt and joined as couples, circling again, and progressively pairing as groups of four, eight, sixteen, and so on, until all the couples had joined in one line. When this dance was over, others followed. One sees in this dance not only the dissolution of the bride and groom's adolescent peer group, but also the couple's reincorporation into the larger community.[60]

The gaiety of a wedding dance fostered public liminality and communal solidarity. All joined in dancing, regardless of age or status, in the line and circle movements of the group. The steps were not particularly important; the social cohesion created was. Particularly popular at such events were the *Vaqueros* and the *Inditas*, round dances in which participants moved around in a circle while someone pantomimed in the center. The work of cowhands was imitated in the *Vaqueros*. The peculiar shuffle that Hispanics associated with the walk of Pueblo Indian women was the focus of the *Inditas*. The lyrics to one *Indita* said:

> The little Indian girls from San Juan
> Beg for bread but are given none
> And so they sit and cry
> In the fields which are nearby.[61]

Of course, I do not wish to suggest that class distinctions were totally obliterated as a result of the public comity that prevailed during wedding dances. Though the night might be dominated by undifferentiated reeling, if the bride and groom had aristocratic pretensions, courtly dances might be stepped intermittently. The *Varsoviana* and the *Cuadrilla* were favored as genteel. Both dances were geometrically planned, balanced, clear, and regular—the quintessence of classical form. Persons did not venture onto the dance floor unless the precise movements were known. In such an instance the distinction between dancer and spectator were clear: the dress, movements, and manners all symbolized class divisions within the congregated group and the dancer's position in the social structure.[62]

The night of merriment was often punctuated by shouts: "they stole the bride." This custom consisted of kinsmen of the bride stealing her from her husband and demanding a ransom for her return. The promise of a future party or dance was often enough to win her back. This rite was truly a final attempt by the bride's kin to symbolically protest their loss and demand compensation for the taking of a productive member. An event that fostered unity between the two kinship groups usually appeased all.[63]

Shortly before the festivities ended and the groom and his bride retired, they were reintegrated into the community, now as married adults. This was accomplished through the *Entrega de Novios* (which literally means to hand over the newlyweds), by which the couple was entrusted to the community's care by their godparents, thus ending the period of ritual liminality. A poet and fiddler were usually hired for the *entrega*. The singer began by summarizing the Genesis myth, noting how the female had been created from Adam's rib. The couple was admonished on the sacredness of marriage, its indissolubility, and the responsibilities and duties they owed each other. "Listen husband," one poet sang, "this cross which Christ has given you may never be abandoned. . . . You too I tell you wife, honor and obey your husband always. Listen both of you, no longer is there father, no longer is there mother, each other is all you have now. . . . Love each other as Christ loves the Church, using Saint Joseph and Mary as your conjugal model." Finally, parents and elders were urged to guide the couple in their new life, "so that the flower of matrimony may never wilt or die." With the *entrega* complete, the party ended, the newlyweds retired, and life returned to normal.[64]

In this chapter we examined the broad jurisdiction the Church enjoyed in defining who were and were not appropriate marriage partners, in protecting the rights of children to express their individualistic desires, and in defining the judicial and sacramental form of marriage. In the next chapter we turn to behavioral level data to ask when, at what age, and with whom New Mexicans married in the colonial period.

9

Marriage—
The Empirical Evidence

At what age did persons marry? Did New Mexicans prefer spouses of a certain age? What was the mean age difference between a bride and a groom? Did men prefer to marry women of similar social status? At what age did slaves marry? To what extent did persons remarry? These are some of the questions answered in this chapter.[1]

Age at Marriage

The age at which a person first married in New Mexico was affected by several factors: legal restrictions, economic conditions, cultural norms, and demographic realities. Both canon and secular law stipulated minimum ages at which individuals could be married. Males under the age of thirteen and females under the age of eleven could not contract a valid marriage because the purpose of conjugal life was procreation and at such a tender age this end seemed unlikely. The marriage records for New Mexico between 1694 and 1846 document only two nuptials where one of the partners was below the minimum age. Doña Antonia de las Ceras in 1697 at age eleven married Don Ramón García Jurado of Santa Fe. Both of Doña Antonia's parents were killed during the Indian revolt of 1696; it was perhaps because of this misfortune that she was allowed to marry so young. During his 1760 episcopal visitation to Santa Fe, Durango's bishop, Dr. Pedro Tamarón y Romeral, said that a fifteen-year-old girl presented him with an annulment petition claiming to have been married at the age of ten. Bishop Tamarón refused to abrogate the marriage because she had not given birth to a child until the age of eleven. Of the 3,540 women who were legally married between 1694 and 1846 and re-

TABLE 9.1

Age at First Marriage for Males and Females, 1690-1846

Ages	Males		Females	
	No.	Pct.	No.	Pct.
11	—		1	
12	—		57	1.6%
13	8	0.2%	138	3.9
14	7	0.2	248	7.0
15	11	0.3	463	13.1
16	32	0.8	487	13.7
17	43	1.1	256	7.2
18	180	4.7	590	16.7
19	168	4.4	243	6.9
20	397	10.4	357	10.1
21	243	6.4	78	2.0
22	455	12.0	155	4.4
23	296	7.8	74	2.1
24	309	8.1	83	2.3
25-29	1,274	33.4	212	6.0
30-39	313	8.1	72	2.0
40-49	52	1.3	26	0.7
50-59	1	0.0	—	
60+	8	0.2	—	
Total	3,798	100.0%	3,540	100.0%

SOURCE: AASF-*DM* Reels 60-79.

ported their age, approximately one out of every four entered marriage by the age of fifteen. Eighty percent of all females who partook of the sacrament had done so by the age of twenty. (See Table 9.1.) No male below the age of thirteen was married in New Mexico during the period under study. José Lucas Mora of Algodones was thirteen when he married María Teodora Gurule in 1844. Seven other men were of José's same age when they married. Josef Cristobal Trujillo was thirteen and his spouse, Josefa Romero, was twelve when they celebrated their 1788 nuptial in Chimayo.[2]

Where one out of every four women had married by the age of fifteen, only seven out of every hundred men had. Males were generally older than females when they married. Approximately one-fourth had a wife by age 20 and all but 10 percent of those who married had done so by the age of 29. Table 9.2 presents New Mexico's population of single people as a percentage of the total population in each age group in 1800 and 1820, and shows more vividly the different ages at which males and females married. In 1800, for example, 72 percent of all males in the age cohort 16 to 24 were still single as opposed to only 40 percent of the females. The 1820 data show that twice as many men as women were still single in the age group 16 to 24. Women married at a younger age than men, and older males competed with one another for younger females.

Economic, sociocultural, and demographic variables also significantly influenced age at first marriage. The amount of spatial mobility, the economic organization of production, and land tenure all influenced the timing of marriage. A cultural preference for class endogamous marriages limited the pool of available partners and could lead to a rise or decline in the mean age at first marriage depending on the ratio of males to females in the "at risk" pool. If, for example, a set age gap between spouses was culturally preferred and the birth rate rose in favor of females, eventually more women than men would enter the marriage market. To marry, women would have to accept younger husbands and break with traditional mores. The loss of a large number of men in war or through conscription could have similar consequences if cultural expectations concerning nuptial age were not altered.

This complex of factors had an effect on the mean age at first marriage for Spanish or Hispanic men and women in New Mexico between 1694 and 1846.[3] The mean at which these single New Mexicans married

TABLE 9.2

Single Population as Percent of Total Population in Age Group, 1800 and 1820

	1800		1820*	
Age	Male	Female	Male	Female
0-6	100%	100%	100%	100%
7-15	99.6	96.7	99.7	99.2
16-24	71.7	40.0	64.8	30.8
25-39	10.8	13.6	9.0	10.0
40-49	5.2	7.6	3.8	0.7
50+	4.2	3.8	2.3	3.0
Total	1,247	1,263	4,300	4,205

SOURCE: AASF-*DM* Reels 60-79.
* Santa Fe and Santa Cruz only.

TABLE 9.3

Mean Age at First Marriage for Males and Females in New Mexico, 1690-1846

	Males				Females			
Years	Mean	% Point Change	Coefficient of Variation	No.	Mean	% Point Change	Coefficient of Variation	No.
1690-99	22.6	—	.171	34	19.0	−1.2	.187	34
1700-09	22.3	−0.3	.195	48	17.8	−1.2	.233	49
1710-19	23.1	+0.8	.246	116	17.7	−0.1	.214	117
1720-29	22.0	−1.1	.197	64	18.7	+1.0	.308	68
1730-39	25.4	+3.4	.304	7	17.4	−1.3	.243	7
—	—	—	—	—	—	—	—	—
1760-69	25.5	—	.229	138	19.4	—	.276	150
1770-79	24.9	−0.6	.223	225	18.6	−0.8	.322	223
1780-89	23.2	−1.7	.183	297	18.2	−0.4	.206	325
1790-99	23.4	+0.2	.192	132	18.5	+0.3	.171	116
1800-09	24.4	+1.0	.231	96	15.5	−3.0	.191	84
1810-19	23.3	−1.1	.157	339	18.3	+2.8	.200	295
1820-29	24.1	+0.8	.161	798	19.5	+1.2	.263	671
1830-39	24.4	+0.3	.172	928	17.7	−1.8	.198	832
1840-46	24.0	−0.4	.302	584	17.9	+0.2	.182	568
Total	24.0		.206	3,806	18.3	+0.4	.232	3,540

One-way analysis of variance: Age by Year--F ratio=5.244 significant to .0000 level.

Eta-squared = .0177

One-way analysis of variance: Age by Year--F ratio=9.158 significant to .0000 level.

Eta-squared = .0351

SOURCE: AASF-*DM* Reels 60-79.

is presented in Table 9.3. Males first married at age 24.0, females at 18.3. The male mean age at marriage was lowest (between 22 and 23 years of age) during the 40 years following the reconquest of the kingdom when the necessity of imposing Spanish domination through population growth was greatest. A young nuptial age guaranteed a high level of fertility and a quick reproduction of the area's population. This reproductive strategy, marked by a low age at marriage, was most efficacious after a famine or epidemic as a way of recovering lost numbers. The highest mean age at marriage for males, 25.5, was reached between 1760 and 1769, a period of relative stability in population growth. The lowest male mean age at first marriage was 22 in 1720–29. Males also married at low mean ages in 1780–89 (23.2) and 1810–19 (23.3) as a result of the smallpox epidemics that broke out in 1780–81 and 1809. The demographic impact of disease similarly explains fluctuations in the female mean age at first marriage. The lowest female mean age, 15.5, was recorded between 1800–1809. A drop in the female mean age from 19.4 during 1760–69, to 18.2 during 1780–89, also bespoke the effects of the smallpox epidemics.[4]

Pueblo Indians enjoyed *privilegios de campana* (literally privileges of the bell) by virtue of residence in Indian parishes. These privileges dispensed them from having to submit to formal matrimonial investigations. Among Hispanics, these investigations are full of vital information on the population. Lacking these, we know very little about those Pueblo Indians who entered Christian matrimony with residents from their own parishes. The friars very sparingly listed these matrimonies in their parish registers, noting only baptismal names, rarely surnames, the names of the witnesses, and little else.

When, however, a Puebloan married someone from a different parish, be it Indian or Spanish, the groom's parish priest was required to consult the bride's parish priest regarding known or hidden impediments to the union. These letters of consultation always contained the marital candidates' full names, sometimes their ages, and the parishes in which they resided, thus allowing us to study Puebloan mean age at first marriage and spatial exogamy. Bear in mind that ecclesiastical records refer only to Christian marriage. The records on the native Pueblo ritual of marriage, discussed at length in Chapter 1, do not exist for this period.

The letters of consultation between parish priests produced age information on 372 Pueblo Indians—206 males, 166 females—between 1694 and 1846. Pueblo men who married someone outside their parish did so at a mean age of 22.8. Pueblo females who did likewise were, on the average, 17.2 years old.

The mean age at which Hispanos married in New Mexico was very similar to that reported for central Mexico. In their study of the town of León, David A. Brading and Celia Wu found that between 1780 and 1789, years marked by the ravages of smallpox, the mean age at which single males married was 21.9 and 18.3 for females. The 18.2 mean age at marriage for New Mexican women was virtually identical to the León study results. The differences were greater among males. New Mexican men, at 23.2 years, were 1.3 years older when they married than León's men.[5]

By comparison with Western European patterns of behavior, New Mexicans first married at much younger ages. Between 1700 and 1849, single Western European males married at 27.7 years (coefficient of variation 0.92); males in New Mexico were 24 (coefficient of variation 0.21). Among females the pattern was even more divergent. New Mexico's

TABLE 9.4

Mean Age at First Marriage by Parental Survival

	Males		Females	
Parental survival	Mean age	No.	Mean age	No.
All marriages	23.8	3,531	17.9	3,112
Both parents alive	23.6	2,337	17.8	2,292
Father dead	24.4	517	17.7	335
Mother dead	23.9	364	18.5	287
Both parents dead	24.1	313	18.5	198

One-way analysis of variance:

$F = 2.353$ for Males with 3/3527 degrees of freedom--Not significant
$F = 3.917$ for Females with 3/3108 df--Not significant
The null hypothesis cannot be rejected in either case

Eta-squared for Males = .002
Eta-squared for Females = .003

SOURCE: AASF-*DM* Reels 60-79

single females married at a mean age of 18.3 (coefficient of variation 0.23); Western European females were 7.1 years older when they married, at an average age of 25.4 (coefficient of variation 0.08). If one examines for comparative purposes the data on age at first marriage in Western Europe between 1330 and 1879, the New Mexican results between 1694 and 1846 most resemble those observed on the continent two centuries earlier.[6]

Marriage, for aristocrats and peasants alike, frequently entailed the pre-mortem division of patrimony. Females brought dowries to marriage, males were given endowments of land and money so that they could create a new household. One would expect that because of the property exchanges that occurred at marriage and the nature of parental supervision over nuptial formation, children whose parents were alive would marry at older ages than those individuals whose parents were deceased. The mean age at which males first married when both parents were alive was 23.6, and for females 17.8 (see Table 9.4). When both parents were dead, males married at 24.1 years of age and females at 18.5. A one-way analysis of variance indicated that the mean ages for males and females were not significantly different and could have been produced by random variation in the data. Parental survival seems not to have been a crucial variable in determining the age at which a person married.

A person's social status also affected nuptial age. An analysis of variance for mean age at first marriage by parental social status is presented in Table 9.5. The results indicate that males of different social standing married at significantly different ages. Sons of commoners married at a mean age of 23.7; sons of the nobility at 24.0. Men whose fathers were titled military officers married at a mean age of 31.2. Significantly different marriage ages were also observed among women of different social status. The average age at marriage for women whose parents were titleless was 18.0, for daughters of the nobility 15.4, and 17.8 for aristocrat/officer's daughters.

The analysis of variance presented for the data in Table 9.5 on marriage and parental status simply tells us that the three category means were statistically different and could not have been the product of random variation. To further study the relationship between social status and average marriage age, a t-test was performed combining nobility and nobility-military and comparing this group to commoners. The t-test is a measure that tells us if category means are statistically different. The results indicate that sons of the aristocracy married on the average seven months younger than commoners did, but these differences were not statistically significant ($t=0.55$, p less than o.6). Among females the differences between the nobility and commoners in mean marriage age were significant ($t=4.33$, p less than .002). Daughters of aristocrats were, on the average, about two-and-one-half years younger than daughters of peasants when they were married.

The various correlates of mean age at first marriage examined here show that parental survival did not affect the mean age at which one mar-

TABLE 9.5

Mean Age at First Marriage by Parental Social Status

	Males		Females	
Parental social status	Mean age	No.	Mean age	No.
No titles	23.7	3,310	18.0	2,943
Both of nobility	24.0	112	15.4	96
Nobility & military	31.2	87	17.8	63

One-way analysis of variance:

$F = 37.875$ for Males with 4/3526 degrees of freedom--Significant at .01 level
$F = 15.119$ for Females with 3/3108 df--Significant at .05 level

Eta-squared for Males = .0412
Eta-squared for Females = .0144

SOURCE: AASF-*DM* Reels 60-79.

ried, and that daughters of the nobility and military officers married at significantly different average ages than did the rest of the population.

Age Difference at Marriage

The age at which one married to an extent determined the tone and tenor of the conjugal relationship that would develop between spouses. When a husband was much older than his wife, the parent-child model of authority would undoubtedly serve as the foundation for the marital bond. As natural law conceded fathers the right to demand unflinching subservience from their children, so too could a husband expect it of his wife. Older male-younger female marriages exaggerated the father-daughter role; older female-younger male unions negated it. If the age gap between spouses was minimal, nuptial life held the potential of developing as a partnership between equals.[7]

New Mexican males generally preferred to marry women who were younger than they were. Men in the 14–20 age group married women of their own age or those who were anywhere from one to three years younger (see Table 9.6). Brides for men in the age group 21–25 were on the average five years younger. Wives of men ages 26–30 were approximately nine years their minors. And when men married at ages 31–35, their spouses were, on the average, fourteen years younger. Older, single men who married when they were 40 to 62 years of age, always selected young women to maximize the likelihood of offspring. Thus Don Salvador Martínez at age 62 took nineteen-year-old Doña Simona Polonia Valdez as his bride in 1761. Vicente Rael de Aguilar at age 50 also followed suit in 1776, taking twenty-two-year-old María Josepha García for his wife. One New Mexican proverb suggested why a woman might be content in marrying a man who was much older than she: "I would rather be the idol of an old man than the slave of a young one."[8]

When women married between the ages of 11 and 26, their husbands were always older. Some women ages 27 and above chose or were married to husbands 10 to 25 years younger. María Baca, for example, was 36 and Francisco Sánchez, her spouse, was 19 when they married in 1763. María de los Reyes Chacón at age 47 entered conjugal life with twenty-seven-year-old Juan Pascal Martínez in 1776.[9]

A man might marry an older woman for several reasons. Older women, those considered past their "prime," might allow themselves to be easily seduced as a way of losing their virtue so that they could then demand marriage. If the social differences were not of marked inequality, matrimony would take place to restore the maiden's integrity. A father might equally arrange the marriage of his son to an older woman for purely eco-

TABLE 9.6

Age of Bride and Groom at First Marriage, by Mean Age of Spouse

Males				Females			
Age of groom	Mean age of bride	No.	Coefficient of variation	Age of bride	Mean age of groom	No.	Coefficient of variation
11	—	—	—	11	18.0	1	—
12	—	—	—	12	20.3	52	.217
13	—	—	—	13	24.1	117	.148
14	16.0	7	.426	14	23.2	215	.212
15	13.6	11	.236	15	22.5	414	.154
16	15.7	23	.121	16	23.6	425	.276
17	16.3	42	.188	17	23.6	217	.138
18	16.5	121	.260	18	23.4	515	.187
19	16.1	135	.170	19	25.0	214	.210
20	18.0	339	.192	20	24.1	323	.187
21	17.8	181	.187	21	21.9	62	.071
22	16.9	350	.165	22	25.6	127	.154
23	18.7	261	.202	23	23.9	50	.117
24	17.3	255	.173	24	24.1	63	.087
25	18.5	560	.232	25	26.5	114	.135
26	17.6	161	.198	26	27.1	28	.131
27	19.7	131	.241	27	21.8	5	.081
28	18.8	137	.235	28	26.5	15	.229
29	19.9	57	.105	29	—	—	—
30	20.4	119	.230	30	27.1	41	.036
31	20.0	11	.163	31	37.0	1	—
32	16.8	13	.130	32	30.0	1	—
33	16.3	13	.228	33	—	—	—
34	21.3	3	.346	34	20.0	1	—
35	17.8	19	.240	35	35.0	1	—
36	23.5	2	.270	36	19.0	1	—
37	25.7	4	.382	37	37.0	1	—
38	18.6	10	.084	38	—	—	—
39	14.0	8	.235	39	—	—	—
40	25.6	16	.185	40	26.2	12	.183
41	—	—	—	41	—	—	—
42	28.0	1	—	42	—	—	—
43	26.0	1	—	43	—	—	—
44	—	—	—	44	—	—	—
45	19.0	8	.102	45	—	—	—
46	18.0	1	—	46	22.0	3	.240
47	16.0	1	—	47	27.0	1	—
48	20.0	1	—	48	—	—	—
49	—	—	—	49	—	—	—
50	—	—	—	50	—	—	—
51	30.0	1	—	51	—	—	—
60	20.0	1	—	60	—	—	—
62	16.0	2	.023	62	—	—	—

SOURCE: AASF-*DM* Reels 60-79.

nomic reasons. Older women would be more likely to control land and movable property that they could bring to a conjugal fund. In such unions the male was clearly the inferior partner. One New Mexican proverb held that: "In the house where the wife holds the wealth, she commands and she also bawls." Additionally, given the rudimentary knowledge Hispanic women had of birth control techniques, marriage to an older woman

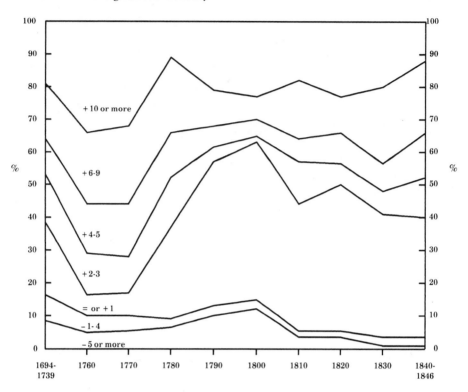

Figure 9.1.   Age Difference at First Marriage Between Husband and Wife in New Mexico, 1694-1846 (N = 5463). Source: AASF–*DM* Reels 60-79.

with fewer fecund years guaranteed a smaller family size. Lessened fecundity, in conjunction with the fact that an older woman would be a more experienced homemaker, induced some men to marry older females. When females were older than their spouses, the chances of conjugal life developing into a partnership based on equality were also more likely.[10]

Examining the temporal distribution of age differences at first marriage between all spouses in New Mexico between 1694 and 1846 (see Figure 9.1), we note that in the period 1694–1739 the proportion of wives who were older than their husbands by five or more years was 9.4 percent. Wives between one and four years older represented 8.1 percent of the total. Spouses of equal age or where the husband was one year older than his wife totaled 22 percent. Grooms two to three years older than their brides comprised 14.8 percent, grooms four to five years older 11.4 percent, and men six years older or more than their brides totaled 34 percent. The major change after 1770 was a large rise in the proportion of persons marrying someone their own age or just one year older. From 22 percent in the years 1694 to 1739, the proportion increased to 28 percent in 1780, 46 percent in 1790, 50 percent in 1800, 38 percent in 1810, 44 percent in 1820, 40 percent in 1830, and 38 percent in 1840. The number of older women marrying younger men (-5 or more) rose slightly between 1780 and 1800, then fell to 1 percent in 1840–46. The most apparent conclusion to be drawn from Figure 9.1 is that the age difference between spouses decreased dramatically after 1770.

The most convincing explanation for why this was so appears to be demographic. A cursory examination of the sex ratio in New Mexico at the end of the eighteenth century indicates that in most towns and hamlets, women outnumbered men. The first date for which a sex ratio can be calculated is 1790. The census for the kingdom that year showed a ratio of .87, or 87 men for every 100 women. In 1794 the sex ratio was .87, and in 1820 it was .94. These results are easy to explain. We mentioned earlier that the majority of Indians who entered New Mexican towns as slaves were women. Women formed the majority of marginalized Pueblo Indians who were exiled from their communities. If we compound this imbalance with the fact that New Mexicans were in a constant state of war with the Apaches and Navajos that surrounded the Rio Grande basin and that more men than women died protecting the area from Indian attacks, the reason for the numeric preponderance of females becomes obvious.[11]

Theoretically, when such an imbalance exists, as it did during the last quarter of the eighteenth and first quarter of the nineteenth centuries, there should be two additional correlates: a drop in the age difference between spouses and a drop in the mean age at first marriage. Since we have examined the statistics on both of these topics, let me reiterate by saying that the highest mean age at first marriage for men, 25.5, occurred between 1760 and 1769. In the next 40 years the mean age for men fluctuated, but perceptibly dropped until it reached its lowest point, 23.3, between 1810 and 1819. A similar pattern was observed among women after 1760. The mean age at first marriage for women between 1760 and 1769 was 19.4, dropping to 15.5 between 1800 and 1809, and finally hovering around 18.3 between 1810 and 1846. At first glance it appears that the narrowing of age differences between spouses at marriage and the decline in the mean age at first marriage occurred at the same time.

Place of Residence at Marriage

In a small face-to-face society where evaluation of one's honor was based on reputation, knowledge of a bride's and groom's family history

TABLE 9.7

Distance in Miles Between Nuptial Candidates' Places of Residence, 1700-1846

Year	0-5 Miles		6-20 Miles		21-40 Miles		41 + Miles		Total Miles	
	No.	Pct.	No.	Pct.	No.	Pct.	No.	Pct.	No.	Pct.
1700-1739*	319	83.8%	8	2.1%	39	10.2%	15	3.9%	381	100%
1760-1779	229	90.9	16	6.3	6	2.4	1	0.4	252	100
1780-1799	411	86.2	38	8.0	18	3.7	10	2.1	477	100
1800-1819	459	86.1	11	2.1	43	8.1	20	3.7	533	100
1820-1846	1,792	94.8	62	3.3	25	1.3	11	0.6	1,890	100
Total	3,210	90.9%	135	3.8%	131	3.7%	57	1.6%	3,533	100

SOURCE: AASF–*DM* Reels 60-79.
 * No data for 1740-1759

was a prerequisite for marriage. Before matrimony could take place, fathers made it their business to know the social status of the possible candidates, their wealth, the number of sheep they owned, their servants, amount of arable land, and so on. Travel restrictions before 1821 made communication between New Mexican villages infrequent, and the constant threat of Navajo, Apache, and Comanche attack discouraged people from moving about freely. As a result of these circumstances most individuals married someone residing in the same village or town. Table 9.7 summarizes the distance between the places of residence of nuptial candidates between 1700 and 1846. Ninety percent of all persons who married chose a spouse who resided in the same town. Another 7.5 percent of marital candidates resided 6 to 40 miles apart, and slightly more than 1 percent of all couples lived more than 40 miles from each other before they married.

Marriages exogamous of place were only a small fraction of each period total listed in Table 9.7. The highest proportion of individuals marrying persons who resided in other villages, 16.2 percent, occurred between 1700 and 1739. The lowest proportion of such marriages, 5.2 percent, took place between 1820 and 1846. Examining these data, one notes that out-marriages were inversely related to year, that is, the greatest number of out-marriages occurred during the early 1700s and the least during the 1820–40 period. Computation of the gamma statistic, a measure of association between two ordinal variables, verifies this intuitive finding. The gamma statistic for year of marriage by distance between places of residence for nuptial candidates was −0.378, significant to the .01 level. Marriageable persons thus had to travel farther during the first half of the eighteenth century to obtain a spouse than they did in the early nineteenth century. A simple examination of the number of Spaniards living in

New Mexico at both times explains the logic of the marriage market. In 1746 New Mexico had a Spanish population that totaled 4,143, by 1842 there were 46,988 people of Spanish descent. During the nineteenth century it was no longer necessary to leave one's place of residence to obtain an acceptable spouse.

The distance one had to travel in New Mexico to obtain a spouse was extremely low in comparison to those patterns observed during the eighteenth century in other regions of New Spain. León Yacher reported that in the central Mexican town of Tlazazalca, Michoacán, only 20 percent of all marriages performed between 1750 and 1800 were place endogamous. The vast majority of persons, 76.1 percent, traveled anywhere from 6 to 20 miles to obtain a spouse. Michael Swann's data on San Juan del Rio and Santiago Papasquiaro, two rural agrarian parishes located near the mining town of Parral in northern Mexico, yielded intermediate levels of marriages exogamous of place. In the 1770s, approximately 32 percent of all nuptials in these two parishes were between individuals from different villages. Nancy Farriss's study of population dynamics in colonial Yucatán, Mexico's far south, reported low levels of marital place exogamy similar to those in New Mexico. On the basis of these studies one can advance a hypothesis regarding the level of mobility due to marriage during the eighteenth century that is radically different from that based on the assumption that society in New Spain's north was fluid and "open." The evidence presented here suggests just the opposite. The highest levels of matrimonial place exogamy were recorded in the highly commercialized centers of central Mexico, intermediate levels of place exogamy were observed in the near north (Durango-Parral), and the lowest levels of mobility occurred in the far south (Yucatán) and the far north (New Mexico).[12]

Marriage records in the Archives of the Archdiocese of Santa Fe contain enough information to study Pueblo out-marriage, or place exogamy. Table 9.8 indicates that between 1694 and 1846, 378 such mar-

TABLE 9.8

Pueblo Indian Exogamous Marriages, 1694-1846

| Groom | Bride | | |
	Pueblo	Spanish	Total
Pueblo	104*	117	221
Spanish	157	—	—
Total	261	—	6,390

SOURCE: AASF–*DM* Reels 60-79.
   * Marriages between residents of different pueblos.

riages occurred. During that period, 221 Pueblo men married women who did not reside in their own pueblo. The women these men took as their brides were rather evenly divided; 104 were Indian women residing in other pueblos, 117 of them resided in nearby Spanish towns. The spouse selections of the 261 Pueblo women who married out were significantly different: 104 married residents from other pueblos, 157 married residents from Spanish towns and villages. Whereas Pueblo men who married out were just as likely to marry a Pueblo Indian from another pueblo as they were a resident from a Spanish settlement, two out of every three Pueblo women married residents from Spanish towns.

The distribution of Hispano out-marriages within the Kingdom of New Mexico clustered around central places in the marketing system, a pattern common to other regions of New Spain. Individuals from hamlets and villages surrounding Albuquerque, Santa Fe, and Santa Cruz were attracted to these towns to obtain spouses (see Figure 9.2). Significant amounts of mobility occurred between Albuquerque and Santa Fe, and Santa Fe and Santa Cruz, but there was little between Santa Cruz and Albuquerque. In other words, the distance one would travel in colonial New Mexico to marry, even considering the frequent communication between marketing centers, rarely exceeded 75 miles.[13]

The spatial distribution of Pueblo Indian out-marriages reflected trends very similar to those found in the Spanish or Hispano population. Table 9.9 lists such marriages by place. When Pueblo women married non-Pueblo residents they tended to choose persons who lived in the largest town nearby, such as Albuquerque, Santa Fe, and Santa Cruz, a pattern also found among Pueblo men. When Puebloans married persons residing in other pueblos, their mates resided within 20 miles. Figure 9.3 displays some of the most common links in Puebloan out-marriages.

Racial Endogamy and Exogamy

When we discussed the meaning of honor-status in Chapter 5, reference was made to the various factors that defined one's *calidad*, or social status. Between 1693 and 1759 (see Table 5.1), social status was primarily equated with civic status, that is, whether one was a land owner or a resident of a particular locality. I proposed that since racial and ethnic differences were so patently obvious in this period, and since mixed bloods of various hues had not yet become a significant number, civil and ecclesiastical officials felt no real need to record more complex distinctions. But starting in 1760 and extending into the 1830s, there was a radical shift in this pattern. Race now became the dominant determinant of social status. I concluded that this change in the documentary evidence re-

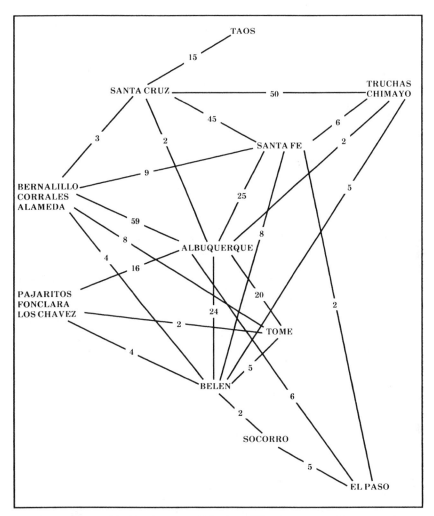

Figure 9.2.   Geographic Distribution and Number of Place Exogamous Marriages, 1700-1846. Source: AASF–*DM* Reels 60-79.

flected an increasing preoccupation over race mixture among New Mexico's nobility and landed peasants, particularly in light of the high levels of illegitimacy that accompanied Indian slavery and the movement of Pueblo women into Spanish towns.

Spanish men throughout the colonial period freely enjoyed intimacies with mixed-blood and Indian women but when they married, they preferred Spanish brides. Marriage was generally isogamic—like married like. The most important criteria in the selection of a spouse was that

TABLE 9.9
Bride's and Groom's Residence in Pueblo Indian Place-Exogamous Marriages, 1694-1846

GROOM \ BRIDE	SAN FELIPE	SANTA ANA	ZIA	SANTO DOMINGO	COCHITI	JEMEZ	TESUQUE	NAMBE	POJOAQUE	SAN ILDEFONSO	SANTA CLARA	SAN JUAN	ISLETA	SANDIA	PICURIS	TAOS	EL PASO	BELEN	TOME / VALENCIA	LOS CHAVES / LOS LENTES	ALBUQUERQUE	ALAMEDA	ALGODONES	PEÑA BLANCA	CAÑADA DE COCHITI	SANTA FE	CHIMAYO / CUNDIYO	SANTA CRUZ	CHAMA	ABIQUIU	SAN MIGUEL DEL VADO	TOTAL
INDIAN PUEBLOS																																
KERES -- SAN FELIPE		4																	3													7
SANTA ANA																																
ZIA						9																										9
SANTO DOMINGO																															4	4
COCHITI						2																										2
TOWA -- JEMEZ																															2	2
TEWA -- TESUQUE										1																	4					5
NAMBE																																
POJOAQUE										1												1				1	4	7	1	1		16
SAN ILDEFONSO											5																	1				6
SANTA CLARA									16																			1				17
SAN JUAN							10		40																		2	2		3		57
TIWA -- ISLETA																		6	15	5	11	1										38
SANDIA													4								30											34
PICURIS									4																		3	5		4		16
TAOS											8																					8
SPANISH TOWNS / VILLAGES																																
EL PASO													1																			1
BELEN													3																			3
TOME / VALENCIA													12																			12
LOS CHAVES / LOS LENTES																																
ALBUQUERQUE											9		34	5																		48
ALAMEDA						2																										2
ALGODONES	7																		7													7
PEÑA BLANCA						4																										4
CAÑADA DE COCHITI						1																										1
SANTA FE	1					3	1	8	17	7	1								1													37
CHIMAYO / CUNDIYO																																
SANTA CRUZ						4		8	5	1					11																	29
CHAMA																																
ABIQUIU						1					4	8																				13
SAN MIGUEL DEL VADO																																
TOTAL	8	4				26	11	16	82	10	26	8	54	5	11			6	18	5	41	2				1	13	16	1	8	6	378

SOURCE: AASF--*DM* Reels 60-79.

GROOM	NUMBER OF MARRIAGES	BRIDE
	10	TESUQUE PUEBLO
	40	POJOAQUE PUEBLO
SAN JUAN PUEBLO	2	CHIMAYO-CUNDIYO
	2	SANTA CRUZ
	3	ABIQUIU
SANTA CLARA PUEBLO	16	POJOAQUE PUEBLO
SANDIA PUEBLO	30	ALBUQUERQUE
	4	ISLETA PUEBLO
	6	BELEN
	15	TOME-VALENCIA
ISLETA PUEBLO	5	LOS CHAVES-LOS LENTES
	11	ALBUQUERQUE
	1	ALAMEDA
	9	SANTA CLARA PUEBLO
ALBUQUERQUE	34	ISLETA PUEBLO
	5	SANDIA PUEBLO
	3	JEMEZ PUEBLO
SANTA FE	8	NAMBE PUEBLO
	17	POJOAQUE PUEBLO
	7	SAN ILDEFONSO PUEBLO
	4	JEMEZ PUEBLO
SANTA CRUZ	8	NAMBE PUEBLO
	5	POJOAQUE PUEBLO
	11	PICURIS PUEBLO

Figure 9.3.   Geographic Distribution and Number of Place–Exogamous Pueblo Indian Marriages, 1694-1846. Source: AASF–*DM* Reels 60-79.

there be equality in social standing. Endogamy, or in-marriage to someone of equal status, was the preferred way of maintaining social boundaries and of restricting communication and interaction between cultural groups. To determine how strictly endogamy was practiced and to what extent hypergamy (a higher status man marrying a lower status woman)

TABLE 9.10

Racial Status Endogamous and Exogamous Marriages in New Mexico, 1694-1846

Years	Total marriages	Endogamous marriages		Exogamous marriages		Contingency coefficient*
		No.	Pct.	No.	Pct.	
1694-1699	51	47	92.9%	4	7.8%	.657
1700-1709	77	72	93.5	5	6.5	.671
1710-1719	152	148	97.3	4	2.7	.690
1720-1729	90	86	95.5	4	4.5	.616
1730-1739	8	8	100	—	0	—
—						
1760-1769	162	130	80.2	32	19.8	.637
1770-1779	266	212	79.7	54	20.3	.587
1780-1789	477	418	87.6	59	12.4	.372
1790-1799	192	180	93.8	12	6.2	.617
1800-1809	162	162	100	—	0	.816
1810-1819	357	349	97.7	8	2.3	.773
1820-1829	1,045	1,013	96.9	32	3.1	.440
1830-1839	1,376	1,376	100	—	0	—
1840-1846	901	901	100	—	0	—
Total	5,316	5,102	96.0%	214	4.0%	

SOURCE: AASF-*DM* Reels 60-79.
  * Maximum value of contingency coefficient = .816.

and hypogamy (lower status man marrying a higher status woman) indicated status mobility and consequently the blurring of racial lines, the races of all marital partners between 1694 and 1846 were statistically analyzed. This population was aggregated into three groups: Spaniards, mixed-bloods, and Indians. Table 9.10 presents the results of the association between the bride's and the groom's racial status at the time of marriage as measured by Pearson's Contingency Coefficient. Pearson's Contingency Coefficient is a statistic of association, which ranges from o (meaning no association) to .816 (perfect association) for a three by three table, and detects the amount of distance between observed frequencies in a population and expected frequencies in a model of statistical independence where no association exists. Between 1694 and 1769 the contingency coefficient was quite high, ranging from .690 to .616. These statistics indicated that the majority of individuals marrying during this period took spouses of similar social status. The fact that the contingency coefficient did not reach its upper limit of .816 shows that endogamy was not absolute and that mixed marriages did occur. As Table 9.14, which also presents the number and percentage of racial endogamous and exogamous marriages, indicates, between 1694 and 1739 there were a handful of individuals who married partners of a lower status.

The contingency coefficient fell sharply after 1760. A statistic of .372 in 1780–89 indicates that many persons were marrying with little regard for race. Table 9.10 shows that between 1760 and 1789 roughly one out of every five marriages was racially exogamous. The rise in the contingency coefficient after 1790, reaching a perfect association at .816 in 1800–1809, is easily explained. Because racial categories started to disappear from matrimonial investigations during the 1790s, after 1800 the only persons who consistently declared a racial status were aristocrats or individuals concerned with their racial pedigree. This is the reason for the high contingency coefficients in the period after 1800. Persons who did not mention their race or for whom it was not reported could not be included in these calculations. This explains why there were relatively few exogamous marriages reported after 1800.

Preferential endogamy was also confirmed by census data. Table 9.11 presents the racial status of marriage partners in Albuquerque in 1750. The intermarriage ratio reported there is an index of the proportion of men who did not marry a partner of their own race. The intermarriage rate for Spanish men was 21.2 percent, indicating that roughly one in five Spanish men married mixed-blood women. Approximately seven out of every ten *mulato* and coyote men married women of a racial status other than their own. And two in five Indian men married non-Indian women. The ratio of observed to expected marriages, that is, the number of marriages that actually took place divided by the number of marriages one would expect to find between partners of any two racial groups, give a hypothesis of complete impartiality, what might be called racial blindness, indicates that like married like. If one reads the diagonal line (i.e., Español/Española, Mulato/Mulata, etc.), then the ratio of observed to expected marriages tended to be higher than one and lower than one in the adjoining cells, indicating the tendency to marry a person of one's own race. A chi-square analysis of a two by two contingency table with Spaniards as one category and all persons of mixed and Indian ancestry collapsed into another tested whether such a result could have occurred randomly. The analysis yielded a statistic of 24.0 (1 degree of freedom), which was extremely significant, indicating that this result was not due simply to chance. We may conclude from this analysis that Spanish men wanted Spanish brides much more than a hypothesis of complete randomness or racial blindness would suggest.

Table 9.12 presents similar data for a one in three sample of the 1790 household census. In 1790, the intermarriage ratio for Spaniards was 13.1 percent, indicating that about one out of every seven Spanish men

Table 9.11

Racial Status of Marriage Partners in Albuquerque in 1750

	Females												Total Males	Inter-marriage Ratio
	Española		Mestiza		Mulata		Coyota		Castiza		India			
Males	No.	O/E	No.	O/E	No.	O/E	No.	O/E	No.	O/E	No.	O/E		
Español	41	78.8	2	3.9	7	13.5	1	1.9	1	1.9			52	21.2
Mulato	13	40.6	1	3.1	9	28.1	7	21.9			2	6.3	32	71.9
Coyote	3	25.0	1	8.3	5	41.7	3	25.0					12	75.0
Indio	3	18.7					3	18.7			10	62.6	16	37.4
Total Females	60		4		21		14		1		12		112	

SOURCE: Biblioteca National de México, Fondo Franciscano 8:81.
NOTE: Includes intermarriage ratio and ratio of observed to expected marriages assuming random mate selection.

TABLE 9.12

Racial Status of Marriage Partners in 1790

| | Females | | | | | | | | | | | | | | |
Males	Española		Mulata		Mestiza		Genízara		Color Quebrada		Coyota		India		Total Males	Inter-marriage Ratio
	No.	O/E	No.	O/E	No.	O/E	No.	O/E	No.	O/E	No.	O/E	No.	O/E		
Español	340	1.62	30	0.39	1	0.27			10	0.91	6	0.44	4	0.05	391	13.1
Mestizo	36	0.49	88	3.22	2	1.52			4	1.01	5	1.02	5	0.19	140	37.2
Mulato			3	2.20	2	30.76			2	10.20					7	71.4
Genízaro			6	0.01	2	11.29	2	13.15			3	4.54	6	1.67	19	89.5
Color Quebrado	8	0.83	5	1.42					5	9.90					18	72.2
Coyote	11	0.79	8	1.57							7	7.75			26	73.1
Indio	5	0.06	6	0.20			4	3.39			5	0.98	127	4.58	147	13.6
Total Females	400		146		7		6		21		26		141		748	

SOURCE: SA 12:319-502.
NOTE: Includes intermarriage ratio and ratio of observed to expected marriages assuming random mate selection.

married mixed-blood or Indian women. Approximately two in five mestizo men married other than mestiza women. The vast majority of *mulato*, *genízaro*, *color quebrado*, and coyote men married women of different racial classifications than their own. Indian men tended to marry Indian women, and as with the Spanish men, only one out of every seven Indian men married a non-Indian. Particularly noteworthy is the fact that in comparison to the marriage patterns observed in Albuquerque in 1750 (Table 9.11), in 1790 Spaniards were marrying out less frequently; 21 percent in 1750 and 13 percent in 1790. The vast majority of racial mixing at both times occurred among mixed bloods. The ratio of observed to expected marriages were all much higher than one on the diagonal, and lower in the adjoining cells, again confirming the finding in Albuquerque in 1750 that like married like. A chi-square analysis of a two by two contingency table with Spaniards and mixed races yielded a statistic of 369 (1 degree of freedom), which was extremely significant, indicating that Spanish men married Spanish brides, thus forcing us to reject the null hypothesis that persons were blind to race in the selection of marriage partners.

Remarriage

The Archives of the Archdiocese of Santa Fe contained information on 1,037 individuals who remarried between 1694 and 1846. Men remarried after the death of a spouse at a mean age of 39.6; women remarried at a mean age of 28.9 (see Table 9.13). Although men quickly remarried after the death of a spouse, women did not. Marcos Montoya in 1709

TABLE 9.13

Mean Age at Remarriage

Ages	Males		Females	
	No.	Pct.	No.	Pct.
15-19	2	0.3%	36	9.7%
20-29	96	15.8	175	47.0
30-39	206	34.0	103	27.7
40-49	191	31.4	57	15.3
50-59	60	9.9	1	0.3
60-69	46	7.6	—	—
70-75	6	1.0	—	—
Total	607	100.0%	372	100.0%
Mean	39.6		28.9	

SOURCE: AASF-*DM* Reels 60-79.

TABLE 9.14

Marital Status of New Mexico's Population

		1790	1792	1794	1811	1817
MEN						
Number		16,389	17,912	18,247	17,727	17,973
Percent	Children	23.8%	23.6	23.3	—	22.2
	Single Adults	13.6%	42.4	41.9	53.2	3.6
	Married	59.3%	29.8	30.3	43.2	72.7
	Widowed	3.3%	4.2	4.5	3.6	1.5
WOMEN						
Number		14,564	15,719	16,009	18,927	18,624
Percent	Children	25.1%	23.3	23.3	—	27.8
	Single Adults	0.2%	33.2	32.7	54.2	0.0
	Married	66.8%	34.0	34.5	40.4	70.2
	Widowed	7.9%	9.5	9.5	5.4	2.0

SOURCES: SA 12:428; SA 21:530; SA 13:560; AASF 53:743-44; SA 18:870.

mourned the death of his wife only seven months before he married Sebastiana Machuca de Vargas. Josefa García de Noriega died in 1824 and eight months later her widower, Juan Cristóbal Cruz, took Margarita Pacheco as his wife. Felipe Vega, a *mulato* slave, was eighteen years old when he lost his first wife. Two years later he remarried, this time to Dominga de la Concepción, Governor Don Francisco Cuervo Valdez's black slave. Dominga too was a widow. Her first husband died when she was thirteen. Ten years passed before she remarried.[14]

For those women who did remarry, the period between the death of their husband and the celebration of a second nuptial was much longer than it was for men. Ana Durán, whose husband was killed by Apaches in 1698, waited seven years before she remarried. Juana de Abeyta remarried in 1725, five years after her first husband's death. Josefa Gabriela de los Angeles, the *mulata* slave of Don Diego de Vargas, was the woman with the shortest reported period of widowhood. Only eight months elapsed between the 1705 death of her husband, Ignacio, and her marriage to the *mulato* slave of Don Antonio Valverde. Table 9.14 presents the marital status of New Mexico's population as a percentage of the total number of persons of each sex. Examining the widowed category, in most periods for which data exists, the ratio of widowers to widows was approximately two to five. By 1811 and 1817 this ratio had been reduced to approximately two to three.[15]

Regardless of their age, men who remarried always chose young brides between the ages of 14 and 22. Captain Alonso del Rio was 53 years old in 1699 when he married fourteen-year-old Rosa María López. Gregorio Benavides at age 48 was 30 years older than his second wife, Juana Candelaria. Miguel Luna, the widower of Juana Leal de Aguilar, was 25 and his bride, María Catarine Valdez, was 15 when they embraced conjugal life in 1772.[16]

A woman's chances of remarriage were greater if her husband died while she was still young. María de la Vega was widowed at age 24. Two years later, in 1698, she married Gabriel de Lira, a fifty-year-old widower from Santa Fe. María Paula González did not mention how many years her husband had been dead when she married seventy-two-year-old Salvador Montoya in 1792. Silvestre Griego and María Dolores Alarid, who had each been widowed, remarried in Albuquerque in 1802. He was 66, she was 25.[17]

A few individuals survived two spouses and married a third time. In popular folklore a third marriage was a sign of physical vigor. The folk song "El Viejo" says:

> Everyone says that I am an old man
> I know not what basis they have for saying that
> I am so fat and robust
> That I can marry three times.

Table 9.15 shows the mean ages at which males and females married for the third time. The 44 men who did so were remarried at a mean age of

TABLE 9.15

Mean Age at Third Marriage

Ages	Males		Females	
	No.	Pct.	No.	Pct.
20-29	1	2.3%	4	28.6%
30-39	21	47.6	2	14.3
40-49	12	27.3	8	57.1
50-59	1	2.3	—	—
60-69	9	20.5	—	—
Total	44	100.0%	14	100.0%
Mean	42.9		36.0	

SOURCE: AASF-*DM* Reels 60-79

42.9, while the 14 females were on the average 36 years old. In 1725 at the age of 80, Antonio Martín of Santa Cruz married for a third time. His bride, Gertrudes Fresquis, was 14. María Josefa Vigil had been widowed twice by the age of 22. In 1816, at the age of 25, she married thirty-eight-year-old Lorenzo Aragón of Valencia.[18]

Francisco Gamos was unique among New Mexico's colonists. He outlived four wives: Sebastiana Marques, Isabel de la Cruz, Ana María, and Gertrudes, a Pawnee Indian. In 1714 he married for the fifth time to nineteen-year-old Francisca Olguín. Unfortunately, Francisco never reported his age.[19]

Slave Marriages

Civil and ecclesiastical law in New Mexico guaranteed Indian slaves the right to marry freely. From evidence presented in Chapter 8, there is no doubt that some slaves exercised that prerogative. Yet, for the majority of these slave unions only meager bits of documentation remain. Of the 6,613 extant marriage investigations for the years 1694 to 1846, only sixteen explicitly identified the candidates as slaves. Five additional slave marriages were discovered in the 1790 census of the kingdom, bringing the total to 21.[20]

Why were so few unions between slaves recorded? A partial answer is found in a statement made by a slave-trader, Pedro León, in 1852. León claimed that "women are freed whenever married—say from 14 to 16—Men ditto from 18 to 20." New Mexicans were permitted to capture and purchase slaves provided they not be kept in bondage for more than ten years. The ten-year restriction was interpreted liberally by owners to mean that point in the life course when an adolescent became an adult—marriage. When an Indian entered a household at the age of eight, manumission usually occurred at eighteen, when the individual was of marriageable age. This broad cultural interpretation of the time limit placed on slavery, I suspect, in part explains why relatively few slave marriages surface in the documentary evidence. Marriage too was a sign of one's social status. Since slaves and ex-slaves owned no property, lived in concubinage and were not concerned about the legitimation of their progeny, they had no real reason for a sacramental matrimony.[21]

What we do know about the slaves that were sacramentally married is rather limited. Males married at a mean age of 29 (N=4) and females at 29.1 (N=8). Slave males were on the average five years older than Hispanic males when they first married. Slave females were approximately eleven years older than Spanish women when they married, and fourteen years older then the daughters of the nobility.

TABLE 9.16

Social Status of Slave Spouses at Marriage, 1690-1846

	Bride		
Groom	Indian Slave	Spanish	Vecina
Indian Slave	11	2	6
Spanish	1	—	—
Vecino	1	—	—

SOURCES: AASF 61:116, 475, 604; AASF 62:240, 256, 347, 461, 752, 772; AASF 63:249, 617; AASF 64:60; AASF 65:510; SA 12:323, 334, 337, 342, 345, 349.

The evidence also suggests that it was easier for male thralls to undertake a marriage than it was for females, thereby escaping explicit slave status. Two-thirds as many female slaves (N=13) as males (N=19) were joined in wedlock. David M. Brugge found that at baptism, 66 percent of all Indian slaves were female and 34 percent male. At death, 94 percent of those persons explicitly identified as slaves were female and only 6 percent were male. Granted, some of this variance can be explained by the fact that a high proportion of male captives were marched to Chihuahua and points beyond for sale while females were kept in New Mexican households as domestics. But equally important in explaining the disproportionate number of males and females at baptism and burial was the unwillingness of masters to allow their female slaves to marry. The marriage of a female slave represented the loss both of an outlet for sexual gratification and an economic asset in terms of workers that the illegitimate children of a thrall represented.[22]

Half of all slaves married slaves (N=11). Most were servants of the same master (see Table 9.16). Nicolás de los Angeles, the slave of Governor Antonio Valverde Cosío, was married in 1718 to Francisca Enríquez, a "free servant" in the same household. Owners may have encouraged unions between their thralls both for the purpose of forestalling flight by lovesick servants and retaining the services of the couple after marriage. For slaves, the sheer proximity of another individual of similar cultural origin offered the only possibility for the development of a close affective bond and sexual intimacy. Seven slaves married persons identified as *vecinos*, landowning citizens with full civic rights.[23]

There were only three slave-Spaniard marriages. In two of those cases the nuptial candidate that claimed Spanish ancestry had an unusual personal history. Pedro Atencio, an *español* bachelor from Santa Cruz, was past his prime at age 51, when he married Isabel, his sister's thirty-year-old slave. José, Don Manuel Armijo's household slave, married María Rosalía González of Tomé in 1822. María claimed to be an *española*, but given that she was illegitimate, with father unknown, she was undoubtedly of modest ancestry. No details remain of the 1779 matrimony between José Armijo, a Ute Indian slave, and the *española* Juana Josefa Baca that might explain their hypogamous alliance.[24]

The impulses that motivated slaves to marry were not unlike those of others in New Mexico—love and personal attraction. "Sentiments of the heart," said Isabel, Manuel Martín's slave, was the reason she wanted to marry Cipriano, the servant of Don Bernardo Roybal. Despite her master's opposition to the match in 1741, Isabel confidently told the governor that she and Cipriano were, in fact, already married. There was, as she stated, "unity of hearts."[25]

The conditions of bondage in which slaves lived forced them to postpone marriage until their masters agreed that the time was right. Thralls rarely married before their late twenties, took spouses of similar social status, and spoke of love as their reason for desiring matrimony.

The empirical evidence presented in this chapter shows that the mean age at first marriage for males and females was relatively low (24 and 18, respectively) and progressively declined during the period under study. The age gap between marital partners narrowed, particularly after 1770, undoubtedly because of low sex ratios; a fact also reflected in lower mean ages at first marriage starting for females in the 1760s and for males in the decades following 1770. Between 1694 and 1759, marriages of status endogamy were the norm. In the decades that followed, up until 1820, Spaniards continued to prefer racially endogamous marriages. Among the popular classes exogamy was more widely practiced due to the blurring of racial boundaries. Parental mortality did not affect the age at which children married in New Mexico, and children of the nobility and officer corps married at older ages than children of the popular classes. Men, regardless of their age, preferred brides between the ages of 11 and 29. And the greatest level of matrimonial place exogamy occurred during the early eighteenth century when New Mexico's population was rather sparse.

The Bourbon Reforms on
the Northern Frontier

The eighteenth century in New Mexico was ushered in by the beat of war drums; drums that beat continually for the rest of the century. The century had been ushered in by the reconquest, but as the Pueblo Indians admitted their defeat and openly submitted to Spanish authority, New Mexico's *españoles* shifted their attention to the *indios bárbaros*, the nomadic Indians. Mounted, armed, and masters now of equestrian hit-and-run tactics, these nomads submerged the province in endless war. The Spaniards defended themselves as best they could and always avenged their losses. New Mexicans said that they simply were chastising Indian obstinacy. But the number of Apache and Comanche prisoners pressed into slavery gave this justification a hollow ring.

New Mexico's defense became an acute preoccupation for the Spanish crown in the eighteenth century primarily because the silver-producing provinces of northern New Spain were at risk. By the middle of the eighteenth century two-thirds of the world's silver was being extracted from the northern Mexican provinces of Nueva Galicia, Nueva Vizcaya, and Nuevo León, and that extraction was keeping Spain solvent. So some solution to the marauding Indians who inhibited orderly trade and communication between the northern provinces had to be found. Equally troubling, though undoubtedly less vexing, was the increasing penetration of its American empire by foreigners, particularly in northern Mexico, at the margins of its most valuable terrain. Spain's xenophobia was noticeably increased in 1763, when, at the end of the French and Indian War (1754–63), Spain acquired from France the trans-Mississippi West and the English took everything east of the river. Spain and England were now face-to-face in North America. Already the French had armed the Comanches and driven them south from Illinois into Apache hunting grounds, a movement that reverberated in New Mexico as heightened levels of Apache attacks. Already English merchants had advanced toward Santa Fe with their wares and Russian trappers were hunting otter in Alta California. How the Spanish crown responded to these threats is the focus of this chapter.[1]

Threats to the Kingdom

In 1759, the third and last Bourbon monarch of Spain, King Charles III, ascended the throne. Faced, as his two predecessors had been, with decreasing revenues from America, with decreasing export volumes in the trans-Atlantic trade, and with what mistakenly appeared to be moribund local economies, Charles III gathered a group of enlightened ministers to help him restore Spain's international prominence. The series of economic, administrative, political, and military reforms, known collectively as the Bourbon Reforms, sought to recolonize Spanish America by increasing taxation, by industrializing, by increasing communications, by colonizing marginal areas, by fortifying defenses, and by stripping corporate bodies such as the Church, the nobility, and sheep breeders of their special status and privileges. If the first conquest of America had dominated the Indians, America's second conquest, as historian John Lynch terms the Bourbon Reforms, dominated the creoles (Spaniards of American birth), destroyed the independent local economies they had built, and placed them in renewed subordination vis-à-vis the imperial economy and overseas trade. Let us see how these goals were accomplished in northern New Spain.[2]

Hostile Indians and foreigners were the chief threats to the prosperity of northern New Spain. To ascertain how best to deal with this problem, in 1765 King Charles III dispatched Cayetano María Pignatelli Rubí Corbera y San Climent (known simply as the Marqués de Rubí) to review New Spain's frontier defenses, especially the internal organization and administration of the presidios. Early in April of 1768, the Marqués de Rubí issued a list of recommendations, urging the king to rearm and to relocate some of the presidios, creating an arc-shaped string of forts at intervals of about 40 leagues running from the mouth of the Rio Concepción in Sonora to the Rio Guadalupe in Texas. Santa Fe and San Antonio, Texas, were beyond this arc. Rubí suggested that these presidios also be buttressed with additional forces.[3]

The New Regulations of Presidios, the essence of Rubí's recommendations, were put into law in 1772. Execution of the law was assigned to Don Hugo O'Connor, the first inspector-commander of presidios. Largely because of his success in relocating presidios and waging all-out war against the Apaches, in 1776 New Spain's northern provinces were unified into one administrative unit, the Internal Provinces, and removed from viceregal control.

Successful as O'Connor had been, the wrath of the nomadic Indians in the north had not been significantly tempered. Whether in Texas, Coahuila, Arizona, Sonora, or New Mexico, the story was the same, reported New Mexico's Governor Fermín de Mendinueta in 1772 and in 1777. The enemy Indians perpetrated "incessant robberies, attacks and murders" so that "in all its regions there is no safe place in which to keep horses or herds of cattle." Between 1771 and 1776, the Indians of Nueva Vizcaya had murdered 1,674 persons (not counting persons killed while traveling or presidio soldiers), had stolen 68,256 head of livestock, had captured 154 persons, and had forced the abandonment of 116 haciendas and ranches.[4]

In response, the first commandante-general of the Internal Provinces, Don Teodoro de Croix, convened a series of war councils in 1778. There he and the provincial governors concluded that the Apaches were their most troublesome enemy and that the eastern half of the frontier would be best protected by forging an alliance with the Comanches against the Lipan, Mescalero, and Natage Apaches. But in 1779, the crown ordered Croix to abandon this strategy and instead to employ gifts as a way of befriending hostile Indian groups, hoping, as had been the case with the Pueblo Indians a century and a half earlier, that Indian debts incurred through gifts would make the Indians increasingly dependent on Spanish manufactured goods and markets. And so the Spanish policy to subdue the *indios bárbaros* in northern New Spain from 1779 to 1821 was to divide and conquer the various tribes, first offering gifts to win alliances, then using allies to help vanquish intractable enemies, and when necessary using military force.[5]

The assault on enemy Indian nations was coupled with a policy to develop the far north's productive capacities and to channel those capacities toward imperial ends. Since the early 1700s New Mexico had been tied to New Spain's market economy at Chihuahua through a yearly mule train that had been created initially to provision the missions. New Mexico's trade items were agricultural goods (corn, wheat, beans, pine nuts), livestock, textiles (woolen socks, blankets), and small amounts of wine, brandy, jewelry and animal pelts. Production levels had never been high and rarely covered the purchase of manufactured and luxury goods from Chihuahua merchants.[6]

Throughout the eighteenth century, Chihuahua's merchants and their agents in El Paso, Albuquerque, Santa Fe, and Santa Cruz held a virtual stranglehold on New Mexico due to its remote and isolated location. Since travel south to Chihuahua from New Mexico was dangerous, cumbersome, time-consuming, and expensive, few individuals had any choice but to consign their products to Chihuahua's mercantile agents. Shortly after the harvest in late October and November the yearly mule train would arrive in New Mexico to pack off that year's production and to unload those items most desired in the province—chocolate, sugar, indigo, jewelry, cloth, hats, hard liquor, and manufactured goods. The balance of trade was always negative; the value of imports usually exceeded the value of exports by about two to one. In 1804 alone, for example, exports amounted to 60,000 pesos, while the value of imported Chihuahua goods reached 112,000 pesos.[7]

New Mexicans repeatedly complained to royal authorities about the unscrupulous practices of Chihuahua's merchants and their agents. So strong was their control over the local economy, claimed the citizens, that they had even managed to impose an imaginary monetary exchange system, which always worked to their advantage. Fray Juan Agustín Morfi in 1778 described how exchange transactions were accomplished by merchants through the use of four different peso values. Instead of the official *peso de plata* (silver peso) valued at eight reales, which rarely circulated in New Mexico, three imaginary coins had been invented: *pesos de proyecto* (pesos based on expected production) pegged at six reales, *pesos a precios antiguos* (pesos according to old prices) worth four reales, and *pesos de la tierra* (pesos in local products) valued at two reales. The complexity of the system frequently baffled New Mexicans and worked to the advantage and profit of the merchant. For example, a merchant could purchase a 32-yard bolt of wool cloth for six silver pesos in Chihuahua, resell it in New Mexico at a price of one peso in local products per yard, and receive back a total worth eight silver pesos. But since the merchant was forced to accept local products in exchange for goods due to the lack of currency, and would accept a string of chile or a bottle of brandy at a peso each (that is, a *peso de la tierra*), his earnings were potentially much higher. For if 32 bottles of brandy were collected for the wool cloth, he could then resell the brandy to other New Mexicans at the price of one silver peso per bottle, making six reales profit on each item for which he paid only one *peso de la tierra*. Again, because hard currency was difficult to secure, the resale of local products might be arranged through payment from a future corn harvest. If this was the case, the merchant would sell at *pesos de precios antiguos*, equivalent to four reales, for each short bushel (*costal*) of grain accepted. Thus for the 32 bottles of brandy, the merchant could collect 51 short bushels of corn, which if resold in Chihuahua could bring 10 reales per short bushel, or a total of 84 pesos in silver for an original investment of six silver pesos on a bolt of cloth.[8]

Father Morfi maintained that this monetary system was particularly detrimental for the Pueblo Indians. In their case the local chief constables (*alcaldes mayores*) were usually in cahoots with mercantile agents or were themselves directly in the employ of Chihuahua merchants. The post of *alcalde mayor* was highly honorific but uncompensated. To profit from their tenure, constables often turned to Chihuahua's merchants, who all too willingly supplied them with a salary, expenses, and advances to further specific economic activities among the Indians. By advancing capital and credit, and by selling goods, seeds, and equipment to the Indians, the alcaldes controlled much of economic life in their districts. Additionally, through the use of the *repartimiento*, a rotational labor levy that the Puebloans were required to perform, the alcaldes could extract labor in excess of their legal due, thereby driving the Indians into financial dependence because they could not attend to their own familial reproductive needs, and precipitating movement off the pueblo into some form of debt peonage in Spanish settlements.[9]

As early as 1750, Fray Carlos Delgado inveighed against such alcalde abuses. He reported how it was common for chief constables to enter the pueblos demanding to buy 1,000 *fanegas* of maize, to force the Indians to transport the maize without recompense, and then to pay only half of what the maize was worth in trinkets. "From this manifest injustice two very serious evils result," wrote Delgado: "first, the unhappy Indians are left without anything to eat for the greater part of the year; and second, in order not to perish of hunger they are forced to go to the mountains and hunt for game or to serve on the ranches or farms for their food alone, leaving the missions abandoned."[10]

Equally disruptive of native communities were the alcaldes' demands for labor, be it constructing buildings, grazing livestock, or transporting goods. Such labor was paid with "only a little ground corn." While employed in such projects, "the Indians must abandon their families and leave their lands uncultivated, and, as a consequence, are dying of hunger during the greater part of the year," declared Delgado. Every year the Indians had to weave "four hundred blankets, or as many woolen sheets"; they had to plant, harvest, and store in granaries maize and wheat; they had to trade tobacco and knives for pelts among the nomadic Indians;

and the women had to spin wool into yarn. If the Indians complained or resisted, the *alcaldes* violated the women and whipped the men. Delgado writes:

> I cannot say it without tears—the officials flog them so pitilessly that, their wrath not being appeased by seeing them shed their blood, they inflict such deep scars upon them that they remain for many years . . . when I went among the heathen to reduce the apostates there were among them some who, with an aggrieved air, showed me their scars, thus giving me to understand that the reason why they fled and did not return to the pale of the church was their fear of these cruel punishments.[11]

Similar alcalde abuses were chronicled by Fray Juan Sanz de Lezaún in 1760, by Fray Pedro Serrano in 1761, and by Fray Juan Agustín de Morfi in 1778. The tenor of their complaints to the crown were poignantly captured in 1751, when Fray Andrés Varo, paraphrasing the prophet Jeremiah, exclaimed: "Oh land and kingdom of New Mexico! So long oppressed, humiliated, and persecuted, so often not governed, but tyrannized over by these unworthy chiefs."[12]

King Charles III responded to the general economic stagnation in northern New Spain by dispatching the Spanish Royal Corps of Engineers in 1765 to map the area thoroughly and to identify its mineral and hydraulic resources. Charts were drawn of the best routes of communication. In anticipation of increased dockings, Alta California's ports were mapped for safer navigation. Methods of increasing New Mexico's livestock and agricultural production were among the numerous proposals they advanced.

The Royal Corps of Engineers in 1768 recommended the refortification of the frontier, the establishment of intra-provincial east-west links, such as between New Mexico, Arizona, and California, and additional north-south links between New Mexico and central Mexico.[13] A major step toward this goal was realized in 1769 when a permanent settlement was established at San Diego, California. Soon thereafter commercial ties between California and New Mexico were created. The fiscal officer of New Spain's treasury in 1789 made explicit the economic intent of these links: "Commerce between California and New Mexico will facilitate the export of their goods and their grain, will contribute to population increase in that area, and will protect them from insults and the enemy ready to invade."[14]

The crown believed that New Mexico would be best developed and retained as part of the empire through a freer and fuller integration into the market economy of Chihuahua. To achieve this, previous trade and travel restrictions were abolished. New Mexican products were given sales tax exemptions at market. Agricultural specialists, veterinarians, and master weavers were sent to the area to upgrade local production and to improve the competitive position of the kingdom's products. Within a few years the frequency of mule trains to and from Chihuahua increased. Coin began to circulate more widely, alleviating some of the abuses perpetrated by merchants through the use of imaginary monetary standards. On December 4, 1786, the *repartimiento* was abolished and *alcaldes mayores* were replaced by intendants, bureaucratic officers who answered directly to the king. And finally, new colonists from north-central Mexico began migrating into the area.[15]

The swelling of New Mexico's population due both to natural increase and state stimulated in-migration resulted in intense land pressure, which was relieved through a series of grants of unoccupied territory. Though at first glance New Mexico's land seemed limitless, the amount of arable land near water was quite limited. The crown recognized the anteriority of Pueblo claims to some of the best watered spots. At the beginning of New Mexico's colonization, each pueblo had been recognized as holding corporately four square leagues or 17,712 acres of inalienable land. Hispanic settlers accommodated themselves to this. Had there been peace in the province, the colonists would have brought more land into production, but a constant state of war against the nomadic Indians had contracted the amount of arable land at precisely the moment that the population was growing. Partible inheritance among the Spanish further complicated the situation. Within three to four generations, plots that once had sustained a family, when divided, no longer provided a livelihood.

Some families with inadequate lands for agriculture turned to livestock production, using the open ranges as pasturage. This too soon created problems. The livestock began overrunning Indian lands. Increased grazing soon depleted available forage. And when this occurred, greener pastures had to be found. In 1748 the settlers of Santa Cruz sought permission from the governor to send their Indian servants in search of land. He granted the permit, cautioning the settlers to keep the distance to these areas at a minimum, or soldiers would not be able to come to their aid against hostile Indians.[16]

The lack of adequate arable land for subsistence seriously began to plague the kingdom in the 1770s. Governor Pedro Fermín de Mendinueta in 1773 informed the viceroy that as a result of this fact, New Mexico's Spanish villagers were being forced to purchase substantial portions of their agricultural needs from Indian producers. A Spanish aversion to physical labor and the lack of lands had placed them at the mercy of the

Puebloans, totally dependent on whatever surplus they wished to sell. Governor Francisco de la Concha further described the severity of the problem in 1789. "Generally the Indians of this province because they possess the best lands live in more comfort than the Spaniards. Many Spaniards are forced to rent land from the Indians to produce their food, and some years, particularly if there is famine or drought, Spaniards are even forced to serve the Indians."[17]

The desire to expand New Mexico's arable land by settling areas that were difficult to protect, resulted in the awarding of *mercedes* (land grants), first to landless emancipated *genízaros*—Indian slaves who had gained their freedom from Hispano households—and later, particularly after 1821, to landless Spaniards. The *genízaros* were resettled on the margins of the kingdom at Belén in 1740, at Abiquiu and Ojo Caliente in 1754, and at San Miguel del Vado in 1794. Aside from ridding Santa Fe, Albuquerque, and Santa Cruz of ex-slaves who were deemed unruly by *españoles*, the authorities hoped that by strategically locating *genízaro* villages as buffers along nomadic Indian raiding routes, the impact of Indian depredations on Spanish towns would be softened. Thus Belén guarded the southern approach to the Rio Grande Valley, Analco, the *genízaro* suburb of Santa Fe, protected the town's eastern approach, Abiquiu and Ojo Caliente the northwest approach to Santa Cruz, and San Miguel the northeast access route to Santa Cruz and Santa Fe.[18]

By the 1770s *genízaros* were perceived as a distinct and dangerous ethnic group, and this explains why they were congregated into their own villages. Spanish and Puebloan society viewed them as marginalized and degraded because of their slave and ex-slave status. They spoke a distinctive (broken) form of Spanish. Fray Carlos Delgado observed that *genízaros* practiced marriage class endogamy, taking "women of their own status and nature." They also "lived in great unity *como si fueran una nación*," as if they were a nation. Indeed, it is interesting to note that at Abiquiu, there is ample documentary evidence to show that the village had a governor, an *alguacil* (constable), and a *fiscal* (church warden), thus resembling in administrative structure not a Spanish town, but an Indian pueblo.[19]

With the emancipation and movement of *genízaros* onto the frontier, they finally had an independent space in which to express their own identity. Some *genízaros* abandoned their Christian baptismal names for what appear to be indigenous ones. Antonio Jiménez called himself "Cuasipe." Miguel Reaño was "Tasago." Juana, the Apache slave of Diego Velásquez, was "Guisachi." *Genízaros* also began to take active roles in the defense of the kingdom. Fray Carlos Delgado reported in 1744 that the *genízaros* at Belén were obliged to "go out and explore the country in pursuit of the enemy, which they do with great bravery and zeal." They are "great soldiers, very warlike and the ones most feared by our enemies," wrote Fray Agustín Morfi in 1782. When Governor Pedro Fermín de Mendinueta gave chase to a band of Apaches in 1777, he dispatched 55 *genízaros* in their pursuit. For their services as soldiers, scouts, and interpreters during the second half of the eighteenth century, *genízaros* solicited and were given special distinctions. Manuel Antonio, a *genízaro*, received a presidio post in 1768. Others must similarly have been honored, for when the authorities in Tomé had to use force to arrest Marcos Sánchez for maltreating his concubine in 1793, he loudly protested: "I am a *genízaro* unworthy of such base treatment."[20]

The Bourbon Reforms instituted by King Charles III had sought to rejuvenate the stagnant imperial economy by increasing revenue collections in America, by increasing trade, and by splintering those powerful colonial interest groups that had the potential to resist monarchical authority. If royal absolutism and the secular state were to reign supreme, those corporate bodies that under the Hapsburg kings had enjoyed extensive privileges and autonomy—the Church, the Inquisition, the nobility, the guilds, the *mesta*—had to be subordinated.

Subordination of the Church

The royal assault on the power of the Church and on the authority of its priests occurred both in the Indian Pueblos and in Spanish settlements. Church-state relations had been rather calm during the first half of the eighteenth century. But in 1761, the scabs were torn off what were now old wounds.[21] The themes in this round of Church-state controversy were identical to those in the 1600s. From the perspective of the governors, who wanted the Franciscans removed from the province so that they could have full reign over the Pueblo Indians, the friars had been remiss in their duties. They claimed that the sons of St. Francis infrequently said Mass and were lax in the administration of the sacraments. They had failed to teach the Indians the Spanish language, were seizing Indian crops and livestock for themselves, and were selling the excess for profit. To relieve the Indians of such abuses the governors recommended that some of the missions be secularized and others consolidated.[22]

The Franciscans hotly contested all of these charges. Certainly there were a few weak and dissolute priests, they claimed, but the majority were models of virtue. The friars administered the sacraments conscientiously and though they had not totally mastered the Indian languages, the Indians did in fact understand Spanish well. With regard to the extortion of Indian property, it simply was not so. Since time immemorial the Indians had freely worked a plot of land designated specifically for the support of their friar. The labor the Indians performed in caring for Church flocks was freely performed. They were being calumniated for profiteering, said the Franciscans. It was the governor and his constables who were guilty of this crime. They were the ones who demanded more labor of the Indians than was permissible by law, not the friars. The false and malicious testimony the governors presented the viceroy was but a ploy to rob the Indians of their true protectors, the Franciscans, and to expose them to unbridled exploitation.[23]

So what was the reality of Pueblo Indian life in the latter half of the eighteenth century? In the preceding 50 years the Franciscans had expended tremendous energy ministering to the Pueblo Indians, instructing them in Christian doctrine and teaching them the rudiments of civilization; all with very little success. The notorious conflicts between Indians and friars over the celebration of indigenous rites, particularly the katsina dance, which had characterized the seventeenth century, did not reoccur primarily because these rituals were now being performed clandestinely. Gone too were the constant Indian complaints of clerical abuse. The friars continually detested Indian idolatry, detested the devil's influence in the Pueblos, but did not engage in vicious iconoclasm to eradicate it.[24]

Assessing the state of New Mexico's Indian missions in 1776, Fray Atanasio Domínguez was quite disheartened by what he saw. "Even at the end of so many years since their reconquest," wrote Domínguez, "the specious title or name of neophytes is still applied to them. This is the reason their condition now is almost the same as it was in the beginning, for generally speaking they have preserved some very indecent, and perhaps superstitious, customs." Domínguez went on to detail how Puebloans ignored their baptismal names and ridiculed each other with them; how they did not pray, cross themselves, or show much devotion to the saints; how when the church bell was rung they would not come willingly to church; and how they performed their church duties "only under compulsion," with resistance and repugnance. According to Domínguez, the Indians continued to perform the scalp dance with considerable gusto despite its prohibition; they refused to give charity or lodging to Spaniards; and when the Puebloans did attend services, they entered the church stark naked. At Taos and Picuris the Indians so disliked their friar, said Domínguez, that "they flee from him like the devil from the cross, and the children even cry, running as if from their cruelest enemy."[25]

Despite nearly two centuries of evangelization, the Pueblo Indians, said Viceroy Revillagigedo in 1793, were "heathens underneath and very given to the vain respect and superstitions of their elders. They have a natural antipathy for everything to do with our sacred religion." Indeed, Fray Atanasio Domínguez was startled to find in 1776 that when Pueblo Indians wanted a priest to pray a Mass, they could not specify their exact intention and instead would say: "You know, that Saint what more good, more big, him you make Mass. I not know, maybe him Virgin, maybe St. Anthony."[26]

Indian comportment at Jémez left Fray Joaquín de Jesús Ruiz equally horror-struck in 1776. Ruiz reported that he had to be constantly vigilant because the Indians would steal "the holy oils and the consecrated water for their superstitions." He had often found girls and boys in church "romping, laughing, and pulling one another by the fringe of their buckskins and blankets, and the women by their girdles, and, during a certain prayer, a nude *fiscal* with his private parts uncovered performing many obscene acts." When the women attended Mass "they spend all the time dedicated to prayer and Mass in gossip, showing one another their glass beads, ribbons, medals, etc., telling who gave them to them or how they obtained them, and other mischief." The young boys and girls were even worse and had to be constantly watched so that they did not "play games and laugh (which they do even under this regime) or play pranks or fall asleep or draw unseemly things upon the walls." Ruiz had forbidden the Indian women from entering the fields to weed during the growing season because when they did, they would "join the older youths in wanton and wicked dalliance." In the two years that Ruiz had been at Jémez, "on three occasions they showed disrespect for me, [and] . . . one went so far as to strike me in the face."[27]

The burlesque that Agustín Guichi, a Pecos cacique, staged in 1760 was emblematic of the contempt the Puebloans showed for Christian ritual. On May 29, 1760, Bishop Pedro Tamarón y Romeral visited Pecos and was greeted with much pomp and circumstance. After Tamarón had finished his inspection of the mission and had departed, Agustín fashioned a bishop's costume for himself, with miter, cope, crosier, and all, and processed through the town mimicking Tamarón. He demanded that the women greet him kneeling in two rows. He distributed blessings, performed confirmations, prayed a high Mass, gave out wheat tortillas as Holy Communion, and presided over several days of debauchery and disorder. Tamarón was scandalized on hearing of these events. However, he felt God had punished this mockery, for shortly afterward a bear mauled Agustín to death.[28]

For all intents and purposes, during the eighteenth century the pueblos evolved quite independently of each other. Though travel between the pueblos was strictly regulated, communication and trade did occur, but how frequently is a difficult question to answer. To travel from one place to another, everyone—Spanish and Indian alike—was required to have a license or passport. Justifiably, as we will shortly see, the kingdom's governors feared Indian rebellion, particularly with the rise of Indian depredations after 1770. By this date too, *españoles* had begun to masquerade as "wild Apaches" to commit heinous crimes. Isidro Barelas of Santa Fe was apprehended in 1800 and sentenced to four years of penal slavery for having raped four Spanish women while disguised as a masked Indian. Dionicio González was sentenced to four years in prison in 1800 too, for stealing a horse and several cows while similarly attired.[29]

Residents of each pueblo had established trade relations with settlers in the Spanish towns and villages nearby and with adjacent pueblos, particularly if the pueblos shared a common language. One can study the network of exchanges between particular pueblos and their neighbors by examining the claims that were made when an administrative review or *visita* of the province was conducted. Governor Don Joaquín Codallos y Rabal conducted such a *visita* in 1745. Here are just a few of the disputes he adjudicated. At Taos the Indians demanded compensation for the livestock, cloth, and skins they had sold to Indians at Santa Clara and Tesuque and to Spaniards residing at Taos, Santa Cruz, Santa Fe, and Embudo. San Juan's Indians pressed claims against Indians at San Ildefonso and Spaniards at Albuquerque, Santa Cruz, and Ojo Caliente. At Isleta Pueblo all the claims were against Spaniards at Albuquerque, Belén, and Valencia or against other residents at Isleta.[30]

Visita evidence shows quite conclusively that trade relations between pueblos and towns occurred with some frequency. Marriage alliances, on the other hand, rarely occurred between individuals from different pueblos or between Pueblo Indians and residents in Spanish towns. In Chapter 4, while discussing eighteenth-century Pueblo demography, we noted that during the eighteenth and early nineteenth centuries Pueblo population grew slowly, at an annual geometric rate of 0.382 percent, in comparison to the Spanish population, which grew at 2.66 percent annually. Since most pueblos experienced negative growth rates, it was of importance to determine if these rates were due to out-migration as might be reflected in marital-place exogamy. To determine this the marriage registers at Zuñi and Cochiti Pueblos were analyzed. These two pueblos were selected because, with an annual geometric growth rate of +5.47 percent and −3.46 percent respectively, the former experienced the greatest growth and the latter the most precipitous decline.

Both extant marriage registers were incomplete. At Zuñi, 275 marriages had been recorded between 1705 and 1775; at Cochiti, 93 marriages had been listed for 1776–1786. Only five Zuñians married residents from other pueblos; none had married Spaniards or mixed-bloods. Magdalena (surnames were rarely listed) married a Hopi named Juan Joseph in 1726. Isabel married another Hopi, also named Joseph, in 1726. Estevan married a Hopi woman named Catharina in 1727. Magdalena married a Tiwa named Gabriel in 1753. And Francisco married a Santa Ana woman named Rosa in 1757. Of the 93 marriages listed in Cochiti's register, 43 were among Spanish residents at the nearby settlement of Cañada de Cochiti. In no case did a Cochiti Indian marry outside the pueblo either to another Indian or to a Hispano.[31]

Several conclusions can be drawn from these results. Those pueblos that experienced population growth in the eighteenth century did not achieve it through in-migration or in-marriages, but through natural increase. Marital-place exogamy was not principally responsible for population decrease at those pueblos that experienced marked decline, though as we saw in Table 9.9, which reported 378 Pueblo Indian place-exogamous marriages between 1694 and 1846, such marriages did contribute to the decline. More significant in producing the high rates of population decline were the factors highlighted in earlier chapters: out-migration due to excessive *repartimiento* labor demands, the expulsion of violated women from their pueblos, and the abandonment of mixed-blood children born to Pueblo women.[32]

Pueblo marriage registers document another interesting pattern. Whereas in the seventeenth century the Franciscan friars were most often the individuals who served as marital godparents (*padrinos*) for Indians, in the eighteenth century this role was primarily filled by the pueblo's civil governor and the interpreter. This illustrates yet again how the role of intermediary between Pueblos and Spanish authorities had shifted from the friars to the Indian civil officers—their Outside Chiefs—during the eighteenth century.

Placid as the Puebloans may have appeared on the surface during the latter half of the 1700s, the reality was quite different. Seditious plots were discovered by Spanish authorities at San Juan Pueblo in 1784, at San Ildefonso in 1793, at Taos in 1810, and among the Tewa and Northern Tiwa (Taos, Picuris) in 1837. The 1793 San Ildefonso plot, aside from being the best documented, is the only case that gives us some sense of what was actually transpiring in the pueblos. In this particular instance, Asencio Peña, a Tewa from San Ildefonso, had invited the governors of San Ildefonso, San Juan, Santa Clara, Poajoque, Nambé, and a handful of other men to discuss a revolt plan. Bentura Piche testified that Miguel Cacage, Miguel Ortiz, and he had opposed the plan, saying that they would only join if Asencio promised "to give us a mountain of corn and wheat and all the foods they ate among the Spanish." Asencio is said to have retorted, "it was true that the God of the Spaniards was powerful, but that his was his equal." In the end, only two men favored rebellion. The plot fizzled. New Mexico's governor got wind of it and had the men brought to Santa Fe to explain the intent of their secret meetings. Asencio, the apparent ring-leader, said that the purpose of their meetings had been to advise his countrymen "to live according to the law of God and to teach their children how to pray and speak Spanish, because there was only one God through whose favor they had food to eat, clothing and possessions . . . and that he had said all of this in Spanish." Flabbergasted by what he heard, Governor Fernando de la Concha rebuked the men for mocking him. "Being morally impossible that the said meetings could have had as their goal the things they say," wrote the governor, "for their conduct was diametrically opposite to what they claim," he had the bunch flogged, fined, and sentenced to public service for up to six months.[33]

The problems the Franciscans had experienced in exerting their authority over the Pueblo Indians during the second half of the eighteenth century were not unlike the problems they would experience with the kingdom's Hispanic population. A chorus of recriminations against the friars began reverberating broadly in the Hispanicized population by the 1770s. Where in 1657 there had been 70 missionaries, by 1792 there were only 16. Where once the friars had been stationed in pairs and had remained in a parish for ten to twelve years, in the 1700s they were stationed alone and were moved almost every year, thus making it much more difficult for them to establish relationships of confidence with their parishioners. New Mexico's missions in the seventeenth century had been the pride of the Province of the Holy Gospel in Mexico City. The fabric of the Franciscan Order had begun to unravel and the flesh had grown weak and flaccid. Service in New Mexico's missions had become a disciplinary stint akin to internal exile. Where death at the hands of the Apaches was so ever present, even profligate priests could ill-afford not to mend their ways.[34]

But they did not, or so claimed the colonists. A group of citizens from Truchas launched a formal complaint against their friar in 1762. The *vecinos* of Santa Cruz did likewise in 1781, as did those in Albuquerque in 1786, Pecos in 1798, Santa Fe in 1801, Picuris in 1809, and Abiquiu and Ojo Caliente in 1820. What they all said was that the friars were failing to perform their priestly duties. They were not saying Mass regularly, preaching, baptizing, hearing confessions, or administering the last rites. The friars were charging such exorbitant fees that they could not afford to be married or buried. Worst of all, some friars were indecorous in their words and deeds.[35]

Fray Francisco Campo Redondo responded to the 1762 charge that he failed to say Mass at Truchas by countering that his accusers were a depraved, disobedient, and "loose-reined" bunch who were trying "to denigrate his person with their vituperations." Yet, in the end, he admitted that he had not said Mass. In another case, New Mexico's vicar determined in 1820 that Fray Teodoro Alcina "was simply not a good person" and had failed to give sermons, perform baptisms, or hear confession. Father Teodoro was immediately transferred to Zuñi, and there the matter ended.[36]

The charge that the priests were extracting excessive fees for marriages and burials, was, on the basis of established fee schedules, simply unwarranted. In 1781 the friars were deprived of all Indian service, both in the form of obventions and labor. Previously the friars had been fed with these obventions; without them they became more rigid in demanding payment for their services. Whereas before 1781 the friars had accepted just about anything a parishioner would offer him in payment, after 1781 they accepted only those products they could easily sell or exchange. Thus Fray José Mariano Rosete y Peralta responded to the accusation that he had overcharged Francisco Olguín for a burial in 1789 by saying that Francisco "had tried to pay me with a well-worn skirt of very poor quality wool; I guess he wanted me to wear it, which I guess I deserve, given the infamies I have suffered." Had Olguín treated him with respect, stated the friar, he might have been more accommodating. But Olguín had rolled a cigarette in church and had lit it with an altar candle. "Such is the state of affairs that even the Indians show the house of God more reverence than the sons of Old Christians," stated Fra José. Fray Diego Muñoz Jurado said in 1781 that he had demanded a different form of payment from Salvador Trujillo for his daughter's burial because "on my saint's day, while accompanied by the chief constable of Santa Cruz he tried to pay me for the burial with a pig. . . . In my view he did this to mock me." Father Diego presented his superiors with the death registers from Santa Cruz parish, proving that in no case had he overcharged for a burial. Quite the contrary, for most burials, the parishioners were still in his debt.[37]

The majority of New Mexico's friars were of educated Spanish origin and regarded the colonists as a rude and crude lot. In 1820, Fray Teodoro Alcina had harangued Abiquiu's citizens from the pulpit, saying that he would "drive them into the ground with censures," and shouting: "Cursed be Abiquiu! Cursed be Abiquiu!" It was. Shortly after Alcina's sermon their crops were destroyed by a hail storm and a locust infestation. Fray Diego Muñoz Jurado explained that he treated his Santa Cruz congregation contemptuously because they behaved "like pagans, entering church as if it were a horse stable, not crossing themselves, kneeling on only one knee like Jews, and remaining covered with their hooded cloaks throughout the Holy Sacrifice of the Mass." He did not care if his congregation complained of the constant surveillance he kept over them because he was simply performing his priestly duties. He had indeed threatened María Sánchez with a stick and kept her standing during one of his surprise visits, because she was "a woman with a venomous and pestilent tongue." "I kept the woman standing during my visit," declared Father Diego, "because if she had been properly educated as a child she would have known that in the presence of a priest, no matter how unworthy or vile he might be, she should stand. Since her parents had not taught her this, I as her pastor tried." [38]

Christ preached that he who was without sin could cast the first stone. If New Mexico's friars had heeded his words, they might not have been so pious in their pursuit of adulterers and fornicators. For the sins they saw in others were also their own. The faithful usually remained silent about these sins because they understood the enormity of the tasks their priests performed. The duty of a priest was to criticize and to inspire, to minister and to administer at the cradle, altar, and grave, to the living and to the dead. He had to educate the children, care for the fabric of the church, stage rituals properly, guard the community from the devil, and secure its relationship with God and with itself. So if several of New Mexico's priests lived in stable concubinage and had authentically earned the title padre, it was not particularly troublesome. It became so when priests began philandering about, seducing boys, nubile virgins, and married women alike.

Fray José de la Santa Cruz Polanco was accused of having caused Pascual Avalos "pollutions" with impure acts during Lent in 1771. He had sodomized Paulino, a *mulato* orphan who he kept locked in his cell. He tried to rape Juana Antonia Trujillo and forced Dominga Rodríguez to have sex with him while she was pregnant. When another woman, María Dolores Trujillo, resisted Fray José's advances by telling him that she was married, the friar coaxed her, saying, "to try, for women, when they wanted to could facilitate everything." The friar left New Mexico quickly with the pretext that he was sick. He was later deprived of his priestly faculties and sentenced to ten years in a cloister for his sins. Fray Ramón Antonio González was denounced for soliciting sex from women in his

Santa Cruz confessional in 1792. Fray Rafael de Benavides, the Vice-Custodian of the New Mexican missions, allegedly fathered several children that same year. And Fray José Benito Pereyro did not hold his tongue when in 1818 he heard that his prelate had ordered Fray Sebastian Alvarez to pay Juana María Laín 60 pesos to help her support the child he had fathered. Fray José told his superior that he knew for fact that Father Alvarez also had commerced with:

María Encarnación and María de García, first cousins of María Guadalupe Valdez who bore a daughter, Manuela Trujillo, María Lain who bore a son, Ana María Fresquis, Rosa Mestas who bore a son, La Roma, La Lupe Sánchez, Antonia Gallego, Ignacia Peña, the daughter of Isidro Medina who bore a son, the daughter of Alejandro Márques who bore a son, Manuela Trujillo, alias la Malinche, Soledad Tenorio.[39]

Given the friars' own failings and their berating of Indian and mixed-blood women as wells of lust and passion who fornicated with little discretion, celebrated sexual perversions, and lived in concubinage, some interesting socio-psychological insights present themselves. Priests were in a particularly contradictory position in the Spanish sex/gender system. As males, priests were socialized to be aggressive and authority figures. They derived their masculinity from the possession of a penis, their virile member. Yet as priests, through their vow of chastity they were symbolically castrated. The tonsure on their head signified this. Rules of religious discipline expected them to be sexually pure, meek, gentle, and Christ-like—behavior more commonly associated with women. A penitent and remorseful Fray Francisco Pulido denounced himself before the Inquisition in 1761 "for committing the sin of sodomy about four or five times out of frailty, having totally lost my senses" with an Indian male servant. Frailty was naturally only a characteristic of women.[40]

A priest's social emasculation was mitigated by the role he played as intermediary between God and mortals. When such power was no longer deemed particularly important, and the friars' status loss was apparent in many realms, what were they to do? What were they to do when men mocked them by giving them skirts and pigs; or when women would not stand in their presence or even listen to what they said? Angered by these facts, Fray Santiago Fernández de Sierra demanded in 1788 that the civil magistrate of Sandía jurisdiction punish the area's citizens for their insolence. Appalled that even the women refused to respect him, he wrote: "this document will bring to your attention how poorly priests are treated here that even the women want to trample and ridicule us."[41]

Fray Santiago's rage was justified on other counts too, for the ritual efficacy of priests was also under attack. Governor Don Fernando de la

Concha in 1794 allegedly said to Don Antonio Ruiz, "these Masses which the friars of New Mexico celebrate are worth as much as those my horse might say: Do you believe that Jesus Christ descends into the hands of those priests?" Don Antonio Ruiz responded that he believed it because he was a faithful Christian. Governor de la Concha responded, "but if these friars live in concubinage, how can Jesus Christ descend into their hands?"[42]

The provincials of the Franciscan Order in Mexico City constantly tried to promote better relations between priests and their communities. They ordered the friars not to employ women as domestics in their convents, to observe their vow of chastity, to hear confessions through some sort of partition, to avoid excess in drinking, gambling, and commerce, in short, to observe all the rules of the Order. Only in this way could the honor of the Franciscan habit and of the Order be preserved. The pleas fell largely on deaf ears, for the priests were far from civilization and did virtually as they pleased.[43]

The Royal Pragmatic on Marriage

This was the socio-historical context in New Mexico within which the Bourbon ecclesiastical policy unfolded. As the Bourbons stimulated the colonial economy on the frontier and streamlined their bureaucratic apparatus, they simultaneously sought to weaken the power of the Church and its clergy. Symbolic of this posture was the expulsion of 2,500 Jesuits from Spanish America in 1767. Pressures to secularize the missions followed, as did rulings to deprive the friars of Indian service, to strip them of ecclesiastical wealth, to curtail their clerical immunities before the civil courts, and to abrogate their legal functions. Particularly poignant in this last respect was the promulgation by King Charles III of the Royal Pragmatic on Marriage, issued on March 23, 1776.

The Royal Pragmatic prohibited the legitimation of unequal unions and required, under pain of disinheritance, formal parental consent to marry for all persons below the age of 25. The decree maintained that wide status disparities between marital candidates were detrimental to the economic prosperity of honorable families and to their social exclusivity. "The blind passions of youth" and egalitarian notions such as those of love were the primary culprits, said King Charles III, for children often moved solely by physical desires, ignored parental dictates on marriage, shirked their responsibilities to their class, and undermined the hierarchy and integrity of the state by marrying persons who were of lower status.[44]

Aiding and abetting this subversion was the Catholic Church. Its enforcement of an individual's liberty to marry freely was leading to the erosion of parental authority over children and to the moral collapse of society. The Church abused the principle of marital freedom when children were joined in matrimony against parental wishes. The clergy had the right to define the rites that constituted matrimony, but had to recognize that marriage was also a civil contract that legitimized progeny, created inheritance and property rights, and was the basis for the accession of honors. As canon law stood, regardless of the endless litigation over property that could ensue from a misalliance, so long as the sacrament was valid, the contract was too. This could not be.[45]

King Charles cautioned parents that the authority to supervise their child's spouse selection should not be interpreted as the right to force a partner upon them. Only grave spiritual and temporal prejudices could result by thwarting honestly desired matrimonies or by celebrating them without the liberty and reciprocal love. Parents could oppose only marriages that offended the honor of the family or jeopardized the integrity of the state. Civil courts would hear all such cases and determine if the opposition was justified.[46]

The Marriage Pragmatic was extended to all of Spain's territories on April 7, 1778, and became law in New Mexico that year. No official copy of the decree or correspondence relating to its publication exists in local archives, but all subsequent legal clarifications and addenda were received and duly acknowledged. The first mention of the implementation of the Pragmatic came on May 20, 1780, when Francisco Romero and María Manuela Gutiérrez presented written parental consent to marry.[47]

The Royal Pragmatic on Marriage can only be understood as part of the state's assertion of its secular authority. Between the Renaissance and the Enlightenment, all Western European states had undertaken reforms to bolster the absolutist state and to thwart the power of the Church. Spain did not undergo these changes primarily because of its role in the Counter-Reformation. With the ascent of Charles III to the throne, all of this changed.

The vision of power Charles III advanced to his subjects was not rooted in abstract notions of divine sanction or those representations of the king as universal head of the Church as articulated in the *Real Patronato de Indias*. The rituals of monarchy celebrated in honor of the Bourbon kings of Spain had defined a new ritual space, separate and clearly distinct from the Church's sacral community. The royal standard was now revered with as much majesty as was shown the Eucharist on the feast of Corpus Christi. We see this very clearly at the Santa Fe celebration of King Ferdinand VI's coronation in 1748. At the tolling of the church's bell on January 24, the town's citizens gathered to process the royal standard through the streets as they always had their reverential objects. "At the head [of the procession] was the infantry regiment, all with bare swords," wrote Fray Lorenzo Antonio Estremera. Following them were the presidio soldiers, then the "distinguished citizens dressed in the best clothes they owned . . . then came the royal standard" carried by the governor. The procession ended with the placement of the standard in the plaza on a velvet cushion under a canopy. Fray Lorenzo writes:

> that night there were many luminaries, with sundry close volleys by the soldiery and divers peals of the bells in our church, so that the atmosphere was filled with rejoicing. Then came a resplendent triumphal chariot with the arms of Spain and an imperial crown and scepter. And riding in this chariot was a personage who acted in three different parts a very learned [panegyric] in praise of our King and Lord don Ferdinand the Sixth, to great acclamations by the people with many huzzas and 'Long live our King and Lord don Ferdinand the Sixth.' This brought the night's festivities to a close.[48]

As we can see from this ritual honoring the remote king, in defining the sacred and the profane, the king's coronation was celebrated in secular space without religious symbols. The terrestrial community increasingly was no longer viewed as a mere reflection of the celestial order. Rather, the patriarchal household became the natural and analogical symbol of good government. As a father exercised his authority and domination within the household over wife, children, servants, and retainers, so the king viewed the state as his private domain, a form of rule Max Weber called "patrimonialism."[49]

The impact of the Caroline Pragmatic on Marriage, both in New Mexico and in the rest of the colonial empire, was to expand the legal scope of parental control and to constrain the power of the clergy to impinge upon it. The principle of matrimonial freedom, which had previously provided adolescents and their confessors with a vehicle to subvert parental dictates, after 1788 proved more difficult, though not impossible. In the case of marriage, the king had allied himself with male heads of households in order to undermine the power of the Church and of the lower clergy.

By depriving the Church of exclusive control over marriage in 1776, the state had expanded the role of the civil judiciary in private life. As might be expected, faced with an assault on their privileges, the clergy sided with youths against their parents and staged a new, albeit futile, tug of war over the liberty of persons to marry the spouse they chose.

In 1781, for example, Miguel Angel Tafoya asked his pastor at Santa Cruz, Fray Diego Muñoz Jurado, to sequester María Rosa Maestas, the daughter of Juan Ignacio Maestas, who would not allow her to marry freely. Father Diego determined that Miguel and María truly wanted to be husband and wife, had exchanged as a token of that desire a *prenda*, and so married them. Juan Maestas and his wife María Sánchez continued to oppose the marriage, even after it had occurred. Availing themselves of the provisions of the Marriage Pragmatic, they disinherited the girl, not allowing her access to any of her clothes or possessions. Hoping to nullify the marriage, they got María Michaela Salazar to place a false impediment to it, claiming that the nuptial was invalid because Miguel Angel Tafoya had given her a previous promise of betrothal. Father Diego smelled a rat and badgered María Michaela until she confessed the truth. Maestas had threatened her with exile from New Mexico if she did not cooperate. Before the ecclesiastical court María Michaela admitted that: "I do not want to bear false witness against Tafoya, nor do I want the devil to take me only to please Juan Maestas." Maestas was thus foiled in his attempt to abrogate the marriage. But Father Diego was not finished. One day when Maestas was out of town, he confronted María Sánchez and seized the clothes she would not give her daughter. Maestas and his wife complained to the governor of the friar's behavior, but no reported action was taken against him.[50]

Fray Francisco Antonio Galforsoso likewise sequestered the daughter of militia captain Don Juan Domingo García and married her to the man she loved in 1792, despite her father's opposition. Don Juan's objections to the union were upheld by the civil court. The groom was of "notorious inequality and vice-ridden behavior," and therefore unfit for a son-in-law. Fray Galforsoso refused to annul the marriage or to return the girl to her father. New Mexico's vice-custodian read the friar the Royal Pragmatic and the canons of the Fourth Council of the Mexican Catholic Church, and still he would not release the girl. Finally, when word of his insubordination reached his superiors, Galforsoso was relieved of his duties and transferred to Mexico City for disciplinary action. Don Juan's daughter was surrendered and her marriage was abrogated.[51]

Economic Reform

The various reforms the Bourbons undertook in New Mexico and northern New Spain to safeguard and develop the area had mixed and contradictory results. On the economic front the policies to stimulate production, mercantile activities, and immigration had the anticipated and desired effects. Where in 1750 New Mexicans had produced roughly 20,000 *fanegas* of wheat, corn, and beans a year, by 1812, Don Pedro Bautista Pino reported that total production reached over 50,000 *fanegas*.[52]

Since the seventeenth century, textile production had been one of the mainstays of New Mexico's economy. Much of the labor and tribute the Spaniards extracted from the Indians had been provided as blankets, shawls, and socks, or through the production of wool into yarn. Large-scale production of textiles thus seemed an appropriate way for the Bourbon ministers to stimulate growth in New Mexico. Various feasibility studies were conducted in the 1770s and 1780s showing how New Mexico had the land, water, and labor necessary to establish *obrajes* (textile mills). But the project never won royal support. To the contrary, the Bourbon trade policies, which allowed European manufactured products to enter America more freely, quickly displaced whatever advantages New Mexico's production previously had enjoyed. European and United States economies of scale in textile production as well as the introduction of larger looms and machine-driven carders and spinners finally undermined New Mexico's position in the Mexican textile market. The establishment of mechanized fabric workshops in Mexico City, Puebla, and Querétaro in the latter quarter of the eighteenth century increased production and lowered prices to such an extent that New Mexican textiles could no longer profitably compete.[53]

Reporting on the state of New Mexico's economy in 1832, Antonio Barreiro succinctly summarized the situation: "There is no demand for New Mexican cotton goods because of the abundance of foreign material of better quality and at much cheaper prices." José Agustín Escudero, a member of the Mexican National Military Statistics Commission, in 1839 explained how New Mexico's textiles had "deteriorated, are of poor quality, and only a few are still exported." The reason for this was a flooding of the market by Anglo merchants with textiles which were:

of a much better quality, attractiveness, and at prices much lower than these same articles from Europe and Asia. Not only do they sell these goods in New Mexico, but also prejudice commerce in other departments, taking them to the two Sonoras, California, Chihuahua, Durango, and a few cities in Coahuila and Texas where they are introduced without great difficulties, and frequently as contraband.

This penetration by Anglo merchants with cheap cloth after 1808 was partially responsible for a shift from textiles to greater agricultural production as New Mexico's main commercial activity.[54]

Livestock production, which before the 1770s had barely met subsistence needs, now began yielding an exportable surplus. Governor Fernando de la Concha estimated the number of New Mexican sheep sold in Chihuahua in 1788 at 15,000 head, valued at "close to 30,000 pesos." Six years later one friar would note that "15 to 20,000 sheep leave this province annually, and there have been some years when up to 25,000 left." If cattle, horses, and mules were added to these figures, the numbers became more substantial. Governor Fernando Chacón in 1803 placed the number of horses and cattle bound for markets in Sonora and Nueva Vizcaya "at more than 600 annually . . . [plus] twenty-five to twenty-six thousand sheep and goats." The first complete picture of New Mexican livestock production comes from 1827. Colonel Antonio Narvona reported that that year there were 5,000 cattle, 240,000 sheep and goats, 550 horses, 2,150 mules, and 300 mares.[55]

For some time now the dominant interpretation of New Mexico's economic history has been a circulationist one that proposes that the economy was "feudal," stagnant, and impervious to change until coinage became the predominate medium of exchange. Flowing from this is the assumption that market penetration and the birth of mercantile capitalism did not occur in New Mexico until 1821 when trade restrictions between the newly independent Mexican nation and the United States were lifted. Then money began to circulate, thus leading to greater economic development. If one accepts such circulationist arguments, the evidence clearly shows that political dates such as 1821 (Mexican Independence) and 1846 (U.S.-Mexico War) were not particularly significant. Rather, the date should be pushed back to the 1770s, to the Bourbon Reforms, when specie began to circulate and to predominate in commercial transactions.

As early as the 1750s merchants and members of New Mexico's nobility were undertaking their economic transactions in hard currency. When Doña María de Roybal gave Don Juan Joseph Moreno power of attorney to settle the estate of her deceased husband on November 15, 1747, she stipulated that Moreno was to collect "5,000 pesos in gold" from Don Joseph Gómez, Don Joseph Pérez de Teran, and Don Gabriel Gutiérrez de Riva. Merchants such as the wealthy Don Clemente Gutiérrez, who resided on his hacienda in Pajaritos, a hamlet just south of Albuquerque, undertook many of their financial matters in hard currency. In 1762, Antonio Armijo demanded and received "20 pesos in gold" for a hide that the merchant Don Clemente Gutiérrez had purchased from him. Later that same year, Governor Velez Cachupín ordered Juan Miguel Alvarez del Castillo to pay Don Clemente Gutiérrez "10 pesos in sealed silver" for a debt incurred through the purchase of a slave. In 1776, Don Miguel Morales of Pajaritos was ordered by the governor to satisfy the debt of 75 sheep, which he owed to Don Miguel Olona of Pojoaque. Morales paid "32 pesos 4 reales in silver."[56]

The payment of salaries to the governor, presidio soldiers, and Franciscan missionaries by the national treasury had always brought a certain amount of hard currency into New Mexico. In a January 28, 1769, letter from Viceroy Marqués de Croix to the governor of New Mexico, the governor was ordered to pay the salaries of the presidio's soldiers in "specie of money." Eleven years later, in 1780, the Commander General of the Internal Provinces, Teodoro de Croix, issued a decree ordering that all items presidio soldiers purchased from local merchants had to be paid for in hard currency and not accepted on credit. His office received too many complaints over excessive prices, interest rates, and fraud. Croix felt that this measure would curb irregularities.[57]

Among the popular classes, it is more difficult to ascertain when and to what extent money was used as a medium of exchange. One clue was discovered in a 1794 report on the general state of confraternities in New Mexico. The document noted that the Confraternity of Our Lady of Mount Carmel in Santa Cruz formerly had charged members one *peso de la tierra* as yearly dues. In 1790 dues were "changed to 2 reales in silver, and if that was too much, then to one real, and in this way we could avoid frauds and differences in payment." Governor Fernando Chacón observed in 1803 that "while many, and in particular the Indians, do not esteem currency very much, in the last three years it has become more widely known in these parts." By 1816, the use of currency in the payment of routine debts was common. The burial account books of San Felipe de Neri Parish in Albuquerque indicated that for the August 30, 1816, funeral of Antonio Chávez, "1 ox and 3 pesos in silver" were paid. At Juan Cristobal Ortega's October 12, 1816, funeral, "6 pesos in coin" were paid. When Don Francisco Durán ended his tenure as accountant for the parish in 1818, the church fund consisted of "197 serapes, 70 sheep, and 41 pesos in silver." The increase in the use of currency by the popular classes in New Mexico after the 1800s was indicative of greater marketing activity and export of native products.[58]

Increased market penetration into New Mexico in the 1770s occurred at a time when local internal conditions, specifically the ecological balance between humans and arable land, were in transition. The granting of *mercedes* to *genízaros* had alleviated some of this pressure and helped to safeguard the frontiers, but population growth continued to outstrip available natural resources. The onset of export agriculture, the promotion of animal husbandry, and increased commercial activity combined to exacerbate the pace of land monetization and concentration. By 1790, a 33 percent sample of that year's household census indicated that 60 percent (N=631) of household heads owned the land they worked, while the other 40 percent (N=420) owned none. Governor Fernando de Chacón estimated the landless heads of households in 1796 at 1,500.[59]

The inevitable upshot of this growth in the landless peasantry due to

TABLE 10.1

Occupational Structure of Albuquerque, Santa Fe,
and Santa Cruz in 1790 and 1827

	1790		1827	
	No.	Pct.	No.	Pct.
Albuquerque				
Farmers	391	65%	397	66%
Craftsmen	151	25	85	14
Merchants	1	—	15	2
Day Laborers	58	10	113	19
Other	—	—	—	—
Total	601	100%	610	100%
Santa Fe				
Farmers	350	85%	467	55%
Craftsmen	28	7	101	12
Merchants	1	—	12	1
Day Laborers	34	8	264	31
Other	—	—	2	—
Total	413	100%	846	100%
Santa Cruz				
Farmers	564	73%	553	57%
Craftsmen	—	—	145	15
Merchants	—	—	19	2
Day Laborers	208	27	239	25
Other	—	—	6	—
Total	772	100%	962	100%

SOURCES: 1790 census in SA, Reel 12:319-502; 1827 census in *Three New Mexico Chronicles*, p. 88.

population increase was the expansion of wage labor. A comparison of the occupational structure of the kingdom in 1790 and 1827 reflects this (see Table 10.1). In 1790 Albuquerque had an adult working population of 601. Sixty-five percent were occupied as farmers (N=391), 25 percent as craftsmen (N=151), and 10 percent as day laborers (N=58). By 1827, 610 persons were listed as full-time workers; 66 percent were farmers (N=397), 14 percent craftsmen (N=85), and 19 percent day laborers (N=113). The 1790 census of Santa Fe listed 413 individuals with occupations. Farmers represented 85 percent (N=350), craftsmen 7 percent (N=28), and day laborers 8 percent (N=34). By 1827, of 846 workers, 55 percent were employed as farmers (N=467), 12 percent as craftsmen (N=101), and 31 percent as day laborers (N=264). The expansion of the day laborers category both in relative size and proportion also occurred in Santa Cruz during this period.[60]

The growth of export-oriented agriculture and livestock production on a highly circumscribed land base worked by landless peasants provided the conditions for the development of debt peonage. As early as 1750 Fray Carlos Delgado had complained that because the governors demanded Pueblo Indian labor at planting and harvest, at the very time when Indians, if they were going to produce adequately for their own sustenance, should be working their fields, "the poor Indians are left without anything to eat for the rest of the year . . . and due to hunger . . . enter into service on a hacienda or rancho, solely to live." Once off their pueblos and in a wage relationship, they soon became so indebted that they could never gain their freedom or return to their homes. *Genízaros* were in a similar predicament, said Fray Juan Agustín Morfi in 1776: "without land, without livestock, without any other manner of subsisting than with their bows and arrows . . . they have surrendered themselves into wage labor and suffer all sorts of tyrannies."[61]

Debt peonage had also begun to afflict Spaniards and mixed-bloods, continued Father Morfi. How this occurred was simple. Families all too frequently purchased many items from merchants with future crops, mortgaging in some cases up to six future harvests. The least bit of difficulty, a sickness, crop failure due to pestilence, or drought "is the lasso which takes them into slavery, and forbids them from ever having any rest for the remainder of their lives," said Morfi. "To enter such a contract it is not necessary to be vice ridden, or wasteful: a marriage, a trip, a burial or the smallest unexpected expense is enough to submerge them in this labyrinth." Governor Juan Bautista de Anza underscored Morfi's statements in 1780, noting that many persons had been forced to sell their children into domestic service because of the droughts New Mexico experienced between 1778 and 1780. Such sales brought only "a few pesos to satisfy their hunger."[62]

The manner in which a labor contract was transformed into debt peonage on New Mexican farms and haciendas was quite simple. First a basic work and salary schedule was established. Mauricio Trujillo entered the service of Don Toribio Ortiz of Santa Fe in the 1760s at a monthly salary of six pesos. Don Joseph García, a merchant in El Paso, retained Luís Tafoya in 1762 "for a salary of 10 pesos a month plus the ration of 3 *almudes* (a ration equal to ¹⁄₂₀ of a *fanega*) of corn and half an *almud* of beans each week." But these wages rarely provided an adequate subsistence. Juan Cruz García of Albuquerque in 1805 told the local justice that his salary did not even purchase the food he needed. His wife worked to feed the family, the "two children we have, one son is already a peon for Don Antonio Ruiz [García's employer] and my daughter was employed by various persons until last winter . . . and for this reason I asked my employer's permission to work at other places so that I could maintain myself for I had not been able to get a food ration from him." When another peon, Josef Bitorio Pallares, could not obtain food for his sick wife in 1805, he asked his employer Don José Antonio Chávez of Los Padillas for half a *fanega* of corn. Don José refused Josef the corn. Josef told his master that the case was urgent and that he would have to obtain the food elsewhere. Don José forbade Josef to leave the hacienda to search for food, but he left anyway. "It caused me considerable work to find him," stated Don José, "and to bring him back here so that he could pay what he owed me or reduce the amount with labor, and having no way of paying the debt, he continued to serve me."[63]

Technically, if a person wanted to leave the service of a particular employer, he could on retiring all his debts. Easier said than done, attested Luís Tafoya in 1766:

I asked my master for an account of my debts and he would only respond that I owed him, never telling me how much. Finally this year I asked him to tell me the specific amount and he said I owed 140 pesos, with which I did not agree seeing that last year I asked him for two barrels of wine, which are worth in this place 40 pesos, as is well known by all, and I found that he charged me 90 pesos each, which equals 180 pesos. I thought this a little heavy for at the time that he gave them to me he did not tell me the price nor did I ask. I did not ask the price because he has always told us that he gives items to his peons at the just price. When I asked about the high price he said that it was because it was aged wine. I told him it was not aged and hardly had been barrelled four months, and even so, aged wine sells for only 40 pesos a barrel. Because of these questions he mistreated me, beat me with a stick . . . and so I escaped to seek justice.

Governor Velez Cachupín ordered Tafoya's master to appear with his ledgers so that he could establish if his prices were "just" or not. The accounts were never examined, for Don Joseph García pardoned Tafoya's debts and sent him on his way before the governor investigated the matter.[64]

The extent of debt peonage on New Mexican farms is difficult to ascertain without more comprehensive study. Yet one index, though at best a rough approximation, can be obtained by examining household struc-

TABLE 10.2

Household Structure in New Mexico, 1790-1845

	1790		1818[a]	
	No.	Pct.	No.	Pct.
Solitaries	48	4.9%	35	5.4%
Co-residing siblings	14	1.4	16	2.5
Single family	777	79.5	517	79.9
Extended family	99	10.1	7	1.1
Multiple families	22	2.3	6	0.9
Augmented families	18	1.8	66	10.2
Total	978	100.0%	647	100.0%

	1823[b]		1845	
	No.	Pct.	No.	Pct.
Solitaries	5	1.8%	64	5.9%
Co-residing siblings	7	2.5	26	2.8
Single family	158	56.4	918	85.1
Extended family	19	6.8	52	4.8
Multiple families	82	29.3	1	0.1
Augmented families	9	3.2	14	1.3
Total	280	100.0%	1075	100.0%

SOURCES: SA, Reel 12:319-502; MA, Reel 3:220-47; Reel 40:361-74.
   [a] Santa Cruz only.
   [b] Santa Fe only.

ture as reported in censuses. Particularly indicative of debt peonage were households that listed multiple families, that is, domestic groups comprised of two or more conjugal families with no apparent kinship link, and augmented families in which nonrelated working age males were residing with a conjugal family. In the multiple family structure, one household head was reported to provide dwelling for different families. The augmented structure similarly detailed the dependence of single males on one household head and when occupation was mentioned for these men listed as *jornaleros* (day wage laborers). The data on household structure from four New Mexican censuses—1790, 1818, 1823, 1845—are presented in Table 10.2. Adding together multiple and augmented families, one notes a rise from 4.1 percent in 1790 to 32.5 percent in 1823, which dropped to 1.4 percent in 1845. The 1845 census showed a very low percent of multiple and augmented families, because the census primarily focused on villages settled through land grants in the 1830s and 1840s. Whereas in the 128 years between 1693 and 1821, only 61 land grants were given to New Mexicans, in the next 25 years (1821–1846) 30 tracts were portioned out.[65]

What all this information on household structure indicates is that by 1818 and 1823 a large number of persons were living in household arrangements that were not typically based on affinity or consanguinity, that had not been of statistical significance in 1790, and that appeared to be some form of wage retainership. Don Leonardo Ortiz of Santa Fe in 1823, for example, listed 27 individuals in his household, who were apparently part of four different families: that headed by Don Leonardo, that of Pedro Sánchez, that of Bartolo Aliri, and that of José María Benavides. Similarly, the household of Matias Sena, located in Santa Fe, reported 23 persons in five nuclear families.[66]

Partidos, livestock rental contracts, were another labor form that came to employ part of New Mexico's landless peasantry at the end of the eighteenth century. In a *partido* the owner of animals would loan them out to different persons for a set number of years, expecting in return that his herd would be increased by a certain amount yearly. Whatever surplus remained after the owner's conditions had been satisfied became the *partidario*, the caretaker's income. A 1760 *partido* contract between Don Juan Vigil of Santa Fe and Ignacio Jaramillo of Albuquerque shows how the relationship functioned. Ignacio Jaramillo accepted 605 newly born sheep from Vigil for the period of five years. Each April Jaramillo was to increase Vigil's flock by 130 sheep and was to turn over 130 bales of wool from the shearing of the sheep. The number of animals shared out in such arrangements varied greatly. Bartolomé Baca in 1819 had 8,000 sheep in *partido*, which yielded him a yearly income of 1,500 *pesos*.[67]

For the *partidario* (the person renting the livestock), profits and risks were always inequitably distributed. The pasturing of livestock produced no more than a subsistence income, if that. Nonetheless, the *partidario* was responsible for the animals and if any loss occurred, had to compensate the owner. *Partido* contracts frequently stipulated that the caretaker would not assume loss due to weather, epidemics, or Indian attacks. When the contract made no note of these conditions, or if negligence could be proven, the *partidario* accepted total risk for the animals and was liable to suit. The 1767 case of Bentura Romero of Nacimiento was particularly tragic. In 1764, Bentura accepted 1,025 sheep from Don Antonio Baca for five years with the condition that he augment the herd by 300 head annually. Bentura noted:

When I received the sheep, I hesitated because they were all very old, but Baca assured me verbally that he would not hold me responsible for losses and as I have always regarded him as a father, I took the sheep, and in this regard I have even given him my children so that they may serve the said Baca, and it has now been about 15 years that he has had one of my sons and one of my daughters, and it would not be just if now I tried to charge for their work, it having been my desire to send them there, how then can he in justice ask me to be responsible for the losses. For in the first year many sheep died because they were old; the next year a hail storm killed 80. After 2 years Baca took back the sheep and broke our contract. In all justice he cannot expect me to pay for these losses.

Felipe Tafoya, Don Antonio Baca's lawyer, argued that Bentura was not a minor and was fully conscious of the state of the sheep when he entered into the *partido*. The sheep had been lost through negligence, claimed Tafoya. The governor of New Mexico in this case ruled that Bentura was not responsible for the loss and that the little property that he did own could not be confiscated—as had already been done by Baca. Bentura's property was to be quickly returned.[68]

The economic effect of the Bourbon Reforms in New Mexico had been to increase the movement of people into the kingdom, to increase New Mexico's communication with marketing centers in northern Mexico, and to promote broad economic development. Much of this had proceeded as planned. The unintended results were that heightened levels of population growth and in-migration swelled the ranks of the landless in New Mexico. The decline in crafts manufacturing, most notably textiles, and the rapid expansion of livestock production exacerbated land pressure and created the conditions for the growth of servile forms of labor such as debt peonage and *partidos*.

Social Change

These economic changes coincided with a period of profound behavioral change as well. We noted in Chapter 9 that at the end of the eighteenth century women outnumbered men in New Mexico by a ratio of 10 to 8. This was due primarily to the New Mexican preference for female Indian slaves, to the number of exiled Pueblo women who entered Spanish households, and to the rates of mortality Spanish men experienced as a result of Indian wars. When there are too many women in a society, theoretically one expects changes in the marriage market. The mean age at first marriage for New Mexican men declined from a high of 25.5 years in 1760–69 to 23.3 years in 1810–19. Female mean age at first marriage went from 19.4 in 1760–69 to 15.5 in 1800–1809. A marked narrowing of the age difference between spouses also occurred during these same years. Whereas between 1690 and 1739 only 22 percent of all persons took a spouse of a similar age or just one year older or younger, by 1800, 50 percent did. It was noted in Chapter 9 that the number and percentage of racially exogamous marriages as reported in Table 9.10 rose after 1760. Between 1694 and 1739 only about 5 percent of all individuals who married did so with a spouse of a different race. From 1760 to 1799 this pattern drastically changed. Now approximately 20 percent, or one out of every five marriages, was to a person of a different race. We noted in Chapter 5 that a consciousness of minute racial differences had not been articulated in New Mexico before 1760 (see Table 5.1). Between 1693 and 1759 only about 5 percent of all marriage partners in New Mexico had been classified by race. But starting in 1760 and continuing to 1800, race became the dominant way in which social status was defined by the powers that be. After 1800 the racial hierarchy lost all intermediate hues and became much more clearly polarized into Spaniards and Indians, much as it had been earlier between 1693 and 1759.

What all of these changes in human behavior indicated—the lowering of mean age at marriage, the narrowing of the age gap between spouses, the increased racial exogamy, the acute racial consciousness—was that the Bourbon policies to develop the north, when combined with local demographic factors, had stimulated a great deal of social mobility. Whereas Bourbon social policy was restrictive—for example, the 1776 Royal Pragmatic on Marriage allowed parents to disinherit disobedient children—its economic policy was expansive. We will soon look at the effects of social mixing and fluidity on New Mexico's nobility, but before we do, let us look at the behavior of youths. My contention is that the behavioral changes discussed above were indicative of changing values and mores concerning the place of the individual in marriage and in the larger local community.

When the friars asked New Mexican men and women why they wished to marry, the most common responses between 1693 and 1790 were religious or obligational. Cristóbal García said in 1702, "I want to put myself in the state of grace." "It is my goal to serve God and no other reason," claimed Gregoria Valverde in 1712. Francisco Durán y Chávez alleged in 1713 that we wanted to marry "for love (amor) of God our Lord." Francisco Saes in 1718 answered "To serve God and save my soul." And marriage was "to greater love and serve God," declared Andrés de la Paz in 1719, as did Doña Gertrudes Durán in 1771.[69]

The first sign of any change in the reasons for desiring marriage appears in a 1798 record. José García of Albuquerque averred that he wanted to marry María López "because of the growing desire (voluntad) that we mutually have for each other." The word voluntad had previously appeared in marital investigations, but only to mean volition, as in the determination that free will was being exercised. María Durán gave the word *voluntad* this meaning when she proclaimed "I marry freely and spontaneously, neither counseled nor coerced, but totally of my own volition."[70]

Beginning in 1800, a flurry of new responses appeared in the matrimonial investigations, which stressed individualism and love as reasons for wishing to marry. Juan José Ramón Gallego, a resident of the Spanish village at Jémez, said in 1810 that he wanted to enter the state of matrimony because "I fell in love (*me enamore*) with Juana María, the daughter of Santiago Aragón." Francisco Xavier Chávez claimed in 1822 that he wanted to marry Feliciano Tafoya "solely because of the love that I will profess for her as my spouse." In 1838, José Rafael Sánchez of Tomé took Gertudes Sánchez as his wife "because of the great love that I have for her." José Torres of Belén in the same year gave "the mutual love that I have with the said [María Serafina Chávez]" as his reason for wishing to marry.[71]

Amor (love) as a verb or noun appeared in New Mexican colonial documents with two different meanings. Reference to Christian love was made throughout the whole period from 1693 to 1846 as a sentiment that had to be displayed out of duty. Good Christians were commanded to love God, neighbor, and self. Thus Francisco Durán y Chávez said he was marrying in 1713 "for love of God." Jacinto Mirado in 1771 expressed "the fatherly love" he had for his adopted daughter. And María Loreta García in 1835 begged her husband, who so mistreated her, to "love me as Christ loves his Church."[72]

Natural love, or love stemming from concupiscence, was the second meaning of the word *amor*. Before 1800, the word was used in this sense only to refer to illicit sexual contact with Indian or *genízara* women, such as seduction, concubinage, and adultery. Antonio Velásquez claimed in 1705 that "I happened to make love [*llegue a enamorar*] to the said Juana de Guadalupe after having known that she had an illicit friendship." Josepha Sedano demanded a divorce from her husband in 1711 because she was tired of feeding him, clothing him and "giving him money to play [cards] and *enamorar*." It is interesting to note that before 1800 mention of concupiscent love occurred only in reference to illicit sexual acts, not as a reason for desiring marriage. After 1800, derivatives of the word *amor* were no longer used to refer to illicit acts, but were replaced with expressions such as "*amistad ilicita*" or "*copula ilicita*."

These statements indicate that by 1800 a love born of passion was sufficient reason for choosing a particular conjugal mate. "The urges of the flesh, human wretchedness and the great love which we have for each other," said José de Jesús Romero in 1845, was the reason he wished to marry Doña Persiliana Salazar and did. By the last quarter of the eighteenth century young men and women were being swept away by love and began choosing marital partners on the basis of affect and desire, at times forsaking family name, honor, and patrimony.[73]

As early as 1776, when King Charles III issued the Royal Pragmatic on Marriage, he had complained about those "blind passions of youth," the egalitarian and individualistic ideology of romantic love. What passed for romantic love in New Mexico was a complex amalgamation of cultural values. The untrammelled expression of libidinous energies, a common romantic love theme, was as ancient to the Southwest as the Pueblo Indians. Among the Indians the celebration of sexual desire was an activity necessary for the harmonic continuation of life.

Indigenous values toward sexuality and the body, which we have discussed throughout this book, blended with European notions of individual will that had been diffused throughout the West as a result of the Protestant Reformation and the Enlightenment. The birth of science eroticized the body and the spread of capitalist relations of production was shattering the bonds of households and families, and creating autonomous forms of labor divorced from domestic patriarchal rule.

The convergence of sexual values and attitudes diffused upward from the Pueblo Indians through mixed-bloods to the Spanish, and outward from Europe to the colonies, infused old symbols with new meanings. When the Pueblo Indians and *genízaros* plied their love magic, stole human hearts, and celebrated rituals to arouse sexual desire, they were employing symbols that became the essence of romantic love. When the friars sang of their mystical love for God, of having their hearts pierced by the arrows of God's love, of being intoxicated with His love, and of being penetrated by their Beloved, they were uttering in sacred tones words that would be desacralized to describe carnal love. And when men spoke of love as bewitching, they were tacitly acknowledging the power of independent action that women came to enjoy in romantic matters.

Increasingly after 1770 New Mexicans celebrated marriages based on love or physical attraction, sexual passion and other quite personal likes and dislikes. Love was an irrational, whimsical and spontaneous desire, oblivious to earthly constraints. Gabriel Prieto, a popular Mexican writer, defined love in 1846 thus: "Love is the soul of the soul; the soul without it is like an eye with a damaged pupil; it is like a machine that motivates matter, it is like an electric shock to a cadaver, upon contact it causes shakes and trembles."[74] In the 1830 folksong "True Love of Lucinda and

Belardo," Lucinda described her love sickness and how she longed for her Belardo:

> What I long for is your love;
> Because the fire in your eyes
> Is like a volcano that burns me;
> I am yearning and you know it,
> If you do not come to me,
> The power of this love will drive me insane.[75]

In a poem another Santa Fe man eloquently described the bewitching power of love.

> Lovely maid come to my arms
> Your brow so pure, that ardent breast I would enfold
> And if some day, maid of bewitching charm
> I could kiss those ruby lips how happy I would be,
> A kiss from those lips, a kiss I pray
> One look from those lovely eyes I beg
> I would see us in ardent embrace
> In ardent and loving embrace I vow
> Your fluttering heartbeats I would feel
> As lip to lip I press you close,
> Kiss for kiss of tenderest love.[76]

Love was considered subversive because it made persons oblivious to status, generational, and sexual hierarchies. An 1851 Mexican medical dictionary described the dangers inherent in such uncontrolled urges.

Dangers of Sexual Life: Though the sexual life leads to the highest virtues and even to sacrifice itself, and to sacrifice of self; yet in it lies a great danger. Unless properly checked it may degenerate into powerful passions and develop the greatest vices. When love is permitted to become an unbridled passion it is like a fire that burns and consumes everything. It is like a pit that swallows all—honor, fortune and happiness.[77]

In an 1837 sermon on lust, the clerical author reached very similar conclusions. "Lust blinds our reason and the rest of our senses; it transforms rational beings into mere animals. It is an evil which very quickly consumes our possessions: our reputation, our honor, money, serenity, health, prudence, liberty: and finally, it is a grave and abominable evil which more than any other leads to a sad death." [78]

Romantic love placed the sexes on a more equal footing in terms of marital formation. Females were in no way emancipated or given the same freedom men enjoyed, but they did increasingly gain some control over their bodies and their sexuality. The cant of love was personal autonomy. The ability to choose a mate or to refuse one, and particularly for women to express their personal pleasures in the matter, were the concrete benefits of love.

The change that had occurred in marriage matters was astutely observed by William Watts Davis, the United States Attorney for New Mexico, in 1853. Describing the arrival of a marriage proposal at the home of a Santa Fe resident, he wrote:

I chanced to call at the home the same evening the letter had been received, and the mother, feeling unusually happy in view of the proposed alliance . . . descanting with considerable eloquence upon the advantages to arise from such a match—that the young man was *mui rico* (very rich) and *mui buen* (very good), with many other words of praise. . . . The mother was quite anxious for the alliance to take place, but told me, in a semiconfidential manner, that her daughter was opposed to the arrangement—a perverseness that the old lady could not understand. . . . I determined to know how the matter stood with the daughter. . . . She told me, with great frankness, that she did not love her suitor, and would not marry him. . . . I counseled treason on the premises, and advised her to have her own way in a matter which was of more importance to her than any one else. She took this course, and the unromantic and unwooing swain was obliged to look elsewhere for a housekeeper. A few evenings afterward I saw the father of the young man at the house, who had come to talk the matter over with the mother; but it did no good, for the young lady had a mind of her own, and neither persuasion nor parental threats could induce her to accede to their wishes.[79]

In nuptial formation women increasingly came to reject mates as easily as they selected them. Fray José de Castro chastised María del Refugio Herrera in 1824 for breaking the promise of marriage she had given to Juan de Jesús Rivera. When the priest asked María why she had changed her mind, she responded: "I have no reason except that previously I wanted to marry him and now I no longer do." Fray José asked the local constable to punish María "as an example to other women, so that they fulfill their contracts and do not promise so easily things they do not plan to deliver." A New Mexican poem from the early nineteenth century made a similar point:

> Without a pretext, without a reason
> Because she changed her mind
> She said good-bye on Tuesday morning.[80]

The saddest case in New Mexico, where a woman's choice pained her lover, was recounted by Felix Esquivel. Although this incident occurred in the 1870s, later than most of the other documentary material presented here, the story illustrates the extent to which the practice of parental imposition of a spouse had changed and the greater freedom females had to decide their futures. The story tells of a woman who had freely decided to marry a man she loved. On the day of the betrothal the groom had too much to eat and drink. When the engagement party was over and while riding on a buggy to church for the celebration of the nuptial, the flatulent groom cut air quite loudly. "Stop this buggy," the bride told her godfather. "Did you not hear that loud and gross fart?" When no one responded, the incensed bride said, "I will never marry such a gross pig!" She called off the nuptial and refused to marry the man for whom she once had proclaimed so much love.[81]

Assessing the changes that occurred in marriage formation among New Mexico's colonists between 1693 and 1846, it is important to remember that although arranged marriage was the norm among the nobility and landed peasantry, love matches, infrequent though they were, did occur, encouraged, aided, and celebrated by the Catholic Church. Marriage in New Mexico was a symbol of social status both to the Pueblo Indians and to the Spanish colonists because of the gifts that had to be gathered for exchange, the feast that had to be staged, and the acceptance of the union that kin and community had to display. If one had no property to transmit to legal heirs, if one did not cherish the cultural ideals of Spanish society, if one valued Pueblo or nomadic Indian conceptions about the meaning of the marital bond, then there was little reason for entertaining a sacramental Christian marriage. For this reason, landless peasants and *genízaros*, and later wage workers, preferred love matches that were rarely legitimized. By the middle of the nineteenth century, due to the acquisition of land and upward mobility by *genízaros*, some of them married to establish their social respectability in the community, but by then, personal motives were more based on love.

The profound behavioral, ideological, and social changes symbolized by the rise of romantic love were deemed by New Mexico's nobility to be an assault on their privileges and their status. For centuries strict patriarchal control over marriage formation had been the rule in order to assure the perpetuation of familial honor and fame and the unequal distribution of the instruments and means of production. To best understand how the nobility expressed its fears about a rapidly changing society, recall the dominant medieval representation of society as a human body. Mary Douglas, in her book *Purity and Danger*, proposed some years ago that when society was conceived organologically, the disruption and blurring of social boundaries was often expressed as pollution fears, the actual body parts or bodily excretions most invoked serving as privileged symbols of those fears.[82]

In patrilineal societies, women's bodies and their issue were routes of entry into social groups. Thus when New Mexico's nobility expressed their concerns over the deterioration of their status and privileges, it was done in the language of pollution as a concern for the integrity of their blood lines and for the protection of their women. As we noted earlier, the aristocratic privileges the conquistadores had bequeathed their children had, by the eighteenth century, come to be seen as an innate quality of their blood. And since maternity was undeniable while paternity was not, aristocracy could only be preserved from pollution by guarding the sexual purity of females and frowning on marriage with members of lower classes. To assure that the latter did not occur, from 1760 clear into the 1820s the nobility begged the Church to allow them to marry close relatives—marriages the Church defined as incestuous—arguing that if they were not allowed to do so they would have to marry racial inferiors and thereby metaphysically taint their pure aristocratic blood.

The exception in canon law that the nobility invoked in their consanguinity dispensation requests was one known as *pro honestis familiis*. Fray José de Vera defined it as: "when both candidates are of illustrious and respected families and in order to conserve the fame and respect of their families, and that the maiden not be forced to marry a man who is not her equal, a consanguine wishes to marry her so as to protect her reputation." Don Pedro Sánchez of Albuquerque availed himself of this point of law in 1761 when he sought marriage with his cousin Doña Efigenia Durán y Chávez. "I cannot find another person with whom to contract marriage who is my blood equal," he said.[83]

"The purity of our families has always been conserved with honor and without mixture with castes; and the love which I have for him," declared Doña Serafina Chávez of Belén, was the reason why she wanted to marry her cousin Don José Torres. When Juan de Jesús Valdez remarried in 1836, he chose María Dolores Trujillo, his deceased wife's first cousin. Curate José Antonio Martínez sought the consanguinity dispensation on the bride's behalf, noting that because she was 31, "she has not had a matrimonial offer from someone who is her equal and her attractiveness is such that she may not receive another; she has always lived a sheltered life and has never given her relatives, with whom she lives, any problems due to imprudence, as is so common among people of another class."[84]

Coupled with their requests to marry close kin, New Mexico's aristocrats consciously tried to force the Church's hand to sanction their incestuous marriages by claiming that the woman had allowed her virginity to be taken. If the marriage was not allowed, the loss of the girl's honor would cause grave public scandal. In those cases, which number 56 out of 215 consanguinity dispensation petitions registered between 1760 and 1819, illicit sex was being used by women, who by tradition were secluded and virginal, in order to obtain the spouses they desired over parental objections, and certainly against the will of the Church.

We can only speculate on how this might have come about. A young man and woman might be aroused by a genuine love for each other and desire matrimony. Knowing that both their parents and the Church would object to the marriage, they might devise a ploy to manipulate familial honor concerns and the clergy's desire to safeguard public morals. The woman might allow her virginity to be taken, claim that her honor had been sullied, and demand marriage to restore it. Under such circumstances parents and the Church would be hard-pressed to acquiesce. In fact, such a ploy was a common resolution to the loss of a woman's honor in Golden Age Spanish theater.[85]

Don Bernardo Veitia used such an argument when he sought a dispensation to his consanguinity impediment in 1805 so that he could marry Doña María Manuela Trujillo. Don Bernardo said that he could not find anyone else to marry who was his equal and "because of scandal and the defamation of the woman . . . we illicitly copulated." Fray José de Vera appeared before the Durango See on the couple's behalf and argued:

they were frail and committed the grave sin on knowing each other carnally, but they did not do it with depraved intentions, or with the belief that the dispensation would be facilitated in this matter, they are not unworthy of a dispensation; they have repented for their acts and have sought the mercy of the Church and hope that the young woman will not remain defamed but will be honored with a dispensation.

The bishop granted the dispensation but sternly admonished New Mexico's faithful against engaging in illicit coition "to facilitate a dispensation."[86]

The concerns voiced by New Mexico's nobility over miscegenation and the necessity of closing ranks to protect their corporate identity were not unique to this region. Throughout Spanish America the sexually exploitative regimes, which had been established on the backs of Indian women, by 1760 had produced an expanding mixed-blood population for whom the ascribed status categories of the conquest were meaningless and dysfunctional. Widespread racial passing and the increasing importance of achieved status garnered through hard work and economic enterprise—anathema to the aristocracy—had begun to erode the primacy of the nobility in local affairs. The intense preoccupation over physically indistinguishable racial hues, which was so intense in New Mexico between 1760 and 1800, served no other purpose but to assuage the fears of the aristocracy. In this respect, restrictive Bourbon social policies that had expanded parental authority over the marriages of their children to quell elite fears over familial and social disorder were quite at odds with Bourbon economic policies. These policies were aimed at destroying the power of provincial nobilities and dismantling the independent local economies they had built and through which they were successfully skirting imperial control and taxation. Economic change triumphed in the short run. It loosened social bonds in society and shattered some of the hierarchies in isolated and tradition-bound New Mexico, facilitating, indeed accelerating, the pace of cultural change. In the long run, however, the Bourbon Reforms only deepened American resentment over colonial status and created the discontent that would result in the Spanish American independence movement between 1810 and 1821.

Epilogue

On February 21, 1821, a young officer named Agustín de Iturbide issued the Plan de Iguala formally declaring Mexico's independence from Spain. The proclamation of Mexico's independence ended what had been over a decade of turbulent revolutionary insurgence throughout Spanish America. Beginning in 1810, one colonial province after another had opted for statehood, until only Cuba and Puerto Rico remained under Spain's imperial control. Throughout Mexico independence was greeted with fanfare and celebration. But in New Mexico, on the remote northern frontier, news of the event only reached the area belatedly and then hardly caused much of a stir. In dusty Santa Fe, Albuquerque, and Santa Cruz, the kingdom's three most populous towns, it was hard to get too excited over Mexican independence. New Mexico had always been far removed from the centers of power, and in the end, political independence meant very little for how New Mexicans organized their lives.

However apathetic New Mexicans were on hearing of their independence, what was cause for elation in 1821 was the abolishment of the strict trade embargo Spain had imposed on the kingdom. Much as the Bourbon Reforms had ushered in sweeping economic and cultural changes in New Mexico in the decades following 1770 and had shattered the region's isolation, the lifting of trade restrictions had a similar effect, further opening the area to commerce and communication, accelerating the tenor and tempo of changes already under way, and leading to increased immigration from, and in time, annexation by the United States.

Anglo merchants who had waited anxiously to exploit the lucrative markets of northern Mexico began arriving in Taos and Santa Fe from late 1821 on, and from there they pushed their cargo-laden caravans south into Chihuahua. William Bucknell, a notorious Indian fighter, was one of the first merchants to travel the road that soon connected Missouri and New Mexico, and which became known as the "Santa Fe Trail." Arriving in November of 1821 with an array of highly coveted manufactured goods, Bucknell quickly sold his wares, reaped a large profit, and by February of 1822 was back in Missouri preparing to repeat the trek. And much like Fray Marcos de Niza in 1539 and his stories of New Mexico's cities of gold, so the stories of Bucknell and his partners inflamed the imagination of others who soon were also blazing trails to Santa Fe.[1]

First came the Anglo merchants plying their wares. Then came the mountain men who found in New Mexico's Rockies an abundant harvest of pelts. Pioneers who wanted wives and land came next. And finally the soldiers came, the famous (or infamous) Army of the West that was to wrap New Mexico in the American flag. Whatever their rank or class, whatever their ambitions or motives, the Yankees, as New Mexico's Hispanos referred to them, preached a social gospel that had a very familiar ring.[2]

Having examined at great length in previous pages the Spanish rhetoric of colonialism, particularly the racist tenets that were advanced to describe and justify the vanquishment and enslavement of New Mexico's various Indian groups, it is not difficult to see a very similar discourse being articulated after 1821, and without doubt for very similar imperial aims. As Anglos gloated about their own moral and cultural superiority, all the time denigrating the Hispanos and Indians they found in New Mexico, they asserted God-given rights of conquest. And much as the Spanish conquistadores and Franciscan friars had lambasted the idolatrous ways of their Indian subjects, so too the nineteenth-century Protestant apostles of American democracy found in New Mexico a depraved people who wallowed in promiscuity, whose devilish fandangos corrupted, and whose addiction to vice had created an indolent and mongrel race. New Mexicans were "peculiarly blessed with ugliness," wrote the American trader Albert Pike in the 1830s. They were, Pike continued, "a lazy gossiping people always lounging on their blankets and smoking cigarillos." For Josiah Gregg, the merchant whose best-selling book *Commerce of the Prairies* so fundamentally forged the image of the Mexican in the American imagination, New Mexicans lived "in darkness and ignorance . . . hav[ing] inherited much of the cruelty and intolerance of their ancestors, and no small portion of their bigotry and fanaticism."[3]

In the war of words that Anglos waged against Mexico for control over New Mexico—prelude to the war of might that would follow in 1846—Hispanos were depicted as "cruel, cowardly, treacherous, immoral, indolent, and backward." Indeed, as the historian Reginald Horsman has argued, when Anglos expounded their expansionist ideology, they claimed that they were divinely destined to greatness and world power and routinely blamed whatever sufferings they inflicted on others to the racial inferiority of their victims and not to their own ruthlessness.[4]

An article in the June 1846 edition of the *Illinois State Register* captured well what was by then a popular representation of the enemy in English-language print. Mexicans were, stated the article's anonymous author, "reptiles in the path of progressive democracy . . . and they must either crawl or be crushed." J. Ross Browne, a popular journalist in his day, echoed a related sentiment in his *Adventures in Apache Country*, when he ascribed Mexican inferiority to three centuries of miscegenation. "Every generation the population grows worse, and the [Mexicans] may now be ranked with their natural compadres—Indians, burros, and coyotes." According to the pseudo-scientific racial theories of the day, persons of mixed racial ancestry inherited not the best characteristics of each race, but the worst. Thus when William Watts Davis, the United States Attorney for New Mexico, noted in 1853 that New Mexico's Hispanos were the products of a long history of racial mixing among Spaniards, Moors, and Indians, he concluded that the effects of such had been extremely deleterious. New Mexicans carried, Davis wrote, "all the vices of those whose homes are washed by the blue waters of the Mediterranean Sea . . . [and all] the cunning and deceit of the Indian."[5]

The Anglos who entered New Mexico after 1821 came to regard the local population as backward and popish. Entry into the Union was necessary, they argued, to uplift the Mexicans and tutor them in the ways of democracy. For centuries they had slavishly shown allegiance to the kings of Spain and had helped the Catholic church grow rich and strong at the expense of its faithful. Entry into the American temple of freedom would be a liberating experience for the New Mexicans. They would, after proper schooling, be granted self-government, a democratic government by and for the people, sanctified by private property, and completely free from established churches.[6]

So it was. The flag-waving apostles of American democracy conquered New Mexico in 1846 exclaiming that their God, the one and only true God, had destined them to inherit the earth and to encompass in their terrestrial domain all the land that connected the Atlantic and the Pacific seas. Never mind territorial rights of anteriority. Never mind the rules of international law. For as John O'Sullivan, one of the principle architects of the expansionist ideology of Manifest Destiny would so poignantly write in 1845: "Away, away with all these cobweb tissues of rights of discovery, exploitation, settlement, contiguity, etc. . . . . [The

American claim] is by the right of our manifest destiny to overspread and to possess the whole of the continent which Providence has given us for the development of the great experiment of liberty and federative self-government entrusted to us."[7]

In 1598 "Padre Jesús" entered the homelands of the Pueblo Indians, and with him came all the cataclysmic changes that would be wrought by the Spanish conquest. Nearly a century later, after the Pueblo Indians had rebelled against their Spanish overlords and had driven them out of the province in 1680, the Spanish again returned. Leading the troops of the reconquest of New Mexico in 1693 was "La Conquistadora," the Virgin Mary, Our Lady of the Conquest. Like Jesus, and then Mary, in the nineteenth century, Liberty, the goddess of the rising American empire, turned her gaze toward New Mexico and brought there a cavalcade of men who stood ready to defend her honor. The arrival of the Anglos in New Mexico initiated an intense cycle of cultural conflict over the very same issues that had pitted the Spanish against the Pueblo Indians—religion, labor, land, and water. We examined those conflicts in seventeenth- and eighteenth-century New Mexico to give historical depth and understanding to the cultural conflicts that would occur in New Mexico in the second half of the nineteenth century—a series of cultural conflicts that are still very much alive in New Mexico to this day.

Reference Matter

Notes

To keep the number of note citations to a manageable level, I have grouped all the references for a given paragraph of text in a single note keyed to the end of the paragraph. Within the resulting note, references are sequential, with semicolons separating multiple references to a single point in text, and periods marking divisions between points. Dates in the text and notes will help make the relationship between statements in the text and the sources on which they are based clear.

The following abbreviations are used in the Notes. For full forms of these and other shortened citations, see the Bibliography following.

AA	*American Anthropologist*
AASF	Archives of the Archdiocese of Santa Fe. (Microfilm edition of 81 reels; cited by reel : frame number).
	BAPT = Baptisms
	DM = Diligencias Matrimoniales
	LD = Loose Documents
	PAT = Patentes
AGN	Archivo General de la Nación (Mexico City, Mexico). (Cited by tomo-expediente : folios)
	ARZO = Arzobispos
	CALIF = Californias
	HIST = Historia
	INQ = Inquisición
	PI = Provincias Internas
	RH = Real Hacienda
BM	Peter P. Forrestal, trans., *Benavides' Memorial of 1630* (Washington, D.C., 1954).
BN	Biblioteca Nacional de México (Mexico City, Mexico).

Cartilla   *Cartilla y doctrina espiritual para la crianza y educación de los novicios que toman el hábito en la orden de N. P. S. Francisco: En la qual brevemente se les enseña lo que deben hacer conforme a la doctrina de N. Seráfico Doctor San Buenaventura, y lo que se usa, y practica en la Santa Provincia del Santo Evangelico* (Mexico, 1775).

CF   Joaquín García Icazbalceta, ed., *Códice Franciscano*, vol. 2 of *Nueva colección de documentos para la historia de México* (Mexico, 1941).

DHNM   *Documentos para servir a la historia del Nuevo México, 1538–1778* (Madrid, 1962).

FEV   J. Manuel Espinosa, ed. and trans., *First Expedition of Vargas into New Mexico, 1692* (Albuquerque, 1940).

HD   Charles W. Hackett, ed. and trans., *Historical Documents Relating to New Mexico, Nueva Vizcaya, and Approaches Thereto, 1773* (Washington, D.C., 1937), vol. 3.

HAHR   *Hispanic American Historical Review.*

HNAI   William G. Sturtevant, general editor, *Handbook of North American Indians* (Washington, D.C., 1979).

HNM   Gaspar Pérez de Villagrá, *History of New Mexico, 1610*, Gilberto Espinosa, trans., (Los Angeles, 1933).

Instrucción   *Instrucción y doctrina de novicios, sacada de la de San Buenaventura* (Mexico, 1738).

MA   Mexican Archives of New Mexico. (Microfilm edition; cited by reel : frame number)

MNM   Eleanor B. Adams and Fray Angélico Chávez, eds. and trans., *The Missions of New Mexico, 1776: A Description by Fray Atanasio Domínguez* (Albuquerque, 1975).

NCE   George P. Hammond and Agapito Rey, eds. and trans., *Narratives of the Coronado Expedition 1540–1542* (Albuquerque, 1940).

NMHR   *New Mexico Historical Review.*

OD   George P. Hammond and Agapito Rey, eds. and trans., *Don Juan de Oñate: Colonizer of New Mexico, 1595–1628* (Albuquerque, 1953), 2 vols.

PIR   Elsie C. Parsons, *Pueblo Indian Religion* (Chicago, 1939), 2 vols.

RBM   Fredrick W. Hodge, George P. Hammond, and Agapito Rey, eds. and trans., *Fray Alonso de Benavides' Revised Memorial of 1634* (Albuquerque, 1945).

RNM   George P. Hammond and Agapito Rey, eds. and trans., *The Rediscovery of New Mexico, 1580–1594: The Explorations of Chamuscado, Espejo, Castaño de Sosa, Morlete, and Leyna de Bonilla and Humaña* (Albuquerque, 1966).

RPI   Charles W. Hackett, ed., *Revolt of the Pueblo Indians of New Mexico and Otermín's Attempted Reconquest, 1680–1682* (Albuquerque, 1942), 2 vols.

SA	Spanish Archives of New Mexico. (Microfilm edition of 23 reels; cited by reel: frame number.)
SAII	Spanish Archives of New Mexico Part II. On deposit at the New Mexico State Records Center and Archives (Santa Fe, New Mexico). (Cited by case number.)
TM	Fray Agustín de Vetancurt, *Teatro Mexicano: Descripción breve de los sucessos exemplares de la Nueva España en el Nuevo Mundo* (Madrid, 1961), 4 vols.
WB	José de Vinck, ed. and trans., *The Works of Bonaventure* (Paterson, N.J., 1960), 6 vols.
WPA	Works Progress Administration. Survey of New Mexican Folklore on deposit at the Museum of New Mexico Library (Santa Fe, New Mexico).

Introduction

1. Collier and Yanagisako, eds., *Gender and Kinship*, pp. 14–50; Ortner and Whitehead, eds., *Sexual Meanings*, pp. 1–2. Those interested in the cultural construction of gender and sexuality should consult Caplan, ed., *The Cultural Construction of Sexuality*; Snitow, et al., eds., *Powers of Desire*; and Vance, ed., *Pleasure and Danger*.

2. Declaration of Pedro García, a Tano Indian, Aug. 25, 1680, *RPI* 1, pp. 24–25.

3. Irwin-Williams, "Post-Pleistocene Archaeology, 7000–2000 B.C.," *HNAI* 9, pp. 31–42; Wormington, *Prehistoric Indians of the Southwest*, pp. 2–26.

4. Woodbury and Zubrow, "Agricultural Beginnings, 2000 B.C.–A.D. 500," *HNAI* 9, pp. 43–60.

5. Gumerman and Haury, "Prehistory: Hohokam," *HNAI* 9, pp. 75–90; Plog, "Prehistory: Western Anasazi," *HNAI* 9, pp. 131–51; Wormington, *Prehistoric Indians*, pp. 27–161. On Anasazi development and kinship structure, see Mindeleff, "Localization," pp. 635–53; Fewkes, *Prehistoric Villages*; Eggan, *Social Organization of the Western Pueblos*, p. 299.

6. Gumerman and Haury, *HNAI* 9, pp. 75–90; Plog, *HNAI* 9, pp. 131–51; Wormington, *Prehistoric Indians*, pp. 27–161. On Anasazi ties with Mesoamerica, see Mathien and McGuire, *Ripples in the Chichimec Sea*.

7. Slatter, "Climate in Pueblo Abandonment of the Chevelon Drainage, Arizona" (Paper presented at the Annual Meeting of the American Anthropological Association, New Orleans, 1973); Martin and Plog, *The Archaeology of Arizona: A Study of the Southwest Region* (Garden City, N.Y., 1973); Cordell, "Predicting Site Abandonment at Wetherill Mesa," *Kiva* 40(1975), pp. 189–202.

8. P. Horgan, *Great River: The Rio Grande in North American History* (Austin, Texas, 1984), p. 22.

9. Longacre, ed., *Pueblo Societies*, p. 3; Kintigh, *Settlement, Subsistence, and Society*, p. xii; Upham, *Polities and Power*, pp. 65, 74.

10. Longacre, ed., *Pueblo Societies*, pp. 2–3; Kintigh, *Settlement, Subsistence and Society*, pp. 1–7; L. Spier, "An Outline for a Chronology of Zuni Ruins," p. 300.

11. Sahlins, *Tribesmen*, pp. vi–viii; M. G. Smith, "Segmentary Lineages," pp. 120–33; Titiev, *Old Oraibi*, p. 68.

12. Kintigh, *Settlement, Subsistence and Society*, p. 117.

13. Fewkes, *Prehistoric Villages*, p. 76. A. Kidder, "Artifacts of Pecos," in *Papers of the Phillips Academy Southwestern Expedition* 6(1932), pp. 57–72; M. E. Lambert, *Pa-ako*; Snow, "Protohistoric Rio Grande Pueblo Economics," pp. 354–77. On the origins of the katsina cult and artistic changes see Schaafsma and Schaafsma, "Pueblo Kachina Cult," pp. 535–45; W. Smith, "Kiva Mural Decorations," pp. 322–75; Hibben, "Mexican Features of Mural Paintings."

14. On the distinction between Eastern and Western Pueblos see Eggan, *Social Organization of the Western Pueblos*; Jorgensen, "Comparative Traditional Economics."

15. Population estimates are from Schroeder, "Pueblos Abandoned in Historic Times."

16. Linguists believe that the origin of the Tanoan family is to be found some 4,500 years ago in eastern Sonora or western Chihuahua in Mexico. From there, sedentary horticulturists slowly made their way north, traveling along the Sierra Madre Occidentál and up the Rio Grande Valley. Lexicostatistical relationships found among Tiwa, Tewa, and Towa vocabulary lists suggest that their separation from a proto-language occurred around A.D. 1400. Piro was an extinct language by the eighteenth century; we know very little about it. On the origins of Tanoan see Jorgensen, *Western Indians*, p. 70; and I. Davis, "Linguistic Clues." On the Tewa see K. Hale and D. Harris, "Historical Linguistics and Archaeology," *HNAI*, 9, pp. 170–77; Schroeder and Matson, eds., *Colony on the Move*, p. 110. On the Tano see Ibid., p. 146; Bandelier, *Final Report of Investigations*, Part 1, p. 125. On Tiguex see Dozier, *Pueblo Indians*, p. 41; A. Bandelier, *Final Report of Investigations*, Part 1, pp. 129–30. On the Piro see Ibid., pp. 130–31.

17. Diego Pérez de Luxán, Relation, *RNM*, p. 181n; Zárate Salmerón, *Relaciones*, p. 93; F. Scholes, "Notes on the Jémez Missions in the Seventeenth Century," *El Palacio* 44(1938), pp. 61–71, 93–102. Adolph Bandelier incorrectly locates Giusewa at the later site of San Diego de la Congregación. See Bandelier, *Final Report of Investigations*, Part 1, pp. 126–27. San Diego was a *reducción* established in 1622 following the abandonment of Giusewa. For detailed analysis of this point see Kubler, *Religious Architecture of New Mexico*, pp. 82–85; and, Charlotte Arnold, "The Mission of San Diego de Jémez," *El Palacio* 27(1930), pp. 118–22.

18. Fox, *The Keresan Bridge*.

19. Schroeder, "Pueblos Abandoned in Historic Times," p. 253.

20. Linguists classify Uto-Aztecan and Tanoan as derivative of the same language phylum, Aztec-Tanoan. Dozier, *Pueblo Indians*, p. 44; J. Terrell, *Pueblos, Gods and Spaniards* (New York, 1973), p. 66.

21. Adolph Bandelier was the first to propose that Pueblo contraction had been due to the arrival of nomads. See Bandelier, "Reports by A. F. Bandelier," pp. 55–98. The identification of these nomads as Athapaskans was proposed by the following authors: Fewkes, "Tusayan Migration Traditions," p. 598; Mat-

thews, *Navaho Legends*; Bourke, "Gentile Organization of the Apaches." The A.D. 1525 arrival date for Athapaskans in New Mexico comes primarily from D. Gunnerson, "The Southern Athabascans: Their Arrival in the Southwest," *El Palacio* 63(1956), pp. 346–65, and "Man and Bison on the Plains in the Protohistoric Period," *Plains Anthropologist* 17(1972): 1–10; Gunnerson and Gunnerson, "Apachean Culture," pp. 7–27. For a review of Athapaskan prehistory in the Southwest see D. Wilcox, "The Entry of Athapaskans into the American Southwest: The Problem Today," D. Gregory, "Western Apache Archaeology: Problems and Approaches," C. Schaafsma, "Early Apacheans in the Southwest: A Review," D. Brugge, "Comments on Athabaskans and Sumas," all in D. Wilcox and W. B. Masse, eds., *The Protohistoric Period in the North American Southwest, A.D. 1450–1700* (Tempe, 1981), pp. 213–320.

22. *NCE*, pp. 26–27, 183n, 186, 235–36, 242, 258, 261, 292–93, 300–301, 310–11; *RNM*, 189, 200, 182. For an identification of the Querechos as Navajos see Bandelier, *Final Report of Investigations*, Part 2, p. 180; and Forbes, *Apache, Navajo and Spaniard*, p. 57. The identification of Querechos as Gila Apaches is found in Schroeder, "Navajo and Apache Relationships." *OD*, p. 345. Zárate Salmerón, *Relaciones*, pp. 94, 88. *RBM*, p. 89. For additional Oñate references to Athapaskans in New Mexico, see *OD*, pp. 480, 484–85.

23. *BM*, p. 45. Jorgensen, "Comparative Traditional Economics," pp. 695–700.

24. Jorgensen, "Comparative Traditional Economics," p. 695.

25. Schroeder, "Pueblos Abandoned in Historic Times." Bandelier, *Final Report of Investigations*, Part 1, p. 34. Forbes, *Apache, Navajo and Spaniard*, p. 139; Informe de Fray Juan Albares, 1707, AGN-PI 36-2:43–45. Schroeder and Matson, "Colony on the Move," p. 160. Percy M. Baldwin, "Fray Marcos' Relación," *NMHR* 1(1928), pp. 211–12. Castañeda, in *NCE*, pp. 234 and 173, 257–58. *OD*, 1, p. 427; Forbes, *Apache, Navajo and Spaniard*, pp. 137, 252–54; Trial of Diego de Peñalosa, 1665, *HD*, pp. 263–64; Zárate Salmerón, *Relaciones*, p. 15; *RBM*, p. 278.

26. A view of Pueblo history that focuses on migrations, factionalism, and enmities can be found in Schroeder, "Shifting for Survival"; and Bandelier, *Final Report of Investigations*, pp. 44–187. On extinct tribal units, see Naylor, "The Extinct Suma of North Chihuahua"; Scholes and Mera, "Some Aspects of the Jumano Problem"; Secoy, "The Identity of the Paduca"; Forbes, "Unknown Athapaskans." There is a pernicious, albeit romantic notion that the Pueblo Indians were "peace-loving" and lived "harmoniously" with their neighbors before European contact and only later became bellicose in self-defense. The archaeological, documentary, and oral evidence does not sustain such a view. If "peace-loving" is to be applied to the Pueblo Indians, the term is appropriate only after the 1696 reconquest of New Mexico when the Pueblos realized that continued overt resistance to Spanish domination would be suicidal. The Pueblo Indians have been characterized as "peace-loving" by J. Sando in "The Pueblo Revolt," *HNAI*, 9, pp. 194–97 and *The Pueblo Indians* (Santa Fe, 1976), especially p. xiii.

27. On the uniqueness of Acoma's origin myth see *PIR*, p. 966.

28. Dozier, "Making Inferences." On ethnohistorical methodology see Axtell, *The European and the Indian*, especially pp. 3–15; and Martin, ed., *The American Indian*.

29. Critiques of historical reconstructions can be found in Clendinnen, *Ambivalent Conquests*, pp. 131–34; Harms, "The Wars of August"; Burns, "The Caste War in the 1970's"; Price, *First-Time*; E. Wolf, *Europe and the People Without History* (Berkeley, 1982).

30. On tribesmen and social inequality see Sahlins, *Tribesmen*; and Collier, *Marriage and Inequality in Classless Societies*. Jorgensen, "Comparative Traditional Economics," pp. 708, 696. A. Ortiz, "Ritual Drama and the Pueblo World View," in Ortiz, ed., *New Perspectives on the Pueblos*, pp. 135–62.

Chapter 1

1. Several versions of Acoma Pueblo's origin myth exist. Here I have used Stirling's *Origin Myth of Acoma*, which is a transcription of a 1928 Bureau of American Ethnology taped interview with several Acoma Indians. The chief Acoma informant learned the origin myth as a youth during his initiation to the Koshari Society, a group of sacred clowns to whom all religious knowledge was entrusted. Other versions of the Acoma emergence myth can be found in White, *The Acoma Indians*; Boas, *Keresan Texts*; D. Ford, "A Creation Myth from Acoma"; J. Gunn, *Schat-Chen*; *PIR*, pp. 242–48; Tyler, *Pueblo Gods and Myths*.

2. Several transliterations of katsina appear in ethnographic literature, including kachina, katcina, cachina, and catzina. The origins and significance of the katsina in Pueblo religion can be found in Dockstader, *The Katchina and the White Man*; Anderson, "The Pueblo Kachina Cult"; Bunzel, *Zuñi Katcinas*; Ellis, "A Pantheon of Kachinas"; Fewkes, "An interpretation of Katcina Worship"; Schaafsma and Schaafsma, "Pueblo Kachina Cult."

3. C. Lévi-Strauss, *Structural Anthropology* (New York, 1963), pp. 220–21.

4. Eliade, *The Myth of the Eternal Return*. My understanding of the relationship between myth and history has been greatly influenced by Sahlins, *The Islands of History*, pp. 56–60; Dumézil, *The Destiny of the Warrior*, pp. 3–11; Vansina, *Oral Tradition as History*, pp. 13–25; Eliade, *Patterns in Comparative Religion*, pp. 388–409.

5. Sahlins, *The Islands of History*, p. 77.

6. Stirling, *Origin Myth of Acoma*, pp. 41–42. White, *The Acoma Indians*, pp. 133–34.

7. My understanding of the politics of gift giving comes largely from Collier, *Marriage and Inequality*, pp. 79–92; R. Ford, "Barter, Gift or Violence"; W. Jacobs, *Wilderness Politics and Gifts*; Mauss, *The Gift*; Sahlins, *Stone Age Economics*, pp. 149–276; Whitehead, "Fertility and Exchange in New Guinea"; Meeker, Barlow, and Lipset, "Culture, Exchange, and Gender."

8. Collier, *Marriage and Inequality*, pp. 103–5.

9. Stirling, *Origin Myth of Acoma*, pp. 2–10. *RBM*, pp. 42–43.

10. Collier, *Marriage and Inequality*, pp. 102–3.

11. Stirling, *Origin Myth of Acoma*, pp. 50–59.

12. *RNM*, p. 86; *PIR*, p. 43.

13. Collier, *Marriage and Inequality*, pp. 71–141.

14. *RNM*, pp. 101–2. Declaration of Marcelo de Espinosa, 1601, *OD*, p. 636.

15. Declaration of Joseph Brondate, 1601, *OD*, p. 627. On marital norms among the Pueblos see also, Declaration of Ginés de Herrera Horta, 1601, *OD*, p. 647; Declaration of Marcelo de Espinosa, 1601, *OD*, p. 636; Bandelier, *Final Report of Investigations*, Part 1, p. 141; M. de la Mota Padilla, *Historia de la Conquista de la Provincia de la Nueva Galicia, Escrita en 1742* (México, 1872), p. 160; Niethammer, *Daughters of the Earth*, pp. 64–66.

16. Pérez de Villagrá, *History of New Mexico*, p. 143. Declaration of Marcelo de Espinosa, 1601, *OD*, p. 636. Declaration of Joseph Brondate, 1601, *OD*, p. 627; Declaration of Captain Juan de Ortega, 1601, *OD*, p. 663. *RMB*, pp. 47, 81; *OD*, pp. 636, 647.

17. *NCE*, p. 174. *RNM*, pp. 193–94. *NCE*, pp. 183, 215.

18. Collier, *Marriage and Inequality*, p. 76.

19. Parsons, "Hopi Mothers and Children," p. 100. *PIR*, p. 182. See also Sjöo and Mor, *The Great Cosmic Mother*.

20. Niethammer, *Daughters of the Earth*, p. 11; Parsons, "Mothers and Children at Zuñi," p. 168; Haeberlin, *The Idea of Fertilization*; Collier, *Marriage and Inequality*, pp. 131–33; Duberman, ed., "Documents in Hopi Indian Sexuality," p. 124.

21. Declaration of Marcelo Espinosa, 1601, *OD*, p. 636.

22. *NCE*, p. 254. *RNM*, pp. 82–84, 172; Scully, *Pueblo: Mountain, Village, Dance*, pp. 1–46.

23. *NCE*, pp. 158, 170–71, 208, 252–55; Horgan, *Great River*, pp. 34, 48–49. Bandelier, *Final Report on Investigations*, Part 1, p. 139; *NCE*, p. 167.

24. *NCE*, p. 254. *RBM*, p. 44.

25. Eggan, *Social Organization of the Western Pueblos*, pp. 231–32, 291–324; Benedict, *Patterns of Culture*, pp. 75–76. *RNM*, p. 86. Fox, *Kinship and Marriage*, p. 90.

26. Parsons, "Mothers and Children at Laguna" and "Tewa Mothers and Children." *PIR*, p. 621.

27. *NCE*, p. 256.

28. Qoyawayma, *No Turning Back*, p. 5; *RNM*, p. 85. On female domestic production, also see *NCE*, pp. 158–59, 183, 252, 255; *RNM*, pp. 85, 172.

29. The gifts women demanded for sex are mentioned numerous places. See *NCE*, p. 248; *RNM*, p. 206; *RBM*, pp. 43–44; *HD* vol. 3, pp. 149, 184; AGN-INQ 587-1: 19, 60, 64, 140.

30. Tyler, *Pueblo Gods and Myths*, p. 81; Hill, "Hermaphrodite and Transvestite in Navaho Culture"; Titiev, *Hopi Indians*, pp. 153, 214–15. Titiev, *Old Oraibi*, p. 206; Hay, "The Hammond Report," p. 20. Ritual copulation is described in *PIR*, pp. 566–67, 644, 805; Affidavits of Kuanwikvaya (1920), Steve Quonestewa (April 14, 1921), Quoyawyma (April 16, 1921), and L. R. McDon-

ald (May 11, 1915) in the National Anthropological Archives, the Smithsonian Institution (Washington, D.C.). Bestiality, fellatio, and phallic clowning are reported in the affidavits of Siventiwa (1920), William H. Pfeifer (November 13, 1920), Blas Casaus (November 7, 1915), Otto Lomauitu (1920), and Emory A. Marks (December 11, 1920) deposited at the National Anthropological Archives.

31. Eliade, *Patterns in Comparative Religion*, pp. 239–64, 331–66. *PIR*, pp. 428–31. Niethammer, *Daughters of the Earth*, p. 11.

32. *NCE*, p. 171. *RNM*, p. 172.

33. Declaration of Fray Nicolás de Chávez, September 18, 1660, AGN-INQ 587-34. Niethammer, *Daughters of the Earth*, p. 213.

34. *PIR*, p. 680.

35. Fewkes, "The Tusayan New-fire Ceremony," p. 447; Titiev, *Old Oraibi*, p. 164.

36. Titiev, *Hopi Indians*, pp. 164–65; Voth, *The Oraibi Marau Ceremony*, p. 32; Duberman, ed., "Documents in Hopi Sexuality," pp. 108–13; *PIR*, pp. 675–82.

37. Titiev, *Hopi Indians*, pp. 166–67; Schlegel, "Male and Female in Hopi Thought and Action."

38. Sahlins, *Stone Age Economics*, pp. 149–276; Whitehead, "Fertility and Exchange in New Guinea."

39. *MNM*, p. 257. Other scalp dances are described and analyzed in *PIR*, pp. 624–25, 644–45; Bunzel, "Zuñi Ritual Poetry," p. 679; Parsons, *The Scalp Ceremonial of Zuñi*.

40. *PRI*, pp. 350–51; White, *The Pueblo of Santo Domingo*, pp. 144–48.

41. White, *New Material from Acoma*, p. 336.

42. Sahlins, *The Islands of History*, p. 38.

43. Schlegel, "Adolescent Socialization," p. 452.

44. *RNM*, p. 85. *NCE*, p. 254.

45. I thank Jane Collier for bringing this point to my attention. See also Yava, *Big Falling Snow*; and Talayesva, *Sun Chief*.

46. This spatial model is best described by Ortiz in *The Tewa World*, pp. 11–28; Stubbs, *Bird's-Eye View of the Pueblos*; Tyler, *Pueblo Gods and Myths*, pp. 169–79.

47. White, *The Acoma Indians*, p. 132. Stephen, *Hopi Journal*, vol. 2, p. 1190n.

48. *RNM*, p. 101; *RBM*, p. 43; *RNM*, pp. 193–94.

49. White, *Pueblo of Santa Ana*, p. 187; Parsons, *Hopi and Zuñi Ceremonialism*, p. 53; Schroeder, "Rio Grande Ethnohistory," p. 51.

50. These three categories of male political life come from Dumézil, *The Destiny of the Warrior* and *The Destiny of a King*.

51. *NCE*, p. 135. *PIR*, p. 169; Titiev, *Old Oraibi*, p. 131.

52. Bellah, "Religious Systems," pp. 227–64; Benedict, *Patterns of Culture*, pp. 54–55; Dozier, *Pueblo Indians of North America*, p. 151.

53. Bellah, "Religious Systems," p. 230. McCluskey, "The Astronomy of the Hopi Indians."

54. *RNM*, p. 78.

55. R. Ford, "An Ecological Perspective on the Eastern Pueblos"; Beaglehole, *Notes on Hopi Economic Life*, pp. 72–81.

56. Benedict, *Patterns of Culture*, pp. 57–129. During the historic period factionalism has rattled the foundations of many pueblos. Population dispersals and town abandonments created by these tensions are explored in *PIR*, pp. 15, 108, 1131, 1137–38, 1094–97; French, *Factionalism in Isleta Pueblo*; Pandey, "Images of Power in a Southwestern Pueblo." The prominent role of clowns (*koshari*) in Pueblo ritual was testament to the consequences of personal over collective will. Clowns turned the world topsy-turvy, behaved without constraint, spoke backwards, ate feces, and drank urine. Some poor clowns did not even know the meaning of sexual intercourse, the symbol of cosmic harmony, and thought the proper orifice for its consummation was the ear. On Pueblo clowning see: "Teaching the Mudheads How to Copulate," in Erdoes and Ortiz, eds., pp. 279–80; Bourke, *Urine Dance of the Zuni Indians*, and *Compilation of Notes and Memoranda*; Duberman, ed., "Documents in Hopi Indian Sexuality," passim.

57. Tyler, *Pueblo Gods and Myths*, p. 219; *PIR*, p. 125.

58. White, *The Acoma Indians*, pp. 45–46.

59. Stirling, *Origin Myth of Acoma*, p. 97. Tyler, *Pueblo Gods and Myths*, p. 213.

60. *PIR*, p. 181. Stephen, "Hopi Tales," p. 6; Cushing, "Origin Myth from Oraibi," p. 166.

61. Stirling, *Origin Myth of Acoma*, pp. 83–90.

62. Ibid. Those interested in the role that secrecy and the distribution of esoteric knowledge plays in creating and perpetuating inequality should consult Brandt, "On Secrecy and the Control of Knowledge," and "The Role of Secrecy in a Pueblo Society."

63. Nabokov, *Indian Running*.

64. Ellis, "Patterns of Aggression"; Woodbury, "A Reconsideration of Pueblo Warfare." Pueblo war societies have been extinct since the seventeenth century. To understand what Pueblo warrior societies may have been like, I studied warfare in other Indian tribes. See Hill, *Navaho Warfare*; Guernsey, "Notes on a Navajo War Dance"; Parsons, "Notes on a Navajo War Dance"; Bandelier, "On the Art of War and Mode of Warfare"; Ellis, "Patterns of Aggression"; Farmer, "Defensive Systems of the Southwest"; Hadlock, "Warfare Among the Northeastern Woodland Indians"; Mishkin, *Rank and Warfare Among the Plains Indians*; M. Smith, "The War Complex of the Plains Indians," and "American Indian Warfare"; Stewart, "Mohave Warfare."

65. *NCE*, p. 249; Bandelier, *Final Report of Investigations*, Part 1, pp. 69–70; *RBM*, p. 44; R. Smith, "Mexican and Anglo-Saxon Traffic in Scalps, Slaves, and Livestock," *West Texas Historical Association Year Book* (1960), pp. 98–115. *RMB*, p. 239n. *PIR*, pp. 467, 875, 923; J. Green, ed., *Zuñi: Selected Writing of Frank Hamilton Cushing* (Lincoln, 1979), passim.

66. Collier, *Marriage and Inequality*, pp. 131–32. *NCE*, p. 184. Ibid., p. 175.

67. Fewkes, "A Few Tusayan Pictographs," pp. 16–17; N. Judd, *The Material Culture of Pueblo Bonito*, p. 278. On phallic/serpentine symbolism see León, "El Culto del Falo"; Stoddard, "Phallic Symbols in America"; Lejeal, "Rites Phalliques."

68. Stirling, *Origin Myth of Acoma*, p. 27. Eliade, *Patterns in Comparative Religion*, p. 164; Haeberlin, *The Idea of Fertilization*, passim; Lummis, *The Man who Married the Moon*, pp. 71–72.

69. NCE, p. 286; Tyler, *Pueblo Gods and Myths*, p. 234. M. Stevenson, "The Zuñi Indians," *Twenty-third Annual Report of the Bureau of American Ethnology* (Washington, D.C., 1901), p. 30; Parsons, *The Social Organization of the Tewa*, pp. 302–3, "Some Aztec and Pueblo Parallels," and "The Zuñi Origin Myth"; Duberman, ed., "Documents in Hopi Indian Sexuality," p. 116. PIR, pp. 1016–17.

70. PIR, p. 173. RNM, p. 99; NCE, pp. 184, 258; PIR, p. 171. Katsina is a Hopi word meaning "respect spirit" (*ka*, respect, and *china*, spirit); the word is used here generically to refer to those cloud-beings known at Taos as *thlatsi* or *thliwa*, at Isleta as *wenin* or *thliwa*, at Jémez as *k'ats'ana* or *dysa*, and to the Tewa as *oxuhwa*. To Frederick Dockstader katsina means "life father" or "spirit father" (from *kachi*, life or spirit, and *na*, father). See Dockstader's *The Kachina and the White Man*, p. 9.

71. Stirling, *Origin Myth of Acoma*, p. 109; White, *The Acoma Indians*, p. 72. Waters, *Masked Gods*, p. 178. On the meaning of prayer sticks see PIR, pp. 270–91; Tyler, *Pueblo Birds and Myths*, p. xii. B. Tedlock has argued that the offering of prayer sticks was an act of sacrifice. The prayer stick was deemed a living person and was often referred to as "sacred younger sister or relative." The deities by accepting the prayer stick took the life and breath of the prayer stick. "The sacrifice is the vehicle of communication of the mediator between these people (the profane) and their gods (the sacred)," writes Tedlock. "The message is the paradox: a life for a life. My life (in surrogate form) for the necessities of my life." See B. Tedlock, "Prayer Stick Sacrifice at Zuñi" (Manuscript in Department of Anthropology, Wesleyan University, Middletown, Conn., 1973).

72. Stirling, *Origin Myth of Acoma*, pp. 108–12; White, *The Acoma Indians*, pp. 71–75. Stirling, *Origin Myth of Acoma*, pp. 50–56. Seventeenth-century katsina initiations are described by Spanish observers in HD, pp. 133–34, 152, 157–58.

73. NCE, pp. 254–55. RNM, p. 178; Zárate de Salmerón, *Relaciónes*, paragraph 74. My translation of Spanish quoted in Bandelier, *Final Report of Investigations*, Part 1, pp. 143. NCE, p. 255. Kivas also served as lodge houses for esoteric societies and as places to house foreign guests. A group of Hopi testified in 1704 that in one of their kivas some men "worked, others chatted, and others played games." The kiva "served as a community center," said Diego Pérez de Luxán in 1582, "and lodging place for strangers." On these points, see "Declaration taken upon the arrival of some Hopi Indians at the Pueblo of Taos, 1704," quoted in Bandelier, *Final Report of Investigations*, Part 1, pp. 143–44; RNM, p. 175; NCE, p. 254.

74. RNM, pp. 99–101. Tyler, *Pueblo Animals*, p. 54.

75. Schele and Miller, *The Blood of Kings*, pp. 175–208; Bishop Diego de Landa noted in the 1560s that the Maya "offered sacrifices of their own blood, sometimes cutting themselves around in pieces and they left them in this way as a sign. Other times they pierced their cheeks, at others their lower lips . . . others slit the superfluous part of the virile member." Another Franciscan colleague of Landa's noted how Maya ritual celebrants cut their penes: "They took a chisel and wooden mallet, placed the one who had to sacrifice himself on a smooth stone slab, took out his penis, and cut in three parts two finger breadths [up], the largest in the center, saying at the same time incantations and words." Both quotes in Tozzer, ed. and trans., *Landa's Relación*, pp. 113–14. See also Clendinnen, *Ambivalent Conquests*, pp. 180–81; Furst, "Fertility, Vision Quest and Auto-Sacrifice"; Joralemon, "Ritual Blood-Sacrifice Among the Ancient Maya." On Aztec bloodletting and genital mutilation see León, "El Culto del Falo"; Lejeal, "Rites Phalliques"; Clendinnen, "The Cost of Courage in Aztec Society."

76. *RNM*, p. 100. *PIR*, pp. 764, 397n. Duberman, "Documents in Hopi Indian Sexuality," pp. 106, 116, 123. Tyler, *Pueblo Animals*, p. 54. Several studies on the Hopi Snake Dance exist: Bourke, *The Snake Dance*; Fewkes, "The Snake Ceremonials at Walpi"; Stephen, *Hopi Journal*; Fergusson, *Dancing Gods*, pp. 145–67.

77. Tyler, *Pueblo Animals*, pp. 32–35; Beaglehole, *Hopi Hunting*, pp. 4–7; Underhill, *Ceremonial Patterns*, p. 30; Scully, *Pueblo*, p. 67.

78. Cushing, *Zuni Fetishes*, p. 15.

79. Tyler, *Pueblo Animals*, pp. 35–36. Beaglehole, *Hopi Hunting*, p. 6.

80. Driving animals into pits, into natural culs de sac, or over mesa tops were also common hunting techniques. Beaglehole, *Hopi Hunting*, p. 8.

81. White, *New Material from Acoma*, p. 336. Stirling, *Origin Myth of Acoma*, pp. 24–25. Beaglehole, *Hopi Hunting*, pp. 7, 11, 13. See also Bonnegjea, "Hunting Superstitions"; Hill, *Agriculture and Hunting Methods*.

82. Schlegel, "Socialization of a Hopi Girl," p. 453.

83. The illnesses and curses associated with various curing societies can be found in *PIR*, pp. 189–92 and Titiev, *Old Oraibi*, p. 241. White, *The Acoma Indians*, pp. 107–27; Underhill, *Ceremonial Patterns*, p. 38; Tyler, *Pueblo Animals*, pp. 184–202; Simmons, *Witchcraft in the Southwest*, pp. 69–95; Parsons, "Witchcraft Among the Pueblos." It should be noted that although women could and still do become *chaianyi*, the Spanish friars and explorers never mentioned them as such. Rather, as shown in chapters 2 and 10, they thought of native women with religious or magical powers as witches.

Most pueblos today have clown societies. They probably existed in the sixteenth century but were not mentioned by the Europeans. I suspect that the Spanish chroniclers could not differentiate between the medicine men and their assistants, the clowns. On Pueblo clowning see Stirling, *Origin Myth of Acoma*, p. 33; Hieb, "Meaning and Mismeaning"; Erdoes and Ortiz, *American Indian Myths and Legends*, pp. 333–86.

84. Collier, *Marriage and Inequality*, pp. 131–33.

85. These "men-women" were known to the Zuñi as *la'mana*, to the Tewa as

quetho, and to the Navajo as *nadle*. They existed among the Keres (Acoma, Laguna, and Santa Ana) and Hopi, but I have not been able to locate their indigenous names. Parsons, "The Zuñi La'Mana"; S. Jacobs, "Comment"; Hill, "The Status of the Hermaphrodite"; Gifford, "Cultural Elements Distribution"; Fewkes, "A Few Tusayan Pictographs," *AA*, 5(1892), p. 11.

86. Male berdache status has been reported in 113 North American Indian Cultures; female berdache in only 30. The Navaho, Western Apache, and Utes are the only Southwestern Indian groups known to have female berdache. The berdache tradition is best studied in Callender and Kochems, "The North American Berdache"; S. Jacobs, "Berdache"; Williams, *The Spirit and the Flesh*. On female berdaches see Whitehead, "The Bow and the Burden Strap." Those interested in the cross-cultural meaning of homoeroticism and homosexuality will find the following works illuminating: Herdt, *Guardians of the Flute, Rituals of Manhood*, and *Ritualized Homosexuality in Melanesia*; Sergent, *Homosexuality in Greek Myth*; Boswell, *Christianity*; Ariès and Béjin, *Western Sexuality*; J. Trevisan, *Perverts in Paradise: Homosexuality in Brazil, from the Colonial Period to the Present* (New York, 1986); E. Blackwood, ed., *The Many Faces of Homosexuality*.

87. *NCE*, pp. 130, 148. "Naufrahios de Alvar Núñez Cabeza de Vaca," quoted in Jonathan Katz, *Gay American History*, p. 285.

88. Fray Juan Agustín Morfi cited in Newcomb, *The Indians of Texas*, p. 74; Hammond, "The Disease of the Scythians." Ibid., pp. 334–36. Eliade, *Mephistopheles and the Androgyne*, pp. 78–124, and *Patterns in Comparative Religion*, pp. 356–61, 419–25.

89. *RNM*, pp. 99–100. Declaration of Don Esteban Clemente, 1660, AGN-INQ 587-1:123. Duberman, ed., "Documents in Hopi Indian Sexuality," p. 116. Hay, "The Hammond Report," p. 18.

90. *NCE*, p. 248. Ibid., pp. 147–48.

Chapter 2

1. *NCE*, p. 145.
2. *NCE*, p. 77.
3. *NCE*, p. 198. Estevanico's adventures are described in Fray Marcos de Niza's Report, *NCE*, pp. 63–82. See also Ibrahim, "Estevan, the Moor of New Mexico"; Terrell, *Estevanico the Black*.
4. Clissold, *The Seven Cities of Cibola*, pp. 14–15.
5. H. Johnson, Jr., *From Reconquest to Empire*, p. 5.
6. Gómara quoted in ibid., p. 49.
7. Leonard, *Books of the Brave*, pp. 1–35.
8. F. Bandelier, trans., *The Journey of Alvar Núñez Cabeza de Vaca*. Bannon, *The Spanish Borderlands*, p. 14.
9. Baldwin, ed. and trans., "Fray Marcos' Relación," pp. 202, 218–19. Hernán Cortés, Francisco Vásquez de Coronado, and Pedro de Castañeda all denounced Fray Marcos as a fantastic liar. Cíbola in 1539 was a village no larger than a square city block and was far from a "city greater than Mexico." Given the timetable and the terrain the friar claimed to have traversed, it does not seem pos-

sible that he ever saw Cíbola. The veracity of Fray Marcos' report is questioned in Sauer, *The Road to Cíbola* and "The Credibility of The Friar Marcos Account"; Wagner "Fr. Marcos de Niza."

10. A. Alton, *The Muster Roll and Equipment of the Expedition of Francisco Vásquez de Coronado* (Ann Arbor, 1939). NCE, pp. 113–14. Bannon, *The Spanish Borderlands*, p. 17. NCE, p. 202.

11. NCE, pp. 164, 205, 170.

12. NCE, pp. 157, 321.

13. NCE, pp. 169, 233, 133–34, 144.

14. NCE, pp. 160, 168–70, 207–9.

15. NCE, p. 214, RNM, pp. 94, 77, 168. NCE, pp. 184, 175.

16. NCE, p. 170; OD, p. 318; NCE, pp. 183, 219; OD, p. 315; NCE, p. 238.

17. HD, p. 149; OD, p. 457; HD, p. 110. NCE, p. 171. Schroeder and Matson, *A Colony on the Move*, p. 87. RNM, p. 79. For other comments on Indian intelligence see RBM, p. 215; NCE, p. 255; HD, p. 122.

18. NCE, p. 221.

19. NCE, pp. 24, 225.

20. NCE, p. 304.

21. NCE, p. 66. Powell, *Soldiers, Indians and Silver*, pp. 1–56.

22. "Ordenanzas de su magestad hechas para los nuevos descubrimientos, conquistas y pacificaciones, Julio de 1573," in Hanke, *History of Latin America Civilization*, vol. 1, pp. 149–52. The ordinances are found in *Colección de Documentos Ineditos relativos al Descubrimiento, Conquista y Organización de las antiguas posesiones Españolas de América y Oceania* (Madrid, 1871), vol. 16, pp. 142–87.

23. Ricard, *The Spiritual Conquest of Mexico*, pp. 2–5.

24. G. Mendieta, *Historia Eclesiástica Indiana*, Lib. 4, cap. 23, p. 104. The eschatological significance of Fray Marcos' discovery is studied in J. Phelan, *The Millennial Kingdom*, pp. 69–80.

25. RNM, p. 109. Ibid., pp. 153–244.

26. OD, pp. 4–9. Don Juan de Oñate was the son of Cristóbal de Oñate who had accompanied Cortés in the conquest of Mexico, had briefly served as the governor of Nueva Galicia, and had helped develop the Zacatecas silver mines. See Chipman, "The Oñate-Moctezuma-Zaldívar Families." OD, pp. 44, 65–68, 390.

27. OD, p. 390. Salazar Inspection, Ibid., pp. 199–308.

28. I owe my understanding of conquest theater to Trexler, "We Think, They Act"; Wachtel, *The Vision of the Vanquished*.

29. FEV, p. 59; and Espinosa, "The Virgin of the Reconquest." M. Simmons, "Tlascalans in the Spanish Borderlands," NMHR 39(1964), pp. 101–10. On Doña Inés see OD, pp. 48, 321. Oñate was quite irritated at Doña Inés because as a Tano-speaking Indian she did not speak any of the other Pueblo languages, and few individuals remembered the details of her 1590 abduction. So much for the calculated ploys of political theater!

30. *HNM*, p. 129. *OD*, p. 315. Trexler, *Public Life in Renaissance Florence*, p. 432. Trexler, "We Think, They Act," p. 191; Bancroft, *History of Arizona and New Mexico*, p. 199.

31. Phelan, *The Millennial Kingdom*, p. 33; Trexler, "We Think, They Act," p. 191. *HNM*, p. 129. *RBM*, pp. 88, 214. *HNM*, p. 136.

32. *OD*, pp. 339, 340.

33. *HNM*, p. 149. This summary of "The Christians and the Moors" is based on several extant versions of the play: WPA 5-5-3:26, 5-5-6:6, 5-5-21. See also T. Pearce, "Los Moros y los Cristianos: Early American Play," *New Folklore Record* 2, pp. 58–65; C. B. Martin, "Medieval Religious Drama in New Mexico," pp. 86, 152; Sister J. McCrossan, *The Role of the Church*, p. 2. The cross as a symbol of the victorious Christ is studied by Aulen, pp. 4–7. *OD*, p. 344.

34. On deserted villages see *OD*, pp. 318–19. On Oñate's reception see *OD*, pp. 322, 394–96.

35. *HNM*, p. 141. *RBM*, pp. 43–44.

36. Testimony of Fray Francisco Zamora, 1601, *OD*, pp. 675–76. Fray Joseph Manuel de Equía y Leronbe to Viceroy, 1734, AGN-INQ 854: 253–56.

37. Declaration of Ginés de Herrera Horta, Marcelo de Espinosa, Joseph Brondate, Juan de Ortega, 1601, *OD*, pp. 647, 644–45, 637, 627, 663.

38. *RNM*, p. 84, my emphasis. On trinkets given as gifts, see *OD*, p. 318.

39. Testimony of Gerónimo Márquez, 1598, *OD*, pp. 430–33.

40. *OD*, pp. 428–451, 354–56, 451–54.

41. Trial of Acoma Indians, *OD*, pp. 464, 466.

42. *OD*, p. 427; *HNM*, p. 264. Fray Alonso de Benavides asserted in 1630 that since the battle at Acoma had occurred on the feast of St. Paul, the saint who had assisted the Christians was not St. James but St. Paul. See *RBM*, pp. 166, 196. *OD*, pp. 477–78.

43. *OD*, pp. 746–60.

44. *OD*, p. 1111. Ibid., pp. 675, 608–18.

45. *OD*, pp. 1004, 1067–68, 1087–91.

46. My understanding of charismatic domination is largely informed by the works of Max Weber. See Eisenstadt, *Max Weber* and Weber, *The Sociology of Religion*.

47. Mendieta, *Historia Eclesiástica Indiana*, Lib. 4, cap. 21, pp. 92–93.

48. *HNM*, p. 140. *RBM*, pp. 57, 58.

49. *RBM*, p. 89. The medicine chest of the 1598 Oñate expedition is described in *OD*, pp. 104–7. Scholes, "The Supply Service of the New Mexican Missions," pp. 93–115, 186–210, 386–404 lists the supplies in the mission infirmaries.

50. *RBM*, pp. 76–77, 300; Defori, *The Martyrs of New Mexico*, p. 33; *TM*, vol. 4, pp. 174–75.

51. *OD*, pp. 139–47; Crosby, *The Columbian Exchange*, p. 88. *RBM*, p. 39.

52. *RBM*, p. 218. G. Hammond and A. Rey, "The Rodríguez Expedition to New Mexico, 1581–1582," *NMHR* 2(1927), p. 345. *OD*, p. 459.

53. Trexler, *Public Life in Renaissance Florence*, pp. 45–84. NCE, p. 79; M. Servín, "Religious Aspects"; *RBM*, pp. 61, 196; *HD*, p. 107.

54. Ross Gordon Montgomery found that the mission church of St. Bernard at Awatovi had been erected over a kiva. See Montgomery, et al., *Franciscan Awatovi*, pp. 64–67. Scholes and Adams, "Inventories of Church Furnishings," p. 34. Montgomery, et al., "Showing that the New Mexico Mission Churches were Seldom or Never Consecrated," in Montgomery, et al., *Franciscan Awatovi*, pp. 273–76.

55. Kubler, *Religious Architecture of New Mexico*, p. 18.

56. My analysis of altar pieces was sparked by a reading of Taylor's "Between Global Process and Local Knowledge." F. de la Maza, "Simbolismo del Retablo de Huejotzingo," *Artes de Mexico* 106(1968), pp. 26–30. Kubler, *Religious Architecture of New Mexico*; MNM; J. E. Espinosa, *Saints in the Valleys*, pp. 89–100; *La Iglesia de Santa Cruz*; J. Kessell, *The Missions of New Mexico Since 1776*; Scholes and Adams, "Inventories of Church Furnishings"; "Supplies for Benavides and Companions going to New Mexico, 1624–1626," in *RBM*, pp. 109–24. For comparative purposes see P. Johnson, *The California Missions*.

57. There were numerous other objects in the sanctuary such as candles, an altar stone, and altar linens, which need not concern us here. On altar furnishings see Montgomery et al., *Franciscan Awatovi*, pp. 191–96. On predella relics see Scholes and Adams, "Inventories of Church Furnishings," pp. 29–30.

58. *RBM*, p. 129; MNM, p. 17; "Observations of Fray Joaquin de Jesus Ruiz, 1776," in Ibid., pp. 308–9.

59. *RBM*, pp. 66, 255; *TM*, vol. 3, p. 268. Ibid., vol. 4, p. 198; Bandelier, *Final Report of Investigations*, Part 1, pp. 258–59; *La Iglesia de Santa Cruz de la Cañada*, p. 65. Excavations of seventeenth-century New Mexican churches confirm the fact that bones were concentrated near the altar. At the Mission of St. Bernard of Clairvaux in Awatovi, archaeologists found 118 burials concentrated near the sanctuary and diminishing in frequency as one moved out from the altar; a clustering also was found at Santa Fe's *parroquia* when it was razed in 1870 to make way for a new church. On these points see A. Ely, "The Excavation and Repair of Quarai Mission"; Montgomery et al., *Franciscan Awatovi*, pp. 54, 59–60, 95–99, 178–80; Kubler, *Religious Architecture of New Mexico*, p. 42. On the importance of burial in sacred space see the controversy over the burials of Sebastian de Sandoval in 1640 and that of Governor Luís de Rosas in 1642. Both are discussed in Scholes, "Church and State," *NMHR* 11, p. 318, and 15, pp. 84–85.

60. *OD*, pp. 309–28. On place names see A. Chávez, "Saint's Names in New Mexico Geography" and "New Mexico Religious Place-Names." On Santiago at Acoma see *OD*, p. 427; *HNM*, p. 264. Benavides' rebuttal is in *RBM*, pp. 166, 196. On apparitions of St. James in the New World see R. Valle, *Santiago en América*.

61. Kubler, *Religious Architecture of New Mexico*, p. 66.

62. My interpretation of the Mass comes largely from Bossy, "The Mass as a Social Institution," pp. 33–34; Hardison, "The Mass as Sacred Drama"; Dugmore, *The Mass*.

63. On the ritual suspension of social inequalities see Turner, *The Ritual Process*, pp. 94–165. I have embraced here the theory of sacrifice expounded by Girard in *Violence and the Sacred*, pp. 1–67, and *The Scapegoat*, pp. 100–111.

64. Bossy, "The Mass as a Social Institution," pp. 48–49. On the *Pax* see *RBM*, p. 129. On pax-boards see Scholes and Adams, "Inventories of Church Furnishings," pp. 27–38; *MNM*, p. 358. Lienhardt, *Social Anthropology*, p. 148, quoted in Bossy, "The Mass as a Social Institution," p. 52.

65. On the importance of Mass to Governor Oñate see *OD*, pp. 312, 314, 317, 321, 322; and *HNM*, pp. 102, 206, 220, 237.

66. *PIR*, pp. 428–29. *RBM*, p. 215; *HD*, pp. 144, 151.

67. *RBM*, p. 83.

68. *RBM*, pp. 220–21.

69. *RBM*, p. 217.

70. *RBM*, pp. 220, 215, 218.

71. *OD*, p. 466. *RBM*, p. 89.

72. *RBM*, p. 42.

73. *RBM*, pp. 89–90, 196. Scholes, "Church and State," pp. 145–46; Zárate Salmerón, *Relaciones*, p. 15.

74. Bynum, *Jesus as Mother*, pp. 82–109.

75. Kubler, *Mexican Architecture*, vol. 1, pp. 4–14; Phelan, *Millennial Kingdom of the Franciscans*, pp. 44–48; Lambert, *Franciscan Poverty*, passim; Bynum, *Jesus as Mother*, pp. 82–109.

76. *Instrucción*; *Cartilla*. St. Bonaventure's various works contained in *WB*.

77. *Instrucción*, pp. 189, preface, 30, 215, 61. "Letter Containing Twenty-five Points to Remember," *WB*, vol. 3, pp. 260, 255.

78. *Instrucción*, pp. 23, 37. Cousins, ed. and trans., "The Life of St. Francis," p. 218.

79. Weinstein and Bell, *Saints and Society*, p. 84. Juan Cirita, a twelfth-century Galician saint, burned off all the flesh from his left arm to rid himself of sexual desires. Heimerad, an eleventh-century Swabian monk, rolled his body on a bed of thorns for similar ends. See ibid., pp. 81–84. "Regla Seráfica," in *Manual Seráfico . . .* (Mexico, 1779), pp. 191–92. Clissold, *The Wisdom of the Spanish Mystics*, p. 61; Weinstein and Bell, *Saints and Society*, pp. 84–87.

80. "The Triple Way," *WB*, vol. 1, p. 66. Lambert, *Franciscan Poverty*, p. 38. Fortini, *Francis of Assisi*, p. 229.

81. In the years following Francis' death, a rich hagiographical lore developed emphasizing how perfectly the *Poverello* had modeled himself after Christ. Their lives were so identical that an antique literary form, the double biography, was resurrected to compare and contrast their lives. Since the Gospels and the various biographies of St. Francis were but fragmentary accounts of each man's life, by printing parallel lives, the gaps in one biography could be filled in by the other, thus giving the reader a fuller knowledge of each man. On this point see Pelikan, *Jesus Through the Ages*, p. 135.

82. Moorman, *A History of the Franciscan Order*, pp. 3–6. Fortini, *Francis of Assisi*, pp. 219–30; L. Little, *Religious Poverty*, pp. 147–48. Clissold, *The Wisdom of St. Francis*, p. 29.

83. Cousins, ed. and trans., "The Life of St. Francis," p. 189. R. Brown, ed. and trans., *The Little Flowers of St. Francis*, p. 192. The most detailed account of the stigmata is "Considerations on the Holy Stigmata," pp. 169–216 in ibid.

84. Bynum, *Jesus as Mother*, pp. 82–109.

85. "The Journey of the Mind to God," *WB*, vol. 1, pp. 13–17. R. Brown, ed. and trans., *Fifty Animal Stories*; Dubos, "Franciscan Conservation." Armstrong, *Saint Francis*, pp. 133–41; Cuthbert, *The Romanticism of St. Francis*, pp. 1–72. V. Oberhauser, "Lamb of God," *New Catholic Encyclopedia* (San Francisco, 1967) vol. 9, pp. 338–42; Cousins, ed. and trans., "The Life of St. Francis," pp. 223, 255–56.

86. Cousins, ed. and trans., "The Life of St. Francis," p. 276. *The Little Flowers of St. Francis* quoted in Armstrong, *Saint Francis*, p. 8. Ozment, *Mysticism and Dissent*, pp. 3–12. St. Paul quoted in P. Zweig, *The Heresy of Self-Love*, pp. 27–28.

87. Cousins, ed. and trans., "The Life of St. Francis," p. 212.

88. Daniel, *The Franciscan Concept*, p. 43. Cousins, ed. and trans., "The Life of St. Francis," p. 268, my emphasis. T. Gilby, "Theology of Martyrdom," *New Catholic Encyclopedia*, vol. 9, p. 315; Daniel, *The Franciscan Concept*, p. 50 and "The Desire for Martyrdom."

89. Leclercq, *Monks and Love*, pp. 27–54, 99–104.

90. *Instrucción*, p. 292. St. Bernard, Sermon on the Canticle of Canticles, 2:2, quoted in R. Whitson, *Mysticism and Ecumenism*, p. 89. Bridal mysticism can also be studied in the work of St. John of the Cross. See Barnstone, ed. and trans., *Poems of Saint John*, pp. 92–105. *Instrucción*, p. 229; St. Bernard, Sermon on the Canticle of Canticles, 31:6, quoted in Whitson, *Mysticism and Ecumenism*, pp. 85–86.

91. "On the Perfection of Life," *WB*, vol. 1, pp. 239–40.

92. "The Mystical Vine," *WB*, vol. 1, p. 156. St. Bernard makes a similar point in Whitson, *Mysticism and Ecumenism*, pp. 71, 91, as does Leclercq, *Monks and Love*, pp. 22–44. Singer, *The Nature of Love*, vol. 1, pp. 183, 206.

93. *Instrucción*, pp. 20, 62; *Cartilla*, p. 73.

94. "The Mystical Vine," *WB*, vol. 1, p. 155. Virginia Reinburg, "Popular Prayers." Inquisitorial records document well those clerical peccadillos of pure unadulterated carnality disguised as mystical marriages. For example, Sister Benedetta Carlini, that seventeenth-century Italian abbess whose stigmata and spiritual marriage Judith Brown has so splendidly described, feigned these physical manifestations of perfection, in part, to gain the sexual affections of her companion, Sister Bartolomea Crivelli. See J. Brown, *Immodest Acts*. Pelikan, *Jesus Through the Ages*, p. 130. Ribalta's painting is housed at the Prado Museum (Madrid, Spain).

95. Singer, *The Nature of Love*, vol. 1, p. 184.

96. *RBM*, pp. 204–5, 143, 219. On the meaning of light and dark in Spanish mysticism see Leborans, *Luz y oscuridad*.

97. *RBM*, pp. 204–5, 143, 43. *RNM*, p. 186. Missionaries throughout the Americas believed that the destruction of native icons was a precondition to conversion. See Tozzer, *Landa's Relación*, pp. 77–78, 108, 110; P. Borges, *Métodos*

misionales, pp. 248–81; T. Motolinía, *History of the Indians of New Spain,* pp. 243–53, 275–78; Ortiz, *The Tewa World,* pp. 93–137.

98. Niethammer, *Daughters of the Earth,* p. 213. Testimony of Ginés de Herrera Horta, 1601, *OD,* vol. 2, pp. 644–45. *NCE,* p. 257.

99. *NCE,* pp. 257, 249; Sánchez, *De sancto matrimonii sacramento,* bk. 9, dispute 16, q. 1, quoted in Flandrin, "Contraception, Marriage," p. 38.

100. Declaration of Fray Nicolás de Chávez, September 18, 1660, AGN-INQ 587:34.

101. Scholes, *Troublous Times,* pp. 15–17, 64–66 and "Church and State," p. 155.

102. *BM,* p. 28; *PIR,* pp. 170–71.

103. J. Sando, "Jémez Pueblo," *HNAI,* vol. 9, pp. 418–29; Kubler (1972), pp. 82–85; Zárate de Salmerón, *Relaciones,* passim. Schroeder, "Pueblos Abandoned in Historic Times," pp. 236–55. The mission typology used here comes from Kubler (1972), pp. 16–17.

104. *RBM,* p. 212. *Summa Theologica,* Question 56: article 3, quoted in S. Gudeman, "The Compadrazgo," p. 49. *CF,* p. 93. *RBM,* p. 219; Scholes, "Documents," p. 199.

105. Mendieta, *Historia Eclesiastica Indiana,* Lib. 3, chp. 28, 91 quoted in P. Barth, *Franciscan Education,* p. 198. I owe much to R. Trexler's brilliant analysis of Christianization in sixteenth-century New Spain for this discussion. See Trexler, "From the Mouths of Babes." The qualities of childhood and adolescence deemed saintly are lucidly discussed in Weinstein and Bell, *Saints and Society,* pp. 19–72; M. Goodich, "Childhood and Adolescence."

106. Ricard, *Spiritual Conquest,* pp. 98–101; McGarry, "Educational Methods"; Canedo, *Evangelización y Conquista,* pp. 169–80. Mendieta, *Historia Eclesiástica Indiana,* vol. 3, pp. 54–105; Foster, ed. and trans., *Motolinía's History,* pp. 243–57; Trexler, "From the Mouths of Babes," pp. 115–35.

107. *RNM,* p. 186.

108. Declarations of the Indians of Taos, October 30, 1638, AGN-INQ 338-22:441–42. Indians were also punished in this manner during the eighteenth century. See SA 8: 133–145. To be buggered is a humiliation equated with emasculation in the gender ideologies of many cultures. See Bullough, "Homosexuality as Submissive Behavior." Millett makes a similar point concerning heterosexual sodomy in *Sexual Politics,* pp. 12–21.

109. *BM,* p. 36.

110. *RBM,* pp. 218, 219.

111. Testimony of Fray Juan de Talaban, 1668, in Scholes, "Documents," p. 199; Petition of Fray Juan de Prada, 1638, *HD,* p. 108.

St. Thomas Aquinas expressed the origin of such maternal symbolism in the *Summa Theologica*: "the child while in the mother's womb receives nourishment not independently, but through the nourishment of its mother, so also children before the use of reason, being as it were in the womb of their mother the Church, receive salvation not by their own act, but by the act of the Church. . . . *The Church, our mother, offers her maternal mouth for her children, that they may imbibe the sacred mysteries.*" Question 68: article 9, quoted in Gudeman, "The Compadrazgo," p. 69 (emphasis in the original). A similar idea is also expressed in the Franciscan novitiate manuals which defined instruction as "the milk which Our Mother [the Church] gives her children." *Instrucción*, preface, n.p.

The popular New Mexican devotions to the Sacred Heart of Jesus and to Christ's Precious Blood stemmed from these feminine maternal images of Christ and the Church. To understand their symbolism we must look at the equivalences drawn in medieval physiology between blood and milk. During pregnancy a fetus was sustained by its mother's blood, in infancy it was suckled on her milk; blood and milk were thus deemed equivalent substances. The soul underwent a developmental cycle akin to Christ's. The infant soul like the infant Christ was weaned on milk. The experience of the adult Christ was the blood of the crucifixion; so for the adult soul. Through the interchangeability of blood and milk Christ nourished souls with his blood, thus giving us images of the Sacred Heart, a pierced heart either suspended by itself in space or radiating in Christ's chest, yielding blood as humanity's nutrient. On this point, consult C. Bynum, *Jesus as Mother*, pp. 132–33. The devotion to Christ's wounds is also closely linked to these ideas.

112. For cases of the friars acting as advocates for women seeking payment for sex, see *HD*, p. 184; AGN-INQ, 587-1: 19, 26, 60, 64, 70, 140. On women cleaning altar linens see *RBM*, p. 148.

113. T. Steele, *Santos and Saints* (Santa Fe, 1974), pp. 181, 183, 187; Wroth, *Christian Images*, pp. 56, 61–63, 78, 99, 101, plates 5, 7, 28, 31, 56, 69.

114. Simmons, *Witchcraft in the Southwest*, p. 89.

115. *RBM*, p. 78. *BM*, p. 27; *RBM*, p. 70.

116. Testimony of Tomé Domínguez, May 21, 1661, AGN-INQ 593: 17.

117. *RBM*, p. 102.

118. *RBM*, pp. 102, 65, 215; Spell, "Music Training"; Spiess, "Instruments in the Missions," and "Benavides and Church Music." On mission education see AASF-LD 53: 153–56 and 53: 108–114; SA 21: 535–42; Matson and Fontana, eds. and trans., *Friar Brigas Reports to the King"*; McGarry, "Educational Methods"; Barth, *Franciscan Education*.

119. Fray Alonso de Molina, *Doctrina Christiana*, CF, pp. 29–74.

120. *CF*, p. 59. Spicer, *Cycles of Conquest*, pp. 290–91.

121. *CF*, p. 59. Forbes, *Apache, Navaho and Spaniard*, p. 96; *OD*, pp. 643–57. On ritual dances see Warman, *La danza*; M. Kirk, *Dancing with Creation*; Karath and Garcia, *Music and Dance*; Champe, *The Matachines Dance*. *CF*, p. 58; Ricard, *The Spiritual Conquest of Mexico*, pp. 176–206.

122. Dussel, *History of the Church*, pp. 64–70.

123. Saint Bonaventure, *The Life of Saint Francis*, pp. 182, 214. Defouri, *The Martyrs of New Mexico*, pp. 8–9.

124. *NCE*, pp. 280, 157; *RBM*, p. 87. *RNM*, p. 197. Schroeder and Matson, *A Colony on the Move*, p. 93.

125. *RBM*, p. 53; *TM*, vol. 3, p. 261. Tedlock, "Prayer Stick Sacrifice at Zuñi."

126. McCrossan, *The Role of the Church*; Stark, *Music of the Spanish Folk*

Plays; A. Espinosa, *The Folklore of Spain*, pp. 201–13; Pazos, "El Teatro Franciscano"; Revello, "Orígenes del teatro religioso"; Trexler, "We Think, They Act," pp. 202–3; Wachtel, *The Vision of the Vanquished*, passim.; Grimes, *Symbol and Conquest*.

127. *RBM*, p. 214. Scholes, "Documents," pp. 196–97. The Taos Indian woman's comment was mentioned to me by Professor Sylvia Rodríguez.

128. Campa, *Spanish Religious Folktheatre*, vol. 2, p. 8. On the nativity plays, see Munro, "The Nativity Plays of New Mexico"; C. Martin, "The Survival of Medieval Religious Drama," pp. 120–40; T. Pearce, "The New Mexican Shepherd's Play," *Western Folklore* 15(1956): 77–88; WPA 5-5-3 No. 16 and 5-5-3 No. 26; Lucero-White, "Los Pastores de Las Vegas"; Rapp, "Pastores." Montezuma's acceptance of Christianity and baptism are memorialized in numerous myths and dramas that have no basis in fact. One suspects that the story was fabricated by the friars to facilitate Indian conversions, for when a monarch or chief accepted Christianity, his subjects and retainers usually followed. Montezuma's failure to accept baptism has been exhaustively studied by Ramirez, "Bautismo de Moteuhzoma II." The dance dramas inspired by Montezuma's baptism can be studied in Champe, *The Matachines Dance*; Kurath, "The Origin of the Pueblo Indian Matachines"; Robb, "The Matachines Dance."

129. *PIR*, pp. 543, 896.

130. Pelikan, *Jesus Through the Ages*, p. 95.

131. *HNM*, p. 110. No complete description of Holy Week services in seventeenth-century New Mexico exists. This account is speculative, based on a compilation of numerous references. Those interested in lenten penitential practices in New Mexico should consult Weigle, *A Penitente Bibliography*, and the nineteenth-century journals of Gregg, *Commerce of the Prairies*, p. 181, and W. Davis, *El Gringo*, p. 346. Also illuminating for comparative purposes are Herrero, *La Semana Santa en Madrid*; Carballo, *Glorias religiosas de Sevilla*; Llompart, "Desfile iconográfico de penitentes españoles" and "Penitencias y penitentes"; Carreras y Candi, *Folklore y costumbres de España*, vol. 3, pp. 507–72. Death carts were common in seventeenth-century Spanish Good Friday processions. See Gonzales de León, *Historia crítica*, p. 189; Stark, "The Origin of the Penitente Death Cart"; Steele, "The Death Cart." On St. Sebastian's cult among the Maya see Bricker, *The Indian Christ*, esp. pp. 143–48; Zimmerman, "The Cult of the Cross"; Nash, "The Passion Play." The central Mexican devotion to St. Sebastian is examined by Fray Agustín Dávila Padilla, *Historia de la Fundación*, vol. 2, pp. 560–66. On the New Mexican St. Sebastian cult see Boyd, *Popular Arts of Spanish New Mexico*, pp. 462–64; Weigle, "Ghostly Flagellants and Doña Sebastiana." H. Thurston and D. Attwater, eds. *Butler's Lives of the Saints* (New York, 1956) vol. 1, pp. 129–30.

New Mexican penitential songs can be studied in Rael, *The New Mexican Alabado*; Ralliere, *Colección de cánticos espirituales* and *Cánticos espirituales con música*; A. Espinosa, "Romances españoles tradicionales."

132. Hearing against Nicolás de Aguilar, May 11, 1663, AGN-INQ 512: 99.

133. "Penitente Papers," Jean Bassett Johnson Papers, Bancroft Library (Berkeley, California), p. 16; Hernández, "Cactus Whips and Wooden Crosses"; Gougaud, *Devotional and Ascetic Practices*, pp. 187–91.

134. Declaration of Fray Nicolas de Villar, September 27, 1661, AGN-INQ 596: 14; McCrossan, *The Role of the Church*, p. 144; Steele, trans., *Holy Week in Tomé*, pp. 128–52. A statue of the *Santo Entierro* is still found in Santa Cruz. See *La Iglesia de Santa Cruz*, pp. 54, 95; J. E. Espinosa, *Saints in the Valleys*, plate 32; Kubler, *Religious Architecture of New Mexico*, plate 112. Similar *Santo Entierro* coffins exist in many colonial Mexican churches. See Rozière, *México*, plates 111, 116, 118, 119, 121.

135. The Maya used ritual knowledge very similarly and I have learned much about their understanding of Christianity from Clendinnen, *Ambivalent Conquests*, pp. 185–87.

136. *RNM*, p. 100. *OD*, p. 664; *RBM*, p. 44. *RBM*, p. 217.

137. *HNM*, p. 110. *RNM*, pp. 72, 75, 77, 79. Wroth, *Christian Images*, pp. 56, 149; Rozière, *México*, plate 25.

138. Declaration of Fray Benito de la Natividad, May 17, 1661, AGN-INQ 573:100.

139. Lummis, *The Land of Poco Tiempo*, p. 68; Rael, *The New Mexican Alabado*, pp. 45, 47; Steele, *Holy Week in Tomé*, p. 74.

140. Fray Francisco de los Angeles, "Obedience and Instruction given to Fray Martín de Valencia and his Twelve Companions . . . 1523," in Chávez, ed. and trans., *The Oroz Codex*, pp. 347–53. *RBM*, p. 66.

141. Wroth, *Christian Images*, plates 37, 65, 76, 95, 98, 137, 153, 164, 198, 191; J. Espinosa, *Saints in the Valleys*, plates 12, 35, 40, 46. On the significance of Christ's genitals in Christian iconography see Steinberg, *The Sexuality of Christ*; Bynum, "The Body of Christ"; Gallop, "Psychoanalytic Criticism." *RBM*, p. 44; *RNM*, pp. 99–101; *OD*, p. 664; Bourke, *The Snake Dance*; Fewkes, "The Snake Ceremonials at Walpi"; León, "El Culto del Falo"; Lejeal, "Rites Phalliques."

142. On penis laceration in Mesoamerica see I. Clendinnen, "Yucatec Maya Women and the Spanish Conquest," *Journal of Social History* 12(1982), pp. 427–42; Tozzer, *Landa's Relación*, p. 114; P. Furst, "Fertility, Vision Quest and Auto Sacrifice," p. 183; Joralemon, "Ritual Blood Sacrifice." On blood as a nutrient in Christian thought see Bynum, "Fast, Feast, and Flesh," *Holy Feast and Holy Fast*, and *Jesus as Mother*, pp. 115–63. Bell makes a similar point in *Holy Anorexia*.

143. Spiro, *Oedipus in the Trobriands*, pp. 6–7.

144. Amon Carter Museum of Western Art, *Santos: An Exhibition of the Religious Folk Art of New Mexico* (Fort Worth, 1964), plate 8; Wroth, *Christian Images*, plates 15, 34, 71, 72, 88, 92, 115, 140, 159, 169, 171; J. E. Espinosa, *Saints in the Valleys*, plates 17, 18. On the cult of the Blessed Virgin Mary in Europe, and particularly her relationship to pagan earth goddesses, see Sharborough, "The Cult of the Mother in Europe"; Berger, *The Goddess Obscured*; Christian, *Apparitions*, pp. 21–22.

145. Phythian-Adams, "Ceremony and the Citizen," pp. 70–71; Bayle, *El Culto de Santísimo*, pp. 193–94. *MNM*, p. 19 n26; Scholes and Adams, "Inventories of Church Furnishings," pp. 27–38; *RBM*, pp. 109–124; Scholes, *Troublous Times*, pp. 21–22, 32 n11. F. Very, *The Spanish Corpus Christi Procession*; Motolinía, *History of the Indians of New Spain*, pp. 101–20. Kantorowicz, *The King's Two Bodies*, pp. 207, 232; Bossy, "The Mass," p. 59. Assessing the long evolutionary changes in the meaning and significance of the Feast of Corpus Christi, Ernst H. Kantorowicz and John Bossy have both argued that in the course of the seventeenth and eighteenth centuries the socially integrative power of the Holy Eucharist was slowly transferred from the feast of Corpus Christi to the rituals of monarchy and secular community. By the early 1800s too, the public power of the host had been eclipsed by very personal and asocial mysticism of individual communicants.

146. Ortiz, *The Tewan World*, passim.

147. *RBM*, p. 34. L. Bloom, "Spain's Investment." See Table 2.1 and *RBM*, p. 34. Petition of Fray Juan de Prada, 1638, *HD*, p. 108. Scholes, "Church and State," p. 324.

148. R. MacMullen, *Christianizing the Roman Empire A.D. 100–400* (New Haven, 1984), p. 5.

149. Scholes, "The Supply Service," passim; *MNM*, pp. 41, 51, 83, 108.

Chapter 3

1. Ullmann, *A History of Political Thought*, pp. 12–13; Ozment, *The Age of Reform*, pp. 135–78.

2. J. Mecham, *Church and State in Latin America* (Chapel Hill, N.C., 1966), pp. 3–12; Farriss, *Crown and Clergy in Colonial Mexico*, pp. 1–28.

3. The provisions of the *patronato* in America are spelled out in Pope Julius II's bull *Universalis ecclesiae*, which can be found in Hernandez, ed., *Colección de bulas*, vol. 1, pp. 24–26. Góngora, *Studies in the Colonial History*, pp. 119–24.

4. Phelan, "Authority and Flexibility," pp. 47–65.

5. Focher, *Itinerario del Misionero en América*, chaps. 11–12, pp. 92–97. Mendieta, *Historia Eclesiástica Indiana*, bk. 1, chaps. 1–4, pp. 13–28. See also Sylvest, *Motifs of Franciscan Mission Theory*, pp. 69–71; Phelan, "Authority and Flexibility," esp. pp. 7–16.

6. A copy of *Omnimoda* and the Quiñones Instruction can be found in Mendieta, *Historia Eclesiástica Indiana*, pp. 30–35, 40–43.

7. "Act of Possession and Submission," 1598, *OD*, pp. 329–31.

8. Kantorowicz, *The King's Two Bodies*, pp. 193–272; Scholes, "Church and State," pp. 328–29.

9. Ibid.; C. Cutter, *The Protector de Indios*, p. 7; Canedo, *Evangelización y Conquista*, p. 97. The European conception of the body politic is best studied in Duby, *The Three Orders*, and in W. Sewell, "Etats, Corps et Ordres: Some Notes on the Social Vocabulary of the French Old Regime," in *Sozialgeschichte Heute*

(Festschrift für Hans Rosenberg zum 70. Geburtstag) (Göttingen, 1974), pp. 49–68. Some years ago Lyle McAlister proposed without much evidence that Europe's three estates (priests, warriors, laborers) were transmuted in New Spain into three racial categories: whites (Spaniards), castes (mixed-bloods), and Indians. Though Professor McAlister's thesis is certainly plausible, he offers no descriptions of a polity so imagined. Glaringly absent in his schemata are the *oratores*, men who pray. See McAlister, "Social Structure and Social Change in New Spain."

10. On the prelacy see Mendieta, *Historia Eclesiástica Indiana*, vol. 2, pp. 32–34; Sylvest, *Motifs of Franciscan Mission Theory*, pp. 77–81. On the Inquisition see Fray Estevan de Perea to Inquisition, Oct. 30, 1633, AGN-INQ 380:231. On the *Cruzada* see Chapman, *Colonial Hispanic America*, pp. 159–60; Scholes, "Church and State," pp. 16–17.

11. West, "The Right of Asylum in New Mexico."

12. Fray Estevan de Perea, 1632, *RBM*, p. 210. S. MacCormack, *Art and Ceremony in Late Antiquity* (Berkeley, 1981), and "Change and Continuity in Late Antiquity: The Ceremony of *Adventus*," *Historia* 21(1971), pp. 721–52. Entrance of Benavides into Santa Fe, *RBM*, pp. 127–29, 94.

13. Duby, *The Three Orders*, pp. 14, 57; de Egaña, *La Teoría*, pp. 20–47.

14. Solórzano Pereira, *Política Indiana* (Madrid, 1776); A. Ribadeneyra, *Manual Compendio*. "Act of Possession and of Submission," 1598, *OD*, pp. 329–31. Farriss, *Crown and Clergy*, pp. 28–38.

15. Scholes, "Civil Government and Society"; Simmons, *Spanish Government in New Mexico*, pp. 159–92.

16. Simmons, *Spanish Government in New Mexico*, pp. 17–20, 66–68, 176–80; C. Cutter, *The Protector de Indios*, passim; Borah, *Justice by Insurance*.

17. Phelan, "Authority and Flexibility," p. 52; Simmons, *Spanish Government in New Mexico*, pp. 68–69.

18. Declaration of Marcelo de Espinosa, *OD*, p. 643. Why the men of distinction returned to New Spain can be studied in the Declarations of Alonso Sánchez, Bernabe de las Casas and Gregorio Cessar, 1601, *OD*, pp. 683–89.

19. Oñate Contract, *OD*, pp. 45–56, *HNM*, p. 274.

20. R. Konetzke, "La Formación"; Góngora, *Studies in the Colonial History*, p. 112; Ladd, *The Mexican Nobility*, pp. 13–23.

21. Góngora, *Studies in the Colonial History*, p. 106.

22. Salazar Inspection, *OD*, pp. 199–308.

23. Chávez, *Origins of New Mexico Families*, pp. 23, 41; Scholes, "The First Decade of the Inquisition," pp. 225, 223. Scholes, "Church and State," p. 308.

24. Scholes, "Civil Government and Society," p. 97.

25. Zárate de Salmerón, *Relaciones*, p. 56. Velasco to Philip III, December 17, 1608, *OD*, p. 1068.

26. Salazar Inspection, *OD*, pp. 247, 252. *OD*, pp. 477–79, 615, 796, 806–7.

27. AGN-HIST 25-3:50–61. *BM*, pp. 23–24. Letter of Estevan de Perea, October 30, 1633, *HD*, p. 130. *RPI*, vol. 1, pp. 142, 146, 153.

28. Zavala, *Los Esclavos Indios*, pp. 179–350. Letter of Alonso Sánchez, February 28, 1599, *OD*, p. 425.

29. Oñate Contract, *OD*, p. 509; Peralta Instructions, *OD*, pp. 1088–89. Lansing B. Bloom, "The Vargas Encomienda," p. 370. *RBM*, pp. 168–77. Testimony of Governor Peñalosa, June 25, 1665, *HD*, p. 258. Declaration of Fray Salvador Guerra, September 22, 1662, *HD*, p. 250. The history of the *encomienda* in central Mexico can be studied in L. Simpson, *The Encomienda in New Spain*. Also enlightening is Góngora, *Studies in the Colonial History*, pp. 127–49.

30. Petition of Fray Juan de Prada Report, September 26, 1638, *HD*, p. 110; Petition of Francisco Martínez de Baeza, February 12, 1639, *HD*, p. 120. Snow, "A Note on Encomienda Economics," pp. 350–51.

31. Fray Martín de Ojacastro to king, October 4, 1543, quoted in Canedo, *Evangelización y Conquista*, p. 97. Ibid. On New Mexican *mercedes* see Van Ness and Van Ness, eds., *Spanish and Mexican Land Grants*; Westphall, *Mercedes Reales*; Leonard, *The Role of the Land Grant*.

32. C. Cutter, *The Protector de Indios*, pp. 5–40.

33. Taylor, "Land and Water Rights"; Keleher, "Law of the New Mexico Land Grant"; M. Jenkins, "Spanish Land Grants in the Tewa Area" and "The Baltasar Baca 'Grant'."

34. Viceregal decree of January 29, 1609, *OD*, pp. 1076–77. Viceroy to king, May 27, 1620, *OD*, pp. 1139–40. *BM*, pp. 23–24.

35. Petition of Fray Juan de la Prada, September 26, 1638, *HD*, p. 108. Petition of Governor Francisco Martínez de Baeza, 1639, *HD*, p. 118.

36. *HD*, p. 324. Letter of Fray Francisco de Ayeta, 1679, *HD*, p. 299. Muster, September 29, 1680, *RPI*, vol. 1, pp. 134–53.

37. *RBM*, p. 68. Margill de Jesús quoted in Boxer, *The Church Militant*, p. 74. See also *BM*, pp. 23–24.

38. Relación de Fray Francisco Pérez Guerta, AGN-INQ 316:152.

39. Scholes, "Church and State," p. 39.

40. Pérez Guerta quoted in Scholes, "Church and State," pp. 42–44. Auto of Santa Fe Cabildo, AGN-PI 1639, 35-5:3.

41. Auto of Santa Fe Cabildo, AGN-PI 1639, 35-5:5. Scholes, "Church and State," pp. 45–47.

42. Declaration of Fray Pedro de Haro de la Cueba, August 22, 1621, AGN-INQ 356:286v; Declaration of Fray Pedro de Ortega, September 2, 1621, AGN-INQ 356:288v. Declaration of Fray Estevan de Perea, January 26, 1626, AGN-INQ 356:264; Declaration of Fray Cristóbal de Quiros, September 3, 1621, AGN-INQ 356:20v. Declaration of Fray Pedro de Ortega, January 27, 1626, AGN-INQ 356:265v; Declaration of Fray Estevan de Perea, August 18, 1621, AGN-INQ 356:282. AGN-INQ 356:256–317 passim. Declaration of Fray Estevan de Perea, August 18, 1621, AGN-INQ 356:282. Declaration of Fray Pedro Zambrano, August 18, 1621, AGN-INQ 356:282; Declaration of Francisco Pérez Granillo, April 20, 1626, AGN-INQ 356:280.

43. Scholes, "Church and State," p. 99. Letter of Fray Juan de Prada, January 15, 1644, quoted in Forbes, *Apache, Navaho, and Spaniard*, p. 131. Report of Fray Pedro Serrano, 1761, *HD*, p. 485.

44. *RBM*, pp. 15–16; Kubler, *Religious Architecture of New Mexico*, p. 8.

45. C. Lange, "Relations of the Southwest with the Plains and Great Basin," *HNAI*, vol. 9, pp. 201–6; Kenner, *New Mexican-Plains Indian Relations*, pp. 13–16.

46. Scholes, "Church and State," pp. 300, 327.

47. Ibid., p. 301.

48. Scholes, "Church and State," p. 324. Testimony of Francisco Salazar, July 5, 1641, quoted in Forbes, *Apache, Navaho, and Spaniard*, p. 132.

49. Petition of Fray Juan de Prada, September 26, 1638, *HD*, p. 108. Testimony of Fray Tomás Manso, 1644, in Scholes, "Church and State," p. 324. Spicer, *Cycles of Conquest*, pp. 290–91.

50. J. Forbes, "The Appearance of the Mounted Indian."

51. Scholes, "Church and State," pp. 324, 332–33.

52. Scholes, "Church and State," pp. 94–95, 242–48.

53. Santa Fe Cabildo to Viceroy, February 14, 1639, *HD*, p. 71.

54. Opinion of Santa Fe Cabildo, February 14, 1639, *HD*, pp. 62, 67.

55. Scholes, "Church and State," p. 328. Letter of Fray Juan de Salas to Franciscan Provincial, September 29, 1643 in Scholes, "Church and State," p. 94.

56. Ibid., pp. 305–6.

57. Opinion of Fiscal Pedro Melián, cited in Forbes, *Apache, Navaho, and Spaniard*, p. 135.

58. Scholes, "Church and State," pp. 323, 324.

59. Ibid., pp. 337–47.

60. Scholes, "Church and State," pp. 78–85.

61. Ibid., pp. 85–87.

62. Petition of Fray Juan de Prada, 1638, *HD*, pp. 106–14; Forbes, *Apache, Navaho, and Spaniard*, pp. 139–41.

63. Declaration of Diego López, December 22, 1681, *RPI*, p. 299. Declaration of Juan Domínguez de Mendoza, December 20, 1681, *RPI*, p. 266. Declaration of Pedro Naranjo, December 19, 1681, *RPI*, pp. 245–46.

64. Testimony of Fray Nicolás de Freitas, January 25, 1661, AGN-INQ 587:1, 65–70.

65. Testimony of Fray Joseph de Espeleta, March 2, 1660, AGN-INQ 587:1–3; Testimony of Fray Juan Ramírez, May 14, 1660, AGN-INQ 587:10; Scholes, *Troublous Times*, pp. 22, 32. Feast of the Blessed Sacrament described in Foster, ed. and trans., *Motolinia's History*, pp. 100–104.

66. Declaration of Fray Juan Ramírez, September 1661, AGN-INQ 593: 249, 255. Reply of Mendizábal to Charges, June 16, 1663, AGN-INQ 594: 130–31.

67. Declaration of Fray Juan Ramírez, September 1661, AGN-INQ 593:250. Scholes, *Troublous Times*, p. 45.

68. Declaration of Fray Juan de Ramírez, September 1661, AGN-INQ 593: 249–53; Scholes, *Troublous Times*, pp. 28, 111. Fray Miguel de Sacristan to Custodian, June 16, 1660, AGN-INQ 587:18; Fray Nicolás de Villar to Custodian, June 14, 1660, AGN-INQ 587:29; Declaration of Fray Nicolás de Chávez,

September 18, 1660, AGN-INQ 587:37; Declaration of Nicolás de Aguilar, May 8, 1663, AGN-INQ 587:223. Declaration of Fray Nicolás de Freitas, January 24, 1661, AGN-INQ 587:85; Declaration of Miguel de Noriega, September 22, 1661, AGN-INQ 593:51; Mendizábal's Reply to Charges, June 1663, AGN-INQ 593:135. Ratification of Miguel Noriega, May 1661, AGN-INQ 593:136.

69. Declaration of Fray Nicolás de Chávez, September 18, 1660, AGN-INQ 587:37; Declaration of Fray García de San Francisco, May 9, 1661, AGN-INQ 593:99. Letter of Fray Nicolás de Freitas, June 18, 1660, AGN-INQ 587:26.

70. Letter of Fray Miguel de Sacristan, June 16, 1660, AGN-INQ 587:22. Declaration of Diego Trujillo, September 22, 1661, AGN-INQ 593:56. Declaration of Fray Nicolás de Freitas, January 24, 1661, AGN-INQ 587:84.

71. Letter of Fray García de San Francisco, December 10, 1660, AGN-INQ 587:116; Letter of Fray Alonso de Posadas, May 23, 1661, AGN-INQ 587:162; Declaration of Nicolás de Aguilar, January 17, 1664, in AGN-INQ 512:139. Letters of Fray Miguel de Sacristan, 1660, AGN-INQ 587:22; Fray Salvador Guerra, 1660, AGN-INQ 587:106; Fray Alonso de Posadas, 1661, AGN-INQ 587:162. Letter of Fray Salvador Guerra, November 20, 1660, AGN-INQ 587:106; Mendizábal Reply to Charges, June 1663, AGN-INQ 573:238. Declaration of Tomé Domínguez, May 21, 1661, AGN-INQ 573:16. Mendizábal Reply to Charges, June 1663, AGN-INQ 573:230; Declaration of Juan Muñoz Polanco, September 1661, AGN-INQ 573:60.

72. Declaration of Esteban Clemente, November 30, 1660, AGN-INQ 587:123. Declaration of Francisco Valencia, May 24, 1661, AGN-INQ 573:23. Declaration of Esteban Clemente, November 30, 1660, AGN-INQ 587:123; Testimony of Fray Nicolás de Freitas, January 24, 1661, AGN-INQ 587:76.

73. Declaration of Fray Nicolás de Chávez, September 18, 1660, AGN-INQ 587:36.

74. Declaration of Fray Nicolás de Freitas, May 8, 1663, AGN-INQ 587:222. AGN-INQ 587:222–23; AGN-INQ 593:99; AGN-INQ 594:167–68; AGN-INQ 587:123; AGN-INQ 587:19.

75. AGN-INQ 388-22:440–42.

76. Declaration of Fray Nicolás de Freitas, February 21, 1671, AGN-INQ 587:82.

77. Letters of Fray Salvador de Guerra, November 20, 1660 and December 1, 1660, AGN-INQ 587:106–121; Declaration of Fray Nicolás de Chávez, September 18, 1661, AGN-INQ 587:35v.

78. Declaration of Miguel Noriega, September 22, 1661, AGN-INQ 593:50–51. Testimony of Nicolás de Aguilar, May 8, 1663, AGN-INQ 587:219–20. Declaration of Mendizábal, June 5, 1660, AGN-INQ 587:165.

79. Reply of Mendizábal to Charges, June 1663, AGN-INQ 594:174–75.

80. Declaration of Andrés Hurtado, September 1661, AGN-INQ 593:251.

81. Scholes, *Troublous Times*, pp. 40–53, 143.

82. Ibid., pp. 128n, 207–44. AGN-INQ 590:513; AGN-INQ 600:155.

83. Scholes, *Troublous Times*, pp. 12–13. Declaration of Nicolás de Aguilar,

May 11, 1663, AGN-INQ 512:99. Inga Clendinnen found a similar pattern of violence at the Franciscan mission of Yucatán. See "Disciplining the Indians."

84. St. Bernard, "Canticle of Canticles," 85:13, quoted in Whitson, *Mysticism and Ecumenism*, pp. 84–85.

85. J. M. Espinosa, *Crusaders of the Rio Grande*, p. 15. Zárate Salmerón, *Relaciones*, pp. 99–100. *TM*, vol. 4, pp. 171–73.

86. *RBM*, pp. 140, 142. María de Jesús Coronel's life is best studied in H. Thurston, *Surprising Mystics*, pp. 122–32; "Sor María de Agreda," *Diccionario Enciclopédico Hispano-Americano* (Barcelona, 1887), vol. 1, p. 603; M. Agreda, *Cartas de la Madre Sor María de Agreda y del Rey Don Felipe IV* (Madrid, 1885–86), 2 vols. Mother María's *Mystical City of God* was widely read in Europe and America, and was published in more than a hundred editions. This book is an account of the life of the Blessed Virgin Mary as dictated to Mother María by the Virgin herself, including her thoughts while still in St. Anne's womb and details of St. Anne and St. Joachim's sex lives. For these heterodox ideas Mother María was prosecuted by the Inquisition. See her *Mystica Ciudad de Dios* (Madrid, 1742), vol. 1, pp. 10, 240–54, 350–66.

87. *TM*, vol. 4, pp. 228–32. Defouri, *The Martyrs of New Mexico*, pp. 53–58.

88. *RBM*, pp. 50–56, 77, 219, 221; Bandelier, "Fray Juan de Padilla"; Defouri, *The Martyrs of New Mexico*, pp. 1–24, 26–27. *TM*, vol. 3, p. 264. *TM*, vol. 4, pp. 174–75. For a comparative analysis of Christian martyrdoms in Japan, see Boxer, *The Christian Century in Japan*, pp. 340–57, and Elison, *Deus Destroyed*.

89. Petition of Fray Francisco de Ayeta, May 10, 1679, *HD*, p. 302; *RBM*, p. 292.

90. *TM*, vol. 4, pp. 286–87; *RBM*, p. 292; Defouri, *The Martyrs of New Mexico*, pp. 35–37; Petition of Fray Francisco de Ayeta, May 10, 1679, *HD*, p. 298. Various authors—Vetancurt, Benavides, Defouri—claim that Fray Pedro de Avila y Ayala was killed at Hawikuh. Fray Francisco de Ayeta said that Fra Pedro died at Abó, and since the two men were in New Mexico at the same time, I have accepted his account as true. *TM*, vol. 3, pp. 274, 281–82.

91. Declarations of Luís de Quintana and Diego López, 1681, *RPI*, vol. 2, pp. 289–90, 300. Declaration of Diego López, 1681, *RPI*, vol. 2, p. 301.

92. Declaration of Jerónimo, a Tigua Indian, January 1, 1682, *RPI*, vol. 2, p. 361. Declaration of Pedro García, a Tagno Indian, August 25, 1680, *RPI*, vol. 1, pp. 24–25. Declaration of Pedro Naranjo, a Queres Indian, December 19, 1681, *RPI*, vol. 2, pp. 246–47.

93. Declaration of Pedro Naranjo, a Queres Indian, 1681, *RPI*, vol. 2, p. 246.

94. Ibid.; Declaration of Luís de Quintana, 1681, *RPI*, vol. 2, p. 295; J. Sando, "The Pueblo Revolt," *HNAI*, vol. 9, 195; A. Chávez, "Pohe-yemo's Representative."

95. Declaration of Luís de Quintana, 1681, *RPI*, vol. 2, p. 295; Otermín Autos, August 9, 1680, *RPI*, vol. 1, pp. 4–5.

96. Otermín Autos, August 9–10, 1680, *RPI*, vol. 1, pp. 1–6.

97. Declaration of Pedro Hidalgo, August 10, 1680, *RPI*, vol. 1, pp. 6–7. Otermín Autos, August 10, 1680, *RPI*, vol. 1, pp. 7–9.

98. Opinion of Cabildo, September 14, 1680, *RPI*, vol. 1, p. 120. Letter of Fray Francisco de Ayeta, 1679, *HD*, p. 299.

99. Otermín Autos, October 9, 1680, *RPI*, vol. 1, pp. 194–95; Muster, September 29, 1680, *RPI*, vol. 1, pp. 134–53.

100. Otermín to Fray Francisco de Ayeta, September 8, 1680, *RPI*, vol. 1, pp. 98–101.

101. Declaration of Josephe, Spanish-speaking Indian, December 19, 1681, *RPI*, vol. 2, pp. 239–40; Otermín Autos, August 13–20, 1680, *RPI*, vol. 1, p. 13. Otermín Autos, August 13–21, 1680, *RPI*, vol. 1, p. 15. Certification of departure, August 21, 1680, *RPI*, vol. 1, p. 19.

102. Opinion of the Santa Fe Cabildo, October 3, 1680, *RPI*, vol. 1, pp. 177–78.

103. Sariñana y Cuenca, *The Franciscan Martyrs*, p. 16; "Carta del Padre Fray Silvestre de Escalante," April 2, 1778, *DHNM*, pp. 305–324; J. Espinosa, *Crusaders of the Rio Grande*, pp. 19–20.

104. Scholes, "Civil Government," p. 96; *RPI*, vol. 1, pp. 21–65.

105. Declaration of Pedro Naranjo, a Queres Indian, December 19, 1681, *RPI*, vol. 2, p. 248.

106. Declaration of Pedro Naranjo, a Queres Indian, December 19, 1681, *RPI*, vol. 2, p. 248. Declaration of Juan, a Tegua Indian, December 18, 1681, *RPI*, vol. 2, p. 235. Declaration of Josephe, Spanish-speaking Indian, December 19, 1681, *RPI*, vol. 2, p. 239; Declaration of Juan Lorenzo, a Queres Indian, December 20, 1681, *RPI*, vol. 2, 251.

107. Declaration of Josephe, a Spanish-speaking Indian, and of Juan Lorenzo, a Queres Indian, December 19–20, 1681, *RPI*, vol. 2, pp. 239–40, 249–52. Declaration of Juan Lorenzo, a Queres Indian, December 20, 1681, *RPI*, vol. 2, p. 251.

108. Otermín Auto, September 13, 1680, *RPI*, vol. 1, 122. Declaration of Pedro Nanboa, an Indian, September 6, 1680, *RPI*, vol. 1, p. 61; Declaration of Pedro García, an Indian, September 6, 1680, *RPI*, vol. 1, p. 62.

109. Declaration of Josephe, Spanish-speaking Indian, December 19, 1681, and Declaration of Juan Lorenzo, a Queres Indian, December 20, 1681, *RPI*, vol. 2, pp. 239–40, 251. Declaration of Pedro Naranjo, a Queres Indian, December 19, 1681, *RPI*, vol. 2, pp. 245–47. Declaration of Juan Lorenzo, a Queres Indian, December 20, 1681, *RPI*, vol. 2, p. 251. Declaration of Pedro García, a Tano Indian, August 25, 1680, *RPI*, vol. 1, pp. 24–25. Declaration of Josephe, Spanish-speaking Indian, December 19, 1681, *RPI*, vol. 2, pp. 239–41.

110. Sierra Letter to Ayeta, September 4, 1680, *RPI*, vol. 1, p. 59. Letter of Friar Juan Alvarez, et al., to viceroy, October 15, 1680, *RPI*, vol. 1, pp. 203–4. Letter of Ayeta to viceroy, August 31, 1680, *RPI*, vol. 1, p. 53.

111. Sariñana y Cuenca, *The Franciscan Martyrs*, pp. 17–18. Staniforth, trans., *Early Christian Writings*, p. 106. I thank Professor Sabine MacCormack for bringing this document to my attention.

112. Scholes, "Documents," p. 195. The impact of the Pueblo Revolt on other Indian groups in northern New Spain is studied in Forbes, *Apache, Navaho, and Spaniard*, pp. 177–224. *RPI*, vol. 1, p. cxxi, and vol. 2, pp. 32–88, 153–83, 190–201.

113. March of the Army from El Paso to Isleta, 1681, *RPI*, vol. 2, pp. 209, 210–12.

114. Declaration of Juan, a Tigua Indian, December 27, 1681, *RPI*, vol. 2, p. 346. *RPI*, vol. 1, p. cxxxvii; Bancroft, *History of Arizona and New Mexico*, p. 185n.

115. Ibid., p. 186n.

116. Schroeder, "Rio Grande Ethnohistory," pp. 41–70.

Chapter 4

1. Stirling, *Origin Myth of Acoma*, pp. 10–13.

2. Vargas' banner mentioned in *FEV*, p. 59. Cortés', Oñate's and Vargas' devotion to Our Lady of Remedies is studied in J. M. Espinosa, "The Virgin of the Reconquest"; A. Chávez, *Our Lady of the Conquest* and "Nuestra Señora del Rosario."

3. *FEV*, p. 91.

4. *FEV*, pp. 96–97.

5. *FEV*, pp. 101–3.

6. J. M. Espinosa, *Crusaders of the Rio Grande*, pp. 114–35. A Spanish version of Don Carlos de Sigüenza y Góngora's *Mercurio Volante* can be found in *DHNM*, pp. 79–111. For an English edition see Leonard, ed. and trans., *The Mercurio Volante*.

7. J. M. Espinosa, *Crusaders of the Rio Grande*, pp. 149–50.

8. *DHNM*, pp. 351–55. It appears that after the Pueblo revolt, the truly zealous Franciscans in the Province of the Holy Gospel turned their attention to new mission fields. In the early 1700s the most challenging task was the Christianization of Texas's Indians, and indeed it is there during the first quarter of the eighteenth century that we find the full flowering of the Franciscan martyrdom tradition that we saw in New Mexico during the previous century.

9. *DHNM*, pp. 352–55; Bancroft, *History of Arizona and New Mexico*, pp. 204–6; J. M. Espinosa, *Crusaders of the Rio Grande*, pp. 136–62.

10. Jones, *Los Paisanos*, pp. 114–16.

11. Bannon, *The Spanish Borderlands*, pp. 92–107.

12. Ibid.

13. Tyler and Taylor, trans., "The Report of Fray Alonso de Posada"; Forbes, "The Appearance of the Mounted Indian"; Roe, "From Dogs to Horses."

14. F. McNitt, *Navajo Wars*, pp. 10–19; Spicer, *Cycles of Conquest*, pp. 211–13.

15. Moorhead, *The Presidio*.

16. AASF-LD 1813, 53:789.

17. *OD*, p. 50. Ladd, *The Mexican Nobility*.

18. Chávez, *Origins of New Mexico Families*, p. xii; AASF-DM Reels 60–79; SA 1790, 12:319–502.

19. On the prohibition of Indian slavery in the New Laws see Zavala, *Los Esclavos Indios*, pp. 107–14, 179–92, 223. The 1680 Compilation of the Laws of the Indies' restrictions on Indian slavery are in Law 1, Title 2, Book 6, and Laws 12, 13, 14, 16 of Book 6, *Recopilación de leyes de los reynos de las Indias* (Madrid, 1681). "Report of Fray Estevan de Perea, 1633," *HD*, p. 130.

20. *RPI*, vol. 1, p. 45; O. Patterson, *Slavery and Social Death*, p. 7.

21. J. Kelley, "Factors Involved in the Abandonment," pp. 384–85.

22. SA 1752, 8:1070–1105. *Recopilación*, Book VII, Laws 3 and 17. AGN-PI 102-8:282; AASF-LD 1716, 51:847; SA 1812, 17:554–57; AASF-LD 1807, 53:650–51. Report of Fray Pedro Serrano, 1761, *HD*, p. 487.

23. *MNM*, pp. 112, 252. "Informe de Fray Pedro Serrano," AGN-HIST 1761, 25-3:50–61.

24. McNitt, *Navajo Wars*, p. 79.

25. Horgan, *Centuries of Santa Fe*, p. 88. SA 1761, 9:410–44; SA 1761, 9:262–67. *HD*, p. 487. NCE, p. 306; Góngora, *Studies in the Colonial History*, p. 130.

26. Brugge, *Navajos in the Catholic Church Records*, pp. 30, 102–4. Morfi, "Desordenes en Nuevo Méjico, 1776," AGN-HIST 1776, 25-8:147; "Descripción de la Provincia, 1773," AGN-HIST 1774, 25-40:340; SA 1820, 20:419; Simmons, *Little Lion of the Southwest*, p. 34.

27. Brugge, *Navajos in the Catholic Church Records*, p. 104. AGN-PI 36-3:310–11; Simmons, "New Mexico's Smallpox Epidemic." Devastating droughts in 1779 and 1780 likewise drove some Pueblo and nomadic Indians into Spanish towns. See AGN-HIST 1779, 25-36:294–95; AGN-HIST 1780, 25-36:288.

28. AGN-HIST 1707, 25-4:62–63. AGN-PI 1761, 36-3:128–29. AGN-HIST 1792, 25-9:151. AGN-HIST 1750, 25-2:31.

29. AASF-BAPT 1:451–61, 472–78, 482–84, 494–502. The matrimonial investigations in the Archives of the Archdiocese of Santa Fe indicate that 997 of 13,204 persons married between 1693 and 1846 were "children of the church" at baptism, thus my 10 percent estimate.

30. Bandelier, *Final Report of Investigations*, part 1, pp. 141–42; *RBM*, p. 81.

31. This discussion of post-revolt Pueblo geography draws extensively on Dozier, *The Pueblo Indians*, pp. 63–67; Schroeder, "Rio Grande Ethnohistory," pp. 56–59; Simmons, "History of Pueblo-Spanish Relations," pp. 186–87.

32. *MNM*, p. 284.

33. Ortiz, *The Tewa World*, p. 69. Simmons, trans. and ed., *Father Juan Agustín de Morfi's Account*, p. 28.

34. Ortiz, *The Tewa World*, pp. 64–66.

35. AGN-PI 36-3:375; AGN-HIST 25-3:39–42; AGN-HIST 25-4:58–59.

36. Isleta Indians vs. Mariano Beitia, 1771, SA 10:662–86. See also Complaint of Santa Clara Indians against their governor, 1788, SA 12:50–54.

37. *FEV*, pp. 1–43, 202–3, 266; J. M. Espinosa, *Crusaders of the Rio Grande*, passim.

38. Much time and ink has been spent by modern anthropologists describing those traits that differentiate the highly acculturated Eastern Puebloans of the Rio Grande Basin and the Western Puebloans, who were on the margins of Spanish New Mexico, resisted colonization, and rather successfully retained their indigenous lifeways. These debates have been rather fruitless primarily because of the underlying assumption of a static and timeless social organization. Miring themselves in kinship terminologies and lists of dances performed here and there, anthropologists have failed to ask the basic historical question that would have explained the variations and patterns they found. What was the impact of the Spanish conquest and colonization across the Pueblo region? This is the question I have engaged throughout this book. For a summary of the Eastern-Western Pueblo debates see Eggan, *Social Organization of the Western Pueblos*. For an excellent discussion of moiety organization among the Tewa see Ortiz, *The Tewa World*.

39. *RPI*, vol. 2, pp. 239–40; E. Parsons, *Tewa Tales* (New York, 1926), p. 108; Parmentier, "The Pueblo Mythological Triangle."

40. SA 1793, 13:237–40.

41. Martin, "The Survival of Medieval Religious Drama in New Mexico," p. 110.

42. Scholes, *Troublous Times*, p. 69. *RBM*, p. 196. Defouri, *The Martyrs of New Mexico*, pp. 20, 30, 61–63. White, *The Acoma Indians*, p. 65. Stirling, *Origin Myth of the Acoma*, pp. 12–13. Ortiz, *The Tewa World*, pp. 47, 92.

43. Kubler, *Religious Architecture*, plates 79, 114, 129, 169, 190.

44. Kirk, "Little Santu of Cíbola," and "Introduction to Zuñi Fetishism"; Parsons, "Nativity Myth" and "Spanish Elements in the Kachina Cult."

45. Chacón to Viceroy, January 26, 1710, AGN-PI 36-3 quoted in Jones, *Pueblo Warriors*, pp. 83–84. Flores to Viceroy, January 20, 1714, and Real de Aguilar, January 23, 1714, both New Mexico Originals at the Bancroft Library as quoted in Kessell, *Kiva, Cross, and Crown*, pp. 313–14.

46. SA 4:841–84.

47. Jones, *Pueblo Warriors*, pp. 87–90. Kessell, *Kiva, Cross, and Crown*, pp. 316–20.

48. Steele, *Santos and Saints*, p. 169 and passim. The retable of San Procopio to which I refer is at the National Gallery of Art, Washington, D.C. See also White, "The Impersonation of Saints."

49. Boxer, *The Church Militant and Iberian Expansion, 1440–1770* (Baltimore, 1978), pp. 2–30; Mendieta, *Historia Eclesiástica Indiana*, bk 4, chap. 23, pp. 103–4.

50. Mendieta, *Historia Eclesiástica Indiana*, bk 3, chaps. 21–24; Bayle, *El Culto del Santísimo*, pp. 461–99; Acosta, *De Procuranda Indorum Salute*, pp. 581–83.

51. D. Cutter, trans., "An Anonymous Statistical Report"; Fray Andrés Varo, "Census of New Mexico, 1749," Biblioteca Nacional de México, Fondo Franciscano, Caja 28, ms 28/522.1; Josiah Gregg quoted in Bloom, "New Mexico," p. 32; Schroeder, "Rio Grande Ethnohistory," p. 62.

52. "Muster of 29 September, 1680," *RPI*, vol. 1, pp. 136–53.

53. Dozier, *The Pueblo Indians*, p. 86.

54. AGN-HIST 25-2:35–36; AGN-HIST 25-2:30–31; AGN-HIST 25-3:30–45; AGN-PI 102-10:323–25; AGN-HIST 25-39:332–37.

55. Carroll and Haggard, eds. and trans. *Three New Mexico Chronicles*, p. 31.

Chapter 5

1. WPA, 5-5-6:6.

2. Peristiany, ed., *Honour and Shame*, pp. 9–17.

3. Hobbes, *Leviathan*, pp. 73, 76. Pitt-Rivers, "Honor."

4. McAlister, "Social Structure," pp. 350–51; E. Lourie, "A Society Organized for War: Medieval Spain," *Past and Present* 35(1966), pp. 54–76.

5. OD, pp. 50–63.

6. Segunda Partida, título 13, ley 17; Segunda Partida, título 13, ley 4; Segunda Partida, título 13, ley 18, all quoted in Baroja, "Honor and Shame," pp. 84–85; *HNM*, p. 250.

7. Zavala, *New Viewpoints*, p. 50. Patterson, *Slavery and Social Death*, pp. 5–13.

8. Patterson, *Slavery and Social Death*, p. 64.

9. M. Chávez quoted in Simmons, *Little Lion of the Southwest*, p. 35. Claude Leví-Strauss asserts that: "The name is an identifying mark which establishes that the individual who is named is a member of a preordained class (a social group in a system of groups, a status by birth in a system of statuses)." *The Savage Mind* (Chicago, 1966), p. 181.

10. A. Chávez, "Genízaros," p. 199. AASF-DM 1715, 61:210. SA 1819, 19:837.

11. SA 1757, 9:160–69. SA 1763, 9:524–26. SA 1765, 9:921.

12. The most intelligent analysis of godparenthood to date is S. Gudeman's "Spiritual Relationships" and "The *Compadrazgo*." Godparenthood statistics adopted from Brugge, *Navajos in the Catholic Church Records*, pp. 104–8.

13. Gudeman and Schwartz, "Baptismal Godparents in Slavery."

14. AASF-LD 1809, 53:703.

15. On respectful forms of address see SA 1751, 8:995–1020; Wainerman, "Family Relations in Argentina." SA 1762, 9:172–78.

16. SA 1751, 8:995–1020.

17. AASF-DM 1777, 63:663–68.

18. Hafen and Hafen, *Old Spanish Trail*, p. 274.

19. Horgan, *Centuries of Santa Fe*, p. 118. AASF-DM 1720, 61:604. SA 1766, 9:922–48. SA 1751, 8:1048.

20. SA 1816, 18:579–603; SA 1751, 8:1033–34, 1045; quote on 8:1045, 8:1033–34.

21. SA 1745, 8:579–85; SA 1774, 10:811–14.

22. SA 1752, 8:1070–1105. AASF-LD 1781, 52:597. SA 1819, 19:866–67.

23. SA 1763, 9:524–26; SA 1766, 9:949–51. Additional cases of slave complaints: SA 1751, 8:1032–48; SA 1766, 9:922–48; SA 1745, 8:579–85;

SA 1741, 8:50–66; SA 1774, 10:811–14. For cases of priests acting as advocates for slaves see: SA 1761, 9:174; SA 1767, 10:231–98; SA 1763, 9:524–26; SA 1766, 9:949–51.

24. Pesos (T) means *pesos de la tierra*, or pesos calculated according to values paid for agricultural goods. Before currency circulated widely in New Mexico a system of equivalents based on silver pesos was used to undertake economic transactions. Two pesos *de la tierra* were equal to one in silver. Hereafter, whenever a "(T)" is placed after a peso amount, it signifies that the amount was calculated in goods. Values in pesos not followed by a "(T)" signify silver pesos. *MNM*, p. 252. SA 1762, 9:262–67. Additional slave purchases are recorded in: SA 1761, 9:410–44; SA 1761, 9:349–51; SA 1713, 21:285–86; AASF-LD 1822, 54:512.

25. *RBM*, p. 44. SA 1788, 12:90–101; SA 1789, 12:238–41.

26. SA 1741, 8:67–95. SA 1761, 9:255–61.

27. SA 1794, 13:475–78.

28. SA 1713, 21:285–86. SA 1748, 8:827–34; SA 1768, 10:446–74; SA 1748, 8:875–77. SA 1747, 8:690; SA 1747, 8:677–707. SA 1780, 11:45–46. See also SA 1767, 10:231–98; SA 1768, 10:446–74; SA 1761, 9:325–37. SA 1768, 10:446–74.

29. AGN-PI 208-15:578–83. AGN-PI 156-4:55–122; SA 1749, 8:875–77; AGN-PI 15-7:8–9; AGN-PI 204-19:460–87. For other slave shipments south see: SA 1716, 5:625–38; AGN-PI 79-1:1–27.

30. *MNM*, p. 42; Morfi, "Desordenes en Nuevo México," AGN-HIST 1778, 25-8:147–48. An English translation of Morfi's report can be found in Simmons, ed. and trans., *Father Juan Agustín Morfi's Account*, pp. 34–35.

31. *MNM*, pp. 42, 259, 126, 208.

32. Martínez quoted in S. Horvath, "The Social and Political Organization of the Genízaros," p. 78; Swadesh, *Los Primeros Pobladores*, p. 45; Ellis, "Tomé and Father J.B.R," p. 94.

33. R. Barcía, *Primer Diccionario*, vol. 1, p. 707.

34. SA 1768, 10:402. SA 1752, 8:1018–20. SA 1773, 10:787.

35. Leach, "Characterization of Caste and Class Systems," p. 19.

36. *RNM*, p. 345; *OD*, p. 315; SA 1749, 9:279. SA 1751, 8:1032.

37. SA 1745, 8:371–80; AASF-LD 1778, 52:493; AASF-LD 1801, 53:349–50.

38. AGN-HIST 25-5:82–90; W. Timmons, "The Population of the El Paso Area."

39. A. Chávez, *Archives of the Archdiocese*, p. 201. AASF-LD 1802, 53:429.

40. SA 1819, 19:822. Tyler, *Pueblo Animals and Myths*, pp. 154–83. "Declaración de los indios de Nuevo México," AGN-PI 1707, 36-3:128–29; SA 1769, 10:594–600. See also the case of the Indians of Sandía Pueblo against Alameda's chief constable in SA 1819, 19:643.

41. P. Pino, *Exposición sucinta y sencilla de la provincia del Nuevo México: hecha por su diputado en Cortes* (Cádiz, 1812), p. 33. A. Chávez, "De Vargas' Negro Drummer." AASF-DM 1697, 60:48; AASF-DM 1705, 60:399. See also B. Young, "The History of the Black."

42. A list of racial categories in colonial Mexico and Peru can be found in Morner, *Race Mixture*, pp. 58–59.

43. *HD*, p. 317. SA 1766, 9:944; SA 1766, 9:960–63; SA 1767, 10: 231–98.

44. A. Lipschütz, *El indoamericanismo*, p. 75. AGN-INQ 1788, 1210: 45–46.

45. AGN-INQ 1734, 854:253, 255–56.

46. Brugge, *Navajos in the Catholic Church Record*, p. 114. AASF-DM Reels 60–79.

47. SA 1766, 9:922–48.

48. W. Borah and S. Cook, "Marriage and Legitimacy in Mexican Culture: Mexico and California," *California Law Review* 54(1966), pp. 959–61; Morner, *Race Mixture*, p. 40. Solórzano quoted in V. Martínez-Alier, *Marriage, Class and Colour*, p. 132. *Diccionario* quoted in A. Lipschütz, *El Problema Racial en la Conquista de América* (México, 1975), p. 240.

49. SA 1768, 10:387–90. SA 1773, 10:752–87. Dress as an encoder of social class has been studied by A. Mazuri, "The Robes of Rebellion"; Barthes, "The Garment System," in *Elements of Semiology*, pp. 25–27; P. Bogatyrev, "Costume as a Sign."

50. Schroeder, "Rio Grande Ethnohistory," p. 48; WPA 5-5-49, 55. SA 1816, 18:579–603.

51. SA 1765, 9:789–820.

52. SA 1745, 8:551–73.

Chapter 6

1. AGN-INQ 1726, 757-25:167–72.

2. SA 1816, 18:579–603.

3. Pitt-Rivers, "Honor," p. 505.

4. Baroja, "Honor and Shame," pp. 81–137; Pitt-Rivers, "Honour and Social Status," in Peristiany, *Honor and Shame*, pp. 21–77; García Valdecasas, *El Hidalgo y El Honor*, pp. 137–264; Castro, *De La Edad Conflictiva*, passim; Davis, *People of the Mediterranean*, pp. 89–100.

5. AGN-INQ 1638, 388-22:440–42; SA 1743, 8:133–45.

6. AASF-LD 1781, 52:569; AGN-INQ 1606, 368:140–42. Pitt-Rivers, *People of the Sierra*, pp. 21–77.

7. AGN-INQ 1726, 757-26:167–72; SA 1793, 13:357–58.

8. AGN-INQ 1804, 1382-190: sin número. The method by which the Virgin Mary conceived was the subject of considerable debate among medieval theologians. It was generally believed that the Holy Spirit had entered Mary's body through some unnatural route. The learned consensus was that impregnation had occurred through the ear. See E. Leach, "Virgin Birth." The most comprehensive study of the different meanings that the cult of the Virgin Mary has assumed over time is Warner, *Alone of All Her Sex*. Several anthropologists have studied the cult of the Virgin of Guadalupe in Mexico to see the ways in which native Indian culture and Spanish culture have been fused to form this national symbol. See

Wolf, "The Virgin of Guadalupe"; J. Lafaye, *Quetzalcoatl and Guadalupe. The Formation of Mexican National Consciousness, 1531–1813* (Chicago, 1976). V. Turner brilliantly analyses the political use of the various devotions to the Virgin Mary during Mexican Independence in "Hidalgo." Attempts to interpret the Virgin Mary as a Jungian archetype can be found in E. Neumann, *The Great Mother: An Analysis of the Archetype* (New York, 1955); E. Stevens, "Marianismo: The Other Face of Machismo in Latin America," in Pescatello, ed., *Female and Male in Latin America*, pp. 90–101. Boxer, in *Mary and Misogyny*, examines the syncretisms that developed when Spanish culture expanded into Latin America and Asia, focusing specifically on women.

9. AASF-LD 1725, 51:955, 962.

10. SA 1766, 9:943; J. Pitt-Rivers, *The Fate of Shechem or the Politics of Sex* (Cambridge, 1977), p. 23.

11. AASF-DM 1700, 61: 209; SA 1805, 15:617; AGN-RH 29-8:2.

12. AASF-DM 1837, 76:586–90.

13. Sánchez, *De sancto matrimonii sacramento* quoted in J. Flandrin, "Contraception, Marriage, and Sexual Relations," pp. 37–38.

14. Pitt-Rivers, *People of the Sierra*, p. 53. AASF-DM 1766, 62:619; AASF-DM 1705, 60:383; AGN-INQ 1663, 594:244; AASF-DM 1702, 60:272.

15. AASF-DM 1845, 79:288.

16. AGN-INQ 1734, 854: 253–56.

17. Manuel Alvarez Papers-notebook. Deposited at the Coronado Room of the University of New Mexico's Zimmerman Library (Albuquerque, New Mexico).

18. AASF-LD 1712, 51:735–58. AASF-DM 1702, 60:270; SA 1816, 18: 579; AASF-DM 1705, 60:376.

19. AASF-DM 1785, 64:618.

20. "Dictamen de Dr. Tembra acerca de la consulta que se hizo sobre si el Cura o cualquier juez eclesiástico puede o debe impedir los matrimonios entre consortes desiguales, celebrados ya esponsales o con juramento de cumplirlos, sin consentimiento paterno," Mexico 1752, Legajo 18, 701, Biblioteca Nacional (Madrid), Manuscritos de América, quoted by Martínez-Alier, *Marriage, Class and Colour*, p. 101.

21. SA 1775, 10:868–72; AASF-LD 1725, 51:952–64.

22. AASF-DM 1736, 62:183–90.

23. AASF-DM 1702, 60:274; AASF-DM 1777, 63:610.

24. AASF-DM 1705, 60:376, 378, 381, 385.

25. SA 1750, 8:963–77; AASF-LD 1775, 52:463–64; SA 1805, 15:1038–39. Other cases not mentioned in the text that conform to the same patterns are AASF-DM 1705, 60:428; AASF-DM 1777, 63:609–11; AASF-LD 1823, 54: 600–602.

26. AASF-DM 1776, 62:514–15.

27. AASF-DM 1705, 60:365, 367.

28. SA 1805, 15:597, 602, 605.

29. SA 1767, 10:4, 8, 23, 24. The role of women as gatherers and repositories of information, often referred to as gossip, has been studied as a form of fe-

male power within the domestic sphere. See S. Harding, "Women and Words in a Spanish Village," in Reiter, ed., *Toward an Anthropology of Women*, pp. 283–308; Bailey, ed., *Gifts and Poison*; Lomnitz and Pérez Lizaur, "The History of a Mexican Urban Family."

30. AASF-LD 1775, 52:457–68.

31. SA 1813, 17:698, 690–91, 702–23.

Chapter 7

1. Oostendorp, *El Conflicto entre el honor y el amor*; Gluckman, *Custom and Conflict in Africa*, pp. 54–80; Goode, "The Theoretical Importance of Love," pp. 45–46; Beigel, "Romantic Love"; Shorter, *The Making of the Modern Family*, pp. 120–67.

2. A. Espinosa, "Spanish Folk-lore in New Mexico," p. 149.

3. AASF-DM 1702, 60:273. AASF-LD 1772, 52:430–32.

4. AASF-LD 1774, 52:449–58.

5. AASF-DM 1786, 64:706–8. The sentence in this case is found in AASF-LD 1786, 52:773–74.

6. P. Bourdieu, "Marriage Strategies as Strategies of Social Reproduction," in Forster and Ranum, eds., *Family and Society* (Baltimore, 1976), p. 122.

7. SA 1775, 10:868–72; SA 1767, 10:4–25.

8. AGN-INQ 1621, 356-1:264–83; AGN-INQ 1640, 425-1:633–44.

9. AASF-DM 1702, 60:260–82.

10. AASF-DM 1708, 60:527–29.

11. AASF-DM 1705, 60:373–90.

12. AASF-DM 1703, 60:302–3. AASF-DM 1802, 66:230–32.

13. AASF-DM 1831, 72:293. AASF-DM 1832, 72:335.

14. AASF-DM 1702, 60:272, 279, 276.

15. AASF-DM 1766, 62:510–11.

16. SA 1763, 9:468–93.

17. SA 1763, 9:524–26. AASF-DM 1705, 60:428. AASF-DM 1705, 60:276. AASF-DM 1705, 60:381. SA 1771, 10:634–57.

18. The suspension of the hierarchical social order and the creation of ritual comity during festivals and rites of passage was first studied by the Belgian folklorist Arnold Van Gennep in 1908 in *The Rites of Passage*. The concept of ritual liminality received its fullest articulation in the works of V. Turner. See Turner, "Betwixt and Between," *The Ritual Process*, and "Variations on a Theme of Liminality," in Moore and Meyerhoff, eds., *Secular Ritual*, pp. 36–52. WPA 5-5-17:7.

19. SA 1813, 17:573–629.

20. SA 1819, 19:911.

21. AGN-RH 291-9:3–6, blanks in the original, date circa 1800.

22. AGN-HIST 25-39:337. SA 1817, 18:811.

23. The potential for festivals to incite violence or to resolve conflict has been studied by E. Le Roy Ladurie in *Carnival in Romans* (New York, 1979).

Chapter 8

1. Aquinas quoted in Gudeman, "The Compadrazgo," p. 49; Fray J. Serra, *Writings* (Washington, D.C., 1955), vol. 3, p. 253.
2. Cramp, *A Text-Book of Popery*, p. 322.
3. McLaughlin, "Equality of Souls"; Bullough and Brundage, *Sexual Practices*.
4. Farriss, *Crown and Clergy*, pp. 1–38.
5. Mans Puigarnau, *Legislación*, vol. 1, pp. 152–73, and *Derecho matrimonial canónico*, pp. 1–84.
6. Escriche, *Diccionario razonado*, pp. 276–77.
7. The intricacies of calculating consanguinity and affinity relations can be found in Herbermann, et al., eds., *The Catholic Encyclopedia*, vol. 4, p. 267. Those interested in a more detailed discussion of consanguinity and affinity impediments should consult R. Gutiérrez, "Marriage, Sex and the Family," pp. 208–48, 340–65.
8. On the function of cousin marriages see R. Murphy and L. Kasdan, "The Structure of Parallel Cousin Marriage," *American Anthropologist* 60(1959), pp. 17–29; Robin Fox, *Kinship and Marriage*, pp. 184–88. AASF-DM 1718, 61:416–20.
9. AASF-DM 1828, 72:142.
10. AASF-DM 1796, 53:196–97.
11. Canon law on religious vows and disparate cult can be found in Escriche, *Diccionario razonado*, pp. 276–77; Mans Puigarnau, *Legislación*, vol. 1, pp. 163–68; Mans Puigarnau, *Derecho matrimonial canónico*, pp. 87–146. On premarital conversion see AASF-DM 1832, 73:302; AASF-DM 1832, 73:353; AASF-DM 1832, 73:400; AASF-DM 1844, 78:1045. James, *Three Years Among the Indians*, p. 82.
12. AGN-INQ 1743, 890:185–97. AASF-DM 1830, 72:86–88.
13. AASF-DM 1781, 52:569–70. Brundage, "The Problem of Impotence." The ideal marriage of Mary and Joseph provided an important exception to the assumption that sex was an essential and intrinsic part of the sacrament. See P. Gold, "The Marriage of Mary and Joseph in the Twelfth-Century Ideology of Marriage," in Bullough and Brundage, *Sexual Practices*, pp. 102–17.
14. AASF-DM 1812, 67:3–8; AASF-LD 1809, 53:699–704.
15. Corbett, *The Roman Law of Marriage*, pp. 24–67.
16. Ibid., pp. 91, 211–48; Joyce, *Christian Marriage*, pp. 41–43.
17. J. Carberry, *The Juridical Form of Marriage*, pp. 7–13.
18. Ibid., pp. 3–6.
19. Joyce, *Christian Marriage*, pp. 9–11; Carberry, *The Juridical Form of Marriage*, pp. 11–17; Godsell, *A History of Marriage*, pp. 221–66.
20. Jedin, *Crisis*, pp. 140–58; Joyce, *Christian Marriage*, pp. 122–23.
21. Ephesians 5:22, 6:9. Flandrin, *Families in Former Times*, pp. 118–19.
22. Flandrin, *Families in Former Times*, p. 122. Matthew 23:9, 10:34–37.
23. AASF-DM 1761, 62:311–14.
24. AASF-DM 1697, 60:40–45.

25. Ots Capdequí, *Instituciones*, pp. 365–66.

26. AGN-PI 1758, 102-8:282. AGN-INQ 1734, 854:253–54.

27. SA 1741, 8:50–66.

28. AASF-DM 1710, 60:680–92.

29. A. Chávez, "A Romeo and Juliet Story in Early New Mexico," *New Mexico Quarterly* 20(1954), pp. 471–80.

30. The role of priests fostering both liberation and accommodation can be studied in Taylor, "The Virgin of Guadalupe in New Spain."

31. Huizinga, *The Waning of the Middle Ages* (Garden City, N.Y., 1949), pp. 77–84. Campa, *Spanish Folk-Poetry*, pp. 29–90; A. Espinosa, "Romancero nuevomejicano," *Revue Hispanique* 33(1915): 446–560.

32. AASF-DM 61:209–12.

33. L. Drummond, "The Cultural Continuum: A Theory of Intersystems," *Man* 15(1980), pp. 352–74.

34. WPA, 5-5-19 No. 26.

35. Campa, *Spanish Folk-Poetry*, p. 203.

36. S. Yanagisako, "Time, Ambiguity, and the Norms of Filial Relations" (unpublished paper, 1980), p. 56.

37. P. Bourdieu, "Marriage strategies as strategies of social reproduction," in R. Forster and C. Ranum, eds., *Family and Society* (Baltimore, 1976), pp. 140–41.

38. Bossy, "The Counter-Reformation."

39. Jaramillo, *Shadows of the Past*, p. 31. Davis, *El Gringo*, p. 280.

40. Laughlin, *Caballeros*, pp. 284–88. "Rural Weddings," WPA 5-5-2:2.

41. AASF-LD 1820, 54:259–61.

42. Van Gennep, *The Rites of Passage*.

43. New Mexico Writers' Project, "Spanish-American Wedding Customs," *El Palacio* 49(1942), pp. 1–5.

44. Belmont, "The Symbolic Function of the Wedding Procession," p. 2. For a thoughtful analysis of the economic functions of trousseau see Schneider, "Trousseau as Treasure." E. De Huff, "People of the Soil," *New Mexico Magazine* 17(1940), p. 48; F. Hawley, "Beyond Taos"; New Mexico Writers' Project, "Spanish-American Wedding Customs," *El Palacio* 49(1942), pp. 1–2; Jaramillo, *Shadows of the Past*, p. 32; Swadesh, *Los Primeros Pobladores*, p. 60.

45. SA 1747, 8:720–35. SA 1792, 13:8–10.

46. SA 1747, 8:720–35; SA 1761, 9:352–85; SA 1767, 10:152–69; SA 1772, 10:717–42; SA 13:8–10; SA 1811, 21:636–54. SA 1749, 8:991–94. Lavrin and Couturier, "Dowries and Wills." The social functions of dowry is studied in cross-cultural context in Goody and Tambiah, *Bridewealth and Dowry*. On the legal disposition of dotal property in Spain and Mexico see J. Ots Capdequí, "Bosquejo histórico" and Chapter 4 of Arrom, "Women and the Family," which deals with inheritance legislation in nineteenth-century Mexico.

47. Dun and Bradstreet Associates Records for New Mexico, 388 (On deposit at the Baker Business Library, Harvard University); SA II, No. 48 Will of Gertudes Armijo.

48. Ots Capdequí, "Bosquejo histórico," pp. 162–82.

49. Edward Westermarck in his monumental *History of Human Marriage* (London, Eng., 1925) proposed that *arrhae* first appeared in Roman ritual as an evolutionary form of bride purchase. In the Roman practice *arrhae* were always presented during the betrothal (*sponsalia*). See Westermarck, vol. 2, pp. 432–595. Goodsell also makes this point in his *History of Marriage and the Family*, (New York, 1934) pp. 124–28. On the functions of *arras* see Frank, Laxalt, and Vosberg, "Inheritance, Marriage, and Dowry Rights"; H. Dillard, "Women in Reconquest Castile: The Fueros of Sepulveda and Cuenca," in S. Mosher Stuard, ed., *Women in Medieval Society*, pp. 71–94.

50. Schneider, "Of Vigilance and Virgins," p. 10.

51. SA 1744, 8:338–42. For similar cases see SA 1818, 19:363–64; AASF-LD 1824, 54:652–53.

52. SA 1747, 8:664–76.

53. AASF-LD 1830, 55:87.

54. AASF-DM 1821, 68:476. Unless otherwise noted, the description of weddings elaborated below come from: WPA 5-5-49:38, WPA 5-5-23:4, WPA 5-5-23:1, WPA 5-5-1:1, WPA 5-5-2:1, WPA 5-5-2:55.

55. C. Morín, "Los libros parroquiales," p. 412; Sánchez-Albornoz, *The Population of Latin America*, p. 118; Yacher, *Marriage, Migration and Racial Mixing*, pp. 28–29; Swann, *Tierra Adentro*, pp. 125–27, 146–47.

56. *Ceremonial y manval sacado del Missal Romano de Pio V. Reformado por la santidad de Clemente VII y Vrbano VIII ajvstado al estilo estrecho, y reformado de los Religiosos Descalcos de N.P.S. Francisco* (México, 1660), pp. 124–30.

57. Baker, *Wedding Customs and Folklore*, pp. 72–76; Fielding, *Strange Customs*, pp. 27–28. Segalen, *Love and Power in the Peasant Family*, p. 27.

58. *MNM*, pp. 30, 244, 351.

59. Espinosa, *España en Nuevo Méjico*, pp. 43–59; Horgan, *Centuries of Santa Fe*, pp. 97–98; "Rural Weddings," WPA 5-5-2:2; Belmont, "The Symbolic Function," pp. 1–7.

60. A discussion of the foods prepared for the wedding feast can be found in H. Thorp, "A Wedding Feast," WPA 5-5-17: 1; W. De Huff, "Fiesta Foods," *New Mexico* 17(1939), pp. 21, 34–36; J. Bourke, "Folk-Foods." On wedding dances see Lucero-White, *Folk Dances*, pp. 16–19.

61. Sedillo, *Mexican and New Mexican Folkdances*, p. 26; WPA 5-5-12:1.

62. Lucero-White, *Folk Dances*, pp. 11, 20–21, 32–36.

63. Edward Westermarck believed that the custom of stealing the bride was quite ancient, reminiscent of barbarian marriage by abduction. See Westermarck, *The History of Human Marriage*, vol. 2, pp. 240–78.

64. Rael, "New Mexico Wedding Songs"; Pérez, "Folk Cycle in a Spanish New Mexican Village," pp. 19–20; M. Austin, "New Mexico Folk Poetry"; Austin, Otero-Warren, and Lucero, "New Mexico Folk Song"; Kittle, "Folk Music of the Upper Rio Grande."

Chapter 9

1. The empirical data contained in this chapter were obtained through an analysis of the *diligenicias matrimoniales,* the matrimonial investigations that every parish priest had to conduct before two individuals could be joined in matrimony. These investigations usually contained extensive genealogical information on the marriage partners, their age at marriage, their social status, whether they were legitimate or illegitimate at birth, and whether they could sign their name. The Archives of the Archdiocese of Santa Fe contain 6,613 extant *diligencias matrimoniales* for the period 1693–1846, with information on approximately 13,226 individuals. This is the data base analyzed here.

2. The effects of age at marriage on fertility can be studied in A. Burguiere, "From Malthus to Max Weber"; Hajnal, "European Marriage Patterns." AASF-DM 1697, 60:10. Adams, *Bishop Tamaron's Visitation,* p. 54. AASF-DM 1844, 78:908; AASF-DM 1788, 65:122.

3. The mean is a measure of central tendency that must be examined cautiously because it gives no indication of the actual spread of the observed marriage ages around the mean. To gauge the amount of dispersion of the observations around the mean, the coefficient of variation has also been included in Table 9.3 for each decade mean. The coefficient of variation is obtained by dividing the standard deviation by the mean. For more detailed information on the coefficient of variation see H. Blalock, *Social Statistics* (New York, 1972), pp. 88–89.

4. Simmons, "New Mexico's Smallpox Epidemic."

5. Brading and Wu, "Population Growth and Crisis," pp. 12–13.

6. Katharine Gaskin, "Age at First Marriage," p. 29. Hajnal, "European Marriage Patterns," pp. 114–15.

7. The emotional relationships created between spouses of widely disparate age has been examined by Shorter, *The Making of the Modern Family,* pp. 154–55; Goody, ed., *The Developmental Cycle,* passim; Bell, *Fate and Honor,* pp. 67–112.

8. AASF-DM 1761, 62:311. AASF-DM 1776, 63:570. For additional old male–younger female marriages see AASF-DM 1777, 63:614; AASF-DM 1841, 77:774. Proverb is in Lucero-White, *The Folklore of New Mexico,* p. 33.

9. AASF-DM 1763, 62:461. AASF-DM 1776, 63:601. For an additional older female–younger male marriage see AASF-DM 1828, 71:576.

10. WPA, 5-5-9:23.

11. SA 1790, 12:428. SA 1794, 13:560. SA 1820, 20:498–99.

12. Yacher, *Marriage, Migration and Racial Mixing,* p. 14. Swann, *Tierra Adentro,* pp. 117–23. Farriss, "Nucleation Versus Dispersal."

13. A. Moreno Toscano, "Economía Regional y Urbanización."

14. AASF-DM 1709, 60:581. AASF-DM 1824, 70:408. AASF-DM 1709, 60:399.

15. AASF-DM 1705, 60:391. AASF-DM 1725, 61:771. AASF-DM 1705, 60:407.

16. AASF-DM 1699, 60:187. AASF-DM 1772, 63:234. AASF-DM 1772, 63:184.

17. AASF-DM 1698, 60:141. AASF-DM 1792, 65:381. AASF-DM 1805, 66:186.

18. Lamar, *Far Southwest*, p. 23. AASF-DM 1714, 61:766. AASF-DM 1816, 67:210.

19. AASF-DM 1714, 61:116.

20. AGN-PI 108-8:282.

21. Hafen and Hafen, *Old Spanish Trail*, p. 274.

22. Brugge, "Some Plains Indians" and *Navajos in the Catholic Church Records*, pp. 109–10.

23. AASF-DM 1718, 61:475.

24. AASF-DM 1767, 62:725. AASF-DM 1822, 68:599. AASF-DM 1779, 64:60.

25. SA 1741, 8:50–66.

Chapter 10

1. Lynch, *The Spanish American Revolutions*, p. 14; Bannon, *The Spanish Borderlands Frontier*, pp. 142, 169.

2. Lynch, *The Spanish American Revolutions*, pp. 1–24.

3. Bannon, *The Spanish Borderlands Frontier*, pp. 172–73.

4. Thomas, ed. and trans., *Forgotten Frontiers*, p. ix. Bannon, *The Spanish Borderlands Frontier*, p. 183.

5. Bannon, *The Spanish Borderlands Frontier*, pp. 186, 221. Loomis and Nasatir, *Pedro Vial*, pp. 3–27.

6. On the mercantile activities of Chihuahua's merchants and their agents in New Mexico see SA 1747, 8:736–47; SA 1762, 9:448–60. Moorhead, *New Mexico's Royal Road*.

7. Ibid. Bannon, *The Spanish Borderlands Frontier*, p. 219.

8. AGN-HIST 1776, 25-8:133–141. Reports and complaints about merchant activities can be found in AGN-HIST 1774, 25-40:338–39; AGN-PI 1788, 254-2:8–23; AGN-HIST 1792, 25-9:155–56; AASF-LD 1794, 53:108–14; SA 1788 12:90–101; SA 1789, 12:238–41; SA 1803, 15:84–91.

9. Lynch, *The Spanish American Revolutions*, p. 9. AGN-HIST 1776, 25-8:133–41.

10. Fray Carlos Delgado, HD, pp. 426–27.

11. Fray Carlos Delgado, HD, pp. 427, 428.

12. Report of Fray Carlos Delgado, AGN-HIST 1750, 25-2:31; Report of Fray Juan Sanz de Lezaún, AGN-HIST 1760, 25-3:40; Report of Fray Pedro Serrano, 1761, HD, pp. 479–500; M. Simmons, trans. and ed., *Father Juan Agustín de Morfi's Account*. Fray Andrés Varo's 1751 comment is quoted in Fray Pedro Serrano's above cited report.

13. Fireman, *The Spanish Royal Corps of Engineers*.

14. AGN-CALIF 1789, 17-7:228. See also the expeditions undertaken in

1774 and 1779 to increase New Mexico-California trade discussed in AGN-HIST 1774, 25-31:252–53. AGN-HIST 1779, 25-36:297.

15. AGN-HIST 1774, 25-31:252–53, AGN-HIST 1779, 25-36:297; AGN-CALIF 1789, 17-7: 228; AGN-CALIF 1801, 17-10: 325–27; SA 1777, 10: 931–33; SA 1778, 10:20–37; J. Escudero, *Noticias estadísticas del estado de Chihuahua* (México, 1862), pp. 37–38. L. Bloom, "Early New Mexico Weaving." Lynch, *The Spanish American Revolutions*, p. 8.

16. SA 1748, 8:808–10.

17. AGN-PI 1773, 152-2:228. AGN-CALIF 1789, 29-3:205. Several other reports noted that Spaniards were in desperate need of land: AASF-LD 1794, 53:109; SA 1795, 21:537; AASF-LD 1795, 53:156; SA 1803, 15:85.

18. *MNM*, p. 42; Dozier, "Making Inferences," p. 85; Simmons, "Patrones de ascentamiento," pp. 82–83.

19. AGN-HIST 1744, 25-25:229; AASF-LD 1782, 52:653.

20. SA 1741, 8:68; SA 1761, 9:336; AASF-DM 1705, 60:376. AGN-HIST 1744, 25-25:229; AGN-HIST 1782, 25-8:147; SA 1777, 10:925; AGN-PI 1768, 102-7:256. SA 1793, 13:346.

21. Henry W. Kelly notes that Fray Andrés Varo had written a report on conditions at New Mexico's missions in 1749, as had Fray Carlos Delgado in 1750, but that these reports sat in Franciscan archives until 1761 when the provincial, Fray Pedro Serrano, relayed them to Viceroy Cruillas with various supporting documents. See Kelly, *Franciscan Missions*, pp. 57–58.

22. A summary of these controversies can be found in *HD*, pp. 35–41, with the supporting documentary evidence in *HD*, pp. 391–487. Eleanor Adams' introduction to Bishop Tamaron's 1760 visitation of New Mexico has an excellent discussion of jurisdictional controversies between the Franciscans and the episcopal see. See Adams, *Bishop Tamaron's Visitation*, pp. 1–33.

23. Ibid.

24. AASF-DM 1798, 66:18.

25. *MNM*, p. 284.

26. *MNM*, pp. 258–59. Conde de Revillagigedo, *Informe sobre las misiones, 1793*, as quoted in Kessell, *Kiva, Cross and Crown*, p. 355.

27. *MNM*, pp. 309, 310, 313.

28. Adams, *Bishop Tamaron's Visitation*, pp. 50–53.

29. For restrictions on travel see the following decrees, SA 1783, 11:610–13; SA 1784, 11:679–86; SA 1790, 12:303–14; SA 1791, 12:349. The cases against Barelas and González are found in SA 1800, 14:575.

30. SA 1745, 8:394–550.

31. AASF, Book of Marriages, Zuñi, 33:1216–56. AASF, Book of Marriages, Cochiti, 27:3–42.

32. One cannot give too much importance to Pueblo Christian marriages for the simple reason that the indigenous rite of marriage was probably of greater importance and frequency. How extensively marital-place exogamy occurred in traditional marriages is impossible to determine for lack of any documentary evidence.

33. SA 1784, 10:623–24; SA 1793, 13:237–240, 241–326; SA 1810,

17:14–16; J. Lecompte, *Rebellion in Rio Arriba* (Albuquerque, 1985). SA 1793, 13:237–40; SA 1793, 13:241–326.

34. AGN-INQ 1771-1787, 1284-13:111–29. SA 1792, 13:90–104; AGN-PI 1792, 161-6:177–238; AASF-LD 1818, 54:14–15.

35. SA 1762; not in microfilm edition of SA but on deposit at the State of New Mexico Record Center (Santa Fe) as Twitchell Document No. 554a; AASF-LD 1781, 52:581–625; AASF-LD 1789, 52:850–53; AASF-LD 1798, 53:234–35; AASF-LD 1801, 53:343–44; AASF-LD 1809, 53:699–704; AASF-LD 1820, 54:224–43; SA 1820, 20:425–32.

36. SA 1762, Twitchell Document No. 554a, on deposit at New Mexico State Records Center. This document is not included in the microfilm edition of the Spanish Archives. SA 1820, 20:425–32.

37. AASF-LD 1789, 52:850–53. AASF-LD 1781, 52:586.

38. AASF-LD 1820, 54:224–43. AASF-LD 1781, 52:594–95.

39. AGN-INQ 1771-1787, 1284-13:111–29. SA 1792, 13:90–104; AGN-PI 1792, 161-6:177–238; AASF-LD 1818, 54:14–15.

40. AGN-INQ 1761, 1042:97.

41. AASF-DM 1788, 65:59.

42. AGN-INQ 1794, 1382-1:1–37.

43. AASF-LD 1784, 52:707–8, 709-12, 714-21; AASF-LD 1791, 52:394–96; AASF-LD 1793, 53:75; AASF-LD 1795, 53:148–49; AASF-LD 1802, 53:447–49, 467–68, 476–78; AASF-LD 1803, 53:514–15; AASF-LD 1809, 53:708–9, 713–15; AASF-LD 1819, 54:117–18, 133–36, 184–85.

44. R. Konetzke, *Colección de Documentos*, 3/1, pp. 401–5.

45. Ibid., pp. 404–5.

46. Ibid., pp. 406–13. The Caroline Pragmatic required all Spaniards and Indians residing in New Spain to obtain explicit parental consent for their marriages. Only "mulattos, blacks, coyotes and individuals of similar castes or races" were exempt, the justification being that illegitimacy was so high among these groups that parental consent might prove difficult to obtain and cause some honorable families embarrassment. By 1781 this position was modified. Mexico's viceroy was ordered to enforce the Pragmatic among mestizos and coyotes as well. On this point see Konetzke, *Colección de Documentos*, 3/2, pp. 476–82. Several other modifications of the Pragmatic were issued to curtail its subversion. On May 26, 1783, the crown ordered that if a father's marriage opposition had been deemed just and rational in the civil courts, neither a mother nor any other relative could reinstate the disobedient child's inheritance. The edict of May 31, 1783, further stipulated that even legally emancipated children—those over age 25—had to seek and obtain parental consent before contracting marriage. Finally, on July 10, soldiers and bureaucrats in Spanish America were given the privilege of marrying without parental consent given the hardships they might experience in obtaining consent. See Ibid., 3/2, pp. 527–30. Copies of these decrees arrived in New Mexico. See SA 11:582–86, 607, 699–708, 727–34.

47. AASF-DM 1780, 64:125.

48. Eleanor B. Adams, "Viva el Rey," *NMHR*, 35(1960), pp. 284–92.

49. Weber, *The Theory of Social and Economic Organization*, pp. 341–54.

50. AASF-LD 1781, 52:594–96, 603–4.

51. AGN-PI 1792, 161–66:117–238.

52. The agricultural production figures here are calculated from known *diezmos*, that is, the royal tenth reported in AGN-HIST 1750, 25-2:29; Carroll and Haggard, eds., *Three New Mexico Chronicles*, p. 35.

53. The proposals to establish textile *obrajes* in New Mexico can be found in AGN-HIST 1776, 25-8:138; AGN-PI 1788, 254-2:10; AGN-PI 1789, 161-9:256–69. On the state of textile production in New Mexico see AASF-LD 1794, 53:108; Bloom, "Early New Mexico Weaving."

54. Carroll and Haggard, eds., *Three New Mexico Chronicles*, p. 39; Archivo Histórico de Hacienda (México), 1839, 117-12:113–15.

55. AGN-PI 1788, 254-2:10. AASF-LD 1794, 53:108. SA 1803, 15:86. Carroll and Haggard, eds., *Three New Mexico Chronicles*, p. 43.

56. SA 1762, 9:343–48. SA 1762, 9:262–67. SA 1776, 10:879–91. A simple tabulation of all the civil court cases before 1800, which settled property disputes through the payment of silver pesos, would reveal the extent to which money was in fact used.

57. M. Moorhead, *The Presidio*, pp. 47–74; SA 1796, 21:542. SA 1769, 10:590. SA 1780, 11:40–43. AGN-PI 1780, 161-5:81–176.

58. AASF-LD 1794, 53:103. SA 1803, 15:90. AASF-LD 1816, 53:959–69.

59. AGN-PI 1773, 152-2:228; AGN-CALIF 1789, 29-3:205; AGN-CALIF 1796, 17-7:226; SA 1803, 15:85.

60. SA 1790, 12:319–502; Carroll and Haggard, eds., *Three New Mexico Chronicles*, p. 88.

61. AGN-HIST 1750, 25-2:29. AGN-HIST 1776, 25-8:147.

62. AGN-HIST 1776, 25-8:133. AGN-HIST 1780, 25-36:288.

63. SA 1765, 9:847. SA 1766, 9:1045. See also the contract of Raphael Pacheco in SA 1767, 9:1058–59. SA 1805, 15:937–39. SA 1805, 15:481–82. See also the cases of Juan Cruz García in SA 1805, 15:940; and Rafael Pacheco in SA 1767, 9:1058.

64. SA 1766, 9:1044–56. For a similar case see Raphael Pacheco's problems with his master as described in SA 1767, 9:1057–88. SA 1766, 9:1044–56.

65. Olen E. Leonard, *The Role of the Land Grant in the Social Organization and Social Processes of a Spanish-American Village in New Mexico* (Albuquerque, 1970), pp. 92–109.

66. MA 1823, 3:220. MA 1823, 3:227.

67. SA 1760, 9:170–71. SA 1819, 19:821. See also the *partido* contracts of Doña Manuela Carrio and Francisco Antonio Chávez in SA 1819, 19:991–1024 and SA 1820, 21:724–27.

68. SA 1820, 21:724–27; SA 1767, 10:170–86.

69. AASF-DM 1702, 60:256; AASF-DM 1712, 61:68; AASF-DM 1713, 61:85; AASF-DM 1718, 61:404; AASF-DM 1719, 61:546; AASF-DM 1771, 63:24.

70. AASF-DM 1798, 66:18.

71. AASF-LD 1810, 53:759; AASF-DM 1822, 68:697; AASF-DM 1838, 76:842; AASF-DM 1838, 76:811.

72. AASF-DM 1713, 61:85; SA 1771, 10:634; AASF-LD 1835, 55:454.

73. AASF-DM 1845, 79:122.

74. Prieto, "El Alma Sin Amor."

75. Archivo Histórico del Instituto Nacional de Anthropología e Historia (México), *Relatos Populares* Legajo 16-3, folio 1a.

76. WPA 5-5-20:8.

77. *Medicología* (México, 1851), p. 122, in BN.

78. Archivo Histórico de Hacienda (México), 291-8:2.

79. W. Davis, *El Gringo*, p. 280.

80. AASF-DM 1824, 69:591; WPA 5-5-12:42.

81. Rael, *Cuentos Españoles*, vol. 1, pp. 88–90.

82. Mauss, "Techniques of the Body"; Douglas, *Purity and Danger*, pp. 137–53. See also Vlahos, *Body, the Ultimate Symbol*.

83. AASF-LD 1813, 53:788. AASF-DM 1761, 62:278–82.

84. AASF-DM 1838, 76:810–17. AASF-DM 1836, 76:540–41. AASF-DM 1836, 76:540–41.

85. Larson, *The Honor Plays of Lope de Vega*, pp. 17–37.

86. AASF-DM 1805, 66:313; AASF-LD 1813, 53:790. For other illustrative cases in which sex was used to obtain a consanguinity dispensation see AASF-DM 1799, 66:72; AASF-DM 1806, 63:381; AASF-DM 1813, 67:43; AASF-DM 1811, 66:513; AASF-DM 1812, 66:621; AASF-DM 1813, 67:41.

Epilogue

1. Bucknell's travel journal to New Mexico can be found in Archer B. Hulbert, ed., *Southwest on the Turquoise Trail: the First Diaries on the Road to Santa Fe* (Denver, 1933), pp. 56–68.

2. Ray A. Billington, *The Far Western Frontier, 1830–1860* (New York, 1956), pp. 1–90.

3. Albert Pike, *Prose Sketches and Poems, Written in the Western Country, with Additional Stories* (Albuquerque, 1967), pp. 275, xv. Gregg, *Commerce of the Prairies*, pp. 141, 154.

4. Raymund A. Paredes, "The Mexican Image in American Travel Literature, 1831–1869," *NMHR* 52 (1977), p. 24. See also *idem*, "The Origins of Anti-Mexican Sentiment in the United States," *New Scholar* 6 (1977), pp. 139–65. Reginald Horsman, *Race and Manifest Destiny: The Origins of American Racial Anglo-Saxonism* (Cambridge, Mass., 1981), pp. 208–28.

5. Horsman, p. 236; J. Ross Browne, *Adventures in the Apache Country* (New York, 1869), p. 172, as quoted in Paredes, "The Mexican Image in American Travel Literature," p. 23; Davis, *El Gringo*, pp. 83, 85.

6. Albert K. Weinberg, *Manifest Destiny; a Study of Nationalist Expansionism in American History* (Baltimore, Md., 1935); Frederick Merk, *Manifest Destiny and Mission in American History* (New York, 1963).

7. Merk, pp. 31–32.

Bibliography

This bibliography includes manuscripts, dissertations, theses, and published works. Citations for unpublished archival material are to be found in the notes.

Acosta, José de. *De Procuranda Indorum Salute*. Madrid, 1952.

Adams, Eleanor B., ed. *Bishop Tamaron's Visitation of New Mexico, 1760*. Albuquerque, 1954.

———, and Fray Angélico Chávez, eds. and trans. *The Missions of New Mexico, 1776: A Description by Fray Atanasio Domínguez*. Albuquerque, 1975.

Anderson, Frank C. "The Pueblo Kachina Cult: A Historical Introduction," *Southwest Journal of Anthropology* 10 (1955): 404–19.

Ariès, Philippe, and Andre Béjin. *Western Sexuality: Practice and Precept in Past and Present Times*. New York, 1986.

Ariès, Philippe, and Jean-Claude Margolin, eds. *Les Jeux à la Renaissance*. Paris, 1982.

Armstrong, Edward A. *Saint Francis: Nature Mystic. The Derivation and Significance of the Nature Stories in the Franciscan Legend*. Berkeley, Calif., 1973.

Arrom, Silvia. "Women and the Family in Mexico City: 1800–1857." Ph.D. diss., Stanford University, 1977.

Aulen, Gustaf. *Christus Victor: An Historical Study of the Three Main Types of the Idea of Atonement*. New York, 1969.

Austin, Mary. "New Mexico Folk Poetry," *El Palacio* 7 (1919): 146–50.

———, Adelina Otero-Warren, and Aurora Lucero. "New Mexico Folk Song," *El Palacio* 7 (1919): 152–59.

Axtell, James. *The European and the Indian: Essays in the Ethnohistory of Colonial North America*. New York, 1981.

Bailey, Frederick G., ed. *Gifts and Poison: The Politics of Reputation*. Oxford, 1971.

Baker, Margaret. *Wedding Customs and Folklore*. London, 1977.

Baldwin, Percy M., ed. and trans. "Fray Marcos' Relación," *NMHR* 1 (1928): 159–223.

Bancroft, Hubert H. *History of Arizona and New Mexico, 1530–1888.* Albuquerque, 1962.

Bandelier, Adolph F. *Final Report of Investigations among the Indians of the Southwestern United States, Part I.* Cambridge, Mass., 1890.

———. *Final Report of Investigations among the Indians of the Southwestern United States, Part II.* Cambridge, Mass., 1892.

———. "Fray Juan de Padilla, the First Catholic Martyr in Eastern Kansas, 1542," *American Catholic Quarterly Review* 15 (1890): 551–65.

———. "On the Art of War and Mode of Warfare of the Ancient Mexicans," *Peabody Museum Annual Report* 2 (1877): 95–161.

———. "Reports by A. F. Bandelier on His Investigations in New Mexico During the Years 1883–84," in *Fifth Annual Report of the Archaeological Institute of America* (Cambridge, Mass., 1884): 55–98.

Bandelier, Fanny, trans. *The Journey of Alvar Núñez Cabeza de Vaca and His Companions from Florida to the Pacific, 1528–1536.* New York, 1905.

Bannon, John F. *The Spanish Borderlands Frontier, 1513–1821.* Albuquerque, 1974.

Barcía, Roque. *Primer Diccionario General Etimológico de la Lengua Española.* Madrid, 1880.

Barns, Thomas C., et al. *Northern New Spain: A Research Guide.* Tucson, 1981.

Barnstone, Willis, ed. and trans. *The Poems of Saint John of the Cross.* New York, 1972.

Baroja, J. Caro. "Honor and Shame: A Historical Account of Several Conflicts," in J. Peristany, ed., *Honor and Shame: The Values of Mediterranean Society* (Chicago, 1965): 81–137.

Barth, Pius J. *Franciscan Education and the Social Order in Spanish North America, 1502–1821.* Chicago, 1950.

Barthes, Roland. *Elements of Semiology.* New York, 1968.

Bayle, Constantino. *El Culto del Santísimo en Indias.* Madrid, 1951.

Beaglehole, Ernest. *Hopi Hunting and Hunting Ritual.* New Haven, Conn., 1936.

———. *Notes on Hopi Economic Life.* New Haven, Conn., 1937.

Beigel, Hugo G. "Romantic Love," *American Sociological Review* 16 (1951): 326–34.

Bell, Rudolph M. *Fate and Honor, Family and Village.* Chicago, 1979.

———. *Holy Anorexia.* Chicago, 1985.

Bellah, Robert N. "Religious Systems," in Evon Z. Voht and Ethel M. Albert, eds. *People of Rimrock: A Study of Values in Five Cultures* (Cambridge, Mass., 1967): 227–64.

Belmont, Nicole. "The Symbolic Function of the Wedding Procession in the Popular Rituals of Marriage," in Robert Forster and Orest A. Ranum, eds. *Ritual, Religion and the Sacred* (Baltimore, 1982): 1–7.

Benedict, Ruth. *Patterns of Culture.* Boston, 1934.

Berger, Pamela. *The Goddess Obscured: Transformation of the Grain Protectress from Goddess to Saint.* Boston, 1985.

Blackwood, Evelyn, ed. *The Many Faces of Homosexuality: Anthropological Approaches to Homosexual Behavior.* New York, 1986.

Bloch, Marc. *French Rural History.* Berkeley, Calif., 1970.

Bloom, Lansing B. "Early New Mexico Weaving," *NMHR* 2 (1927): 228–35.

———. "A Glimpse of New Mexico in 1620," *NMHR* 3 (1928): 357–80.

———. "New Mexico Under Mexican Administration 1821–1846," *Old Santa Fe* 1 (1913): 3–49.

———. "The Royal Order of 1620 to Custodian Fray Estevan de Perea," *NMHR* 5 (1930): 288–98.

———. "Spain's Investment in New Mexico Under the Hapsburgs," *The Americas* 1 (1945): 3–14.

———. "The Vargas Encomienda," *NMHR* 14 (1939): 366–417.

Boas, Franz. *Keresan Texts.* New York, 1928.

Bogatyrev, Petr. "Costume as a Sign," in *The Functions of Folk Costume in Moravian Slovakia* (The Hague, 1971): 80–89.

Bonaventure, Saint. *The Life of Saint Francis.* New York, 1978.

Bonnegjea, B. "Hunting Superstitions of the American Aborigines," *International Congress of Americanists* 32 (1934): 167–84.

Borah, Woodrow. *Justice by Insurance: The General Indian Court of Colonial Mexico and the Legal Aides of the Half-Real.* Berkeley, Calif., 1983.

Borges, Pedro. *Métodos misionales en la cristianización de América, siglo XVI.* Madrid, 1960.

Borker, Ruth. "To Honor Her Head: Hats as a Symbol of Women's Position in Three Evangelical Churches in Edinburgh, Scotland," in Hoch-Smith and Spring, eds., *Women in Ritual and Symbolic Roles*: 55–74.

Bossy, John. *Christianity in the West, 1400–1700.* Oxford, 1985.

———. "The Counter-Reformation and the People of Catholic Europe," *Past and Present* 47 (1970): 51–70.

———. "The Mass as a Social Institution, 1200–1700," *Past and Present* 100 (1983): 33–50.

Boswell, John. *Christianity, Social Tolerance and Homosexuality.* Chicago, 1980.

Bourke, John G. *Compilation of Notes and Memoranda Bearing Upon the Use of Human Ordure and Human Urine in Rites of Religious or Semi-Religious Character.* Washington, D.C., 1888.

———. "The Folk-Foods of the Rio Grande Valley and of Northern Mexico," *Journal of American Folklore* 8 (1895): 41–71.

———. "Notes upon the Gentile Organization of the Apaches of Arizona," *Journal of American Folklore* 3 (1890): 113–24.

———. *The Snake Dance of the Moquis of Arizona.* New York, 1884.

———. *The Urine Dance of the Zuni Indians of New Mexico.* Privately printed, 1920.

Boxer, Charles R. *The Christian Century in Japan, 1549–1650.* Berkeley, Calif., 1951.

———. *The Church Militant and Iberian Expansion, 1440–1770.* Baltimore, 1978.

―――. *Mary and Misogyny: Women in Iberian Expansion Overseas, 1415–1815*. London, 1975.

Boyd, E. *Popular Arts of Spanish New Mexico*. Santa Fe, 1974.

Brading, David A., and Celia Wu. "Population Growth and Crisis: León, 1720–1860," *Journal of Latin American Studies* 5 (1973): 12–13.

Brandt, Elizabeth. "On Secrecy and the Control of Knowledge: Taos Pueblo," in Stanton K. Tefft, ed., *Secrecy: A Cross-Cultural Perspective* (New York, 1980): 123–46.

―――. "The Role of Secrecy in a Pueblo Society," in T. C. Blackburn, ed., *Flowers of the Wind: Papers on Ritual, Myth and Symbolism in California and the Southwest* (Socorro, N.M., 1977): 11–28.

Bricker, Victoria R. *The Indian Christ, The Indian King*. Austin, Texas, 1981.

Brigas, Fray Diego Miguel. *Friar Brigas Reports to the King: Methods of Indoctrination on the Frontier of New Spain 1796–97*. Tucson, 1977.

Brown, Judith C. *Immodest Acts: The Life of a Lesbian Nun in Renaissance Italy*. Oxford, 1986.

Brown, Raphael. *Fifty Animal Stories of St. Francis*. New York, 1962.

―――, ed. and trans. *The Little Flowers of St. Francis*. Garden City, N.Y., 1958.

Brugge, David M. *Navajos in the Catholic Church Records of New Mexico 1694–1875*. Window Rock, Ariz., 1968.

―――. "Some Plains Indians in the Church Records of New Mexico," *Plains Anthropologist* 10 (1965): 181–89.

Brundage, James A. "The Problem of Impotence," in Vern L. Bullough and James A. Brundage, eds., *Sexual Practices and the Medieval Church* (Buffalo, 1982): 135–40.

Bullough, Vern L. "Homosexuality as Submissive Behavior: Examples from Mythology," *Journal of Sex Research* 9 (1973): 283–88.

―――, and James A. Brundage, eds. *Sexual Practices and the Medieval Church*. Buffalo, 1982.

Bunzel, Ruth. *Zuñi Katcinas*. Washington, D.C., 1932.

―――. "Zuñi Ritual Poetry," in *Forty-seventh Annual Report of the Bureau of American Ethnology* (Washington, D.C., 1929): 679–90.

Burguière, André. "From Malthus to Max Weber: Belated Marriage and the Spirit of Enterprise," in Robert Forster and Orest A. Ranum, eds., *Family and Society* (Baltimore, 1976): 237–50.

Burns, Allan F. "The Caste War in the 1970's: Present-Day Accounts from Village Quintana Roo," in Grant D. Jones, ed., *Anthropology and History in Yucatan* (Austin, Texas, 1977): 259–74.

Bynum, Caroline W. "The Body of Christ in the Later Middle Age: A Reply to Leo Steinberg," *Renaissance Quarterly* 39 (1986): 399–439.

―――. "Fast, Feast, and Flesh: The Religious Significance of Food to Medieval Women," *Representations* 11 (1985): 1–25.

―――. *Holy Feast and Holy Fast: The Religious Significance of Food to Medieval Women*. Berkeley, Calif., 1987.

————. *Jesus as Mother: Studies in the Spirituality of the High Middle Ages.* Berkeley, Calif., 1982.

Callahan, William J. *Honor, Commerce and Industry in Eighteenth-Century Spain.* Boston, 1972.

Callender, Charles, and Lee M. Kochems. "The North American Berdache," *Current Anthropology* 24 (1983): 443–70.

Campa, Arthur L. *Spanish Folk-Poetry in New Mexico.* Albuquerque, 1946.

————. *Spanish Religious Folktheatre in the Southwest.* Albuquerque, 1943.

Canedo, Lino Gómez. *Evangelización y Conquista: Experiencia Franciscana en Hispanoamérica.* Mexico City, 1977.

Capdequí, *see* Ots Capdequí.

Caplan, Pat, ed. *The Cultural Construction of Sexuality.* London, 1987.

Carballo, José Bermejo. *Glorias religiosas de Sevilla o noticia descriptiva de todas las cofradías de penitencia, sangre y luz formadas en esta ciudad.* Seville, 1882.

Carberry, John J. *The Juridical Form of Marriage.* Washington, D.C., 1934.

Carreras y Candi, F. *Folklore y costumbres de España.* Barcelona, 1931.

Carroll, H. Bailey, and J. Villasana Haggard, eds. *Three New Mexico Chronicles.* Albuquerque, 1942.

Castro, Américo. *De La Edad Conflictiva: Crisis de la Cultura Española en el Siglo XVII.* Madrid, 1972.

————. *España y su Historia: Cristianos, Moros y Judios.* Barcelona, 1983.

————. *The Spaniards: An Introduction to Their History.* Berkeley, Calif., 1971.

Champe, Flavia Waters. *The Matachines Dance of the Upper Rio Grande: History, Music, and Choreography.* Lincoln, Neb., 1983.

Chapman, Donald. *Colonial Hispanic America: A History.* New York, 1933.

Chávez, Fray Angélico. *Archives of the Archdiocese of Santa Fe, 1678–1900.* Washington, D.C., 1957.

————. "De Vargas' Negro Drummer," *El Palacio* 54 (1949): 128–35.

————. "Genízaros," in *Handbook of North American Indians* (Washington, D.C., 1979): vol. 9, pp. 198–200.

————. "New Mexico Religious Place-Names Other than Those of Saints," *El Palacio* 57 (1950): 23–26.

————. "Nuestra Señora del Rosario La Conquistadora," *NMHR* 23 (1948): 94–128, 177–216.

————. *Origins of New Mexico Families.* Santa Fe, 1975.

————. *Our Lady of the Conquest.* Albuquerque, 1948.

————. "Pohe-yemo's Representative and the Pueblo Revolt of 1680," *NMHR* 42 (1967): 85–126.

————. "Saint's Names in New Mexico Geography," *El Palacio* 56 (1949): 323–35.

————. "El Vicario Don Santiago Roybal," *El Palacio* 55 (1948): 231–52.

————. ed. and trans. *The Oroz Codex.* Washington, D.C., 1972.

Chipman, Donald. "The Oñate-Moctezuma-Zaldívar Families of Northern New Spain," *NMHR* 52 (1957): 297–310.

Christian, William A., Jr. *Apparitions in Late Medieval and Renaissance Spain.* Princeton, 1981.

Clendinnen, Inga. *Ambivalent Conquests: Maya and Spaniard in Yucatan, 1517–1570.* Cambridge, Eng., 1987.

———. "The Cost of Courage in Aztec Society," *Past and Present* 107 (1985): 44–89.

———. "Disciplining the Indians: Franciscan Ideology and Missionary Violence in Sixteenth-Century Yucatan," *Past and Present* 94 (1982): 27–48.

———. "Franciscan Missionaries in Sixteenth-Century Mexico," in Jim Obelkevich, ed., *Disciplines of Faith: Studies in Religion, Politics, and Patriarchy* (London, Eng., 1987): 229–45.

Clissold, Stephen. *The Seven Cities of Cibola.* New York, 1962.

———. *The Wisdom of St. Francis and His Companions.* New York, 1978.

———. *The Wisdom of the Spanish Mystics.* New York, 1977.

Cohn, Norman. *The Pursuit of the Millennium.* New York, 1977.

Collier, Jane. *Marriage and Inequality in Classless Societies.* Stanford, Calif., 1988.

———, and Sylvia Yanagisako, eds. *Gender and Kinship: Essays Toward a Unified Analysis.* Stanford, Calif., 1987.

Congar, Yves M. J. *I Believe in the Holy Spirit.* New York, 1984.

Corbett, Percy E. *The Roman Law of Marriage.* Oxford, 1930.

Cousins, E., ed. and trans. "The Life of St. Francis," in *Bonaventure.* New York, 1978.

Cramp, James Mockett. *A Text-Book of Popery; Comprising a Brief History of the Council of Trent.* New York, 1831.

Crosby, Alfred W. *The Columbian Exchange: Biological and Cultural Consequences of 1492.* Westport, Conn., 1972.

Cushing, Frank H. "Origin Myth from Oraibi," *Journal of American Folk-Lore* 36 (1923): 163–70.

———. *Zuni Fetishes.* Flagstaff, 1966.

Cuthbert, Father, O.S.F.C. *The Romanticism of St. Francis.* New York, 1915.

Cutter, Charles R. *The Protector de Indios in Colonial New Mexico 1659–1821.* Albuquerque, 1986.

Cutter, Donald, trans. "An Anonymous Statistical Report on New Mexico in 1765," *NMHR* 50 (1975): 347–52.

Dabney, William M., and Josiah C. Russell, eds. *Dargan Historical Essays.* Albuquerque, 1952.

Daniel, E. Randolph. "The Desire for Martyrdom: A Leitmotiv of St. Bonaventure," *Franciscan Studies* 32 (1972): 74–87.

———. *The Franciscan Concept of Mission in the High Middle Ages.* Lexington, Ky., 1975.

Davis, David Brion. *The Problem of Slavery in Western Culture.* Ithaca, N.Y., 1966.

Davis, Irvine. "Linguistic Clues to Northern Rio Grande Prehistory," *El Palacio* 66 (1959): 73–84.

Davis, J. *People of the Mediterranean.* London, 1977.

Davis, John, ed. *Religious Organization and Religious Experience.* New York, 1982.

Davis, William W. *El Gringo: Or New Mexico and Her People.* New York, 1857.

Defouri, James B. *The Martyrs of New Mexico: A Brief Account of the Lives and Deaths of the Earliest Missionaries in the Territory.* Las Vegas, N.M., 1893.

Defourneaux, Marcelin. *Daily Life in Spain in the Golden Age.* Stanford, Calif., 1979.

Denziger, Heinrich J. D. *The Sources of Catholic Dogma.* St. Louis, 1957.

Díaz del Castillo, Bernal. *Historia Verdadera de la Conquista de la Nueva España.* Mexico City, 1955.

Di Peso, Charles C., John B. Rinaldo, and Gloria J. Fenner. *Casas Grandes, a Fallen Trading Center of the Gran Chichimeca.* Flagstaff, 1974.

Dockstader, Frederick J. *The Katchina and the White Man.* Albuquerque, 1985.

Douglas, Mary. *Purity and Danger: An Analysis of Concepts of Pollution and Taboo.* London, 1970.

———. *Witchcraft, Confessions and Accusations.* London, 1970.

Dozier, Edward. "Factionalism at Santa Clara Pueblo," *Ethnology* 5 (1969): 172–85.

———. "Making Inferences from the Present to the Past," in W. Longacre, ed., *Reconstructing Prehistoric Pueblo Societies* (Albuquerque, 1970): 202–13.

———. *The Pueblo Indians of North America.* New York, 1970.

Duberman, Martin, ed. "Documents in Hopi Indian Sexuality: Imperialism, Culture and Resistance," *Radical History Review* 20 (1979): 81–124.

Dubos, René. "Franciscan Conservation versus Benedictine Stewardship," in David and Eileen Spring, eds., *Ecology and Religion in History* (New York, 1974): 114–136.

Duby, Georges. *The Three Orders: Feudal Society Imagined.* Chicago, 1980.

Dugmore, C. W. *The Mass and the English Reformers.* London, 1958.

Dumézil, Georges. *The Destiny of a King.* Chicago, 1973.

———. *The Destiny of the Warrior.* Chicago, 1970.

Dussel, Enrique D. *A History of the Church in Latin America: Colonialism to Liberation (1492–1979).* Grand Rapids, Mich., 1981.

Egaña, Antonio de. *La Teoría de Regio Vicariato Español en Indias.* Rome, 1958.

Eggan, Fred. *The Social Organization of the Western Pueblos.* Chicago, 1950.

Eisenstadt, S. N. *Max Weber on Charisma and Institution Building.* Chicago, 1968.

Eliade, Mircea. *Mephistopheles and the Androgyne: Studies in Religious Myth and Symbol.* New York, 1965.

———. *The Myth of the Eternal Return.* New York, 1954.

———. *Patterns in Comparative Religion.* New York, 1974.

Elison, George. *Deus Destroyed: The Image of Christianity in Early Modern Japan.* Cambridge, Mass., 1973.

Ellis, Florence Hawley. "A Pantheon of Kachinas," *New Mexico Magazine* 53 (1975): 13–28.

———. "Patterns of Aggression and the War Cult in Southwestern Pueblos," *Southwestern Journal of Anthropology* 7 (1951): 177–201.

———. "Tomé and Father J. B. R.," *NMHR* 30 (1955): 89–114.

Ely, A. G. "The Excavation and Repair of Quarai Mission." M.A. thesis, University of New Mexico, 1935.

Erdoes, Richard, and Alfonso Ortiz, eds. *American Indian Myths and Legends.* New York, 1984.

Escriche, Joaquín. *Diccionario razonado de legislación civil, penal, comercial y forense.* Valencia, 1838.

Espinosa, Aurelio M. *España en Nuevo Méjico.* New York, 1937.

———. *The Folklore of Spain in the American Southwest.* Norman, Okla., 1985.

———. "Romances españoles tradicionales que cantan y recitan los indios de los pueblos de Nuevo Méjico," *Boletín de la Biblioteca de Menéndez y Pelayo* 14 (1932): 98–109.

———. "Spanish Folk-lore in New Mexico," *NMHR* 1 (1926): 135–55.

Espinosa, J. Manuel. *Crusaders of the Rio Grande: The Story of Don Diego de Vargas and the Reconquest and Refounding of New Mexico.* Chicago, 1942.

———. "Notes on the Lineage of Don Diego de Vargas," *NMHR* 10 (1935): 112–20.

———. "The Virgin of the Reconquest of New Mexico," *Mid-America* 18 (1936): 79–87.

———, ed. and trans. *First Expedition of Vargas into New Mexico, 1692.* Albuquerque, 1940.

Espinosa, José E. *Saints in the Valleys: Christian Sacred Images in the History, Life and Folk Art of Spanish New Mexico.* Albuquerque, 1960.

Farmer, Malcolm F. "A Suggested Typology for Defensive Systems of the Southwest," *Southwestern Journal of Anthropology* 13 (1957): 249–67.

Farriss, Nancy M. *Crown and Clergy in Colonial Mexico 1759–1821: The Crisis of Ecclesiastical Privilege.* London, 1968.

———. "Nucleation Versus Dispersal: The Dynamics of Population Movement in Colonial Yucatan," *HAHR* 58 (1978): 187–216.

Fergusson, Erna. *Dancing Gods: Indian Ceremonials of New Mexico and Arizona.* Albuquerque, 1966.

Fernández, *see* Giménez Fernández.

Fewkes, Jesse Walter. "A Few Tusayan Pictographs," *American Anthropologist* 5 (1892): 9–26.

———. "An Interpretation of Katcina Worship," *Journal of American Folklore* 14 (1901): 81–94.

———. *Prehistoric Villages, Castles, and Towns of Southwestern Colorado.* Washington, D.C., 1919.

———. "The Snake Ceremonials at Walpi," *Journal of American Ethnology and Archaeology* 5 (1894): 19–42.

———. "Tusayan Migration Traditions," in *Nineteenth Annual Report of the Bureau of American Ethnology* (Washington, D.C., 1900): 573–634.

———. "The Tusayan New-fire Ceremony," *Proceedings of the Boston Society of Natural History* 26 (1895): 440–47.

Fielding, William. *Strange Customs of Courtship and Marriage.* Garden City, N.Y., 1960.

Fireman, Janet. *The Spanish Royal Corps of Engineers in the Western Borderlands: Instrument of Bourbon Reform, 1764 to 1815.* Glendale, Calif., 1977.

Firth, Raymond. *Symbols: Public and Private.* Ithaca, N.Y., 1975.

Flandrin, Jean-Louis. "Contraception, Marriage, and Sexual Relations in the Christian West," in Robert Forster and Orest A. Ranum, eds., *Biology of Man in History* (Baltimore, 1975): 15–38.

———. *Families in Former Times.* Cambridge, Eng., 1979.

Focher, Fray Juan. *Itinerario del Misionero en América.* Madrid, 1960.

Forbes, Jack D. *Apache, Navaho and Spaniard.* Norman, Okla., 1960.

———. "The Appearance of the Mounted Indian in Northern New Mexico and the Southwest, to 1680," *Southwestern Journal of Anthropology* 15 (1959): 189–212.

———. "Unknown Athapaskans: The Identification of the Jano, Jocome, Suma, Manso, and Other Indian Tribes of the Southwest," *Ethnohistory* 4 (1959): 59–82.

Ford, Daryll C. "A Creation Myth from Acoma," *Folk-Lore* 41 (1930): 359–87.

Ford, Richard I. "An Ecological Perspective on the Eastern Pueblos," in Ortiz, ed., *New Perspectives on the Pueblos*: 1–18.

———. "Barter, Gift or Violence: An Analysis of Tewa Inter-tribal Exchange," in E. Wilmsen, ed., *Social Exchange and Interaction* (Ann Arbor, Mich., 1972): 21–46.

Forrestal, Peter P., trans., *Benavides' Memorial of 1630.* Washington, D.C., 1954.

Fortini, Arnaldo. *Francis of Assisi.* New York, 1981.

Foster, Elizabeth Andros, ed. and trans. *Motolinia's History of the Indians of New Spain.* Albuquerque, 1950.

Fox, Robin. *The Keresan Bridge.* London, 1967.

———. *Kinship and Marriage.* London, 1967.

Franciscan Order. *Cartilla y doctrina espiritual para la crianza y educación de los novicios que toman el hábito en la orden de N. P. S. Francisco: En la qual brevemente se les enseña lo que deben hacer conforme a la doctrina de N. Seráfico Doctor San Buenaventura, y a lo que se usa, y practica en la Santa Provincia del Santo Evangelio.* Mexico City, 1775.

———. *Instrucción y doctrina de novicios, Sacada de la de San Buenaventura.* Mexico City, 1738.

Frank, Roslyn M., Monique Laxalt, and Nancy Vosberg. "Inheritance, Marriage, and Dowry Rights in the Navarrese and French Basque Law Codes," in *Proceedings of the Fourth Annual Meeting of the Western Society for French History* (1976): 22–31.

French, David H. *Factionalism in Isleta Pueblo*. Seattle, 1966.

Freud, Sigmund. *The Future of an Illusion*. New York, 1951.

———. *The Standard Edition of the Complete Psychological Works of Sigmund Freud*. London, 1957.

Freyre, Gilberto. "The Patriarchal Basis of Brazilian Society," in Joseph Maier and Richard W. Weatherhead, eds., *Politics of Change in Latin America* (New York, 1964): 155–73.

Furst, Peter T. "Fertility, Vision Quest and Auto-Sacrifice: Some Thoughts on Ritual Blood-Letting Among the Maya," in M. Greene Robertson, ed., *The Art, Iconography and Dynastic History of Palenque, Part III* (Pebble Beach, Calif., 1976): 183–89.

Gallop, Jane. "Psychoanalytic Criticism: Some Intimate Questions," *Art in America* 72 (1984): 9–15.

García Icazbalceta, Joaquín. *Nueva Colección de Documentos para la Historia de México*. Mexico City, 1941.

Gaskin, Katharine. "Age at First Marriage in Europe before 1850: A Summary of Family Reconstitution Data," *Journal of Family History* 3 (1978): 23–33.

Gerhard, Peter. *The Northern Frontier of New Spain*. Princeton, N.J., 1982.

Gifford, E. W. "Cultural Elements Distribution: XII Apache-Pueblo," *University of California Anthropological Records* 4 (1940): 4–90.

Giménez Fernández, Manuel. *El Concilio IV Mejicano*. Seville, 1939.

Girard, René. *The Scapegoat*. Baltimore, 1986.

———. *Violence and the Sacred*. Ithaca, N.Y., 1977.

Gluckman, Max. *Custom and Conflict in Africa*. Oxford, 1955.

———, ed. *Essays on the Ritual of Social Relations*. Manchester, Eng., 1962.

Góngora, Mario. *Studies in the Colonial History of Spanish America*. Cambridge, Eng., 1975.

Gonzales de León, Félix. *Historia crítica y descriptiva de la cofradías de Sevilla*. Seville, 1852.

Goode, William J. "The Theoretical Importance of Love," *American Sociological Review* 24 (1959): 38–47.

Goodich, Michael. "Childhood and Adolescence among Thirteenth Century Saints," *History of Childhood Quarterly* 1 (1973): 286–95.

Goodsell, Willystine. *A History of Marriage and the Family*. New York, 1934.

Goodwin, A., ed. *The European Nobility in the Eighteenth Century*. London, 1953.

Goody, Jack, ed. *The Developmental Cycle in Domestic Groups*. Cambridge, Eng., 1958.

Goody, Jack, and S. J. Tambiah. *Bridewealth and Dowry*. Cambridge, Eng., 1973.

Gougaud, L. *Devotional and Ascetic Practices in the Middle Ages*. London, 1927.

Gregg, Josiah. *Commerce of the Prairies*. Norman, Okla., 1954.

Grimes, Ronald L. *Symbol and Conquest: Public Ritual and Drama in Santa Fe, New Mexico*. Ithaca, N.Y., 1976.

Gudeman, Stephen. "The Compadrazgo as a Reflection of the Natural and Spiritual Person," in *Proceedings of the Royal Anthropological Institute of Great Britain and Ireland* (1971): 43–49.

——. "Spiritual Relationships and Selecting a Godparent," *Man* 10 (1975): 221–37.

——, and Stuart B. Schwartz, "Baptismal Godparents in Slavery: Cleansing Original Sin in Eighteenth-Century Bahia," in Raymond T. Smith, ed., *Interpreting Kinship Ideology and Practice in Latin America* (Chapel Hill, N.C., 1984): 35–58.

Guernsey, S. J. "Notes on a Navajo War Dance," *American Anthropologist* 22 (1920): 304–7.

Gumerman, George, and Emil W. Haury, "Prehistory: Hohokam," in *Handbook of North American Indians* (Washington, D.C., 1979): vol. 9, pp. 79–90.

Gunn, John M. *Schat-Chen; History, Traditions and Narratives of the Queres Indians of Laguna and Acoma*. Albuquerque, 1917.

Gunnerson, James H., and Dolores A. Gunnerson. "Apachean Culture: A Study of Unity and Diversity," in Keith H. Basso and Morris E. Opler, eds., *Apachean Culture, History and Ethnology* (Tucson, 1971): 7–27.

Gutiérrez, Ramón A. "Marriage, Sex and the Family: Social Change in Colonial New Mexico City." Ph.D. diss., University of Wisconsin, 1980.

Guttentag, Marcia, and Paul Secord. *Too Many Women? The Sex Ratio*. Beverly Hills, Calif., 1983.

Hackett, Charles W., ed. and trans. *Historical Documents Relating to New Mexico, Nueva Vizcaya, and Approaches Thereto, 1773*, vol. 3. Washington, D.C., 1937.

——. *Revolt of the Pueblo Indians of New Mexico and Otermín's Attempted Reconquest, 1680–1682*. Albuquerque, 1942. 2 vols.

Hadlock, Wendel S. "Warfare among the Northeastern Woodland Indians," *American Anthropologist* 45 (1947): 204–21.

Haeberlin, K. H. *The Idea of Fertilization in the Culture of the Pueblo Indians*. New York, 1916.

Hafen, LeRoy R., and Ann W. Hafen. *Old Spanish Trail: Santa Fe to Los Angeles*. Glendale, Calif., 1954.

Hajnal, J. "European Marriage Patterns in Perspective," in D. V. Glass and D. E. C. Eversley, eds., *Population in History: Essays in Historical Demography* (London, 1965): 101–46.

Hallenbeck, Cleve. *Land of the Conquistadores*. Caldwell, Idaho, 1950.

Hallpike, C. R. "Social Hair," in Ted Polhemus, ed., *The Body Reader: Social Aspects of the Human Body* (New York, 1978): 134–48.

Hammond, George P., and Agapito Rey, eds. and trans. *Don Juan de Oñate: Colonizer of New Mexico, 1595–1628*. Albuquerque, 1953. 2 vols.

——. *Narratives of the Coronado Expedition, 1540–1542*. Albuquerque, 1940.

——. *The Rediscovery of New Mexico, 1580–1594: The Explorations of Chumascado, Espejo, Castaño de Sosa, Morlete, and Leyna de Bonilla and Humana*. Albuquerque, 1966.

Hammond, William A. "The Disease of the Scythians (*Morbus Feminarum*) and Certain Analogous Conditions," *American Journal of Neurology and Psychiatry* 1 (1882): 339–55.

Hanke, Lewis. *History of Latin America Civilization, Sources and Interpretation.* Boston, 1967.

Hardison, O. B. "The Mass as Sacred Drama," in *Christian Rite and Christian Drama in the Middle Ages: Essays in the Origin and Early History of Modern Drama* (Baltimore, 1965): 35–79.

Harms, Robert W. "The Wars of August: Diagonal Narratives in African History," *American Historical Review* 88 (1983): 809–34.

Hawley, Florence. "Beyond Taos," *New Mexico* 19 (1941): 14–39.

Hay, Henry. "The Hammond Report," *One Institute Quarterly* 6 (1963): 6–21.

Henderson, Alice C. *Brothers of Light.* New York, 1937.

Herbermann, Charles G., et al., eds. *The Catholic Encyclopedia.* New York, 1907.

Herdt, Gilbert H. *Guardians of the Flute: Idioms of Masculinity.* New York, 1981.

———. *Rituals of Manhood: Male Initiation in Papua New Guinea.* Berkeley, Calif., 1982.

———. *Ritualized Homosexuality in Melanesia.* Berkeley, Calif., 1984.

Hernáez, Francisco J., ed. *Colección de bulas, breves y otros documentos relativos a la iglesia de América y Filipinas.* Brussels, 1879.

Hernández, Juan. "Cactus Whips and Wooden Crosses," *Journal of American Folklore* 76 (1963): 216–24.

Herrero, M. *La Semana Santa en Madrid en el Siglo XVII.* Madrid, 1935.

Hibben, Fred. "Mexican Features of Mural Paintings at Pottery Mound," *Archaeology* 20 (1967): 84–87.

Hieb, Louis A. "Meaning and Mismeaning: Toward an Understanding of the Ritual Clown," in Alfonso Ortiz, ed., *New Perspectives on the Pueblos* (Albuquerque, 1972): 163–95.

Hill, W. W. *The Agriculture and Hunting Methods of the Navajo Indians.* New Haven, Conn., 1938.

———. *Navaho Warfare.* New Haven, Conn., 1936.

———. "The Status of the Hermaphrodite and Transvestite in Navaho Culture," *American Anthropologist* 37 (1935): 273–79.

Hobbes, Thomas. *Leviathan: Or the Matter, Forme and Power of a Commonwealth Ecclesiastical and Civil.* New York, 1974.

Hocart, Arthur M. *Kingship.* London, 1927.

Hoch-Smith, Judith, and Anita Spring, eds., *Women in Ritual and Symbolic Roles.* New York, 1978.

Hodge, Frederick W., George P. Hammond, and Agapito Rey, eds. and trans. *Fray Alonso de Benavides' Revised Memorial of 1634.* Albuquerque, 1945.

Honig, Edwin. *Calderón and the Seizures of Honor.* Cambridge, Mass., 1972.

Horgan, Paul. *Centuries of Santa Fe.* Santa Fe, 1956.

———. *Great River: The Rio Grande in North American History.* Austin, Texas, 1984.

Horvath, Steven M. "The Social and Political Organization of the Genízaros of Plaza de Nuestra Señora de Los Dolores de Belén, New Mexico, 1740–1812." Ph.D. diss., Brown University, 1979.

Ibrahim, Shirley D. "Estevan, the Moor of New Mexico: An Experiment in Point of View." Ed.D. diss., East Texas State University, 1978.

Icazbalceta, Joaquín García, ed. *Códice Franciscano*, vol. 2 of *Nueva colección de documentos para la historia de México*. Mexico City, 1941.

Israel, J. I. *Race, Class and Politics in Colonial Mexico, 1610–1670*. London, 1975.

Jacobs, Sue-Ellen. "Berdache: A Brief Review of the Literature," *Colorado Anthropologist* 1 (1968): 25–40.

———. "Comment," *Current Anthropology* 24 (1983): 459–60.

Jacobs, Wilbur R. *Wilderness Politics and Gifts: The Northern Colonial Frontier, 1748–1763*. Lincoln, Neb., 1950.

James, Thomas. *Three Years among the Indians and the Mexicans*. Waterloo, Ill., 1846.

Jaramillo, Cleofas M. *Shadows of the Past*. Santa Fe, 1941.

Jedin, Hubert. *Crisis and Closure of the Council of Trent*. London, 1967.

Jenkins, Myra Ellen. "The Baltasar Baca 'Grant': History of an Encroachment," *El Palacio* 68 (1961): 47–64.

———. "Spanish Land Grants in the Tewa Area," *NMHR* 47 (1972): 113–50.

Johnson, Harold B., Jr. *From Reconquest to Empire: The Iberian Background to Latin American History*. New York, 1970.

Johnson, Paul C. *The California Missions*. Menlo Park, Calif., 1981.

Jones, Oakah L. *Los Paisanos: Spanish Settlers on the Northern Frontier of New Spain*. Norman, Okla., 1979.

———. *Pueblo Warriors and Spanish Conquest*. Norman, Okla., 1966.

Joralemon, David. "Ritual Blood-Sacrifice among the Ancient Maya," in M. Greene Robertson, ed., *Primera Mesa Redonda de Palenque, Part II*. (Pebble Beach, Calif., 1974): 59–75.

Jorgensen, Joseph G. "Comparative Traditional Economics and Ecological Adaptations," in *Handbook of North American Indians*: vol. 10, pp. 684–710.

———. *Western Indians: Comparative Environments, Languages, and Cultures of 172 Western American Indian Tribes*. San Francisco, 1980.

Joyce, George H. *Christian Marriage: An Historical and Doctrinal Society*. London, 1948.

Judd, N. M. *The Material Culture of Pueblo Bonito*. Washington, D.C., 1954.

Kantorowicz, Ernst H. *The King's Two Bodies: A Study in Mediaeval Political Theology*. Princeton, N.J., 1957.

Kaplan, Steven L., ed. *Understanding Popular Culture*. Berlin, 1984.

Karath, Gertrude P., and Antonio García. *Music and Dance of the Tewa Pueblos*. Santa Fe, 1970.

Katz, Jonathan. *Gay American History*. New York, 1976.

Keleher, William A. "Law of the New Mexico Land Grant," *NMHR* 4 (1929): 350–71.

Kelley, Charles J. "Factors Involved in the Abandonment of Certain Peripheral Southwestern Settlements," *American Anthropologist* 54 (1952): 356–87.

Kelly, Henry K. *Franciscan Missions of New Mexico City, 1740–1760*. Albuquerque, 1941.

Kenner, Charles L. *A History of New Mexican-Plains Indian Relations*. Norman, Okla., 1969.

Kessell, John L. *Kiva, Cross and Crown: The Pecos Indians and New Mexico, 1540–1840*. Albuquerque, 1987.

———. *The Missions of New Mexico Since 1776*. Albuquerque, 1980.

Kintigh, Keith W. *Settlement, Subsistence, and Society in Late Zuni Prehistory*. Tucson, 1985.

Kirk, Sister Martha Ann. *Dancing With Creation: Mexican and Native American Dance in Christian Worship and Education*. Saratoga, Calif., 1983.

Kirk, Ruth F. "Introduction to Zuni Fetishism," *El Palacio* 50 (1943): 117–29, 146–59.

———. "Little Santu of Cibola," *New Mexico Magazine* 18 (1940): 16–17, 35–38.

Kittle, J. L. "Folk Music of the Upper Rio Grande," *Southwest Review* 30 (1945): 192–95.

Kluckhohn, Clyde. *Navaho Witchcraft*. Boston, 1967.

Konetzke, Richard. *Colección de Documentos para la Historia de la Formación Social de Hispanoamérica, 1493–1810*. Madrid, 1956–62.

———. "La Formación de la nobleza en Indias," *Estudios Americanos* 10 (1951): 329–57.

Kubler, George. *Mexican Architecture of the Sixteenth Century*. New Haven, Conn., 1948.

———. *Religious Architecture of New Mexico*. Albuquerque, 1972.

Kurath, Gertrude P. "The Origin of the Pueblo Indian Matachines," *El Palacio* 64 (1957): 259–64.

La Iglesia de Santa Cruz de la Cañada, 1733–1983. Santa Cruz, N.M., 1983.

Ladd, Doris M. *The Mexican Nobility at Independence, 1780–1826*. Austin, Texas, 1976.

Lamar, Howard R. *The Far Southwest, 1846–1912: A Territorial History*. New Haven, Conn., 1966.

Lambert, Malcolm D. *Franciscan Poverty: The Doctrine of the Absolute Poverty of Christ and the Apostles in the Franciscan Order, 1210–1323*. London, 1961.

Lambert, Marjorie E. *Pa-ako; Archaeological Chronicle of an Indian Village in North Central New Mexico*. Santa Fe, 1954.

Larson, Donald R. *The Honor Plays of Lope de Vega*. Cambridge, Mass., 1977.

Laughlin, Ruth. *Caballeros: The Romance of Santa Fe and the Southwest*. Caldwell, Idaho, 1931.

Lavrin, Asunción, and Edith Couturier. "Dowries and Wills: A View of Women's Socioeconomic Role in Colonial Guadalajara and Puebla, 1640–1790," *HAHR* 59 (1979): 280–304.

Leach, Edmund. "Characterization of Caste and Class Systems," in A. de Reuck and J. Knight, eds., *Caste and Race: Comparative Approaches* (London, 1967): 19–25.

———. "Magic Hair," in John C. Middleton, ed., *Myth and Cosmos: Readings in Mythology and Symbolism* (Garden City, N.Y., 1967): 77–108.

———. "Virgin Birth," *Proceedings of the Royal Anthropological Institute* (1966): 39–49.

Leborans, María Jesús Fernández. *Luz y oscuridad en la mística española.* Madrid, 1978.

Leclercq, Jean. *Monks and Love in Twelfth-Century France: Psychohistorical Essays.* Oxford, 1979.

Lejeal, León. "Rites Phalliques, Origine du Théâtre et des Sacrifices Humaines à Mexico," *Journal de la Societé des Americanistes* 2 (1905): 341–43.

León, Nicolás. "El Culto del Falo en el México Precolombino," *Anales del Museo Nacional* 1 (1904): 278–80.

Leonard, Irving A. *Books of the Brave.* New York, 1964.

———, ed. and trans. *The Mercurio Volante of Don Carlos de Sigüenza y Góngora. An Account of the First Expedition of Don Diego de Vargas into New Mexico in 1692.* Los Angeles, 1932.

Leonard, Olen. *The Role of the Land Grant in the Social Organization and Social Processes of a Spanish-American Village in New Mexico.* Albuquerque, 1970.

Lienhardt, Godfrey. *Social Anthropology.* Oxford, 1976.

Lipschütz, Alejandro. *El indoamericanismo y el problema racial en las Américas.* Santiago, 1944.

Little, Lester K. *Religious Poverty and the Profit Economy in Medieval Europe.* Ithaca, N.Y., 1978.

Llompart, C. R. Gabriel. "Desfile iconográfico de penitentes españoles (siglos XVI a XX)," *Revista de la Dialectología y Tradiciones Populares* 25 (1969): 31–51.

———. "Penitencias y penitentes en la pintura y en la piedad catalana bajomedievales." *Revista de la Dialoectología y Tradiciones Populares* 28 (1972): 229–49.

Lomnitz, Larissa Alder, and Marisol Pérez Lizaur. "The History of a Mexican Urban Family," *Journal of Family History* 3 (1978): 392–409.

Longacre, William A., ed. *Reconstructing Prehistoric Pueblo Societies.* Albuquerque, 1970.

Loomis, Noel, and Abraham Nasatir. *Pedro Vial and the Roads to Santa Fe.* Norman, Okla., 1967.

Lucero-White, Aurora. *Folk Dances of the Spanish Colonials of New Mexico.* Santa Fe, 1940.

———. *The Folklore of New Mexico.* Santa Fe, 1941.

———. "Los Pastores de Las Vegas." M.A. thesis, New Mexico Normal University, Las Vegas, 1932.

Lummis, Charles F. *The Land of Poco Tiempo.* New York, 1893.

———. *The Man Who Married the Moon and Other Pueblo Folktales.* New York, 1894.

Lynch, John. *Spain Under the Hapsburgs.* Oxford, 1981.

———. *The Spanish American Revolutions, 1808–1826.* New York, 1973.

Maier, Joseph, and Richard W. Weatherhead, eds. *Politics of Change in Latin America.* New York, 1964.

Maltz, Daniel N. "The Bride of Christ Is Filled with His Spirit," in Hoch-Smith and Spring, eds., *Women in Ritual and Symbolic Roles:* 27–44.

Mans Puigarnau, Jaime M. *Derecho matrimonial canónico.* Barcelona, 1951.

———. *Legislación, jurisprudencia y formularios sobre el matrimonio canónico.* Barcelona, 1951.

Martin, Calvin, ed. *The American Indian and the Problem of History.* New York, 1987.

Martin, Charles Basil. "The Survival of Medieval Religious Drama in New Mexico." Ph.D. diss., University of Missouri, 1959.

Martin, John Rupert. *Baroque.* New York, 1977.

Martínez-Alier, Verena. *Marriage, Class and Colour in Nineteenth Century Cuba.* Cambridge, Eng., 1974.

Mathien, Frances Joan, and Randall H. McGuire. *Ripples in the Chichimec Sea: New Considerations of Southwestern-Mesoamerican Interactions.* Carbondale, Ill., 1986.

Matson, Daniel S., and Bernard L. Fontana, eds. and trans. *Friar Brigas Reports to the King: Methods of Indoctrination on the Frontier of New Spain, 1796–97.* Tucson, 1977.

Matthews, Washington. *Navaho Legends.* New York, 1897.

Mauss, Marcel. *The Gift: Forms and Functions of Exchange in Archaic Societies.* New York, 1967.

———. "Techniques of the Body," *Economy and Society* 2 (1973): 70–87.

MacCormack, Sabine. *Art and Ceremony in Late Antiquity.* Berkeley, Calif., 1981.

———. "Change and Continuity in Late Antiquity: The Ceremony of *Adventus*," *Historia* 21 (1971): 721–52.

Mazuri, Ali. "The Robes of Rebellion: Sex, Dress and Politics in Africa," *Encounter* 34 (1970): 19–30.

McAlister, Lyle. "Social Structure and Social Change in New Spain," *HAHR* 43 (1963): 349–70.

McCluskey, Stephen C. "The Astronomy of the Hopi Indians," *Journal for the History of Astronomy* 8 (1977): 174–95.

McCrossan, Sister Joseph Marie. *The Role of the Church and the Folk in the Development of Early Drama in New Mexico.* Philadelphia, 1948.

McGarry, Daniel D. "Educational Methods of the Franciscans in Spanish California," *The Americas* 6 (1950): 335–58.

McLaughlin, Eleanor Commo. "Equality of Souls, Inequality of Sexes: Women in Medieval Theology," in R. Ruether, ed., *Religion and Sexism* (New York, 1974): 213–66.

McNitt, Frank. *Navajo Wars: Military Campaigns, Slave Raids and Reprisals.* Albuquerque, 1972.

Meeker, Michael E., Kathleen Barlow, and David M. Lipset. "Culture, Exchange, and Gender: Lessons from the Murik," *Cultural Anthropology* 1 (1986): 6–73.

Mendieta, Fray Gerónimo de. *Historia Eclesiástica Indiana*. Mexico City, 1945.

Meyer, Michael C. *Water in the Hispanic Southwest: A Social and Legal History, 1550–1850*. Tucson, 1984.

Middleton, John C., ed. *Myth and Cosmos: Readings in Mythology and Symbolism*. Garden City, N.Y., 1967.

Miers, Suzanne, and Igor Kopytoff, eds. *Slavery in Africa: Historical and Anthropological Perspectives*. Madison, Wisc., 1977.

Millett, Kate. *Sexual Politics*. New York, 1963.

Mindeleff, Cosmos. "Localization of Tusayan Clans," *19th Annual Report of the Bureau of American Ethnology* (Washington, D.C., 1900): 635–53.

Mishkin, Bernard. *Rank and Warfare among the Plains Indians*. New York, 1940.

Mitterauer, Michael, and Reinhard Sieder. *The European Family: Patriarchy to Partnership from the Middle Ages to the Present*. Oxford, 1982.

Montgomery, Ross Gordon, Watson Smith, and John Otis Brew. *Franciscan Awatovi: The Excavation and Conjectural Reconstruction of a 17th-Century Spanish Mission Establishment at a Hopi Indian Town in Northeastern Arizona*. Cambridge, Mass., 1949.

Moorhead, Max L. *New Mexico's Royal Road: Trade and Travel on the Chihuahua Trail*. Norman, Okla., 1958.

———. *The Presidio: Bastion of the Spanish Borderlands*. Norman, Okla., 1975.

Moorman, John. *A History of the Franciscan Order from its Origins to the Year 1517*. Oxford, 1968.

Morín, Claude. "Los libros parroquiales como fuente para la historia demográfica y social novohispana," *Historia Mexicana* 21 (1972): 412–19.

Mörner, Magnus. *Race Mixture in the History of Latin America*. Boston, 1967.

Motolinia, T. *History of the Indians of New Spain*. Albuquerque, 1950.

Munro, Edwin C. "The Nativity Plays of New Mexico." M.A. thesis, University of New Mexico, 1940.

Nabokov, Peter. *Indian Running*. New York, 1981.

Nash, June. "The Passion Play in Maya Indian Communities," *Comparative Studies in Society and History* 10 (1967): 318–27.

Naylor, Thomas. "The Extinct Suma of North Chihuahua: Their Origin, Cultural Identity, and Disappearance," *The Artifact* 7 (1969): 1–14.

Newcomb, W. W. *The Indians of Texas from Prehistoric to Modern Times*. Austin, Texas, 1961.

New Mexico Writers' Project. "Spanish-American Wedding Customs," *El Palacio* 49 (1942): 1–5.

Nida, Eugene A. "Mariology in Latin America," in William A. Smalley, ed., *Readings in Missionary Anthropology* (Pasadena, Calif., 1974): 17–25.

Niethammer, Carolyn. *Daughters of the Earth: The Lives and Legends of American Indian Women*. New York, 1977.

Noonan, John T., Jr. *Power to Dissolve: Lawyers and Marriages in the Courts of the Roman Curia.* Cambridge, Mass., 1972.

Oostendorp, H. T. *El Conflicto entre el honor y el amor en la literatura española hasta el siglo XVII.* The Hague, 1962.

Ortiz, Alfonso. *The Tewa World: Space, Time, Being, and Becoming in a Pueblo Society.* Chicago, 1969.

———, ed. *New Perspectives on the Pueblos.* Albuquerque, 1972.

Ortner, Sherry, and Harriet Whitehead, eds. *Sexual Meanings: The Cultural Construction of Gender and Sexuality.* Cambridge, Eng., 1981.

Ots Capdequí, José María. "Bosquejo histórico de los derechos de la mujer casada en la legislación de Indias," *Revista General de Legislación y Jurisprudencia* 132 (1918): 162–82.

———. *Instituciones Sociales de la América Española en el Periodo Colonial.* La Plata, Argentina, 1934.

Ozment, Steven E. *The Age of Reform, 1250–1550.* New Haven, Conn., 1980.

———. *Mysticism and Dissent: Religious Ideology and Social Protest in the Sixteenth Century.* New Haven, Conn., 1973.

Padilla, Fray Agustín Dávila. *Historia de la Fundación y Discurso de la Provincia de Santiago de México, de la Orden de Predicadores, por las Vidas de sus Varones Insignes y Casas Notables de Nueva España.* Belgium, 1634.

Pandey, Triloki Nath. "Images of Power in a Southwestern Pueblo," in Raymond D. Fogelson and Richard N. Adams, eds., *The Anthropology of Power* (New York, 1977): 195–216.

Pare, Peter. "The Doctrine of the Holy Spirit in the Western Church," *Theology* 12 (1948): 293–300.

Parmentier, Richard J. "The Pueblo Mythological Triangle: Poseyemu, Montezuma, and Jesus in the Pueblos," *Handbook of North American Indians*: vol. 9, pp. 609–22.

Parsons, Elsie C. "Hopi Mothers and Children," *Man* 21 (1921): 100.

———. *Hopi and Zuñi Ceremonialism.* Menasha, Wisc., 1933.

———. "Mothers and Children at Laguna," *Man* 19 (1919): 34–38.

———. "Mothers and Children at Zuñi," *Man* 19 (1919): 168.

———. "Nativity Myth at Laguna and Zuñi," *Journal of American Folk-Lore* 31 (1918): 256–63.

———. "Notes on a Navajo War Dance," *American Anthropologist* 21 (1919): 465–68.

———. "The Origin Myth of Zuñi," *Journal of American Folklore* 36 (1923): 135–62.

———. *Pueblo Indian Religion.* Chicago, 1939. 2 vols.

———. *The Scalp Ceremonial of Zuñi.* Menasha, Wisc., 1924.

———. *The Social Organization of the Tewa.* Menasha, Wisc., 1929.

———. "Spanish Elements in the Kachina Cult of the Pueblos," *Proceedings of the 23rd International Congress of Americanists* (London, 1928): 582–603.

———. "Tewa Mothers and Children," *Man* 24 (1924): 148–58.

————. "Witchcraft among the Pueblos: Indian or Spanish," *Man* 27 (1927): 106–12, 125–28.

————. "The Zuñi La'Mana," *American Anthropologist* 18 (1916): 521–28.

Patterson, Orlando. *Slavery and Social Death: A Comparative Study*. Cambridge, Mass., 1982.

Pazos, Manuel R. "El Teatro Franciscano en México durante el siglo XVI," *Archivo Ibero-Americano* 11 (1951): 129–89.

Pelikan, Jaroslav. *Jesus Through the Ages: His Place in the History of Culture*. New Haven, Conn., 1985.

Pérez, Salvador. "Folk Cycle in a Spanish New Mexican Village: Customs and Ceremonies of Birth, Marriage, and Death." M.A. thesis, University of New Mexico, 1949.

Pérez de Villagrá, Gaspar. *History of New Mexico*. Los Angeles, 1933.

Peristiany, J., ed. *Honour and Shame: The Values of Mediterranean Society*. Chicago, 1965.

Pescatello, Ann, ed. *Female and Male in Latin America*. Pittsburgh, 1973.

Phelan, John Leddy. "Authority and Flexibility in the Spanish Imperial Bureaucracy," *Administrative Science Quarterly* 5 (1960): 47–65.

————. *The Millennial Kingdom of the Franciscans in the New World*. Berkeley, Calif., 1970.

Phythian-Adams, Charles. "Ceremony and the Citizen: The Communal Year at Coventry, 1450–1550," in Peter Clark and Paul Slack, eds., *Crisis and Order in English Towns, 1500–1700* (Toronto, 1972): 57–85.

Pitt-Rivers, Julian. "Honor," in *International Encyclopedia of the Social Sciences* (New York, 1968): 503–11.

————. *The People of the Sierra*. Chicago, 1966.

Plog, Fred. "Prehistory: Western Anasazi," *Handbook of North American Indians*: vol. 9, pp. 131–51.

Polhemus, Ted., ed. *The Body Reader: Social Aspects of the Human Body*. New York, 1978.

Powell, Philip W. *Soldiers, Indians and Silver: The Northward Advance of New Spain, 1550–1600*. Berkeley, Calif., 1952.

Price, Richard. *First-Time: The Historical Vision of an Afro-American People*. Baltimore, 1983.

Prieto, Gabriel. "El Alma Sin Amor," *Revista Mexicana* 8 (1846): 186–87, contained in BN, Colección La Fragua, vol. 474, no. 5044.

Puigarnau, *see* Mans Puigarnau.

Qoyawayma, Polingaysi. *No Turning Back: A True Account of a Hopi Indian Girl's Struggle to Bridge the Gap Between the World of Her People and the World of the White Man*. Albuquerque, 1964.

Rael, Juan B. *Cuentos Españoles de Colorado y Nuevo Méjico*. Stanford, Calif., 1957.

————. *The New Mexican Alabado*. Stanford, Calif., 1951.

————. "New Mexico Wedding Songs," *Southern Folklore Quarterly* 4 (1940): 55–72.

Ralliere, J. B. *Cánticos espirituales con música.* Las Vegas, N.M., 1916.
———. *Colección de cánticos espirituales.* Las Vegas, N.M., 1892.
Ramírez, José Fernando. "Bautismo de Moteuhzoma II, Noveno Rey de México," *Boletín de la Sociedad Mexicana de Geografía y Estadística* 1a epoca, 10 (1863): 23–57.
Ramiro, Juan Tejada y, ed. *Colección de Canones y de todos los concilios de la iglesia de España y de América.* Madrid, 1849–55.
Rapp, I. H. "Pastores," *El Palacio* 11 (1921): 151–63.
Reinburg, Virginia. "Popular Prayers in Late Medieval and Reformation France." Ph.D. diss., Princeton University, 1985.
Reiter, Rayna R., ed. *Toward an Anthropology of Women.* New York, 1975.
Revello, José Tore. "Origines del teatro religioso en la América colonial," *Razón y Fe* 135 (1947): 220–34, 335–47.
Ribadeneyra, Antonio. *Manual Compendio de el Regio Patronato Indiano.* Madrid, 1755.
Ricard, Robert. *The Spiritual Conquest of Mexico.* Berkeley, Calif., 1966.
Robb, John Donald. "The Matachines Dance—a Ritual Folk Dance," *Western Folklore* 20 (1961): 87–101.
Roe, Frank G. "From Dogs to Horses among the Western Indian Tribes," *Proceedings and Transactions of the Royal Society of Canada* 33 (1939): 209–75.
Rozière, Sonia de la. *México: Angustia de sus Cristos.* Mexico City, 1967.
Sahlins, Marshall. *The Islands of History.* Chicago, 1985.
———. *Stone Age Economics.* Chicago, 1972.
———. *Tribesmen.* Englewood Cliffs, N.J., 1968.
Sánchez, Tomás. *De sancto matrimonii sacramento.* Antwerp, 1607.
Sánchez-Albornoz, Nicolás. *The Population of Latin America: A History.* Berkeley, Calif., 1974.
Sariñana y Cuenca, Fray Ysidro. *The Franciscan Martyrs of 1680: Funeral Oration over the Twenty-one Franciscan Missionaries Killed by the Pueblo Indians, August 10, 1680.* Santa Fe, 1906.
Sauer, Carl O. "The Credibility of The Friar Marcos Account," *NMHR* 16 (1941): 233–43.
———. *The Road to Cibola.* Berkeley, Calif., 1932.
Schaafsma, Polly, and Curtis Schaafsma. "Evidence for the Origins of the Pueblo Kachina Cult as Suggested by Southwestern Rock Art," *American Antiquity* 39 (1974): 535–45.
Schele, Linda, and Mary Ellen Miller. *The Blood of Kings: Dynasty and Ritual in Maya Art.* Fort Worth, Texas, 1986.
Schlegel, Alice. "The Adolescent Socialization of a Hopi Girl," *Ethnology* 12 (1973): 452–67.
———. "Male and Female in Hopi Thought and Action," in Alice Schlegel, ed., *Sexual Stratification: A Cross Cultural View* (New York, 1977): 245–69.

Schneider, Jane. "Of Vigilance and Virgins: Honor, Shame and Access to Resources in Mediterranean Societies," *Ethnology* 10 (1971): 10–26.

———. "Trousseau as Treasure: Some Contradictions of Late Nineteenth-Century Change in Sicily," in Eric Ross, ed., *Beyond the Myths of Culture* (New York, 1980): 323–56.

Scholes, France V. "Church and State in New Mexico, 1610–1650," *NMHR* 11 (1936): 9–76, 145–78, 283–94, 297–349, and 15 (1940): 78–106.

———. "Civil Government and Society in New Mexico in the Seventeenth Century," *NMHR* 10 (1935): 71–111.

———. "Documents for the History of the New Mexican Missions in the Seventeenth Century," *NMHR* 4 (1929): 195–99.

———. "The First Decade of the Inquisition in New Mexico," *NMHR* 10 (1935): 195–241.

———. "The Supply Service of the New Mexican Missions in the Seventeenth Century," *NMHR* 5 (1930): 93–404.

———. *Troublous Times in New Mexico, 1659–1670.* Albuquerque, 1942.

———, and Eleanor B. Adams. "Inventories of Church Furnishings in Some of the New Mexico Missions, 1672," in William M. Dabney and Josiah C. Russell, eds., *Dargan Historical Essays* (Albuquerque, 1952): 27–38.

———, and Lansing B. Bloom. "Friar Personnel and Mission Chronology, 1598–1629," *NMHR* 19 (1944): 319–36; "Friar Personnel and Mission Chronology, Part II," *NMHR* 20 (1945): 58–82.

———, and H. P. Mera. "Some Aspects of the Jumano Problem," *Contributions to American Anthropology and History—The Carnegie Institution* 523 (1940): 273–99.

Schroeder, Albert H. "Navajo and Apache Relationships West of the Rio Grande," *El Palacio* 70 (1963): 5–23.

———. "Pueblos Abandoned in Historic Times," *Handbook of North American Indians*: vol. 9, pp. 236–54.

———. "Rio Grande Ethnohistory," in Ortiz, ed., *New Perspectives on the Pueblos*: 41–70.

———. "Shifting for Survival in the Spanish Southwest," in D. Weber, ed., *New Spain's Northern Frontier* (Albuquerque, 1979): 239–55.

Schroeder, Albert H., and Daniel S. Matson, eds., *A Colony on the Move: Gaspar Costaño de Sosa's Journal, 1590–1591.* Santa Fe, 1965.

Scully, Vincent. *Pueblo: Mountain, Village, Dance.* New York, 1972.

Secoy, Frank R. "The Identity of the Paduca: An Ethnohistorical Analysis," *American Anthropologist* 53 (1951): 525–42.

Sedillo, Mela. *Mexican and New Mexican Folkdances.* Albuquerque, 1935.

Segalen, Martine. *Love and Power in the Peasant Family: Rural France in the Nineteenth Century.* Chicago, 1983.

Sergent, Bernard. *Homosexuality in Greek Myth.* Boston, 1986.

Servín, Manuel. "Religious Aspects of Symbolic Acts of Sovereignty," *The Americas* 13 (1957): 255–68.

Sharborough, Stephen. "The Cult of the Mother in Europe: The Transformation of the Symbolism of Woman." Ph.D. diss., University of California, Los Angeles, 1977.

Shorter, Edward. *The Making of the Modern Family.* New York, 1975.

Simmons, Marc. "History of Pueblo-Spanish Relations to 1821," *Handbook of North American Indians*: vol. 9, pp. 178–93.

———. *Little Lion of the Southwest.* Chicago, 1973.

———. "New Mexico's Smallpox Epidemic of 1780–1781," *NMHR* 41 (1966): 319–26.

———. "Patrones de ascentamiento y planes de las aldeas en Nuevo México en la época colonial," in David J. Weber, ed., *El México Perdido* (Mexico City, 1976): 82–83.

———. *Spanish Government in New Mexico.* Albuquerque, 1968.

———. *Witchcraft in the Southwest: Spanish and Indian Supernaturalism on the Rio Grande.* Flagstaff, 1974.

———, ed. and trans. *Father Juan Agustín Morfi's Account of Disorders in New Mexico, 1778.* Isleta Pueblo, N.M., 1977.

Simpson, Lesley Byrd. *The Encomienda in New Spain: The Beginnings in Spanish Mexico.* Berkeley, Calif., 1950.

Singer, Irving. *The Nature of Love: Plato to Luther.* Chicago, 1984.

Sjöo, Monica, and Barbara Mor. *The Great Cosmic Mother: Rediscovering the Religion of the Earth.* New York, 1987.

Smith, M. G. "Segmentary Lineages," in *Corporations and Society* (London, 1974): 120–33.

Smith, Miriam Y. "American Indian Warfare," *Transactions of the New York Academy of Sciences*, Series 2, 13 (1951): 348–65.

———. "The War Complex of the Plains Indians," *Proceedings of the American Philosophical Society* 78 (1938): 425–64.

Smith, W. "Kiva mural decorations at Awatovi and Kawaika-a," *Papers of the Peabody Museum of American Archaeology and Ethnology* 37 (1952): 322–75.

Snitow, Ann, Christine Stansell, and Sharon Thompson, eds. *Powers of Desire: The Politics of Sexuality.* New York, 1983.

Snow, David H. "A Note on Encomienda Economics in Seventeenth-Century New Mexico," in Weigle, ed., *Hispanic Arts and Ethnohistory in the Southwest*: 350–59.

———. "Protohistoric Rio Grande Pueblo Economics: A Review of Trends," in D. Wilcox and W. Masse, eds., *The Protohistoric Period in the North American Southwest, A.D. 1450–1700* (Tempe, Ariz., 1981): 354–77.

Solórzano Pereira, Juan de. *Política Indiana.* Madrid, 1776.

Spell, Lota M. "Music Training in New Mexico in the Seventeenth Century," *NMHR* 2 (1927): 27–36.

Spicer, Edward. *Cycles of Conquest: The Impact of Spain, Mexico, and the United States on the Indians of the Southwest, 1533–1960.* Tucson, 1962.

Spier, Leslie. "An Outline for a Chronology of Zuni Ruins," *Anthropological Papers of the American Museum of Natural History* 18 (1917): 205–331.

Spiess, Lincoln B. "Benavides and Church Music in the Early Seventeenth Century," *Journal of the American Musicological Society* 17 (1964): 105–30.

———. "Instruments in the Missions of New Mexico, 1598–1680," *NMHR* 40 (1965): 27–42.

Spiro, Melford E. *Oedipus in the Trobriands*. Chicago, 1982.

Spring, David, and Eileen Spring, eds. *Ecology and Religion in History*. New York, 1974.

Staniforth, Maxwell, trans. *Early Christian Writings*. Harmondsworth, Eng., 1968.

Stark, Louisa R. "The Origin of the Penitente Death Cart," *Journal of American Folklore* 84 (1971): 304–10.

Stark, Richard B. *Music of the Spanish Folk Plays in New Mexico*. Santa Fe, 1969.

Steele, Thomas J. "The Death Cart: Its Place Among the Santos of New Mexico," *Colorado Magazine* 55 (1978): 1–14.

———. *Saints and Santos*. Santa Fe, 1974.

———, trans. *Holy Week in Tomé: A New Mexico Passion Play*. Santa Fe, 1976.

Steinberg, Leo. *The Sexuality of Christ in Renaissance Art and Modern Oblivion*. New York, 1983.

Stephen, Alexander M. *Hopi Journal*. New York, 1936.

———. "Hopi Tales," *Journal of American Folk-Lore* 42 (1929): 2–72.

Stewart, Kenneth M. "Mohave Warfare," *Southwestern Journal of Anthropology* 3 (1947): 257–78.

Stirling, Matthew W. *Origin Myth of Acoma and Other Records*. Washington, D.C., 1942.

Stoddard, H. L. "Phallic Symbols in America," *American Antiquarian and Oriental Journal* 27 (1905): 281–94.

Stubbs, Stanley. *Bird's-Eye View of the Pueblos*. Norman, Okla., 1950.

Sturtevant, William G., gen. ed. *Handbook of North American Indians*. Washington, D.C., 1979.

Swadesh, Frances Leon. *Los Primeros Pobladores: Hispanic Americans of the Ute Frontier*. Notre Dame, Ind., 1974.

Swann, Micahel M. *Tierra Adentro: Settlement and Society in Colonial Durango*. Boulder, Colo., 1982.

Sylvest, Edwin Edward. *Motifs of Franciscan Mission Theory in Sixteenth Century New Spain: Province of the Holy Gospel*. Washington, D.C., 1975.

Talayesva, Don C. *Sun Chief: The Autobiography of a Hopi Indian*. New Haven, Conn., 1942.

Taylor, William B. "Between Global Process and Local Knowledge: An Inquiry into Early Latin American Social History, 1500–1900," in Zunz, ed., *Reliving the Past: The Worlds of Social History*: 115–90.

———. "Land and Water Rights in the Viceroyalty of New Spain," *NMHR* 50 (1975): 189–212.

———. "The Virgin of Guadalupe in New Spain: An Inquiry into the Social History of Marian Devotion," *American Ethnologist* 14 (1987): 9–33.

Tedlock, Barbara. "Prayer Stick Sacrifice at Zuñi." Manuscript in Department of Anthropology, Wesleyan University, Middletown, Conn., 1971.

Terrell, John Upton. *Estevanico the Black*. Los Angeles, 1968.

Thomas, Alfred, ed. and trans. *Forgotten Frontiers; A Study of the Spanish Indian Policy of Don Juan Bautista de Anza, Governor of New Mexico, 1777–1787*. Norman, Okla., 1932.

Thurston, Herbert. *Surprising Mystics*. Chicago, 1955.

Timmons, William H. "The Population of the El Paso Area—A Census of 1784," *NMHR* 52 (1977): 311–16.

Titiev, Mischa. *The Hopi Indians of Old Oraibi*. Ann Arbor, Mich., 1972.

———. *Old Oraibi: A Study of the Hopi Indians of the Third Mesa*. Cambridge, Mass., 1944.

Todorov, Tzvetan. *The Conquest of America: The Question of the Other*. New York, 1984.

Toscano, Alejandra Moreno. "Economía Regional y Urbanización: Tres ejemplos de Relación entre Ciudades y Regiones en Nueva España a Finales del Siglo XVIII," in *Urbanización y Proceso Social en América*. (Mexico City, 1972): 197–217.

Tozzer, Alfred M. *Landa's Relación de las Cosas de Yucatán: a Translation*. Cambridge, Mass., 1941.

Trexler, Richard. "From the Mouths of Babes: Christianization by Children in 16th Century New Spain," in John Davis, ed., *Religious Organization and Religious Experience*: 115–35.

———. *Public Life in Renaissance Florence*. New York, 1980.

———. "Ritual in Florence: Adolescence and Salvation in the Renaissance," in Trinkaus and Oberman, eds., *The Pursuit of Holiness in Late Medieval and Renaissance Religion*: 200–264.

———. "La Vie ludique dans la Nouvelle-Espagne—l'empereur et ses trois rois," in Ariès and Margolin, eds., *Les Jeux à la Renaissance*: 81–93.

———. "We Think, They Act: Clerical Readings of Missionary Theatre in 16th Century New Spain," in Kaplan, ed., *Understanding Popular Culture*: 189–228.

Trinkaus, Charles, and Heiko A. Oberman, eds. *The Pursuit of Holiness in Late Medieval and Renaissance Religion*. Leiden, 1974.

Turner, Victor W. "Betwixt and Between: The Liminal Period in *Rites of Passage*," in William A. Lessa and Evon Z. Vogt, eds., *Reader in Comparative Religion: An Anthropological Approach* (New York, 1972): 338–39.

———. "Hidalgo: History as Social Drama," in his *Dramas, Fields, and Metaphors: Symbolic Action in Human Society* (Ithaca, N.Y., 1974): 98–155.

———. *The Ritual Process: Structure and Anti-Structure*. Ithaca, N.Y., 1969.

Tyler, Hamilton A. *Pueblo Animals and Myths*. Norman, Okla., 1975.

———. *Pueblo Birds and Myths*. Norman, Okla., 1979.

———. *Pueblo Gods and Myths*. Norman, Okla., 1964.

Tyler, S. Lyman, and H. Daniel Taylor, trans. "The Report of Fray Alonso de Posada in Relation to Quivira and Teguayo," *NMHR* 33 (1958): 301–3.

Ullmann, Walter. *A History of Political Thought: The Middle Ages*. Baltimore, 1965.

Underhill, Ruth M. *Ceremonial Patterns in the Greater Southwest*. Seattle, 1948.

Upham, Steadman. *Polities and Power: An Economic and Political History of the Western Pueblo*. New York, 1982.

Valdecasas, Alfonso García. *El Hidalgo y El Honor*. Madrid, 1948.

Valdez, Facundo. "Vergüenza," in Paul Kutsche, ed., *The Survival of Spanish American Villages* (Colorado Springs, 1979): 99–106.

Valle, Rafael Heliodoro. *Santiago en América*. Mexico City, 1946.

Vance, Carole S., ed. *Pleasure and Danger: Exploring Female Sexuality*. Boston, 1984.

Van Gennep, Arnold. *The Rites of Passage*. Chicago, 1960.

Van Ness, John R., and Christine M. Van Ness, eds. *Spanish and Mexican Land Grants in New Mexico and Colorado*. Santa Fe, 1980.

Vansina, Jan. *Oral Tradition as History*. Madison, Wisc., 1985.

Ventancurt, Fray Agustín de. *Teatro Mexicano: Descripción breve de los sucesos ejemplares de la Nueva España en el Nuevo Mundo*. Madrid, 1961. 4 vols.

Very, Francis G. *The Spanish Corpus Christi Procession: A Literary and Folkloric Study*. Valencia, 1962.

Vinck, José de, ed. and trans. *The Works of Bonaventure*. Paterson, N.J., 1960. 6 vols.

Vlahos, Olivia. *Body, the Ultimate Symbol*. New York, 1979.

Voth, H. R. *The Oraibi Marau Ceremony*. Chicago, 1912.

Wachtel, Nathan. *The Vision of the Vanquished: The Spanish Conquest of Peru through Indian Eyes, 1530–1570*. New York, 1977.

Wagner, Henry R. "Fray Marcos de Niza," *NMHR* 9 (1934): 184–227.

Wainerman, Catalina H. "Family Relations in Argentina: Diachrony and Synchrony," *Journal of Family History* 3 (1978): 410–21.

Warman, Arturo. *La danza de moros y cristianos*. Mexico City, 1972.

Warner, Marina. *Alone of All Her Sex: The Myth and the Cult of the Virgin Mary*. New York, 1976.

Waters, Frank. *Masked Gods: Navaho and Pueblo Ceremonialism*. New York, 1950.

Watson, Curtis Brown. *Shakespeare and the Renaissance Concept of Honor*. Princeton, N.J., 1960.

Weber, Max. *The Sociology of Religion*. Boston, 1963.

———. *The Theory of Social and Economic Organization*. New York, 1964.

Weigle, Marta. *Brothers of Light, Brothers of Blood. The Penitentes of the Southwest*. Albuquerque, 1976.

———. "Ghostly Flagellants and Doña Sebastiana: Two Legends of the Penitente Brotherhood," *Western Folklore* 36 (1977): 133–47.

———. *A Penitente Bibliography*. Albuquerque, 1975.

———, ed. *Hispanic Arts and Ethnohistory in the Southwest*. Santa Fe, 1983.

Weinstein, Donald. *Savonarola and Florence: Prophecy and Patriotism in the Renaissance*. Princeton, N.J., 1970.

———, and Rudolph M. Bell. *Saints and Society: Two Worlds of Western Civilization, 1000–1700*. Chicago, 1982.

West, Elizabeth Howard. "The Right of Asylum in New Mexico in the Seventeenth and Eighteenth Centuries," *HAHR* 8 (1928): 357–91.

Westermarck, Edward. *The History of Human Marriage*. London, Eng., 1925. 2 vols.

Westphall, Victor. *Mercedes Reales: Hispanic Land Grants of the Upper Rio Grande Region*. Albuquerque, 1983.

White, Leslie A. *The Acoma Indians*. Washington, D.C., 1932.

———. "The Impersonation of Saints among the Pueblos," *Papers of the Michigan Academy of Science, Arts and Letters* 27 (1941): 559–64.

———. *New Material from Acoma*. Washington, 1943.

———. *The Pueblo of Santa Ana, New Mexico*. Menasha, Wisc., 1942.

———. *The Pueblo of Santo Domingo, New Mexico*. Menasha, Wisc., 1935.

Whitehead, Harriet. "The Bow and the Burden Strap: A New Look at Institutionalized Homosexuality in Native North America," in Ortner and Whitehead, eds., *Sexual Meanings*: 80–115.

———. "Fertility and Exchange in New Guinea," in Collier and Yanagisako, eds., *Gender and Kinship*: 244–70.

Whitson, Robley E. *Mysticism and Ecumenism*. New York, 1966.

Williams, Walter L. *The Spirit and the Flesh: Sexual Diversity in American Indian Culture*. Boston, 1986.

Wolf, Eric P. "Society and Symbols in Latin Europe and in the Islamic Near East: Some Comparisons," *Anthropology Quarterly* 42 (1969): 287–301.

———. "The Virgin of Guadalupe: A Mexican National Symbol," *Journal of American Folklore* 71 (1958): 34–39.

———, and Sidney R. Mintz. "An Analysis of Ritual Co-parenthood (*compadrazgo*)," *Southwestern Journal of Anthropology* 6 (1950): 341–68.

Woodbury, Richard. "A Reconsideration of Pueblo Warfare in the Southwestern United States," *Actas del XXXIII Congreso Internacional de Americanistas* 2 (1959): 124–33.

Wormington, H. Marie. *Prehistoric Indians of the Southwest*. Denver, 1975.

Wroth, William. *Christian Images in Hispanic New Mexico: The Taylor Museum Collection of Santos*. Colorado Springs, 1982.

Wyatt-Brown, Bertram. *Southern Honor: Ethics and Behavior in the Old South*. New York, 1982.

Yacher, León. *Marriage, Migration and Racial Mixing in Colonial Tlazazalca (Michoacán, Mexico), 1750–1800*, Department of Geography Discussion Paper No. 32, Syracuse University (Syracuse, N.Y., 1977).

Yava, Albert. *Big Falling Snow: A Tewa-Hopi Indian's Life and Times, and the History and Traditions of His People*. New York, 1978.

Young, Brian Alexander. "The History of the Black in New Mexico from the Sixteenth Century through the Nineteenth Century Pioneer Period." M.A. thesis, University of New Mexico, 1969.

Zárate, Diego López de. *Breve Descripción Genealógica de la llustre Quanto Antiquissima Case de los Vargas de Madrid*. Madrid, 1970.

Zárate Salmerón, Fray Jerónimo. *Relaciones*. Albuquerque, 1966.

Zavala, Silvio. *Los Esclavos Indios en Nueva España*. Mexico City, 1967.

———. *New Viewpoints on the Spanish Colonization of America*. Philadelphia, 1943.

Zimmerman, Charlotte. "The Cult of the Cross: An Analysis of Cosmology and Catholicism in Quintana Roo," *History of Religions* 3 (1963): 50–71.

Zunz, Oliver, ed. *Reliving the Past: The Worlds of Social History*. Chapel Hill, N.C., 1985.

Zweig, Paul. *The Heresy of Self-Love: A Study of Subversive Individualism*. New York, 1968.

Index

Library of Congress Cataloging-in-Publication Data

Gutiérrez, Ramón A., 1951–
    When Jesus came, the corn mothers went away: marriage, sexuality, and power in New Mexico, 1500–1846 / Ramón A. Gutiérrez.
    p.   cm.
    Includes bibliographical references.
    ISBN 0-8047-1816-4 (cloth):
    ISBN 0-8047-1832-6 (paperback)
    1. Marriage—New Mexico—History.   2. Pueblo Indians—Social conditions.   3. Pueblo Indians—Sexual behavior.   I. Title.
HQ835.N6G88   1990
306.81′09789—dc20   90-9512
                                                      CIP

♾ This book was printed on acid-free paper.